KU-185-027

CHRISTOPHER PITTS
DANIEL McCROHAN

SHANGHAI
CITY GUIDE

INTRODUCING SHÀNGHǍI

Enjoy cocktails at stylish TMSK bar (p182)

The engine of China's future, Shànghǎi dazzles, beckoning millions with promises of reinvention and glamour. Some see it as the city that finally launched the country out of a rut of centuries-old traditions; others portray it as the place where an ancient culture was traded in for materialism and calculated ambition. Either way, its influence on modern China has been enormous.

Now two decades in the making, postcommunist Shànghǎi is an unpolished mixture of old concession architecture and giant towers, flash restaurants and tiny dumpling stands, bargain boutiques and the latest fashion. Above all, Shànghǎi is electrified with youthful optimism and opportunity. Business may drive the city with a cracking whip, but there's plenty to keep visitors busy here, from nonstop shopping to skyscraper-hopping to standout art and fantastic eats.

Shànghǎi exudes a style that's unlike anywhere else. Often portrayed as a blend of East and West, the city, with its voracious appetite for new ideas, is above all cosmopolitan and cutting edge. It's a place to taste a future that's just around the bend, to hang on to the roller-coaster ride of change, to hunt down the ghosts of old alleyways, the vanishing remnants of a debauched past and the creations of the next generation. For dealmakers, bargain hunters, in-the-know foodies and those who just want to ride the crest of China's emerging wave, Shànghǎi is the place to be.

SHÀNGHǍI LIFE

LIGHT, HEAT, POWER.

Mao Dun, *Midnight*, a novel of 1930s Shànghǎi

Shànghǎi has nearly 19 million residents (unofficial counts are even higher) looking to find their way in the new economy. For the vast majority – rich, poor, migrant, middle class – the single defining element of the city lifestyle is hard work. You only need to look out your window at night to deduce how the city has grown with such incredible rapidity: scattered across the horizon are the intermittent flashes of spot welders working round-the-clock shifts on construction sites. Tied to hard work is mounting stress and a mobile phone affixed permanently to one ear, but the Shanghainese are starting to enjoy their money too.

The lure of a middle-class lifestyle is one of the city's principal attractions for Chinese, even if it's currently unattainable for the majority. Consumerism extends beyond such middle-class essentials (car, apartment) to more frivolous purchases – the latest fashions and gadgets are very important – and even those without the cash to spend are swept up in Shànghǎi's penchant for ostentation.

But with change comes instability, and the megalopolis can be an intense and stressful place for many, especially the millions who don't have the right connections or enough savings to get over the hump. Education, health care and retirement are issues that all 21st-century governments have to deal with, but in China the system has gone from almost complete socialism to dog-eat-dog capitalism in a compressed space of about two decades. As a cosmopolitan city and financial centre, Shànghǎi has improved immeasurably, but social care in new China has yet to find its feet.

Nevertheless, with jobs offering the highest salaries in the country and thousands of overseas Chinese choosing to return to Shànghǎi every year, there's no doubting that this city is China's golden land of opportunity. For the people who live here, that's enough for the moment. Their pride in their city is palpable.

Customs House (p70) lights up the Bund at night

HIGHLIGHTS

THE BUND 外滩

The Bund's majestic sweep is a monument to the pursuit of spectacular wealth. Even if the concession-era architecture is now dwarfed by an ever-expanding forest of high-rises, its symbolism still sums up Shànghǎi in a jewel-encrusted nutshell.

❶ Wining & Dining
For a taste of sophisticated Shànghǎi (p156)

❷ Cruise the Huangpu or Hop on the Ferry to Pǔdōng
Size up the city, east and west (p65)

❸ East Nanjing Road
Bright lights, big crowds (p64)

❶ Shanghai Urban Planning Exhibition Hall
Welcome to the year 2020 (p74)

❷ Shanghai Museum
Simply put, the best museum in China (p72)

❸ Dumplings
You haven't done Shànghǎi until you've had dumplings (p159)

PEOPLE'S SQUARE人民广场

If the city has a nerve centre, People's Square is it: an open expanse peppered with museums, ringed with supertowers and lorded over by the stoic city hall. Below ground, Shànghǎi's frenetic energy reaches full crescendo with the endless crowds hurrying through the metro interchange.

FRENCH CONCESSION法租界

The Paris of the East? Not quite, and yet the Concession's heart is in the right place: this is where you come to discover the Shanghainese joie de vivre. Here, the emphasis is less on making money and more on spending it on food, fashion and fun.

1 Xīntiāndì
Food, fashion and communism: from Shànghǎi with love (p90)

2 Taikang Road Art Centre
Explore old alleyways and quirky boutiques (p85)

3 Nightlife
...or shake your booty at one of the many clubs and bars (p190)

4 Spa Therapy
Balance your inner *qi* (energy) with a traditional massage...(p196)

5 Wandering the Backstreets
Go from art galleries to art deco (p95)

6 Have You Eaten Yet?
From fusion cuisine to frog hotpots, the Concession's got it all (p161)

❶ Bargain Hunting
Haggle for an array of Shànghǎi souvenirs
(p140)

❷ Walking the Old Town
Twisting alleyways, hanging laundry and the
sound of sizzling woks (p83)

❸ Yuyuan Gardens & Bazaar
Get lost in the traditional gardens, but skip the
weekends (p78)

OLD TOWN南市

For some, the Old Town's beleaguered charms are the most alluring part of a
Shànghǎi visit – antique markets, traditional street life and a handful of temples are
a fitting contrast to the city's future-now mantra.

JÌNG'ĀN静安区

This area is an entertaining combination of Shànghǎi's classiest street, West Nanjing Rd, and an up-and-coming neighbourhood that still retains a rough-edged feel. Far to the north is M50, the factory-area-turned gallery-space; close by is the city's most impressive place of worship, the Jade Buddha Temple.

❶ M50
Postindustrial chic and the latest in Chinese art (p97)

❷ Jade Buddha Temple
In Shànghǎi, even the Buddhas are jewels (p100)

❸ Nightlife
Catch the spectacle of an acrobatics show (p188)

PǓDŌNG浦东

Shànghǎi's money-making flair turned farmland into a shimmering constellation of high-rise towers in the space of little over a decade. The Pǔdōng skyline is exactly what China wants to see when it looks in the mirror.

❶ Shanghai History Museum
Pǔdōng tips its hat to the past (p110)

❷ Skyscrapers
Leave gravity behind (p46)

1 **Qībǎo**
Traditional China – a hop, skip and metro ride away (p131)

2 **Bike Tours**
Sign up for a two-wheeled tour around town (p196)

3 **Gallery Tours**
Check out the art exhibitions in the city's independent galleries (p94)

OFF THE BEATEN PATH

There are plenty of adventurous ways to discover the 'hai, from cycling through the city at night and hunting for antiques to learning about traditional handicrafts in Qībǎo, walking the old Jewish ghetto and going on a gallery tour.

EXCURSIONS

Had more urban frenzy than you think you can handle? Fear not. Cute canal towns, cool mountain retreats, centres of ancient Chinese culture and even a Buddhist island are all just a short trip from the megacity sprawl.

❶ Sūzhōu's Gardens
Contemplate the harmony of rocks, pavilions and pools (p230)

❷ West Lake
Cycle your way around this classical Chinese landscape (p222)

❸ Canal Towns
Float back in time to the Qing dynasty (p235)

CONTENTS

THE AUTHORS

Christopher Pitts

A Philadelphia native, Chris started off his university years studying classical Chinese poetry before a week in 1990s Shànghǎi (en route to school in Kūnmíng) abruptly changed his focus to the idiosyncrasies of modern China. After spending several years in Asia memorising Chinese characters, he abruptly traded it all in and moved to Paris, where he currently lives with his family: Perrine, Elliot and Céleste. He works as a freelance writer, editor and translator for a number of publishers, including Columbia University Press, and has contributed to three editions of Lonely Planet's *China*. Visit his website at www.christopherpitts.net.

Chris was the coordinating author of this guide, and wrote the following chapters: Introducing Shànghǎi, Highlights, Neighbourhoods, Shopping, Eating, Drinking, Entertainment, Transport and Directory.

Daniel McCrohan

Daniel's writing career kicked off with a seven-year spell in London as a news and sports journalist before his first taste of China – as a backpacker in 2004 – proved too delicious to ignore. He soon decided there was more to life than interviewing footballers, so upped sticks and moved to China, where he has lived ever since. Initially spending time in Shànghǎi – studying Chinese and teaching English – Daniel later moved to Běijīng, where he now lives with his wife, Taotao, in a courtyard house in one of the capital's historic *hútòng* (narrow alleyways). Daniel's frequent travels across China – 22 provinces and counting – rekindled his love of writing, and he began contributing travel articles to publications in China and the UK before joining Lonely Planet in 2007. This is his fourth Lonely Planet assignment. He has also coauthored *China*.

For this guide, Daniel wrote the following chapters: Getting Started, Background, Architecture, Sleeping and Excursions.

GETTING STARTED

In terms of culture and facilities, Shànghǎi is about as close to the West as you can get on mainland China, but it is, nevertheless, still China and for the first-time visitor the city can throw up a number of surprises. English, for example, is hardly spoken at all outside backpacker hostels, top-notch hotels and expat friendly Western-style bars and restaurants. Our Language section (p270) may help if you get stuck. Getting around is far easier than in most Chinese cities, but it's still advisable to carry the business card of the hotel you are staying in, with its address in Chinese. Shànghǎi can be expensive (see Costs & Money, p20), but if you're willing to mime your way through ordering meals at restaurants with Chinese-only menus, and are happy to give taxis – and Western bars – a miss, you'll spend surprisingly little. Apart from getting a visa (p267), the only thing you really need to think about before you leave is when to visit. See below for some ideas, then check out our Itinerary Builder (p60) for suggestions on what to do once you arrive.

WHEN TO GO

The best seasons to visit Shànghǎi are spring (March to mid-May), as the city warms up from a cold winter, and autumn (late September to mid-November), when the heat of summer pleasantly subsides. Although Shànghǎi has grown warmer in winter over recent years (snow is rare these days), winter (mid-November to February) is generally miserable with most heating coming from reverse-cycle air-con (central heating is rare). Summer (June to September) is fiercely hot, and the humidity combines with the crowds to rapidly sap energy, although this is the peak tourist season.

All hell breaks loose in late January/early February when the Spring Festival (Chinese New Year) hits town and swamps the transport infrastructure with domestic travellers. It's only a three-day festival but is generally extended to a week by including weekend days. Likewise, National Day (around October 1) is a three-day holiday stretched out to last one week. While being here during these times – especially for the fireworks extravaganza that is Spring Festival – can be fun, unless you have a particular fondness for big crowds and long queues it's best to avoid being on the road or doing too much sightseeing at these times.

Peruse the following Festivals section to cherry-pick events that float your boat. See the Climate section (p53) for more information on the weather in Shànghǎi.

FESTIVALS

Apart from the festivals listed below and the holidays outlined in the Directory chapter, other events include the Shanghai International Fashion Culture Festival, in March or April, and the Shanghai International Tea Culture Festival at the end of April. If you fancy something stronger, the Shanghai Beer Festival staggers into town around the end of July. Of less interest to foreign visitors are the Nanhui Peach Blossom Festival in mid-April, the Osmanthus Festival (near Guilin Park) in September or October, and the Tangerine Festival in early November. Children will particularly enjoy the Anting Kite Festival, held in nearby Āntíng (安亭; Jiādìng district) in mid-April. The Shanghai Tourism Festival kicks off in mid-September with a parade down Middle Huaihai Rd or East Nanjing Rd, and offers a wide variety of cultural programs. The Shanghai Masters 1000 is a significant tournament on the tennis calendar, attracting many of the big names in world tennis. Previously known as the Tennis Masters Cup, it is held every October in the magnificent Qi Zhong Stadium (5500 Yuanjiang Rd) in Mǐnháng district.

Special prayers are held at Buddhist and Taoist temples on days when the moon is either full or just a sliver. According to the Chinese lunar calendar, the lunar month begins with the new moon, while the full moon occurs 15 and 16 days later; some Chinese Buddhists observe a vegetarian diet on the occasions of the new moon and full moon.

January & February

WESTERN NEW YEAR 1 Jan
元旦 Yuándàn

Longhua Temple (p121) has excellent New Year celebrations, with dragon and lion dances. At New Year the abbot strikes the bell 108 times while the monks beat on gongs and offer prayers for the forthcoming year. The Western New Year is celebrated in bars citywide on New Year's Eve.

SPRING FESTIVAL
14 Feb 2010, 3 Feb 2011, 23 Jan 2012
春节 **Chūn Jié**

Also called the Chinese New Year, the Spring Festival is the equivalent of Christmas in the Chinese calendar. Families get together to feast on *jiǎozi* (dumplings), exchange gifts, vegetate in front of the TV, visit friends and take a long holiday. Locals also pay crucial New Year visits (*bàinián*) to their bosses, seniors and elders. The festival traditionally commences on the first day of the first moon of the traditional lunar calendar, but a high-octane month-long build-up – featuring a crescendo of red and gold decorations festooning shopping malls and the inescapable onset of seasonal Cantopop ditties – gets everyone hyped up much earlier. An explosion of fireworks at midnight welcomes the New Year and wards off bad spirits, while special services are held at Longhua Temple (p121) and Jing'an Temple (p102). Top Chinese restaurants are booked out well in advance for *niányèfàn* (New Year's Eve dinner). Families paste red couplets on their doors and hand out *hóngbāo*, red envelopes stuffed with money. Another explosion of firecrackers on the fifth day of the New Year heralds the arrival of the God of Wealth.

This can be a bad time if you are on the road – planes are booked out by overseas Chinese, ticket prices soar, trains are packed with migrant workers returning home, and hotels are booked solid. If you are in China at this time, book your room in advance, don't expect to get much business done and sit tight until the chaos is over.

LANTERN FESTIVAL
28 Feb 2010, 17 Feb 2011, 6 Feb 2012, 24 Feb 2013
元宵节 **Yuánxiāo Jié**

Not a public holiday, but this is a colourful time to visit Shànghǎi, especially the Yuyuan Gardens (p78). Families get together, make *yuánxiāo* (also called *tāngyuán*) delicious dumplings of glutinous rice with a variety of sweet fillings and sometimes hang out paper lanterns. The festival falls on the 15th day of the first lunar month.

VALENTINE'S DAY
14th February

情人节 **Qíngrén Jié**

The traditional Chinese festival for lovers – held on the seventh day of the seventh lunar month (七夕; *qīxì*) – has been usurped by the Western celebration. Valentine's Day is taken seriously by Shànghǎi suitors as an occasion for a massive blowout: it's the chance to get their true love that Cartier wristwatch or diamond ring she has been hankering for, although a bunch of 11 roses (symbolising loyalty) could do the trick. If you plan to eat out, insist on an early reservation as popular restaurants will be stuffed with dewy-eyed lovers.

March & April

SHANGHAI INTERNATIONAL LITERARY FESTIVAL
上海国际文学艺术节 **Shànghǎi Guójì Wénxué Yìshù Jié**

To counter Shànghǎi's drift towards philistinism, this highly popular festival for bibliophiles and literati alike is staged in the Glamour Bar (p179) in March or April, with a range of international and local authors in attendance. Tickets for the 2009 event cost Y65 per day including one drink.

BIRTHDAY OF GUANYIN
2 Apr 2010, 22 Mar 2011, 10 Mar 2012, 29 Mar 2013
观世音生日 **Guānshìyīn Shēngrì**

Guanyin is the Buddhist Goddess of Mercy, much revered in China for her boundless compassion. The goddess (more strictly a Bodhisattva or a Buddha-to-be) goes under a variety of aliases: Guanshiyin, literally meaning 'Observing the Cries of the World', is her formal name, but she is also called Guanzizai, Guanyin Dashi and Guanyin Pusa or, in Sanskrit, Avalokiteshvara. Generally, but not exclusively worshipped by women (especially those eager to bear children), Guanyin has her birthday on the 19th day of the second moon, an excellent time to visit Buddhist temples or the Buddhist island of Pǔtuóshān (p238).

TOMB SWEEPING DAY
5 Apr (4 Apr in leap years)

清明节 **Qīng Míng Jié**

Now a public holiday, Qīng Míng Jié occurs close to Easter every year, when over six million Shanghainese visit the graves of their dearly departed relatives, clean the grave sites and worship their ancestors. Flowers (particularly magnolias, the city flower) are often placed on tombs and 'ghost money' is burnt (for use in the afterworld).

THE EXPO EFFECT

In terms of economic and social impact, World Expo (世博会; shìbóhuì) is the third-largest event on the planet (after the Olympic Games and the FIFA World Cup), and in May 2010 it comes to Shànghǎi with the slogan 'Better City, Better Life'. The government directed a staggering 4.2 billion US dollars towards hosting the event which is expected to attract 70 million visitors, making it the biggest Expo in the event's almost 160-year history. Whether it turns out to be a success or not remains to be seen – some experts predict it will run-up losses of 120 million US dollars – but one thing is certain, its effect on the city of Shànghǎi cannot be ignored. Subway line extensions, new river ferry services, a new river tunnel, five magnificent state-of-the-art structures, including the showpiece China Pavilion, and a complete transformation of Shànghǎi's world-famous esplanade, the Bund, will all be lasting legacies of Expo 2010, as will the controversial relocation of an estimated 18,000 families. Here's our quick-look guide to what all the fuss is about:

When?

From 1 May to 31 October, 2010.

Where?

Across a 5-sq-km site straddling both sides of the Huangpu River between Nanpu Bridge and Lupu Bridge (Map pp62–3). Most of the site will be on the eastern side of the river, in Pǔdōng district, and will be linked to Pǔxī (west of the river) by subway lines 7, 8 and 13, by new ferry services and by the Y3.4 billion South Xizang Rd Tunnel.

Participants

At the time of research, more than 190 countries and over 40 international organisations had signed up to take part. Around 70 million visitors were expected, including 3.5 million foreigners.

Stuff To Do

Most participating bodies will have specially made pavilions showcasing their cultural, economic and technological strengths. As well as being able to judge which looks the coolest – Australia's Ayers Rock lookalike perhaps? UK's 'hairy' cube? Or maybe Belgium's 'brain cell'? – visitors can also peruse interactive exhibitions and watch performances galore. More than 100 different shows a day are planned.

LONGHUA TEMPLE FAIR

16 Apr 2010, 5 Apr 2011, 24 Mar 2012, 12 Apr 2013

龙华寺庙会 **Lónghuá Sìmiào Huì**

The two-week fair coincides with the blossoming of the local peach trees and kicks off on the third day of the third lunar month.

FORMULA ONE (F1)

☎ 6982 6999; www.icsh.sh.cn; 2000 Yining Rd, Jiādìng

The slick Shanghai International Circuit has hosted F1's Chinese Grand Prix every year since 2004. The original seven-year contract to host the event was due to expire after the 2010 grand prix, set for 18 April. At the time of research it was still unclear whether or not the contract would be renewed.

May & June

DRAGON BOAT FESTIVAL

16 Jun 2010, 6 Jun 2011, 23 Jun 2012, 12 Jun 2013

端午节 **Duānwǔ Jié**

Like Tomb Sweeping Day, this is also now a public holiday. It commemorates the death of Qu Yuan, a 3rd-century-BC poet-statesman who drowned himself to protest against the corrupt government. It is celebrated on the fifth day of the fifth lunar month with boat races along the Huangpu River, Suzhou Creek and Dianshan Lake.

SHANGHAI INTERNATIONAL FILM FESTIVAL

上海国际电影节 **Shànghǎi Guójì Diànyǐng Jié**

☎ 6253 7115; www.siff.com

With screenings at various cinemas (p189) around Shànghǎi, the movie-going festival brings a range of international and locally produced films to town in June. Remember to check whether the film you plan to see is being shown in its original language (原版; yuàn bǎn), in Chinese (中文版; zhōngwén bǎn) or in English (英文版; yīngwén bǎn).

September & October

MID-AUTUMN FESTIVAL

22 Sep 2010, 12 Sep 2011, 30 Sep 2012, 19 Sep 2013

中秋节 **Zhōngqiū Jié**

Another newcomer to the recently overhauled public holiday calendar, this age-old festival, also known as the Mooncake Festival, is the time to give and receive delicious moon cakes stuffed with bean paste, egg yolk, coconut, walnuts and the like. Gazing

How Much?

Standard-day tickets cost Y160 for one day. Peak-day tickets are Y200. Peak days are the first three Expo days, the first week in October and the last Expo week. Three-day (Y400) and seven-day (Y900) tickets are also available, but don't cover peak days.

And When It's All Over?

Most of the pavilions were designed to be temporary and will be dismantled by May 2011 at the latest, but five eye-catching permanent structures will remain – the China Pavilion (the red upturned triangle), the Expo Boulevard (the long glass-roofed, three-storey walkway that will be the main entrance to the Expo site), the Themes Pavilion (the large warehouse structure with glass ridges), the World Expo Centre (the long rectangular structure looking not unlike a giant glass matchbox) and the Expo Performance Centre (the giant flying saucer). The 22 new ferries were planned to stay running after Expo leaves town and, of course, the new subway lines and very expensive tunnel will remain.

Controversies

Costs aside, the main controversy was the relocation of around 55,000 residents to make way for the Expo site. Most were moved to two purpose-built developments – one nearby in Pǔdōng, the other not so nearby in Mǐnháng district in west Shànghǎi. Official sources said the relocation went smoothly but, according to the Hong Kong–based group Chinese League of Victims, some residents were bullied into moving – sometimes physically – after not being offered fair relocation packages.

Expo Extras

- A ban on smoking in public places was planned to be enforced throughout the duration of World Expo.
- Shànghǎi's former Communist Party chief, Chen Liangyu, was largely credited as being the man who brought World Expo to Shànghǎi following the city's successful bid in 2002. In 2008 he was sentenced to 18 years in prison on charges of financial fraud, abuse of power and accepting bribery.

at the moon, eating duck and lighting fireworks are popular activities; it's also a traditional holiday for lovers. The festival, now a one-day public holiday, takes place on the 15th day of the eighth lunar month.

HALLOWEEN   31 Oct
万圣节 Wànshèng Jié

One of a handful of imported Western festivals, spooky Halloween is increasingly popular with young Chinese. Pumpkins, seasonal outfits and masks pile up at large supermarkets and stores, while parties are held at expat-oriented bars and restaurants.

SHANGHAI BIENNALE   Sep–Nov 2010, 2012
上海双年展 Shànghǎi Shuāngniánzhǎn
☎ 6327 2829; www.shanghaibiennale.org

Held once every two years, this popular international arts festival takes place at the Shanghai Art Museum (p75).

CHINA INTERNATIONAL ARTS FESTIVAL
中国上海国际艺术节 Zhōngguó Shànghǎi Guójì Yìshù Jié
www.artsbird.com

A month-long program of cultural events in October and November, which includes the Shanghai Art Fair, a varied programme of international music, dance, opera and acrobatics, and exhibitions of the Shanghai Biennale (left).

November & December

SHANGHAI INTERNATIONAL MARATHON   Nov
上海国际马拉松赛 Shànghǎi Guójì Mǎlāsōng Sài
www.shmarathon.com

Held on the last Sunday of November, this annual event attracts around 20,000 runners. It starts at the Bund, and events include a half-marathon and a 4.5km 'health race'.

CHRISTMAS DAY   Dec 25
圣诞节 Shèngdàn Jié

Not an official Chinese festival perhaps, but Christmas is nevertheless a major milestone on the commercial calendar, and Shànghǎi's big shopping zones sparkle with decorations and glisten with (fake) snow. The white stuff does occasionally fall and Father Christmas (shèngdàn lǎorén; 圣诞老人) can be seen around town. Christmas is celebrated more by expats and young Chinese, rather than by more elderly locals. Christmas services can be attended at churches in town. 'Merry Christmas' in Chinese is *'shèngdàn kuàilè!'* (圣诞快乐!).

COSTS & MONEY

Shànghǎi is one of China's most expensive cities. If you frequent expat-oriented restaurants, bars and supermarkets, you can quickly wind up paying the same as in the West.

Otherwise, accommodation is likely to be your greatest expense, with prices ranging from around Y50 for a dorm bed to over Y2000 a night in the best five-star hotels (although discounting in midrange and top-end hotels is standard so always ask for the discounted rate).

Local restaurants offer fantastic value if you can decipher a Chinese menu. For some help, see the menu decoder in our language section (p270). Set-lunch specials or department-store food courts in the city also offer excellent value, where one person can dine for around Y30. Meals at more expensive restaurants will cost anywhere from Y60 to Y600; aim for set meals rather than dining à la carte. Check the bill carefully, and remember tipping is not expected apart from at top-end restaurants.

Cafes and bars are expensive, so expect to pay around Y30 for a cup of fresh coffee, or Y40 for the smallest of beers.

Travelling by metro and bus can keep transport costs down, although taxis are plentiful and, by Western standards, inexpensive.

Be alert to scams (p265), or your holiday costs could start soaring.

HOW MUCH?

Short-hop metro ticket **Y3**

Taxi flag fall **Y11**

Meal in a small Chinese restaurant **Y25, including drinks**

Meal in a top-end international restaurant **from Y200, plus drinks**

Bananas from street-side stall **Y2/kg**

0.5L bottle of mineral water **Y2**

Big bottle of local beer from corner shop **Y3-5**

Small bottle of local beer in bar **Y40**

Local map from hawker **Y5**

Cricket in a cage from a wayside peddler **Y5**

Lamb skewer **Y3-6**

Litre of petrol **Y6**

INTERNET RESOURCES

For more on the media in China, see p55.

City Weekend (www.cityweekend.com.cn/shanghai) Popular expat magazine's comprehensive listings website. News stories can be weak.

CTrip (www.english.ctrip.com) Still one of the best websites for ticketing and hotel bookings in China.

Expat Shanghai (www.expatsh.com) OK intro to Shànghǎi.

Learn Chinese with the BBC (www.bbc.co.uk/languages/chinese) Very useful introduction to learning Mandarin Chinese, with video.

Shanghai Daily (www.shanghaidaily.com) English-language newspaper's website.

Shanghai Expat (www.shanghaiexpat.com) Does exactly what it says on the tin. Includes a resourceful forum.

Shanghaiist (www.shanghaiist.com) Excellent source for news and reviews.

Smart Shanghai (www.smartshanghai.com) Good quality listings website with forum.

Tales of Old China (www.talesofoldchina.com) Lots of reading on Old Shànghǎi, with the text of hard-to-find books online.

That's Shanghai (www.shanghai.urbanatomy.com) So-so website from one of Shànghǎi's popular expat magazines.

Popular Blogs

Andy Best (www.kungfuology.com/andybest) News and views about the Shànghǎi music scene.

Shanghai Scrap (www.shanghaiscrap.com) Very well researched blog from American writer/journalist Adam Minter.

Wangjianshuo (www.wangjianshuo.com) Chinese blogger's English-language site.

SUSTAINABLE SHÀNGHǍI

Environmental degradation in Shànghǎi is a natural consequence of rapid industrialisation and the ongoing construction boom; ecological awareness remains embryonic. There is little visitors can do to mitigate this, but a few measures exist where visitors can make a contribution. Avoid eating the Chinese sturgeon, the Yangtze crocodile or other endangered animals that may be dished up to impress. Shark's fin soup should also be avoided, if it's genuine. Try to invest in a pair of your own chopsticks (to protect the forests of bamboo that are felled to make disposable chopsticks) and try to resist from using the film-wrapped plate-bowl-cutlery-glass combos that are becoming increasingly popular in restaurants across China. You could also consider hiring a bicycle (p245) to get about town. See p54 for more information.

BACKGROUND

HISTORY
EARLY BEGINNINGS
Up until around the 7th century AD, Shànghǎi was little more than marshland. At that time, the area was known as Shēn, 申, (after Chunshen Jun, 春申君, a local nobleman from the 3rd century BC) or Hù, 沪, (after a type of bamboo fishing trap used by fisherman in the area). The character hù, 沪, is still used today to identify the city – on car number plates, for example – while the city's main football team is known as Shanghai Shenhua (上海申花).

The earliest mention of the name Shànghǎi occurs in the 11th century AD and refers to the small settlement that sprang up at the confluence of the Shanghai River (long since vanished) and the Huangpu River (黄浦江; Huángpǔ Jiāng). Shànghǎi was upgraded from village status to market town in 1074, and became a city in 1297 after establishing itself as the major port in the area.

In 1553 a 9m-high, 5km-long defensive wall was built around the small city to fend off Japanese pirates raiding the coast (the wall was pulled down in 1912), and by the late 17th century Shànghǎi supported a population of 50,000, sustained on cotton production, fishing and, thanks to its excellent location at the head of the Yangzi River (长江; Cháng Jiāng), trade in silk and tea.

IT ALL STARTED WITH A LITTLE BIT OF OPIUM
During the early years of the Qing dynasty (1644–1911), the British East India Company and its later incarnations were trading in the only port open to the West, Canton (now Guǎngzhōu; 广州), south of Shànghǎi. British purchases of tea, silk and porcelain outweighed Chinese purchases of wool and spices, so by the late 18th century the British had decided to balance the books by slipping into India to swap (at a profit) silver for opium with which to purchase Chinese goods. The British passion for tea was increasingly matched by China's craving for opium (鸦片; yāpiàn), the drug that would virtually single-handedly create latter-day Shànghǎi and earn the city its bipolar reputation as the splendid 'Paris of the East' and infamous 'Whore of the Orient'.

From a mercantile point of view, the trade in opium – known as 'foreign mud' in China – was an astonishing success, rapidly worming its way into every nook and cranny of Chinese society. Highly addictive and widely available thanks to the prolific efforts of British traders, the drug – smoked via a pipe – quickly became the drug of choice for all sections of the Chinese public from the lowliest and most menial upwards. Jardine & Matheson's highly lucrative trade empire was founded on the opium business.

No other commodity became so uniquely associated with all of Shànghǎi's spectacular peaks and troughs. Opium became the driving force behind the city's unstoppable rise, and its descent into debauchery: from Shànghǎi's affluent taipans (powerful foreign businessmen) and lucrative hongs (business houses) to its piercing inequalities, its wanton netherworld of prostitution and vice, violent criminal gangs, corrupt police forces and the city's cartographic constitution of concessions, settlements and Chinese districts.

TIMELINE

453–221 BC	AD 960–1126	1553
Warring States period: the earliest imperial records date from this period, although Neolithic discoveries in Songze, Qīngpǔ County, suggest human settlement of the region 5900 years ago.	Chinese fleeing the Mongols during the Song dynasty boost the region's population, spurring Shànghǎi on to become the county seat of Jiāngsū in 1291.	The city wall around Shànghǎi's Old Town is first constructed to fend off Japanese pirates. Nine metres high and 5km around, the wall stands until the fall of the Qing dynasty, when it is demolished.

The Opium War between Great Britain and China was similarly fought in the drug's name and as a pretext to extract the concessions that British opium traders had sought from China. The Treaty of Nanking that concluded the First Opium War in 1842 was Shànghǎi's moment of reckoning, for its signing spelt the death of old Shànghǎi and the birth of the wild, lawless and spectacularly prosperous endeavour that would rise up over the Huangpu River.

THE ILLEGITIMATE BIRTH OF SHÀNGHǍI

The Treaty of Nanking stipulated, among other things, peace between China and Britain; security and protection of British persons and property; the opening of Canton, Fúzhōu (福州), Xiàmén (厦门), Níngbō (宁波) and Shànghǎi, as well as residence for foreigners and consulates in those cities (for the purpose of trade); fair import and export tariffs; the possession of Hong Kong (香港, Xiāng Gǎng), and an indemnity of US$18 million. Ironically enough, the trade of opium, legal or otherwise, never entered into the treaty.

Following Great Britain's lead, other countries were quick to join in, including the US and France. In 1843 the first British consul moved into a local house in the Old Town, signalling a foreign presence in the city that would last for the next 100 years.

Of the five port cities, Shànghǎi was the most prosperous due to its superb geographical location, capital edge and marginal interference from the Chinese government. Trade and businesses boomed, and by 1850 the foreign settlements housed more than 100 merchants, missionaries and physicians, three-quarters of them British. In 1844, 44 foreign ships made regular trade with China. By 1849, 133 ships lined the shores and by 1855, 437 foreign ships clogged the ports.

Foreigners were divided into three concessions. The original British Concession was north of Bubbling Well Road (now West Nanjing Road). The American Concession began life in Hóngkǒu District after Bishop William Boone had set up a mission there. These two concessions later joined to form one large area known as the International Settlement. The French, meanwhile, set up their own settlement south of the British one, and to the west of the Old Town, in an area which is still referred to by English speakers as the French Concession.

From regulation to sanitation, everything in Shànghǎi was vested in the foreign oligarchies of the Municipal Council and the Conseil d'Administration Municipale, a pattern that was to last as long as the settlements. It was not until the early 1920s that Chinese and Japanese residents (eventually the two largest groups in the settlements) were allowed even limited representation on the council.

From the start, Shànghǎi's *raison d'être* was trade. Still sailing to the West were silks, tea and porcelain, and 30,000 chests of opium were being delivered into China annually. Soon great Hong Kong trading houses like Butterfield & Swire and Jardine & Matheson set up shop, and trade in opium, silk and tea gradually shifted to textiles, real estate, banking, insurance and shipping. Banks in particular boomed; soon all of China's loans, debts and indemnity payments were funnelled through Shànghǎi. Buying and selling was handled by Chinese middlemen, known as *compradors* (from the Portuguese), from Canton and Níngbō, who formed a rare link between the Chinese and foreign worlds. The city attracted immigrants and entrepreneurs from across China, and overseas capital and expertise pooled in the burgeoning metropolis.

Foreign ideas were similarly imported. By the 1880s, huge numbers of proselytising American Protestants were saving souls in Shànghǎi, while the erudite Jesuits oversaw a flourishing settlement in Xújiāhuì (徐家汇), called Siccawei (or Zikawei).

1685	1793	1823
A customs house is opened in Shànghǎi for the first time.	Lord Macartney, George III's envoy to the imperial court of China, is rebuffed by the Qianlong emperor in Chéngdé, sinking British hopes of expanding legitimate trade relations with the 'Middle Kingdom'.	By now the British are swapping roughly 7000 chests of opium annually – with about 140 pounds of opium per chest, enough to keep one million addicts happy – compared with 1000 chests in 1773.

RECOMMENDED READING: SHÀNGHǍI'S HISTORY

- *Building Shanghai: The Story of China's Gateway*, Edward Denison & Guang Yu Ren. Beautifully illustrated with some fabulous photos and old maps, this book uses Shànghǎi's wealth of fine architecture as its focus for discussion on the city's chequered history.
- *Global Shanghai, 1850–2010: A History in Fragments*, Jeffrey N Wasserstrom. Seven pivotal years, each 25 years apart, are hand-picked by the highly regarded Wasserstrom to discuss globalisation in Shànghǎi's past, present and future.
- *In Search of Old Shanghai*, Pan Ling. A rundown on who was who and what was what back in the bad-old days. At 140 pages, it's an easy read and an excellent introduction to the city's murky past.
- *Secret War in Shanghai*, Bernard Wasserstein. A denser, sometimes heavy-going look at 'treachery, subversion and collaboration in the Second World War'. The real joy of the book is its fascinating cast of characters, such as 'abortionist, brothel-owner and sexual extortionist' Dr Albert Miorini; 'monkey expert, narcotics dealer and friend of Errol Flynn' Hermann Erben; the British gunrunner General 'One-Arm' Sutton; and 'journalist, aviator and pimp' Hilaire du Berrier.
- *Shanghai*, Harriet Sergeant. A portrait of the city in its heyday, efficiently combining first-hand accounts with extensive spade work and lively reconstruction.
- *Shanghai: Crucible of Modern China*, Betty Peh-T'i Wei. This is a more detailed history of the city until 1943. *Old Shanghai*, by the same author, is a shorter, easier read.
- *Shanghai: The Rise and Fall of a Decadent City 1842–1949*, Stella Dong. Thoroughly researched, rip-roaring profile of the city's good-old bad-old days, but Dong's fondness for transcribing Chinese in old-fashioned Wade-Giles Romanisation over Pinyin transliteration can be a drag.
- *Through the Looking Glass: China's Foreign Journalists from Opium Wars to Mao*, Paul French. An unusual look at China from the 1820s to 1949 as seen through the eyes of foreign correspondents of the time. Includes much material on many of Shànghǎi's larger-than-life characters.

Gradually sedan chairs and single-wheeled carts gave way to rickshaws and carriages, the former imported from Japan in 1874. Shànghǎi lurched into the modern age with gaslights (1865), electricity (1882), motorcars (1895), a cinema and an electric tram (1908), and its first bus (1922).

The Manchu in Běijīng gave only cursory glances to the growth of Shànghǎi as all eyes focused on the continued survival of the Qing dynasty, under threat from a barrage of insurgencies that arose from within the rapidly radicalising confines of the Middle Kingdom.

THE REBELLIOUS YOUTH

Wreathed in opium, sucked dry by local militia, crippled by taxes, bullied by foreign interests and increasingly exposed to Western ideas, Shànghǎi's population was stirring, and anti-Manchu rebellions began to erupt. The first major rebellion to impact on Shànghǎi was the Taiping (太平 – literally 'Supreme Peace'), led by the Hakka visionary Hong Xiuquan. The uprising, which led to 20 million deaths, goes down as the bloodiest in human history.

Hong claimed to have ascended to heaven and received a new set of internal organs by a golden-bearded Jehovah, which he used to battle the evil spirits of the world with his elder brother Jesus Christ. Hong's distorted Christian ideology dates from his contact with Christian missionaries in Canton and an identification of his surname (洪; Hóng, meaning 'flood') with the Old Testament deluge. Sensing himself chosen, Hong saw the Manchu as devils to be exterminated and set about recruiting converts to establish a Heavenly Kingdom in China. The rebels burst out of Jīntián

1839	1842	1849
Tensions between England and China come to a head when British merchants are arrested and forced to watch three million pounds of raw opium being flushed out to sea. Merchants begin demanding compensation from the British government.	On 29 August Sir Henry Pottinger signs the Treaty of Nanking aboard the *Cornwallis* on the Yangtze River, prising open China's doors and securing Hong Kong.	The French establish their own settlement, known as the French Concession, to the south of the British Concession and beyond the walls of the Chinese Old Town.

SHANGHAIED

If New York was so good they named it twice, then Shànghǎi was so bad they made it an undesirable verb. To shanghai, or 'render insensible by drugs or opium, and ship on a vessel wanting hands', dates from the habit of press-ganging sailors. Men, many of whom were found drunk in 'Blood Alley' (off modern-day Jinling Rd), were forced onto ships, which then set sail, leaving the comatose sailors no choice but to make up the deficient crew numbers when they sobered up.

village in Guǎngxī (广西) in 1851, swept through Guìzhōu (贵州) and succeeded in taking Nánjīng (南京) three years later, where they established their Heavenly Capital (天京; Tiānjīng).

With the Taiping-inspired Small Swords Society entrenched in the Old Town and fearing the seizure of Shànghǎi, the foreign residents organised the Shanghai Volunteer Corps, a force that would repeatedly protect the interests of foreigners in Shànghǎi.

The Taiping threatened again in 1860 but were beaten back from Shànghǎi by the mercenary armies of Frederick Townsend Ward, an American adventurer hired by the Qing government who was eventually killed in Sōngjiāng in 1862. British and Qing forces joined to defeat the rebels, the Europeans preferring to deal with a corrupt and weak Qing government than with a powerful, united China governed by the Taiping. The Taiping originally banked on the support of the Western powers, but Westerners were ultimately repelled by Hong's heretical concoction.

As rebellions ravaged the countryside, hundreds of thousands of refugees poured into the safety of Shànghǎi's concessions, setting up home alongside the foreigners and sparking a real-estate boom (p49) that spurred on Shànghǎi's rapid urbanisation and made the fortunes of many of Shànghǎi's entrepreneurs.

As imperial control loosened, the encroaching Western powers moved in to pick off China's colonial 'possessions' in Indochina and Korea. National humiliation and a growing xenophobia – partly generated by a distrust of Christian missionaries and their activities – spawned the anti-Western Boxer Rebellion, championed in its later stages by the empress dowager, Cixi.

The Boxers were quelled by Western and Japanese troops – who went on to sack Běijīng's Summer Palace – in 1900, but not before the legation quarter in the capital had been devastated. Empress Cixi and her entourage fled to Xī'ān (西安), but returned to Běijīng to face massive indemnities strapped onto the Qing government by the foreign powers.

The weakened state of the country, the death of the empress dowager and the legion of conspiring secret societies marked the end of the tottering Qing dynasty. Shànghǎi renounced the Qing by declaring independence on the wave of public revolt that swept China in 1911, and all men were instructed to shear off their *queues* (long pigtails that symbolised subjection to Manchu authority). But despite the momentous end to China's final dynasty – one that had ruled China for almost 250 years – insular Shànghǎi carried out business as usual, relatively unaffected by the fall of the Qing or the upheavals of WWI. As the rest of China descended into a bedlam of fighting warlords and plunged into darkness, Shànghǎi emerged as a modern industrial city.

'PARIS OF THE EAST' REACHES ITS PEAK

By the first decade of the 20th century, Shànghǎi's population had swelled to one million. As the most elite and cosmopolitan of China's cities, Shànghǎi ensnared capitalists and intellectuals alike, with literature and cinema thriving in the ferment as Chinese intellectuals began to ponder the fate of a modern China.

1859	1860s	1882
By now virtually half of all British troops stationed in Shànghǎi suffer from venereal disease. The diseases are introduced to Shànghǎi by Westerners and disseminated by the city's rampant prostitution industry.	Cotton emerges as Shànghǎi's chief export.	Shànghǎi's first large beauty pageant for prostitutes is held. The pageant is held every year until 1930.

The foreigners had effectively plucked out prime locations and, using their ever-increasing wealth, the result of cheap labour, they established exclusive communities designed after their own countries and dovetailing with their needs. Vice and crime continued to flourish, assisted by the absence of a paramount police force. The multiple jurisdictions, each representing the laws of the various settlements and the Chinese city, meant that criminals could simply move from one area to another to elude arrest.

Exploited in workhouse conditions, crippled by hunger and poverty, sold into slavery and excluded from the city's high life created by the foreigners, the poor of Shànghǎi developed an appetite for resistance. Intellectuals and students, provoked by the startling inequalities between rich and poor, were perfect receptacles for the many outside influences circulating in the concessions. The communist manifesto was translated into Chinese and swiftly caught on among secret societies.

In light of the intense dislike that many Chinese felt for foreigners, it seems ironic that fundamental ideals stemmed from overseas inspirations. Shànghǎi, with its vast proletariat (30,000 textile workers alone) and student population, had become the communists' hope for revolution, and the first meeting of the Chinese Communist Party, when Mao Zedong was present, was held in July 1921 in a French Concession house (p91). Elsewhere political violence was growing.

In May 1925 resentment spilled over when a Chinese worker was killed in a clash with a Japanese mill manager. In the ensuing demonstrations the British opened fire and 12 Chinese were killed. In protest, 150,000 workers went on strike, which was later seen as a defining moment marking the decline of Western prestige and power.

Strikes and a curfew paralysed the city as the Kuomintang under Chiang Kaishek (with the help of communist supporters under Zhou Enlai) wrested Shànghǎi from the Chinese warlord Sun Chaofang.

Kaishek's aim was not focused on the settlements or even the warlords, but rather his erstwhile allies, the communists, whom he then betrayed in an act of breathtaking perfidy. Backed by Shànghǎi bankers and armed by Shànghǎi's top gangster Du Yuesheng (see boxed text, p28), Chiang Kaishek armed gangsters, suited them up in Kuomintang uniforms and launched a surprise attack on the striking workers' militia. Du's machine guns were turned on 100,000 workers taking to the streets, killing as many as 5000. In the ensuing period, known as the White Terror, 12,000 communists were executed in three weeks. Zhou Enlai and other communists fled to Wǔhàn (武汉), leaving Shànghǎi in the hands of the warlords, the wealthy and the Kuomintang.

Nestled away safely in a world of selectively structured law and cruel capitalism, by the 1930s Shànghǎi had reached its economic zenith and was soon to begin its fatal downwards slide. Shànghǎi had become a modern city equipped with art-deco cinemas and apartment blocks, the hottest bands and the latest fashions – a place of great energy where 'two cultures met and neither prevailed'. Chinese magazines carried ads for Quaker Oats, Colgate and Kodak, while Chinese girls, dressed in traditional qípáo (Chinese-style dresses), advertised American cigarettes. Shànghǎi's modernity was symbolised by the Bund, Shànghǎi's Wall Street, a place of feverish trading and an unabashed playground for Western business sophisticates. To this day the strip alongside the Huangpu River remains the city's most eloquent reminder that modern Shànghǎi is a very foreign invention.

1882	1912	1921
Shànghǎi – and China – is electrified for the very first time by the British-founded Shanghai Electric Company. Shànghǎi's first electricity-producing plant generates 654kw and the Bund is illuminated by electric lights the following year.	Republicans pull down Shànghǎi's ancient city walls to break links with the ousted Qing dynasty. Representatives from 17 provinces gather in Nánjīng to establish the Provisional Republican Government of China with Sun Yatsen as president.	The first meeting of the Chinese Communist Party (CCP), formed by Marxist groups advised by the Soviet Comintern, takes place in Shànghǎi.

SHÀNGHǍI'S RUSSIANS

In the 1920s and '30s, as China's youth looked to revolutionary Russia for their future, 25,000 White Russians fled for their lives, travelling first to Siberia or Central Asia and then along the railroads to China. Many congregated in Manchuria before being pushed on to Shànghǎi by the Sino-Japanese War. By 1935 they formed the city's second-largest foreign community after the Japanese.

The refugees scraped the highest rungs of Tsarist society, from generals and aristocrats to poets and princesses, but all had to find a way to survive. The wealthy sold off their jewellery piece by piece. Moscow's musicians played in Shànghǎi's hotel bands, and ballerinas from St Petersburg quickly learned how to charge by the dance. The men took whatever jobs they could find: as riding instructors or, more commonly, bodyguards, guarding the wealthy against rival gangs and kidnapping.

Ave Joffre (Huaihai Rd) became the heart of the White Russian community, and was lined with Cyrillic signs and cafes serving Shànghǎi borscht, blini and black bread. There were Russian cinemas, printing presses and even rival revolutionary and Tsarist newspapers. White Russians kept the Russian diplomats on their toes with their regular attempts to storm the Bolshevik Russian embassy, just north of the Bund.

Yet beneath the glamour was deep despair and poverty. White Russians were stateless and so, unlike other foreigners in Shànghǎi, were subject to Chinese laws and prisons. Those without money or skills took the city's lowest jobs, or resorted to begging for alms from the Chinese. Others became prostitutes or ended up as drunks lying on street corners. The British looked down on the Russians, believing they 'lowered the tone', but used the men ('real tough nuts') in the Volunteer Corps.

In 1949 the Russians were forced to flee their second communist revolution in 22 years. There are few signs of Mother Russia in Shànghǎi these days, save for the original Russian embassy, the French Concession's attractive Russian Orthodox Mission Church (p94), and the odd Russian cabaret act flirting with the ghosts of the past.

The 'Paris of the East' and 'Whore of the Orient' became an increasingly exotic port of call. Flush with foreign cash and requiring neither visa nor passport for entrance, Shànghǎi became home to the movers and the shakers, the down-and-out and on-the-run. It offered a place of refuge and a fresh start and rejected no one. Everyone who came to Shànghǎi, it was said, had something to hide.

By 1934 the world's fifth-largest city was home to the tallest buildings in Asia, boasting more cars in one city than the rest of China put together, and providing a haven for more than 70,000 foreigners among a population of three million. The city had become three times as crowded as London, and the cosmopolitan mix of people was unequalled anywhere in the world. Between 1931 and 1941, 20,000 Jews took refuge in Shànghǎi, only to be forced into Japanese war ghettos, and to flee again in 1949. Adding to the mix was a huge influx of Russians seeking sanctuary from the Bolshevik Revolution of 1917. In 1895 the Japanese had gained treaty rights and by 1915 had become Shànghǎi's largest non-Chinese group, turning Hóngkǒu into a de-facto Japanese Concession.

THE DEATH OF OLD SHÀNGHǍI

Following Japan's invasion of Manchuria in 1931, with anti-Japanese sentiment inflamed and Chinese nationalistic fervour on the rise, the Japanese seized the opportunity to protect their interests. Warships brought in tens of thousands of Japanese troops, who proceeded to take on

1927	1930s	1930s
Chiang Kaishek takes control of Shànghǎi in March, an event soon followed by his 'White Terror', a brutal slaughter of communists, left-wing sympathisers and labour leaders, also known as the 'Shànghǎi Massacre'.	Blood Alley – a sordid domain of whorehouses, seedy bars and all-night vice in the Bund area – is the destination of choice for drunken sailors on shore leave.	Cosmopolitan Shànghǎi is the world's fifth-largest city (the largest in the Far East), supporting a population of four million. Opium use declines as it goes out of fashion, partly dislodged by growing cigarette consumption.

and defeat the Chinese 19th Route army in Zhábĕi (闸北). The Japanese conducted an aerial-bombing campaign against the district, levelling most of its buildings.

After Japan's full-scale invasion of China in 1937, Chiang Kaishek took a rare stand in Shànghǎi and the city bled for it. The Japanese lost 40,000 men, the Chinese anywhere from 100,000 to 250,000.

The International Settlements were not immune to the fighting, and after Chinese aircraft accidentally bombed the Bund and Nanjing Rd, most foreign residents reacted not by fighting, as perhaps they would have done for a colony, but by evacuation. Four million Chinese refugees were not so lucky.

After intense house-to-house fighting, the Japanese invaders finally subdued Shànghǎi in November, allowing their soldiers to proceed to Sūzhōu before advancing on Nánjīng for their infamous occupation of the city. Under Japanese rule the easy glamour of Shànghǎi's heyday was replaced by a dark cloud of political assassinations, abductions, gunrunning and fear. Espionage by the Japanese, the nationalists, the British and the Americans for wartime information was rife. The rich were abducted and fleeced. Japanese racketeers set up opium halls in the so-called Badlands in the western outskirts of the city, and violent gangs ran rabid.

By December 1941 the hostilities between Japan and the allied powers had intensified abroad, giving the Japanese incentive to take over the foreign settlements in Shànghǎi. Suspect foreigners were taken off for interrogation and torture in notorious prisons such as the Bridgehouse, where JB Powell, editor of the *China Weekly Review*, lost all 10 toes to gangrene. Prisoners were forced to sit for hours in the cold, with heads lowered, facing Tokyo.

The British and American troops had abandoned Shànghǎi in 1942 to concentrate their energies elsewhere, and the British and American governments, unable to overtake the Japanese, signed over their rights of the foreign settlements to Chiang Kaishek in Chóngqìng in 1943, bringing to a close a century of foreign influence.

After the Japanese surrender in 1945, a few foreigners, released from their internment, tried to sweep out their Tudor homes and carry on as before, but priorities and politics had shifted. The gangs, con men, dignitaries, merchants, and anyone who could, had already made their escape to Hong Kong. Those who remained had to cope with biting inflation of 1100%.

By 1948 the Kuomintang was on the edge of defeat in their civil war with the communists, and hundreds of thousands of Kuomintang troops joined sides with Mao Zedong's forces. In May, Chen Yi led the Red Army troops into Shànghǎi, and by October all the major cities in southern China had fallen to the communists.

In Bĕijīng on 1 October 1949, Mao Zedong stood atop the Gate of Heavenly Peace, announced that the Chinese people had stood up, and proclaimed the foundation of the People's Republic of China (PRC). Chiang Kaishek then fled to the island of Formosa (Taiwan), taking with him what was left of his air force and navy, to set up the Republic of China (ROC), naming his new capital Taipei (台北, Táibĕi).

THE PEOPLE'S REPUBLIC

The birth of the PRC marked the end of 105 years of 'the paradise for adventurers'. The PRC dried up 200,000 opium addicts, shut down Shànghǎi's infamous brothels and 're-educated' 30,000 prostitutes, eradicated the slums, slowed inflation and eliminated child labour – no easy task. The state took over Shànghǎi's faltering businesses, the racecourse became the obligatory People's Park (p75), and Shànghǎi fell uniformly into step with the rest of China. Under Bĕijīng's stern hand, the decadence disappeared and the splendour similarly faded.

1931	1935	1937
In September the Japanese invade Manchuria and extend control over the entire area by December. Shànghǎi's Chinese react with a boycott of Japanese goods, and a Japanese monk is killed.	By now 25,000 White Russians have flocked to Shànghǎi, turning the French Concession into Little Moscow.	In an event known as Bloody Saturday, bombs fall on the foreign concessions for the first time on 14 August, killing more than 2000 in separate explosions at the Cathay Hotel, the Palace Hotel and Nanjing Rd.

GREEN GANG GANGSTERS

In Shànghǎi's climate of hedonist freedoms, political ambiguities and capitalist free-for-all, it was perhaps inevitable that Shànghǎi should spawn China's most powerful mobsters. Ironically, in 1930s Shànghǎi the most binding laws were those of the underworld, with their blood oaths, secret signals and strict code of honour. China's modern-day triads and Snakeheads owe much of their form to their Shanghainese predecessors.

One of Shànghǎi's early gangsters was Huang Jinrong, or 'Pockmarked' Huang, who had the enviable position of being the most powerful gangster in Shànghǎi, while at the same time holding the highest rank in the French Concession police force. Now sadly closed, Great World (大世界; Dà Shìjiè) opened in 1917 as a place for acrobats and nightclub stars to rival the existing New World building on Nanjing Rd. It soon became a centre for the bizarre and the burlesque under the seedy control of Huang Jinrong in the 1930s before being commandeered as a refugee centre during World War II.

Another famous underworld figure was Cassia Ma, the Night Soil Queen, who founded a huge empire on the collection of human waste, which was ferried upriver to be sold as fertiliser at a large profit.

The real godfather of the Shànghǎi underworld, however, was Du Yuesheng, or 'Big-Eared' Du as he was known to anyone brave enough to say it to his face. Born in Pǔdōng, Du soon moved across the river and was recruited into the Green Gang (青帮; Qīngbāng), where he worked for Huang. He gained fame by setting up an early opium cartel with the rival Red Gang, and rose through the ranks. By 1927 Du was the head of the Green Gang and in control of the city's prostitution, drug running, protection and labour rackets. Du's special genius was to kidnap the rich and then to negotiate their release, taking half of the ransom money as commission. With an estimated 20,000 men at his beck and call, Du travelled everywhere in a bullet-proof sedan, like a Chinese Al Capone, protected by armed bodyguards crouched on the running boards.

His control of the labour rackets led to contacts with warlords and politicians. In 1927 Du played a major part in Chiang Kaishek's anticommunist massacre and later became adviser to the Kuomintang. A fervent nationalist, his money supplied the anti-Japanese resistance movement.

Yet Du always seemed to crave respectability. In 1931 he was elected to the Municipal Council and was known for years as the unofficial mayor of Shànghǎi. He became a Christian halfway through his life and somehow ended up best known as a philanthropist. When the British poet WH Auden visited Shànghǎi in 1937, Du was head of the Chinese Red Cross!

During the Japanese occupation of Shànghǎi, Du fled to the city of Chóngqìng (Chungking). After the war he settled in Hong Kong, where he died, a multimillionaire, in 1951.

These days you can stay in Du's former Shànghǎi pad, now the Donghu Hotel (p209), or in the building once used as offices by him and Huang, now the exquisite Mansion Hotel (p207). Alternatively seek out Du's one-time summer retreat in Mògānshān (p238), now a Radisson hotel.

Yet the communists, essentially a peasant regime, remained suspicious of Shànghǎi. The group lacked the experience necessary to run a big city and they resented Shànghǎi's former leadership, which they always regarded as a den of foreign imperialist-inspired iniquity, a constant reminder of national humiliation and the former headquarters of the Kuomintang.

Perhaps because of this, Shànghǎi, in its determination to prove communist loyalty, became a hotbed of political extremism and played a major role in the Cultural Revolution, the decade of political turmoil that lasted from 1966 to 1976 (although its most ferocious period ended in 1969). Sidelined in Běijīng, it was to Shànghǎi that Mao turned in an attempt to reinvigorate the revolution and claw his way back into power. For most of a decade the city was the power base of the prime movers of the Cultural Revolution, the Gang of Four: Wang Hongwen; Yao Wenyuan (editor of *Shanghai Liberation Army Daily*); Zhang Chunqiao (Shànghǎi's Director of Propaganda); and Jiang Qing, wife of Mao (and failed Shànghǎi movie actress

1938	1943	1945
Twenty thousand Jews arrive in Shànghǎi, fleeing persecution in Europe.	The Japanese round up 7600 allied nationals into eight internment camps as the formal foreign presence in Shànghǎi ends.	Following the Japanese surrender, the Kuomintang takes back Shànghǎi, fusing the International Settlement and French Concession and the rest of Shànghǎi into the Nationalist Administration, closing treaty ports and revoking foreign trading and self-governing rights.

formerly known as Lan Ping, who used her position to exact revenge on former colleagues at Shànghǎi Film Studios).

Encouraged by Mao, a rally of one million Red Guards marched through People's Square, a force of anarchy that resulted in the ousting of the mayor. Competing Red Guards tried to outdo each other in revolutionary fervour – Shanghainese who had any contacts with foreigners (and who didn't?) were criticised, forced to wear dunce caps, denounced and sometimes killed.

Most extraordinarily, in 1966 a People's Commune, modelled on the Paris Commune of the 19th century, was set up in Shànghǎi. (The Paris Commune was set up in 1871 and controlled Paris for two months. It planned to introduce socialist reforms such as turning over management of factories to workers' associations.) The Shanghai commune, headed by Zhang Chunqiao from headquarters in the Peace Hotel, lasted just three weeks before Mao, sensing that the anarchy had gone too far, ordered the army to put an end to it.

As the Cultural Revolution unfolded, between 1966 and 1970, one million of Shànghǎi's youth were sent to the countryside. Shànghǎi's industries closed, the Bund was renamed Revolution Blvd and the road opposite the closed Soviet consulate became Anti-Revisionist St. At one point there was even a plan to change the (revolutionary) red of the city's traffic lights to mean 'go'.

In the revolutionary chaos and a bid to destroy the 'four olds' (old customs, old habits, old culture and old thinking), Chinese religion (p34) was devastated. Temples were destroyed or converted to factories, priests were conscripted to make umbrellas, monks were sent to labour in the countryside where they often perished, and believers were prohibited from worship. Posters of Chairman Mao were posted over the doors of the Jing'an Temple (p102) to stop Red Guards bursting in, and an image of Mao was even added to the St Nicholas Church (p92) on Gaolan Rd. Amid all the chaos, Shànghǎi's concession architecture stood largely preserved, their wealthy occupants merely fading memories of a vanished era.

In 1976, after the death of Mao, the Gang of Four was overthrown and imprisoned. Accused of everything from forging Mao's statements to hindering earthquake relief efforts, the gang's members were arrested on 6 October 1976 and tried in 1980. Jiang Qing remained unrepentant, hurling abuse at her judges and holding famously to the line that she 'was Chairman Mao's dog – whoever he told me to bite, I bit.' Jiang Qing's death sentence was commuted and she lived under house arrest until 1991, when she committed suicide by hanging.

When the Cultural Revolution lost steam, pragmatists such as Zhou Enlai began to look for ways to restore normalcy. In 1972 US president Richard Nixon signed the Shanghai Communiqué at the Jinjiang Hotel. The agreement provided a foundation for increased trade between the US and China, and marked a turning point in China's foreign relations. With the doors of China finally reopened to the West in 1979, and with Deng Xiaoping at the helm, China set a course of pragmatic reforms towards economic reconstruction, which would result in consistently strong annual growth rates.

In communist China, however, the rush of economic reform generated very little in the way of political reform. Corruption and inflation led to widespread social unrest, which in 1989 resulted in the bloody demonstrations in Běijīng's Tiananmen Square.

The demonstrations overtaking the capital spread to Shànghǎi. In the days leading up to 4 June tens of thousands of students – holding banners demanding, among other things, democracy and freedom – marched from their respective universities to People's Square. Hundreds went on hunger strike. Workers joined students to bring chaos to the city by instigating road blocks across more than 100 Shànghǎi streets. But city mayor Zhu Rongji was praised for his

1949	1966	1972
Hyperinflation means that one US dollar is worth 23,280,000 *yuán*. Communist forces take Shànghǎi and the establishment of the People's Republic of China is proclaimed by a triumphant Mao Zedong.	The Cultural Revolution is launched from Shànghǎi; eventually one million Shanghainese are sent to the countryside. St Ignatius Church finds new employment as a grain store while Jing'an Temple becomes a plastics factory.	President Nixon visits Shànghǎi, as China rejoins the world.

handling of events. In stark contrast to leaders in Běijīng, he decided not to take a heavy-handed approach. 'The municipal government was careful: The rallies continued. Police disappeared from the streets, and no tanks came. The city government sent a message by doing nothing.' (*Unstately Power,* Lynn T White, 1999). According to White, the only serious incident during all the unrest was on 6 June when a train outside Shanghai Station ran into demonstrators who were trying to block it. Eight people were killed and 30 were injured.

THE RECENT PAST

Speeding on cruise control along a highway of its own making, Shànghǎi has in recent years effortlessly outstripped every other city in China, bar celebrated rival Hong Kong. Popping Shànghǎi into any conversation abroad prompts a flood of superlatives, agitated adjectives and breathless hyperbole. Reading the international papers, Shànghǎi can do no wrong. Wherever you look, the smart money is flooding into Shànghǎi, to help it pen the next chapter in the city's dazzling chronicle.

The government has declared its aim to make Shànghǎi the financial centre of Asia. Nothing would satisfy the central government more than for Shànghǎi to replace Hong Kong as China's frontier of the future, swinging the spotlight of attention from the ex-colony on to a home-grown success story. The Shànghǎi Chinese love to compare themselves with Hong Kong; the Huangpu River city is still several years behind its southern rival but is catching up at breathtaking speed.

In 1990 the central government began pouring money into Shànghǎi. By the mid-1990s more than a quarter (some sources say half) of the world's high-rise cranes were wheeling over Shànghǎi. As the 20th century drew to a close, the city had built two metro lines, a lightrailway system, a US$2 billion international airport in Pǔdōng, a US$2 billion elevated highway, several convention centres, two giant bridges, several underground tunnels and a whole new city (Pǔdōng).

Served by two airports and the world's first MagLev train – designed to sum up Shànghǎi as an ultramodern path-breaker – Shànghǎi's denizens now command some of the highest salaries in China. Runaway property prices have furnished a new class with money to burn, despite a nationwide property tax launched in 2005 to hit speculators. Swelling numbers of residents now dwell in gated villa communities, rewarding a life of hard graft with an enviably middle-class standard of living.

Having grown faster than virtually any other Chinese city in the past two decades, Shànghǎi remains the pot of gold at the end of the rainbow for China's swarming migrant workers, who now constitute almost four million of the city's total population of 19 million.

In recent years, a gradual Disneyfication of Shànghǎi has also crept in. The almost-too-perfect Xīntiāndì (p90) is like a fancy epitaph to the city's once ubiquitous, rough-around-the-edges *shíkùmén* (stone-gate house; p49). Skyscraper-filled Pǔdōng, meanwhile, will always look like what developers thought Shànghǎi *should* look like.

The winds of change have long billowed down Nanjing Rd. For all its economic triumphs and the eager speculation of the past decade Shànghǎi is not immune to the historical forces that buffet modern China. Visitors like to see Shànghǎi as a fledgling Singapore or even a Hong Kong, a city-state construct somehow doing its own thing. The future of Shànghǎi, however, is closely enmeshed with nationwide trends way beyond its control. Shànghǎi is rich, but this has been of little consolation to the land's 750-million-strong peasantry. With a population of 39 million, Guìzhōu province in China's southwest has a GDP a mere one ninth of Shànghǎi's.

1976	1989	1990
Mao Zedong dies in September – the same year as the Tángshān earthquake – preparing the way for a rehabilitated Deng Xiaoping to assume leadership of the PRC.	Antigovernment demonstrations in Shànghǎi's People's Square mirror similar protests in Běijīng's Tiananmen Square; the demonstrations are broken up and the brief Beijing Spring comes to an end.	Vegetable-growing Pǔdōng discovers it will become a Special Economic Zone (SEZ). The decade continues to throw money and construction cranes at the district, converting it from flat farmland into one of the world's most ultramodern urban landscapes.

SHÀNGHǍI VICE

Underneath the glitz and glamour of 1930s Shànghǎi lay a pool of sweat, blood and crushing poverty. In the words of a British resident, Shànghǎi was violent, disreputable, snobbish, mercenary and corrupt – 'a discredit to all concerned'. 'If God allows Shànghǎi to endure', said the missionaries, 'He will owe Sodom and Gomorrah an apology.' Others agreed: 'Shànghǎi is a city of 48-storey skyscrapers built upon 24 layers of hell,' wrote Chinese author Xia Yan.

The city was often a place of horrific cruelty and brutal violence. After the Small Swords Rebellion, 66 heads, even those of elderly women and children, were stuck up on the city walls. In 1927 striking workers were beheaded and their heads put in cages. Up to 80,000 rickshaw pullers worked the littered streets until they dropped, while overcrowded factory workers routinely died of lead and mercury poisoning. In 1934 life expectancy of the Chinese in Shànghǎi stood at 27. In 1937 municipal refuse workers picked up 20,000 corpses off the streets.

Shànghǎi offered the purely synthetic pleasures of civilisation. Prostitution ran the gamut from the high-class escorts in the clubs of the International Settlement and 'flowers' of the Fuzhou Rd teahouses, to the *yějī*, or 'wild chickens', of Hóngkǒu, who prowled the streets and back alleys. The 'saltwater sisters' from Guǎngdōng specialised in foreigners fresh off the boats. Lowest of the low were the 'nail sheds' of Zhapei, so called because their services were meant to be as fast as driving nails. Lists of the city's 100 top-ranking prostitutes were drawn up annually and listed next to the names of 668 brothels, which went by such names as the 'Alley of Concentrated Happiness'.

Prostitution was not the exclusive domain of the Chinese. The traditional roles were reversed when White Russians turned to prostitution and Chinese men could be seen flaunting Western women. An American madam ran Gracie's, the most famous foreign brothel in town, at 52 Jiangsu Rd, in a strip of brothels called 'The Line'.

Linked to prostitution was opium. At the turn of the century Shànghǎi boasted 1500 opium dens (known locally as 'swallows' nests') and 80 shops openly selling opium. Even some hotels, it is said, supplied heroin on room service, 'served on a tray like afternoon tea'. Opium financed the early British trading houses and most of the buildings on the Bund. Later it funded Chinese gangsters, warlord armies and Kuomintang military expeditions. It was true that the police in the French Concession kept a close eye on the drug trade, but only to ensure that they got a reasonable slice of the profits. Not that there was much they could do even if they had wanted to; it was said that a wanted man in 1930s Shànghǎi need only pop into the neighbouring concession to avoid a warrant for his arrest.

The Communist Party has continued to hunt for a system that can protect the underprivileged and impoverished while encouraging those with ambition to realise their dreams.

Perhaps alarmed by Shànghǎi's economic supremacy, Běijīng has made attempts to curb the city's influence. In March 2007 Xi Jinping was chosen as the new Shanghai Communist Party secretary after Chen Liangyu was dismissed from his post on corruption charges and later handed an 18-year prison sentence. The choice of Xi was seen by many as a victory for president Hu Jintao as he replaced an influential member of the Jiang Zemin–allied Shànghǎi clique with an official loyal to his tenure. Xi has since been promoted to vice president of the PRC.

Shànghǎi has been busy recasting itself as a global city, but it still lacks the *bon vivant* romantic allure of Paris, the multicultural vibrancy of London or the creative zest of New York. At times spectacular, Shànghǎi can seem like the latest thing, a city about the here-and-now and a future in the making, but also a work in progress, if not a metropolitan-sized construction site. Shànghǎi's triumphant skyline is certainly something to write home about, but the city's creative flatline and aversion to spontaneity still guarantee that many expats arrive to make money, and move on.

It does not really matter whether Shànghǎi has the biggest or the best, as the city has charted its own successful path – due to its unique history, location and sense of purpose – while other

2004	2008	2010
The world's first commercially operating MagLev train begins scorching across Pǔdōng. Plans to connect Běijīng and Shànghǎi are later put to sleep.	World markets crash, finally slowing down Shànghǎi's previously stratospheric rates of economic growth.	The finishing touches are laid to the massive redevelopment of huge swathes of the city in preparation for hosting World Expo.

TOP SHÀNGHǍI BIOGRAPHIES

- *Captive in Shanghai,* Hugh Collar. This is a fascinating personal account of life in the Japanese internment camps in the early 1940s. It's published by Oxford University Press, but is pretty hard to get your hands on.
- *Daughter of Shanghai,* Tsai Chin. This book has less to say about Shànghǎi but is still a good read. Daughter of one of China's most-famous Běijīng opera stars, Chin left Shànghǎi in 1949 and later starred in the film *The World of Suzie Wong* (as the original 'China doll') and in the *Joy Luck Club*. This memoir bridges two worlds during two different times.
- *Life and Death in Shanghai,* Nien Cheng. A classic account of the Cultural Revolution and one of the few biographies with a Shànghǎi angle.
- *The Life, Loves and Adventures of Emily Hahn,* Ken Cuthbertson. A look at the bizarre life of Emily Hahn, who passed through Shànghǎi in 1935 (accompanied by her pet gibbon, Mr Mills), got hooked on opium and became the concubine of a Chinese poet.
- *Red Azalea,* Anchee Min. A sometimes racy account of growing up in Shànghǎi in the 1950s and 1960s amid the turmoil of the Cultural Revolution.

parts of China have simply looked on. But behind the percentile leaps and glittering statistics are questions about Shànghǎi's ultimate destination. Besides solutions to problems such as transport infrastructure or how to build the world's tallest buildings, perhaps the city should be considering how to become a *true* exemplar for the 21st century? As long as China remains authoritarian and uncompromising in its politics, Shànghǎi will remain a city that can certainly dazzle, but struggles to illuminate.

CULTURE

Like Hong Kong, Shànghǎi maintains a deep underlay of traditional Chinese practices and beliefs beneath its often superficial modern guise. Chinese society is conservative, conformist and resilient to change, despite the simplistic presentation of Shànghǎi as a rapidly Westernising city where designer labels have long been the new face of town. Awareness of this underlying adherence to Chinese tradition – despite one's first impressions of a city enamoured with all things foreign – should be noted by business travellers in particular.

That said, the Shanghainese are less bound to the Chinese traditions of gift giving and elaborate ceremonies, and Shànghǎi weddings are often quite bereft of traditional Chinese practices. According to the Shanghainese, the reason for this pragmatic individualism is that for over 100 years Shànghǎi has been a magnet for refugees and fortune seekers, all forced to look out for themselves in a competitive, tough environment.

Despite this individualism, at the heart of Shànghǎi society is the family, a tight-knit unit that is highly idealised. Confucian in design, the Chinese family follows a hierarchy from father to youngest child, although the structure is less strict and rigid than the South Korea example. The Confucian template is quite loose, but filial obedience – despite the wayward behaviour of the internet generation – is far more marked in Shànghǎi than in the West. The instinctive Chinese impression that they are more a unit rather than a collection of individuals encourages family cohesion and a dampening of rebellious impulses. This helps explain why resistance to the Communist monopoly is so hesitant and ambivalent. In rebellion – whether it's taking on corrupt local officials or staging a demonstration against land confiscation – the Chinese will bide their time until critical mass with fellow sympathisers is achieved.

IDENTITY

Shànghǎi's reputation as a melting pot of East and West gained currency during the century of Western domination of the city from 1841 to 1949, when Shànghǎi was considered a 'foreign adventurer's playground'. Shanghainese nowadays are proud of their cosmopolitan history and culture, but other Chinese sometimes interpret this pride as snobbery, and the dalliance with Western culture as a loss of authentic Chinese values.

To the Shanghainese, however, other Chinese are at best *wàidìrén* (外地人; outlanders), at worst *tǔbāozi* (土包子; country bumpkins). On the other hand, Shànghǎi people of all ages generally welcome foreigners, especially Westerners, to the city, and the city government has set a goal of 5% foreign residents in order to become an 'international city'.

As ever in China, language (p36) plays a supreme role in forging an exclusive identity, and the Shànghǎi dialect traditionally created a deep common bond between locals, especially in the face of large influxes of immigrants coming to the city to work. Some suggest this may be slowly changing, however, as standard Mandarin, now used in Shànghǎi schools, tightens its grip (see the boxed text, p37).

Chinese people from other parts of China describe the people of Shànghǎi as pragmatic and stingy. Observing those very same traits that others see in them, the Shanghainese describe themselves as modern and individualistic. Going Dutch on a meal in Běijīng may be unheard of, but in Shànghǎi it is far from taboo – this is one of the few cities in China where most people would rather split the bill at a restaurant than fight for the honour of paying for the entire party.

Shànghǎi society also has its own set of internal divisions and stereotypes. The leafy west end of Shànghǎi, once home to rich foreigners and Chinese tycoons, is still known as Shànghǎi's 'high corner'. The industrial northeast, outside the boundaries of the old foreign concessions, is the 'low corner'. Low-corner Shànghǎi also became home to most of Shànghǎi's poor migrants from the north of the Jiāngsū province, who filled many of the dirty and dangerous trades in prerevolutionary days. Their descendants maintain a distinctive dialect, as well as their own cultural identity. Newer divisions in Shànghǎi are overtaking these old ones, however. 'White-collar' professionals with foreign MBAs are the new elite, sipping cocktails at chic retro bars, while working-class Shanghainese can only afford to stroll past and watch.

Local affiliations aside, as Han Chinese (汉族; Hànzú), the Shanghainese share in the myths and legends associated with their folk. The Shanghainese may consider themselves superior to the Chinese of Běijīng or Hong Kong, but at heart they remain Han Chinese.

CULTURAL HINTS & TIPS

Shànghǎi, like China before it, is not much of a meritocracy: those with *guānxì* (关系; connections) call the shots. Businesspeople invest endless hours in cultivating and massaging (networking) their *guānxì*, normally through business dinners, gift-giving and banqueting. Intractable proposals can suddenly get the green light when discussed over a plate of abalone, a bottle of whisky and a carton of cigarettes.

It helps to understand 'face'. Face can be loosely described as status, ego or self-respect, and is by no means alien to foreigners. Losing face (丢面子; *diūmiànzi*) is about making someone look stupid or being forced to back down in front of others, and you should take care to avoid it. In the West it's important; in China, it's critical. Circumvent a problem with smiling persistence rather than tackling it straight on, and always give your adversary a way out. Avoid direct criticisms of people. Venting your rage in public and trying to make someone lose face will cause the Chinese to dig in their heels and only worsen your situation. Business travellers should take note here as success can hinge on this issue. Don't lose sight of your own 'face' however – things should be reciprocal.

Linked to face are displays of respect and politeness (礼貌; *lǐmào*). Always offer gifts, cigarettes and food several times, and expect them to be refused several times before finally being accepted. It's good to refer to elders with the appellation *lǎo*, which means 'old'; for example, *lǎo* Wang means Old Mr Wang (remember that Chinese put their surnames first, thus Wang Zenghao is Mr Wang). You may find the old classic; 'My English is no good,' – 'No, it is very good,' – 'No, my English is no good,' repeated ad nauseam. Chinese convey respect by handing over business cards with the thumb and first finger of both hands. Another way of showing respect to prospective partners is to show them to the door of your office and even the entry of your building when they leave. They will probably say '*bié sòng wǒ le,*' (don't see me off), but you should insist.

High-density levels and a high tolerance for crowding mean that personal space is generally not a highly valued commodity in Shànghǎi. No one is ever going to get a lot of personal space in a country of 1.3 billion people, but the reasons for this are as much cultural as they are physical. Chinese rarely have that sacrosanct 30cm halo of private space around them that foreigners expect. For example, don't expect someone to walk out of your path if you are headed on a collision course. And when you are standing right in front of a museum exhibit or notice board don't be surprised if someone squeezes into the space between you and the plate glass, blocking out your view. Car drivers refuse to give way, so standoffs become a sheer battle of wills.

Whether it's an evening meal out or a day at the park, the Chinese have a preference for things being '*rènao*' (literally 'hot and noisy') or lively. This helps explain the penchant for cacophonous banquets and top-volume karaoke sessions. The Shànghǎi Chinese also put ostentatiousness high on the list. All of this helps explain why Chinese restaurants are often such large, bright, brash and deeply unromantic places.

EDUCATION

As a result of China's Confucian heritage, the teacher is venerated and obediently respected by pupils. The reverence of teachers creates a sense of efficient order and harmony in the classroom and encourages academic excellence in Shànghǎi and other cities across China (and abroad).

China never quite shrugged off its love-hate affair with the cripplingly hard imperial examination system, inaugurated in the Tang dynasty, and do-or-die competitiveness among Shànghǎi's scholars continues undiminished. The one-child system has further heaped pressure on Shànghǎi's teeny academic shoulders. Every year, as the *gāokǎo* (university entrance examinations) approaches, hopeful parents flock to the Confucius Temple to light incense in hope of a nod from the sage of sages. At exam time, students and their parents avoid taxis with a 'four' or 'six' in the registration number ('four' throughout China chimes with the word for death, while 'six' in the Shànghǎi dialect resembles the word for 'fall'). A mushrooming pharmaceutical industry steps in to supply expensive brain-boosting drugs to parents anxious to unleash their children's full mental powers.

Education in Shànghǎi is patriotic and is marked by a semiregimented theme, as pupils are drilled in the advantages of uniform behaviour and exacting discipline. Not surprisingly, there are downsides to this culture of conformity. The absence of political debate in Chinese society can be partially traced back to the classroom taboos on questioning the teacher, as children learn to agree with what they are told. Foreign teaching staff in Shànghǎi frequently complain that students are very reluctant to debate either what they read in textbooks or are taught by lecturers. Shànghǎi students excel at absorbing information by rote learning, but are disadvantaged at disputing information or adopting arguments that counter accepted wisdom. Even when encouraged to adopt a contrary stance, a powerful resistance to debate influences students to agree with collective opinion.

Neither is the conformist atmosphere of Shànghǎi schools – and China's schools in general – conducive to thinking out-of-the-box or creative problem solving. The majority of high-school students aim to study economics or business, subjects ideally suited to linear thinking. Creative subjects remain sidelined.

This partly explains why China suffers the world's largest brain drain. A recent study discovered that seven out of 10 Chinese studying in universities overseas fail to return to their homeland for work. Another reason for this reluctance to return is China's one-child policy: Chinese living abroad can have any number of children. A further reason is China's disinclination to being a meritocracy, with career advancement in China still often depending on *guānxì* (connections).

RELIGION

Just over 30 years ago religion was still banned in China, but there are now five officially recognised faiths – Buddhism, Protestant Christian, Catholic Christian, Islam and Taoism.

Figures for numbers of believers are continually disputed, but an unprecedentedly large survey, carried out by Horizon Research Consultancy Group between 2005 and 2007, found that between just 14% and 18% of China's population admitted to being religious. If correct,

DOS & DON'TS

- When receiving a gift, put it aside to open later to avoid appearing greedy.
- Take your shoes off when entering a Chinese person's home.
- When presenting your business card, proffer it with the first finger and thumb of both hands (thumbs on top). Cards should be received in the same manner.
- Don't plunge your chopsticks upright into your rice, but lay them down on your plate or on the chopstick rest.
- When beckoning to someone, wave them over with your palm down, motioning to yourself.
- Always hand your cigarettes around in social situations.
- You rarely see Chinese pecking each other on the cheek when meeting, so try to refrain.
- Don't insist on paying for the dinner or bar bill if your fellow diner appears determined.
- Avoid writing in red ink, unless correcting an exam, as the colour is used for letters of protest and conveys unfriendliness.

LOCAL VOICES: WE'RE MORE REFINED THAN BEIJINGERS

Born and bred in Shànghǎi, 21-year-old Chen Feng spent much of his late teens in Běijīng, training with China's national swimming team, before returning to Shànghǎi in 2008 to pursue a career in international trade.

What do you like most about Shànghǎi? The food. Personally, food is my favourite thing in life.
So, what's your favourite food? Dim sum, of course, and noodles. I also love crab, but my favourite dish is *hóngshāoròu* (红烧肉, braised pork), only I like it cooked so it's *very* sweet, just like my mum cooks it.
Is there anything you don't like about Shànghǎi? Sometimes it's too sophisticated. Too many people here focus on things that are too small – they argue and fight over small things. People are a bit selfish. In the old days many families would share one house and they would argue over something really small like which pot they could use in the kitchen. It's not the same in Běijīng. In Běijīng a stranger might say to you, 'Hey, brother, let's go for a drink.' In Shànghǎi, you don't hear this. People often say, 'It's great to do business with a Shànghǎi person. It's not so great to live next door to one."
So, what are the main differences between Běijīng and Shànghǎi? Běijīng is a great big city, but Shànghǎi is smaller in so many ways. This makes the people more refined here. Look at the food portions: in Shànghǎi they are tiny, in Běijīng, huge. In Shànghǎi, if I go for dinner with a friend we order four or five starters. If you do that in Běijīng you won't be able to eat anything else!
Is Shànghǎi a good city for sports enthusiasts? Of course! Yao Ming (the NBA's tallest basketball player) and Liu Xiang (former 110m hurdles Olympic champion) both come from here. Shànghǎi has some of the best sports facilities in China, and its sports teams often get the best results in the country. It's easy to find places to play any sport here, although I think prices in the centre of Shànghǎi are more expensive than other cities.

this would make China one of the least religiously affiliated countries on earth. In comparison, the figure for the USA is thought to be around 83%.

Buddhism accounts for the vast majority of believers (around 11–16% of the population, according to the survey), with Christianity (2–4%), Islam (around 1%) and Taoism (less than 1%) trailing some distance behind. However, many commentators believe the figures are considerably higher if you include nonregistered groups such as the so-called house churches of Chinese Christians. Figures of around 80 million for Christians alone are sometimes posited, which would equate to about 6% of the population, two or three times the number found by the Horizon survey.

What is generally agreed, however, is that religion, and Christianity in particular, is growing rapidly in China. And Shànghǎi is no exception.

Efforts by the Chinese Communist Party (CCP) to replace religion with its own secular tenets have been undercut by the startling volte-face on its very own credo during the decades of reform since 1979. The yawning gap between rich and poor, and the failure of the Party to protect the destitute and powerless left a spiritual hole that has been increasingly filled by other beliefs that offer salvation. Traditionally belonging to Buddhist, Taoist or Confucian belief systems – and occasionally all three – the Shànghǎi Chinese have not yet abandoned superstition, despite the decades of wrenching modernisation that followed hard on the heels of the heathen Mao era.

By wiping the slate clean, Mao Zedong allowed Christianity – which has had an indecisive presence in China since the 8th century – to flourish in a land of people who suddenly found themselves unsure of what to believe in. Christianity had been banned before, during the Qing dynasty, but following the 1842 Treaty of Nanking, Catholic missionaries were able to re-enter the country at Shànghǎi. French Jesuits built their headquarters on the edge of the city, and soon after built Shànghǎi's first cathedral, a wooden predecessor to St Ignatius (p124) that was completed in 1910. Catholicism – and Christianity in general – grew steadily and by the outbreak of World War I, Chinese Catholics were thought to number more than one million. These days most Shànghǎi Christians are thought to belong to nonregistered house churches, rather than the state-recognised Protestant or Catholic churches, so the precise number of Christians is very difficult to gauge.

Buddhism in Shànghǎi goes way back. The Jing'an Temple, for example, was originally built in AD 247 on a site close to the current temple (p102). There are now dozens of active temples across the city, the premier one being the Jade Buddha Temple (p100), also the headquarters of the Shanghai Institute of Buddhism.

Recent reorganisation of Chinese public holidays saw two more Taoist festivals – Tomb Sweeping Day (p17; 清明节; Qīngmíng Jié) and Dragon Boat Festival (p18; 端午节; Duānwǔ Jié) – added to the public holiday calendar. On these days, and during Spring Festival and Mid-Autumn Festival – Taoism's two other major celebrations – Shànghǎi's 20-odd Taoist temples are particularly lively places to visit. Baiyun Temple (p83), in the Old Town, is the headquarters of the Shanghai Taoist Association.

Shànghǎi's first mosque was built 600 years ago in Sōngjiāng district, 25km west of the city centre, and is still an active place of worship, although most of the Muslim population moved to Shànghǎi proper during the Opium Wars. Today, Shànghǎi's Muslims number around 100,000 and there are six active mosques in the city, Peach Garden Mosque (p83) in the Old Town being the principal one.

Although not one of the four officially recognised religions in China, Judaism has had a fascinating role in the make up of Shànghǎi. Like Christianity, the religion has had a presence in China since around the 8th century, but it wasn't until the 1800s that the first of three distinct waves of Jewish immigrants came to Shànghǎi. Jewish businessmen, such as the hugely influential Sassoons and Kadoories, arrived from West Asia, particularly Baghdad, and soon started financing the building of some of the city's now famous concession architecture. The second wave, fleeing persecution in Russia, arrived in the early 1900s. Most settled in north China, but many fled to Shànghǎi after the Japanese invasion of Manchuria in the 1930s. The third wave came from those fleeing Nazi Germany at a time when Shànghǎi was under Japanese occupation. Numbering 20,000, these stateless refugees were forced to live in the so-called Shànghǎi ghetto, a one-sq-mile area in the very poor district of Hóngkǒu. Conditions were dire, but established Jewish families and Jewish charities abroad contributed to their welfare. This area now houses the Shanghai Jewish Refugees Museum in the recently restored Ohel Moishe Synagogue (p115). Although neither of Shànghǎi's two remaining synagogues are active places of worship, Shànghǎi does have an active Jewish community, numbering around 2,000 people. For more details, visit www.chinajewish.org.

LANGUAGE

Spoken by 13 million people, Shanghainese (Shànghǎihuà in Mandarin) belongs to the Wu dialect, named after the kingdom of Wu in present-day Jiāngsū province. To Mandarin or Cantonese speakers, Shanghainese sounds odd, perhaps because it is a more archaic branch of Chinese. Furthermore, the tonal system of Shanghainese differs considerably from Mandarin and Cantonese, displaying closer similarities to African tonal languages.

TONING DOWN SHÀNGHǍIHUÀ

One hundred years ago, the Shànghǎi dialect was spoken with eight tones, but these days locals in the city proper get by with firing off a mere five. This is no economy measure along the lines of simplified written Chinese: the Shànghǎi dialect (Shànghǎihuà) is enduring a combined assault from the rapid influx of workers from outside town and the increased promotion of the Mandarin (Pǔtōnghuà) dialect. The lingo is under attack and old-timers are in a huff.

Prior to the Communist ascendancy, China was a fragmented linguistic mosaic of dialect areas with no lingua franca to bind the whole together. These dialect areas – such as Shànghǎi – still exist, but Mandarin has been pedalled throughout the land as a utilitarian common tongue. In Shànghǎi – as in the rest of the land – Mandarin is everywhere: it's the official language in schools, TV and radio transmissions and it's the language of choice for locals chatting to out-of-towners.

The Shànghǎi dialect has consequently been adulterated with the slang and pronunciation of Mandarin. Fewer and fewer young Shanghainese are now able to yak away in the pure Shànghǎi dialect. Instead, most youths in Shànghǎi gabble in Shànghǎihuà heavily seasoned with Mandarin pronunciation – much to the horror of the old guard. The most perfectly preserved forms of Shànghǎihuà survive in rural areas around Shànghǎi, where Mandarin has less of a toehold.

Few foreigners who live in Shànghǎi speak the dialect properly, although a much larger number can understand it. The dialect has yet to be properly Romanised – unlike Cantonese – which makes learning an arduous task for outsiders. And with the increasing number of immigrant Chinese from all over China arriving in Shànghǎi and the growing dominance of Mandarin, learning Shànghǎihuà is perhaps for the specialist.

A DYING DIALECT?

Like those from many parts of China, the Shànghǎi people are extremely proud of their own unique take on the Chinese language. Shanghainese is an ancient form of the Wu dialect and is thought to still be spoken by about 14 million people. But it's almost never used outside the region and some residents, particularly the older ones, fear for its future as standard Mandarin tightens its linguistic grip. Less than 10 years ago, it was standard practise for Shànghǎi's students to be taught in Shanghainese. At the same time they would have separate Mandarin classes in much the same way that students in some English-speaking countries might have French classes. These days, however, the roles are reversed, with classes being taught in Mandarin.

Chen Feng, a 21-year-old Shànghǎi resident we spoke with during our latest trip to the city (see boxed text, p35), said, 'We are losing our Shanghainese language. Young children don't speak Shanghainese anymore, only Mandarin. If we don't continue speaking it to our children, it will be lost. My generation only speak Shanghainese together, but I have a cousin who's five and doesn't speak any Shanghainese. If you heard two people my age or older walking down the street talking together in Mandarin it would be weird. But if those two people were children, under 10 years old, it would be weird if they were speaking Shanghainese.'

A marked Japanese sound to the Shànghǎi dialect can also be heard. As the dialect is rarely heard on radio or TV and failed to make the transition to pop songs in the way Cantonese did, Shanghainese has a very small fan base among non-native speakers. With increasing immigration into Shànghǎi by speakers of other dialects, this trend is unlikely to be reversed. Furthermore, because of the growing prevalence of Mandarin and the absence of a standard form of Shanghainese, the dialect is constantly transforming and is quite different from how it was spoken just a few generations ago, while some Shànghǎi residents fear for its future altogether (see boxed text, above). For an introduction to Mandarin, refer to the Language chapter (p270).

ARTS

Despite Shànghǎi's hedonistic and decadent past, the contemporary arts scene is something of an exasperating conundrum. Given its reputation for fashionable excess and flamboyant showiness, an invigorating art world would seal Shànghǎi's copper-bottomed standing as a glamorous destination. Yet a manifest reluctance in Shànghǎi's creative milieu stifles the vital frisson that fires up the world's eminent art capitals. Don't expect to be tripping over street-side performance artists, sidestepping wild-haired poets handing out flyers or clawing change from your pocket for itinerant jazz bands.

Revolutionary credentials aside, Shànghǎi is neither alternative nor left-field; it is predictable in its ambitions and the bespectacled white-collar worker serves as an unlikely urban hero. Like the Chinese intelligentsia, artists attract suspicion among the *lǎobǎixìng* (common people). As the white-hot crucible of China's economic overdrive, Shànghǎi funnels its energies into money-making, realising epic steel and concrete infrastructure projects rather than nurturing bohemian creativity. Abstract musings raise eyebrows, so both artist and dreamer are seen as unfortunate outsiders. Blame it on the one-child policy, the matter-of-fact educational system or the universal Shànghǎi dream to own a Porsche SUV, but Shànghǎi is a lonely city for the creatively inclined. Despite its more authoritarian bent, grittier Běijīng tends to pull in and hang on to China's creative idealists.

But art and prosperity being familiar bedfellows, there is actually no shortage of art galleries in Shànghǎi, as a generation of newly rich local art buyers becomes eager to fill spaces on their walls. If art gazing tops your list of priorities, you'll have plenty to keep you busy. See our Visual Arts section (p39).

LITERATURE

Energised by a vibrant literary scene, Shànghǎi in the 1920s and '30s cast itself as a veritable publishing-industry hub. Sheltered from the censorship of Nationalists and warlords by the foreign settlements, and stimulated by the city's new-fangled modernity and flood of foreign ideas, Shànghǎi hosted a golden era in modern Chinese literature.

RECOMMENDED READING: SHÀNGHĂI FICTION

- *Candy*, Mian Mian. A hip take on modern Shànghăi life, penned by a former heroin addict musing on complicated sexual affairs, suicide and drug addiction in Shēnzhèn and Shànghăi. Applauded for its urban underground tone but sensational more for its framing of postadolescent themes in contemporary China.
- *Death of a Red Heroine*, Qiu Xiaolong. Despite some stilted dialogue, this well-received crime novel offers a street-level view of the social changes engulfing Shànghăi in 1990. It is the first mystery in the Inspector Chen series, which had expanded to six titles in 2009.
- *Empire of the Sun*, JG Ballard. An astonishingly well-written and poignant tale based on the author's internment as a child in a Japanese POW camp in Shànghăi, subsequently made into a film by Steven Spielberg.
- *Master of Rain*, Tom Bradby. Atmospheric, noirish detective story set in the swinging Shànghăi of the '20s. 'Pockmarked' Huang, a brutally murdered Russian prostitute and a naive British investigator come together for a real page-turner.
- *Midnight*, Mao Dun. In the opening scene of *Midnight*, conservative Confucian Old Man Wu visits his son's home in Shànghăi. The sight of modern women, in high-slit skirts and revealing blouses literally shocks him to death. A famed presentation of the social mores of 1920s Shànghăi.
- *Shanghai: Electric and Lurid City*, Barbara Baker. An excellent anthology of more than 50 passages of writing about Shànghăi, from its pretreaty port days to the eve of the 21st century.
- *Shanghai Girls*, Lisa Lee. A moving novel about two beautiful sisters whose lives as high-flying models in 1930s Shànghăi are transformed when their father decides to repay his gambling debts by selling them to a family in Los Angeles.
- *The Distant Land of My Father*, Bo Caldwell. A moving portrayal of the relationship between a daughter and father, and of betrayal and reconciliation, commencing in 1930s Shànghăi.
- *The Painter from Shanghai*, Jennifer Cody Epstein. Highly-acclaimed debut novel based on the remarkable life of child prostitute turned painter Pan Yuliang.
- *The Sing-Song Girls of Shanghai*, Han Bangqing. Delving deeply into the lives of courtesans and prostitutes in *fin de siècle* Shànghăi, this absorbing novel was first published in 1892 but only recently translated into English.
- *When Red is Black*, Qiu Xiaolong. Realistic detective story that packs plenty of literary muscle. A follow-up Inspector Chen novel (see *Death of a Red Heroine*) and great snapshot of the changing city seen through Chinese eyes.
- *When We Were Orphans*, Kazuo Ishiguro. Subtle and absorbing portrayal of an English detective who sets out to solve the case of his parents' disappearance in Shànghăi, climaxing in war-shattered Hóngkŏu.

Although born in Shàoxīng, Lu Xun (see the boxed text, p119), China's greatest modern writer, lived in Shànghăi from 1927 until his death of tuberculosis in 1936. The highly influential modernist author dragged Chinese literature into the modern era and was one of the first founders of the Shànghăi-based League of Left-wing Writers. His most famous work, the 1921 novella *The True Story of Ah Q* (阿Q正传, *Ā Q zhèngzhuàn*) – a satirical look at early 20th-century China – is considered a modern masterpiece and was the first piece of literature to fully utilise vernacular Chinese. An English translation can be bought at the bookshop in the museum beside his tomb (p117). Admirers of Lu Xun can also visit his Shànghăi residence (p118).

Mao Dun (real name Shen Yanbing), an active leftist writer in the 1930s, penned *Midnight* (*Zǐyè*), one of the most famous novels about Shànghăi (see the boxed text, p38). *Rainbow* (1992), by the same author, tells the tale of a young girl from a traditional family background who travels to Shànghăi on a journey of political awakening.

Ding Ling, whose most famous oeuvre is *The Diary of Miss Sophie*, lived in Shànghăi, as for a time did the writers Yu Dafu and Ba Jin. Writers were not immune to political dangers; Lu Xun's friend Rou Shi was murdered by the Kuomintang in February 1931.

Eileen Chang (Zhang Ailing, 1920–95) is one of the writers most closely connected to Shànghăi, certainly among overseas Chinese. Born in Shànghăi, she lived in the city only from 1942 to 1948, before moving to Hong Kong and then the USA. Seeped in the city's details and moods, her books capture the essence of Shànghăi. Chang's most famous books include *The Rouge of the North, The Faded Flower, Red Rose and White Rose, The Golden Lock* and *Love in a Fallen City*. Her 1979 novella *Lust, Caution* was made into an award-winning film, directed by Ang Lee (*Crouching Tiger Hidden Dragon, Brokeback Mountain*), in 2007.

Contemporary voices are sparser. The most respected Shànghăi writer today is Wang Anyi, whose bestselling novels (in China) include *Love on a Barren Mountain, Baotown* and *Song of Everlasting Sorrow*, the last detailing the story of a Shanghainese beauty-pageant winner from 1940 to the present. Wang also wrote the script for Chen Kaige's film *Temptress Moon*.

More recently, several high-school dropouts gained notoriety, beginning with Mian Mian, who vividly described the marginalised underbelly of China in *Candy* (see the boxed text, opposite). Less known in the West is Han Han, who skyrocketed to fame before his 18th birthday with his novel *The Third Way,* a searing critique of China's educational system (p34). He inspired awe and disgust simultaneously by turning down a scholarship to the prestigious Fudan University in order to race cars in Běijīng.

VISUAL ARTS

Even if the city's artistic output remains limited, there is a growing gallery and art-museum scene here and it's an exciting place to learn more about contemporary Chinese art in general.

Your first stop should certainly be M50 (p97), Shànghǎi's most cutting-edge art district, housed in warehouses across the river from Shanghai Train Station. Another excellent art centre, focusing more on contemporary sculpture, is the huge complex known as Red Town, near Jiaotong University. The stand-out gallery here is the cavernous Shanghai Sculpture Space (p127). More mainstream, but very impressive nonetheless, is Shanghai Museum of Contemporary Art, or MOCA (p75), located in People's Park. Nearby, Shanghai Art Museum (p75), is housed in a fabulous neoclassical clocktower building and also has some fine exhibitions. With its trendy Bund address, Shanghai Gallery of Art (p66) attracts big-name artists and chic clientele, while a stroll around the quaint alleys of Taikang Rd Art Centre (p85), with its cafes, boutiques and smattering of decent small galleries, can be a lot of fun.

Further afield, the Shanghai Duolun Museum of Modern Art (p116) in Hóngkǒu, and the Zendai Museum of Modern Art (p113) over in Pǔdōng are sometimes worth visiting. The Centre Pompidou, France's premier modern art museum, has been negotiating the opening of a new branch in Shanghai since 2007. It was originally supposed to open in 2010, but at press time the plan was still on hold.

It's worth noting that commercial Chinese art in Běijīng and Shànghǎi is moulded by Western needs and expectations, which binds artistic subject matter within narrow and predictable horizons. Politically risqué themes – Chairman Mao still crops up in art works like some weary old prop and the clash between socialism and China's commercial cravings is another tiresome topic – do little to confront universal themes or push the envelope. It also occasionally promotes mediocrity, which is not where art in Shànghǎi should be heading. Political references merely accentuate the here-and-now context of Chinese art, concepts that will rapidly date.

Contemporary Shanghainese artists to take note of include Pu Jie, with his colourful pop-art depictions of Shànghǎi, video-installation artists Shi Yong and Hu Jieming, and Wu Yiming, who creates calmer, more impressionistic works.

More traditional art comes from the southern suburb of Jīnshān, which has its own school of untrained 'peasant' painters who have been turning out colourful and vibrant paintings for years. Their works have their roots in local embroidery designs and have no perspective. The themes are mostly rural and domestic scenes full of details of everyday life. You can see a selection of paintings from the Jīnshān area in several shops in the Old Town's Old Street (p140), or you can head out to Jīnshān itself.

The Shanghai Biennale (p19) has been held in November every two years since 1996, though the exhibits are watered down by government censors. Related fringe shows spring up around the same time, however, and are often of more interest. Outside Biennale years the China

top picks

GALLERIES

- M50 (p97) The best, most cutting-edge art centre in the city, with over 30 independent studios and galleries.
- Red Town (红坊; Hóngfāng; www.redtown570 .com; Map pp128–9; 570 West Huaihai Rd; 淮海西路570号; ⏰ 10am-4pm Tue-Sun) Huge outdoor space plus a number of converted factories including the excellent Shanghai Sculpture Space (p127).
- Taikang Rd Art Centre (p85) Galleries plus cafes, restaurants and boutiques, all clustered together in a maze of narrow lanes. Also known as Tiánzǐfáng.
- Shanghai Gallery of Art (p66) The Three on the Bund address means big-name exhibitions and chic clientele.

International Arts Festival (p19) is an event held in November that brings traditional and modern (Western and Chinese) art, artists and galleries together.

MUSIC

Shànghǎi had a buzzing live-music scene in the 1930s, featuring everything from jazz divas to émigré Russian troubadours, but for a long time now it's been sadly dominated by Filipino cover bands and saccharine-sweet Canto-pop. Things are changing, though, and while Shànghǎi's live music scene still lags behind Běijīng's, there are a couple of cracking small venues in town where you can catch local bands, the best of which is Yùyīntáng (p192). Melting Pot (p192) is also decent. The only sizeable venue in town is the Zhijiang Dream Factory (p192) which attracts more established bands from all over.

Top Floor Circus, who play anything from folk to punk are legendary on the Shànghǎi music scene. If they're playing while you're in town, do your best to get a ticket. The rock band Hard Queen are another very successful outfit and worth catching live. Others worth checking out include Pinkberry (rock) and Cold Fairyland, who play rock mixed with sounds from traditional Chinese instruments. Torturing Nurse, meanwhile, who make unusual and extremely loud sounds rather than music as such, are China's leading 'noise' band. Check out www.noishanghai .org to find out where they're playing.

For the low-down on who's playing where, grab a free copy of the monthly entertainment magazines *That's Shanghai* (www.urbanantomy.com) or *City Weekend* (www.cityweekend.com.cn/shanghai), or check their websites. Also check out Smart Shanghai (www.smartshanghai.com).

Shànghǎi's once world famous jazz scene isn't quite what it was, but there are still a number of places around town where you can sample the sounds of the 1930s. For details, see p192.

Classical Chinese-music performances are staged from time to time in Shànghǎi. The *èrhú* is a two-stringed fiddle that is tuned to a low register, providing a soft, melancholy tone. The *húqín* is a higher pitched two-stringed viola. The *yuèqín*, a sort of moon-shaped four-stringed guitar, has a soft tone and is used to support the *èrhú*. Other instruments you may come across are the *shēng* (reed flute), *pípá* (lute), *gǔzhēng* (zither) and *xiāo* (vertical flute).

The Conservatory of Music is a prestigious clearing house of Chinese talent. One of its most famous former students is Liao Changyong, a world-class baritone who has performed with Placido Domingo, among others. For classical music venues in Shànghǎi, see p193.

CINEMA

The first screening of any film in China happened in 1896 in the garden of a Shànghǎi teahouse when Spanish entrepreneur Galen Bocca showed a series of one-reel films to astonished audiences. The city's first cinema opened up in 1908, but before films could reach their glamorous peak

RECOMMENDED VIEWING: SHÀNGHǍI ON SCREEN

- *Empire of the Sun*, 1987. Steven Spielberg's film based on JG Ballard's autobiographical account of his internment in Shànghǎi as a child during WWII (also see boxed text, p38).
- *Park Shanghai*, 2009. Shot mostly on top of a Shànghǎi tower block while a school reunion party goes on in a karaoke bar below, Kevin Kai Huang's debut film - nominated at the Moscow Film Festival - contrasts the brash, confident image of Shànghǎi's sleek city skyline with the film's tale of 30-something malaise.
- *Shanghai Express*, 1932. One of the world's top-grossing films in 1932–3, this is probably the most famous Shànghǎi-related movie, though the link is tenuous. Based on the real-life hijacking of foreigners on a Běijīng–Shànghǎi train in 1923, it won an Oscar for best cinematography and a best-director nomination for Josef von Sternberg, though it created a strong backlash in China. It features Marlene Dietrich purring the immortal and enigmatic line: 'It took more than one man to change my name to Shanghai Lily.'
- *Shanghai Triad (Yáo a Yáo! Yáo Dào Wàipó Qiáo)*, 1995. Zhang Yimou's stylish take on Shànghǎi's 1930s gangster scene, starring China's most famous art-house actress, Gong Li.
- *Suzhou River (Sūzhōu Hé)*, 2000. A disturbing and obsessive narrative of love in modern Shànghǎi. The plot is heavy at times, but director Ye Lou's vision of Shànghǎi – gritty, disillusioned and duplicitous – is an excellent portrayal of the real city that lies behind the glamorous facade.

WORTH A PEEK: OTHER GALLERIES

- **Andrew James Art** (安杰当代艺术画廊 Ānjié Dāngdài Yìshù Huàláng; Map pp98–9; ☎ 5228 7550; www .andrewjamesart.com; 39 North Maoming Rd; 茂名北路39号; ⏲ 11am-7pm Tues-Sun; Ⓜ West Nanjing Rd) Set in an old villa, this private gallery has some big openings and focuses on Chinese and Asian artists. The quality here is often very high.
- **Contrasts** (p67) Decorative house ware, furniture, sculptures, paintings and rotating exhibitions of contemporary artists.
- **Deke Erh Art Center** (p85) Fantastic warehouse exhibit space set up by Shànghǎi's cultural *tour de force*, Deke Erh.
- **Grand Cinema Gallery** (大剧院画廊; Dà Jùyuàn Huàláng; Map pp66–7; ☎ 6327 4260; 216 West Nanjing Rd; 南京西路216号; ⏲ Tue-Sun 10.30am-5.30pm; Ⓜ People's Sq) Old cinema-related photos and memorabilia. Attached to the Grand Cinema.
- **Shanghai Chinese Painting Institute** (上海中国画院; Shànghǎi Zhōngguó Huàyuàn; Map pp86–7; ☎ 6474 9977; 197 Yueyang Rd; 岳阳路197号 Ⓜ Hengshan Rd) Occasionally has major exhibitions.
- **ShanghART** (p94) One of a new crop of contemporary art galleries that have moved into intimate French Concession villas.
- **Studio Rouge** (红寨; Hóng Zhài; Map pp98–9; ☎ 6323 0833; Floor 1 Building 7, 50 Moganshan Rd; 莫干山路50号; Ⓜ Shanghai Train St) Recently moved premises to M50, this is a good primer to the contemporary Shànghǎi art scene.
- **Wan Fung Art Gallery** (p123) Modern Chinese paintings completed in traditional style and displayed in a gorgeous setting on the ground floor of the old Jesuit library.

in the 1930s, film-makers had to convince the distrustful Shanghainese that it was worth their hard-earned cash. The first cinema owners shrewdly ran a few minutes of film, cut the reel and went around collecting money from patrons who wanted to see the rest. Soon hooked, the city boasted more than 35 cinemas and over 140 film companies by 1930.

The 1932 Japanese bombing of the Shànghǎi district of Hóngkǒu had a big affect on the industry as an underlying patriotic fervour took hold, epitomised by films coming out of the Lianhua Studio, with its close connections to Chiang Kaishek's Nationalist Party.

Shànghǎi's golden age reached its peak in 1937 with the release of *Street Angel*, a powerful drama about two sisters who flee the Japanese in north-east China and end up as prostitutes in Shànghǎi, and *Crossroads*, a clever comedy about four unemployed graduates. There was still time, however, after WWII and before the CCP took over in 1949, for a final flowering. *A Spring River Flows East*, dubbed the *Gone with the Wind* of Chinese cinema, and *Springtime in a Small Town*, another wartime tear jerker, remain popular films today.

The Cathay Theatre (Map pp86–7) on Huaihai Rd and the Grand Theatre (p76) are among art deco cinemas that survive from that Golden Age, while The Old Film Café (p116), in Hóngkǒu, housed in a beautiful three-storey brick building with charming wooden interior, shows old Shànghǎi films on demand, although when we last visited only one – *Crossroads* (十字街头, *Shízì Jiētóu*) – had English subtitles.

For a scholarly look at old Shànghǎi cinema try the book *Cinema and Urban Culture in Shanghai 1922–1943*, edited by Zhang Yingjin.

The sun seems to have set on Shànghǎi's cinemas. Theatres and cinemas in town sold 200 million tickets in 1979, but that number was down to below 40 million by 1996. Today's moviegoers are even scarcer, as DVD piracy and internet downloads make the economics of domestic film-making increasingly dubious.

More innovative film studios in Xī'ān and Běijīng have captured much of the international acclaim of contemporary Chinese film. Coproductions have been more successful for the Shanghai Film Studios, which in 2001 moved from its central location in Xújiāhuì to the far western city district of Sōngjiāng.

One critical success was *The Red Violin*, a coproduction between Canada and Shànghǎi. Shànghǎi-born Vivian Wu (Wu Junmei; *The Last Emperor, The Pillow Book*) returned to her native city with her husband, director Oscar L Costo, in order to focus on their production company, MARdeORO Films. It produced the well-received *Shanghai Red*, starring Wu and

Ge You (*Farewell My Concubine, To Live*), in 2006. Another actress hailing from Shànghǎi is Joan Chen (Chen Chong), who started her career at the Shanghai Film Studios in the late 1970s and gained international fame in David Lynch's *Twin Peaks*.

Shànghǎi's independent films are scarce. Look out for Ye Lou's *Suzhou River (Sūzhōu Hé)* and Andrew Chen's *Shanghai Panic (Wǒmen Hàipà)*. Both were shot with digital camcorders and are notable for showing a decidedly unglamorous and more realistic side of the city.

Chen Yifei's 1920s period drama, *The Barber* (aka *The Music Box*), was released posthumously in 2006, while Taiwanese-born Oscar-winning director Ang Lee (*Crouching Tiger Hidden Dragon, Brokeback Mountain*) released *Lust, Caution* in 2007. A controversial tale of sex and espionage set in WWII-Shànghǎi, and based on the 1979 novella by Eileen Chang, the award-winning film was heavily censored for its mainland China release.

On-going censorship isn't the only problem facing Chinese cinema these days, as a lack of cinemas, the high price of tickets and a thriving pirate DVD market all continue to hamper the industry.

CHINESE OPERA & THEATRE

Contemporary Chinese opera, of which the most famous is Beijing opera (京剧; *Jīngjù*), has a continuous history of some 900 years. Evolving from a convergence of comic and ballad traditions in the Northern Song period, Chinese opera brought together a disparate range of forms: acrobatics, martial arts, poetic arias and stylised dance.

Over 100 varieties of opera exist in China today and many are performed in Shànghǎi. Shanghainese opera (沪剧; *Hùjù*), sometimes called flower-drum opera, is performed in the local dialect (p36) and has its origins in the folk songs of Pǔdōng. Yueju opera (越剧; *Yuèjù*) was born in and around Shàoxīng County in neighbouring Zhèjiāng (the ancient state of Yue) in the early 20th century. *Yuèjù* roles are normally played by women. Kunju opera (昆剧; *Kūnjù*) or Kunqu opera (昆曲; *Kūnqǔ*) originates from Kūnshān, near Sūzhōu (p229) in neighbouring Jiāngsū.

Operas were usually performed by travelling troupes who had a low social status in traditional Chinese society. Chinese law forbade mixed-sex performances, forcing actors to act out roles of the opposite sex. Opera troupes were frequently associated with homosexuality in the

---

SHÀNGHǍI IN HOLLYWOOD

Western cinema has been so fixated with Shànghǎi over the years that Shànghǎi films are practically a genre unto themselves. In many, Shànghǎi is a mere backdrop, brought in whenever a bit of mystery, allure or plain sleaze is required. Shànghǎi never even appears in Hitchcock's *East of Shanghai*, Orson Welles' *Lady from Shanghai* or Charlie Chaplin's *Shanghaied*.

Armageddon Bruce Willis, Ben Affleck, Steve Buscemi et al save the earth from meteoric devastation, but not before a quaint and romanticised version of Shànghǎi makes a cameo appearance, only to be wiped out by an asteroid impact in this 1998 spectacular.

Code 46 Shànghǎi serves as a futuristic backdrop to Michael Winterbottom's 2003 sci-fi thriller/love story starring Tim Robbins.

Godzilla: Final Wars The Oriental Pearl TV Tower is toppled during the giant lizard's latest – and possibly final – stomp in this 2004 effort from director Ryuhei Kitamura.

Mission Impossible III Indestructible agent Ethan Hunt (Tom Cruise) finds himself transported to Shànghǎi for his latest improbable caper. The shots of canal-side 'Shànghǎi' are actually filmed in Xītáng and Zhōuzhuāng, so if you go looking for them in Pǔxī, you won't find them. The film famously upset Chinese censors for its shots of laundry draped out to dry from bamboo poles and the suggestion that ex-PLA security guards were not paragons of efficiency.

The Painted Veil Excellent period tale of marital crisis unfolding against a backdrop of 1920s Shànghǎi and cholera-ridden Guǎngxī province, starring Edward Norton and Naomi Watts.

Shanghai Surprise Madonna defies the praise she won for 1985's *Desperately Seeking Susan* with this 1986 turkey, starring alongside then-hubby Sean Penn.

The White Countess Limp romantic drama framed against the Shànghǎi of the 1930s, starring Ralph Fiennes and Natasha Richardson.

public imagination, contributing further to their lowly social status.

Formerly, opera was performed mostly on open-air stages in markets, streets, teahouses or temple courtyards. The shrill singing and loud percussion were designed to be heard over the public throng, prompting American writer PJ O'Rourke to say it was 'as if a truck full of wind chimes collided with a stack of empty drums during a birdcall contest'.

Opera performances usually take place on a bare stage, with the actors taking on stylised stock characters who are instantly recognisable to the audience. Most stories are derived from classical literature and Chinese mythology and tell of disasters, natural calamities, intrigues or rebellions. The musicians usually sit on the stage in plain clothes and play without written scores.

China's most legendary 20th-century opera star was Mei Lanfang, who allegedly performed privately for several of Shànghǎi's gangland bosses in the 1930s. The most central venue for appreciating Chinese opera in Shànghǎi is the Yifu Theatre (p189) on Fuzhou Rd.

The lower Yangzi region has a long tradition of storytelling, farce, comic talk and mimicking, all of which were traditionally performed in teahouses. Hángzhōu (p220) and Sūzhōu (p229) have their own variants. *Píngtán* balladry is a mix of *pínghuà* (Sūzhōu-style storytelling) and *táncí* (ballad singing), accompanied by the *pípá* (lute) and *sānxián* (banjo). You can hear samples of various Chinese operas and *píngtán* at the Shanghai History Museum (p110) in Pǔdōng, or at the Pingtan Museum (p231) in Sūzhōu, although daily performances here had just been suspended when we last visited.

MUSEUMS

- Metersbonwe Costume Museum (p66)
- Shanghai Art Museum (p75) Lovely building with lashings of period features and an inimitable museum space.
- Shanghai History Museum (p110) Entertaining primer for getting a handle on Shànghǎi's flamboyant and chequered past.
- Shanghai Museum (p72) Fabulous museum on Chinese culture in a unique *dǐng* (a three-legged food vessel used for cooking and serving)-shaped building.
- Shanghai Urban Planning Exhibition Hall (p74) Some great photos of old Shanghai plus a mind-boggling scale model of the whole city.

ECONOMY

For those who weren't aware of it before, the sheer size and incredible potential of China's economy was brought sharply into focus by the global financial crisis of 2008. As one of the few major world governments to be in the privileged position of presiding over an economy that was actually in credit, China's government reacted exceptionally quickly, launching unprecedented billion dollar economic stimulus measures in an attempt to offset the huge drop in exports caused by markets crashing in debt-ridden Western countries. It became clear for all to see that China was a major world economic player, and while Shànghǎi may not be pulling the strings in terms of decision making, the financial muscle of this massive city continues to have a huge influence.

Combined with the provinces of Zhèjiāng and Jiāngsū, the Shànghǎi region accounts for almost a third of China's exports. This area's 2008 GDP totalled a staggering US$958 billion – almost 22% of China's total GDP, placing the region alone in 15th position, just below Australia, in many world GDP rankings. Before the financial crisis, Shànghǎi's economy had been expanding at an incredible rate of 12% each year. Growth figures slowed dramatically after the crash. Shànghǎi saw just 5.6% growth in the first half of 2009, for example, showing just how intrinsically linked the city was to the flagging global economy (China as a whole grew 7.1%), but these figures were still highly impressive by international, recession-struck standards over the same period.

Left out from China's first round of economic reforms in the 1980s, Shànghǎi's economic renaissance dates from 1990, when it became an autonomous municipality and Pǔdōng was established as a special economic zone. In 1992 Deng Xiaoping gave the seal of approval to Shànghǎi's redevelopment during his 'southern tour'. Until then 80% of the city's revenue went straight into Běijīng's pockets. Economic reforms and restructuring massively boosted

Shànghǎi's GDP, and a flood of foreign investment poured into the city. With average per capita incomes of around US$4400, its residents now enjoy some of China's highest salaries, residents for whom doing business and making money seems to run in the blood. Běijīng folk may be generous, erudite and hospitable, but it's the Shanghainese – with their notorious stinginess and obsession with status – who focus their energies on creating wealth.

With gambling illegal in mainland China, China's addiction to making a legal bet – Macau's casino revenues have outstripped Las Vegas, largely thanks to the hordes of mainland high-rollers sweeping into town – helps fuel stock-market speculation as well as rampant property investment. The latest hot stocks and tips are text messaged about town like there's no tomorrow as everyone *chǎogǔ* (literally 'fries stocks' – playing the stock market). True, the Shanghai Stock Exchange's key index had fallen from its peak in 2007 to a near record low just 12 months later as the global economic downturn took its toll on market sentiment, but figures had already started bouncing back in 2009, with stock exchange turnover growing 28.2% in the first half of the year.

Shànghǎi's traditional rivalry with Hong Kong continues unabated, and the gap in living standards continues to close rapidly. Shànghǎi is hoping the 2010 World Expo will be the final boost needed to hoist it into the category of top-flight world city. If it was a mere construction contest, Shànghǎi's sheer ability to stack cement and reinforced concrete would win it the cup, but Hong Kong's particular advantages – take its first-rate transport infrastructure, well-nurtured international status, dependable rule of law, established business culture, flair with the English language and even its more diverse topography and breezy island getaways – keep it in the lead.

Perhaps Shànghǎi's strongest plus point is its youth and enthusiasm. Compared to its rival – where a growing staleness is apparent – a palpable buzz is in the air. Shànghǎi's energy and zest could carry it across the line, but this would depend on political and social stability. Hong Kong's myriad freedoms, uncensored media, firm line on corruption and protection of intellectual-property rights could also give it the stamina for the long haul.

Industry & Foreign Investment

Saturated with foreign capital, a quarter of all China's foreign investment gushes into Shànghǎi and the neighbouring water-logged provinces of Jiāngsū and Zhèjiāng. This proved to be to its detriment in the heat of the 2008 financial crisis as foreign investment dropped off significantly, denting Shànghǎi's economy in the process. But the long-term view that the world's economic polarity is swinging east still remains. More than 500 multinational companies continue to base themselves in Shànghǎi, showing a commitment to the city and the faith installed in its ability to ride out the storm and emerge as a major global financial centre.

Economic Problems

Seen from the river, towering above their couchant guardian warships, the semi-skyscrapers of the Bund present, impressively, the facade of a great city. But it is only a facade.

Christopher Isherwood, 1937

Christopher Isherwood's poignant reflection may mull over the facade of the Bund, but today's Pǔdōng skyline generates similar qualms. Behind the deafening hype – in which the Western media plays a significant role – lies the economic reality of a nation ambivalent and divided about its reformist path and fearful of its recent history. Well-to-do citizens of Shànghǎi may be transfixed by the dazzling vapour trail left by the city's meteoric rise, but the 'lost generation' have more mundane concerns. Behind the incessant images of a strident Shànghǎi lies an assortment of more pear-shaped economic scenarios. Many of today's over-50s who endured the horrors of the Cultural Revolution found themselves either too old to benefit from capitalist reforms or saw their iron rice bowl cradle-to-grave securities smashed.

Shànghǎi is not some kind of Singapore – a city-state divorced from another country. It is not even a Hong Kong operating under a 'One Country, Two Systems' arrangement. It is an intrinsic part of China, and as such it is buffeted by the social and political currents that course through the land. Much of the frothy excitement about Shànghǎi bubbles up from its context as a city embedded within a communist state, a contradiction simply too startling for pundits to

(Continued on page 53)

1933

大上海

ARCHITECTURE IN SHÀNGHĂI

看看大上海

走进博

Duolun Road Cultural Street (p116)

ARCHITECTURE IN SHÀNGHǍI

The imposing skyline of the French Concession district (p85)

The ever more dazzling array of glittering skyscrapers may be the star attraction in modern Shànghǎi, but this city has been flexing its ample construction muscles throughout its chequered past. This has left it with a montage of architectural designs with more diversity than many first-time visitors imagine.

Shànghǎi is particularly rich in concession architecture – the Bund being a fabulous highlight – and the city's unique indigenous buildings – *shíkùmén* (stone-gate houses) – can still be found in quiet *lòngtáng* (lanes), scattered around north and west Shànghǎi. Religious buildings also play their part, with some strikingly attractive temples, charming old churches and synagogues to be found.

But it's Shànghǎi's soaring superstructures that steal the headlines, for both the right and wrong reasons. This city boasts some of the tallest skyscrapers in the world, but their rise is often another's demise as swaths of old Shànghǎi continue to be felled to make way for tower blocks that, more often than not, fall into a growing pool of uninspiring, high-rise dross. Thankfully, some architects have their heads screwed on, meaning there are a handful of stand-out designs, as brilliantly eye-catching as they are unbelievably tall.

SHÀNGHǍI RISING

Let's face it: if we're talking architecture (which we are), Shànghǎi is all about skyscrapers. Concession-era garden villas may well be exceedingly charming, and strolling down an alleyway in the Old Town can be a lot of fun, but in terms of pure, adrenalin-charged 'wowability', the big boys win hands down.

Shànghǎi's head-spinning, space-age forest of terrifyingly tall towers has come to define a confident and brash, modern China in the way that the Bund (p68) forever recalls the indignity of foreign encroachment. Although still some way behind the likes of Hong Kong and New York in the world skyscraper charts, and now eclipsed by Dubai in the whoppers-under-construction rankings, Shànghǎi still boasts an enormous and ever-growing number of neck craners.

The last time we totted them up, the city had 982 high-rise buildings (more than 12 floors), 32 of which were over 200m tall. Another 121 were under construction (11 are 200m plus), and a further 43 had been approved (six are 200m plus). At the time of research, Shànghǎi had the world's third- and 10th-tallest buildings, and another even taller one on the way. (All figures have been verified by construction data experts Emporis Standards Committee.)

Sadly, the results of this 20-year-long construction craze are often hit-and-miss – there are a lot of mind-numbingly dull tower blocks out there – but notable exceptions do exist.

For almost 10 years, the tallest building in Shànghǎi was the beautiful, 421m-tall, pagoda-like Jinmao Tower (p109). Replete with symbolism, it has 88 floors (eight being the ultimate lucky number to the Chinese), while its 13 stepped bands allude to Buddhist imagery.

In 2008, though, Jinmao was usurped by its new next-door neighbour, the striking Shanghai World Financial Center (p107), a 492m-tall bottle-opener lookalike that, for now at least, is the world's third-tallest building (see the boxed text, below).

By the end of 2014, however, these two will seem like titches when, if all goes to plan, the

World Financial Center (p107), Jinmao Tower (p109)

unusual 632m-tall twisting structure of the Shanghai Tower is unveiled beside them, becoming the world's tallest building (outside Dubai, of course).

For an example of one the designers got wrong, look no further than the gaudy, nay hideous, Oriental Pearl TV Tower (p110), a 468m-tall tower whose shocking-pink bauble design wouldn't look out of place as runner-up in a high-school architecture contest.

Over the other side of the river, overlooking People's Park, a glorious, gleaming tower, known as Tomorrow Square (p76), proves eye-catching Shànghǎi skyscrapers don't have to built in Pǔdōng.

WORLD'S TALLEST SKYSCRAPERS

Name	Height	City	Completed
Burj Dubai	818m	Dubai, UAE	2009
Taipei 101	509m	Taipei, Taiwan	2004
Shanghai World Financial Centre	492m	Shànghǎi, China	2008

Coming soon

Name	Height	City	Due to be completed
Shanghai Tower	632m	Shànghǎi, China	2014
Pentominium	618m	Dubai, UAE	2011
Guangzhou TV & Sightseeing Tower	610m	Guǎngzhōu, China	2010

Traditional Chinese architecture meets the 21st century at the Shanghai Grand Theatre (p194)

...BUT SIZE ISN'T EVERYTHING

The likes of the Jinmao Tower may take all the glory, but some of Shanghai's best-looking contemporary buildings are distinctly low-rise.

A stroll around People's Square will take you past three of the city's most eye-catching designs. The Shanghai Urban Planning Exhibition Hall (p74) is capped with a distinctive roof with four 'florets'. Supposed to symbolise budding magnolias, the city's flower, they actually make the building look like *Star Wars* droid R2-D2 doing a head stand.

Nearby Shanghai Grand Theatre (p194) combines Chinese sweeping eaves with a futuristic employment of plastic and glass. Think trendy giant ashtray and you won't be far off. Opposite this pair is the wonderfully designed Shanghai Museum (p72), made to resemble an ancient Chinese vessel known as a *dǐng*.

The World Expo (p18) gave architects another excuse to let their imaginations run wild, and the upturned red pyramid design of the China Pavilion is a notable highlight.

Customs House (p70)

CONCESSION ARCHITECTURE

For many foreign visitors, Shànghǎi's architectural vision of the China-to-be is a mere side salad to the feast of historic architecture lining the Bund and beyond. The remnants of old Shànghǎi, these buildings are a part of the city's genetic code and are inseparable from its sense of identity as the former 'Paris of the East'.

The Bund (p64) – Shànghǎi's most famous esplanade of concession buildings – was built on unstable foundations due to the leaching mud of the Huangpu River. Bund buildings were first built on concrete rafts that were fixed onto wood pilings, which were allowed to sink into the mud. Because of the lack of qualified architects, some of the earliest Western-style buildings in Shànghǎi were partially built in Hong Kong, shipped to Shànghǎi, then assembled on site.

In the 1920s the British architectural firm of Palmer & Turner designed many of Shànghǎi's major buildings (13 buildings on the Bund alone), including the neoclassical Hongkong and Shanghai Banking Corporation (HSBC) building (p70), the Bank of China building (p69), the Yokohama Specie Bank, Grosvenor House (Jinjiang Hotel; p208) and the Customs House (p70). For more on the Bund buildings, see our walking tour (p68).

Although the Bund contains the lion's share of Shànghǎi's neoclassical designs, arguably the most impressive is the Shanghai Art Museum (p75) in People's Square. This beautiful red-brick building with a clock tower once formed part of the main stand at the old racecourse.

Interior of the HSBC building (p70), the Bund

Shanghai Museum (p72)

Old Shànghǎi's other main architect was Ladislaus Hudec (1893–1958), a Hungarian who came to Shànghǎi in 1918 after escaping en route to a Russian prisoner-of-war camp in Siberia. The Moore Memorial Church (p76), Woo Villa (p105), Park Hotel (p76) and Shanghai Grand Theatre (p194) all owe their creation to Hudec.

The late 1920s saw the Shànghǎi arrival of art deco and its sophisticated, modish expressions of the machine age. It was one of Shànghǎi's architectural high-water marks, with the city boasting more art deco buildings than any other city in the world. For a comprehensive low-down on the style, read *Shanghai Art Deco* by Deke Erh and Tess Johnston.

Art deco buildings of note include the Peace Hotel (p204), the Woo Villa (p105), the Paramount Ballroom (p103), Broadway Mansions (p214), the Cathay Theatre (p190), the Liza Building at 99 East Nanjing Rd, the Savoy Apartments at 209 Changshu Rd, the Picardie Apartments (now the Hengshan Hotel) on the corner of Hengshan Rd and Wanping Rd, the Embankment Building (p120) and the Bank of China building (p69), but there are dozens of others.

The tree-lined streets of the French Concession house a delightful collection of magnificent residential villa architecture, much of which has been well preserved. See our French Concession walking tour (p95).

LÒNGTÁNG & SHÍKÙMÉN 弄堂、石库门

In the same way that Běijīng's most authentic features survive among its gorgeous *hútòng* (narrow alleyways), so Shànghǎi's *lòngtáng* (or *lǐlòng*) are the city's principal indigenous urban architectural feature. *Lòngtáng* are the back alleys that form the building blocks of living, breathing communities, supplying a warm and charming counterpoint to the abstract and machinelike skyscrapers rising over the city. Sadly, these alleys, and their signature buildings, the *shíkùmén*, have pitted little more than a feeble resistance against developers who have toppled swaths of *shíkùmén* to make way for more glittering projects.

The *shíkùmén* 'restoration' project – called *Jiànyèlǐ* (建业里) – on West Jianguo Rd is a recent example of development work in an area occupied by the houses. This area, built during the 1930s, was until recently one of Shànghǎi's largest blocks of *shíkùmén* housing. Billboards put up around the area promised that 'the historic *shíkùmén* buildings will be restored to their

Aerial view of a traditional lòngtáng

original beauty'. The area was then cordoned off with high metal fences and completely flattened before rebuilding began using some of the old bricks.

HISTORY & DESIGN

Following the strife of the Taiping Rebellion (p23) in 1853, some 20,000 Chinese fled into the International Settlements. Sensing a newly arrived cash cow, the British decided to scrap the law forbidding Chinese from renting property in the concessions, and foreigners from developing real estate. British and French speculators built hundreds of houses in what became Shànghǎi's biggest real-estate boom.

The result was the *shíkùmén*, a unique mixture of East and West that was a successful meeting of the Chinese courtyard house and English terraced housing. Such buildings made up 60% of Shànghǎi's housing between the 1850s and the 1940s.

Typical *shíkùmén* houses were two to three storeys tall and fronted by an imposing stone-gate frame topped with a decorated lintel

WHERE TO FIND SHÍKÙMÉN

As well as the ones listed here, check out our Walking Tours on p95, p104 and p119.

Old Town

Zhuangjia St (庄家街; Map p79, B3) Bursting with Old Town textures, this narrow market street southeast of Peach Garden Mosque has a number of historical *shíkùmén*, some with beautifully carved lintels.

Danfeng Rd (丹凤路; Map p79, C2) Despite being a stone's throw from the very touristy Yuyuan Gardens, this alley retains some genuine Old Town charm.

Hóngkǒu & North Shànghǎi

Shanyin Rd (山阴路; Map p116, B1) Pleasant tree-lined street with a number of *shíkùmén*-filled alleyways branching off it.

Zhoushan Rd (舟山路; Map p116, C2) You'll find *shíkùmén* housing all along this street, especially at its southern end. The market street of Dongyuhang Rd (东余杭路), which it crosses, also has some interesting *shíkùmén* entrances to alleyway housing.

Panlong St (蟠龙街; Map p116, B3) This small lane off Zhapu Rd has a long row of unusual pillar-fronted *shíkùmén*. The tiny alleys at the far end are fun to explore.

French Concession

Nanchang Rd (南昌路; Map pp86–7, F2) This typical tree-lined French Concession avenue has a number of *shíkùmén* buildings, most of which are now cute little boutique shops. For the still-lived-in version, look for alleyway 212 on the north side of the road's eastern end.

Taikang Road Art Centre (泰康路艺术中心; Map pp86–7, H2) This vast maze of beautifully restored alleyway housing between Taikang Rd (泰康路) and Middle Jianguo Rd (建国中路) has maintained its local-community feel, despite the art galleries and wi-fi cafes moving in.

Jìng'ān

319 Jiaozhou Rd (胶州路319号; Map pp98–9, D5) You can find a charming row of rundown *shíkùmén* on your left, before you reach Le Tour Traveler's Rest Youth Hostel.

enclosing two stout wooden doors (frequently black), each decorated with a bronze handle. The lintel was sometimes elaborately carved with a dictum in Chinese, usually four characters long. At the entrance to the alley was usually a *yānzhǐdiàn* (烟纸店) – literally a 'tobacco and paper shop' – where residents could pick up provisions round the clock.

Shíkùmén were originally designed to house one family, but Shànghǎi's growth and socialist reorientation led to them being sublet to many families, each of which shared a kitchen and outside bathroom to complement the *mǎtǒng* (chamber pot). For the Shanghainese, a single-family kitchen and separate bedrooms remained a dream until the 1990s.

RELIGIOUS ARCHITECTURE

After the horrifying destruction of religious beliefs, practices and architecture that characterised the Cultural Revolution, religion is, slowly but surely, making a comeback in Shànghǎi (p34) – as it is nationwide – and many of the most impressive religious buildings are once more active places of worship. Don't expect to be bowled over by religious fervour – this isn't India – and be aware that most of the buildings you see will have been heavily restored, or even completely rebuilt. Nevertheless, you'll find some charming, calming city retreats as well as an interesting mix of architectural styles.

TEMPLES 寺庙

The place of prayer for Buddhist, Taoist or Confucian worshippers, Chinese *sìmiào* (temples) tend to follow a strict, schematic pattern. Most importantly, all are laid out on a north–south axis in a series of halls, with the main door of each hall facing south.

One striking difference from Christian churches is the temples' open plan, with buildings interspersed with breezy open-air courtyards. This allows the climate to permeate; seasons therefore play an essential role in defining a temple's disposition. The open-air layout furthermore allows the *qì* (气; energy) to circulate, dispersing stale air and allowing incense to be burned liberally.

Jade Buddha Temple (p100), one of Shànghǎi's few Buddhist places of worship

Buddhist temples of architectural note include the Jade Buddha Temple (p100), with its striking yellow-and-red walls, the Jing'an Temple (p102), a recent rebuild of one of Shànghǎi's first temples (c AD 247), and the Fazangjiang Temple (p83), a recently restored yellow-walled complex originally built in 1923 that has some unusual art deco touches.

Standout Taoist temples include the Temple of the Town God (p81), with its fine carvings, and the Baiyun Temple (p83), rebuilt in 2004 with attractive port-red walls. Both are in the Old Town, also home to the large Confucian Temple (p81), lovingly restored in the 1990s after taking a battering during the Cultural Revolution.

CHURCHES

St Ignatius Cathedral (p124) is Shànghǎi's standout Christian building. Originally built in 1904 it suffered hits during the Cultural Revolution (losing its spires and at one stage being used a grain warehouse), but was beautifully restored in 2002 with a few local touches (note the Chinese characters in the stained-glass windows).

Other churches of note are the beautiful Russian Orthodox Mission Church (p94), with its blue domes; the pretty Dongjiadu Catholic Church (p82), Shànghǎi's oldest church (c 1853); and the delightful St Joseph's Church (c 1862; p71), with its Gothic spires, now located within the grounds of a school.

MOSQUES

The main active mosque in Shànghǎi is the Peach Garden Mosque (p83), built in the Old Town in 1917. Whilst not particularly impressive architecturally, it is nevertheless an interesting mix of styles with its neoclassical-like facade, Islamic green domes and mixture of Arabic lettering and Chinese characters. For something more impressive, catch a train from Shanghai South station to Sōngjiāng (松江; Y10, 20 minutes), 25km west of the city centre, where you'll find Songjiang Mosque (松江清真寺; Sōngjiāng Qīngzhēnsì), Shànghǎi's oldest mosque, within walking distance of the station. Originally built in the 14th century, its current, distinctly Chinese design is a product of renovations made during the Ming dynasty.

SYNAGOGUES

Of the seven synagogues once built in Shànghǎi, only two remain. The recently renovated Ohel Moishe Synagogue (p115) is now the Shanghai Jewish Refugees Museum. Of more authentic charm is the rather neglected, ivy-cloaked Ohel Rachel Synagogue (Map pp98–9) in Jing'ān, which, built in 1920, was Shànghǎi's first synagogue.

St Ignatius Cathedral (p124)

pass by. But it is the state – the inflexible, communist government of China – that needs a full appraisal if we can even begin to guess at Shànghǎi's economic future. Will Shànghǎi continue to spearhead the galvanisation of China to superpower status or will it become a symbol of what-might-have-been in a climate of abrupt economic reversal?

They may be bandied around like medals, but shimmering GDP growth figures – which despite slipping to a 17-year low of 6.1% at the start of 2009 were still enviable when compared to same-time US and European growth rates – only tell part of the story. The eventual political hue of this one-party state has yet to finally set as the spectrum shifts from Marxist-Leninist Utopianism to Marxist–Thatcherism. Communist China is far less socialist than nations like the UK, where a fully functioning welfare state protects the underprivileged. In terms of free housing, education, health care or unemployment benefit, China today is far more coldly capitalist than sympathetically socialist.

Běijīng's fondness for coercive governance and excessive control-freakiness nurtures festering, unresolved social grievances. Amid all the uncertainty, what is definite is that popular faith in the Communist Party – its mandate to rule – is hardwired to continuing economic growth. This is a fragile symbiosis. The Chinese people cannot simply vote out the government, so faltering economic growth could expose the Communist Party's tenacity to retain power in the event of protests.

Pure economic problems in China traditionally range from sluggish domestic consumption and a high savings rate to an export-led economy and an overdependence on foreign investment. The government's massive financial rescue package and accompanying support measures were aimed at addressing such problems, but it is still too early to say whether this will have the effect of boosting domestic consumption enough to reduce China's reliance on exports in the long run.

China remains resilient in the face of any pessimistic prognoses. A long list of books have mused on China's coming economic demise, attempting to prick the bubble of expectation hanging over the country. Gordon Chang's eight-year-old polemic *The Coming Collapse of China* predicted a 2006 economic meltdown that failed to materialise. Kerry Brown's well-written *Struggling Giant: China in the 21st Century*, sees Brown apply his rich experience living and working in China to determine – in often humorous fashion – the startling incongruities of this land. *Mr China: A Memoir* by Tim Clissold is an hysterically honest account of how to lose money big time in China. However, for perhaps one of the most respected and well-researched recent accounts on China's economy, look for the award-winning *China Shakes the World* by James Kynge, former Beijing bureau-in-chief at the *Financial Times*.

Only time will tell if measures such as China's major economic stimulus packages will turn out to be a long-term success but they already had positive affects by the start of 2009. Car sales in China, for example, increased to US levels thanks to demand-stimulating policies such as discounts on new cars if old ones were traded in, and tax cuts on small-car purchases. Healthcare spending also received a much-needed boost with the hope of reducing the need to save for costly medical expenses thereby increasing household expenditure and thus consumption. However, many of these measures were only initially put in place for one year and some market analysts believe that for the growth in domestic consumption to be sustainable, significantly more money needs to be pumped into the social welfare system in order for domestic demand to remain healthy.

ENVIRONMENT & PLANNING
CLIMATE
Shànghǎi's humid subtropical climate means it is often grey and overcast here, so don't bank on clear blue skies at any time of the year. With a mean temperature of around 18°C, the city starts the year shivering in midwinter, when temperatures can drop below freezing and vistas are grey and misty. The Shànghǎi cold is not the dry, biting cold of Běijīng, but a clammy chill that seeps into the bones. Few apartments have central heating in winter, so heating comes from reverse-cycle air-conditioning, if at all.

Spring brings warming days and blossom to town, making March to mid-May probably one of the best times to visit weather-wise. As the weather warms, Shànghǎi residents take to wandering about town in pyjamas. Autumn (late September to mid-November) is also very pleasant, but it can still be very hot in September.

Summer may be the peak travel season, but the hot and humid weather makes conditions outside uncomfortable, with temperatures sometimes as high as 40°C (104°F) in July and August. The heat – a damp saunalike heat – is draining. June brings 'plum rains', saturating downpours that send pedestrians scrambling for cover as streets turn to rivers. Expect to see umbrellas in profusion on both wet and dry days, though, as Shànghǎi girls prefer their fair skin to be shielded from the sun's rays. Cooling winds blow into town in September and the temperature begins to slide, but watch out for sudden stingingly hot days at the tail end of summer, affectionately known as the Autumnal Tiger (*qiūlǎohǔ*). By December the thermal underwear is being unpacked. Rain is heaviest between June and September, but falls throughout the year.

In short, you'll need long johns and down jackets for winter, an ice cube for each armpit in summer and an umbrella handy at all times. See the When to Go section (p16) for more information on the best times to visit Shànghǎi.

Green Shànghǎi

In its ambition to morph into a fully international city in the twinkling of a construction-dust-inflamed eye, Shànghǎi was straining the limits of its environmental integrity even before the 2008 financial crisis refocused the priorities of world governments. An urgent need to increase domestic consumption, after the world-markets crash caused a sharp fall in export demand, inevitably diluted the importance of environmental concerns, but China has still been making bold claims in an attempt to improve its green credentials.

The government plans, for example, to increase use of solar and wind power over the next decade so that by 2020 one-fifth of China's energy needs will be met by renewable sources. In Shànghǎi, there are plans to bring drinkable tap water to 10 million residents by 2012. At present, Shanghainese would only neck water straight from the tap at gun point.

Recent setbacks have done little to instill confidence in China's ecological initiatives. Dōngtān on Chongming Island, north of Shànghǎi, was to become the world's first ecologically sustainable city, designed to accommodate half a million people in time for the start of World Expo. But poor planning led to the project being widely regarded as a flop, and by the start of 2009 it was showing no signs of getting off the ground.

One area showing promise has been the car sector. In early 2009, Běijīng unveiled a series of measures aimed at accelerating the development of greener transport, setting targets to produce half a million clean energy vehicles by 2011. Hybrid cars, such as BYD's FD3M – China's first mass-produced plug-in hybrid – which went on sale in December 2008, are also starting to make some headway.

But Shànghǎi clearly still has a lot of work to do. With four times the number of people per sq km living here than in New York, drains carry more than five million tons of industrial waste and untreated sewage into the mouth of the Yangzi each day. Shànghǎi's restaurants throw away an estimated 673 million polystyrene boxes and 1.3 billion bamboo chopsticks a year.

And China as a whole still uses energy at an extraordinarily inefficient rate – 10 times that of the developed world. In industrial production, it is estimated that China uses three times the world energy average to generate US$1 of GDP. To produce US$10,000 worth of goods, China uses seven times the amount of resources as Japan. Ten percent of China's GDP is frittered away by pollution and environmental degradation. China has also become a climate-change heavyweight and has overtaken the USA as the world's largest emitter of carbon dioxide.

Shànghǎi has one of the worst air qualities of all Chinese cities. Windy days are much clearer than still days, however. Cars generate 70% to 80% of air pollution, and vehicle numbers continue to multiply. And since 16 of the world's 20 most-polluted cities are in China (according to the Washington-based Worldwatch Institute) and the realisation that China's environmental problems are both national and international (acid rain and dust from China falls on Japan, and up to 25% of atmospheric pollution in Los Angeles originates in China, according to figures), Shànghǎi has its work cut out trying to stay clean.

A major hindrance is the absence of a grassroots, proactive green movement. Shànghǎi is being effectively prettified, with green cover increasing towards a target of 35%, and slowly cleaned up, with large fleets of buses running on natural gas and considerably less airborne construction dust compared to recent years, but it will still take years to clean everything up.

See the Getting Started chapter for more info on sustainability, (p20).

Urban Planning & Development

Over the past two decades, Shànghǎi has grown faster than any other world city and now houses almost 19 million people (a third of the population of the UK). To accommodate the vast influx of economic migrants, the city's size has expanded sixfold since the early 1990s. And with the state owning all land, urban development in Shànghǎi moves at a famously rapid rate compared to the snail's pace of similar projects in the West. For more on Shànghǎi's skyscrapers see our all singing and dancing full-colour section on the city's standout Architecture (p46).

The new deep-water container port at Yángshān, linked to the mainland by a 32.5km bridge, has made Shànghǎi the world's busiest port city in terms of cargo volume. Completed in 2007, the colossal 36km-long Hangzhou Bay Bridge links Níngbō in Zhèjiāng province with Jiāxīng, south of Shànghǎi. It is the world's longest cross-bay bridge.

GOVERNMENT & POLITICS

Shànghǎi has long courted extremism in politics and has served as a barometer for the mood of the nation. The Chinese Communist Party was formed here back in 1921 (p91). Mao Zedong cast the first stone of the Cultural Revolution in Shànghǎi by publishing in the city's newspapers a piece of political rhetoric he had been unable to get published in Běijīng. The Gang of Four had its power base here while the Shanghai People's Commune, modelled along the lines of the Paris Commune and established in February 1967, lasted a mere month before being closed down.

Things are different these days, and in its sixth decade of communist rule, Shànghǎi has become politically apathetic. With no forum for open political debate and strict taboos on questioning government policy, most Shànghǎi Chinese instead get their heads down and work, exceptionally hard, to forge an economic future for themselves and security for their families. There are few ways of dealing with political realities, and demonstrations tend to occur only if they dovetail with the government's agenda (eg anti-Japanese riots).

In a knowledge-based economy, censorship creates mammoth disadvantages. And it is still rife. Charter 08, a democracy document that circulated on the internet towards end of 2008 and that was signed by prominent Chinese citizens inside and outside the government, ended in a number of arrests. Běijīng's continued stringent control of information hugely impinges on China's ability to fully involve itself in the world. Many believe that one of net results of this is the frequent proliferation of mediocrity. China's educational system (p34) effectively sedates truly enquiring minds and stifles inventiveness.

Corruption – one of the principle complaints of the Tiananmen Square protesters in 1989 – survives as a powerful grievance. The indignant cannot count on a free press or a free and fair legal system to represent their complaints against corrupt activities, nor do they have the option of political activity. One high-profile move in recent years which suggested Běijīng was trying to deal with high-level corruption (while attempting to curb Shànghǎi's power) was the arrest and sentencing of city party-secretary Chen Liangyu.

As one of China's four municipalities (the others being Běijīng, Tiānjīn and Chóngqìng), Shànghǎi is headed by the mayor of Shànghǎi, although the Shànghǎi (Communist) party chief holds as much, if not more power. In 2006, Chen, the then party chief was sacked for corruption, raising international eyebrows. Born locally, Chen had been a member of the Shànghǎi clique, an informal group of politicians assembled by former President Jiang Zemin, who before his rise to president, had previously held both the Shànghǎi mayor and Shànghǎi party chief positions. Chen's duties were initially taken over by city mayor Han Zheng before the position was given to Xi Jinping, a close ally of President Hu Jintao, who has never been a member of the Shànghǎi clique. Yu Zhengsheng now holds the post following Xi Jinping's promotion to Vice President of China. Chen, meanwhile, has been sentenced to 18 years in prison.

MEDIA

Shànghǎi (along with the rest of China, bar Hong Kong) has a media system that differs hugely from that to which Westerners are accustomed. It's no secret that the CCP uses media as a propaganda tool – the country's most powerful monitoring body is actually called the Communist Party's Central Propaganda Department (CPD) – to promote its own political achievements while simultaneously dismissing bad news. The party line is crudely channelled into the full variety of media, from war films on TV to newspaper commentaries, radio news programs and internet sites. It all gets very numbing for visitors, even after only a very brief exposure.

The two main censoring agencies that report to the CPD are the General Administration of Press and Publication (GAPP), which deals with the written press, and the State Administration of Radio, Film, and Television (SARFT), its broadcast equivalent. Under the watchful eye of the CPD, these two agencies make sure content promotes and remains consistent with party doctrine. Guidelines are given to heads of media outlets who, in turn, ditch controversial stories and decide how delicate topics will be covered. Journalists who do not follow the rules can face reprisals. In fact, even publicizing the rules invites punishment, as in the case of Shi Tao, a journalist who, according to media watchdog Reporters Without Borders, was detained in 2004 and is now serving a 10-year sentence for posting an online summary describing the CPD's instructions for how to report on the 15-year anniversary of the Tiananmen Square crackdown.

Every year, China finds itself near the bottom of the Reporters Without Borders annual World Press Freedom index. According to the Committee to Protect Journalists, China tops the world league for jailing reporters. The social impact of this cannot be underestimated: in the absence of hard facts and balanced analysis, even intelligent and cynical Shànghǎi readers find themselves repeating pro-China mantras at the drop of a hat. Constant propaganda has created a marked absence of independent thinking among the Chinese – the Shànghǎi Chinese included.

With such limitations on what can be reported, many newspapers opt for tabloid-style content, where celebrity gossip shares the page with graphic accounts of homicides and UFO abductions.

A major lifeline is the blogosphere, where young, modern Chinese get to grips with the issues that affect them. China has now overtaken the USA as the world's most populous internet nation, and the internet – along with mobile phone technology – has emerged as the principal tool for circumventing media restrictions despite the enormous reach of the filtering system known as the Great Firewall of China that blocks websites deemed hostile to the Communist Party's interests. The list of popular websites that have been blocked from time to time over the past few years includes Hotmail, Twitter and YouTube.

For a less censored slant on stories making the news in China, visit www.danwei.org. To see what Chinese netizens make of the latest headlines, go to www.chinasmack.com.

For more on Shànghǎi websites and blogs, see p20. See p20 for more information on newspapers and magazines.

FASHION

The Shanghainese have the reputation of being the most fashionable people in China. 'There's nothing the Cantonese won't eat,' so one version of a popular Chinese saying goes, 'and nothing the Shanghainese won't wear'. Although you're still quite likely to see locals wandering around their neighbourhood dressed in clearly very comfortable, but extremely uncool pyjamas and slippers, Shànghǎi does have breathtaking, voguish pockets and the petite figures of Shànghǎi *xiǎojiě* (young women) can ooze glamour in even the cheapest and trashiest of skirts and blouses.

The city government has optimistically declared its goal to make Shànghǎi a fashion centre to rank alongside Tokyo, London, New York and Paris. In reality, though, the city still has a long way to go just to catch up with its own 1930s fashion scene, when images of Chinese women clad in figure-hugging *qípáo* (cheongsams) gave rise to its epithet as the 'Paris of the East'. Shanghai Fashion Week is a biannual event showcasing the work of local, national and international designers. There is also the city-sponsored month-long International Fashion Culture Festival in March or April.

On the street, Chinese-language lifestyle magazines such as *Shanghai Tatler*, *Elle*, *Vogue*, *Harper's Bazaar* and *Marie Claire* crowd every corner newsstand and the latest mobile phone has taken on almost religious importance. Christian Dior, Gucci and Louis Vuitton shops glut Shànghǎi's top-end malls, while trendy boutiques line French Concession streets such as Changle Rd, Xinle Rd and Nanchang Rd.

See the Shopping chapter for more information, p136.

NEIGHBOURHOODS

top picks

What's your recommendation? lonelyplanet.com/shanghai

NEIGHBOURHOODS

Central Shànghǎi is geographically and existentially cleaved into two hefty chunks by the busy waters of the winding Huangpu River (黄浦江; Huángpǔ Jiāng), with Pǔxī (浦西; west of the Huangpu River) and Pǔdōng (浦东; east of the Huangpu River) locked in a face-off to define the city. In crossing the river from west to east, you leave the elegant traces of Shànghǎi's lavish and notorious past behind in Pǔxī and step into Pǔdōng, a vertical cityscape carried into the clouds by its own brash self-confidence.

> 'Without Běijīng's clear-cut focus and archaic core, modern-day Shànghǎi still owes much to the layout of its original concessions.'

Shànghǎi's cultural centre of gravity – where its heritage, historic architecture, snappy commercial zones, talk-of-the-town restaurants, bars and must-see sights conveniently converge – is Pǔxī, a huge area fragmented into a rambling mosaic of districts. Some have unmistakable personalities and persuasions, but others are more low-key. For this reason, we have divided the book up into neighbourhoods, some of which reflect an area's historic integrity that may or may not overlap with Shànghǎi's official district jigsaw.

Without Běijīng's clear-cut focus and archaic core, modern-day Shànghǎi still owes much to the layout of its original concessions. Shànghǎi's most iconic zone is the Bund, where the city's most puffed-up historic architecture shares the limelight with a gaggle of top-league restaurants, bars and exclusive hotels. The last helpfully can be found in abundance, in all budget brackets from shoestring to landmark. The People's Square area to the west marks the geographic centre of town and the western terminus of East Nanjing Rd's shopping maelstrom.

The ragged Old Town lies south of the Bund, near the southwestern shore of the Huangpu River. Stretching west of the Old Town is the elegant French Concession, with its stylish charm, leafy backstreets and voguish boutiques.

North of the French Concession extends the vibrant commercial district of Jìng'ān, an expat-friendly domain focused on the bustling West Nanjing Rd, with an abundance of period architecture, malls, top-end hotels and appealing *lòngtáng* architecture (p49).

Needing little introduction, Pǔdōng on the east side of the Huangpu River is a dazzling panorama of high-altitude five-star hotels, banks, MagLev trains, megamalls and neon advertising set to the constant roar of construction. The most visible side of Pǔdōng is new-fangled newcomer Lùjiāzuǐ, from where Century Ave thrusts towards Century Park (p113).

Hóngkǒu and north Shànghǎi reach north of the Bund into a tattier and grittier realm of old lanes and working class textures; it's currently a hot redevelopment area.

The south and west of Shànghǎi, divided into the neighbourhoods Xújiāhuì, Chángníng, Gǔběi and Hóngqiáo, are mostly of interest to long-term residents.

Most arriving travellers stick to taxis (p248), the metro (p247) or bicycles (p245) to move about town; walking large distances is shattering, buses are user-hostile for foreigners and car hire is a no-go for tourists.

CITY OF 10,000 CHANGES

Shànghǎi exists in a state of continual transformation; as the *I Ching* once put it, unrelenting change is the one constant you can rely on. The 2010 World Expo was the most recent catalyst for a major city overhaul, and, in addition to US$14.5 billion in transportation upgrades, numerous sights were in the process of opening (or being renovated) as we went to press. These include: the Bund (p64, transformed into a pedestrian area), new Suzhou Creek boat tours (p103), the Shanghai Museum of Folk Collectibles (p81), the Cool Docks (p82), the Shanghai World Financial Center (p107), the Ohel Moishe Synagogue (p115), Fisherman's Wharf (p119) and the Chinese Wushu Museum (p119) as well as the pavilions at the World Expo site (p18), some of which will be permanent structures.

ITINERARY BUILDER

Shànghǎi conveniently bundles most of its sights and must-do activities into the fashionable parts of Pǔxī. Although sooner or later you'll find yourself east of the river in Pǔdōng, your prime dining, drinking, sightseeing and socialising will be concentrated west of the Huangpu waters. A handful of more further-flung sights gives you the chance to cast your net wider.

AREA	ACTIVITIES	Sights	Shopping	Eating
	The Bund	The Bund (p64) Cruise the Huangpu (p65) Metersbonwe Costume Museum (p66)	Annabel Lee (p138) Blue Shanghai White (p138) Suzhou Cobblers (p139)	Tiandi (p157) South Memory (p158) Jean Georges (p157)
	People's Square	Shanghai Museum (p72) Shanghai Urban Planning Exhibition Hall (p74) MOCA Shanghai (p75)	Shanghai Museum Art Store (p139) Shanghai No 1 Food Store (p139)	Yang's Fry Dumplings (p159) Xiǎo Nán Guó (p159) Nina's Sichuan House (p159)
	Old Town	Yuyuan Gardens (p78) Chenxiangge Nunnery (p81) Dongjiadu Cathedral backstreets (p82)	Old Street (p140) Shiliupu Fabric Market (p139) Dongtai Road Antique Market (p140)	Sōngyuèlóu (p161) Nanxiang Steamed Bun Restaurant (p160) Mingtang Organic Dining (p160)
	French Concession	Taikang Rd Art Centre (p85) Xīntiāndì (p90) French Concession backstreets (p95)	Taikang Road Art Centre (p141) Clothing boutiques (p141) Spin (p142)	T8 (p161) Bǎoluó Jiǔlóu (p166) Sichuan Citizen (p168)
	Jìng'ān	M50 (p97) Jade Buddha Temple (p100) Lìlòng walking tour (p104)	Fenshine Fashion & Accessories Plaza (p146) Amy Lin's Pearls (p146) Art Deco (p146)	Fu 1039 (p170) Lynn (p170) Vegetarian Lifestyle (p172)
	Pǔdōng & Century Avenue Area	Shanghai World Financial Center (p107) Jinmao Tower (p109) Shanghai History Museum (p110)	AP Xinyang Fashion & Gifts Market (p147)	On 56 (p173) South Beauty (p173) Element Fresh (p171)
	Hóngkǒu & North Shànghǎi	Ohel Moishe Synagogue (p115) Post Museum (p116) Lu Xun Memorial Hall (p117)	Qipu Market (p147) Electronics Market (p147) Duolun Road Cultural Street (p116)	Factory (p174) Afanti Restaurant (p174)
	Xújiāhuì & South Shànghǎi	Longhua Temple & Pagoda (p121) CY Tung Maritime Museum (p121) Qībǎo (p131)	Grand Gateway (p148) Henry Antique Warehouse (p148)	Grand Gateway (p148) Shanghai Uncle (p174) Xinjiang Fengwei Restaurant (p175)

HOW TO USE THIS TABLE

The table below allows you to plan a day's worth of activities in any area of the city. Simply select which area you wish to explore, and then mix and match from the corresponding listings to build your day. The first item in each cell represents a well-known highlight of the area, while the other items are more off-the-beaten-track gems.

Drinking	Entertainment	Sleeping
Glamour Bar (p179) New Heights (p179) Captain's Bar (p178)	Glamour Bar (p179) House of Blues and Jazz (p193) Cabaret (p192)	Westin Shanghai (p203) Peace Hotel (p204) Ming Town Hiker Youth Hostel (p206)
Barbarossa (p178) 789 Nanjing Lu Bar (p179) Kathleen's 5 (p159)	Yifu Theatre (p189) Shanghai Grand Theatre (p194) Peace Cinema (p190)	JW Marriott Tomorrow Square (p203) Shangfu Holiday Hotel (p205) Ming Town E-tour Youth Hostel (p206)
Old Shanghai Teahouse (p180) Fat Olive (p160)	D2 (p190)	
Cotton's (p181) TMSK (p182) Citizen Café (p183)	Shelter (p191) Melting Pot (p192) Zapata's (p183)	Mansion Hotel (p207) Lapis Casa (p209) Quintet (p210)
Spot (p184) Café 85°C (p184) I Love Shanghai (p184)	Shanghai Centre Theatre (p188) Muse (p191) Apsara Spa (p197)	Jia Shanghai (p211) URBN (p211) Le Tour Traveler's Rest (p212)
Cloud 9 (p184) 100 Century Avenue (p184) Blue Frog (p172)	Oriental Art Center (p193) Stellar Cinema City (p190) SISU Cycling Club (p197)	Grand Hyatt (p212) St Regis Shanghai (p213) Park Hyatt (p213)
Vue (p179) Factory (p174) Old Film Café (p185)	Chinatown (p193) Shanghai Circus World (p188)	Broadway Mansions (p214) Astor House Hotel (p214) Koala Garden House (p215)
		Asset Hotel (p216)

SHANGHAI CITY

To Formula One
Grand Prix

Shanghai
West Train
Station
上海火车站

Zhongtan Rd

Pengpu
Xincun
彭浦新村

Hutai Rd

Lingshi Rd

Pǔtuó

To Shanghai International
Golf & Country Club

Wuning Rd 武宁路

Caoyang Rd
曹杨路

Jinshajiang Rd 金沙江路

Jinshajiang Rd
金沙江路站

East China
Normal
University

Jing'ān

Jing'an Park

Jing'an Park

Songhong Rd
松虹路

Beixinjing
北新泾

Changning Rd 长宁路

Changfeng Park

Zhongshan
Park
中山公园

Tianshan
Park
天山公园

Chángníng

Xianxia Rd

Dongua
University
东华大学

Middle Huaihai Rd

Hongqiao
Airport
虹桥机场

Longxi Rd

Hongqiao
Central
Garden
虹桥中心花园

W Huaihai Rd

Jiaotong
University
交通大学

Xújiāhuì

Wuyi Rd

Hongqiao Rd

Guyang Rd

Gǔběi

W Yan'an Rd

W Zhongshan Rd

Xúhuì

Wuzhong Rd

Cáohéjīng

Caohejing
Development
Zone
漕河泾开发区

Guilin Rd
桂林路

Cabxi
Park
漕溪公园

Longhua
Park
龙华公园

Zhongshan No 2 Rd

A9 Expressway

Minhang

A20 Expressway

Hechuan Rd

Shanghai
Normal University
上海师范大学

Kepu
Park

Caobao Rd

Shilong Rd
石龙路

Longwu Rd

Xingzhong Rd
兴中路

Qihao
七宝站

To Dino Beach (1km);
Shanghai Yinqixing
Indoor Skiing

Shanghai
South Train
Station

17

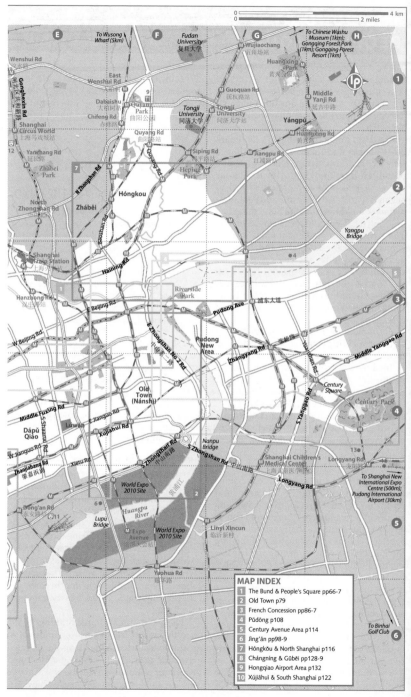

THE BUND & PEOPLE'S SQUARE 外滩、人民广场

Drinking p178; Eating p156; Shopping p137; Sleeping p203

Exuding a gravitas and pomposity that Pǔdōng across the river could never muster, the iconic stone buildings of the Bund (外滩; Wàitān; pronounced 'bunned' in English) typify colonial-era Shànghǎi. More than any other Shànghǎi streetscape, the Bund is a boastful reminder of the city's cosmopolitan and decadent heyday and is the first port of call for most visitors to Shànghǎi.

The area, home to Shànghǎi's landmark hotels, banks and financial houses, slipped into a coma during the communist tenure post-1949. It was only in the 1990s, after the pervasive effects of economic reform had begun to penetrate the grime and soot of its hallmark buildings, that the Bund sensed an uplifting renaissance in the Huangpu breeze. The strip has become enamoured with its stupendous real-estate value and exclusive pedigree, and today the city's most exclusive boutiques, restaurants and hotels see the Bund as the only place to be. Price tags and restaurant bills here are closer to Hong Kong or New York than the rest of mainland China.

top picks

THE BUND

- The Bund (left) Stroll along Shànghǎi's original monument to money.
- Views of Pǔdōng (p178) Watch Pǔdōng light up through a martini glass.
- River cruise (opposite) Cruise the Huangpu River to size up the city, east and west.
- East Nanjing Road (p137) Plunge into the neon-lit crowds.
- Metersbonwe Costume Museum (p66) And now for something completely different...

The streets leading west from the waterfront form a gritty commercial district housed in the shells of concession-era buildings, mixed in with new apartment complexes and hotels. Even the most casual of wanders in this area, defined by a tatty grandeur, divulge sudden architectural gems; see the walking tour (p68) for pointers. Beyond this is People's Square (p72), the de facto city centre. Here you'll find a clutch of museums, the city hall, a park and Shànghǎi's busiest metro junction.

Linking the Bund with People's Sq is East Nanjing Rd, once China's most famous shopping street. It's now home to a bonanza of retail shops, gaudy neon signs, popular hotels and determined English-speaking girls latching onto foreign men, seeking kick-backs from cafes they drag their victims to. If you don't mind the crowds, it's a fun walk.

THE BUND 外滩

Mainland China's most iconic concession-era backdrop and a source of intense local pride (tinged with regret for its reverberating echoes of foreign encroachment and subjugation), the Bund is Shànghǎi's standout spectacle. Coming to Shànghǎi and missing the Bund is like visiting Běijīng and bypassing the Forbidden City or the Great Wall.

Originally a towpath for dragging barges of rice, the Bund gets its Anglo-Indian name from the embankments built up to discourage flooding (a *band* is an embankment in Hindi). It became the seat of foreign power in the early 20th century and presented a grand facade of ostentatious buildings to those arriving in Shànghǎi by river.

The Bund was once situated only a few feet from the water, but in the mid-1990s the road was widened and a 771m-long flood barrier was built (the river now lies above the level of Nanjing Rd due to subsidence), which now serves as a promenade. Then, in 2009, the majority of traffic was diverted underground (although there are still six lanes), with the aim of making the area more pedestrian-friendly. The renovation project, which was nearing completion as this book went to press, will add more park space and should be a considerable improvement on the previous traffic-clogged East Zhongshan No 1 road.

The Bund offers a horde of things to do. See the walking tour (p68) for a rundown of the architecture. Amble along the elevated riverside promenade beside the Huangpu River for visions of Pǔdōng and China's tireless tourist boom: boisterous hawkers, toy sellers, the endless squawk of '*Huānyíng Guānglín*' ('Welcome') and coin-operated telescopes aimed across the river. Otherwise take a boat trip (right) on the Huangpu River and survey both the aristocratic architecture of the Bund and the brash steel and glass horizon of Pǔdōng, or simply cross the river by ferry (p247). The area is pretty much open round the clock, but it's at its best in the early morning, when locals are out practising taichi, or in the early evening, when both sides of the river are lit up and the majesty of the waterfront is at its grandest. Historic buildings along the Bund and throughout Shànghǎi are affixed with plaques from the Shanghai Municipal Government proclaiming their historic value in both English and Chinese (although the English translations are generally quite meagre).

The Bund is a public space so there's no entry charge and you can wander at will, but some buildings are more accessible than others. Retail centres, restaurants and bars are found at Nos 3, 5, 6, 9 and 18, with more shopping arcades to come.

For a rundown of some of the buildings north of the Bund in Hóngkǒu close to Suzhou Creek, turn to the Hóngkǒu and north Shànghǎi walking tour (p119). For exhaustive coverage of the Bund and its buildings, try to get your hands on a copy of Peter Hibbard's *The Bund Shanghai: China Faces West* (Odyssey Guides), available in many bookstores citywide.

HUANGPU PARK

Map pp66-7

黄浦公园 **Huángpǔ Gōngyuán**

Ⓜ **East Nanjing Rd**

Shànghǎi's – indeed China's – very first public park was laid out in 1886 by a Scottish gardener shipped out to Shànghǎi especially for that purpose. Originally called the Public Gardens, the park today is famously deformed by its anachronistic Monument to the People's Heroes (人民英雄纪念塔; Rénmín Yīngxióng Jìniàntǎ), underneath which is the Bund History Museum (外滩历史纪念馆; Wàitān Lìshǐ Jìniànguǎn; admission free; ☉ 9am-4pm), undergoing renovation at the time of writing.

HUANGPU RIVER CRUISE

Map pp66-7

黄浦江游览 **Huángpǔ Jiāng Yóulǎn**

☎ 6374 4461; 219-239 East Zhongshan No 2 Rd; 中山东二路219-239号; Ⓜ **East Nanjing Rd**

The Huangpu River offers staggering views of the Bund and riverfront activity. Tour boats pass an enormous variety of craft – freighters, bulk carriers, roll-on roll-off ships, sculling sampans, giant cranes and massive floating TV advertisements. Most tour boats depart from the docks on the south end of the Bund, near East Jinling Rd, where tickets can be purchased; popular 30-minute cruises also depart hourly from the Pearl Dock (明珠码头; Míngzhū Mǎtou; Map p108; 1 Century Ave) in Lùjiāzuǐ.

The river trip is big business with a medley of operators offering cruises. Tickets are Y50/70 for the one-hour day/night cruise to Yangpu Bridge (杨浦大桥; Yángpǔ Dàqiáo; Map pp62–3). Other boat trips lasso in both Yangpu Bridge and Nanpu Bridge (南浦大桥; Nánpǔ Dàqiáo; Map p79). The 3½-hour cruise up to the mouth of the Yangzi River at Wúsōngkǒu (吴淞口) costs Y150.

Depending on your enthusiasm for loading-cranes, the night cruises are more scenic, though boat traffic during the day is interesting. Departure times vary depending on which trip you take, but there are generally morning, afternoon and evening departures; boats to Wúsōngkǒu generally leave at 2pm.

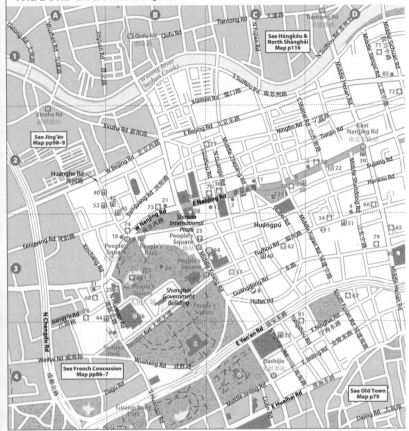

METERSBONWE COSTUME MUSEUM

Map pp66–7

美特斯邦威服饰博物馆 **Měitèsībāngwēi Fúshì Bówùguǎn**

☎ 6352 7801; www.mbmuseum.org; 5th fl, 387 East Nanjing Rd; 南京东路387号5楼; admission free; ⏲ 10am-10pm; Ⓜ East Nanjing Rd

This captivating private museum was opened by the owner of Chinese fashion giant Metersbonwe to display the traditional attire of Han Chinese and ethnic groups from around the country. The collection is enormous (not everything is on display) and ranges from Emperor Qianlong's dragon robes and Shànghǎi *qípáo* (cheongsam dress) to delicate embroidery from China's southwest and even an outfit made of salmon skin. It's located on the fifth floor of their flagship store (those who want to take a look at today's youth fashion may also be interested in checking out the store – Metersbonwe has over 1800 locations across China).

SHANGHAI GALLERY OF ART

Map pp66-7

上海沪申画廊 **Shànghǎi Hùshēn Huàláng**

☎ 6321 5757; www.threeonthebund.com; 3rd fl, Three on the Bund, 3 East Zhongshan No 1 Rd; 中山东1路3号3楼; ⏲ 11am-9pm; Ⓜ East Nanjing Rd

Shànghǎi's handiest (and perhaps trendiest) art gallery finds itself sandwiched between two floors at Three on the Bund, and introduces you to Shànghǎi's effortless marriage of contemporary art and *haute couture*. Pop in for glimpses of high-brow and conceptual Chinese art, and a taste of the gallery's

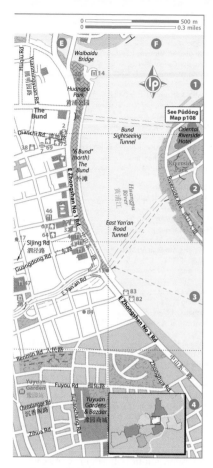

gallery website states: 'SHANGHAI is THE center of an electro DECO revolution......... it is the FIRST 21st-Century BOUNDARY URBan SPACestation.'

BUND MUSEUM
Map pp66-7

外滩博物馆 **Wàitān Bówùguǎn**
1 East Zhongshan No 2 Rd; 中山东二路1号; admission free; ☉ 9am-5pm; Ⓜ **East Nanjing Rd**
The modest museum at the Meteorological Signal Tower (外滩信号台; Wàitān Xìnhào Tái; also called the Gutzlaff Signal Tower) contains a small scattering of ground-floor historical photographs. Originally a wooden tower, this version was built in 1907 as a meteorological relay station set up by the tireless Shànghǎi Jesuits. The tower was moved southeast by 22.4m in the mid-1990s. Head up the staircase to the 2nd floor where a bar has cashed in on the monuments' unique character and spot-on views from its terrace a further floor above.

BUND SIGHTSEEING TUNNEL
Map pp66-7

外滩观光隧道 **Wàitān Guānguāng Suìdào**
☎ 5888 6000; **300 East Zhongshan No 1 Rd**; 中山东一路300号; 1-way/return Y40/50; ☉ 8am-10.30pm summer, to 10pm winter; Ⓜ **East Nanjing Rd**
A 647m voyage with entertainment from budget effects, garish lighting and dreadful props, the Bund Sightseeing Tunnel is a transport mode that guarantees to get you to Pǔdōng in an altered state. Stepping

rarefied atmosphere and manifestly exclusive inclinations.

CONTRASTS
Map pp66-7

对比窗艺廊 **Duìbǐchuāng Yìláng**
☎ 6323 1989; www.contrastsgallery.com; **181 Middle Jiangxi Rd**; 江西中路181号; ☉ 10am-10pm; Ⓜ **East Nanjing Rd**
This art gallery is most notable for its owner, the Hong Kong–raised, London-educated property heiress and socialite Pearl Lam, who has a string of galleries around the world and is one of the more influential figures in China's contemporary art and design scene. Known for her iconoclastic tastes, the exhibits here are supposed to be provocative but can be somewhat uneven. As the

TRANSPORT: THE BUND & PEOPLE'S SQUARE

Metro The Bund is a five-minute walk east from the East Nanjing Rd stop (lines 2 and 10). People's Sq is the city's main transfer station and is the intersection for lines 1, 2 and 8.

Ferry Goes from the south end of the Bund to Lùjiāzuǐ in Pǔdōng; see p247.

Bund Sightseeing Tunnel Runs from the Bund to Pǔdōng under the Huangpu River; see above for details.

Tourist 'Train' Runs the length of East Nanjing Rd's pedestrianised section (tickets Y2) from Middle Henan Rd to the Shanghai No 1 Department Store.

THE BUND & PEOPLE'S SQUARE

from the trains at the terminus, visitors are visibly nonplussed, their disbelief surpassed only by those with return tickets. Connoisseurs of unabashed cheesiness will love it.

SHANGHAI MUSEUM OF NATURAL HISTORY Map pp66–7

上海自然博物馆 Shànghǎi Zìrán Bówùguǎn
☎ 6321 3548; 260 East Yan'an Rd; 延安东路 260号; admission Y5; ☺ 9am-4.30pm Tue-Sun (last tickets sold 3.30pm); Ⓜ East Nanjing Rd
Located in the former Cotton Exchange Building (built in 1923), the exhibits at this dusty and gloomy museum haven't been touched since the 1950s – now that's something! It is easily the city's most forlorn attraction and is horribly out of date, but, like the Bund Sightseeing Tunnel, it's a bizarre experience and it has its fans. The museum's former chairman, the gangster Du Yuesheng (p28), built the dramatic red-brick building across East Yan'an Rd as the Chung Wai Bank (with a private bullet-proof elevator). It's all expected to go soon, though. City officials feel it's something of an embarrassment and a new natural history museum (more in line with post-1950s scientific theories) is scheduled to open in the Jìng'ān district in 2012.

THE BUND & AROUND
Walking Tour

1 Broadway Mansions The brick pile of Broadway Mansions (p214) gauntly rises north of Suzhou Creek, not far from the Russian Consulate-General and the Astor House Hotel (p214). Head south over Waibaidu Bridge (Garden Bridge) – over which trams used to glide – with Huangpu Park (p65) to your east.

THE BUND & PEOPLE'S SQUARE

2 Bank of China Building Opposite Huangpu Park is the old Glen Line Shipping building (No 28; later the German Consulate) and the former headquarters of early opium traders Jardine Matheson (No 27). Standing on the site of the former German Club Concordia, the imposing Bank of China Building (No 23) was built in 1937. The Bank of China was the first bank with government backing (originally established as the Qing Imperial Bank in 1897); their national headquarters moved from Běijīng to Shànghǎi in 1928,

NO DOGS OR CHINESE

A notorious sign at Huangpu Park (p65), then called the Public Gardens, apocryphally declared 'No dogs or Chinese allowed'. Although this widely promoted notice never actually existed, the general gist of the wording hits the mark. A series of regulations was indeed posted outside the gardens listing 10 rules governing use of the park. The first regulation noted that 'The gardens are for the use of the foreign community', while the fourth ruled that 'Dogs and bicycles are not admitted'. Chinese were indeed barred from the park (as expressed in the first regulation), an injustice that gave rise to the canard. The bluntly worded sign has however become firmly embedded in the Chinese consciousness. Bruce Lee destroys a Shànghǎi park sign declaring 'No dogs and Chinese allowed' with a flying kick in *Fist of Fury* and Chinese history books cite the insult as further evidence of Chinese humiliation at the hands of foreigners. For a thorough academic examination of the subject, hunt down *Shanghai's 'Dogs and Chinese not Admitted' Sign: Legend, History and Contemporary Symbol* by Robert A Bickers and Jeffrey N Wasserstrom, published in the *China Quarterly*, No 142 (June 1995).

a reflection of the growing importance of Shànghǎi as a financial centre. In the 1920s the bank established residential compounds for its employees that peculiarly foreshadowed communism's *dānwèi* (work unit) organisation.

3 Peace Hotel Lording it over the corner of East Nanjing Rd and the Bund, the landmark Fairmont Peace Hotel at No 20, constructed between 1926 and 1929 (and closed for renovations at the time of writing), was built as the Cathay by Victor Sassoon, and originally occupied only the 4th to 7th floors of the Sassoon house. It wasn't for the hoi polloi, with a guest list including Charlie Chaplin, George Bernard Shaw and Noel Coward, who penned *Private Lives* here in four days in 1930 when he had the flu. Sassoon himself spent weekdays in his personal suite on the top floor with 360-degree views. The hotel was renamed the Peace Hotel in 1956, and later used as a base during the Cultural Revolution. Even if you are not a guest, pop in for a glimpse of the former art-deco grandeur – hopefully fully restored during the renovations.

4 Bund 18 An assortment of high-profile tenants has occupied Bund 18 (外滩十八号; Wàitān Shíbāhào), originally the Chartered Bank of India and Australia, but it's so exclu-sive it's virtually a ghost town. Seventh-floor Bar Rouge (p178) is only open in the evening, but has excellent views of Pǔdōng and the straining Atlas figures holding up the roof of the adjacent former home of the *North China Daily News* (No 17), once the main English-language newspaper in China. Today No 17 is again home to American Insurance International, the first of the Bund's original tenants (who left en masse in 1949) to return to its former home.

5 Customs House Three buildings down, the Customs House (No 13) was erected in 1925 as one of the most important buildings on the Bund. Capping the building was the largest clock face in Asia and 'Big Ching', a bell modelled on London's Big Ben. Clocks were by no means new to China, but Shànghǎi was the first city where they gained widespread acceptance and the lives of the masses became dictated by a regulated, common schedule. The bell was dismantled in the Cultural Revolution and replaced by loudspeakers that blasted out revolutionary slogans and songs. The original customs jetty stood across from the building, on the Huangpu River.

6 Hongkong & Shanghai Banking Corporation (HSBC) Adjacent to the Customs House, the Hongkong and Shanghai Banking Corpora-

---

tion (HSBC) building was constructed in 1923, when it was the second-largest bank in the world and 'the finest building east of Suez'. One of the pair of bronze lions that once guarded the entrance can now be found in the Shanghai History Museum (p110). The bank was first established in Hong Kong in 1864 and in Shànghǎi in 1865 to finance trade, and soon became one of the richest in Shànghǎi, arranging the indemnity paid after the Boxer Uprising. Enter and marvel at the beautiful mosaic ceiling, featuring the 12 zodiac signs and the world's eight great banking centres. If you'd like to take a break, try Bund 12 Café (p179) on the 2nd floor inside; exit and re-enter using the north entrance.

7 Shanghai Club Passing the upscale retail outlets at No 9, No 6, No 5 and Three on the Bund brings you to the city's most famous bastion of British snobbery, the Shanghai Club (No 2). It had 20 rooms for residents, but its most famous accoutrement was its bar – at 33m said to be the longest in the world. Foreign businessmen would sit here according to rank (no Chinese or women were allowed in the club), with the taipans (foreign heads of a business) closest to the view of the Bund. The building has long-been empty though it's slated to become a boutique hotel in the near future.

8 Meteorological Signal Tower Past the McBain Building at No 1 is the 49m-tall Meteorological Signal Tower, originally built in 1908 opposite the French consulate and now housing the modest Bund Museum (p67). A bar is on the 2nd floor, with seating on the terrace.

9 St Joseph's Church Walk west along East Yan'an Rd (延安中路), which originally marked the dividing line between the international and French concessions, before strolling south along South Sichuan Rd (四川南路) to the Gothic spires of St Joseph's Church (若瑟堂; Ruòsè Táng; 36 South Sichuan Rd). The French church was consecrated in 1862 and is now surrounded by a school, through which you can occasionally gain access.

10 Golden Cage Heading north up Middle Sichuan Rd (四川中路), pop in and examine the splendid gold ceiling mosaics and stunning stained glass of the former Golden Cage at No 93 on the corner with Guangdong Rd (广东路), once home to the captive concubines of

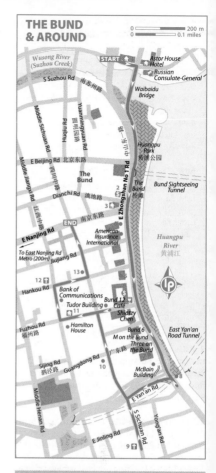

THE BUND & AROUND

WALK FACTS

Start Broadway Mansions (M Tiantong Rd/East Nanjing Rd)
End East Nanjing Rd
Distance 3km
Time 2½ hours
Fuel stop Bund 12 Café (p179)

a colourful Chinese entrepreneur. At Fuzhou Rd (福州路) head east to look at the Tudor building at No 44, the former offices of Calbeck Macgregor & Co.

11 Metropole Hotel Backtrack west until you reach the corner of Fuzhou Rd and Middle Jiangxi Rd (江西中路), where the complimentary architecture of the Hamilton House

The naming of streets in Shànghǎi once depended on which concession they belonged to, French or English, except for the central area of the city where the streets were given the names of Chinese cities and provinces. While the foreign names have disappeared, streets named after Chinese places have been retained: those named after other Chinese cities are oriented east–west and those named after provinces north–south. Below are some of Shànghǎi's former street names:

Now	Then
East Yan'an Rd	Edward VII Ave
Fanyu Rd	Columbia Rd
Fenyang Rd	Rue Pichon
Gaolan Rd	Rue Corneille
Guangdong Rd	Canton Rd
Huaihai Rd	Ave Joffre
Jiangsu Rd	Edinburgh Rd
Jinling Rd	Ave Foch
Jinshan Rd	Astor Rd
Tongren Rd	Hardoon Rd
West Nanjing Rd	Bubbling Well Rd
Xiangshan Rd	Rue Molière
Xinhua Rd	Amherst Rd

(福州大楼; Fúzhōu Dàlóu) and the Metropole Hotel (新城饭店; Xīnchéng Fàndiàn), both built around 1934 on the orders of Victor Sassoon, create an engaging balance.

12 Trinity Cathedral Turn north onto Middle Jiangxi Rd past the Bank of Communications at No 200 – pop in and see the marble interior – to the corner of Hankou Rd (汉口路). The red-brick building on the northwest corner is Trinity Cathedral (1869), known to the Chinese as the Red Temple (红庙; Hóng Miào).

13 Guangdong Development Bank

Walk east along Hankou Rd, once a street of publishers and presses. At the corner with Sichuan Rd lies the elegant portico of the Guangdong Development Bank, formerly the Joint Savings Society Bank (1928) and designed by Ladislaus Hudec (p49). Walking north brings you to East Nanjing Rd (南京东路).

PEOPLE'S SQUARE
人民广场

Every communist metropolis worth its salt has an imposing public square at its heart, and Shànghǎi has People's Square (Rénmín Guǎngchǎng; Map pp66–7), aka Renmin Square. Although Shànghǎi has no clearly defined focal point, the square serves as an acknowledged geographic and cultural hub and centre of gravity – especially as metro lines 1, 2 and 8 intersect here at the city's busiest subway junction.

Much less austere and regimented than Běijīng's crypto-Stalinist Tiananmen Square, People's Square is free of the rigid geometry and paranoia of the capital's more notorious rectangle, but crowds can be intense. By avoiding symmetry, People's Square is also far more relaxed than Tiananmen Square. Shànghǎi's essential shapelessness finds expression in the square's lack of clear equilibrium, while Tiananmen Square in many ways echoes the shape of the Forbidden City and the concentric ring-roads that radiate from it. Other marked differences are that People's Square is overlooked by stratospheric skyscrapers (Tiananmen Square is not) and it has emerged as a snazzy platform for culture, entertainment and the arts in Shànghǎi.

People's Square is also a fun place to relax and watch people strolling, flying kites and even waltzing in front of the musical fountain. Beneath the square lurk a huge subterranean shopping plaza and a warren of corridors linking the numerous entrances of the metro station.

The building anchoring the west of the square is the French-designed Shanghai Grand Theatre (p194), Shànghǎi's premier venue for the performing arts. To the northeast end of the square is the equally impressive Shanghai Urban Planning Exhibition Hall (p74). Sandwiched between the two is the austere Shanghai Government Building, while in the south of the square is the distinctive form of the Shanghai Museum (below). Overlooking all of this is the unique form of Tomorrow Square (p76). Housing the JW Marriott hotel (p203), the rocketing tower of Tomorrow Square is one of Shànghǎi's most electrifying edifices, by day or by night. Other lofty buildings on the periphery of the square include the UFO-topped Radisson Hotel Shanghai New World and the double-antenna Brilliance Shimao International Plaza (Le Royal Meridien).

Although its skyline is dominated by new-generation five-star hotels, the occasional cheap hostel brings the exclusive area within reach of the frugal and budget-minded. See the Sleeping chapter (p203) for suggestions.

SHANGHAI MUSEUM Map pp66-7
上海博物馆 Shànghǎi Bówùguǎn
☎ 6372 3500; www.shanghaimuseum.net; 201 Renmin Ave (entrance on East Yan'an Rd); 人民

大道201号; admission free; audio tour Y40 plus passport or deposit Y400; ⊙ 9am-5pm Mon-Fri (last entry 4pm); Ⓜ People's Sq

Rocked slightly from its jealously guarded throne by the 2006 unveiling of Běijīng's tip-top Capital Museum, the monarch of mainland China's museum world remains one of Shànghǎi's highlight attractions. Anyone even remotely interested in traditional China should spend at least half a day here, if not the whole day. A primer of Chinese civilisation recounted via 120,000 exhibits, the intelligently designed museum guides you through the pages of Chinese history.

Make sure to get here early, as queues can get quite long on busy days. Also note that the entrance is on East Yan'an Rd and not People's Square (that's the exit). Before you go in, admire the exterior of the building. Designed to recall an ancient bronze *dīng* (a three-legged food vessel used for cooking and serving), the building also echoes the shape of a famous bronze mirror from the Han dynasty, exhibited within the museum.

The most famous collection of the museum is the Ancient Chinese Bronzes Gallery (see the boxed text, p75), but if you're pressed for time, start with the Ancient Chinese Ceramics Gallery, which covers a wide variety of styles from different dynasties and is much more than a stereotypical collection of blue-and-white Qing pieces. Pick up a museum floor plan from the help desk prior to navigating the galleries.

Exhibits in the Ancient Chinese Sculpture Gallery range from stonework of the Qin and Han dynasties to Buddhist stucco sculpture, which was influenced by the Central Asian styles that travelled the Silk Rd. Note that sculptures displayed were almost all painted, but only scraps of pigment survive. Carvings meditate predominantly on Sakyamuni Buddha, as well as images of his disciples, gentle Bodhisattvas and fierce-looking *lokapalas* (Buddhist protectors).

The Ancient Chinese Ceramics Gallery is one of the largest and most fascinating. Exhibits include 6000-year-old pottery from the Neolithic Songze culture excavated from just outside Shànghǎi, *sāncǎi* (polychrome) pottery of the Tang, and the enormous variety of porcelain ('china') produced by the Qing. Don't worry if you don't know your 'ewer with overhead handles in *dòucǎi*' from your 'brush-holder with *fěncǎi* design',

it's all part of a luxurious learning curve. Many pieces originated at the Jǐngdézhèn kilns in Jiāngxī, one of the principal centres of ceramics production in China, where craftspeople perfected the vivid cobalt blues that first appeared in the Yuan dynasty. Look out for the 'celadon vase with ancient bronze design' (Qianlong period) and the delightful, white Ming dynasty *déhuà* (white-glazed porcelain) statues of Guanyin, the Goddess of Mercy. Angled mirrors beneath each piece reveal the mark on the foot.

The Chinese Painting Gallery leads visitors through various styles of traditional Chinese art, with many pieces dwelling on idealised landscapes. At first glance many appear to be similar, but upon closer inspection you'll realise that there is a vast array of techniques used to depict the natural world. There are some true masterpieces here, such as Ni Zan's *Streams in the Mountains* (1364) and Wu Wei's *Back from Fishing in the Autumn River* (15th century). The Ming collection is particularly strong. Scroll paintings are 'read' right to left.

The Calligraphy Gallery is unfathomable for those who don't read Chinese, although anyone can enjoy the purely aesthetic balance of Chinese brush artistry. The display covers everything from inscribed bamboo strips and Shang oracle bones to the various scripts such as seal script, official script and the more abstract cursive script, a challenge to read even for Chinese, as it dispenses with many of the strokes.

top picks

PEOPLE'S SQUARE

- Shanghai Museum (opposite) Contemplate its masterpieces .
- Shanghai Urban Planning Exhibition Hall (p74) Propel your consciousness into the year 2020.
- South Yunnan Rd & Huanghe Rd (p160) Stain your shirt (but don't burn your tongue) eating dumplings here.
- Shanghai Museum of Contemporary Art (p75) Delve into current art trends at this zesty museum.
- Shanghai Grand Theatre (p194) Catch a first-class performance.

The Ancient Chinese Jade Gallery reveals the transformation of jade use from early mystical symbols (such as the *bì*, or 'jade discs', used to worship heaven), to ritual weapons and jewellery. Exhibit 414 is a remarkable totem, with an engraved phoenix carrying a human head. Bamboo drills, abrasive sand and garnets crushed in water were used to shape some of the pieces, which date back over 5000 years.

When it comes to the Coin Gallery it's tempting to keep moving. But do look for the earliest coins on display, which are pierced with a hole so they could be carried by string; some older coins are shaped like keys or knives.

The Ming & Qing Furniture Gallery features rose- and sandalwood furniture of the elegant Ming dynasty, and heavier, more baroque examples from the Qing dynasty. Several mock offices and reception rooms offer a glimpse of wealthy Chinese home life.

Save something for the Minority Nationalities Art Gallery, introducing you to the diversity of China's 55 non-Han ethnic groups, totalling some 40 million people. Displays vary from the salmon fish-skin suit of the Hezhen in Hēilóngjiāng and the furs of the Siberian Oroqen, to the embroidery and batik of Guìzhōu's Miao and Dong, the Middle-Eastern satin robes of the Uighurs and the wild hairstyles of the former slave-owning Yi. Handicrafts include Miao silverware, Yi lacquer work, Tibetan cham festival masks and Nuo opera masks from Guìzhōu.

The audio guide is well worth the Y40 (Y400 deposit, or your passport). It highlights particularly interesting exhibits and has good gallery overviews and general background information. Photos can be taken in most halls (without a tripod).

The excellent museum shop sells postcards, a rich array of books and faithful replicas of the museum's ceramics and other pieces. There are a few overpriced shops and teahouses inside the museum, as well as an attached snack bar, cloakroom and an ATM. Seats are provided outside galleries on each floor in case museum lethargy strikes.

SHANGHAI URBAN PLANNING EXHIBITION HALL

Map pp66-7

上海城市规划展示馆 **Shànghǎi Chéngshì Guīhuà Zhǎnshìguǎn**

☎ 6318 4477; 100 Renmin Ave (entrance on Middle Xizang Rd); 人民大道100号; adult/student Y30/Y15; ☯ 9am-5pm Tue-Thu (last entry 4pm), to 6pm Fri-Sun (last entry 5pm); Ⓜ People's Sq

Some cities romanticise their past, others promise good times in the present, but only in China are you expected to visit places that haven't even been built yet. The idea is akin to the city patting itself on the back for a job not yet done, but even still, the Urban Planning Exhibition Hall has its moments. The third floor features Shànghǎi's idealised future (aka the 'Master Plan'), with an incredible model layout of the megalopolis-to-come plus a dizzying Virtual World 3D wraparound tour complete with celebratory fireworks. Balancing out the forward-looking

SUZHOU CREEK 苏州河

Also called the Wusong River (吴淞江; Wúsōng Jiāng), Suzhou Creek – its waters originating in famous Lake Tai (Tài Hú) in Jiāngsū province before belching into the Huangpu River just north of the Bund – has undergone a massive clean-up in recent years. Years of pollution and untreated sewage had transformed the river into a notoriously squalid Dickensian eyesore. In the 1920s and 1930s, gangsters would fling corpses into the river to rot. Rapid industrialisation brought distinctive hues and off-the-scale pH factors to the murky waters; residents would reel from the stench rising from its fetid surface and shut their windows, but that didn't stop many from falling ill. With the creek draining into the Huangpu River, from where much of Shànghǎi's drinking water is drawn, action was finally taken to cleanse the river in 1998 with a Y1.3 billion, decade-long program. Due for completion by the start of the 2010, the project aims to prevent pollutants from flooding into the creek, and sewage facilities in the vicinity are undergoing full repairs. Further work will involve silt-dredging and restoration of the river floodwall, while the area has also benefited from gradual gentrification and prettifying patches of greenery. Artists have also flocked into the neighbouring warehouse and factory areas such as around M50 (p97), which has become commercially dynamic and is where property prices have rocketed. The acid test could be the fish – long repelled by the foul stream – that have been released into the waters again. If they don't go belly up, fingers are crossed that an ecosystem can flourish once more.

BRONZES IN THE SHANGHAI MUSEUM

The Shanghai Museum is famed worldwide for its collection of bronzes, some of which date from the 21st century BC. China reached the apex of bronze production in the late Shang (1700–1100 BC) and Western Zhou (1100–771 BC) dynasties, though a second flowering blossomed during the Middle Spring and Autumn (722–481 BC) and Warring States (453–221 BC) periods.

When appreciating the bronzes, remember that they would have originally been a dazzling golden colour. Oxidisation has given them their characteristic dull green patina.

Their remarkable range of shapes and versatility is striking, revealing the significance of bronze in ritual ancestor worship and, later, everyday life. Vessels range in shape from *hú* (wine bottle), *jué* (wine pourer with spout), *gū* (goblet), *bēi* (wine jar), *zūn* (wine vessel), *yǎn* (steamer), *guǐ* (round food vessel used for rice and grain), *pán* (water vessel) and assorted wine pots known as *zhī*, *hé* and *yǒu*. The hooks visible on several pots originally supported a cloth bag for filtering hot wine.

The most important ritual bronzes are *dǐng* (three- or four-legged food vessels used for cooking and serving). The number of *dǐng* an official was allowed strictly depended on imperial rank. Some ceremonial bronzes are vast, such as the 200kg *dǐng* on display.

Decoration is an intrinsic element of their beauty. The most common design is the stylised animal motif, depicting dragons, lions and the phoenix. This was replaced in the 10th century BC by zigzags (representing thunder) and cloud designs, and later, geometric shapes. Subsequently, decoration spread to finlike appendages, studs and relief carvings. As bronzes lost their ritual significance, decorative scenes from daily life made an appearance. Later still, stamped moulds, lost wax techniques and piece moulds enabled designs to become ever more complex.

An especially creative use of bronze is evident in the *zhōng* (bells), each of which produces two notes. Up until the Han dynasty (206 BC–AD 220), bronze bells were China's chief musical instrument; traditional bell concerts are still held occasionally in Shànghǎi. Other examples of bronze use include 3000-year-old weapons such as *dāo* (daggers), *yuè* (axes) and *máo* (spears and swords) forged from two metals. Also displayed are bronzes collected from minority nationalities such as the Yi from southwest China, with their characteristic ox motifs, the Ba from Sichuān, the Central Asian Xiongnu (Kushan), with their camel and tiger motifs, and bronze drums from Guǎngxī.

exhibits are photos and maps of historic Shànghǎi.

SHANGHAI MUSEUM OF CONTEMPORARY ART (MOCA SHANGHAI)
Map pp66-7

上海当代艺术馆 **Shànghǎi Dāngdài Yìshùguǎn**
☎ 6327 9900; People's Park; 人民公园; adult/student Y20/10, rates vary depending on exhibition; ⏰ 10am-6pm Thu-Tue, Wed to 10pm; Ⓜ People's Sq

A recent opening that has grabbed the bull by the horns on steering the world contemporary art scene to Shànghǎi, this nonprofit museum collection has an all-glass home to maximise natural sunlight (when it cuts through the clouds), a tip-top location in People's Park (right) and a fresh, invigorating approach to exhibiting contemporary artwork. One recent installation countered the Urban Planning Exhibition Hall's rosy vision of Shànghǎi with a scale-model urban dystopia – complete with car wrecks, endless traffic jams and decaying buildings. On the top floor is the funky Art Lab Café with terrace.

SHANGHAI ART MUSEUM
Map pp66-7

上海美术馆 **Shànghǎi Měishùguǎn**
☎ 6327 2829; 325 West Nanjing Rd; 南京西路 325号; adult/student Y20/5; ⏰ 9am-5pm (last entry 4pm); Ⓜ People's Sq

Venue of the Shanghai Biennale (p19), this museum is located within the former British racecourse club building next to People's Park. Refreshingly cool in summer, the interior galleries are suited to appreciating art, displayed in well-illuminated alcoves and a voluminous sense of space. It's also worth noting the ceiling details and other period features, including the horse-head design on the balustrades and the art deco chandeliers, original to the 1933 building. Unfortunately, the quality of the exhibitions is inconsistent. English captions are sporadic at best.

PEOPLE'S PARK
Map pp66-7

人民公园 **Rénmín Gōngyuán**
admission free; ⏰ 6am-6pm; Ⓜ People's Sq

Occupying the site of the colonial racetrack (which became a holding camp during

WWII), People's Park is a green refuge from Shànghǎi's fume-ridden roads, with its Shanghai Museum of Contemporary Art; p75) and pond-side bar, Barbarossa (p178), all overlooked by Tomorrow Square, the Shanghai Art Museum and the Park Hotel. If you're in Shànghǎi in June, join the photographers ringing the gorgeous pink lotuses that flower in the pond. On weekend mornings an unofficial matchmaking market is held here, where parents show up with their children's CVs (but without the children) in an attempt to find a suitably successful spouse.

TOMORROW SQUARE
Map pp66-7
明天广场 Míngtiān Guǎngchǎng
399 West Nanjing Rd; 南京西路399号;
Ⓜ People's Sq

This stupendous tower – designed by John Portman & Associates and completed in October 2003 – seizes the Shànghǎi zeitgeist with dramatic aplomb. Resembling a sci-fi corporation headquarters, the stratospheric building is given further lift by the stylistic awkwardness of nearby rivals: chiefly the Radisson Hotel Shanghai New World, which looks like a gigantic UFO has swivelled down from the sky to screw itself onto its roof. Tomorrow Sq houses Shànghǎi's highest serviced apartments while the foyer of the JW Marriott Tomorrow Square (p203) debuts on the 38th floor. Pop up to put People's Sq in the proper perspective.

top picks

IT'S FREE

Hard up in Huángpǔ? Fill your time with these five freebies.

- Visit the Shanghai Museum (p72), the best place on the mainland to see traditional Chinese art.
- Size up contemporary Chinese art at M50 (p97).
- Admire traditional dress from around the Middle Kingdom at the Metersbonwe Costume Museum (p66).
- Saunter round the French Concession (p85) or take any one of our comprehensive walking tours (listed after each neighbourhood).
- Stop by the Post Museum (p116) and take in the vistas from the rooftop garden.

PARK HOTEL
Map pp66-7
国际饭店 Guójì Fàndiàn
170 West Nanjing Rd; 南京西路170号;
Ⓜ People's Sq

Designed by Hungarian architect Ladislaus Hudec and erected as a bank in 1934, the Park Hotel (p204) was Shànghǎi's tallest building until the 1980s, when shoulder-padded architects first started squinting hopefully in the direction of Pǔdōng. Back in the days when building height had a different meaning, it was rumoured your hat would fall off if you looked at the roof. Peruse the foyer for its art deco overture and wander further east along Nanjing Rd to the Pacific Hotel (p204), formerly the China United Apartment Building, also equipped with some lovely lobby details.

Other Sights

Opened in 1936, the Shanghai No 1 Department Store (上海市第一百货商店; Shànghǎi Shì Dìyī Bǎihuò Shāngdiàn; Map pp66–7; 800 East Nanjing Rd; 南京东路800号; ⏲ 9.30am-10pm; Ⓜ People's Sq) was formerly known as the Sun Company and was one of East Nanjing Rd's big department stores (with Wing On, Sun Sun and Sincere) and the first equipped with an escalator. Today it averages 150,000 shoppers a day over 11 levels of merchandise.

The Moore Memorial Church (沐恩堂; Mù'ēn Táng; Map pp66–7; 316 Middle Xizang Rd; Ⓜ People's Sq), designed by Ladislaus Hudec, is the standout red-brick Christian edifice east of People's Square.

West of the Park Hotel (above), the Grand Cinema (大光明电影院; Dàguāngmíng Diànyǐngyuàn; Map pp66–7; 216 West Nanjing Rd; Ⓜ People's Sq) is a further art deco veteran, also designed by Hudec and was Shànghǎi's premier theatre in the 1930s.

The waxworks at Madame Tussauds (上海杜莎夫人蜡像馆; Shànghǎi Dùshā Fūrén Làxiàngguǎn; Map pp66–7; West Nanjing Rd; adult/student Y135/100, 2 adults plus 1 child Y260; Ⓜ People's Sq) are largely aimed at locals and cost a lot, but could make do when one of Shànghǎi's notorious summer downpours inundates town.

At the corner of East Yan'an Rd and Middle Xizang Rd stands Great World (大世界; Dà Shìjiè; Map pp66–7; Ⓜ People's Sq), a place for acrobats and nightlife stars that was opened in 1917 to rival the existing New World on Nanjing Rd. In the 1930s it was taken over by the gangster Pockmarked Huang and became a six-floor house of ill-repute before eventual rehabilitation under the communists during the Mao years. Renovations are ongoing, but there's no word as to when it will reopen or what the future function will be.

Drinking p180; Eating p160; Shopping p139; Sleeping p206

Known to Shànghǎi locals as Nán Shì (Southern City), the Old Town is the most traditionally Chinese area of Shànghǎi, along with Qībǎo (p131). With most of historic Shànghǎi only dating as far back as the mid-19th century, the Old Town has long been an intriguing catchment area of old-fashioned textures, tatty charm and musty temples, although sifting the genuine from the repro is tricky. Sitting as it does on a piece of coveted real estate, and with many inhabitants considering the buildings old and rundown, it is not surprising that much of the area has been bulldozed to provide room for developers to build upwards. But for glimpses of old Shànghǎi – that of the Chinese, not the foreigners – the remaining Old Town backstreets with their crowded lanes, dark alleyways and hanging laundry are the places to explore.

Before Shànghǎi went global, the town was just one of many trading hubs strung out along the eastern seaboard of China. The circular layout of the Old Town still reflects the footprint of its old 5km-long city walls, flung up to defend against marauding Japanese pirates. The 16th-century city wall was eventually torn down in 1912, but the bastion's outline can be seen in the circular path of Renmin and Zhonghua Rds. Middle Fangbang Rd was once a canal running through the centre of the town from a small harbour at the eastern Dongpu Gate.

Most visitors come to the Old Town to battle the crowds at the traditional Chinese Yuyuan Gardens (below) before downing a pot of Chinese tea, haggling at the attached bazaar and sifting hopefully through knick-knacks on Old Street (p140) and at the Dongtai Rd Antique Market (p140). Those interested in traditional architecture will enjoy the area for its assortment of modest Confucian, Taoist, Buddhist and Muslim places of worship. Keep in mind that most of the central area has been (or is in the process of being) torn down. The most interesting areas to wander now are well off the beaten track and include the western stretch of Dongjiadu Rd and the alleys north of the Confucian Temple (p81). The Old Town's rickety, narrow streets house few hotels, so not many travellers overnight in the district.

top picks

OLD TOWN

- Yuyuan Gardens & Bazaar (left) Get lost in the traditional Yuyuan Gardens & Bazaar, but avoid the weekend surge.
- Get shopping! (p140, p139, p140) Faux antiques, tailor-made clothes and souvenirs – how can you resist?
- Walking (p83) Join our Old Town walking tour for a journey through the Old Town's backstreets.
- Backstreets (p81, p82) Explore the backstreets around the Confucian Temple or Dongjiadu Cathedral.
- Temple hopping (p81, p81, p83) Temple hop through the Old Town for a typically Chinese religious melange – there are places of worship for Buddhists, Taoists and Muslims.

YUYUAN GARDENS & BAZAAR
Map p79

豫园、豫园商城 Yùyuán & Yùyuán Shāngchéng
adult/child Y30/10; 8.30am-5.30pm (last tickets sold at 5pm); Ⓜ Yuyuan Garden

With its shaded alcoves, glittering pools churning with carp, pavilions, pines sprouting wistfully from rockeries, whispering bamboo, jasmine clumps, stony recesses and roving bands of Japanese tourists, the Yuyuan Gardens are one of Shànghǎi's topnotch sights. With over 1000 visitors daily, securing an early-morning visit is advisable. See p232 for background information on Chinese gardens. The adjacent bazaar is arguably tacky, but great for a browse, if you can ignore the surrounding sales roar and the fake-Rolex pushers. Look out for the lāyángpiàn (拉洋片) performer, a fashionable form of entertainment in 1920s Shànghǎi. Weekends at both the gardens and the bazaar can be overpowering. Pick up a map of the bazaar at the tourist office (p267) or follow the signs for orientation.

The Yuyuan Gardens were founded by the Pan family, who were rich Ming dynasty officials. The gardens took 18 years (from 1559 to 1577) to be nurtured into existence, only to be ransacked during the Opium War in 1842, when British officers

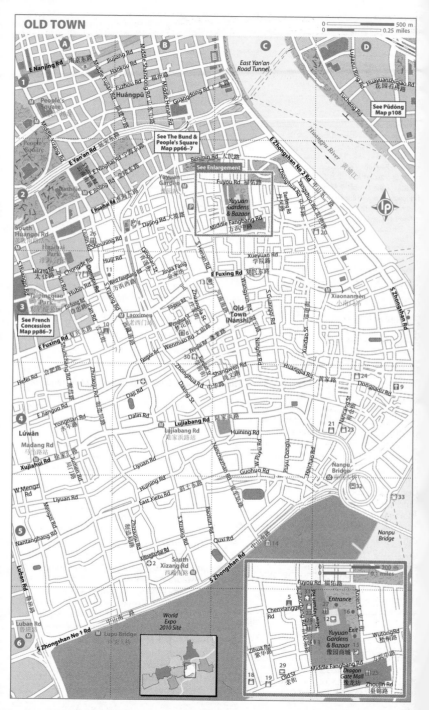

OLD TOWN

0 — 500 m
0 — 0.25 miles

E Nanjing Rd 南京东路

Jiujiang Rd

Hankou Rd

Middle Shandong Rd

Middle Fujian Rd

Fuzhou Rd 福州路

Huángpǔ

Guangdong Rd 广东路

Middle Henan Rd

East Yan'an Road Tunnel

See Púdōng Map p108

Huayuanshiqiao Rd 花园石桥路

Lujiazui Ring Rd

Fucheng Rd

People's Square

E Yan'an Rd

People's Square

E Yan'an Rd

E Ningbo Rd 宁波东路

Middle Xizang Rd

E Jinling Rd 金陵东路

E Zhongshan No 2 Rd 中山二路

Zhongshan Rd

Yangshuo Rd 扬州路

See The Bund & People's Square Map pp66–7

Renmin Rd 人民路

Huángpǔ River 黄浦江

See Enlargement

Fuyou Rd 福佑路

Yuyuan Garden 豫园

Yuyuan Gardens & Bazaar

Nashijie

E Huaihai Rd 淮海东路

Dajing Rd 大境路

Dantang Rd

Baoyu Rd

P

20

South Huangpi Rd 黄陂南路

S Huangpi Rd

Haizhai Rd 海潮路

Taicang Rd 太仓路

Chongde Rd

Dongtai Rd

Baohuning Rd

Liuhe Rd

Qipulu St

S Henan Rd

Xueyuan Rd 学院路

Wangyun Rd

Huji Rd

Jinlia Fang

E Fuxing Rd 复兴东路

Taipingqiao Park 太平桥公园

See French Concession Map pp86–7

E Fuxing Rd 复兴东路

Xizang Rd

Dufeng Rd

13

Jiagu Rd

Zhonghua Rd

S Guangqi Rd

Old Town (Nánshì)

Ninghai Rd

Xiaonanmen 小南门

S Zhongshan Rd

7

Laoximen 老西门

Menghua Rd

Wenmiao Rd

6

Penglai Rd 蓬莱路

Fanghua Rd

Shangwen Rd 尚文路

Xundao St

Huangjia Rd 黄家路

24

Dongjiadu Rd

9

Hefei Rd 合肥路

Zhaojiabang Rd

Zhonghua Rd 中华路

30

Dajing Rd

Daxing St

21

23

Lùwān

Yongnian Rd 永年路

Dalin Rd

Lujiabang Rd

Lujiabang Rd 陆家浜路站

Huining Rd

Nangubang Rd

Pudong

Nanpu Bridge 南浦大桥

Xujiahui Rd

Madang Rd 马当路站

Xujiahui Rd

Liyuan Rd

Huining Rd

Guohuo Rd

32

W Mengzi Rd

Mengzi Rd

Liyuan Rd

East Xietu Rd

S Xizang Rd

Baoduin Rd

Quxi Rd

Nanpu Bridge

33

Nanpu Bridge

Nantangbang Rd

Xietu Rd

Kuangjiazhai Rd

2

South Xizang Rd 西藏南路

S Zhongshan Rd 中山南路

14

Luban Rd

Luban Rd 鲁班路

World Expo 2010 Site

Luban Rd

S Zhongshan No 1 Rd 中山南一路

Lupu Bridge 卢浦大桥

6

Enlargement

0 — 200 m
0 — 0.1 miles

Fuyou Rd 福佑路

5

31

27

Jiujiang Rd

Anren St

Entrance

16

Chenxiangge Rd

Jiujiang Rd

17

Yuyuan Gardens & Bazaar 豫园商城

Exit

15

Wutong Rd 梧桐路

Zihua Rd 紫华路

29

Old St 老街

Dragon Gate Mall 豫龙坊

18

19

Middle Fangbang Rd 方浜中路

25

Zhoujin Rd 筹锦路

OLD TOWN

were barracked here, and again during the Taiping Rebellion, this time by the French in reprisal for attacks on their nearby concession. Today the gardens have been restored and are a fine example of Ming garden design – if you can see through the camera-wielding crowds that blot them out, that is. Though the gardens are small, they seem much bigger due to an ingenious use of rocks and alcoves. The spring and summer blossoms bring a fragrant and floral aspect to the gardens, especially in the heavy petals of its *Magnolia grandiflora*, Shànghǎi's flower. Other trees include the Luohan pine, bristling with thick needles, willows, ginkgos and cherry trees.

A handy map depicting the layout of the gardens can be found just inside the entrance. Keep an eye out for the Exquisite Jade Rock (玉玲珑; Yù Línglóng), which was destined for the imperial court in Běijīng until the boat sank outside Shànghǎi, and the Hall of Heralding Spring (点春堂; Diǎnchūn Táng), which in 1853 was the headquarters of the Small Swords Society (which may have been one reason why the gardens were spared revolutionary violence in the

1960s). Note also the beautiful stage, dating from 1888, with its gilded carved ceiling and excellent acoustics. The two shiny pavilions in the eastern corner were only added in 2003.

Next to the entrance to the Yuyuan Gardens is the Mid-Lake Pavilion Teahouse (湖心亭; Húxīntíng; ⏰ 8.30am-9.30pm; tea downstairs/upstairs Y25/50), once part of the gardens and now one of the most famous teahouses in China, visited by Queen Elizabeth II and Bill Clinton among others. The zigzag causeway is designed to thwart spirits (and trap tourists), who can only travel in straight lines.

Surrounding all this is the restored bazaar area, where scores of speciality shops and restaurants – including the Nanxiang Steamed Bun Restaurant (p160) – jostle over narrow laneways and small squares in a mock 'ye olde Cathay' setting. If you can handle the surging crowds it's a great stop for lunch and a spot of souvenir shopping.

Just outside the bazaar is Old Street (p140), known more prosaically as Middle Fangbang Rd, a busy strip lined with slightly better souvenir and curio shops.

CHENXIANGGE NUNNERY Map p79
沉香阁 Chénxiāng Gé

29 Chenxiangge Rd; 沉香阁路29号; admission
Y5; ⏰ 7am-4pm; Ⓜ Yuyuan Garden

Sheltering a community of around 40 dark-brown-clothed nuns from the *chénhǎi* (Sea of Dust) – what Buddhists call the mortal world, but which could equally refer to Shànghǎi's murky atmosphere – this gorgeous yellow-walled temple is a tranquil portal to a devout existence far from the city's frantic temporal realm. The Hall of Heavenly Kings (天王殿; Tiānwáng Diàn) envelops an arrangement of four gilded Heavenly Kings and a slightly androgynous form of Maitreya. The sacred aura is completed by the muttering of prayers and chanting of hymns filling the Great Treasure Hall (大雄宝殿; Dàxióng Bǎodiàn), where a statue of Sakyamuni (Buddha) is flanked by two rows of nine *luóhàn* (arhat). The rear courtyard is lovingly decked out with flowers, pines and ornamental trees, while a sign reading 'This way up to the Guanyin Tower' (观音楼; Guānyīn Lóu; admission Y2; ⏰ 7am-3pm) guides you to the temple's signature sight – a glittering effigy of the compassionate goddess carved from *chenxiang* wood (Chinese eaglewood) and seated in *lalitasana* posture.

CONFUCIAN TEMPLE Map p79
文庙 Wén Miào

215 Wenmiao Rd; 文庙路215号; admission Y10;
⏰ 9am-5pm (last entry 4.30pm); Ⓜ Laoximen

Most historic Chinese towns boast a temple dedicated to Confucius, although the iconoclastic spasms of the Cultural Revolution left many battered and bruised. A modest and pretty retreat, this well-tended temple to the dictum-coining sage is cultivated with maples, pines, magnolias and birdsong. Originally dating to 1294, when the Mongols held sway through China, the temple moved to its current site in 1855, at a time when Christian Taiping rebels were sending much of China skywards in sheets of flame. The layout is typically Confucian, its few worshippers complemented by ancient and venerable trees, including a 300-year-old elm. The towering Kuixing Pavilion (Kuíxīng Gé) in the west is named after the God of the Literati. The main hall for worshipping Confucius is Dacheng Hall (Dàchéng Diàn), complete with twin eaves and a statue of the sage outside. The magnolias on either side of

its main door are garlanded with ribbons left by the devout. In line with Confucius championing of learning, a busy second-hand market of (largely Chinese language) books is held in the temple every Sunday morning.

TEMPLE OF THE TOWN GOD Map p79
城隍庙 Chénghuáng Miào

Yuyuan Bazaar (off Middle Fangbang Rd); admission
Y10; ⏰ 8.30am-4.30pm; Ⓜ Yuyuan Garden

Chinese towns traditionally came with a Taoist Temple of the Town God, but many fell victim to periodic upheaval. Originally dating to the early 15th century, this particular temple was badly damaged during the Cultural Revolution and later restored. Note the fine carvings on the roof as you enter to the main hall, dedicated to Huo Guang, a Han dynasty general, flanked by rows of effigies representing both martial and civil virtues. Exit the hall north and peek into the multifaith hall on your right dedicated to three female deities, Guanyin (Buddhist), Tianhou and Yanmu Niangniang (Taoist). Gazing fiercely over offerings of fruit from the rear hall is the red-faced and bearded Town God himself.

SHANGHAI MUSEUM OF FOLK COLLECTIBLES
Map p79

上海民间收藏品陈列馆 Shànghǎi Mínjiān
Shōucángpǐn Chénlièguǎn

1551 South Zhongshan Rd; 中山南路1551号;
☎ 6313 5582; admission Y4; ⏰ 9am-4pm;
Ⓜ South Xizang Rd

Located near the outskirts of the World Expo site and housed in the magnificent

---

TRANSPORT: OLD TOWN

Metro Line 10 runs from East Nanjing Rd to the French Concession, passing under the Old Town. The central Yuyuan Garden station is close to most sights. Line 8, which runs south from People's Sq to the World Expo grounds, intersects with line 10 at Laoximen (near the Confucian Temple), line 9 at Lujiabang Rd, and line 4 at South Xizang Rd. Line 9 runs along the Old Town's southern edge and into Pǔdōng with a station at Xiaonanmen.

Bus Route 11 circles the Old Town, following Renmin Rd and Zhonghua Rd; bus 66 travels along Henan Rd, connecting the Old Town with East Nanjing Rd.

Sanshan Guildhall (built in 1909), this fascinating museum allows an exploration of Shànghǎi via the medium of collectibles, from cigarette lighters to ceramics and cruelly exquisite-looking miniature shoes for bound feet. At the time of writing it was undergoing a massive renovation, with a brand-new hall set to open in 2010.

FLOWER, BIRD, FISH & INSECT MARKET Map p79
万商花鸟鱼虫市场 Wànshāng Huā Niǎo Yú Chóng Shìchǎng
South Xizang Rd; 西藏南路; Ⓜ Laoximen
One of the few remaining traditional markets in town, this is the spot to go shopping for city-sized pets. There are all sorts of critters for sale, but it's the insects that are the most remarkable. Crickets come in a variety of sizes and are sold in woven bamboo cages; pick one up for under Y30.

DONGJIADU CATHEDRAL
Map p79
董家渡教堂 Dǒngjiādù Jiàotáng
175 Dongjiadu Rd; 董家渡路175号; admission free; Ⓜ Nanpu Bridge
Just outside the Old Town, this magnificent cathedral is Shànghǎi's oldest church, built by Spanish Jesuits in 1853. A splendid sight, the church was located within a famously Catholic area of Shànghǎi and is generally open if you want to view the interior (ring

the bell at the side door). Follow Dongjiadu Rd west for an absorbing stroll through the bustling garment district – assuming it's still standing.

LUPU BRIDGE
Map pp62-3
卢浦大桥 Lúpǔ Dàqiáo
905 Luban Rd; 鲁班路905号; admission Y68; Ⓜ Luban Rd, then bus No 17 (1 stop)
For aerial views of the World Expo grounds or for those interested in observing the extent of Shànghǎi's massive sprawl, climb up to a viewing platform at the apex of the city's longest suspension bridge. The entrance is located at the end of Luban Rd (under the bridge). It's one elevator ride and an additional 367 wind-blown steps to the top. If you take a taxi, insist on the address; the bridge is 4km long and the driver will probably have no idea what you are looking for.

COOL DOCKS
Map p79
时尚老码头 Shíshàng Lǎomǎtou
479 South Zhongshan Rd; 中山南路479号; Ⓜ Xiaonanmen
A recent development project often billed as Xīntiāndì 2, the Cool Docks consist of several *shíkùmén* (stone-gate houses) surrounded by red-brick warehouses, near (but not quite on) the waterfront. Perhaps

because it had the misfortune to open just as the economic recession hit, most of the retail shops and restaurants (with the exception of the club D2, p190) had still failed to take off as 'in' destinations as we went to press.

DAJING PAVILION
Map p79
大境阁 Dàjìng Gé
Dajing Rd; 大境路; admission Y5; ☉ 9am-4pm; Ⓜ Dashijie

Dating from 1815, this pavilion contains the only preserved section of the 5km-long city walls. They were originally erected in 1553, to protect the city against pirates, but were felled in 1912. A Chinese-language-only exhibition on the history of the Old Town is on the ground floor, along with an interesting scale model depicting the walled district during the reign of Qing emperor Tongzhi. You can climb up to the restored battlements and wander through a collection of halls, otherwise there's not much to see.

BAIYUN TEMPLE
Map p79
白云观 Báiyún Guàn
239 Dajing Rd; 大境路239号; admission Y5; ☉ 8am-4.30pm; Ⓜ Dashijie

Relocated from southwest of the Old Town, the port-red Taoist Baiyun (White Cloud) Temple seems separated from Dajing Pavilion (p83) by Dajing Lane and fronted by an entrance with twin eaves. Though nowhere near as big as its Běijīng namesake, the temple is worth a peek for its colossal effigy of the Jade Emperor (玉皇大帝; Yùhuáng Dàdì) up the steps in the Xiaobao Hall (霄宝殿; Xiāobǎo Diàn), seated between two walls studded with smaller deities.

FAZANGJIANG TEMPLE
Map p79
法藏讲寺 Fǎzàngjiǎng Sì
271 Ji'an Rd; 吉安路271号; admission Y5; ☉ 7.30am-4pm; Ⓜ Laoximen

This simple but very active temple is curiously accessed from the west rather than the south, where the entrance to Buddhist temples usually lies. The main hall, restored with new doors, encloses a large modern statue of Sakyamuni, seated lily-top between two walls glinting with gilded *luóhàn* (arhat). Other lesser halls include a trinity of golden Buddhist effigies and a small shrine to the Buddhist God of the Underworld, Dizang Wang.

PEACH GARDEN MOSQUE
Map p79
小桃园清真寺 Xiǎotáoyuán Qīngzhēnsì
52 Xiaotaoyuan Rd; 小桃园路52号; ☉ 8am-7pm; Ⓜ Laoximen/Yuyuan Garden

Originally dating to 1917, this famous mosque is the city's main place of worship for Shànghǎi's Muslims. Fridays are the best time to visit, when the faithful stream in to pray at lunch and a large market is held outside the entrance.

OLD TOWN
Walking Tour

1 Chenxiangge Nunnery Begin by visiting the lovely Chenxiangge Nunnery (p81) on Chenxiangge Rd (沉香阁路), a retreat from the surrounding clamour.

2 Wangyima Alley Clarity attained, exit the temple and weave south down Wangyima Alley (王医马弄), a small and typical Old Town alley immediately facing you. Follow the alley, then turn west along Zhongwangyima

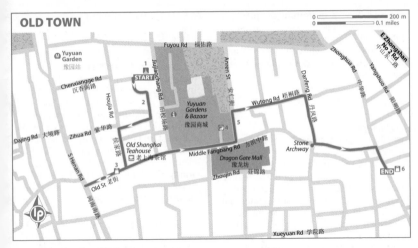

OLD TOWN

OLD TOWN

0 — 200 m
0 — 0.1 miles

Alley (中王医马弄) to follow Zihua Rd (紫华路) before turning south onto Houjia Rd (侯家路).

3 Old Street Wander along Middle Fangbang Rd (方浜中路) – once a canal and also known as Old Street (p140) – and browse for Tibetan jewellery, tea pots and prints of 1930s poster advertisements. Alternatively, break for a pot of refreshing oolong tea at the Old Shanghai Teahouse (p180).

4 Temple of the Town God Head east down Old Street passing the Yuyuan Bazaar to pay your respects to the red-faced town protector at the Temple of the Town God (p81).

5 Anren St Upon exiting, continue east down Middle Fangbang Rd and then turn north at the KFC onto Anren St (安仁街). Wend your way past the outdoor mah jong and Chinese chess matches, then turn east onto Wutong Rd (梧桐路) and then south on Danfeng Rd (丹凤路), a pinched lane frequently dressed with hanging washing. Note the lovely old doorways on Danfeng Rd, such as the carved red brick gateway at No 193.

6 Shiliupu Fabric Market Exit Danfeng Rd, turning east onto Middle Fangbang Rd at the old stone archway (四牌楼; sì páilou). Stroll down the boisterous shopping street, filled with snack stands, clothing shops and booming stereo systems. As long as the eastern part of town remains standing over the next few years, there are plenty of little alleyways to explore here, particularly off to the south. When you reach the end of Middle Fangbang Rd, cross Zhonghua Rd (which marks the eastern boundary of the old city wall) to the Shiliupu Fabric Market (p139) for a tailor-made shirt, dress or jacket.

FRENCH CONCESSION 法租界

Drinking p180; Eating p161; Shopping p140; Sleeping p207

If you want to see the city's best profile, the French Concession is Shànghǎi sunny side up, at its coolest, hippest and most elegant. Once home to the bulk of Shànghǎi's adventurers, revolutionaries, gangsters, prostitutes and writers – though ironically many of them weren't French but British, American, White Russian and Chinese – the French Concession (also once called Frenchtown) is the most graceful part of Pǔxī. Shànghǎi's erstwhile reputation as the 'Paris of the East' largely stems from its tree-lined avenues, the 1920s mansions and the French-influenced architecture of this district.

The sky isn't fragmented with skyscrapers, and the identikit Pǔdōng-style street planning is a world away from the concession's shady, European-styled streets. This is the most desirable area to live in for those who can't exist without period features and genteel low-rise street charms. Real-estate prices have done a spectacular upwards parabola over the past decade; house price tags in the smartest areas here wouldn't look out of place in London's most fashionable districts.

The name captures the colonial-style personality and Old World refinement that characterises the district. It's a foreign construction, so the name 'French Concession' brings blank looks from many Shànghǎi Chinese, who refer to this swathe as an amalgam of the Lúwān district (卢湾区) and more elegant chunks of the districts of Xúhuì (徐汇区), Chángníng (长宁区) and Jìng'ān (静安区).

top picks

FRENCH CONCESSION

- Walking tour (p95) Wander or cycle the Concession-era backstreets in low gear.
- Taikang Road Art Centre (left) Delve into lived-in charm and trendy boutiques.
- Shikumen Open House Museum (p91) Explore the interior of a stone-gate house.
- Xīntiāndì (p90) Food, fashion and…communism?
- Propaganda Poster Art Centre (p92) The East is still red.

The French Concession's chic and tirelessly inventive restaurant and bar scene means you never need to stray far for epicurean requirements. The area is also home to the lion's share of Shànghǎi's nightlife and shopping venues, while a generous crop of recommended hotels – across the budget range – can ease a pillow under your head. The district also outclasses the rest of town when it comes to walks and bike rides. Jump on two wheels and be insistently pulled along leafy streets by its infectious charms.

The central traffic artery is Huaihai Rd (淮海路), west of Old Town and named after a decisive battle that ended with the communists routing the Kuomintang during the Civil War.

TAIKANG ROAD ART CENTRE
Map pp86–7
田子坊、泰康路艺术中心 Tiánzǐfáng, Tàikāng Lù Yìshù Zhōngxīn;
Lane 210, Taikang Rd; 泰康路210弄;
Ⓜ Dapuqiao

Xīntiāndì (p90) and Taikang Rd are based on a similar idea – an entertainment complex housed within a layout of traditional lòngtáng alleyways – but when it comes to genuine charm and vibrancy, Taikang Rd is the one that delivers. Also known as Tiánzǐfáng, this community of design studios, wi-fi cafes, and boutiques is the perfect antidote to Shànghǎi's oversized malls and intimidating skyscrapers. With families still residing in neighbouring buildings, a community mood survives, and

the area's relative transport isolation has prevented it from being utterly swamped by tour groups.

There are three main north–south lanes (Nos 210, 248, 274) criss-crossed by irregular east–west alleyways, which makes exploration slightly disorienting and fun. On the main lane is the excellent Deke Erh Art Centre (Érdōngqiáng Yìshù Zhōngxīn; No 2, Lane 210; Ⓨ 9am-10pm), owned by local photographer and author Deke Erh, who also runs the Old China Hand Reading Room (p94). A fantastic range of books on Shànghǎi (many are collaborations by Deke Erh and Shànghǎi resident Tess Johnston) are on display. Another gallery to seek out is Unique Hill (Qígāng Cǎotáng; No 10, Lane 210), which has a collection of old Shànghǎi photos and posters. Also on the

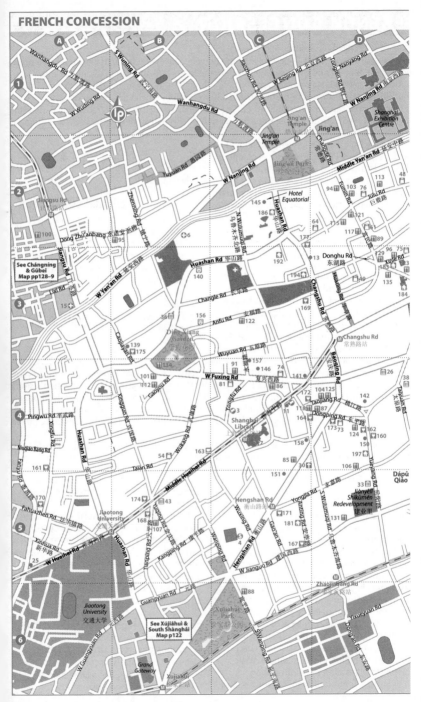

FRENCH CONCESSION

A B C D

1

Wanhangdu Rd 万航渡路
S Wuning Rd 武宁南路
Jiaohui Rd 胶州路
Beijing Rd 北京西路
Tongren Rd 铜仁路
Nanyang Rd 南阳路
W Nanjing Rd 南京西路
Shanghai Exhibition Centre
W Wuding Rd
Wanhangdu Rd
Jing'an Temple
Jing'an
Jing'an Temple
Yuyuan Rd 愚园路

2

Jiangsu Rd
Jing'an Park
W Nanjing Rd
Middle Yan'an Rd 延安中路
100
113 48
94 103 76
Juhu Rd 巨鹿路
Funmin Rd
Dong Zhu'anbang 东诸安浜路
95
Zhenning Rd 镇宁路
Hotel Equatorial
145
186
N Wulumuqi Rd 乌鲁木齐北路
Huashan Rd 华山路
64
51
121
117
89
6
96 75
29
Little Rd
185
13 Donghu Rd 东湖路
177
192
135
184
See Chángníng & Gúběi Map pp128–9
Jiangsu Rd
Lixi Rd
140
194
Changshu Rd 常熟路

3

15
Huashan Rd
W Yan'an Rd 延安西路
Caojiaban Rd
Changle Rd 长乐路
36
156
Anfu Rd 安福路
122
Changshu Rd 常熟路
169
Ding Xiang Garden 丁香花园
139
175
134
Wuyuan Rd 五原路
Changshu Rd
Baoqing Rd
26
38
101
112
Gaoyou Rd
91 157
146 74
W Fuxing Rd
141
81
86
104 125
Taojiang Rd 桃江路
142
172
87
11
Dongping Rd 东平路
16

4

Pingwu Rd 平武路
Xinguo Rd
Fanyu Rd 番禺路
Xingfu Rd
Huashan Rd
Wukang Rd 武康路
Fuxing Rd
Shanghai Library
3
73
173
124
162
160
150
Niuqiao Bang Rd
161
54
163
158
85
30
106
197
Taian Rd
151
Dápù Qiáo

5

Fahuazhen Rd 法华镇路
170
174
43
Middle Huaihai Rd 淮海中路
Mengshan Rd 蘅山路
171
181
33
Jiànyèli Shikùmén Redevelopment 建业里
131
25
W Huaihai Rd 淮海西路
Jiaotong University
168
107
Huashan Rd
Tianping Rd
Wanping Rd
Kangping Rd
Hengshan Rd 蘅山路
Yongjia Rd 永嘉路
S Wulumuqi Rd
Gao'an Rd
167
W Jianguo Rd 建国西路
4
Xinhua Rd 新华路

6

W Guangyuan Rd 光元西路
Jiaotong University 交通大学
Guangyuan Rd 元元路
See Xújiāhuì & South Shànghái Map p122
Xujiahui Park 徐家汇公园
88
Zhaojiabang Rd 肇嘉浜路
S Wanping Rd
Tixueyuan Rd 体育院路
Grand Gateway
Xujiahui
Xujiahui

86

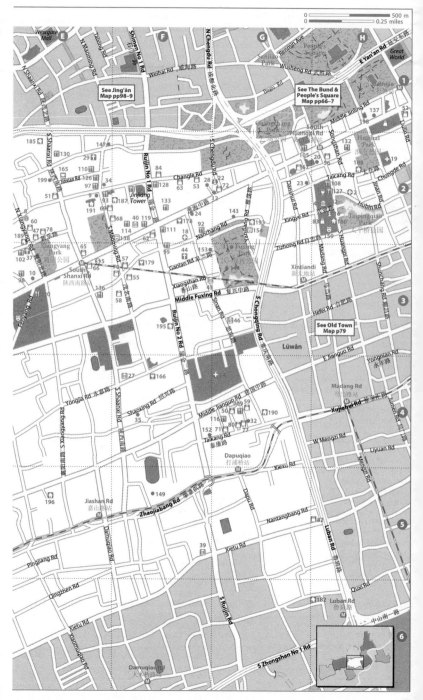

FRENCH CONCESSION

INFORMATION

American Consulate-General 美国领事馆 1 C4
Arrail Dental 瑞尔齿科 2 H2
Eastday B@r 东方网点 .... (see 62)
European Union Chamber of Commerce in
　China 中国欧盟商会 .... (see 20)
German Consulate 德国领事馆 3 C4
HSBC 24-hr ATM 汇丰银行取款机 4 C5
HSBC 24-hr ATM 汇丰银行取款机 5 E3
Huadong Hospital 华东医院外宾门诊 6 B2
Huashan Hospital 华山医院 7 C3
Huashi Pharmacy 华山药店 .... (see 7)
Jidu Kongjian Internet Café 极度空间网吧 8 E2
Jinjiang Tours 锦江旅行社 9 E2
K Wah Center 嘉华中心 10 E3
Kitchen...at Huaihai 11 C4
Kodak Express 柯达 12 G2
Mandarin Center 文化研习中心 13 D3
New Zealand Consulate-General
　新西兰领事馆 .... (see 21)
Post Office 邮局 .... (see 16)
Ruijin Hospital 瑞金医院 14 G4
Shanghai Chiropractic & Osteopathic Clinic
　上海脊椎医疗中心 15 A3
Shanghai Information Centre for
　International Visitors 上海国际访问者中心 16 H2
Shanghai Library 上海图书馆 17 C4
Shanghai Qigong Institute 上海气功研究所 18 F2
Shuguang Hospital 曙光医院 19 H2
Shui On Plaza 瑞安广场 20 H2
The Centre 世纪商贸广场 21 C3
Tourist Information & Service Centre
　旅游咨询服务中心 22 G2
UPS 优必送 23 G2
Watson's 屈臣氏 24 F2
Watson's 屈臣氏 .... (see 187)
Wuyao Pharmacy 五药大药房 25 A5

SIGHTS
(pp85–96)

140 sqm 26 D4
Art Labor 27 F4
Centre of Jewish Studies Shanghai
　上海犹太研究中心 28 F2
Christ the King Church 君王天主堂 29 E2
Community Church 国际礼拜堂 30 C4
Deke Erh Art Centre 尔冬强艺术中心 .... (see 77)
Fuxing Park 复兴公园 31 G3
International Artists' Factory
　艺术创作设计中心 32 G4
James Cohan Gallery 33 D5
Lyceum Theatre 兰馨大戏院 34 E2
Moller House 马勒别墅 .... (see 185)
Old China Hand Reading Room 汉源书店 35 F4
Propaganda Poster Art Centre
　宣画年画艺术中心 36 B3
Russian Orthodox Mission Church
　东正教圣母大堂 37 E3
Shanghai Arts & Crafts Museum
　上海工艺美术博物馆 38 D4
Shanghai Museum of Public Security
　上海公安博物馆 39 F5
ShanghART 香格纳画廊 40 F2
Shikumen Open House Museum
　石库门屋里厢 41 H2

Site of the 1st National Congress of CCP
　中共一大会址纪念馆 42 H2
Song Qingling's Former Residence 宋庆龄故居 43 B5
St Nicholas Church 圣尼古拉斯教堂 44 F3
Sun Yatsen's Former Residence 孙中山故居 45 F3
Unique Hill Gallery 奇岗草堂 .... (see 109)
Zhou Enlai's Former Residence 周恩来故居 46 G3

SHOPPING 🛍
(pp140–5)

100 Change & Insect 百变虫 .... (see 70)
100 Change & Insect 百变虫 47 E2
Annabel Lee .... (see 108)
Ba Yan Ka La 巴颜喀拉 .... (see 54)
Brocade Country 锦绣纺 48 D2
Chaterhouse .... (see 79)
Chinese Printed Blue Nankeen Exhibition Hall
　中国蓝印花布馆 49 D3
Chouchou Chic 喆缤豆小童生活馆 50 G4
Chouchou Chic 喆缤豆小童生活馆 51 E2
City Shop 城市超市 .... (see 66)
Cybermart 赛博数码广场 52 H1
Elbis Hungi 53 F2
eno .... (see 53)
EsyDragon 石怡集 .... (see 77)
Feel Shanghai 金粉世家 .... (see 77)
Ferguson Lane 武康亭 54 B4
Fúlíntáng's 福林堂 .... (see 83)
Harvest 上海盈穰坊工作室 .... (see 77)
Heping Finery 和平旗袍专卖店 55 F3
Hong Kong Plaza 香港广场 56 H2
Huā Yàng Nián Huá 花样年华 57 F3
Huifeng Tea Shop 汇丰茶庄 58 F3
I Life Design .... (see 77)
Insh 玩场 59 G4
Jip .... (see 77)
Joma .... (see 77)
Jùnměizǔ 俊美组 60 E2
La Vie 生织坊 .... (see 109)
La Vie 生 .... (see 84)
Liúligōngfáng 琉璃工房 .... (see 176)
Madame Mao's Dowry 毛太设计 61 D2
MANifesto .... (see 114)
New Hualian Commercial Building 新华联大厦 62 F2
NoD .... (see 41)
Not Just Silver .... (see 77)
One By One 63 F2
Pacific Department Store 太平洋百货商场 .... (see 20)
Paramita 波罗蜜多西藏工艺品 64 D2
Parkson Department Store 百盛购物中心 65 E3
Printemps Shanghai 上海巴黎春天百货 66 E3
Propaganda Poster Art Centre
　宣画年画艺术中心 .... (see 36)
Shanghai Central Plaza 中环广场 67 G2
Shanghai Museum Art Store
　上海博物馆艺术品商店 .... (see 108)
Shanghai Tang 上海滩 68 F2
Shanghai Tang 上海滩 .... (see 176)
Shanghai Trio 上海组合 .... (see 108)
Shiatzy Chen 夏姿 69 E2
Shirt Flag 衫旗帜 70 F3
Shirt Flag 衫旗帜 .... (see 109)
Shokay 71 G4
Silk King 真丝商厦 72 G2
Simply Life 逸居生活 .... (see 41)

FRENCH CONCESSION

(Continued on next page)

main lane is the International Artists' Factory (Yìshù Chuàngzuò Shèjì Zhōngxīn), which is home to a collection of design studios and the popular Wuyi Chinese Kungfu Centre (p196).

Of course the real activity here is shopping, and the recent explosion of creative start-ups makes for some interesting finds (see p140). Elsewhere, a growing band of cool cafes – such as Kommune (p168), Ginger (p165) and Origin (p165) – can sort out lunch or drinks, get you online and take the weight off your feet. Don't bother looking for Chinese food here; there isn't any.

XĪNTIĀNDÌ
Map pp86–7
新天地

www.xintiandi.com; 2 blocks enclosed within Taicang, Zizhong, Madang & South Huangpi Rds; Ⓜ South Huangpi Rd/Xintiandi

Xīntiāndì hasn't even been around for a decade yet and already it's a Shànghǎi icon. An upscale entertainment complex modelled on traditional alleyway (lòngtáng) homes, this was the first development in the city to prove that historic architecture does, in fact, have economic value. Elsewhere that might sound like a no-brainer, but in 21st-century China, which is head-over-heels for the bulldozer, it came as quite a revelation. Well-heeled shoppers and al fresco diners keep the place busy until late, and if you're looking for a memorable meal (p161) or a browse through some of Shànghǎi's more fashionable boutiques (p141), you're in the right place.

The heart of the complex, divided into a pedestrianised north and south block, consists of largely rebuilt traditional shíkùmén houses, brought bang up-to-date with a stylish modern spin. (For more on shíkùmén see p49.) But while the layout suggests a flavour of yesteryear, you should not expect much in the cultural realm. Xīntiāndì doesn't deliver any of the lived-in charm of the Taikang Road Art Centre (p85) or the creaking, rickety simplicity of the Old Town. Beyond two worthwhile sights – the Shikumen Open House Museum (below) and the Site of the 1st National Congress of the CCP (right) – it's best for strolling the prettified alleyways and enjoying a summer evening over drinks or a meal. Pick up an orientation map at the Shanghai Information Centre for International Visitors (Xīntiāndì South Block, Bldg 2) on Xingye Rd.

SHIKUMEN OPEN HOUSE MUSEUM
Map pp86-7

石库门屋里厢 Shíkùmén Wūlǐxiāng

☎ 3307 0337; Xīntiāndì North Block, Bldg 25; 太仓路181弄新天地北里25号楼; admission Y20; ⏰ 10.30am-10.30pm Sun-Thu, 11am-11pm Fri & Sat; Ⓜ South Huangpi Rd/Xintiandi

Arranged over two floors and entered via Xingye Rd in Xīntiāndì (opposite), this fascinating exhibition invites you into a typical *shíkùmén* household, decked out with period furniture. The ground floor arrangement contains a courtyard, entrance hall, bedroom, study and lounge, small kitchen to the rear and natural illumination spilling down from light wells *(tiānjǐng)* above. The small and frequently north-facing wedge-shaped *tíngzijiān* room on the landing almost at the top of the stairs between the 1st and 2nd floors was a common feature of *shíkùmén*, and was often rented out. The main bedrooms are all on the 2nd floor, linked together by doors.

SITE OF THE 1ST NATIONAL CONGRESS OF THE CCP Map pp86-7

中共一大会址纪念馆 Zhōnggòng Yīdàhuìzhǐ Jìniànguǎn

☎ 5383 2171; Xīntiāndì North Block, 76 Xingye Rd; 兴业路76号; admission free; ⏰ 9am-5pm (last entry 4pm); Ⓜ South Huangpi Rd/Xintiandi

On 23 July 1921 the Chinese Communist Party (CCP) was founded in this French Concession house (then 106 Rue Wantz), and in one fell swoop converted this unassuming *shíkùmén* block into one of Chinese communism's holiest shrines.

The dizzying Marxist spin of the museum commentary is a salutary reminder that Shànghǎi remains part of the world's largest communist nation. The certainties of that era – whether you sympathise with *Mǎlièzhǔyì* (Marxism-Leninism) or not – exude a nostalgic appeal in today's Shànghǎi, where ideology of any shade is fervently shunned.

Beyond the communist narcissism, there's little to see, although historians will enjoy ruminating on the site's historic momentousness.

On the ground floor you can be present in the room where the whole Party began, actually the house of the delegate Li Hanjun. Up the marble stairs in the 'Exhibition of Historical Relics Showing the Founding of the Communist Party of China' is a highly patriotic hymn to early Chinese communist history with exhibits such as the Chinese translation of Mary E Marcy's *The ABC of Das Kapital by Marx*.

Obtain a ticket (free) and enter on Xingye Rd.

THE SOONG FAMILY

The Soongs probably wielded more influence and power over modern China than any other family. The father of the family, Charlie Soong, grew up in Hǎinán and after an American evangelical education, finally settled in Shànghǎi. He began to print Bibles and money, becoming a wealthy businessman and developing ties with secret societies, during which time he became good friends with Sun Yatsen (Sun Zhongshan). Charlie had three daughters and a son.

Soong Ailing – said to be the first Chinese girl in Shànghǎi to own a bicycle – married HH Kung, the wealthy descendent of Confucius, Bank of China head and later finance minister of the Republic of China. Soong Meiling (May-ling) became the third wife of Chiang Kaishek (Kuomintang leader and future president of the Republic of China) in 1928. She went to the USA during the Japanese occupation of China and fled to Taiwan with Chiang after the communist victory. Much to the disapproval of her father, Soong Qingling (more commonly known as Song Qingling) married Sun Yatsen, 30 years her elder, studied in Moscow and was the only member of the family to live in China after 1949, until her death in 1981. TV Soong, Charlie's only son, served as the Republic of China's finance minister and premier, becoming the richest man of his generation.

Mainland Chinese say that of the three daughters, one loved money (Ailing), one loved power (Meiling) but only Qingling loved China. Among them, the siblings stewed up a heady brew of fascism and communism.

Song Qingling died in Běijīng and is buried at the Song Qingling Mausoleum (p127) in Shànghǎi. Her sister Meiling declined the invitation to return to China to attend the funeral; she died in the USA in October 2003, aged 105.

PROPAGANDA POSTER ART CENTRE

Map pp86–7

宣传画年画艺术中心 Xuānchuánhuà Niánhuà Yìshù Zhōngxīn

☎ 6211 1845; Room B-OC, President Mansion, 868 Huashan Rd; 华山路868号B-OC室; admission Y20; ☯ 10am-4.30pm; Ⓜ Jiangsu Rd

If phalanxes of red tractors, bumper harvests, muscled peasants and lantern-jawed proletariats fire you up, this small gallery in the bowels of a residential block should intoxicate. The collection of 3000 original posters from the 1950s, '60s and '70s – the golden age of Maoist poster production – will have you weak-kneed at the cartoon world of anti-US defiance. The centre divides into a showroom and a shop featuring posters and postcards for sale. Once you find the main entrance, a guard will pop a small business card with a map on it into your hands and point you the way. Head around the back of the apartment blocks to Building B and take the lift to the basement. It is a good idea to phone ahead (they speak some English) before heading out here to make sure they're open.

SHANGHAI ARTS & CRAFTS MUSEUM

Map pp86–7

上海工艺美术博物馆 Shànghǎi Gōngyì Měishù Bówùguǎn

☎ 6437 2509; 79 Fenyang Rd; 汾阳路79路; admission Y8; ☯ 9am-4pm; Ⓜ Changshu Rd

Repositioned as a museum, this arts and crafts institute displays traditional crafts such as embroidery, paper cutting, lacquer work, jade cutting and lantern making. Watch traditional crafts being performed live by craftspeople and admire the wonderfully wrought exhibits, from jade, to ivory to inkstones and beyond. It's hard not to suspect that the collections were arranged to herd visitors through the overpriced ground-floor shops (foreign exchange assisted). The highlight is quite possibly the building itself, built in 1905, and its ample lawn out back.

ST NICHOLAS CHURCH

Map pp86–7

圣尼古拉斯教堂 Shèngnígǔlāsī Jiàotáng 16 Gaolan Rd; 皋兰路16号; Ⓜ South Huangpi Rd

A short walk west along Gaolan Rd from Fuxing Park (below) is rewarded by the distinctive shape of the vacant and now derelict St Nicholas Church, one of Shànghǎi's small band of Russian Orthodox houses of worship, built to service the huge influx of Russians who arrived in Shànghǎi in the 1930s (see boxed text, p26). The church, dating from 1934, has a typically varied CV, ranging from shrine to washing-machine factory and French restaurant (the latter re-called by the inscription 'Ashanti Dome' on the plaque embedded above the door). It was spared destruction during the Cultural Revolution by a portrait of Mao Zedong, hung strategically from its dome. It was not open to the public at the time of writing.

FUXING PARK Map pp86–7

复兴公园 Fùxīng Gōngyuán

☯ 5am-6pm; Ⓜ South Shanxi Rd/Xintiandi

This leafy park, laid out by the French in 1909 and later used by the Japanese as a parade ground in the late 1930s, remains one of the city's more pleasant. There is always plenty to see here – the park is a refuge for the elderly and a practising field for itinerant musicians, chess players, people walking backwards and slow-moving taichi types. Heavily shaded by big-leafed wutong trees, it's an excellent place to take a seat and escape the summer sun and there's even a popular kiddies playground. Wreathed in the laughter of children, the huge stony-faced busts of Karl Marx and Friedrich Engels gaze out from a seemingly redundant epoch, and nobody seems to notice.

SUN YATSEN'S FORMER RESIDENCE

Map pp86–7

孙中山故居 Sūn Zhōngshān Gùjū

☎ 6437 2954; 7 Xiangshan Rd; 香山路7号; admission Y20; ☯ 9am-4pm; Ⓜ South Shanxi Rd/Xintiandi

China is awash with Sun Yatsen (Sun Zhongshan) memorabilia and this is one of several former dwellings nationwide. Countless Chinese cities evoke the celebrated Father of Modern China (Guófù) with a Zhongshan Park, Zhongshan Rd, or both. Sun lived here on Rue Molière for six years from 1918 to 1924, supported by overseas Chinese funds. After Sun's death, his wife, Song Qingling (1893–1981), continued to live here until 1937, constantly watched by Kuomintang plain-clothes officers and the French police. The two-storey house is set back from the street and is furnished as it was back in Sun's days, though it was looted by the Japanese during WWII. The entry price gets you a brief tour of the house in English.

ZHOU ENLAI'S FORMER RESIDENCE
Map pp86-7
周恩来故居 Zhōu Ēnlái Gùjū
☎ 6473 0420; 73 Sinan Rd; 思南路73号; admission free; ⏰ 9am-4pm; Ⓜ South Shanxi Rd/Xintiandi

In 1946 Zhou Enlai, the urbane and much-loved (although some swear he was even more sly than Mao) first premier of the People's Republic of China, lived in this former French Concession Spanish villa at 107 (now 73) Sinan Rd. Zhou was then head of the Communist Party's Shànghǎi office, and spent much of his time giving press conferences and dodging Kuomintang agents who spied on him from across the road.

There's not much to see these days except spartan beds and stern-looking desks, but the charming neighbourhood, with its lovely old houses, is a great place to wander around.

SONG QINGLING'S FORMER RESIDENCE
Map pp86-7
宋庆龄故居 Sōng Qìnglíng Gùjū
☎ 6474 7183; 1843 Middle Huaihai Rd; 淮海中路1843号; admission Y20; ⏰ 9am-4.30pm; Ⓜ Jiatong University

Built in the 1920s by a Greek shipping magnate, this building became home to the wife of Dr Sun Yatsen from 1948 to 1963 (see boxed text, p91). Size up two of her black limousines (one a gift from Stalin) in the garage and pad about the house, eyeing its period furnishings. It's all a bit neglected, with threadbare carpets and peeling paint, and in need of tender loving care. The highlight is the gorgeous garden out back, with tall magnolias and camphor trees towering over a delightful lawn, where Song entertained her guests with conversation and tea.

LOCAL VOICES: SHANG STYLE

Elfa Huang, 27, studied fashion design in university and owns one of the many boutiques on Changle Rd.

How long have you had your store? Four years. I opened it right after I graduated from university. I sell a mixture of international brands – from Hong Kong and Korea – and Chinese brands. I have thought about designing my own clothing, but I'm not ready for that yet.

Do you think Shànghǎi is the most fashionable city in China? Of course! Shànghǎi has been the most fashionable place in China for a long time now. It's part of our history. I think this is because Shanghainese, the young Shanghainese, are more open to new ideas from other parts of the world. Another important thing is that today foreign brands are all based in Shànghǎi. We have more access to new styles. And women here can afford to care a lot about their appearance because they are more independent. In Shànghǎi, women are equal with men. All of my friends think this way. We don't need to depend on men, so we can be more demanding of them.

Who are your most common customers? How much does an average customer spend at one time? Most women are 20 to 30 years old and they are at least middle class – they have money to spend. On average I'd say they spend between Y700 to Y1000 per visit. But over the past two years I've had more customers from other provinces; I'm speaking Mandarin [as opposed to Shanghainese] more and more now.

What do you do in your free time? Umm…I go shopping! And on the weekends sometimes I go dancing at Muse (p191).

How many pairs of shoes do you own? Around thirty.

If you could change one thing in Shànghǎi, what would it be? Nothing! I'm quite satisfied with my life here.

SHANGHAI MUSEUM OF PUBLIC SECURITY
Map pp86-7

上海公安博物馆 **Shànghǎi Gōng'ān Bówùguǎn**

☎ 6472 0256; www.policemuseum.com.cn; 518 South Ruijin Rd; 瑞金南路518号; admission Y8; ⏰ 9am-4pm Mon-Sat; Ⓜ Dapuqiao

It may sound turgid and dull, but this museum has some gems among the inevitable displays on traffic control and post-Liberation security milestones. The gold pistols of Sun Yatsen and 1930s gangster Huang Jinrong are worth hunting down amid the fine collection of Al Capone-style machine- and pen-guns, and look out for the collection of hand-painted business cards once dispensed by the city's top *jìnǚ* (prostitutes).

MOLLER HOUSE
Map pp86-7

马勒别墅 **Mǎlè Biéshù**

30 South Shaanxi Rd; 陕西南路30号; Ⓜ South Shanxi Rd

One of Shànghǎi's most whimsical buildings, the Scandinavian-influenced gothic peaks of the Moller House could double as the Munsters' holiday home. The Swedish owner and horse-racing fan, Eric Moller, owned the Moller Line. Previously home to the Communist Youth League, the building now houses a hotel, the Hengshan Moller Villa (p209). Fancifully perhaps, legend attests that a fortune teller warned Moller that tragedy would befall him on the house's completion, so the tycoon dragged out its construction (until 1949). Moller clung on for a few years before dying in a plane crash in 1954.

LYCEUM THEATRE Map pp86-7

兰心大戏院 **Lánxīn Dàxìyuàn**

☎ 6217 8530; 57 South Maoming Rd; 茂名南路 57号; Ⓜ South Shanxi Rd

Completed in 1930, this art deco theatre is one of the oldest in Shànghǎi and once housed the British-run Shanghai Amateur Dramatic Society. All manner of acts are staged here, but they're in Chinese only.

RUSSIAN ORTHODOX MISSION CHURCH Map pp86-7

东正教圣母大堂 **Dōngzhèngjiào Shèngmǔ Dàtáng**

55 Xinle Rd; 新乐路55号; Ⓜ South Shanxi Rd

Built in 1934, the lovely blue-domed church was built for the huge influx of Russian worshippers (p26) to Shànghǎi in the 1930s. It is currently closed to the public. The Grape Restaurant (p169) is adjacent to the church.

OLD CHINA HAND READING ROOM
Map pp86-7

汉源书店 **Hànyuán Shūdiàn**

☎ 6473 2526; 27 Shaoxing Rd; 绍兴路27号; ⏰ 10am-midnight; Ⓜ South Shanxi Rd/Dapuqiao

Opened by Shànghǎi photographer and publisher Deke Erh, the Old China Hand Reading Room is a bright space stuffed with antique furnishings and bookshelves, the highlight being a collection of illustrated books on Shànghǎi (published by Old China Hand Press), which you can browse through or purchase. There's also tea, coffee (from Y30) and wi-fi access.

COMMUNITY CHURCH Map pp86-7

国际礼拜堂 **Guójì Lǐbài Táng**

☎ 6437 6576; 53 Hengshan Rd; 衡山路53号; Ⓜ Hengshan Rd

Shànghǎi's largest and most popular church, this nondenominational ivy-cloaked church was flung up in 1924. There are no cheesy Chinese Catholic frills and the church lawn is a gorgeous expanse of green, while the lush tangle of plant life adds to the sense of pleasant refuge. Services are regularly held on Sundays (7.30am and 10am).

FRENCH CONCESSION
Walking Tour

1 Shíkùmén From South Huangpi Rd metro station, walk south through the rebuilt shíkùmén (p49) of Xīntiāndì (p90) and visit the Shiku-

men Open House Museum (p91) and the anachronistic Site of the 1st National Congress of the CCP (p91).

2 St Nicholas Church Follow Xingye Rd west, cross South Chongqing Rd and continue along Nanchang Rd. Meeting cafe-lined Yandang Rd, head south and pass through Fuxing Park (p92) to exit the park at its west. Continue west along Gaolan Rd for a glance at the former Russian Orthodox St Nicholas Church (p92), built in 1933 in dedication to the murdered tsar of Russia.

3 Sun Yatsen & Zhou Enlai's Former Residences Walk south down Sinan Rd to Sun Yatsen's Former Residence (p92), a characteristic old villa. A short walk south is Zhou Enlai's Former Residence (p93).

4 Ruijin Hotel Head west along Middle Fuxing Rd to Ruijin No 2 Rd and south to the Ruijin Hotel (p209), the former Morriss estate and home to the founder of the *North China Daily News*. You can stroll around the eastern half of the complex, but unfortunately the western half was demolished to make room for a new hotel tower.

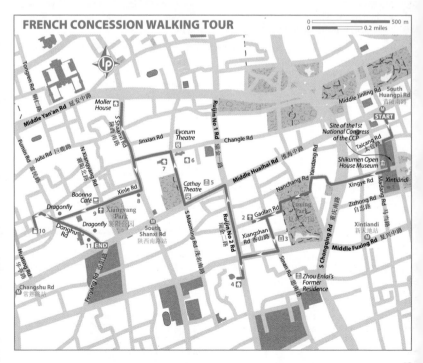

FRENCH CONCESSION WALKING TOUR

5 ShanghART Follow Ruijin No 1 Rd north to Middle Huaihai Rd and cross to the northern side. Head west until you reach the 1920s twin villas and garden at No 796 (formerly the residence of a Shànghǎi middleman or *comprador*), which houses a luxurious new branch of the ShangART gallery (p94). Afterwards, continue west along Middle Huaihai Rd, and turn north onto South Maoming Rd at the 1932 Cathay Theatre (p190).

6 Jinjiang Hotel North of here rises the historic 1931 Jinjiang Hotel (p208). Shànghǎi's diplomatic community was held under house arrest here in 1941 when the Japanese took control of the city. At the southern end of the complex is the plush 1930s apartment block, the Grosvenor House (贵宾楼; Guìbīnlóu).

7 Okura Garden Hotel Shanghai Across Maoming Rd is the Okura Garden Hotel Shanghai (p208), originally constructed in 1926 as the Cercle Sportif Français. The eastern entrance of the hotel features a gold mosaic statuary niche and the original staircase leading up to the ballroom with its beautiful stained-glass ceiling piece.

8 Xinle Rd At the Lyceum Theatre (p94) head west along Changle Rd. The fairytale-like Hengshan Moller Villa (p209) is north up South Shaanxi Rd

at No 30 and makes for a good detour. Otherwise, turn south on South Shaanxi Rd and then west onto Xinle Rd (p141), a premier shopping street.

9 Russian Orthodox Mission Church On the corner of Xinle Rd and Xiangyang Rd is the lovely blue-domed Russian Orthodox Mission Church (p94), built in 1934 and recently renovated (but unfortunately closed to the public).

10 Chinese Printed Blue Nankeen Exhibition Hall Keep walking along Xinle Rd to the junction with Donghu Rd and turn right onto Changle Rd. Hidden down Lane 637 is the Chinese Printed Blue Nankeen Exhibition Hall (p144). There are a number of 1930s *lòngtáng* in this area, including one across the street at Lane 764.

11 Big-Eared Du's Former Residence Backtracking, walk south down Donghu Rd past one of the former houses of the gangster Du Yuesheng (杜月笙故居; Dù Yuèshēng Gùjū) hidden behind elegant art deco gates at the corner. Look out for two branches of Dragonfly (p197) along the way – if you want a massage, they might be able to squeeze you in.

Drinking p183; Eating p170; Shopping p146; Sleeping p211

In the early days of the International Settlement, West Nanjing Rd was known as Bubbling Well Rd and its far western end marked where the city stopped and the countryside began. By the 1920s, the fields were being swallowed up by the rapidly expanding city and Bubbling Well Rd was one of Shànghǎi's busiest and most exclusive streets. Apart from its name, not much has changed since then. The main thoroughfare of today's Jìng'ān district, West Nanjing Rd, is now home to some of the city's priciest malls, high-end shops and five-star hotels.

Pǔdōng may have taller towers and the French Concession more charisma, but this part of Jìng'ān is still the city's most exclusive neighbourhood. Even the skyscrapers here blend together – a change from the disjointed skyline in other districts – while the traditional *lìlòng* (alleyways) are unexpectedly well preserved. The heart of all the consumer action is the Shanghai Centre, a focal point both for tourists and the many expats who work in the area. Inside the complex are airline offices, consulates, supermarkets, restaurants, cafes, bars and the Portman Ritz-Carlton.

top picks

JÌNG'ĀN

- M50 (left) Contemplate the artwork at the post-industrial M50.
- Jade Buddha Temple (p100) Admire Song dynasty architecture and a superlative jade Buddha.
- Walking tour (p104) Visit the old alleyways featured on our walking tour.
- Nightlife (p191, p192) Bust a move at Muse or rock it at the Zhijiang Dream Factory.
- Shanghai Centre Theatre (p188) Catch the acrobats at the Shanghai Centre Theatre.

But head north of West Nanjing Rd and you're plunged into a grittier and more absorbing section of Jìng'ān, which takes its name from the ancient temple (p102). Walk north along bustling Jiangning or North Shaanxi Rds for a taste of an authentic working-class Shànghǎi neighbourhood. Like Hóngkǒu (p115), this area is primed for development and a burst of new nightlife venues and shopping complexes – some of which have not succeeded – hint at bigger things to come. The dining options here have long been first-rate, and those on a culinary tour of Shànghǎi should definitely squeeze it in to the itinerary.

M50 Map pp98–9

M50创意产业集聚区 M Wǔshí Chuàngyì Chǎnyè Jíjùqū
50 Moganshan Rd; 莫干山路50号; M Shanghai Train Station or taxi

Chinese contemporary art has been the hottest thing in the art world for the past decade and there's no sign of the boom ending, with collectors around the world paying record prices for the work of top artists like Zhang Xiaogang (whose paintings sold for a total of US$57 million in 2007). Běijīng may dominate the art scene in China, but Shànghǎi has its own thriving gallery subculture, centred on this complex of industrial buildings down dusty Moganshan Rd in the north of town.

Although many of the artists who originally established the enclave are long gone, it is well worth putting aside a half-day to poke around the many galleries here. There's some challenging, innovative art

as well as work that won't last, and there are places to sip coffee and eat noodles once you run out of steam. Most galleries are open from 10am to 6pm; some close on Monday. Maps are available at the main entrance (try the security guard if you can't find them).

The most established gallery here, the 10-year old ShanghART (Xiānggénà Huàláng; ☎ 6359 3923; www.shanghartgallery.com; Bldg 16 & 18) has a big, dramatic space to show the work of some of the 40 artists it represents. The top-notch and provocative island6 (☎ 6227 7856; www.island6.org; 2nd fl, Bldg 6) focuses on collaborative works created in a studio behind the gallery. OFoto (☎ 6298 5416; 2nd fl, Bldg 13) features China-related photography exhibitions. Other notable galleries include Art Scene (Yìshùjìng Huàláng; ☎ 6277 4940; 2nd fl, Bldg 4) and twocities (☎ 5252 1518; www.twocitiesgallery.com; 2nd fl, Bldg 0), the latter of which specialises

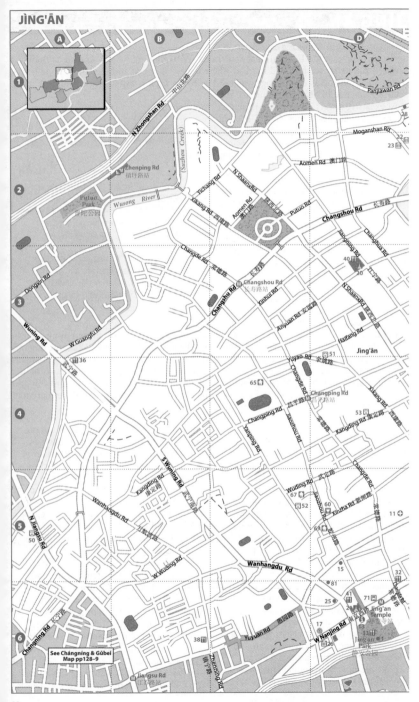

JÌNG'ĀN

A   B   C   D

N Zhongshan Rd 中山北路

Panjiawan Rd

Moganshan Rd

Zhenping Rd 镇坪路站

23

Aomen Rd 澳门路

Putuo
Park
普陀公园

Wusong River

(Suzhou Creek)

Yichang Rd

N Shaanxi Rd

Xikang Rd 西康路

Aomen Rd 澳门路

Putuo Rd

Changshou Rd 长寿路

Jiangning Rd

Changhua Rd

Dongan Rd

Changde Rd 常德路

40
20

Changshou Rd 长寿路

Changshou Rd
长寿路站

Wuning Rd

Changshou Rd 长寿路

Xinhui Rd

Anyuan Rd 安远路

N Shaanxi Rd 陕西北路

W Guangfu Rd

Haifang Rd

36

Jìng'ān

Yuyao Rd 余姚路

51

Changde Rd

65

Changping Rd

Changping Rd 昌平路站

Xikang Rd

53

Kangding Rd 康定路

Changde Rd

Changping Rd

Haofang Rd

Yanping Rd

S Wuning Rd

Kangding Rd 康定路

Wanhangdu Rd 万航渡路

Wuding Rd 武定路

67
52

60

Xinzha Rd 新闸路

11

69

N Jiangsu Rd

50

W Wuding Rd

Wanhangdu Rd

15

81

32

41 71

25

Changning Rd 长宁路

See Chángníng & Gǔběi
Map pp128–9

38

Yuyao Rd 愚园路

Zhenning Rd

W Nanjing Rd 南京西路

17

26

Jing'an
Temple

Jìng'ān
Park

Jiangsu Rd 江苏路站

98

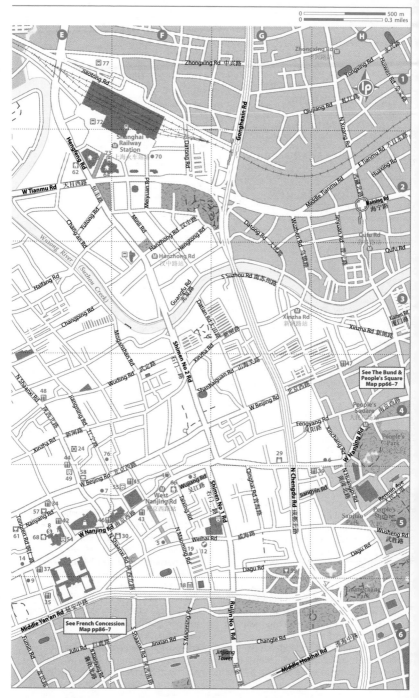

JÌNG'ĀN

in 3D art. Across the street is m97 (☎ 6266 1597; www.m97gallery.com; 2nd fl, 97 Moganshan Rd; ⏰ 10.30am-6.30pm Tue-Sun), an innovative photography gallery.

Gentrification was inevitable, and you can now also browse shops like Shirt Flag (Bldg 17; p143), Art Deco (Bldg 7; p146) as well as several clothing boutiques. When your legs finally give way, take a seat at Bandu Cabin (p192), which provides drinks, peanut butter sandwiches (Y12) and noodles (Y18) as well as traditional Chinese music concerts (Saturdays from 8pm). Other evening entertainment includes Image Tunnel (p189), which has slideshows and independent Chinese films, and twocities (p97), which holds improv jazz concerts once or twice a month (Friday at 7.30pm).

JADE BUDDHA TEMPLE
Map pp98–9
玉佛寺 Yùfó Sì

☎ 6266 3668; cnr Anyuan Rd & Jiangning Rd; 安远路和江宁路拐角; admission Y20; ⏰ 8am-4.30pm; 🚍 19 from Broadway Mansions along Tiantong Rd, Ⓜ Changshou Rd
Built between 1911 and 1918 in Song dynasty style, this active place of worship is one of Shànghǎi's few Buddhist temples. The Hall of Heavenly Kings (天王殿; Tiānwáng Diàn) contains its namesake kings and a splendid statue of the laughing Buddha back-to-back with a fabulous effigy of Weituo, the guardian of Buddhism.

Festooned with red lanterns, the first courtyard is paved with slabs etched with lotus flowers and leads to the

JÌNG'ĀN

twin-eaved Great Treasure Hall (大雄宝殿; Dàxióng Bǎodiàn), where worshippers pray to the past, present and future Buddhas, which are seated on splendidly carved thrones. Also lodged within the hall are the temple's drum and bell that would normally be hung within separate towers, and a copper-coloured statue of Guanyin stands at the rear.

Follow the left-hand corridor beyond the main hall and you will pass a chamber where Buddhist services are held. At the very rear of the temple is the recently built 10,000 Buddhas Hall, where Buddhist services and lectures are held.

But the absolute centrepiece of the temple is its 1.9m-high pale-green jade Buddha, seated upstairs in his own hall. It is

said that Hui Gen (Wei Ken, a Pǔtuóshān monk) travelled to Myanmar (Burma)

TRANSPORT: JÌNG'ĀN

Metro Line 2 runs east–west and stops at People's Sq, West Nanjing Rd, Jing'an Temple and Jiangsu Rd. Line 7 runs north–south and intersects with line 2 at Jing'an Temple and line 1 at Changshu Rd in the French Concession.

Bus Bus 19 links the North Bund area to the Jade Buddha Temple area; catch it at the intersection of Tiantong Rd and North Sichuan Rd. Bus 112 zigzags north from the southern end of People's Sq to West Nanjing Rd, and up Jiangning Rd to the Jade Buddha Temple.

In its bid to totally refashion itself as a Brave New World futuropolis, Shànghăi is deeply at odds with its more mundane communist heritage. The colourless residue of the communist period – still nominally the presiding epoch lest we forget – still lurks among the swell and neon of the town like a record at the bottom of the pile that no one plays any more. Nonetheless, nostalgic middle-aged Chinese on the 'Red Tour' (红色旅游; Hóngsè Lǚyóu) of town get dewy eyed at several places of note.

China's communist bandwagon first rolled out from the Site of the 1st National Congress of the CCP (p91), one of communist China's holiest places of pilgrimage, possibly on par with Mao Zedong's birthplace at Sháoshān in Húnán province.

A palpable reverence hangs over the Former Residence of Mao Zedong (Map pp98–9), which includes his bedroom, study and photos of the ex-Chairman doing his thing, but for foreigners the highlight is the well-tended and very pretty shíkùmén building itself. It was closed for renovation at the time of writing. Others on the Chairman Mao trail can take a look at the building at 168 Anyi Rd (安义路168号) where the Great Helmsman once stayed in 1920.

Visits to Fuxing Park (p92) turn up anachronistic statues of Karl Marx and Friedrich Engels, godfathers to China's communist dry run. Astonishingly, the effigies were only carved in 1985, when Marxist dogma in Shànghăi was already irreversibly pear-shaped.

The Shanghai Exhibition Centre (p104) is a classic example of socialist bravado, and for a lavish blast of hardcore communist spin, pop into the Propaganda Poster Art Centre (p92). Then visit another notable stop on the heritage trail (though the architecture may be concession era), Zhou Enlai's Former Residence (p93).

via Tibet, lugged five jade Buddhas back to China and then went off in search of alms to build a temple for them. Two of the Buddhas ended up in Shànghăi. The beautiful seated effigy of Sakyamuni, clearly Southeast Asian in style, gazes out from a cabinet. Visitors are not able to approach the statue, but can admire it from a distance. An additional charge of Y10 is levied to see the statue (photographs aren't allowed).

A similarly elegant jade reclining Buddha can be found downstairs, opposite a much larger copy in stone. A black-faced statue of Guanyin is ensconced within another hall, and a large vegetarian restaurant (☎ 6266 5596; 999 Jiangning Rd; 江宁路999号; dishes from Y18) is attached to the temple.

In February, during the Lunar New Year, the temple is very busy, as some 20,000 Chinese Buddhists throng to pray for prosperity. The surrounding shops and the many hawkers can supply everything you need to generate good luck, including bundles of spirit money to burn in incense pots. This is one of Shànghăi's top sights; expect crowds.

JING'AN TEMPLE
Map pp98-9
静安寺 Jìng'ān Sì
☎ 5213 1586; 1686-1688 West Nanjing Rd; 南京西路1686-1688号; admission Y20; ⓥ 7.30am-5pm; Ⓜ Jing'an Temple

The Jing'an Temple (Temple of Tranquillity) was originally built in AD 247 but was largely destroyed in 1851. Khi Vehdu, who ran the Jing'an Temple in the 1930s, was one of the most remarkable figures of the time. The nearly 2m-tall abbot had a large following and each of his seven concubines had a house and a car. The temple was shorn of its Buddhist statues in the Cultural Revolution and turned into a plastics factory.

Restoration has been ongoing since 1999, but while the city has managed to add nine new metro lines and countless skyscrapers since then, the temple remains unfinished. It's largely synthetic in feel, but there is a small stream of devotees who file in throughout the day, and the silhouettes of traditionally upturned eaves set against the nearby supertowers are photogenic in their own way. Underneath the main hall (unfinished at the time of writing) is a storage room that serves as a makeshift worship area.

Good times to visit include the Festival of Bathing Buddha on the 8th day of the 4th lunar month and at the full moon.

Opposite is newly remodelled Jing'an Park, formerly Bubbling Park Cemetery, which is worth a stroll, while just round the corner and up Huashan Rd is the distinctive art deco Paramount Ballroom (opposite), built in 1932 and visited by Charlie Chaplin in 1936. See the Walking Tour for directions there.

PARAMOUNT BALLROOM Map pp98-9
百乐门 Bǎilèmén
☎ 6249 8866; 218 Yuyuan Rd; 豫园路218号; afternoon tea dances Y80, evening ballroom dancing Y100; ⏲ 1pm-12.30am; Ⓜ Jing'an Temple
This old art deco theatre was the biggest nightclub in the 1930s, and today has sedate tea dances in the afternoon to the sounds of old-school jazz and tango, as well as ballroom dancing in the evening. It makes for a nice nostalgia trip for those with a sense of humour. Dance partners are Y35 to Y45 for 10 minutes.

SUZHOU CREEK BOAT TOURS
Map pp98-9
M50创意产业集聚区 M Wǔshí Chuàngyì Chǎnyè Jíjùqū
50 Moganshan Rd; 莫干山路50号; Ⓜ Shanghai Train Station or taxi

New boat tours along Suzhou Creek, which has benefited from a decade-long clean-up project, were scheduled to begin service in April 2010. Tours are expected to take in several new museums, including the Matchbox Museum (2521 West Guangfu Rd; 光复西路2521号), the Coin Museum (17 West Guangfu Rd, inside the Shanghai Mint; 光复西路17号上海造币厂内) and the Silk Museum (289 Aomen Rd; 澳门路289号; admission free), actually tours of a silk factory. Boats will leave from W Guangfu Rd in western Jing'an, running for a 10km stretch along Suzhou Creek to the M50 art galleries (it will be easiest to find more information about the tours at M50). There are plans to extend the tour to Waibaidu Bridge, on the Bund, in the future. This may be geared more toward tour groups than individual travellers, so scout it out before making plans.

LOCAL VOICES: ART-HOUSE CINEMA

Han Yuqi, 46, is an art professor at Shanghai Technical University. She founded Image Tunnel in 2005 as a place to screen independent Chinese films and was one of the original artists who helped transform the M50 industrial complex into art studios.

What is your favourite Shànghǎi film? Oh, there are so many... Let me tell you, there are a lot of Shanghainese who have never seen old movies. In 2005, I showed some silent films here, and one of my friends said, 'I have no interest in watching a movie with Ruan Lingyu [a famous Chinese actress from the 1930s], I want to see something modern'. So I was really worried before I showed the films – there were two silent films, three hours long – I was afraid that everyone would lose interest and leave right away. But, in fact, not a single person left! Those silent films were really well done. Afterwards, everyone said, 'Wow, Ruan Lingyu, she is really an amazing actress!' Old films and contemporary films are quite different from each other, but I really hope that more people learn to appreciate these old films.

What about modern cinema? Contemporary Shànghǎi is interesting too – I believe that there are so many good films that come out of Shànghǎi because there are so many unusual stories that take place here. Take my studio for example. There's a famous mystery writer, Cai Jun (蔡骏), who several years ago wrote a book called *The 19th Level of Hell* – in China, we usually say hell has 18 levels, but his book was about the 19th level. Anyway, in 2005 he came to find me in order to give me a copy of his book. I didn't know him and I had no interest in reading it – it's for kids, I don't have time to read that stuff – but he kept on hanging around here, which I thought was kind of strange. Finally in 2007, when we were putting together an e-zine, one of the young designers told me, 'Do you know why he keeps on hanging around here, Professor Han? It's because you're in building No 19, and he's obsessed with the number 19.' Then on July 24 of that year – his novel had already been made into a movie (*Nakara 19*) and we were screening it here – it was here on that day that he met the woman he fell in love with and eventually married. All because of the number 19. There are so many unusual stories like this in Shànghǎi.

What do you think about Shànghǎi? You might think that this city has a lot of drawbacks – there's no peace and quiet, there's all this construction that's always going on – but there are a lot of opportunities. For instance, every day I can create new things, exhibit new works. There are a lot of young people here, especially at M50, they come and they do a lot of projects with the artists, so I think it's really interesting. For instance a young graphic designer may come and help you do something – we publish e-zines and websites – so there are a lot of opportunities for collaboration with the younger generation.

Tell me one thing you would like to change in Shànghǎi. The people! I mean, I would like to change the Chinese attitude toward art. Because of historical circumstances, most Chinese don't think of spending money on art. Our tradition has always been: save, save, save; don't spend money on unnecessary things. But young Chinese are different. So artists are now concentrating on cultivating a new market. Selling our own work is not the primary goal; what we want is for a new market to develop in the future.

THE GREAT JEWISH FAMILIES

The Sassoon family consisted of generations of shrewd businesspeople from Baghdad to Bombay, whose achievements brought them wealth, knighthoods and far-reaching influence. Though it was David Sassoon who initiated cotton trading out of Bombay (now Mumbai) to China, and son Elias Sassoon who had the ingenuity to buy and build his own warehouses in Shànghǎi, it was Sir Victor Sassoon (1881–1961) who finally amassed the family fortune and enjoyed his wealth during Shànghǎi's heyday. Victor concentrated his energies on buying up Shànghǎi's land and building offices, apartments and warehouses. At one time Victor Sassoon owned an estimated 1900 buildings in Shànghǎi. Victor left Shànghǎi in 1941, returning only briefly after the war to tidy up the business, and then he and his assets relocated to the Bahamas. He had plenty of affairs but remained a bachelor until he finally married his American nurse when he was 70. Today the Sassoon legacy lives on in the historic Fairmont Peace Hotel (p204) and Sassoon Mansion (Map p132; known to Sassoon as 'Eve') – now the Cypress Hotel in Hóngqiáo – each the site of some infamously raucous Sassoon soirées. For one of his celebrated fancy dress parties, he requested guests to come dressed as if shipwrecked.

The company of David Sassoon & Sons gave rise to several other notables in Shànghǎi, among them Silas Hardoon and Elly Kadoorie. Hardoon began his illustrious career as a night guard and later, in 1880, as manager of David Sassoon & Sons. Two years later he set out to do business on his own and promptly went bust. His second independent business venture in 1920 proved successful and Silas Hardoon made a name for himself in real estate. In his father's memory he built the Beth Aharon Synagogue near Suzhou Creek, which later served as a shelter for Polish Jews who had fled Europe. It has since been demolished. Once a well-respected member of both the French and International Councils, Hardoon's reputation turned scandalous when he took a Eurasian wife, Luo Jialing, and adopted a crowd of multicultural children. He then began to study Buddhism. His estate, including the school he had erected (now the grounds of the Shanghai Exhibition Centre) went up in smoke during the Sino-Japanese war. At the time of his death in 1931, he was the richest man in Shànghǎi.

Like Silas Hardoon, Elly Kadoorie began a career with David Sassoon & Sons in 1880 and he too broke away and amassed a fortune – in real estate, banking and rubber production. His famous mansion is the result of too much money left in the hands of an unreliable architect; after returning from three years in England, Kadoorie found a 19.5m-high ballroom aglow with 5.4m chandeliers and enough imported marble to warrant the name Marble Hall. Architecture detectives can still visit the staircases and peek at the ballroom of the former mansion, once the site of Shànghǎi's most extravagant balls and now home to the Children's Palace (Map pp98–9; 64 West Yan'an Rd); see also opposite. Kadoorie died the year the communists took power; you can visit his mausoleum in the International Cemetery (Map pp128–9; Hongqiao Rd).

With their immense wealth, many Jewish families were pivotal in aiding the thousands of refugees who fled to Shànghǎi. The Kadoorie family resides in Hong Kong and is still involved in charity work.

ANDREW JAMES ART Map pp98-9
安杰当代艺术画廊 **Ānjié Dāngdài Yìshù Huàláng**
☎ 5228 7550; www.andrewjamesart.com; 39 North Maoming Rd; 茂名北路39号; ⏰ 11am-7pm Tue-Sun; Ⓜ West Nanjing Rd
This private art gallery is set in an old villa with two decent-sized showrooms. There are some big openings here and the quality of the work (with a focus on Chinese and Asian artists) is generally very high.

SHANGHAI EXHIBITION CENTRE
Map pp98-9
上海展览中心 **Shànghǎi Zhǎnlǎn Zhōngxīn**
☎ 6279 0279; 1000 Middle Yan'an Rd; 延安中路 1000号; Ⓜ Jing'an Temple
The hulking great monolith of the Shanghai Exhibition Centre can be seen from West Nanjing Rd. It was built as the Palace of Sino-Soviet Friendship, a friendship that soon turned to ideological rivalry and even the brink of war in the 1960s. Architectural buffs will appreciate its monumentality and unsubtle, bold Bolshevik strokes – there was a time when Pǔdōng was set to look like this.

The site of the Exhibition Centre was originally the gardens of the Jewish millionaire Silas Hardoon (see the boxed text, above).

JÌNG'ĀN
Walking Tour
1 Lǐlòng houses Stroll east along leafy *lǐlòng*-strewn Yuyuan Rd (愚园路) from its junction with Zhenning Rd (镇宁路), a starting point around 500m east of Jiangsu Rd metro station. On the south side of the road at No 611 (611弄) is a gorgeous alleyway of red brick *lǐlòng* houses overlooking quaint gardens.

2 New lǐlòng houses Cross the road to look at the modern-style *lǐlòng* houses at Wenyuan Fang (文元坊), built in 1938, at No 608 (608弄) before continuing east to peruse the new-style *lǐlòng* houses at Zhōngshí Xīncūn (中实新村; 579弄). *Lǐlòng* houses with art deco detailing can be discovered across the road at No 576 (576弄).

3 Bubbling Well Lane The fabulous brick and carved stone gateway to Bubbling Well Lane (湧泉坊) further east at No 395 (395弄) leads to a series of handsome stuccoed houses, at the end of which stands a distinctive old brick building with arched windows and crazily arranged brickwork. Continue east and turn into No 361 (361弄) Yugucun (愚谷村), a wisteria-shaded alleyway of new-style *lǐlòng* houses that threads through to West Nanjing Rd.

4 Shanghai Children's Palace Walk east on West Nanjing Rd and you will see the large two-storey building on the south side of the road at No 1799. This is the Shanghai Children's Palace (少年宫; admission Y20; ☉ 8am-6pm Wed-Sun), formerly the Kadoorie House, named after its wealthy Jewish owner. You can buy a ticket to explore the building, built in 1924, from the ticket office on the eastern side of the building.

5 Paramount Ballroom Continue walking east to Wanhangdu Rd (万航渡路) and head north to one of Shànghǎi's foremost art deco structures, the magnificent Paramount Ballroom (p103), which just a few decades ago was the run-down Red Capital cinema. The ballroom continues its tradition of providing paid dancers for the partnerless.

6 Jing'an Temple Cross the road, continue along Yuyuan Rd to take the first right down the pedestrian street running down to Jing'an Temple (p102) with its towering monument topped with four golden lions seated back to back.

7 Shanghai Exhibition Centre After wandering through pleasant Jing'an Park (p102) stroll east along the south side of West Nanjing Rd to the socialist styling of the Shanghai Exhibition Centre (opposite). Cross to the other side of the road and admire the grand residence at 1418 West Nanjing Rd, built in 1926.

8 Woo Villa Saunter north up Tongren Rd (铜仁路) to the art deco Woo Villa (aka the Green House), a private residence designed by Ladislaus Hudec that's been turned into a restaurant. Across West Beijing Rd, note the art deco gateway to the Shanghai Children's Hospital. On the other side of Tongren Rd

WALK FACTS

Start **Corner of Zhenning Rd and Yuyuan Rd**

End **Méilóngzhèn Jiǔjiā**

Distance **4.5km**

Time **Three hours**

Fuel stop **Element Fresh (p171) or Plum (p106)**

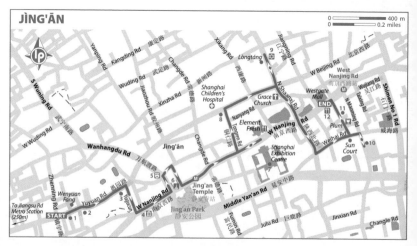

are the Avenue Apartments, also designed by Hudec.

9 Ohel Rachel Synagogue Head east along West Beijing Rd and then north along North Shaanxi Rd to the ivy-cloaked Ohel Rachel Synagogue (boxed text, p104) at No 500. Across the way stand some *lòngtáng* (Lane No 493) and *shíkùmén* houses that were undergoing restoration at the time of writing.

10 Former Residence of Mao Zedong Walk south past Grace Church (怀恩堂; Huái'ēn Táng), built in 1942, at No 375 North Shaanxi Rd and turn east onto Weihai Rd (威海路). Beyond Sun Court (651 Weihai Rd), a hefty brick apartment block flung up in the 1920s, turn right onto North Maoming Rd and explore the lovingly preserved *shíkùmén*

architecture of the Former Residence of Mao Zedong (boxed text, p102), also undergoing restoration at the time of writing.

11 Bubbling Well Road Apartments Return to Sun Court and walk north up Bubbling Well Road Apartments (静安别墅; Jìng'ān Biéshù) directly opposite, a gorgeous *lòngtáng* with rows of new-style *lǐlòng* houses with balconies, built between 1928 and 1932. Get a feel for the interiors at Plum (No 37, Lane 652; 652弄37号; tea Y25; ⏰ 11am-8pm Tue-Sun), a tiny gallery-cum-cafe.

12 Méilóngzhèn Jiǔjiā Reaching West Nanjing Rd, head west to the magnificent architecture of the restaurant Méilóngzhèn Jiǔjiā (p171). To return to the metro system, the West Nanjing Rd metro station is a short walk to the east.

Drinking p184; Eating p173; Shopping p146; Sleeping p212

Pŭdōng is a Chinese place name that many Westerners know before setting foot in Shànghǎi and its vertical skyline is one of China's most photographed entities. More than 1.5 times larger than urban Shànghǎi, the Pudong New Area (浦东新区; Pŭdōng Xīnqū) takes up the eastern bank of the Huangpu River. Before 1990 – when development plans were first trumpeted – Pŭdōng was 350 sq km of boggy farmland that supplied Shànghǎi's markets with vegies. Before that it was home to the *godowns* (warehouses) and *compradors* (buyers or middlemen) of Shànghǎi's foreign trading companies. Today the only things sprouting out of the ground are skyscrapers, and Pŭdōng has become Shànghǎi's and China's economic powerhouse.

Charisma – part and parcel of Pŭxī to the west – has missed the boat across the Huangpu River and panache only exists in frugal pockets, but the sparkling panorama of Pŭdōng testifies to the swagger of China, Inc. The enclave belongs to a future age where MagLevs glide swiftly into a universe of skyscrapers and multilane highways. History is not strong here: time – with fins on – goes in one direction only in Pŭdōng and the sumptuousness of Shànghǎi's past can only be perceived by squinting through the haze at the Bund across the water. The hit-and-miss architecture may make Pŭdōng little more than a tourist curiosity but it serves as a convenient contrast to the cultural highs of Pŭxī.

top picks

PŬDŌNG & CENTURY AVENUE AREA

- **Shanghai World Financial Center** (left) Ascend to the heavens on the world's highest observation deck.
- **Riverside Promenade** (p110) Stroll along the river and enjoy the views back to the Bund.
- **Shanghai History Museum** (p110) Visit this fun museum for a taste of old Shànghǎi.
- **Faking it** (p147) Start spending at the mother of all fake markets in the Science & Technology Museum metro station.
- **Cloud 9** (p184) Admire the curvature of the earth from this bar at the Grand Hyatt.

The high-rise area directly across from the Bund is the Lujiazui Finance and Trade Zone, where China's largest stock market (the Shanghai Stock Exchange) is located. From the unmistakable Oriental Pearl TV Tower, the eight-lane-wide Century Ave runs over 4km to Century Park. Here you'll find the Shanghai Science and Technology Museum, Pŭdōng's government building and the Oriental Art Center, set around Century Sq. Further out is the huge new International Expo Hall and the MagLev train terminus near the Longyang Rd metro stop.

For the visitor, the main attractions are the high-altitude observation decks, hotels, restaurants and bars in the Jinmao Tower and the Shanghai World Financial Center. Also of note is the Shanghai History Museum and the views back to the Bund from the relatively peaceful Riverside Promenade. So, what's up next for Pŭdōng? You guessed it – another skyscraper. Aiming for a 2014 completion date, the 128-storey Shanghai Tower will one day dwarf the rest of Lùjiāzuǐ at a towering height of 632m.

SHANGHAI WORLD FINANCIAL CENTER

Map p108

上海环球金融中心 **Shànghǎi Huánqiú Jīnróng Zhōngxīn**

☎ 5878 0101; 100 Century Ave; 世纪大道 100号; observation deck adult 94th/97th/100th fl Y100/110/150, under-18yr Y70/80/100, child 0.8-1.4m Y50/70/75; ⏱ 8am-11pm (last entry 10pm); Ⓜ Lujiazui Rd

Completed in 2008, China's tallest building (492m) was never able to grab the much coveted and elusive crown of 'world's tallest building' and has instead had to settle for the title of 'world's highest observation deck'. There are actually three observation decks, the top two (located at the bottom and top of the trapezoid) of which are known as Sky Walks. There is room for debate as to whether the top Sky Walk (474m) is the best spot for Shanghigh views, though. The hexagonal space is bright and futuristic, and some of the floor is transparent glass (a very nice touch), but the lack of a 360-degree sweep – windows only face west or east – is something of a detractor in comparison with the facing Jinmao Tower. But then again,

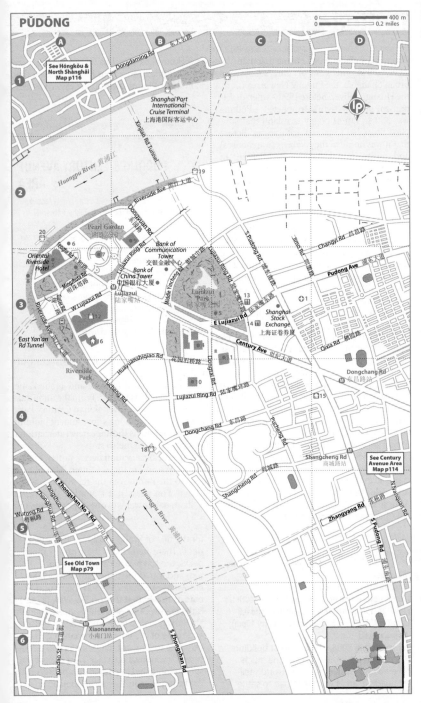

PŬDŌNG

0 — 400 m
0 — 0.2 miles

A   东大名路

B   **C**   **D**

Dongdaming Rd

Shanghai Port
International
Cruise Terminal
上海港国际客运中心

See Hóngkǒu &
North Shànghǎi
Map p116

Huangpu River 黄浦江

Xinjian Rd Tunnel

19

Riverside Ave 滨江大道

Pearl Garden
明珠公园

Dongyuan Rd
东园路

Bank of
Communication
Tower
交银金融中心

Oriental
Riverside
Hotel

Fenghe Rd 丰和路

Lujiazui Ring Rd 陆家嘴环路

Bank of
China Tower
中国银行大厦

Middle Yincheng Rd 银城中路

Lujiazui Ring Rd 陆家嘴环路

Lujiazui
陆家嘴站

Mingzhu Rd
明珠塔路

Guta Rd
古塔路

W Lujiazui Rd

E Lujiazui Rd

Lujiazui
Park
陆家嘴公园

13

5

Shanghai
Stock
Exchange
上海证券交易所

4

S Pudong Rd 浦东南路

Jilin Rd 吉林路

Changyi Rd 昌邑路

Jima Rd 即墨路

Pudong Ave 浦东大道

1

Riverside Ave 滨江大道

East Yan'an
Rd Tunnel

12

16

Riverside
Park

Huayuanshiqiao Rd 花园石桥路

Fucheng Rd 富城路

Dongtai Rd

0

Lujiazui Ring Rd 陆家嘴环路

11

Century Ave 世纪大道

Qida Rd 栖霞路

Dongchang Rd
东昌路

15

Dongchang Rd 东昌路

18

Fucheng Rd

Shangcheng Rd
商城路

Shangcheng Rd

See Century
Avenue Area
Map p114

E Zhongshan No 2 Rd

Wutong Rd
梧桐路

Yangshuo Rd 杨硕路

Zhonghua Rd 中华路

Huangpu River 黄浦江

Zhangyang Rd

S Pudong Rd 浦东南路

N Nanquan Rd

See Old Town
Map p79

Xiaonanmen
小南门

JS Depux

S Zhongshan Rd

1
2
3
4
5
6

TRANSPORT: PŬDŌNG

Metro Line 2 can whisk you through several stations in Pŭdōng, including Lujiazui, Century Ave and the Science & Technology Museum. Line 9 runs through the southern part of the French Concession and on to Century Avenue. Lines 4 and 6 also cut through Pŭdōng, but are less useful for travellers. All four lines meet at Century Avenue.

Ferry Ferries run regularly between Pŭxi and Pŭdōng for the six-minute trip across the river (Y2). It's a 10-minute walk to the Jinmao Tower from the dock.

Taxi A taxi ride will cost you around Y25 as you'll have to pay the Y15 tunnel toll heading eastwards. There is a useful taxi queue in front of the Science & Technology Museum.

Bund Sightseeing Tunnel Travel underneath the Huangpu River in a tunnel (p67) dedicated to kitsch.

---

you do get to look down on the top of the Jinmao, which might be worth the ticket price alone. If lines are long, head up to the building's 91st-floor restaurant-bar 100 Century Avenue (p184) instead. Access to the observation deck is on the west side of the building off Haixin Rd; access to the Park Hyatt (p213) is on the south side of the building.

JINMAO TOWER
Map p108

金茂大厦 Jīnmào Dàshà

☎ 5047 5101; 88 Century Ave; 世纪大道 88号; adult/student/child 0.8-1.2m Y88/60/45; ☉ 8.30am-10pm; Ⓜ Lujiazui Rd

In a city of dubious contemporary architecture, the colossal Jinmao Tower stands out for its winning design. It's essentially an office block (owned by the Ministry of Foreign Trade and Economic Cooperation) with the high-altitude Grand Hyatt (p212) renting space from the 53rd to 87th floors. The eye-catching stepped design is loosely inspired by a traditional Chinese subject, the pagoda. If you want to see Shànghăi in a splendid nutshell, travel in the elevators to the 88th-floor observation deck, accessed from the separate podium building to the side of the main tower. Time your visit at dusk for both day and

---

night views. Alternatively, sample the same view through the carbonated fizz of a gin and tonic at Cloud 9 (p184) on the 87th floor of the Grand Hyatt (accessed on the south side of the building), and photograph the hotel's astonishing barrel-vaulted atrium.

ORIENTAL PEARL TV TOWER Map p108
东方明珠广播电视塔 Dōngfāng Míngzhū Guǎngbō Diànshì Tǎ

☎ 5879 1888; ⊙ 8am-10pm; Ⓜ Lujiazui Rd

Love it or hate it, this 468m-tall poured-concrete tripod tower has become a symbol of Pǔdōng and of Shànghǎi's renaissance. While it may have been stylistically eclipsed by many of the more recent skyscrapers, it remains the most iconic building in the city. The huge edifice is dazzling when illuminated at night and you can always join the queue for high-altitude views of Shànghǎi. The tower is most notable for its excellent Shanghai History Museum (right), located in the basement. The long lines are matched by a complex ticketing system:

Ticket	Price	Includes
A	Y150	bottom, middle & top bauble plus Municipal History Museum
B	Y135	bottom & middle bauble plus Municipal History Museum
CY	100	middle bauble plus Municipal History Museum
D	Y250/280	ticket A plus lunch/dinner; lunch 11am-2pm, dinner 5-9pm
EY	50-70	boat tours from the dock (10am-8pm)
F	Y35	Shanghai History Museum

Children from 1m to 1.4m are charged half price. The boat tours (p65) on the Huangpu operate from the Pearl Dock (明珠码头; Míngzhū

Mǎtou; 1 Century Ave), next to the Oriental Pearl TV Tower.

SHANGHAI HISTORY MUSEUM
Map p108
上海城市历史发展陈列馆 Shànghǎi Chéng-shi Lìshǐ Fāzhǎn Chénlièguǎn

☎ 5879 8888; Oriental Pearl TV Tower basement; admission Y35, English audio tour Y30; ⊙ 8am-9.30pm; Ⓜ Lujiazui Rd; ♿

The entire family will enjoy this sophisticated and informative museum with a fun presentation on old Shànghǎi. The city's transport domain is the first for examination, and you can size up an antique bus, an old wheelbarrow taxi and an ornate sedan chair. Learn how the city prospered on the back of the cotton trade and junk transportation, when it was known as 'Little Sūzhōu'. Life-size models of traditional shops are staffed by realistic waxworks, and a wealth of historical detail abounds, including a boundary stone from the International Settlement and one of the bronze lions that originally guarded the entrance to the HSBC bank on the Bund. Some exhibits are hands-on or accompanied by creative video presentations. Hunt down the detailed replica of the Dangui Teahouse and look out for the public phones that you can dial up to listen to old operas.

RIVERSIDE PROMENADE
Map p108
滨江大道 Bīnjiāng Dàdào; ⊙ 6.30am-11pm; Ⓜ Lujiazui Rd

Hands down the best stroll in Pǔdōng, the sections of promenade alongside Riverside Ave on the eastern bank of the river offer splendid views to the Bund across the way and choicely positioned cafes looking out over the water. Sections of the promenade are covered in the Pŭdōng walking tour (right).

LUJIAZUI DEVELOPMENT SHOWROOM Map p108
陆家嘴民俗馆 Lùjiāzuǐ Mínsúguǎn
☎ 5887 9964; 15 East Lujiazui Rd; 陆家嘴东路 15号; admission Y5; ☯ 8.30am-8pm; Ⓜ Lujiazui Rd
Undergoing renovation at the time of writing, this exhibition of photos, folk life and recent development in Pŭdōng, on the edge of Lujiazui Park, is mildly diverting but it's the historic building itself – unique in a forest of skyscrapers – that stands out. Built in 1914 to 1917 as the residence of a rich merchant, Chen Guichun, it has both a main hall and interior courtyard.

SHANGHAI OCEAN AQUARIUM
Map p108
上海海洋水族馆 Shànghǎi Hǎiyáng Shuǐzúguǎn
☎ 5877 9988; www.sh-aquarium.com; 1388 Lujiazui Ring Rd; 陆家嘴环路1388号; adult/child Y120/80; ☯ 9am-6pm, last tickets sold at 5.30pm; Ⓜ Lujiazui Rd; ♿
Education meets entertainment in this slick and intelligently designed aquarium that children will love. Join them on a tour through the aquatic environments from the Yangzi River to Australia, South America, the frigid ecosystems of the Antarctic and to the flourishing marine life of coral reefs. The 155m-long underwater clear viewing tunnel has gobsmacking views.

NATURAL WILD INSECT KINGDOM
Map p108
大自然野生昆虫馆 Dà Zìrán Yěshēng Kūnchóng Guǎn
☎ 5840 6950; 1 Fenghe Rd; 丰和路1号; adult/child Y40/25; ☯ 9am-5pm; Ⓜ Lujiazui Rd; ♿
Aimed at kids, this collection of creepy-crawlies includes a chance to handle the hairy beasts. It's one that could be missed unless your kids have a special interest.

PŬDŌNG
Walking Tour
1 Oriental Pearl TV Tower Looming above you like a sci-fi control tower a short walk from the Lujiazui Rd metro station is the Oriental Pearl TV Tower (opposite), one of Lùjiāzuǐ's most opinion-dividing edifices. The absorbing Shanghai History Museum (opposite) on the basement level is definitely worth exploration.

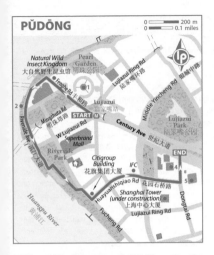

PŬDŌNG

0 ——— 200 m
0 ——— 0.1 miles

WALK FACTS

Start Lujiazui Rd metro station

End Shanghai World Financial Center

Distance 3.5km

Time Two hours

Fuel stop Stop for an ice cream on the Riverside Promenade

2 Riverside Promenade Walk up Fenghe Rd (丰和路) past the Natural Wild Insect Kingdom (p111) on your right and turn left onto Riverside Park to reach a section of the Riverside Promenade (p110) for glorious images of the Bund across the water. Have your camera primed for action.

3 Pudong Shangri-La Hotel Tower Two Walk along a further excellent stretch of the Riverside Promenade before cutting through Riverside Park and coming out onto Fucheng Rd (富城路) by the Citigroup Building. Note the dramatic form of Tower Two of the Pudong Shangri-La hotel (p213), one of Pŭdōng's most distinctive pieces of architecture.

4 Jinmao Tower Immediately after the Citigroup Building, turn onto Huayuanshiqiao Rd (花园石桥路) to walk past the twin towers of the IFC (International Financial Centre) on your left and then the construction site for the new Shanghai Tower (p47) on your right before reaching the magnificent Jinmao Tower (p109). You're spoiled for high-altitude views – you can either ascend to the 88th-floor observation deck here or cross the street to the world's highest observation deck (100th floor) in the Shanghai World Financial Center.

5 Shanghai World Financial Center Virtually blotting out the sun next door is the dominating form of the Shanghai World Financial Center (p107). Once ear-marked to be the world's tallest building, the tower's hesitant construction schedule put it behind other competitors. Head up to the observation deck or the bar 100 Century Avenue (p184) in the Park Hyatt. To return to metro line 2, the Lujiazui Rd metro stop is a short walk west along Century Ave.

CENTURY AVENUE AREA

Shopping p146; Sleeping p213

Part of Pǔdōng and immediately southeast of the frantic, concrete-splattered domain of Lùjiāzuǐ, is the area surrounding Century Ave as it blazes its ozone-enriched trail to Century Park. Synthetic, totally modern and thin on style, the area is chiefly notable for its sights, including Century Park (below), the Shanghai Science and Technology Museum (below), the Zendai Museum of Modern Art (below), the Qinciyang Temple (below), a gigantic underground fake market (p147) and a selection of fine hotels.

For transport in the Century Ave area, see the box on p109.

SHANGHAI SCIENCE & TECHNOLOGY MUSEUM

Map p114

上海科技馆 **Shànghǎi Kējìguǎn**

☎ 6862 2000; www.sstm.org.cn; 2000 Century Ave; 世纪大道2000号; **adult/child over 1.2m/child under 1.2m Y60/45/20;** ☻ 9am-5.15pm Tue-Sun, last tickets sold 4.30pm; Ⓜ Science & Technology Museum; ♿

This impressive space-age building aims at providing a fun educational experience. Kids will like the Light of Wisdom hall, with its hands-on science experiments, and the audiovisual rides (including an earthquake simulator) are fun but draw long queues. Surprisingly, there is nothing on Chinese science and technology (this is, after all, the land that brought us fireworks and the rudder).

There are four theatres (two IMAX, one 4D and one outer space), that show themed films throughout the day (tickets Y20 to Y40; 15 to 40 minutes). When you need a break there's a good food court for lunch; get your hand stamped with a pass if you want to return to the exhibits.

ZENDAI MUSEUM OF MODERN ART (ZENDAI MOMA)

Map p114

证大现代艺术馆 **Zhèngdà Xiàndài Yìshùguǎn**

☎ 5033 9801; www.zendaiart.com; No 28, Lane 199, Fangdian Rd; 芳甸路199弄28号; **adult/student Y20/5, Wed free;** ☻ 10am-6pm Tue & Thu-Sun, to 9pm Wed; Ⓜ Science & Technology Museum

This newish, small-scale museum delivers an invigorating shot in the arm to Shànghǎi's ever-flexing art scene. The emphasis is on contemporary exhibitions in a highly modern art space; the effect is a sophisticated and cool haven for fashionable aesthetes. Tours (in Chinese), lectures, concerts and other activities are part of the overall production. There's a great selection of restaurants on the plaza outside.

CENTURY PARK

Map pp62-3

世纪公园 **Shìjì Gōngyuán**

1001 Jinxiu Rd; 锦绣路1001号; **admission Y10;** ☻ 7am-6pm; Ⓜ Century Park; ♿

Shànghǎi's largest park at the eastern end of Century Ave is strong on hard edges and synthetic lines, but there's a great central lake with boat hire (Y40 per hour), and bicycle hire (Y30 to Y80 per hour) for getting around all the paths. Children will enjoy themselves, and the spacious paved area between the Science and Technology Museum and the park is great for flying kites (for sale from hawkers) and rollerblading.

QINCIYANG TEMPLE

Map p114

钦赐仰殿 **Qīncìyǎng Diàn**

476 Yuanshen Rd; 源深路476号; **admission Y5;** ☻ 6.30am-4pm; Ⓜ Yuanshen Stadium

Shànghǎi's largest Taoist temple is, perhaps surprisingly, located in Pǔdōng. It's worth a perusal for its massive trinity of Taoist gods in the Hall of the Three Clear Ones (三清殿; Sānqīng Diàn), although the temple architecture is all recent (at the southern end of the temple grounds are what appears to be older, semidestroyed temple halls). At the rear of the temple is the humungous Hall for the Storing of Scriptures (藏经殿; Cángjīng Diàn) and up the stairs above the side halls is a huge glittering gathering of 61 gilded Taoist generals.

CENTURY AVENUE AREA

INFORMATION	
PSB 公安局	1 D3

SIGHTS	(pp113–4)
Century Park 世纪公园	2 D4
Qinciyang Temple 钦赐仰殿	3 B2
Shanghai Science & Technology Museum 上海科技馆	4 C3
Zendai Museum of Modern Art (MOMA) 证大现代艺术馆	5 D3

SHOPPING	(pp146–7)
Amy Lin's Pearls 艾敏林氏珍珠	(see 6)
AP Xinyang Fashion & Gift Market 亚大新阳服饰礼品市场	6 C3
Carrefour 家乐福	(see 5)

EATING	(p174)
Shanghai Uncle 海上阿叔	7 A3

ENTERTAINMENT	(pp188–99)
Oriental Art Center 上海东方艺术中心	8 C3

SLEEPING	(pp213–14)
Hidden Garden Youth Hostel 大隐国际青年旅舍	9 B1
Holiday Inn Pudong 浦东假日酒店	10 B3
Novotel Atlantis 海神诺富特大酒店	11 A1
St Regis Shanghai 瑞吉红塔大酒店	12 B3
Zhongdian Hotel 中电大酒店	13 A3

TRANSPORT	(pp241–51)
Taxi Queue 出租车招呼站	14 C3

Drinking p185; Eating p174; Shopping p147; Sleeping p214

North of Suzhou Creek is one of the hot new areas in Shànghăi. Hóngkŏu (or the North Bund) hasn't entirely come into its own yet, but it is well on its way, with a handful of hip new hotels, restaurants and entertainment venues all opening in 2009. Originally the American Settlement, it merged with the British Settlement in 1863 to form the International Settlement and was a prosperous section of the city. But by the beginning of the 20th century, it was divided between the slums of Zhábĕi and Hóngkŏu, which was home to 30,000 Japanese and known as 'Little Tokyo'.

The area continued to decline in the following years; it was a popular place for gangsters to go to ground, while Zhábĕi became infamous for its sweatshops and factories. In 1932 Japanese troops occupied Hóngkŏu and reduced Zhábĕi to rubble while battling Chinese soldiers from the Red Army. Up to 14,000 people died. During WWII, Hóngkŏu was home to thousands of Jewish refugees, mostly from Germany, who transformed 'Little Tokyo' into 'Little Vienna'.

top picks

HÓNGKŎU & NORTH SHÀNGHĂI

- Ohel Moishe Synagogue (left) Walk the streets of the old Jewish neighbourhood, once Shànghăi's 'Little Vienna', culminating in this synagogue.
- Qipu Market (p147) Attention shoppers: all clothing is going for Y50. Today only!
- Post Museum (p116) The pony express, red China stamps and the official postal hymn.
- Factory (p174) Find out what's cookin' at the next generation's cultural kitchen.
- Burlesque (p193) Shànghăi goes risqué at Chinatown.

Today, Zhábĕi is still working class. Many of its residents have come to Shànghăi from nearby provinces like Ănhuī and Jiāngsū. There's not much to see in terms of sights, but there's plenty of interesting street life. In Hóngkŏu, there are still run-down terraced houses and a few art deco structures. One interesting building is 1933 (10 Shajing Rd; 沙泾路10号), an old abattoir that has been transformed into a shopping complex (unfortunately the shops themselves are of little interest). It's across from the Factory (p174).

OHEL MOISHE SYNAGOGUE
Map p116

摩西会堂 Móxī Huìtáng
☎ 6541 5008; 62 Changyang Rd; 长阳路62号; admission Y50; 9am-5pm; Ⓜ Dalian Rd

This synagogue was built by the Russian Ashkenazi Jewish community in 1927 and lies in the heart of the 1940s Jewish ghetto (see the boxed text, p118). Today it houses the new Shanghai Jewish Refugees Museum, which is an excellent introduction to the lives of the approximately 20,000 Central European refugees who fled to Shànghăi to escape the Nazis. You can also visit the synagogue.

For a mini walking tour of the surrounding streets, turn right outside the synagogue, then right again past the former Jewish tenements of Zhoushan Rd, once the commercial heart of the district. At Huoshan Rd turn left to visit Huoshan Park and the memorial plaque erected for the visit of Yitzak Rabin in the late 1990s.

Head back southwest along Huoshan Rd (formerly Wayside Rd) past the art deco facade of the former Broadway Theatre (at No 57, now the Dajinlong Restaurant), with its rooftop Vienna Café, to the Ocean Hotel. Turn right up Haimen Rd (Muirhead Rd), past Changyang Rd, to what was once a row of Jewish shops and a kosher delicatessen.

At the top of the road (crossing with Kunming Rd) you'll see the large, renovated Xiahai Buddhist Monastery (Xiàhăi Miào; Kunming Rd; 昆明路; admission Y5; 7am-4pm); take a right turn, then another right, down Zhoushan Rd (formerly Ward Rd) once again to complete the circle back to the synagogue.

Zhoushan Rd is also home to the British-built Ward Road Jail, once Shànghăi's biggest. Used by the Japanese during WWII, it's still

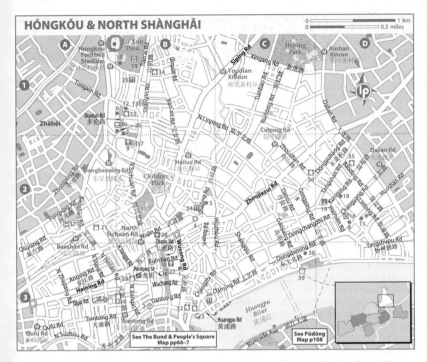

functioning as a prison and is probably as close as you'll get, or would want to get, to a Chinese detention facility. You can catch bus 33 here from the Bund.

If you're interested in learning more about Hóngkŏu's Jewish heritage contact Dvir Bar-Gal, an Israeli Shànghǎi resident who offers informative tours (☎ 130 021 467 02; www.shanghai-jews.com; tour Y400) of the area.

POST MUSEUM
Map p116
邮政博物馆 Yóuzhèng Bówùguǎn
2nd fl, 250 North Suzhou Rd; 北苏州路250号 2楼; admission free; 🕙 **9am-5pm (last entry 4pm)**
It may sound like a yawner, but the Post Museum is actually a pretty interesting place. It explores postal history in imperial China, which dates back to the 1st millennium BC and used an extensive pony express to relay messages; Marco Polo estimated there were 10,000 postal stations in 13th-century China. Tap your foot to China's official postal hymn (*The Song of the Mail Swan Geese*) and check out the collection of pre- and post-Liberation stamps (1888–1978) in a special climate-controlled room. On the 5th floor

(after you exit) is a rooftop garden with panoramic views of the Shànghǎi skyline.

DUOLUN ROAD CULTURAL STREET
Map p116
多伦文化名人街 Duōlún Wénhuà Míngrén Jiē
Ⓜ **Dongbaoxing Rd**
This nicely restored street of fine old houses, just off North Sichuan Rd, was once home to several of China's most famous writers (as well as several Kuomintang generals), when the road was known as Doulean Rd. Today it is lined with art-supply stores, curio shops, galleries, teahouses and cafes, although it is fairly sleepy by Shànghǎi standards.

Looking like a 1960s university physics block, the Shanghai Duolun Museum of Modern Art (Shànghǎi Duōlún Xiàndài Měishùguǎn; ☎ 6587 6902; 27 Duolun Rd; 多伦路27号; adult/student Y10/5; 🕙 10am-5pm Tue-Sun) has a focus on experimental contemporary art, with a good range of art books and an empty cafe on the 6th floor. Further along the street, the 1928 brick Hongde Temple (Hóngdé Táng; ☎ 5696 1196; 59 Duolun Rd; 多伦路59号) was built in a Chinese style as the Great Virtue Church; note the Chinese-style bell tower. Come Sunday morning, it's worth clambering upstairs to catch a church service (7.30am & 9.30am Sun).

The main appeal of the street is its galleries and antique shops, including Dashanghai (181 Duolun Rd; 多伦路181号), a marvellous deluge of Mao-era badges and posters, old records, photos, books, typewriters and assorted Shànghǎi bric-a-brac from the decadent days. With a bit of exploration you are bound to dig up something.

The League of Left-Wing Writers was established down a side alley on 2 March 1930. Today the building serves as a political museum (No 2, Lane 201, Duolun Rd; 多伦路 201弄2号; adult/student Y5/3; 9am-4pm Tue-Sun), perhaps worth a look for the architecture alone. Also wander down this alley for some lovely old architecture, pigeons in coops and further small alleyway openings.

Duolun Rd ends in another Kuomintang residence, the Moorish-looking Kong Residence (Kǒng Gōngguǎn; 250 Duolun Rd; 多伦路 250号; no entry), built in 1924.

If you need a break, try the Old Film Café (p185), next to the 18.2m-high Xishi Bell Tower

(Xīshí Zhōnglóu) at the bend in the road. There's a statue of Charlie Chaplin outside.

LU XUN MEMORIAL HALL Map p116

鲁迅纪念馆 Lǔ Xùn Jìniànguǎn

☎ 6540 2288; Lu Xun Park, 2288 North Sichuan Rd; 鲁迅公园内，四川北路2288号; admission free; 9am-4pm; M Hongkou Football Stadium

An excellent museum, this modern hall charts the life and creative output of Lu Xun with photographs, first editions, videos

TRANSPORT: HÓNGKǑU & NORTH SHÀNGHǍI

Metro Line 10 runs north from East Nanjing Rd up to Fudan University, passing the Tiantong Rd, North Sichuan Rd and Hailun Rd stations. Line 3 also runs north, offering access to Duolun Rd and Lu Xun Park. Lines 4 and 8 loop east–west. Main interchange stations are Baoshan Rd (lines 3 and 4), Hailun Rd (lines 4 and 10) and Hongkou Football Stadium (lines 3 and 8).

Bus Buses 22, 37 and 135 run up Dongdaming Rd and back down Changyang and Dongchanghzhi Rds.

SHÀNGHǍI'S JEWS

Shànghǎi has two centuries of strong Jewish connections. Established Middle Eastern Sephardic Jewish families such as the Hardoons, Ezras, Kadoories and Sassoons built their fortunes in Shànghǎi, establishing at least seven synagogues and many Jewish hospitals and schools (see the boxed text, p104). It was Victor Sassoon who famously remarked: 'There is only one race greater than the Jews and that's the Derby'.

A second group of Jews, this time Ashkenazi, arrived via Siberia, Hǎ'ěrbīn and Tiānjīn from Russia after anti-Jewish programs in 1906. The biggest influx, however, came between 1933 and 1941, when 30,000 mostly Ashkenazi Jews arrived from Europe by boat from Italy or by train via Siberia. Many had been issued with visas to cross China by Ho Fengshan, Chinese consul-general in Vienna, who was recently honoured as the 'Chinese Schindler'.

Shànghǎi was one of the few safe havens for Jews fleeing the Holocaust in Europe as it required neither a passport nor visa to stay. Gestapo agents followed the refugees and, in 1942, tried to persuade the Japanese to build death camps on Chongming Island. Instead, in 1943, the Japanese forced Jews to move into a 'Designated Area for Stateless Refugees' in Hóngkǒu.

The Jewish ghetto (stateless Russians didn't have to live here) became home to Jews from all walks of life. It grew to shelter a synagogue, schools, a local paper, hospitals and enough cafes, rooftop gardens and restaurants to gain the epithet 'Little Vienna'. Those Jews who held jobs in the French Concession had to secure passes from the Japanese, specifically the notoriously unpredictable and violent Mr Goya. Poorer refugees were forced to bunk down in cramped hostels known as *Heime*, and had to rely on the generosity of others. As the wealthy Anglophile Jewish trading families left in 1941, the situation grew even tighter. Still, the refugees heard of events in distant Europe and realised that they were the lucky ones.

Today there are a few remainders of Jewish life in Shànghǎi, such as the Ohel Moishe Synagogue (p115) and the former Jewish Club (1932) in the grounds of the Conservatory of Music (p194), where concerts are still performed. The Ohel Rachel Synagogue (Yóutài Jiàotáng; Map pp98–9; 500 North Shaanxi Rd) was built by Jacob Elias Sassoon in the late 19th century and was restored for Hillary Clinton's 1998 visit. Unfortunately it remains closed to the public. Nearby are the remains of the school founded on the grounds by Horace Kadoorie.

For information and pricey tours of Jewish Shànghǎi, contact the Centre of Jewish Studies Shanghai (上海犹太研究中心; Shànghǎi Yóutài Yánjiū Zhōngxīn; Map pp86–7; ☎ 5306 0606 ext 2476; www.cjss.org.cn; Room 476, No 7, Lane 622, Middle Huaihai Rd; 淮海中路622弄7号476屋; tour US$80; ☉ 9am-4pm). The centre offers one-day tours (for groups only) of Jewish Shànghǎi with English- and Hebrew-speaking guides and also has a fine library of books and periodicals.

and waxworks. Detailed English captions throughout. The museum bookshop sells Lu Xun's stories in English, French and German.

LU XUN FORMER RESIDENCE Map p116
鲁迅故居 Lǔxùn Gùjū

☎ 5666 2608; No 9, Lane 132, Shanyin Rd; 山阴路132弄9号; adult/child Y8/4; ☉ 9am-4pm; Ⓜ Dongbaoxing Rd

Lu Xun buffs will adore ferreting around this three-floor domicile on lovely Shanyin Rd, where an English-speaking guide can fill you in on all the bits and bobs. Attracted by the city's progressiveness and literary scene, Lu Xun moved to Shànghǎi in 1927; this was his final residence, from 1933 to 1936. Don't overlook wandering along Shanyin Rd and peeking into its lovely alleyways and traditional *lòngtáng* houses (for example at Nos 41 to 50, Lane 180, Shanyin Rd).

LU XUN PARK
Map p116

鲁迅公园 Lǔ Xùn Gōngyuán

146 East Jiangwan Rd; 江湾东路146号; admission free; ☉ 6am-6pm; Ⓜ Hongkou Football Stadium

Especially gorgeous in spring and summer when the trees are in blossom, Lu Xun Park is one of the city's most pleasant parks, with elderly Chinese practising taichi or ballroom dancing, and even the occasional retired opera singer giving a free performance. The English corner on Sunday mornings is one of the largest in all of Shànghǎi and a good place to chat to locals in English. You can take boats out onto the small lake.

The park used to be called Hongkou Park but was renamed because it holds Lu Xun's Tomb, moved here from the International Cemetery in 1956, on the 20th anniversary of his death. Mao himself inscribed the memorial calligraphy.

HERMAN'S WHARF Map pp62-3

渔人码头 Yúrén Mǎtou
Yangshupu Rd; 杨树浦路; ferry or Ⓜ **Yangshupu Rd then taxi**

A place to come eat sourdough bread and watch frolicking sea lions? Probably not, though you might confuse it with the Shànghǎi restaurant of the same name (which does serve clam chowder). This new attraction is scheduled to open in 2010 and will host a fishing museum and entertainment/shopping complex. The local government has promoted it as a top tourist attraction, but check the online reviews before you head up here. It should be served by a new ferry line.

GONGQING FOREST PARK

off Map pp62-3

共青森林公园 Gòngqīng Sēnlín Gōngyuán
☎ 6574 0586; www.shgqsl.com; 2000 Jungong Rd; 军工路2000号; admission Y15; ☼ 6am-5pm (last entry 4pm); Ⓜ Nengjiang Rd; ♿

The miserly lawn space in most of Shànghǎi's synthetic parks can leave one cold, but this vast expanse of forested parkland on the western shore of the Huangpu River is a leafy, wooded and tranquil slice of countryside in town. This is about as wild as you get in Pǔxī, with acres of willows, *luohan* pines, magnolias, hibiscus and nary a skyscraper in sight. Aim to spend half if not a whole day picnicking and wandering around this huge area, or hop into one of the buggies (Y10) for express tours around the grounds. Children will whoop at the sight of the roller coaster (Y20), rock climbing wall (Y20), adventure ground and fun fair. There's also a pricey football pitch (Y400 per hour), angling, views over Huangpu River, electric powered boats (Y30 per hour) on the lakes and horseriding. If you want to spend the night in the park, there's the Gongqing Forest Resort (共青森林度假村; Gòngqīng Sēnlín Dùjiàcūn; ☎ 6588 1572; 2300 Jungong Rd; 军工路2300号; d Y180-200). It gets busy at weekends. The Nengjiang Rd station near the northern terminus of metro line 8 will get you close to the western edge of the park.

CHINESE WUSHU MUSEUM

off Map pp62-3

中国武术博物馆 Zhōngguó Wǔshù Bówùguǎn
☎ 5125 3213; Shanghai University of Sports, 650 Qingyuanhuan Rd; 清源环路650号上海体育

学校内; admission free; ☼ 9-11am & 1-4pm Wed & Sat; Ⓜ Nengjiang Rd

Kung fu and *bāguàzhǎng* ('eight trigram palm', an internal martial art) fanatics may want to check this one out, if only for the weapons collection. The three halls here feature a history of Chinese martial arts, various weaponry and an audio-visual exhibit. The museum has collected some 2500 items from 18 Chinese provinces, but only 500 are on display. Call first to make an appointment.

HÓNGKǑU & NORTH SHÀNGHǍI

Walking Tour

1 Hongkew Methodist Church This walk begins at the 1923 Hongkew Methodist Church (景灵堂; Jǐnglíng Táng; 135 Kunshan Rd; 昆山路135号), where Chiang Kaishek married Soong Meiling (see boxed text, p91). The church seats roughly 2000 worshippers during its early morning Sunday service. It's generally closed to the public, but the caretaker may let you in.

2 Young Allen Court West along Kunshan Rd on the corner with Zhapu Rd (乍浦路) stands Young Allen Court (260 Zhapu Rd), a distinctive brick building constructed in 1923. Walk down the side of the alley for views of its three-storey architecture and the rear of the adjacent church towards the end.

3 Shíkùmén Stroll north along Zhapu Rd from Kunshan Rd and pop into the first pinched alley at No 313 (乍浦路313弄)

LU XUN

Lu Xun (born Zhou Shuren; 1881–1936) is one of China's most famous writers and is often regarded as the originator of modern Chinese literature. Part of China's May 4 literary movement, his main achievement was to break from the classical literary traditions of the past – unintelligible to most Chinese – to create a modern vernacular literature. He was also a fierce critic of China's social ills, which led to him being canonised by the communist hierarchy even though he was never a member of the Party. Lu Xun's most famous works are *A Madman's Diary*, *The True Story of Ah Q* and *Kong Yi Ji*. These are presented in two collections: *Call to Arms* and *Wandering*, both of which still make excellent reading today.

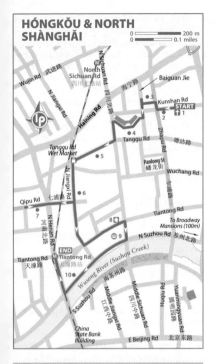

HÓNGKǑU & NORTH SHÀNGHǍI

0 — 200 m
0 — 0.1 miles

on your left. You will pass a line of typical *shíkùmén*, all decorated with distinctively carved lintels. Emerging from the alley, turn right along Baiguan Jie (百官街) for a short walk north to admire a further cluster of *shíkùmén* through the archway on your right.

4 Kunshan Huayuan Rd Walk south along Baiguan Jie and pass the modern art deco–style apartment block at 227 Kunshan Rd on the corner. Slightly further south, turn west into Kunshan Huayuan Rd (昆山花园路), the first alley on your right, leaving Kunshan Park to your east. Note the lovely four-storey red brick houses on your right as you walk west along the alley.

5 Lǐlòng Exit the alley onto North Sichuan Rd and walk south to turn west in Tanggu Rd (塘沽路). At the time of writing construction cranes were wheeling above the plot to the north, building a large tower, while the south edge of the road remains typified by low, two-storey ramshackle dwellings and small dishevelled *lǐlòng* such as Guangxing Li (广兴里) at No 597.

6 North Jiangxi Rd The Tanggu Rd Wet Market is worth a wander before heading south down North Jiangxi Rd, passing several *lǐlòng* to your east, including Taihua Li (泰华里) at No 192. North Jiangxi Rd is stuffed with pedestrians, beggars, chefs with steamers, kebab sellers and *málàtàng* (麻辣烫; spicy soup with meat and vegetables) vendors. Note the distinctive old house at No 174, with the full-form characters 爱莲坊 (Ailian Lane) above the door.

7 Qipu Market You will soon run into pushy vendors dragging foreigners towards outlets in the vicinity of Qipu Market (p147) along Qipu Rd. Keep an eye on your belongings as pickpockets mill about the crowded streets and foreigners are high priority targets.

8 New Asia Hotel When you reach Tiantong Rd (天潼路), stroll east to the New Asia Hotel (新亚大酒店; Xīnyà Dàjiǔdiàn; 422 Tiantong Rd; 天潼路422号) at No 422, one of Shànghǎi's rich brood of extant art deco wonders.

9 Main post office Right across the road is the pompous main post office, a grand building topped with a cupola and clock tower, ornamented with bronze statues coated in a green patina. Directly facing you as you cross the road is the entrance to the Post Museum (p116). Even if you don't visit the museum, you can still head up to the rooftop garden for skyline views.

10 Embankment Building Exiting the post office, consider wandering across the bridge to the other side of the river where strips of greenery prettify Suzhou Creek (boxed text, p74) and excellent views reach out to Broadway Mansions (p214) and Lùjiāzuǐ. West along North Suzhou Rd from the Post Office is the Embankment Building (河滨大厦; Hébīn Dàshà) at No 400, designed by architects Palmer & Turner and dating from the 1930s.

Eating p174; Shopping p148; Sleeping p215

Bordering the southwestern end of the French Concession, Xújiāhuì was known to 1930s expats as Zicawei or Sicawei. Originally a Jesuit settlement dating back to the 17th century, there's still a strong Catholic flavour to the neighbourhood, with the magnificent Bibliotheca Zi-Ka-Wei (p123) and St Ignatius Cathedral (p124) holding firm against the ever-encroaching office blocks.

Nevertheless, Xújiāhuì is more of a monument to capitalism than Catholicism these days. The area is dominated by giant shopping malls and department stores that circle a five-way intersection that's insanely busy even by Shànghǎi standards. It's one of the most popular shopping areas in the city and packed at weekends.

A short walk northeast is the pleasant Xujiahui Park. To the northwest is Jiaotong University, one of Shànghǎi's best. Head south on North Caoxi Rd and you reach the Shanghai Stadium, the city's biggest venue for sporting events and big-league pop concerts. Just beyond that is one of the world's largest outlets of Ikea.

top picks

XÚJIĀHUÌ & SOUTH SHÀNGHǍI

- **Longhua Temple & Pagoda** (left) Explore the oldest monastery in Shànghǎi.
- **CY Tung Maritime Museum** (below) Learn about the great explorer and admiral Zheng He.
- **Bibliotheca Zi-Ka-Wei** (p123) Take a Saturday tour around one of the finest libraries in China.
- **Xinjiang Fengwei Restaurant** (p175) Spend a night celebrating Uighur-style at one of the liveliest spots in town; dancing is optional, but the black beer compulsory.
- **Dino Beach** (p124) Cool off in Asia's largest wave pool.

South Shànghǎi is home to the impressive and ancient Longhua Temple (below), as well as a couple of amusement parks that are great places to take kids who are rebelling against sightseeing.

LONGHUA TEMPLE & PAGODA
Map p122

龙华寺、龙华塔 **Lónghuá Sì & Lónghuá Tǎ**
☎ 6457 6327; 2853 Longhua Rd; 龙华路2853号;
admission Y10; ⏱ 7am-4.30pm; Ⓜ Longcao Rd,
🚌 44 from Xujiahui

Southwest of central Shànghǎi, close to the river, this is the oldest and largest monastery in Shànghǎi. Said to date from the 10th century, it has been much renovated. *Lónghuá* refers to the pipal tree under which Buddha achieved enlightenment.

There are five main halls, starting with the Laughing Buddha Hall. To either side of the entrance are a bell and a drum tower. The temple is famed for its 6500kg bell, which was cast in 1894. There are several side buildings to explore, including the Thousand Luohan Hall, in which is arrayed a huge legion of glittering arhat. A large effigy of Sakyamuni seated on a lotus flower is contained within the main hall – the Great Treasure Hall. Beyond the main hall are a vegetarian restaurant and a further imposing hall – the Sanshengbao Hall – with a golden trinity of Buddhist statues.

Opposite the temple entrance rises the much-restored seven-storey, 44m-high Longhua Pagoda, originally built in AD 977. Visitors are not allowed to climb the pagoda, but a sprawl of stalls selling snacks and souvenirs fans out in the vicinity. Across the road is a further complex of fast-food outlets.

The best time to visit is during the Longhua Temple Fair, in the third month of the lunar calendar (usually during April or May).

CY TUNG MARITIME MUSEUM
Map p122

董浩云航运博物馆 **Dǒng Hàoyún Hángyùn Bówùguǎn**
☎ 6293 3035; Jiaotong University campus, 1954
Huashan Rd; 华山路1954号交通大学内;
admission free; ⏱ 1.30-5pm Tue-Sun; Ⓜ Jiaotong
University

Named after the Shànghǎi-born shipping magnate, this small but fascinating

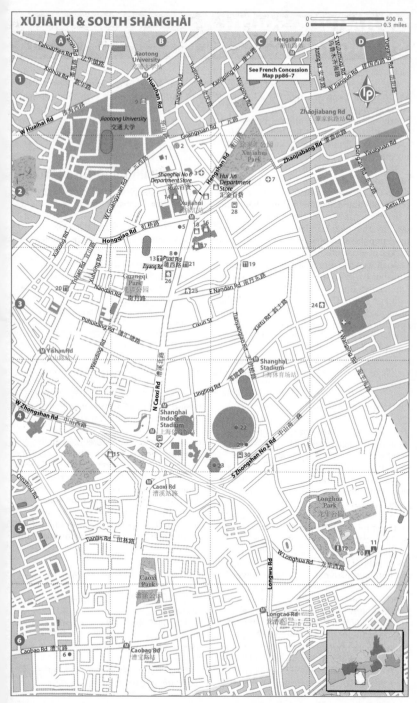

0 ____ 500 m
0 ____ 0.3 miles

Fahuazhen Rd 法华镇路
Fanyu Rd 番禺路
让华镇路
Xinhua Rd 新华路

Jiaotong University
交通大学

Hengshan Rd 衡山路

S Wulumuqi Rd 乌鲁木齐南路

Anting Rd 安亭路

Yongkang Rd 永康路

See French Concession
Map pp86–7

W Huaihai Rd 淮海西路

Huashan Rd 华山路

Tianping Rd 天平路

Kangping Rd 康平路

Wanping Rd 宛平路

Zhaojiabang Rd 肇家浜路站 M

Guangyuan Rd 元路

徐家汇 公园
Xujiahui
Park

Zhaojiabang Rd 肇家浜路

Dong'an Rd 东安路

Yixueyuan Rd 医学院路

9 ♨ ⊞ 2
♨ 1

Hengshan Rd 衡山路

Hui Jin
Department
Store
汇金百货

♨ 7

Xietu Rd

Shanghai No 6
Department Store
第六百货

14 ♨
Xujiahui
徐家汇

28

W Guanqyuan Rd 元路

Xutong Rd

Hongqiao Rd 虹桥路

♨ 5   18 ♨
♨ 17

♨ 8   ⊞ 19
13 ⊞ Puxi Rd
蒲西路
⊞ 21
26 ♨
♨ 25

Ziyang Rd

20 ⊞
Guangqi
Park
光启公园

Naqdan Rd
南丹路

E Nandan Rd 南丹东路

24 ⊞

Puhuitang Rd 蒲汇塘路

Cixin St

Tianyaoqiao Rd

Xietu Rd 斜土路

Wanping Rd

Yishan Rd M
宜山路站

Weining Rd

N Caoxi Rd 漕溪北路

Lingling Rd

Shanghai
Stadium
上海体育场站 M

W Zhongshan Rd 中山西路

Shanghai
Indoor
Stadium
上海体育馆
⊞ 27

♨ 22

29 ●
⊞ 30

S Zhongshan No 2 Rd 中山南二路

♨ 23

⊞ 15

Caoxi Rd
漕溪路

Longhua
Park
龙华公园

Qinzhou Rd

♨ 12
10 ⊞ 11 ⊞

Tianlin Rd 田林路

W Longhua Rd 龙华西路

Longwu Rd

Caoxi
Park
漕溪公园

Longcao Rd

Caobao Rd 漕宝路
♨ 6

Caobao Rd
漕宝路

museum explores the little-known world of Chinese maritime history, with model ships, maps of early trade routes, and a video. A large portion of the 1st floor is devoted to Zheng He, the 15th-century admiral and explorer who was born a Hui Muslim in Yúnnán, was later captured and made a eunuch at the Ming court, and eventually went on to command vast Chinese fleets on journeys to east Africa, India and the Persian Gulf.

BIBLIOTHECA ZI-KA-WEI

Map p122

徐家汇藏书楼 **Xújiāhuì Cángshūlóu**
☎ 6487 4095 ext 208; 80 North Caoxi Rd; 漕溪北路80号; ☽ **library tour 2-4pm Sat**; Ⓜ **Xujiahui**

Among the several Jesuit monuments littering Xújiāhuì is the imposing St Ignatius Catholic Library, the Bibliotheca Zi-Ka-Wei, established in 1847 by the local Jesuit mission. Home to 560,000 volumes in Greek, Latin and other languages, the edifice consists of two buildings, with the library itself housed in the lower, two-

storey, east-facing building that partially arches over the pavement. There are free guided tours of the highlight main library (Dà Shūfáng) on Saturday afternoons. English-speaking guides are on hand to take you through a truly magnificent collection of antiquarian tomes, arranged in a beautiful historic library laid out on one floor with a gallery above. Wander past rare books on ecclesiastical history, *Philosphica*, *Res Sinenses* (Things Chinese) and other erudite branches of Jesuit learning. The 15-minute tours are limited to 10 people per group, so it's best to phone ahead to book and ensure you don't miss out. Photography is not allowed.

TRANSPORT: XÚJIĀHUÌ & SOUTH SHÀNGHǍI

Metro Lines 1, 3, 4 and 9 run through the district. Xiujiahui (lines 1 and 9) and Shanghai Indoor Stadium (lines 1, 3 and 4) are the main interchange stations. Line 1 runs through the French Concession and down to the South Shanghai Train Station.

CHINESE CHRISTIANS

Shànghǎi has at least 140,000 Catholics, largely due to its history of Jesuit communities. St Ignatius Cathedral (below) is the largest in the city. Relations between the government and the Chinese Catholic Church are uneasy, as the church refuses to disown the Pope as its leader. Nor does China's one-child policy sit well with the Catholic stand on abortion. For this reason, the Vatican maintains diplomatic relations with Taiwan, much to China's consternation. For more on Christianity in China, see p34.

To see or take part in prayer, Catholics can visit the Christ the King Church (君王天主堂; Jūnwáng Tiānzhǔtáng; Map pp86–7; cnr Julu Rd & Maoming Rd), St Ignatius Cathedral or the splendid Catholic Church (p131) in Qībǎo. Protestants can visit the lively Community Church (p94), with Sunday school for children and a small nursery for toddlers. There is also a growing flock of modern, newly built churches throughout Shànghǎi, including in Pǔdōng. There are also other marvellous Catholic churches in Zhujiajiao (p235) and an old Protestant church in Hángzhōu (p227).

ST IGNATIUS CATHEDRAL
Map p122
徐家汇天主教堂 Xújiāhuì Tiānzhǔtáng
☎ 6438 4632; 158 Puxi Rd; 蒲西路158号; ☽ 1-4.30pm Sat & Sun;
Ⓜ Xujiahui

Southwest of the Bibliotheca Zi-Ka-Wei, the dignified twin-spired St Ignatius Cathedral (1904) is a major Xújiāhuì landmark, its ecclesiastical form reflected in much of the local architecture. A long span of gothic arches, its nave is ornamented on the outside with rows of menacing gargoyles. Much of the stained glass is missing, but colourful replacements (some with Chinese inscriptions) have been installed to recreate the cathedral's original glory.

Mass is held on Sunday at 6am, 7.30am, 10am and 6pm; on weekdays at 7am and on Saturday at 6pm (and the first Friday of the month at 6pm). Across North Caoxi Rd is the former St Ignatius Convent, now reinvented for diners as the Ye Olde Station Restaurant (p175).

SHANGHAI BOTANICAL GARDENS
Map pp62-3
上海植物园 Shànghǎi Zhíwùyuán
☎ 5436 3369; 997 Longwu Rd; 龙吴路997号; admission Y15; ☽ 7am-5pm;
Ⓜ Shilong Rd

The location just off the busy and polluted Longwu Rd is hardly idyllic, but the Botanical Gardens offer an escape from Shànghǎi's synthetic cityscape. The Tropicarium gives you the chance to get close to tropical flora, and once inside, you can take the lift to the 6th floor for an impressive view of the gardens. Some of the flower arrangements are a little twee, but the place is well-maintained and bustling with visitors.

The northern side of the gardens has a dusty memorial temple, originally built in 1728. It's dedicated to Huang Daopo, who supposedly kick-started Shànghǎi's cotton industry by bringing the knowledge of spinning and weaving to the region from Hǎinán.

JINJIANG AMUSEMENT PARK
Map p221
锦江乐园 Jǐnjiāng Lèyuán
☎ 5493 7999; 201 Hongmei Rd; 虹梅路201号; admission Y70; ☽ 9am-10pm summer, to 5pm winter;
Ⓜ Jinjiang Park; ♿

Roller coasters, rides and a huge Ferris wheel are all here in this amusement park. It's a bit out of town, but easy to get to, as it has its own metro station.

DINO BEACH
off Map pp62-3
热带风暴 Rèdài Fēngbào
☎ 6478 3333; 78 Xinzhen Rd; 新镇路78号; admission Mon, Tue & Thu Y120, Wed & Fri Y150, Sat & Sun Y200, child under 1.2m free; ☽ 2-11pm Mon & 10am-11pm Tue-Sun Jun-Sep;
Ⓜ Xinzhuang then bus 763 or 163; ♿

Way down south in Mǐnháng district, this popular summer place has a beach, a wave pool, water slides and tube hire to beat the Shànghǎi summer heat and keeps going late. But it's absolutely heaving at weekends. You can also take a cab here from Qībǎo (p131).

NEIGHBOURHOODS XÚJIĀHUÌ & SOUTH SHANGHAI

MARTYRS MEMORIAL

Map p122

龙华烈士陵园 Lónghuá Lièshì Língyuán
Longhua Rd; 龙华路; admission Y1, memorial hall
Y5; ⊙ 6am-5pm, museum 9am-4pm; Ⓜ Longcao
Rd, ⛟ 44 from Xújiāhuì

Next to the Longhua Temple, this park
marks the site of an old Kuomintang prison,
where 800 communists, intellectuals and
political agitators were executed between
1928 and 1937. You can take a modern underground tunnel to the original jailhouses
and the small execution ground. Scattered
throughout the manicured lawns are epic
sculptures of workers and soldiers, depicted
in true socialist realism art style. During
WWII this area was a Japanese internment
camp and airfield, as depicted in the JG
Ballard novel and Spielberg film *Empire of
the Sun*.

GUILIN PARK

Map pp62-3

桂林公园 Guìlín Gōngyuán
☎ 6483 0915; Caobao Rd; 漕宝路; admission
free; ⊙ 6am-6pm; Ⓜ Shanghai South Train
Station

This park probably isn't worth a special
visit but it's a pleasant enough place. It's
famous for its spring blossoms, gardens
and because it houses the former residence
(1932) of the gangster 'Pockmarked' Huang
Jinrong. It's now a teahouse.

XÚJIĀHUÌ & SOUTH SHÀNGHǍI
Walking Tour

1 Xuhui Middle School From Xujiahui
metro station, exit on the south side of Hongqiao Rd (虹桥路) to admire the red brick form
of the historic Xuhui Middle School (徐汇中学;
Xúhuì Zhōngxué).

2 Bibliotheca Zi-Ka-Wei Retracing your
steps and walking south onto North Caoxi
Rd (曹溪北路) will take you underneath
the upper floor of the north building of the
Jesuit-built Bibliotheca Zi-Ka-Wei (p123), partially
built over the footpath. Adjacent to the magnificent library to the south is the Priest's
Residence.

3 St Ignatius Cathedral Across North
Caoxi Rd stands a former convent which

belonged to the Helpers of the Holy Souls,
now serving as Ye Olde Station Restaurant (p175).
Continue on the west side of North Caoxi
Rd to turn into Puxi Rd and approach St
Ignatius Cathedral (opposite), its cool interior a
welcome respite from the relentless Shànghǎi
summer heat.

4 Former Major Seminary Just south of
the cathedral at 166 Puxi Rd is the Jesuit-built
Xujiahui Observatory, now part of the Shang-
hai Meteorological Bureau. Continue along North
Caoxi Rd and turn west into East Nandan
Rd (南丹东路) where you will see a further
Jesuit-constructed building on the far side of
the road, the former Major Seminary.

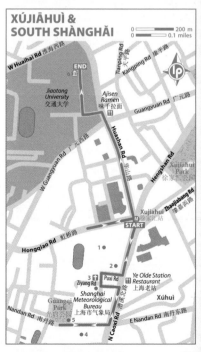

XÚJIĀHUÌ &
SOUTH SHÀNGHǍI

XU GUANGQI

Xújiāhuì ('the Xu family gathering') is named after Xu Guangqi (1562–1633), a Chinese renaissance man. Xu was an early student of astronomy, agronomy and the calendar, and he established a meteorological observatory that relayed its information to the tower on the Bund. He was then converted to Catholicism by Matteo Ricci and baptised with the name Paul. Xu became a high official in the Ming court and bequeathed land to found a Jesuit community, which eventually led to the construction of St Ignatius Cathedral. Xu's tomb can still be visited in nearby Guangqi Park (Map p122), next to the modern-day Shanghai Meteorological Bureau, and stands as an inspirational symbol of Shànghǎi's openness to accept foreign ideas.

5 Guangqi Park Escape the streets by wandering around pleasant Guangqi Park (see boxed text, above), named after the Catholic scholar Xu Guangqi whose tomb lies within the park.

6 CY Tung Maritime Museum Return to Xujiahui metro station and consider walking up Huashan Rd (华山路) to the CY Tung Maritime Museum (p121) in the grounds of Jiaotong University, appreciating the splendid university architecture, including the magnificent Library Building, before returning to Xujiahui metro station along Huashan Rd.

Eating p176; Shopping p148; Sleeping p216

Sometimes confused with the Hóngqiáo airport area, which is a separate neighbourhood, Chángníng is out in the west of Shànghǎi and begins where the French Concession ends. Gǔběi lies to the south of it, with West Yan'an Rd acting as a rough dividing line between the two areas. Both Chángníng and Gǔběi are dominated by uninspiring office blocks, big roads, various commercial enterprises and shopping malls, as well as more apartment complexes, which are home to Shànghǎi's new middle class, long-term expats and the mistresses of wealthy businessmen. Gǔběi thus has some of the city's best Western-style supermarkets, as well as pockets of Korean, Japanese and Western restaurants and a selection of international schools.

Many visitors just pass through on their way to or from Hongqiao Airport (Map p132), which handles domestic flights.

SHANGHAI SCULPTURE SPACE

Map pp128–9

上海城市雕塑艺术中心 Shànghǎi Chéngshì Diāosù Yìsù Zhōngxin

570 West Huaihai Rd; 淮海西路570号; 10am-5pm Tue-Sun; Ⓜ Hongqiao Rd

The No 10 Steel Factory has come to life again with an enormous display of large-scale sculpture pieces, set among the offices, studios and cafes of the Red Town Creative Cluster. The quality of the art varies, but it's a fun walk and offers an interesting glimpse at one of Shànghǎi's recent redevelopment projects.

SONG QINGLING MAUSOLEUM

Map pp128-9

宋庆龄陵园 Sōng Qìnglíng Língyuán

☎ 6474 7183; 21 Songyuan Rd; 宋园路21号; adult/student Y20/10; 9am-5pm, last entry 4.30pm; Ⓜ Hongqiao Rd

Despite its hard-edged communist layout, this green park is excellent for a stroll and for escaping the relentless Gǔběi skyline. Song Qingling (boxed text, p91) herself is interred in a low-key tomb here, but she is memorialised in the Song Qingling Exhibition Hall (宋庆龄陈列馆; Sòng Qìnglíng Chénlièguǎn) straight ahead from the main entrance, which itself looks like a Chinese imperial tomb. Among the displays of Song memorabilia – including her black qípáo – is a telling photograph of Marxist Westerners reading from Mao's *Little Red Book* back in the days when it was politically fashionable. The international cemetery here also contains a host of foreign gravestones, including those of Jewish, Vietnamese and Western settlers of Shànghǎi.

CHANGFENG OCEAN WORLD

Map pp62-3

长风海底世界 Chángfēng Hǎidǐ Shìjiè

☎ 6233 8888; Gate No 4, Changfeng Park, 451 Daduhe Rd; 大渡河路451号长风公园4号门; adult/child Y130/90; 9am-5pm; Ⓜ Loushanguan Rd then taxi;

Adults may find this subterranean aquarium dank, dingy and dear, but the little people will adore the clownfish and shark tunnel. Children under 1m get in for free.

ZHONGSHAN PARK

Map pp128-9

中山公园 Zhōngshān Gōngyuán

780 Changning Rd; 长宁路780号; admission Fundazzle Y35; 6am-6pm, Fundazzle 9am-5pm; Ⓜ Zhongshan Park;

Known as Jessfield Park to the British, this is a moderately interesting park located in the

top picks

CHÁNGNÍNG, GǓBĚI & HÓNGQIÁO

- Qībǎo (p131) Visit the narrow alleyways of the ancient town for a glimpse of old China in modern Shànghǎi.
- Yùyīntáng (p192) Rock out at Shànghǎi's premier music venue.
- Antique warehouses (p148) Take a day to tour the antique warehouses of Hongqiao; you might find that Qing dynasty piece you were looking for.
- Happy Valley Amusement Park (p131) Get in touch with your inner child.
- Shanghai Zoo (p132) Enjoy the manicured lawns and the animals.

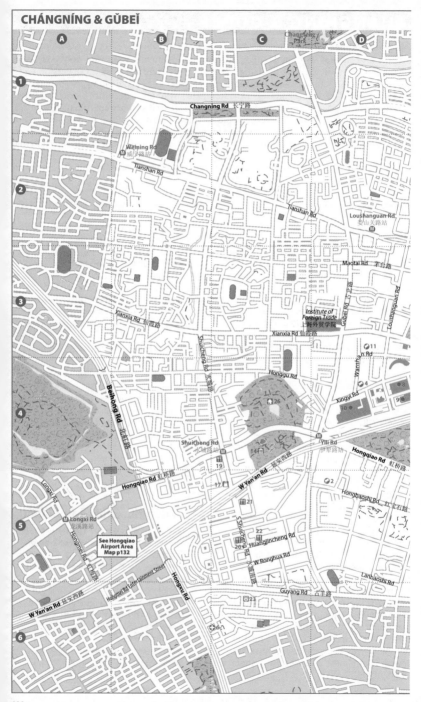

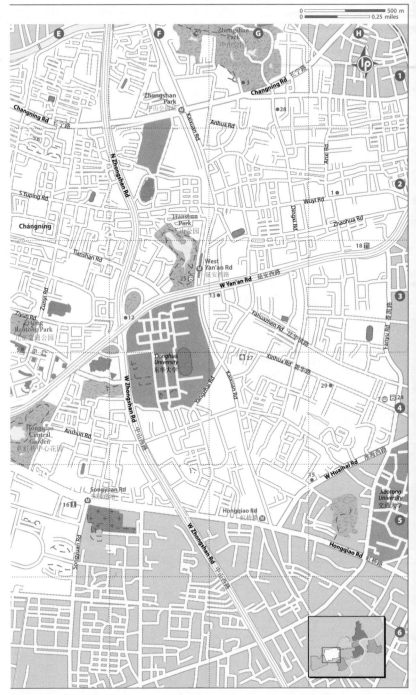

CHÁNGNÍNG & GǓBĚI

TRANSPORT: CHÁNGNÍNG & GǓBĚI

Metro Lines 2 and 10 run east–west through the area (line 10 is more central) while lines 3 and 4 mirror each other, running north–south.

north east, in the former 'Badlands' area of 1930s Shànghǎi. Kids will like Fundazzle (翻斗乐; Fāndǒulè), an adventure playground with slides, mazes and tunnels.

LIU HAISU ART GALLERY
Map pp128–9

刘海粟美术馆 Liú Hǎisù Měishùguǎn
☎ 6270 1018; 1660 Hongqiao Rd; 虹桥路 1660号; ◷ 9am-4pm Tue-Sun;
Ⓜ Shuicheng Rd

This hulking gallery exhibits works of the eponymous painter, as well as often impressive visiting exhibitions, with the Chine Antiques (p148) store in the lobby.

Drinking p185; Eating p176; Shopping p148; Sleeping p216

This area was once countryside and a playground for the rich to retreat to at weekends. The old Sassoon country estate is now the Cypress Hotel, while the Shanghai Zoo (p132) sits on what was once the British Golf Club. It's thin on sights, but the district has some handy hotels for those who aim to be near the airport. Qībǎo (below), a traditional Chinese town, is located south of the district. There are also a lot of family activities in the area. Metro lines 2 and 10 converge west of the airport at the new Hongqiao Transport Hub, which will also be the site of the high-speed Shànghǎi–Běijīng express train, although its estimated completion date isn't until 2014.

QĪBǍO Map pp62-3
七宝

☎ 6461 5208; 2 Minzhu Rd; Minhang district; 闵行区民主路2号; admission Y30; ☺ sights 8.30am-4.30pm; Ⓜ Qibao

The *gǔzhèn* (ancient town) of Qībǎo – literally 'Seven Treasures' – in Shànghǎi's Minhang district dates back to the Northern Song dynasty (AD 960–1127). Easily reached from town, the ancient settlement prospered during the Ming and Qing dynasties. Today it's overrun with Chinese visitors, but is also littered with traditional, historic architecture, threaded by small, busy alleyways and cut by a picturesque canal. If you can blot out the crowds, then Qībǎo brings you some of the flavours of old China.

A visit to Qībǎo also gets you out of the centre of Shànghǎi – trading heaving flyovers for arched bridges, and wide streets for pinched alleyways – closer to the feel of rural China, where locals still raise eyebrows and stare at foreigners. Vestiges of village handicrafts survive, including traditional wooden bucket makers, a traditional distillery and a remarkable miniature carving museum.

The best strategy is to just wander the streets, though the ticket office will provide you with a map with the nine official sights marked on it (all included in the through ticket). The best of the bunch include the Cotton Textile Mill, the Shadow Puppet Museum (☺ performances 1-3pm Wed & Sun), Zhou's Miniature Carving House and the Old Wine Shop (still an active distillery). Half-hour boat rides (per person Y10; ☺ 8.30am-5pm) along the picturesque canal slowly ferry passengers from Number One Bridge to upstream Dōngtángtān (东塘滩) and back. It's also worth ferreting out the decrepit Catholic Church (天主教堂; Tiānzhǔ Jiàotáng; 50 Nan St), adjacent to a convent off Nan St, south of the canal. The single-spire edifice dates back to 1867. It isn't on the official map, but you can reach it down an alley off Yutang St.

Souvenir hunters and diners will be agog at the choice of shops and eateries simply stuffed along the narrow streets. Wander along Bei Dajie north of the canal for a plethora of small shops selling fans, dolls, tea and wooden handicrafts from traditional two-storey dwellings. Nan Dajie is full of snacks and small eateries like No 14, which sells sweet *tāng yuán* dumplings and No 19, which is a rarely seen traditional teahouse. The Old Wine Shop (No 21) has a quieter second-floor restaurant (dishes Y10-38, local wine from Y11) overlooking the street. A taxi from the centre of Shànghǎi costs Y50 to Y60; otherwise take metro line 9.

HAPPY VALLEY AMUSEMENT PARK
Map p221

欢乐谷 Huānlè Gǔ

☎ 5779 9127; www.happyvalley.com.cn, in Chinese; Linyin Ave, Sheshan, Songjiang County; 松江区佘山林荫大道; admission adult/child 1.2-1.4m Y200/100; Ⓜ Sheshan; ♿

Happy Valley is a wildly popular national amusement park with four locations around China. This one opened in late

TRANSPORT: HONGQIAO AIRPORT AREA

Metro Lines 2 and 10 run east–west through the area, converging at Hongqiao Airport and terminating at the Hongqiao Transport Hub. Line 9 is to the south and passes through Qībǎo and terminates at Sōngjiāng town.

HONGQIAO AIRPORT AREA

2009. The rides in other parks get good
reviews; the Shànghǎi branch will even
have a dive machine and the country's
first wooden roller coaster, the Fireball.
It's located in Songjiang county, in the
town of Sheshan.

SHANGHAI ZOO Map p132
上海动物园 Shànghǎi Dòngwùyuán
☎ 6268 7775; www.shanghaizoo.cn; 2381 Hongqiao Rd; 虹桥路2381号; adult/child under 1.2
m/child Y30/free/24; ⏰ 6.30am-5.30pm Apr-Sep,
7am-5pm Oct-Mar; Ⓜ Shanghai Zoo; ♿

As Chinese zoos go, this is just about the best there is, and it makes for a good day out for those who have kids in tow. There's a decent selection of beasts – from woolly twin-humped Bactrian camels to spindly legged giraffes, gorillas, lions, lots of different monkeys, giant pandas and polar bears – but some of the enclosures they're housed in are less than ideal. The Shànghǎi folk flock here to enjoy one of the city's most picturesque and well-tended acreages of green grass. Picnic-goers dive onto the lawns for a spot of sun, while electric tour buggies (tour Y10; 8.30am-4.30pm) whirr along shaded paths through old-growth woods every 10 to 15 minutes. There's a lovely Children's Zoo, where the little ones can shower chubby piglets and billy goats with handfuls of grain, go fishing for goldfish or ride the ponies. The whole menagerie is navigable on foot with a map (Y1) from the information kiosk at the entrance or by following the signs. The elephant show (10am-3.30pm,

every 30 min) will have most adults cringing, but kids will surely adore handing out sticks of sugar cane to be scooped up by inquisitive trunks.

Not far from the zoo, in the grounds of the Cypress Hotel, is the former Sassoon Mansion (see boxed text, p104).

SHANGHAI YINQIXING INDOOR SKIING
off Map pp62-3
银七星市内滑雪场 Yínqīxīng Shìnèi Huáxuěchǎng
☎ 5485 3248; 1835 Qixing Rd, Xinzhuang; 莘庄七星路1835号; per hr Mon-Thu Y98, Fri & Sat Y118; 9.30am-10.30pm Mon-Thu, to 1am Fri & Sat; M Xinzhuang;
The slope is aimed at first-timers so don't expect anything overly long or steep, but children will love it. The snowboard park is more challenging. To get there take the metro to Xinzhuang and hop in a taxi or catch the free shuttle bus (every 30 minutes).

top picks

What's your recommendation? lonelyplanet.com/shanghai

It would not be an exaggeration to say that some people come to Shànghǎi specifically to shop. What the city lacks in terms of historic sights, it makes up for with its fashion-forward attitude and great bargains. You could probably create an entire itinerary devoted solely to the art of retail therapy, and even those who disdain shopping in any other situation may find themselves pulled into the fray. 'You like this T-shirt? Y90. OK, three T-shirts for Y90...OK, best price! You give me best price!' With dealmakers at every turn, it will take even the most thrifty personalities every ounce of willpower not to spend a few *kuài* at some point. And once you start, there's no going back.

But Shànghǎi shopping is more than just bargain hunting. The city has reinvented itself as an Asian centre for fashion and design, and there are some real treasures to hunt down, especially as more and more independent boutiques continue to appear each year. During lunch breaks and after work, the city's shopping centres swarm with people. Women in particular are superstylish by Chinese standards and take great care in developing their own look.

All that is good news for visitors, who can usually find a wide selection of clothes for cheaper than back home. But shopping in Shànghǎi is not for the faint-hearted. Even in the more upmarket malls like Grand Gateway (p148), the press of people when a sale is on can be intimidating – watching a crowd of Shanghainese pick their way through a pile of discounted items is like watching a plague of locusts devour a field of crops.

If you're just in town for a couple of days, head to the Old Town for interesting souvenirs and custom-tailored clothing. The French Concession has cool little boutiques that sell funky ceramics, clothing, memorabilia, faux antiques – you name it. The Taikang Rd Art Centre (p141) is a particularly good spot to spend the day. Pearls are another great Shànghǎi purchase, but remember that knock-offs are ubiquitous and much of what you see for sale may be a forgery (in particular, antiques). Dodging the fake Rolex salesmen who pop up out of nowhere is, in fact, a quintessential Shànghǎi experience. Try and make time too for a visit to the Qipu Market (p147), where Shànghǎi's masses buy their clothes. Prepare to push and be pushed, watch out for flying elbows and marvel at the sight of people who literally fight for their right to shop.

SHOPPING TIPS

Generally, shops are open from 10am to 9pm daily, though government-run stores often close at 6pm while smaller boutiques may not open until noon. Nonstandard opening hours are listed in the reviews. Yuyuan Bazaar and Dongtai Rd Antique Market are both best visited early in the day.

In larger stores, after you've selected an item the sales assistant will write a ticket, then send you to the cashier, who will collect your money and send you right back to the salesperson, who will have your items bagged. It rarely happens that the wrong item ends up in the bag, but it's worth checking.

Most department stores will exchange items with a receipt, though smaller shops and markets have an 'every sale is final' clause. To save yourself a headache, make sure you scrutinise the item carefully. Always try on clothing before buying. Also make sure you have a legible receipt and get a business card.

HAGGLING

While prices in formal stores are supposed to be standardised, it never hurts to ask for a discount. In the markets, haggling over prices is all part of the shopping experience. In fact, many vendors are genuinely upset when shoppers refuse to partake in the bargaining game.

The most common method of haggling is for the vendor to display the price on a calculator and hand the calculator to you. You then laugh and punch in 25% to 30% of their price, the vendor shakes their head and emits a cry that suggests you just insulted their ancestors, comes down a little and gives the calculator back to you. This goes on until the price drops by about 50%. At some of the more touristy places, like Yuyuan Bazaar, vendors will go as low as 30% of the original price. A lot of vendors have learned to say 'final price', but this rarely holds true.

If you're short on patience, offer around 35% to 40% of the asking price and when it is refused, smile, shrug and walk away to a nearby stall selling exactly the same thing. Most times the vendor will chase you down and agree to your price, but you could walk away empty-handed. If you're bargaining for fake goods, then haggle hard. It's always best to conduct business with one person and not a group; no Chinese is going to be out-bargained and lose face in front of a crowd of their own.

Do bear in mind though, that the point of the process is to achieve a mutually acceptable price and not to screw the vendor into the ground. It's always best to smile, which will help keep negotiations light even if you don't ultimately agree on a price. Get angry, and you not only lose face but give foreigners a bad name. Remember that the Y10 you're haggling over is a little less than US$1.50 and probably worth spending if you're taken with the item.

If negotiating in pidgin Chinese, be very careful of similar-sounding numbers, like 14 (shísì) and 40 (sìshí), and 108 (yībǎilíngbā) and 180 (yībǎibā), as these offer great potential for misunderstanding, deliberate or otherwise. Note that Chinese shops advertise the final sale price and it is marked as a proportion; for example, a 20% discount will be marked as 打8折. But given the prices in China, you get ripped off only if you end up buying something you didn't really want in the first place.

SHIPPING & CUSTOMS

Most reputable shops will take care of insurance, customs and shipping for larger items, though find out first exactly what the dealer covers. Separate charges may materialise for handling, packaging, customs duty and quarantine, driving the shipping charges above the price of the item! Also consider how much it will cost to get the goods from the shipping port to your home.

Technically, nothing over 200 years old can be taken out of China, but you'll be very lucky if you come across any antiques in Shànghǎi that old. If you are buying a reproduction, make sure the dealer provides paperwork stating that it is not an antique. Dealers should also provide the proper receipts and paperwork for any antiques. Keep the receipts along with the business card of the dealer, just in case.

Shipping clothing, curios and household items on your own is generally not a problem and China Post has an excellent packing system for airmailing light items.

THE BUND & PEOPLE'S SQUARE
外滩、人民广场

Linking the Bund with People's Sq is East Nanjing Rd, formerly known as Nanking Rd. It was once the most famous shopping street not just in China, but in all of Asia. In the 1920s the department stores Sincere, Wing On, Sun Sun and Da Sun imported luxury goods from London, Paris and New York and revolutionised the retail experience with new concepts such as window displays, advertising campaigns and customer service. These days, it's less exclusive (in fact it can be downright tacky) and can

WHERE CAN I FIND...

Seekers of curios are warned that many of those to be found in the Chinese city are excellent imitations of the authentic article.

All About Shanghai; A Standard Guidebook, 1934

- Faux antiques and souvenirs? Dongtai Rd Antique Market (p140), Fuyou Antique Market (p140), Old Street (p140) and Hóngqiáo warehouses (p148).
- Local fashion? Taikang Rd Art Centre (p141) and the French Concession streets featured in the Best Boutiques box (p141).
- Tailor-made clothing and fabric? Shiliupu Fabric Market (p139) and South Bund Fabric Market (p140).
- Discount clothing and accessories? Fenshine Fashion & Accessories Plaza (p146), AP Xinyang Fashion & Gifts Market (p147) and Qipu Market (p147).
- Real pearls? Amy Lin's Pearls (p146) and Hongqiao International Pearl City (p149).
- Tea? See the Tea Tasting box (p146).
- Ethnic handicrafts? Brocade Country (p144), Paramita (p144) and Skylight (p145).
- Electronics? Cybermart (p144), Electronics Market (p147) and Xingguang Photography Equipment (p144).

SHOPPING THE BUND & PEOPLE'S SQUARE

137

no longer compete with the stores elsewhere in the city. But millions of Chinese continue to visit anyway, if only for the historical associations, and a good hunt can lead to some intriguing purchases. For something a little different, the parallel streets of Fuzhou Rd and Jinling Rd sell (respectively) Chinese art supplies and musical instruments. Underneath People's Sq is a maze of former bomb shelters that have been transformed into a downmarket shopping centre known as D-Mall. The Bund itself is all about luxury shopping, but only some of the brands are local.

THE BUND
ANNABEL LEE
Map pp66-7   Accessories

安梨家居 Ānlí Jiājū

☎ 6445 8218; No 1, Lane 8, East Zhongshan No 1 Rd; 中山东一路8弄1号; ☻ 10am-10pm; Ⓜ East Nanjing Rd

This elegant shop sells a range of soft-coloured accessories in silk, linen and cashmere, many of which feature delicate and stylish embroidery. Peruse the collection of shawls (Y2800), scarves (Y580), table runners and evening bags (Y160). Another branch is at Xīntiāndì (Map pp86–7; North Block, Bldg 3).

DUOYUNXUAN ART SHOP
Map pp66-7   Art

朵云轩 Duǒyún Xuān

☎ 6360 6475; 422 East Nanjing Rd; 南京东路422号; ☻ 9.30am-9.30pm; Ⓜ East Nanjing Rd

A multistorey, traditional-looking building (look for the two enormous calligraphy brushes outside) with an excellent selection of art and calligraphy supplies. The 2nd floor is one of the best places for heavy art books, both international and Chinese, and the 3rd floor houses antiques and some excellent calligraphy and brush-painting galleries. You can get your own chop made here.

FOREIGN LANGUAGES BOOKSTORE
Map pp66-7   Books

外文书店 Wàiwén Shūdiàn

☎ 6322 3200; 390 Fuzhou Rd; 福州路390号; ☻ 9.30am-6pm Sun-Thu, 9.30am-7pm Fri & Sat; Ⓜ East Nanjing Rd

The days when the selection of titles at these government-sponsored bookstores ran from Dickens to Sherlock Holmes are long gone. There's now an ever-expanding

range of fiction and nonfiction upstairs, as well as an impressive selection of Lonely Planet guides on the ground floor (though they sometimes refuse to stock the China guide). It's a good place to come for titles and maps on Shànghǎi. There is a small branch in Gǔběi (Map pp128–9; 71 South Shuicheng Rd; 水城南路71号; Ⓜ Shuicheng Rd).

BLUE SHANGHAI WHITE
Map pp66-7   Handicrafts

海晨 Hǎi Chén

☎ 6352 2222; Unit 103, 17 Fuzhou Rd; 福州路17号103室; ☻ 10.30am-6.30pm; Ⓜ East Nanjing Rd

Just off the Bund, this little boutique is a great place to browse for a contemporary take on a traditional art form. It sells a tasteful selection of hand-painted porcelain tea cups, teapots and vases, displayed together with the store's ingeniously designed wooden furniture.

SHIATZY CHEN
Map pp66-7   Clothes

夏姿 Xià Zī

☎ 6321 9155; 9 East Zhongshan No 1 Rd; 中山东一路9号; ☻ 10am-10pm; Ⓜ East Nanjing Rd

One of the top names in Asian haute couture, Taiwanese designer Shiatzy Chen finds her inspiration in traditional Chinese aesthetics. The exclusive collections (women's and men's apparel) at her Bund 9 flagship store display a painstaking attention to detail and cross cultural boundaries with grace. Another branch is at the entrance to the Jinjiang Hotel (Map pp86–7; Unit D, 59 South Maoming Rd; 茂名南路59号D座) in the French Concession.

SILK KING Map pp66-7   Silk, Fabric

真丝大王 Zhēnsī Dàwáng

☎ 6321 1869; www.silkking.com; 66 East Nanjing Rd; 南京东路66号; ☻ 10am-10pm; Ⓜ East Nanjing Rd

The city's largest fabric chain sells attractive silk from Y158 per metre, although prices can go far higher. In-store tailors can make you a custom-fit qípáo (cheongsam), shirt or jacket in three to 10 days for around Y1800. Twenty-four-hour rush jobs are also possible. There are numerous branches around Shànghǎi, including one on Middle Huaihai Rd (Map pp86–7; 588 Middle Huaihai Rd; 淮海中路588号; Ⓜ South Huangpi Rd).

SUZHOU COBBLERS Map pp66–7 · Shoes
上海起想艺术品 **Shànghǎi Qǐxiǎng Yìshùpǐn**
☎ 6321 7087; Unit 101, 17 Fuzhou Rd; 福州路17号
101室; ⏱ 10.30am-6.30pm; Ⓜ East Nanjing Rd
Right off the Bund, this cute boutique sells
exquisite, hand-embroidered silk slippers.
Patterns and colours are based on the fashions of the 1930s, and as far as the owner,
Huang Mengqi, is concerned, the products
are one of a kind. Her shop also sells hand-
made bags, hats and toys.

YUNHONG CHOPSTICKS SHOP
Map pp66–7 · Souvenirs
韵泓筷子店 **Yùnhóng Kuàizi Diàn**
☎ 6322 0207; 387 East Nanjing Rd; 南京东路
387号; ⏱ 9am-10.30pm; Ⓜ East Nanjing Rd
The Běijīng arts-and-crafts people have
opened up this smart little shop selling
designer chopsticks (from Y12 to Y1650)
for everyone from your four-year-old to
the sophisticated aunt who loves to throw
extravagant dinner parties. You might even
find a set for yourself.

PEOPLE'S SQUARE
SHANGHAI MUSEUM ART STORE
Map pp66–7 · Art
上海博物馆艺术品商店 **Shànghǎi Bówùguǎn
Yìshùpǐn Shāngdiàn**
☎ 6327 4514; 201 Renmin Ave (entrance on East
Yan'an Rd); 人民大道201号; ⏱ 9am-4pm;
Ⓜ People's Sq
Attached to the Shanghai Museum (p72), this
high-quality store offers refreshing variety
from the usual tourist souvenirs. Apart from
the excellent range of books on Chinese
art, architecture, ceramics and calligraphy,
there is a good selection of quality cards,
prints and slides. The annexe shop sells fine
imitations of some of the ceramic pieces
on display in the Ceramics Gallery (as well
as scarves and bags). Another branch is
at Xīntiāndì (Map pp86–7; Xīntiāndì North Block, 123
Taicang Rd; ⏱ 11am-8.30pm), near the corner of
Taicang Rd and South Huangpi Rd.

RAFFLES CITY
Map pp66–7 · Mall
来福士广场 **Láifúshì Guǎngchǎng**
☎ 6340 3600; 268 Middle Xizang Rd; 西藏中路
268号; ⏱ 10am-10pm; Ⓜ People's Sq
A seven-floor, nonsmoking, Singapore-
owned mall that specialises in medium-level
Western brands like Levi's, Miss Sixty and

Quiksilver. There are also electronics and toy
shops here, as well as food courts with noodle and pizza places, and a juice bar (水果吧;
shuǐguǒ bā) and Watson's in the basement.

SHANGHAI NO 1 FOOD STORE
Map pp66–7 · Food
上海市第一食品商店 **Shànghǎi Shì Dìyī
Shípǐn Shāngdiàn**
720 East Nanjing Rd; 南京东路720号;
⏱ 9.30am-10pm; Ⓜ People's Sq
Brave the crowds here to check out the
amazing variety of dried mushrooms,
ginseng and sea cucumber, as well as more
tempting snacks like sunflower seeds,
nuts, dried fruit, moon cakes and tea. Built
in 1926, this used to be Sun Sun, one of
Shànghǎi's big department stores.

OLD TOWN 南市
Although it wasn't originally set up as a shopping district, Yuyuan Bazaar (p78) has become
exactly that. All souvenirs can be found here
or on the bordering Old Street, along with
some alleged antiques and interesting shops
specialising in things such as fans, scissors
and walking sticks. The Shiliupu Fabric Market (below) and the South Bund Fabric Market
(p140) are both fine places to go in search of
inexpensive fabric or have a dress or shirt
tailor made.

TONG HAN CHUN TRADITIONAL
MEDICINE STORE Map p79 · Chinese Medicine
童涵春堂 **Tóng Hán Chūn Táng**
☎ 6355 0308; 20 New Yuyuan Rd; 上海豫园
新路20号; ⏱ 8am-9pm; Ⓜ Yuyuan Garden
A fantastic old emporium of elixirs, infu-
sions and remedies, this place has been in
business since 1783. There's a huge range
here, including modern medication, but it's
all labelled in Chinese and there's not much
English spoken so you'll need a translator.
On the 3rd floor, traditional-Chinese-
medicine (TCM) doctors offer consultations
(you'll need an appointment).

SHILIUPU FABRIC MARKET
Map p79 · Fabric
十六铺面料城 **Shíliùpù Miànliào Chéng**
☎ 6330 1043; 2 Zhonghua Rd; 中华路2号;
⏱ 8.30am-6.30pm; Ⓜ Xiaonanmen
Having silk shirts, dresses and cashmere
coats tailor-made for a song is one of
Shànghǎi's great indulgences. This

three-storey building, one of several fabric markets in the city, is conveniently located near the Yuyuan Bazaar. It's a far cheaper source of silk than places like Silk King (p138), with prices no higher than Y200 per metre. There are many other types of fabric here, from wool and velvet to synthetic, but the quality of the material varies, so shop around. Most places can fill an order in 24 hours if needed, but it's best to count on at least three days.

SOUTH BUND FABRIC MARKET
Map p79   Fabric
南外滩轻纺面料市场 **Nán Wàitān Qīngfǎng Miànliào Shìchǎng**
399 Lujiabang Rd; 陆家浜路399号; ☻ 8.30am-6pm; Ⓜ Nanpu Bridge
This old building with over 100 hundred stalls is similar to the Shiliupu Fabric Market (p139), with an atmospheric location not far from the markets and tailoring shops along Dongjiadu Rd. It's further out of the way, but more popular with expats.

ZHEJIANG HUZHOU BEDDING FACTORY Map p79   Silk, Fabric
浙江湖州床上用品厂 **Zhèjiāng Húzhōu Chuángshàng Yòngpǐn Chǎng**
☎ 139 1855 2501; 89 Waicangqiao St; 外仓桥街89号; ☻ 8.30am-6.30pm; Ⓜ Nanpu Bridge
The 'factory' is no more than a large outdoor workbench where family members measure out and comb silk quilts (蚕丝被; *cánsī bèi*) right on the street. A popular Shànghǎi purchase, silk quilts (comforters) are lighter weight and more breathable than their down counterparts. They are sold by density (1.5kg or 2kg are reasonable choices). The prices are fixed (Y650 for a 2kg queen-sized quilt) and cheaper than anywhere else in town. They also sell their quilts at the Wangjia Docks Fabric Market (王家码头丝绸面料市场; Wángjiā Mǎtou Sīchóu Miànliào Shìchǎng; 191 Nancang St; 南仓街191号), across from the South Bund Fabric Market (above).

DONGTAI ROAD ANTIQUE MARKET
Map p79   Souvenirs
东台路古玩市场 **Dōngtái Lù Gǔwán Shìchǎng**
☎ 5582 5254; Dongtai Rd; 东台路; ☻ 9am-6pm; Ⓜ Laoximen
A block west of South Xizang Rd, this market street has over 100 stalls spread over both Dongtai Rd and Liuhekou Rd. The 'antique' stalls sell some interesting items

among the inevitable Mao memorabilia, including ceramics, old Shànghǎi calendar posters, pocket watches, paintings and a host of other collectables. Haggle hard here as it's all vastly overpriced – prices fold to half almost immediately. Most of the items sold here are mass-produced for the market. A good rule of thumb: if you like the look of something and can get a fair price for it, buy it for what it is and not as an antique.

FUYOU ANTIQUE MARKET
Map p79   Antiques, Souvenirs
福佑工艺品市场 **Fúyòu Gōngyìpǐn Shìchǎng**
459 Middle Fangbang Rd; 方浜中路459号; Ⓜ Yuyuan Garden
There's a permanent antique market here on the 1st and 2nd floors, but the place really gets humming for the 'ghost market' on Sunday at dawn, when sellers from the countryside fill up all four floors and then some. The range is good, but again, there's a lot of junk, so you need a shrewd eye if you don't want to pay too much over the odds.

OLD STREET Map p79   Souvenirs
老街 **Lǎo Jiē**
Middle Fangbang Rd; 方浜中路; Ⓜ Yuyuan Garden
This renovated Qing dynasty stretch of Fangbang Rd is lined with specialist tourist shops. This is an excellent place for souvenirs and the vendors here are less pushy than at Yuyuan Bazaar. The wide range of best finds include shadow puppets (at No 363); jade jewellery (No 367); a collection of memorabilia from the Old Shanghai Teahouse (p180; No 385), including reproduced calendar posters (Y10) and 'liberate Taiwan' matchboxes (Y5); bags and embroidered fabric (No 397); old illustrated books and calligraphy manuals (No 408); kites (No 417); Yixing teapots (No 419); old poster advertisements and bank notes (No 423); and Tibetan jewellery (No 424).

FRENCH CONCESSION
法租界

Huaihai Rd in the French Concession area is definitely *the* modern shopping street in Shànghǎi. Shops start in the east (near South Huangpi Rd metro) with a succession of towering department stores and global chains

BEST FASHION BOUTIQUES

There are boutiques on almost every corner in the French Concession. But around the South Shanxi Rd metro station there a few blocks in particular that are a must for serious clothes shoppers. Afternoon and evening are the best hours for browsing: some smaller shops don't open their doors until noon, but most stay open until 10pm.

- Changle Rd (Map pp86–7) Young designers and emerging local brands have taken over a one-block stretch of Changle Rd east of Ruijin No 1 Rd. Check out La Vie (p143), Elbis Hungi (No 139-18), eno (No 139-23) and One by One (No 141-10/12) to see where local fashion is headed. West of Ruijin No 1 Rd are traditional tailors and Chouchou Chic (p142).
- Xinle Rd (Map pp86–7) This two-block stretch has less high-end fashion than Changle Rd but ultimately greater variety. Pop into The Thing (p144), 100 Change & Insect (p142), and Source (No 158) for a taste of the 'Hai's urban style. Bargain hunters should look for Jùnměizǔ (p143) around the corner.
- South Maoming Rd (Map pp86–7) South of Huaihai Rd is custom-tailored traditional women's clothing (like qípáo – cheongsam); north of Huaihai Rd is high-end men's clothing, tailoring and shoes.

following one after the other. From here, Dongtai Rd Antique Market (opposite) and Xīntiāndì (right) are only a short walk away. Near the central stretch around South Shaanxi Rd are many of the boutiques where young Shanghainese go shopping for clothes and shoes. The enjoyable Taikang Rd Art Centre (below) is probably the best shopping experience in the area (if not the city) but make sure to give yourself plenty of time to hunt down smaller stores like Spin (p142), Ba Yan Ka La (p142) and Brocade Country (p144), which are all further west.

SHANGHAI TRIO

Map pp86-7   Accessories, Clothes

上海组合 **Shànghǎi Zǔhé**

☎ 6355 2974; Xīntiāndì North Block, No 4-5 (entrance on Taicang Rd); 太仓路181弄新天地北里单元4-5; ☻ 10.30am-10pm; M South Huangpi Rd/Xintiandi

Ravissant! C'est tout moi! French women go crazy for the chic eco-friendly fabrics here, which incorporate traditional Chinese motifs into much of the collection. Among the finds: cute children's clothes, purses, scarves and quilt (duvet) covers.

TAIKANG ROAD ART CENTRE

Map pp86-7   Accessories, Clothes, Souvenirs

田子坊、泰康路艺术中心 **Tiánzǐfáng, Tàikāng Lù Yìshù Zhōngxīn**

Taikang Rd; 泰康路; M Dapuqiao

Burrow into the lǐlòng (alleys) here for a rewarding haul of creative boutiques, selling everything from hip jewellery and yak-wool scarves to retro communist dinnerware. Feel Shanghai (Unit 110, No 3, Lane 210; ☻ 10am-8pm) is the place to pick up a tailored traditional wàitào (short Chinese jacket) or qípáo, while further along is Harvest (International

Artists Factory, Unit 118, No 3, Lane 210; ☻ 10am-6pm), which sells Miao embroidery from southwest China. The courtyard at No 7 Lane 210 (aka The Yard) features Himalayan jewellery and tapestries at Joma (Unit 6) and local fashion designers at La Vie (p143) and I Life Design (Unit 11). Nearby Insh (p143) is another Shànghǎi brand with a younger look. Jip (No 51, Lane 210; ☻ 9.30am-7pm) comes in with eye-catching, modern jewellery for men, while Not Just Silver (No 10, Lane 210; ☻ 9.30am-6.30pm) sells its jewellery from a lovely old residence with a magnificent tiled floor. The vibrant and colourful selection of crafts at Esydragon (No 20, Lane 210; ☻ 10am-7pm) makes for excellent gifts; Zhenchalin Tea (p145) has Chinese herbal teas in nifty packaging. Other standout stores are Chouchou Chic (children's clothes; p142), Shokay (yak products; p143), Springhead (folk art; p145) and Urban Tribe (fashion; p144).

XĪNTIĀNDÌ

Map pp86-7   Accessories, Clothes, Souvenirs

新天地

cnr Taicang & Madang Rds; 太仓路与马当路路口; ☻ 11am-11pm; M South Huangpi Rd/Xintiandi

There are few bargains to be had at Xīntiāndì, but even window shoppers can make a fun afternoon of it here. The North Block is the place to browse, with embroidered accessories from Annabel Lee (p138), eco-friendly fabrics from Shanghai Trio (left), iridescent glass creations at Liúligōngfáng (p142) and mod jewellery from NoD (Bldg 25), in addition to home furnishings at Simply Life (p145) and a branch of the Shanghai Museum Art Store (p139). The South Block has only one boutique – Fúlíntáng's (Bldg 1) herbal remedies and *pu-erh* teas – but the mall at the southern end, with import stores like Hong Kong's IT, beckons shopaholics onward.

LIÚLIGŌNGFÁNG

Map pp86-7   Art
琉璃工房
☎ 6326 2223; Xīntiāndì North Block, Bldg 11; 太仓路181弄新天地北里11号楼; ⏱ 11am-10pm; Ⓜ South Huangpi Rd/Xintiandi
If you like the decor at TMSK (p182) you'll definitely want to check out this one-of-a-kind crystal-art shop next door, where you can marvel at iridescent cast-glass creations such as a contemplative monk (Y1165) and exquisite earrings (Y600) and pendants (Y520). There are nine branches around town.

SMALL SMALL MUSEUM

Map pp86-7   Art
牛心 Niúxīn
☎ 5404 8085; 20 Donghu Rd; 东湖路20号; ⏱ 11am-8pm; Ⓜ South Shanxi Rd
Hidden behind el Willy (p162) is this eccentric Japanese shop, which rents out 12in-by-12in boxes to Shànghǎi artists and designers. It's as much a study in personalities as it is a place to shop for gifts – some people cram their box full, others choose to highlight just one or two creations. Items on sale range from the hokey (Shànghǎi pet photos) to the unusual (kimono fabrics) to the quotidian (candles).

BA YAN KA LA

Map pp86-7   Beauty
巴颜喀拉 Bā Yán Kā Lā
☎ 6126 7600; Ferguson Lane, Unit B1-b, 376 Wukang Rd; 武康路376号武康新里B1-b室; ⏱ 10am-9pm; Ⓜ Shanghai Library
Taking its name from the Tibetan mountain range that separates the Yellow and Yangzi watersheds, Ba Yan Ka La offers a line of natural beauty products derived from Chinese herbs. Goji berry (skin revitalisation), lotus seed (skin nourishment) and mulberry (detoxification) are all familiar ingredients in TCM, although the products here are considerably more appealing than the medicinal forms. The scented candles, shampoos, Tibetan (crystal of wisdom) bath salts and facial scrubs can also be found in spas and hotels around town.

CHATERHOUSE Map pp86-7   Books
☎ 6391 8237; Shop B1-E, Times Square, 93 Middle Huaihai Rd; 淮海中路93号, 上海时代广场B1-E; ⏱ 10am-10pm; Ⓜ South Huangpi Rd or Dashijie
Bookworms greeted the arrival of this chain with a cheer. There's a good range of new Western fiction and nonfiction, and it also has a strong selection of children's books and magazines. Another branch is in the Shanghai Centre (Map pp98-9; ☎ 6279 7633; Unit 104, 1376 West Nanjing Rd; 南京西路1376号104室; ⏱ 9am-9pm).

SPIN Map pp86-7   Ceramics
旋 Xuán
☎ 6279 2545; Bldg 3, 758 Julu Rd; 巨鹿路758号3号楼; ⏱ 11am-9.30pm; Ⓜ Jing'an Temple
Chinese porcelain hasn't developed artistically since at least the Qing dynasty, and much of what you see for sale these days is clunky, soulless and devoid of originality. Fortunately, a new generation of designers has started picking up the slack, trying to restore artistic integrity to Jǐngdézhèn ceramics. Spin, which provides the chinaware for Shintori Null II (p161), does an excellent job of bringing China up to speed with its oblong tea cups (Y35), twisted sake sets (Y180) and all manner of cool plates, chopstick holders and 'kung fu' and 'exploded pillar' vases (Y240).

100 CHANGE & INSECT Map pp86-7   Shoes
百变虫 Bǎibiànchóng
☎ 5404 0767; 76 Xinle Rd; 新乐路76号; ⏱ 10.30am-10.30pm; Ⓜ South Shanxi Rd
Strange name, funky footwear – this is the place for those who want their heels to be seen in the dark. Browse Hong Kong designs covered in rhinestones, sequins, pink glitter, and silver and gold accents. They have men's shoes too. There's another location at 318 Nanchang Rd (Map pp86–7).

CHOUCHOU CHIC

Map pp86-7   Clothes
喆缤豆小童生活馆 Zhébīndòu Xiǎotóng Shēnghuó Guǎn
☎ 5403 5626; 162-8 South Shaanxi Rd (entrance on Changle Rd); 陕西南路162-8号; Ⓜ South Shanxi Rd
French-Chinese hybrid Chouchou Chic sells kids' clothes (ages 0 to 8) that are infinitely cuter than what you find at the souvenir stalls. Most of the clothing is Western-style, but you can find some attractive

floral-patterned fabrics and Chinese-style cotton dresses as well. Prices start at Y148. Another shop is at the Taikang Road Art Centre (p141; No 47, Lane 248).

HEPING FINERY
Map pp86-7 · Clothes

和平旗袍专卖店 **Hépíng Qípáo Zhuānmài Diàn**
☎ 6473 9043; 161 South Maoming Rd; 茂名南路161号; ☽ 9.30am-9.30pm; Ⓜ South Shanxi Rd

This tiny store offers cheaper tailor-made *qípáo* (from Y880) than most of its nearby competitors. It does silk shirts, dresses and jackets as well. Most of the patterns incorporate large embroidered flowers in their design. Custom-fit clothing only takes two to three days to make.

HUĀ YÀNG NIÁN HUÁ
Map pp86-7 · Clothes

花样年华
☎ 6415 6765; 145 South Maoming Rd; 茂名南路145号; ☽ 9am-10pm; Ⓜ South Shanxi Rd

Huā Yàng Nián Huá takes its name from the Chinese title of the Wong Kar Wai movie *In the Mood for Love*, which featured Hong Kong actress Maggie Cheung in an array of stunning *qípáo*. Fittingly, they make fine tailor-made *qípáo* here from Y1200, but there's no guarantee you'll look like Ms Cheung once you slip one on.

INSH
Map pp86-7 · Clothes

玩场 **Wán Chǎng**
☎ 6466 5249; Taikang Rd Art Centre, No 11A, Lane 210, Taikang Rd; 泰康路210弄11A号; ☽ 10.30am-9pm; Ⓜ Dapuqiao

Contemporary fashion with a bohemian twist is what's on offer at this trendy place, created by local designer Helen Lee. Come here for cute patterned bags (Y398), T-shirts (Y158) and stylish jackets. The designs are fun and aimed firmly at the younger crowd.

JÙNMĚIZǓ
Map pp86-7 · Clothes

俊美组
☎ 5403 5291; 95 North Xiangyang Rd; 襄阳北路95号; ☽ 10am-10pm; Ⓜ South Shanxi Rd

Hunt through the racks for brand-name markdowns (shirts, pants and shoes), selling from Y30 to Y200. The collection is all over the place, but you'll definitely find some bargains here.

LA VIE
Map pp86-7 · Clothes

生 **Shēng**
☎ 6445 3585; Taikang Rd Art Centre, the Yard, Unit 13, No 7, Lane 210, Taikang Rd; 泰康路210弄7号13室; ☽ 10.30am-8.30pm; Ⓜ Dapuqiao

Jenny Ji has made a name for herself with her stylish take on street fashion, including patterned jeans and nicely cut shirts. None of it comes cheap, though: jeans start at Y6900 and even the T-shirts go for Y3200. Another shop is on Changle Road (Map pp86–7; 306 Changle Rd; 长乐路306号).

SHANGHAI TANG
Map pp86-7 · Clothes

上海滩 **Shànghǎi Tān**
☎ 6384 1601; Xīntiāndì North Block, Bldg 15; 太仓路181弄新天地北里15号楼; ☽ 10am-midnight; Ⓜ South Huangpi Rd

Hong Kong-based Shanghai Tang flies the flag for the Middle Kingdom in the world of high-end fashion. The designs are classic Chinese with a twist, incorporating fluorescent colours, traditional motifs and luxury fabrics like silk and cashmere into the clothes and accessories. More affordable items include the slinky tops (from Y1500) and the scarves (Y985), but if you have to ask the price of an item here you can't afford it. There are other branches in the Jinjiang Hotel complex (p208) and Pudong Shangri-La (p213).

SHIRT FLAG
Map pp86-7 · Clothes

衫旗帜 **Shān Qí Zhì**
☎ 5465 3011; 330 Nanchang Rd; 南昌路330号; ☽ 10.30am-10pm; Ⓜ South Shanxi Rd

Purveyors of the finest T-shirts on the mainland, Shirt Flag specialises in witty designs like its Angry Panda series, giving an ironic twist to Maoist propaganda and later party slogans such as the 'Four Modernisations'. Prices start at Y198 and unlike many Chinese T-shirts, they won't shrink two sizes the first time you wash them. There are six branches around town, including at M50 (p97; Bldg 17) and the Taikang Road Art Centre (p141; The Yard, Unit 8, No 7, Lane 210).

SHOKAY
Map pp86-7 · Clothes

☎ 5466 0907; Taikang Rd Art Centre, No 9, Lane 274, Taikang Rd; 泰康路274弄9号田子坊; ☽ 9.30am-6.30pm; Ⓜ Dapuqiao

If the sign outside ('100% yak!') doesn't catch your attention, we don't know what will. Shokay is one of the few places in the world where you can pick up hand-knit clothing made entirely out of, yup, yak wool – which is a surprisingly soft, supple material. A nonprofit organisation, they support Tibetan herders (who gather the wool) and Chongming Island farmers (who do the knitting) and use revenue to help Chinese minority groups start their own businesses. Scarves start at Y980.

THE THING Map pp86-7   Clothes
☎ 5404 3607; 60 Xinle Rd; 新乐路60号;
☺ 11am-10pm; Ⓜ South Shanxi Rd
The Thing specialises in inexpensive Shànghǎi urbanwear, selling hoodies (Y180), messenger bags (Y299), shoes and Chinglish T-shirts (Y100).

URBAN TRIBE Map pp86-7   Clothes
城市山民 Chéngshì Shānmín
☎ 6433 5366; 133 West Fuxing Rd; 复兴西路133号;
☺ 10am-10pm; Ⓜ Shanghai Library
Urban Tribe is the only contemporary Shànghǎi label to draw inspiration from the ethnic groups of China and Southeast Asia. The collection of loose-fitting blouses, pants and jackets are made of natural fabrics and are a refreshing departure from the city's on-the-go attitude and usual taste for flamboyance. Be sure to also look through their collection of photographs and silver jewellery. A tea garden is located behind the store. A smaller outlet is in the Taikang Road Art Centre (p141; No 14, Lane 248).

CYBERMART Map pp86-7   Electronics
赛博数码广场 Sàibó Shùmǎ Guǎngchǎng
1 Middle Huaihai Rd; 淮海中路1号; ☺ 10am-8pm;
Ⓜ Dashijie
Cybermart is the most central and reliable location for all sorts of gadgetry, including DVD players, iPods, laptops, digital cameras and camcorders, as well as blank CDs, memory sticks and software. It's essentially two floors of independent stalls so you won't get a store guarantee, but you may find some deals. You can definitely bargain, but don't expect enormous discounts.

XINGGUANG PHOTOGRAPHY EQUIPMENT Map pp86-7   Electronics, Photography
星光摄影器材城 Xīngguāng Shèyǐng Qìcái Chéng
288 Luban Rd; 淮海中路288号; ☺ 7am-7pm;
Ⓜ Dapuqiao/Luban Rd
There are three main floors of photography equipment here, and while prices vary (you

need to bargain; no guarantees) you can still expect to find some good buys. Digital cameras are everywhere, but photography buffs will be most interested in sorting through the various lenses, tripods and bags. A real find is the Shen-Hao (申豪) shop on the 4th floor, which sells their hard-to-find field cameras. A repair shop is on the 3rd floor.

CHINESE PRINTED BLUE NANKEEN EXHIBITION HALL Map pp86-7   Fabric
中国蓝印花布馆 Zhōngguó Lán Yìnhuābù Guǎn
☎ 5403 7947; No 24, Lane 637, Changle Rd; 长乐路637弄24号; ☺ 9am-5pm; Ⓜ Changshu Rd
Follow the blue signs through a maze of courtyards until you see bolts of blue cloth drying in the yard. Originally produced in Jiāngsū, Zhèjiāng and Guìzhōu provinces, this blue-and-white cotton fabric (sometimes called blue calico) is similar to batik, and is coloured using a starch-resist method and indigo dye bath. This museum and shop, started by Japanese artist Kubo Mase, displays and sells items made by hand, from the cloth right down to the buttons. It has been in business for 20 years, takes pride in quality and does not give discounts. You could visit as part of our French Concession walking tour (p95).

BROCADE COUNTRY
Map pp86-7   Handicrafts
锦绣纺 Jǐnxiù Fǎng
☎ 6279 2677; 616 Julu Rd; 巨鹿路616号;
☺ 10.30am-7pm; Ⓜ Changshu Rd
Peruse an exquisite collection of minority handicrafts from China's southwest, most of which are second-hand (ie not made for the tourist trade) and personally selected by the owner Liu Xiaolan, a Guìzhōu native. Items for sale include embroidered wall hangings (some of which were originally baby carriers), sashes, shoes and hats, as well as silver jewellery. The butterfly, a homonym for 'mother' in the Miao language, is a popular motif.

PARAMITA Map pp86-7   Handicrafts
波罗蜜多西藏工艺品 Bōluómìduō Xīzàng Gōngyìpǐn
☎ 6248 2148; 850-1 Julu Rd; 巨鹿路850-1号;
☺ 10am-10pm; Ⓜ Changshu Rd/Jing'an Temple
If you can't make it to Tibet, at least swing by Paramita for its inspiring collection of souvenirs, including yak-bone amulets (Y90), masks, jewellery, framed mandalas

and other Buddhist treasures from the Himalayas. It's a nonprofit organisation, founded to help Tibetans with minimal education find employment.

SKYLIGHT Map pp86-7 Handicrafts
天籁 Tiān Lài

☎ 6473 5610; 28 West Fuxing Rd; 复兴西路28号; ⏱ 9.30am-9pm; Ⓜ Changshu Rd

Sneak into this lovely little incense-perfumed nook opposite the Iranian consulate for its small haul of hand-crafted Tibetan jewellery, antiques and furniture. There are also a few exquisite *thangka* – sacred Buddhist paintings on silk – and colour photographs taken by the owner during his voyages across the Tibetan plateau.

SIMPLY LIFE Map pp86-7 Homewares
逸居生活 Yìjū Shēnghuó

☎ 6387 5100; Unit 101, North Block Xīntiāndì, 159 Madang Rd; 马当路159号新天地北里101单元; ⏱ 10.30am-10pm; Ⓜ South Huangpi Rd/Xintiandi

Come here for upmarket household knick-knacks, including hand-painted tea sets, crockery and pottery, all of which is locally made. There's a smaller branch on Dongping Rd (Map pp86-7; ☎ 3406 0509; 9 Dongping Rd; 东平路9号; Ⓜ Changshu Rd).

MADAME MAO'S DOWRY
Map pp86-7 Souvenirs
毛太设计 Máotài Shèjì

☎ 5403 3551; 207 Fumin Rd; 富民路207号; ⏱ 10am-7pm; Ⓜ Jing'an Temple

Everyone needs some Revolution-era collector's items somewhere in the house. What better way to brighten up the foyer than with a bust of the Chairman? Or why not make a statement in the kitchen with a poster of happy socialist workers? If reminiscing of the Mao days leaves you cold, peruse the apolitical designer items: antique furniture, modern ceramics, vintage clothing and T-shirts from Shirt Flag (p143).

PROPAGANDA POSTER ART CENTRE
Map pp86-7 Art, Souvenirs
上海宣传画艺术中心 Shànghǎi Xuānchuánhuà Yìshù Zhōngxīn

☎ 6211 1845, 1390 184 1246; Room B-OC, 868 Huashan Rd; 华山路868号B-OC房间; admission Y20; ⏱ 9am-4pm; taxi

If socialist art is your thing, check out this gallery which houses a huge collection of propaganda posters. Increasingly prized by collectors, some of them are very rare and prices are correspondingly high. The cheapest start at around Y1000. But there are also lots of cartoons and memorabilia, which are more affordable. Mr Yang, who runs the place, speaks good English and will show you around. Ask to see his collection of *dàzìbào*, the hand-written posters used to denounce people during the Cultural Revolution. This is the only place on the mainland you'll see them; most young Chinese have never seen one. The beautiful calligraphy makes for a huge contrast with the violence of the language the writers used. See p92 for more details on this place.

SPRINGHEAD
Map pp86-7 Handicrafts, Souvenirs
根源 Gēnyuán

☎ 6473 9837; Taikang Rd Art Centre, No 17, Lane 274, Taikang Rd; 泰康路274弄17号田子坊; ⏱ 9am-10pm; Ⓜ Dapuqiao

This handicrafts shop has an intriguing collection of folk-art prints as well as diaries, paper cuts and communist-era enamel mugs and bowls (Y35). A nearby branch (No 26, Lane 274) continues the retro theme with propaganda poster reproductions (Y10 to Y20) from the 1960s.

YĚ HUǑ HÙWÀI YÒNGPǏN DIÀN
Map pp86-7 Outdoor Gear
野火户外用品店

☎ 5386 0591; 296 Changle Rd; 长乐路296号; ⏱ 10.30am-10pm; Ⓜ South Shanxi Rd

A great store for outdoor gear. Osprey packs and Vasque boots are available, in addition to quality Gore-Tex clothing, tents and sleeping bags.

ZHENCHALIN TEA Map pp86-7 Tea
臻茶林 Zhēnchálín

☎ 6473 0507; Taikang Rd Art Centre, No 13, Lane 210, Taikang Rd; 泰康路210弄13号田子坊; ⏱ 10am-8pm; Ⓜ Dapuqiao

From the entrance this looks like just another tea shop, but poke around inside and you'll find specially blended herbal teas (Y40) from Ayako, a TCM-certified nutritionist. Peruse the hand-wrapped *pu-erh* teas, ceramic and crystal teaware, and water-colour postcards of Shànghǎi while staff ply you with tiny cups of ginseng oolong to keep you lingering.

JÌNG'ĀN 静安区

West Nanjing Rd is more upmarket and elitist than the eastern end. It's home to the high-end Western fashion brands and luxury items, as well as Shànghǎi's most exclusive malls, like Plaza 66 (恒隆广场; Hénglóng Guǎngchǎng; 1266 West Nanjing Rd; 南京西路1266号). Behind People's Sq is Dagu Rd, which has a number of large DVD stores.

ART DECO

Map pp98-9   Antiques

凹凸家具库 **Āotū Jiājù Kù**

☎ 6277 8927; Bldg 7, 50 Moganshan Rd; 莫干山路50号7号楼; ☽ 10am-7pm; Ⓜ Shanghai Train Station

For stylish period furnishings that match the Peace Hotel's streamlined aplomb, stop by artist Ding Yi's gallery in the M50 complex (p97). His standout antique collection includes folding screens, armoires, tables and chairs, with a few vintage poster girls on the walls to help recapture the 1930s magic. Chairs start at around Y1200.

FENSHINE FASHION & ACCESSORIES PLAZA Map pp98-9 Clothes

风翔服饰礼品广场 **Fèngxiáng Fúshì Lǐpǐn Guǎngchǎng**

580 West Nanjing Rd; 南京西路580号; ☽ 9am-9pm; Ⓜ West Nanjing Rd

This unassuming-looking building is the best location to pick up quality knock-offs, with hundreds of stalls spread across two floors. Scavenge for bags, belts, jackets, shoes, suitcases, sunglasses, ties, T-shirts and electronics. Amy Lin's Pearls (right) is located here. Bargain hard.

AMY LIN'S PEARLS Map pp98-9 Pearls

艾敏林氏珍珠 **Àimǐn Línshì Zhēnzhū**

☎ 5228 2372; Room 30, 3rd fl, 580 West Nanjing Rd; 南京西路580号3楼30号; ☽ 10am-8pm; Ⓜ West Nanjing Rd

The most reliable retailer of pearls of all colours and sizes. Both freshwater pearls (from Y80), including prized black Zhèjiāng pearls (from Y3000), and saltwater pearls (from Y200) are available here. The staff speak English and will string your selection for you. They do jade and jewellery too. Another shop is in the AP Xinyang Fashion & Gifts Market (Map p114).

JINGDEZHEN PORCELAIN ARTWARE

Map pp98-9   Porcelain

景德镇艺术瓷器 **Jǐngdézhèn Yìshù Cíqì**

☎ 6253 8865; 212 North Shaanxi Rd; 陕西北路212号; ☽ 10am-10pm; Ⓜ West Nanjing Rd

This is one of the best places for traditional Chinese porcelain. Blue-and-white vases, plates, teapots and cups are some of the many choices available. Credit cards are accepted, and shipping overseas can be arranged.

PǓDŌNG & CENTURY AVENUE AREA 浦东

As the district heats up, more and more strip malls and department stores are opening along South Pudong Rd, Zhangyang Rd and Century Ave. Further out, all the material goods you'll ever need in one lifetime are found in the market in Science & Technology Museum metro station (opposite). There is also a Carrefour (p156) and shopping plaza

---

TEA TASTING

It may be a rather clichéd choice, but there's no doubt that a Yixing teapot and a package of oolong tea makes for a convenient gift. But how do you go about a purchase? Two things to remember: first, taste (品尝; pǐncháng) and compare several different teas – flavours vary widely, and there's no point in buying a premium grade if you don't like it. Tasting is free (免费; miǎnfèi) and fun, but it's good form to make some sort of purchase afterwards. Second, tea is generally priced by the jīn (500g; 斤), which may be more tea than you can finish in a year. Purchase several liǎng (50g; 两) instead – divide the list price by ten for an idea of the final cost. Some of the different types of tea for sale include oolong (wūlóng), green (lù), flower (huā), and pu-erh (pǔ'ěr) – true connoisseurs have a different teapot for each type of tea.

Try the following stores.

Huifeng Tea Shop (汇丰茶庄; Huìfēng Cházhuāng; Map pp86–7; 124 South Maoming Rd; 茂名南路124号; ☽ 9am-9.30pm; Ⓜ South Shanxi Rd)

Yányè Míngchá (严叶茗茶; Map pp86–7; 170 Fumin Rd; 富民路170号; ☽ 8am-10pm; Ⓜ Jing'an Temple)

Zhenchalin Tea (p145)

located next to the Zendai Museum of Modern Art (p113).

SUPERBRAND MALL

Map p108   Mall

正大广场 **Zhèngdà Guǎngchǎng**

☎ 6887 7888; 168 West Lujiazui Rd; 陆家嘴西路168号; ⏰ 10am-10pm; Ⓜ Lujiazui Rd
The most popular mall in the area, this behemoth is always busy. It's most notable for its dining options, which range from the 10th-floor restaurant South Beauty (p173), which has great Bund views, to the food court in the basement. There's also a supermarket in the basement, a kid's arcade on the 6th floor and a cinema and ice-skating rink (Y70 for two hours) on the 8th floor.

AP XINYANG FASHION & GIFTS MARKET

Map p108   Souvenirs

亚太新阳服饰礼品市场 **Yàtài Xīnyáng Fúshì Lǐpǐn Shìchǎng**

⏰ 10am-8pm; Ⓜ Science & Technology Museum
Below ground in the Science & Technology Museum metro station is Shànghǎi's largest collection of shopping stalls, which includes a branch of the Shiliupu Fabric Market (p139) and an entire separate market place devoted exclusively to pearls. Amy Lin's Pearls (opposite) also has a shop in the main area (A3-66). There is a vast selection here, including shoes, sports equipment, T-shirts, toys, electronics, Indian saris, jeans…well, you get the picture. Make sure to bargain hard.

HÓNGKǑU & NORTH SHÀNGHǍI

虹口区、北上海

Head for the area north of Suzhou Creek to see where the masses shop. Factory (p174) also has a small collection of locally designed items for sale.

QIPU MARKET
Map p116   Clothes

七浦服装市场 **Qīpǔ Fúzhuāng Shìchǎng**
168 & 183 Qipu Rd; 七浦路168 & 183号;
⏰ 5am-5pm (west side), 7am-7pm (east side);
Ⓜ Tiantong Rd
Qipu Market is where ordinary Shànghǎi goes shopping for clothes. Consisting of two rundown, rabbit warren–like depart-

ment stores surrounding the North Henan Rd intersection, it's one big 'everything must go now' sale here. This ain't Plaza 66 (opposite), so do as the locals do and push through the hordes of people searching for T-shirts, shoes, tank tops, dresses, shorts, pretty much any item of clothing you can find for around Y50. It's exhausting and exhilarating in equal measure and very Shànghǎi. Haggle here; you should be paying at least 50% below the asking price.

ELECTRONICS MARKET
Map p116   Electronics

电子市场 **Diànzǐ Shìchǎng**
Qiujiang Rd; 虬江路; ⏰ 9.30am-5.30pm;
Ⓜ Baoshan Rd
If you want to put together your own computer, replace a processor, soup up an

CLOTHING SIZES

The measurements below are approximate. Remember that Chinese sizes are far smaller than Western ones; an extra large in China is equivalent to a size 10 in the US or size 12 in the UK. Always try on clothes before buying them.

Women's clothing

Aus/UK	8	10	12	14	16	18
Europe	36	38	40	42	44	46
Japan	5	7	9	11	13	15
USA	6	8	10	12	14	16

Women's shoes

Aus/USA	5	6	7	8	9	10
Europe	35	36	37	38	39	40
France only	35	36	38	39	40	42
Japan	22	23	24	25	26	27
UK	3½	4½	5½	6½	7½	8½

Men's clothing

Aus	92	96	100	104	108	112
Europe	46	48	50	52	54	56
Japan	S		M	M		L
UK/USA	35	36	37	38	39	40

Men's shirts (collar sizes)

Aus/Japan	38	39	40	41	42	43
Europe	38	39	40	41	42	43
UK/USA	15	15½	16	16½	17	17½

Men's shoes

Aus/UK	7	8	9	10	11	12
Europe	41	42	43	44½	46	47
Japan	26	27	27½	28	29	30
USA	7½	8½	9½	10½	11½	12½

SHOPPING HÓNGKǑU & NORTH SHÀNGHǍI

MP3 player or score a pair of speakers for the apartment, try this market located right under the elevated train tracks that lead into Baoshan Rd metro. It's a Cybermart for people who don't mind the lack of a guarantee or receipt. Prices are low and negotiable (DVD players go from Y150 up), but how long everything will last is another matter.

XÚJIĀHUÌ & SOUTH SHÀNGHĂI
徐家汇、南上海

Xújiāhuì is best known for its collection of department stores and malls that ring an insanely busy intersection. Don't try crossing the roads; use the underground metro tunnels to get to the stores.

METRO CITY

Map p122   Electronics

美罗城 **Měiluó Chéng**

☎ 6426 8380; 1111 Zhaojiabang Rd; 肇嘉浜路 1111号; ⏰ 10am-10pm; Ⓜ Xujiahui

Half of this mall is about technology, selling electronics, computers and software; the other half is all about fun, with a Sega arcade and a Megabite (boxed text, p158) in the basement and Kodak Cinema World (p190) on the 5th floor. Next door is the Pacific Digital Plaza (1117 Zhaojiabang Rd), another electronics emporium that spreads across two buildings.

GRAND GATEWAY

Map p122   Mall

港汇广场 **Gǎnghuì Guǎngchǎng**

☎ 6407 0111; 1 Hongqiao Rd; 虹桥路1号; ⏰ 10am-10pm; Ⓜ Xujiahui

Possibly the most popular mall in the city, Grand Gateway is a vast airy space with a decent range of Western brands like Agnes B, Benetton, Diesel, DKNY, Jack Jones and Levi's, as well as a big selection of cosmetics and sports gear. The complex also has an excellent range of restaurants on the 5th and 6th floors and an outside food strip, with outlets of Crystal Jade (p165), Element Fresh (p171) and Wagas (p172) among numerous other options.

CHÁNGNÍNG, GŬBĚI & HONGQIAO AIRPORT AREA 长宁、古北

The western part of town boasts the city's best selection of antique furniture shops. Many of these can direct you to even larger warehouses further west on the Huqingping Hwy. The shops listed in this section all offer a certificate of authenticity, accept credit cards and can handle shipping and customs for you. In this area you'll also find the biggest and best-stocked Carrefour (p156) in Shànghǎi.

CHINE ANTIQUES

Map pp128-9   Antiques

☎ 6270 1023; 1665 Hongqiao Rd; 虹桥路 1665号; ⏰ 10am-7.30pm; Ⓜ Shuicheng Rd

This is one of the glossiest antique stores, with prices at the higher end of the spectrum. This branch is at the Liu Haisu Art Gallery (p130) and there's a warehouse on the western outskirts. A small branch office in the Old Town (Map p79; ☎ 6387 4100; 38 Liuhekou Rd; 浏河口路38号), just off Dongtai Rd, can direct you to another warehouse a couple of minutes' walk away.

GUYI ANTIQUE FURNITURE

Map pp62-3   Antiques

古意古典家具有限公司 **Gǔyì Gǔdiǎn Jiājù Yǒuxiàngōngsī**

☎ 5422 2479; No 59, Lane 175, Wanyuan Rd; 万源路175弄59号; ⏰ 9.30am-6pm; Ⓜ Hechuan Rd

There aren't many genuine antiques here, but there are a lot of good-quality reproductions and it's especially strong on screens, cabinets and desks. They speak English.

HENRY ANTIQUE WAREHOUSE

Map p132   Antiques

亨利古典家具 **Hēnglì Gǔdiǎn Jiājù**

☎ 6401 0831; www.h-antique.com; 3rd fl, Bldg 2, 359 Hongzhong Rd; 虹中路359号2号楼3层; ⏰ 9am-6pm; taxi

This enormous showroom, with more than 2000 high-quality antique pieces, both large and small, is a good first stop for antique hunters. It's down a lane off Hongzhong Rd in a not-so-obvious location; look for the signs. The Traditional Furniture research department of Tongji University is based here.

ZHŌNGZHŌNG JIĀYUÁN JIĀJU

Map p132   Antiques

中国古典家具艺术精品总汇

☎ 6406 4066; 3050 Hechuan Rd; 合川路3050号;
☾ 8am-8pm; taxi

There are more pieces, including hundreds
of wooden screens, here under one roof
than anyone can take the time for. Ask to
see all the rooms (about 15!), including the
unrestored pieces in the warehouse, but
only if you have a spare day or two. The
sales staff are slicker and prices slightly
higher than at some other places in town,
but if you're looking for something specific, they might just have it.

HONGQIAO INTERNATIONAL PEARL
CITY Map p132   Pearls

虹桥国际珍珠城 Hóngqiáo Guójì Zhēnzhū
Chéng

☎ 6465 0183; 2nd fl, Hongqiao Craft Market,
3721 Hongmei Rd; 虹梅路3721号虹桥市场
2楼; ☾ 10am-9pm; taxi

Popular with the local expats, the 2nd floor
of this market has a smaller selection of
freshwater and saltwater pearls than Amy
Lin's Pearls (p146), but is worth a browse. It's a
relaxed atmosphere and you can bargain
here. On the 1st floor there are clothes
and golf gear, on the 3rd floor carpets and
luggage.

top picks

What's your recommendation? lonelyplanet.com/shanghai

EATING

Shànghǎi is most alive at the end of the day, when workers pour out of the offices, the neon flickers on and the restaurants begin to fill up. As in the rest of China, food is at the centre of social life here, and even the most straight-laced individuals loosen their ties once dinner is served. Restaurants are where people go to meet friends or dates, to hold family reunions, to celebrate or drown their sorrows and to clinch business deals. It's over a meal that the Chinese are at their most relaxed and sociable, and, suffice it to say, eating out is one of Shànghǎi's great highlights. If you get a chance to eat with the locals, jump at it.

In true Shànghǎi style, today's restaurant scene is a reflection of the city's craving for foreign trends and tastes, whether they come in the form of Hunanese chilli peppers or French *amuse-bouche* (bite-sized hors d'ouevre courses). Most visitors will be interested in the Chinese end of the spectrum, of course, for that's where the best cooking is as well as the most variety. On a single strip you might find Shanghainese seafood, explosively hot Sichuanese, a Cantonese tea restaurant and MSG-free Taiwanese soup noodles – and that's just on your first night out. Still, Shànghǎi has become a magnet for both global superchefs and less-established international talents trying to make a name for themselves, and it's worth taking note of their presence; there are some fine meals to be had here.

But while a dinner overlooking the Huangpu River or safe in the Xīntiāndì bubble makes for a nice treat, real foodies know that the best restaurants in China are often where you least expect to find them. Part of the fun of eating out in Shànghǎi is stumbling across those tiny places in malls, metro stations or down backstreets that offer an unexpectedly memorable dining experience. Nor should you be put off by eating in chain restaurants; many of Shànghǎi's better eateries have branches scattered across town. The downside of this admirable lack of snobbery is that Chinese restaurants aren't great for romantic meals; they're often brightly lit, large and noisy, with in-your-face waiting staff. If you want a romantic soirée, go international.

Of course, the major obstacle for foreigners trying to enjoying authentic Chinese meals has long been the indecipherable menus that can be as thick and overwhelming as a 14th-century martial-arts novel. But Shànghǎi continues to improve on this account, and we are happy to state that almost all of the places listed in this chapter have English menus (some also have picture menus which are an enormous help) unless noted, and although they aren't always as comprehensive (or comprehensible) as the Chinese version, you'll no longer feel trapped into ordering *kung pao* chicken at every meal. In any case, if you see a dish on someone else's table that looks absolutely delicious, just point at it when the waiter comes – no one will think you're being rude. Shànghǎi's restaurants reward the adventurous, so be brave, because some of your most memorable experiences will be culinary ones. Just do what the Shanghainese do and dig in with those chopsticks.

ETIQUETTE

Strict rules of etiquette don't apply to Chinese dining; table manners are relaxed and get more so as the meal unfolds and the drinks flow. Meals commence in Confucian fashion – with good intentions, harmonic arrangement of chopsticks and a clean tablecloth – before spiralling into total Taoist mayhem, fuelled by incessant toasts with *báijiǔ* (a white spirit) or beer and furious smoking all round. Large groups in particular wreak havoc wherever they dine, with vast quantities of food often strewn across and under the table at the end of a meal.

A typical dining scenario sees a group of people seated at a round table, often with one person ordering on everyone's behalf. At Chinese restaurants, group diners never order their own dishes, but instead a selection of dishes embracing both *ròu* (meat) and *cài* (vegetables) are chosen for everyone to share. Rice normally comes at the end of the meal. If you want it before, just ask. At large tables, dishes are placed on a lazy Susan, so the food revolves to each diner, occasionally knocking over full glasses of beer and causing consternation.

The mainland Chinese dig their chopsticks into communal dishes (in Hong Kong, people are more fastidious), although some dishes are ladled out with spoons. Don't worry too much about your chopstick technique; many Chinese are equally fazed by knives and forks. There's no shame in being defeated by a dumpling or bamboozled by broccoli.

In smarter restaurants, you'll be given plastic or bamboo chopsticks. Cheaper places use disposable chopsticks, which are more hygienic but not great for the environment. China gets through 45 billion pairs annually, which is a lot of bamboo. (Shànghǎi, like many Chinese cities, now imposes a tax on disposable chopsticks.) Whatever type you use, don't point them at people and don't stick them upright in bowls of rice; it's a portent of death.

Remember to fill your neighbours' tea cups when they are empty, or beer glasses, as yours will be filled by them. You can thank the pourer by gently tapping your middle finger on the table. It's considered bad manners to serve yourself tea or any drink without serving others first. The Chinese toast each other much more than in the West, often each time they drink. A toast is conducted by raising your glass in both hands in the direction of the toastee and crying out *gānbēi*, literally 'dry the glass'. That's the cue to drain your glass in one hit.

Nonsmokers can find China's restaurants a trial (smoking is an essential part of the Chinese banquet experience), although Shànghǎi has gone out on a limb and asked that some 6000 restaurants and hotels go nonsmoking by 2010, with more to follow. It seems highly unlikely that regular restaurants will bother to enforce this regulation, though most upscale places will probably have at least a nonsmoking section in place by the time this guide is published. If you do smoke, hand your cigarettes around as Chinese smokers are generous to the last.

Chinese toothpick etiquette is similar to that of neighbouring Asian countries. One hand wields the toothpick while the other shields the mouth from prying eyes. Coping with the bill also requires some skill. The Chinese like to compete to pay, but don't argue too much as the person who extended the invitation will inevitably foot the bill.

Staff are not used to diners leafing at length through the menu at the door. You may have to take a seat and scope the menu; you can always get up and leave if you don't like the look of it. Chinese waiting staff hover annoyingly at the elbow while you read the menu, but there's nothing wrong with saying *wǒ huì jiào nǐ* (I'll call you).

SHÀNGHǍI CUISINE

Shànghǎi cuisine is influenced by neighbouring Zhèjiāng and Jiāngsū, and is defined, along with Sūzhōu and Hángzhōu cuisines, as Yángzhōu

top picks

SHANGHAINESE RESTAURANTS

You can't leave Shànghǎi without trying hairy crab, eel and jellyfish. Or can you?

- **Bǎoluó Jiǔlóu** (p166) Pandemonium and lip-smackingly good lemon-drizzled eel – experience the Shànghǎi buzz at its no-frills best.
- **Yang's Fry Dumplings** (p159) Dumplings hot off the wok.
- **Fu 1039** (p170) Drunken shrimp, hidden villa.
- **Jíshì Jiǔlóu** (p165) All the classics, just like *pópo* (grandma) used to make.
- **Lánxīn Cāntīng** (p168) A family-run hole-in-the-wall = yum!
- **Lynn** (p170) Shanghainese meets Cantonese and everyone's a winner.
- **Xiǎo Nán Guó** (p159) Stylish chain where the price is right.

or Huáiyáng cuisine. It is generally sweeter and oilier than China's other cuisines.

Shànghǎi's position as a major port at the head of the Yangzi Delta means that the cuisine features plenty of fish and seafood, especially cod, river eel and shrimp. The word for fish (*yú*) is a homonym for 'plenty' or 'surplus', and fish is a mandatory dish for most banquets and celebrations.

Common Shanghainese fish dishes include *sōngrén yùmǐ* (pine nuts and sweet corn), *guìyú* (steamed Mandarin fish), *lúyú* (Songjiang perch), *chāngyú* (pomfret), and *huángyú* (yellow croaker). Fish is usually *qīngzhēng* (steamed) but can be stir-fried, pan-fried or grilled. Crab-roe dumplings are another Shanghainese luxury. Both fish and seafood are usually priced by weight, either per 50g or 500g.

Squirrel-shaped Mandarin fish is a famous dish from Sūzhōu. The dish dates from a political assassination during the Warring States period (453–221 BC), when a dagger was hidden in the thick sauce until the assassin struck.

Several restaurants specialise in *xiánjī* (cold salty chicken), which tastes better than it sounds. *Zuìjī* (drunken chicken) is marinated in Shàoxīng rice wine. *Bāo* (clay pot) meals are braised for a long time in their own casserole dish. Shànghǎi's most famous snack is *xiǎolóngbāo* – small dumplings with a meaty interior, bathed in a scalding juice.

Vegetarian dishes include *dòufu* (bean curd), *sōngrén yùmǐ* (pine nuts and sweet corn), *mèn dòufu* (braised bean curd) and various types of mushrooms, including *xiānggū báicài* (mushrooms surrounded by baby bok choy). *Hǔpí jiānjiāo* (tiger skin chillies) is a delicious dish of stir-fried green peppers, seared in a wok and served in a sweet chilli sauce.

Dàzháxiè (hairy crabs) are a Shànghǎi speciality between October and December. They are eaten with soy, ginger and vinegar and downed with warm Shàoxīng rice wine. The crab is thought to increase the body's *yīn*, or coldness, and so rice wine is taken lukewarm to add *yáng*. Aficionados say that the best crabs come from Yangcheng Lake and are black with hairy feet. Male and female crabs are supposed to be eaten together. They are delicious but can be fiddly to eat. The body opens via a little tab on the underside (don't eat the gills or the stomach).

VEGETARIANS & VEGANS

Chīzhāi (vegetarianism) became something of a snobbish fad in Shànghǎi in the 1930s, when it was linked to Taoist and Buddhist groups. It's now undergoing a minor revival, although there's nothing like the huge vegetarian and vegan populations in countries such as the UK or the USA. Beyond Buddhist reasons, very few Chinese give up meat as an ethical choice. But there are a growing band of vegetarian restaurants in Shànghǎi, while monasteries (such as the Jade Buddha Temple, p100) all have good vegetarian restaurants.

SNACKS

Shànghǎi has some great snacks (*xiǎo chī*, literally 'little eats') and it's worth trying out as many of them as possible. They are cheap and quick, and there's no need to labour through any 15-page Chinese menus. Traditional snacks are becoming harder to come by though; visit the food streets (p160) for the best selection.

Look out for *xiǎolóngbāo* (literally 'little steamer buns'), Shànghǎi's favourite dumpling – copied everywhere else in China, but only true to form here. There's an art to eating them as they're full of scalding broth – the trick is to avoid both burning your tongue and staining your shirt. Tradition actually attributes the invention of the dumpling – filled with pork, and in more upmarket establishments, with pork and crab – to Nánxiāng, a village north of Shànghǎi city. Dumplings are normally bought by the *lóng* (steamer basket), though large versions are sold individually for about Y1 each.

Another Shanghainese speciality is *shēngjiān*, similar to *guōtiē* (pot stickers) and fried in a black pan with a wooden lid. Again, watch out for the palate-scorching scalding oil. Several Shanghainese restaurants serve *luóbosībǐng* (fried turnip cakes), which make a good beer snack. On the sweet side are *tāng yuán* (also known as *yuán xiāo*), a small glutinous rice ball filled with black sesame paste, red bean paste or another sweet filling that's traditionally eaten during the Lantern Festival, and is absolutely delicious. You can find them easily in Qìbǎo (p131) at any time of year.

Shuǐjiǎo (dumplings), which originated in northern China, are perhaps best described as Chinese ravioli – stuffed with pork, spring onion and greens. They are sometimes served by the bowl in a soup, or alternatively dry, by weight (250g, or half a *jīn*, is normally enough). Locals mix *làjiāo* (chilli), *cù* (vinegar) and *jiàngyóu* (soy sauce) in a little bowl according to taste and dip the dumplings in. Note that vinegar and soy sauce look almost identical, although vinegar is slightly lighter in colour. The slippery little guys can be tricky to eat with chopsticks so don't wear your best shirt as you'll get sprayed in soy sauce whenever you accidentally drop them in the bowl. *Shuǐjiǎo* are often created by family minifactories – one person stretches the pastry, another makes the filling and a third spoons the filling into the pastry, finishing it off with a little twist.

A hugely popular winter meal is *huǒguō* (hotpot), with several chain restaurants cornering the market. There are two varieties of hotpot: Sìchuān and Mongolian. A typical Sìchuān version is the circular *yuānyāng* hotpot, compartmentalised into hot (red) and mild (creamy-coloured) sections, into which you plunge vegetables and meats. Plucking the cooked chunks from the broth, diners douse them in spicy sauces and then tuck in. It's a sweat-inducing experience that should be done with a group. Mongolian hotpots differ in both appearance and flavour. These are typically a brass pot with a central stove, focusing on thin slices of lamb and vegetables with a nonspicy broth. Again, they are accompanied by sauces. Mongolian- and Korean-inspired barbecued meats are also popular.

Other street snacks include *chòu dòufu* (stinky tofu; the sharp aroma of which brings tears to the eyes), *yángròuchuàn* (lamb kebabs) and *dìguā* (baked sweet potatoes). Also look out for *málàtàng*, a spicy soup into which are chucked loads of mushrooms, *dòufu*, cabbage, fish balls and noodles.

Keep an eye open for *sōnghuādàn* (thousand-year eggs), duck eggs that are covered in straw and stored underground for long periods of time – the traditional recipe has them soaked in horse urine before burial! The yolk becomes green and the white becomes jelly. More interesting snacks available at markets include chickens' feet, pigs' ears, pigs' trotters and even pigs' faces.

The Chinese are masters at adding variety to vegetarian cooking and, to the bemusement of Western vegetarians, they like to create so-called 'mock meat' dishes. Chinese vegetarian food is based on *dòufu* (bean curd), to which crafty chefs add their magic. Not only is it made to taste like any meaty food you could possibly think of, it's also made to resemble it; a dish sculptured to look like spare ribs or fish can be created with layered pieces of dried bean curd, or fashioned from mashed taro root or mushrooms.

DESSERTS & SWEETS

The Chinese do not generally eat dessert, but fruit – typically *xīguā* (watermelon) or *chéng* (oranges) – often concludes a good meal. Ice cream can be ordered in some places, but in general sweet desserts are consumed as snacks and are seldom available in restaurants.

An exception to the rule are caramelised fruits, such as *básī píngguǒ* (caramelised apple), *básī xiāngjiāo* (caramelised banana) and even *básī tǔdòu* (caramelised potato), which you can find in several restaurants. Other sweeties include *tāngyuán* (small, sweet, glutinous balls, traditionally from Níngbō, filled with red bean paste, black sesame paste or something similarly sweet), *bīngshā* (literally 'frozen sand', shaved ice and syrup), *bābǎofàn* (a sweet, sticky rice pudding known as eight-treasures rice), and various types of steamed buns filled with sweet bean paste.

Bīngtáng húlu (toffee crab apples) and *cǎoméi* (strawberries) on a stick are favoured winter treats. *Lìzi* (roast chestnuts), sold from the roadside, are also popular in winter and wayside *bàomǐhuā* (popcorn) sellers are a common sight. The Shanghainese are fond of *dàntà* (egg tarts), and Shànghǎi's bakeries also stock a wide range of Western cakes, tarts and breads.

Several shops around the Yuyuan Gardens (p78) have been selling pear-syrup sweets since 1894.

PRACTICALITIES
Opening Hours

In general, the Chinese eat earlier than Westerners. Restaurants serve lunch from 11am to 2pm and then often close until 5pm, when the dinner crowd starts arriving, and then carry on serving until 10pm. Smaller restaurants are more flexible, and if you're

top picks

VEGETARIAN & HEALTH-FOOD RESTAURANTS

- **Vegetarian Lifestyle** (p172) Hip, delicious and…surprise! It's organic too.
- **Element Fresh** (p171) Snappy gourmet sandwiches and killer smoothies.
- **Gōngdélín** (p173) Austere vegetarian beneath honeycombed lamps.
- **Longhua Temple** (p121) and **Jade Buddha Temple** (p100) These temple restaurants have been doing this for hundreds of years.
- **Sōngyuèlóu** (p161) Shànghǎi's oldest vegie joint, still going strong on a diet of tofu and soup.

hungry out of hours they'll be happy to accommodate you. Shànghǎi also stays up late, so there are plenty of spots where you can dine at the wee hours. Popular places open 24 hours, or close to it, include Bǎoluó Jiǔlóu (p166), Bellagio Café (p165), the Changle Rd outlet of Bì Fēng Táng (p170), Yī Jiā Yī (p169) and the Velvet Lounge (p183). Nonstandard opening hours are included in the individual restaurant reviews.

How Much?

Compared with other major cities such as Tokyo, Hong Kong, New York or Paris, Shànghǎi can be a bargain. People coming from other areas in China, however – even Běijīng – may be shocked at the prices; Shànghǎi is the most expensive city on the mainland, and the street food so common elsewhere in the country continues to disappear. Basic backstreet noodle and dumpling shops continue to hang on in some parts of the city, where you can eat for about Y10, and dishes at mall food courts and noodle chains (like Ajisen) generally start at around Y30. In general, though, count on spending about Y60 for a decent Chinese meal, which will include two to three dishes plus rice. A nice dinner for two will probably run anywhere from Y160 to Y200, while the fanciest meals in the city can easily top Y500 per head. If you choose to frequent midrange Western restaurants and bars, expect to pay about what you'd pay back home (eg Y80 for a burger). Remember that only top-end places take credit cards, so make sure you have enough cash on you.

Booking Tables

The economic recession dampened the passion for eating out, but you should still reserve anywhere that is popular. At high-end restaurants like T8 (p161), Jean Georges (opposite) and M on The Bund (opposite), it's sometimes necessary to book a week ahead if you want a decent table with a view, especially if there's a big event like the Shanghai International Film Festival or the Formula One Grand Prix happening. Generally though, a couple of days in advance is OK. At other spots, a day ahead is normally fine. Even if you don't have a reservation, most places will do their best to squeeze you in after a wait.

Tipping & Service

If there's one dining experience that drives foreigners in Shànghǎi crazy, it's the service. To be fair, some Shanghainese seem to have a natural surliness that rivals Parisian waiters in days of yore, but more often than not, the real problem behind most service complaints is the language barrier. Remember that many wait staff will only have a minimal command of English, and unless you are able to hold your own in Mandarin (or Shanghainese), there will inevitably be a few mix-ups and scowling faces somewhere along the way. Occasionally a waiter or waitress will be so intimidated by a non-Chinese-speaking customer that they will, unfortunately, completely ignore you, especially if it's a busy night.

Tipping is mostly not done in Shànghǎi. If you do tip in a local restaurant, you might wind up with some good-natured soul running after you because they think you've forgotten your change. High-end international restaurants are another matter and while tipping is not obligatory, it is encouraged. Hotel restaurants automatically add a 15% service charge.

Self-Catering

Shànghǎi has more than 5000 convenience stores, and most of them are open 24 hours. The most common supermarkets are Lawson, Kedi and Allday. A step up are the growing number of local supermarkets such as Hualian, Lianhua, Homegain (Jiādélì) and Tops (Dǐngdǐngxiān). Short-term visitors will find

PRICE RANGE FOR RESTAURANTS

YYY	over Y160 a meal
YY	Y60-160 a meal
Y	up to Y60 a meal

most of what they need at these places. Long-term visitors will need to look elsewhere for bread, dairy products, wine and meat. French hypermarket Carrefour and the local City Shop are good places to start. One convenient supermarket is in the basement of the Parkson department store (Map pp86–7) at Middle Huaihai Rd and South Shaanxi Rd. There's another, smaller supermarket in the basement of the Westgate Mall (Map pp98–9).

CARREFOUR Map pp128-9   Supermarket
家乐福 Jiālèfú
☎ 6278 1944; www.carrefour.com.cn; 268 Shuicheng Rd; 水城路268号; ⏱ 7.30am-10pm; Ⓜ Shuicheng Rd
This French chain is currently the only foreign supermarket that actually turns a profit and at nights and weekends the place is packed, largely because prices are the same as those in Chinese supermarkets. You can find everything from imported wines and French bread to cheap bikes and crockery. The Gǔběi branch has the widest range of Western food. There are currently nineteen branches in the greater Shànghǎi area, including one north of Zhongshan Park in Pǔtuó (Map pp98–9; ☎ 800-620 0565; 20 Wuning Rd; 武宁路20号); and another in Pǔdōng (Map p114; ☎ 800-820 0871; 185 Fangdian Rd; 方甸路185号).

CITY SHOP Map pp98-9   Supermarket
城市超市 Chéngshì Chāoshì
☎ 6215 0418 (all branches); www.cityshop.com.cn; Shanghai Centre, 1376 West Nanjing Rd; 南京西路1376号; ⏱ 8am-10pm; Ⓜ Jing'an Temple
For all those imported goodies you just can't get anywhere else – at a price. The Shanghai Centre branch offers 50% off bakery items after 7pm. There are seven branches, including ones in Times Square (Map pp86–7; basement, 99 Middle Huaihai Rd; 淮海中路99号B1) and Hóngqiáo (Map p132; 3211 Hongmei Rd; 虹梅路3211号). Free delivery service.

THE BUND & PEOPLE'S SQUARE
外滩、人民广场

The Bund is Shànghǎi's epicentre of global chic. This is where international superchefs and hotel restaurants vying for China's first Michelin star have established themselves. While the settings are often spectacular, there's far less diversity here than in the French

Concession. Count on spending a minimum Y300 to Y400 per head at any of the top Bund-side restaurants, unless you go for a *prix fixe* (fixed price) lunch.

Many local eateries are in malls (p158) or designated food streets; try Zhapu Rd, Huanghe Rd or Yunnan Rd (p160) for old-school Shànghǎi.

THE BUND

M ON THE BUND Map pp66-7   Continental YYY
米氏西餐厅 Mǐshì Xīcāntīng
☎ 6350 9988; 7th fl, 20 Guangdong Rd; 广东路 20号7楼; mains from Y188, 2-/3-course set lunch Y176/224; ⏰ 11.30-2.30pm, 6-10.30pm; Ⓜ East Nanjing Rd

M exudes a timelessness and level of sophistication that surpasses the flash and fireworks of many other upscale Shànghǎi restaurants. The menu isn't radical, but that's the question that it seems to ask you – do you really need to break new culinary ground just to enjoy dinner? Crispy suckling pig (Y258) and Florentine steak (Y298) are, after all, simply delicious just the way they are. The art deco dining room and 7th-floor terrace are equally gorgeous – reserve well in advance. Finish off with drinks in the Glamour Bar (p179).

WHAMPOA CLUB
Map pp66-7   Shanghainese YYY
黄浦会 Huángpǔ Huì
☎ 6321 3737; 5th fl, Three on the Bund, 3 East Zhongshan No 1 Rd; 中山东一路3号5楼; dishes Y88-208; ⏰ 11.30am-2.30pm & 6-11pm; Ⓜ East Nanjing Rd

This nouveau Shanghainese joint has a 'wow' interior, replete with gilded chairs, pastel-tinted room dividers and a ceiling-to-floor crystal chandelier. But while no one argues over the decor, not everyone agrees on the food. It's audacious – almond and cocoa fried ribs (Y88), chrysanthemum and duck soup (Y48), chocolate curry ice cream (Y28) – but the kitchen can be inconsistent for such a high-class restaurant. Book ahead.

JEAN GEORGES Map pp66-7   Fusion YYY
法国餐厅 Fǎguó Cāntīng
☎ 6321 7733; 4th fl, Three on the Bund, 3 East Zhongshan No 1 Rd; 中山东一路3号4楼; mains from Y148, 3-course lunch Y188; ⏰ 11.30am-2.30pm, 6-11pm; Ⓜ East Nanjing Rd
Somewhere between Gotham City and new Shànghǎi is Jean Georges Vongerichten's

dimly lit, copper-appliquéd temple to gastronomy. The menu is slightly less daring now with Lam Ming Kin at the helm (JG currently has 19 restaurants in his empire and is mostly in NYC), but there are some divine palate-pleasers here, such as foie gras brûlée with sour cherries and candied pistachios, crab with mango and cumin crisps, and beef tenderloin in a miso-red wine sauce. It's divided into casual and formal (set dinner only, Y538) dining rooms at night, but not for lunch, when you can get a window table with relatively little hassle. Reserve.

TIANDI Map pp66-7   Chinese YYY
天地一家 Tiāndì Yìjiā
☎ 6329 7333; 3rd fl, Bund 6, 6 East Zhongshan No 1 Rd; 中山东一路6号3楼; dishes from Y48-208, set lunches Y58/88/128; ⏰ 11.30am-2.30pm, 6-11pm; Ⓜ East Nanjing Rd
Sultry jazz standards set the tone at this new Bund 6 restaurant, which boasts an enticing if unlikely Běijīng-Cantonese culinary pairing. Duck breast with mango and asparagus (Y68), sweet-and-sour prawns (Y138), and quick-fried lamb and scallions rolled in pancakes are some of the contemporary fare on offer. If you come for lunch, look out for the marvellous (albeit calorie-laden) deep-fried prawns with popped wheat. Reserve.

SHANGHAI GRANDMOTHER
Map pp66-7   Chinese Y
上海姥姥 Shànghǎi Lǎolao
☎ 6321 6613; 70 Fuzhou Rd; 福州路70号; dishes from Y20; Ⓜ East Nanjing Rd
This packed home-style eatery is within easy striking distance of the Bund and perfect for a casual lunch or dinner. You can't go wrong with the classics here: fried tomato and egg (Y20), Grandmother's braised pork and three-cup chicken rarely disappoint. It may look like a tourist trap from the outside, but it's not: even the local foodies on www.dianping.com give it the thumbs up.

DOLAR SHOP Map pp98-9   Hotpot Y
豆捞坊 Dòulāo Fáng
☎ 6351 7077; 5th fl, Hongyi Plaza, 299 East Nanjing Rd; 南京东路299号宏伊国际广场 5楼; hotpot from Y60; ⏰ 11am-11pm; Ⓜ East Nanjing Road
Hotpot is a favourite across China, especially in the winter months, but this top-notch

MEGAFOOD

It may not be something to post up on your blog, but eating in a mall is a quintessential Shànghǎi food experience. The city's omnipresent shopping centres cater to everybody; inside you'll usually find an inexpensive food court, a juice bar, lunch spots popular with office workers and high-end restaurants where clients are entertained over gourmet dinners.

Food courts are a good bet for visitors as they have a diversity of choice – Japanese teppan-yaki, Korean barbecue, Cantonese, hotpot and noodles – and are easy to navigate – just point at what you want. The most successful food court is Megabite (Map pp66–7; 大食代; Dàshídài; meal from Y30; ⏰ 10am-10pm), with innumerable Shànghǎi locations – the one on the 6th floor of Raffles City (p139) overlooking People's Square is kind of cool. Pay up-front at the entrance (Y5 deposit) and hand over your card to the vendor of your choice.

Other handy malls for visitors include Hongyi Plaza (Map pp66–7; 宏伊国际广场; 299 East Nanjing Road), which is close to the Bund and has some outstanding Chinese restaurants such as South Memory (below); the Dragon Gate Mall (p161), across from the Yuyuan Bazaar; and the colossal Superbrand Mall (p147) in Pǔdōng, which has restaurants spread across all 10 floors (plus some in the basements).

chain is popular with the locals no matter what the season because of the quality ingredients and the big range of sauces (Y4), essential to hotpot dining, which you can mix yourself at the sauce bar. The procedure is simple; you cook your own choice of food in the hotpot at your table and add the sauce to your taste. The home-made meatballs (pork or beef; Y18 to Y22) are great and there's seafood and vegies (from Y6) as well. There are other branches, mostly in shopping malls, around the city.

SOUTH MEMORY Map pp66-7   Hunanese Y
望湘园 Wàng Xiāng Yuán
☎ 6360 2797; 6th fl, Hongyi Plaza, 299 East Nanjing Rd; 南京东路299号宏伊国际广场6楼; dishes from Y22; ⏰ 11.30am-2.30pm, 5-9.30pm;
Ⓜ East Nanjing Rd

The latest addition to the Húnán dining scene, South Memory is a stone's throw from the waterfront and has a range of spicy hotpots, including bamboo shoots and smoked pork (Y48) and the more mysterious tea-shrub fungi (Y48). Note that the hotpots here are actually gānguò (dry pots) and are served in a miniwok without broth; one is enough for two moderately hungry people. It's absolutely jammed at lunchtime, so arrive early to get a window seat.

XÌNGHUĀ LÓU Map pp66-7   Dim Sum Y
杏花楼
☎ 6355 3777; 343 Fuzhou Rd; 福州路343号; dim sum from Y5, dishes from Y28; ⏰ 7.30am-9pm;
Ⓜ East Nanjing Rd

This old-school dinosaur has been pumping out quality Cantonese dishes and dim sum since the reign of Emperor Xianfeng (r 1851–61). OK, it's been state run for the

past 60 years or so, but somehow they found the motivation to give the place a total makeover, transforming the enterprise into a comfortable 2nd-floor restaurant. Cantonese dim sum, noodle soups and other dishes are on offer, and the afternoon tea (green, flower and black; pot from Y5) may be the cheapest in town.

AJISEN Map pp66-7   Noodles Y
味千拉面 Wèiqiān Lāmiàn
☎ 6360 7194; Basement, Hongyi Plaza, 299 East Nanjing Rd; 南京东路299号宏伊国际广场地下一层; noodles from Y30; ⏰ 11am-10pm;
Ⓜ East Nanjing Rd

Simply hopping come meal time, this Japanese ramen chain escorts diners to the noodle dish of their choice via easy-to-use photo menus and diligent squads of staff in regulation black T-shirt and jeans. Dishes perfectly resemble their photo menu images, so two thumbs up for that. This is possibly the most popular chain in Shànghǎi, with 83 locations around town and growing. In the event you're having trouble finding a branch, try the nearest mall. Handy outlets are located at Pǔdōng's Superbrand Mall (8th fl; p147), the main train station and even at Pudong International Airport.

PEOPLE'S SQUARE
人民广场

WÁNG BǍOHÉ JIǓJIĀ
Map pp66-7   Shanghainese YYY
王宝和酒家
☎ 6322 3673; 603 Fuzhou Rd; 福州路603号; set menu from Y350; ⏰ 11am-1pm, 5-8.30pm;
Ⓜ People's Square

Over 250 years old, this restaurant is a Shànghǎi institution. Its fame rests on its extravagant selection of crab dishes and its popularity reaches an apex during hairy-crab season (October to December). Most diners opt for one of the all-crabs-must-die banquets (Y350 to Y880), but if you're new to hairy crab, you might want to give it a try elsewhere before shelling out for an eight-course meal – it's debatable as to whether this place is still top-rate. Be sure to reserve.

KATHLEEN'S 5

Map pp66-7   Fusion YYY

赛玛西餐厅 **Sàimǎ Xīcāntīng**

☎ 6327 2221; 5th fl, Shanghai Art Museum, 325 West Nanjing Rd; 南京西路325号上海美术馆5楼; mains Y210-290, 2-/3-course set lunch Y120/140, afternoon tea Y78; ⓨ 11.30am-3pm, 5.30-10.30pm; Ⓜ People's Square

Kathleen's 5 is all about the location: it's set on the roof of the gorgeous Shanghai Art Museum (p75) in a glass-encased dining area, providing great leafy views of the park during the day, and People's Square's bright blinking towers by night. The menu here has changed from standard American to more inventive creations – jewfish with coconut milk and coriander pesto (Y210) or grilled prawns in sea-urchin sauce (Y230). The separate bar is a popular, if pricey spot, especially if you can grab a seat on the outside terrace.

XIĂO NÁN GUÓ

Map pp66-7   Shanghainese YY

小南国

☎ 3208 9777; 214-216 Huanghe Rd; 黄河路214-216号; dishes from Y22; ⓨ 11am-2pm & 5-10pm; Ⓜ People's Square

Even with the smart banquet halls and classy presentation, this is still one of Shànghǎi's more affordable (and delicious) chains. First-rate dishes include pork trotters braised for six hours (Y48–88), the crab clay-pot with glass noodles, deep-fried snake and the usual run of Shanghainese dumplings and noodles (Y12–38). It's a good place for group meals. Other branches are located in the French Concession (Map pp86–7; 4th fl, Dichan Bldg, 9 Donghu Rd; 东湖路9号地产大厦4楼) and in Pǔdōng's Superbrand Mall (p147; 9th fl). It's also known as Shanghai Spring.

NINA'S SICHUAN HOUSE

Map pp66-7   Sichuanese YY

蜀菜行家 **Shǔcài Hángjiā**

☎ 6375 8598; 227 North Huangpi Rd, inside Central Plaza; 黄陂北路227号; dishes Y15-88; Ⓜ People's Square

Nina's is as authentic as they come, with lines out the door and few foreigners in on the secret. It also has the best English menu in Shànghǎi: the entire text appears to have been penned by the Google translation machine. The salt-fried meat (Y22) and fiery water-cooked beef (Y29) are pretty much what they claim to be (and excellent at that), but what about the 'fish joss-stick dish dragon Jia' (Y17)? That's apparently a fancy way of saying fish-flavoured egg-plant. The 'almond in the United States fry cow' (Y88) is another winning description, but for those who can take the heat, we recommend a giant bowl of spicy black river fish (Y78). There's another branch in the No 1 Department Store (p139; 5th fl).

WÚYUÈ RÉNJIĀ

Map pp66-7   Noodles Y

吴越人家

☎ 6322 1842; 479 East Nanjing Rd; 南京东路479号; noodles from Y8; ⓨ 9am-10.30pm; Ⓜ East Nanjing Rd

Hidden in a side-street basement off East Nanjing Rd, this cool little place serves great bowls of Suzhou noodles in an old-style teahouse. Choose between *tāng* (soupy) or *gān* (dry) noodles; in either case the flavouring comes on a side plate. The excellent *xiābào shànbēi miàn* comes with shrimp and fried eels (Y17). There are also branches in the French Concession (Map pp86–7; No 10, Lane 706, Middle Huaihai Rd; 淮海中路706弄10号) and Hóngkǒu (Map p116; Huangdu Rd; 黄渡路), south of Lu Xun Park.

YANG'S FRY DUMPLINGS

Map pp66-7   Dumplings Y

小杨生煎馆 **Xiǎoyáng Shēngjiān Guǎn**

101 Huanghe Rd; 黄河路101号; Y4 per *liǎng* (两; 4 dumplings); Ⓜ People's Square

The city's most famous sesame-seed-and-scallion-coated fried dumplings (生煎; *shēngjiān*) unquestionably belong to Yang's. Lines here can stretch to the horizon as eager diners wait for their scalding *shēngjiān* to be dished out onto vintage communist-era enamel dishes – this isn't some sort of retro fashion statement, they just never bothered to upgrade the tableware. Order at the left counter – eight dumplings and a soup (汤; *tāng*) should be enough – then join the queue on the right to pick up your order. Another branch is located in Jìng'ān (Map pp98–9; 678 North Shaanxi Rd; 陕西北路678号).

OLD TOWN 南市

The Yuyuan Gardens area is hardly a dining destination in itself, but if you're visiting the Old Town you needn't go hungry as there's plenty of snack food, a couple of famous old restaurants and, of course, a brand-new mall.

top picks

FOOD STREETS

Shànghǎi's food streets are gradually being erased from the map, but a few remain hanging on by their fingertips – they're great places to wander both because of the variety of food and the atmosphere. There was talk of transforming Yunnan Rd into a night market in 2010; see for yourself what's become of it at sunset.

- Huanghe Rd (Map pp66–7) With a prime central location near People's Park, Huanghe Rd covers all the bases from cheap lunches to late-night post-theatre snacks. You'll find large restaurants like Qiánlóng Měishí (No 72), but Huanghe Rd is best for dumplings – get 'em fried at Yang's (No 97, p159), boiled northern style at Manchurian Dumplings (哈尔滨水饺; Hā'ěrbīn Shuǐjiǎo; No 101) or served up in bamboo steamers across the road at Jiajia Soup Dumplings (佳家汤包; No 90).

- Yunnan Rd Food Street (Map pp66–7) Yunnan Rd has some interesting speciality restaurants and is just the spot for an authentic meal after museum hopping at People's Square. Look out for Shaanxi dumplings at No 15 and five-fragrance dim sum at Wǔ Fāng Zhāi (五芳斋; No 28). You can also get Peking duck (No 100), salted chicken and Uighur kebabs here.

- Zhapu Rd (Map p116) A short walk north of the Bund, Zhapu Rd has a variety of local restaurants, but west along Tanggu Rd are smaller mom-and-pop shops and local dumpling stands – it's the cheapest place to eat within walking distance of Shànghǎi's most-prized strip of real estate.

MINGTANG ORGANIC DINING

Map p79   Chinese YY
名唐有机粤菜 Míngtáng Yǒujī Yuècài
☎ 6152 6668; Unit 102-106, Bldg 2, Cool Docks, 479 South Zhongshan Rd; 中山南路479号老码头广场2号楼102-106室; dishes Y48-128, weekday set lunch Y38-58; Ⓜ Xiaonanmen
The only restaurant in the Cool Docks (p82) that seems to have taken off, Mingtang's earth-coloured tones provide a soothing counterpoint to Shànghǎi's frenetic energy. The menu (new-wave Chinese) has a selection of organic vegetables, free-range poultry and lots of seafood. Favourites include the fried prawns with apple thousand-island dressing (Y98), roast Mongolian lamb with potato cakes (Y128) and almond-papaya chilled cake (Y32) for dessert.

NANXIANG STEAMED BUN
RESTAURANT Map p79   Dumplings YY
南翔馒头店 Nánxiáng Mántou Diàn
378 Fuyou Rd, Yuyuan Bazaar; 豫园商城福佑路378号; 16 dumplings takeaway Y12, 6 dumplings upstairs from Y25, set menu Y60; Ⓨ 10am-9pm; Ⓜ Yuyuan Garden
Shànghǎi's most famous dumpling restaurant divides the purists, who love the place, and the younger crowd, who think it's an overrated tourist trap. Decide for yourself how the *xiǎolóngbāo* (see the boxed text, p154) rate, but be forewarned that hordes of visitors descend on the place and you won't even get near it on weekends. There are three dining halls upstairs, with the prices escalating (and crowds diminishing) in each room. The takeaway deal is comparable to what you pay elsewhere for *xiǎolóngbāo*, but the queue snakes halfway around the Yuyuan Bazaar.

FAT OLIVE Map p79   Mediterranean YY
☎ 6334 3288; 6th fl, 228 South Xizang Rd (enter through the Fraser Residence on Shouning Rd); 西藏南路228号6楼; wine per glass from Y35, meze from Y28, pita burgers Y68; Ⓨ 11am-1pm; Ⓜ Dashijie; �ⓦ
Nestled among office towers and residential suites, the Fat Olive has a cosy outdoor deck overlooking the Old Town to the south. The brainchild of chef David Laris (of Three on the Bund fame), it serves Greek-style meze (olives, feta, tzatziki and pita burgers) accompanied by a decent selection of New World wines that go for as low as Y100 a bottle. This is a prime summer-lounging locale.

DRAGON GATE MALL Map p79   Chinese Y

豫龙坊 **Yùlóngfáng**

Middle Fangbang Rd; 方浜中路; dishes from Y10;
⏰ 9am-11pm; Ⓜ Yuyuan Garden

True, eating in a mall isn't *quite* the same as wandering amid the chaos of the Yuyuan Bazaar, but if you've had enough of the push and pull of the crowds, this spot is a lifesaver. Noodle restaurants, a food court and juice bar are on the basement level while a branch of Din Tai Fung (p164) is on the second floor, thumbing its nose at Nanxiang's *xiǎolóngbāo* across the way. The enormous dragon-arch fountain marks the entrance.

SŌNGYUÈLÓU Map p79   Chinese, Vegetarian Y

松月楼

☎ 6355 3630; 99 Jiujiaochang Rd; 旧校场路 99号; steamer of dumplings from Y7, dishes from Y25; ⏰ 7am-7.30pm; Ⓜ Yuyuan Garden; Ⓥ

Shànghǎi's oldest vegie restaurant, dating back to 1910, this place offers a far cheaper and more authentic dining experience than most of the tourist-saturated restaurants in the area. Unless you're conversant in Mandarin, you'll want to dine upstairs, where an English menu is provided. There's the usual mix of tofu masquerading as meat – for starters, sample the sweet and spicy Hangzhou 'beef' and chilli peppers (杭椒牛柳; Hángjiāo niúliǔ).

FRENCH CONCESSION
法租界

The French Concession is where it's at when it comes to eating, and whatever it is that you're craving, you'll probably be able to find it here. Tongue-tingling Sichuanese? Check. Wild Yunnanese mushrooms? Check. Wacky *maki* rolls? Check. Fancy fusion food? Double check.

Taojiang Rd, Dongping Rd, Fumin Rd and Xīntiāndì are the main culinary hotspots in town, and with dozens of choices between them, you'd have to eat out every night for a year to try them all. Well, what are you waiting for?

T8 Map pp86-7   Fusion YYY

☎ 6355 8999; Bldg 8 North Block Xīntiāndì, Lane 181 Taicang Rd; 太仓路181弄新天地北里8号楼; mains Y198-Y398, 2-/3-course set lunch Mon-Fri Y168/198, Sat & Sun Y198/228; ⏰ 11.30am-2.30pm & 6.30-11.30pm; Ⓜ South Huangpi Rd/Xintiandi

top picks

REGIONAL CHINESE

Travel China without ever leaving the French Concession.

- Crystal Jade (p165) Skip brunch at the Portman, come here for dim sum instead.
- Dì Shuǐ Dòng (p166) Countryside cookin' and Hunanese hot peppers.
- Dōngběi Rén (p169) The Manchurian candidate does dumplings.
- Sāngù Niúwā (p169) C'mon, admit it. You've never had frog hotpot before, have you?
- Sichuan Citizen (p168) Singe your tastebuds, then kill the pain with a peppercorn.
- Southern Barbarian (p167) Barbarian-shmarbarian – Yunnanese cuisine is a culinary treasure.

T8 is designed for seduction, which it does exceptionally well. The renovated grey-brick *shíkùmén* (stone-gate house) is the perfect setting for the dark, warm interior, decorated with antique Chinese cabinets, carved wooden screens and the striking feng shui–driven entrance. The menu is 'modern Mediterranean with Asian accents' – T8's signature dish is Sìchuān high pie with yellow coriander bisque (Y238). Shànghǎi's celebs love this place. Reserve.

CHINOISE STORY

Map pp86-7   Shanghainese YYY

锦庐 **Jǐnlú**

☎ 6445 1717; 59 South Maoming Rd; 茂名南路 748号; dishes Y30-158; Ⓜ South Shanxi Rd

A curvaceous beauty set in the Jinjiang Hotel complex, the Chinoise Story is a study in style, where art deco architecture meets Philippe Starck design. Shanghainese cuisine gets a reworking here and the dishes are every bit as stunning as the four dining areas: the wasabi smoked salmon is presented as rose petals (Y48) and even common fare like the lion's head meatball (Y36) is given a touch of class.

SHINTORI NULL II Map pp86-7   Fusion YYY

新都里无二店 **Xīndūlǐ Wú'èr Diàn**

☎ 5404 5252; 803 Julu Rd; 巨鹿路803号; dishes Y50-160; ⏰ 6-10.30pm; Ⓜ Jing'an Temple

The warehouse industrial-chic interior here resembles a set from a Peter Greenaway film, from the eye-catching open kitchen, which looks like it should house Hannibal Lector, to the sleek staff running around like an army of ninjas. The dishes – Beijing duck rolls (Y75), cold noodles served in an ice bowl (Y70), beef steak on *pu-erh* leaves (Y160) – are excellent, but they maintain the minimalist theme, so make sure to order more than one. Finish off with black sesame seed ice cream (Y65). Reserve.

EL WILLY Map pp86-7 Spanish YYY

☎ 54045757; 20 Donghu Rd; 东湖路20号; tapas Y45-165, mains Y165-198; ⏰ 11am-11pm; Ⓜ South Shanxi Rd

The unstoppable energy of colourful-sock-wearing Barcelona chef Willy fuels this restored 1920s villa, which ups its charms with a bold selection of 'sexy wines' and even 'sexy mini pizzas' (Y69). The temptations continue throughout the menu, from the creative tapas – red snapper, gazpacho and avocado (Y98) and foie gras, green apple and smoked eel (Y75) – to succulent main dishes such as black truffle and pumpkin creamy rice (Y185, serves two). Reserve.

AZUL/VIVA/VARGAS GRILL

Map pp86-7 Fusion YYY

☎ 6433 1172; 18 Dongping Rd; 东平路18号; tapas Y40-80, mains Y80-200, weekend brunch Y120; ⏰ 11am-11pm; Ⓜ Changshu Rd

Peruvian restaurateur Eduardo Vargas specialises in hip fusion food with the flavours of South America prominent. Rough-hewn stone seating and shimmery gold and violet decor sets the scene at the downstairs tapas bar, Azul, where the Latin influence is to the fore thanks to the Peruvian beef tapas (Y65), prawn ceviche (marinated raw seafood) with orange sauce (Y70) and margaritas. On the 2nd floor is Viva, which is more of a restaurant, despite the couches to recline on. A new addition, the Vargas Grill (☎ 6437 0136; mains Y150-400; ⏰ dinner), has opened on the 3rd floor. The weekend brunch here is a good deal. Reserve.

MESA Map pp86-7 Fusion YYY

魅莎 Mèishā

☎ 6289 9108; 748 Julu Rd; 巨鹿路748号; mains Y128-198; ⏰ 11am-3pm & 6-11pm Mon-Fri, 9.30am-11pm Sat & Sun; Ⓜ Jing'an Temple

For fine dining in a casual atmosphere, Mesa is your spot. The former factory has been renovated just enough to be *en*

vogue, but touches such as exposed steel support beams remind you to leave the tie at home. The menu appears to have roots somewhere in France, but it has since adapted to its own distinctive Australasian niche: crispy duck in an apple-fig glaze and oven-roasted sea bass with *chèvre* (goat's milk cheese) risotto are among the temptations. The megapopular weekend brunches (from Y80) are kid-friendly too. Upstairs is the swish bar Manifesto (p181). Reserve.

CHENG CHENG'S ART SALON

Map pp86-7 Shanghainese YY

成成餐厅 Chéngchéng Cāntīng

☎ 5306 5462; 30 Donghu Rd; 东湖路30号; dishes Y48-128; ⏰ 11am-2.30pm & 5-10pm; Ⓜ South Shanxi Rd

Squeezed in alongside Donghu Road's heavy hitters, Cheng Cheng distinguishes itself with a funky, colourful interior full of antique furnishings and large oil paintings (for sale). The food is mostly Shanghainese, with a few Sìchuān favourites thrown in to keep risk-averse *lǎowài* (foreigners) happy. There's talk of Beijing-opera performances in the evenings, but they've yet to materialise. There's a smaller cafe-style branch (Map pp86–7; ☎ 5306 5462; 164 Nanchang Rd; 南昌路164号).

YÈ SHANGHAI Map pp62-3 Shanghainese YY

夜上海

☎ 6311 2323; North Block Xīntiāndì, 338 South Huangpi Rd; 黄陂南路338号新天地北里; dishes from Y42; ⏰ 11.30am-2.30pm & 6-10.30pm; Ⓜ South Huangpi Rd/Xintiandi

Yè offers sophisticated, unchallenging Shanghainese cuisine in classy surroundings, which makes it a favourite with visitors. The drunken chicken and smoked fish starters are an excellent overture to local flavours, the crispy duck comes with thick pancakes (Y88 for half a duck) and the sautéed string beans and bamboo shoots (Y48) doesn't disappoint either. There's an extensive wine list starting at Y190 a bottle.

LOST HEAVEN Map pp86-7 Yunnanese YY

花马天堂 Huāmǎ Tiāntáng

☎ 6433 5126; 38 Gaoyou Rd; 高邮路38号; dishes from Y40; ⏰ 11.30am-2pm & 5.30-10.30pm; Ⓜ Shanghai Library

In a town of notoriously fickle diners, Lost Heaven has maintained its status as one of the most fashionable eateries longer than many restaurants have managed to stay open. Located on a quiet street in Shànghǎi's most desirable neighbourhood, it's stylish and atmospheric with subdued red lighting and a giant Buddha dominating the main dining area. The Yunnanese food is delicately flavoured and nicely presented, although purists will bemoan the way some dishes, such as the Dali chicken with green pepper and onion (Y60), aren't as spicy as they should be. The Yunnan vegetable cakes (Y40) come with a salsa-like garnish and make a fantastic starter. Reserve.

PǏNCHUĀN Map pp86-7   Sichuanese YY
品川
☎ 6437 9361; 47 Taojiang Rd; 桃江路47号; dishes Y39-85; ⏱ 11am-2pm & 5-11pm; M Changshu Rd
Fire fiends love Sìchuān cooking, where the sophistication goes far beyond merely smothering everything with hot peppers. The telltale blend of chillies and peppercorns is best summed up in two words: *là* (spicy) and *má* (numbing). Even though Pǐnchuān has hit the upscale button repeatedly in the past few years, this is still a fine place to experience the tongue tingling. Try the sliced beef in spicy sauce (Y69), baked spare ribs with peanuts (Y79) or *làzi jī* (spicy chicken). The duck with sticky rice (Y79) will help mitigate the damage to your tastebuds. Reserve.

TAIRYO Map pp86-7   Japanese YY
大渔 Dàyú
☎ 5382 8818; 2nd fl, 139 Ruijin No 1 Rd; 瑞金1路139号2楼; teppan-yaki from Y20, buffet Y150; ⏱ 11am-midnight; M South Shanxi Rd
All-you-can-eat deals are popular in Shànghǎi, but nothing compares to Tairyo's teppan-yaki steak house. The cooks here may lack the *savoir flair* of true teppan-yaki chefs, but no one seems to be complaining. Don't limit yourself to the grill; there's also excellent sashimi and pitchers of sake – all included in the buffet – so start working up an appetite. There's another branch at the Hong Kong Plaza (Map pp86-7; 3rd fl, 283 Middle Huaihai Rd; 淮海中路283号香港广场南3楼).

A FUTURE PERFECT
Map pp86-7   Continental YY
☎ 6248 8020; No 16, Lane 351, Huashan Rd; 华山路351弄16号; lunch Y76-96, dinner Y98-188; ⏱ 7am-11pm; M Jing'an Temple/Changshu Rd
A hang-out for hip grammarians and those who miss the cafes back home, A Future Perfect relies on fresh ingredients to keep the menu enticing throughout the day. Try the Strammer Max breakfast (two eggs on chive-buttered farmer's bread; Y48), one of the superb salads (from Y48), the veal *piccata* and gnocchi with caper-lemon butter (Y188) or a simple blue-cheese burger (Y98). There's a fair amount of attitude floating around this place, but that's all part of the vibe. It's inside the Old House Inn (p210).

LITTLE FACE Map pp86-7   Thai/Indian YY
☎ 6466 4328; 3rd fl, 30 Donghu Rd; 东湖路30号3楼; dishes Y60-120; ⏱ 5.30-1am; M South Shanxi Rd
Little Face is a daring fusion of what were once two separate restaurants (Lan Na Thai and Hazara). With both cuisines it could be a slightly schizophrenic experience, but the Thai-Indian combination works: you can pair samosas (Y40) with a green curry (Y75) or papaya salad (Y45) with Tandoori lamb kebabs (Y80) and flavours are mostly complementary. Ochre-coloured walls, candlelit tables and a collection of Asian antiques set the scene for intimate dining. Stop off at the trendy 2nd-floor bar (p181) for drinks.

DES LYS Map pp86-7   French YY
德丽滋 Délìzī
☎ 5404 5077; 178 Xinle Rd; 新乐路178号; mains from Y58; ⏱ 9am-midnight; M Changshu Rd
The closest thing in Shànghǎi to a genuine bistro, young French expats flock here for the *confit de canard* (duck confit) in foie-gras

top picks

ECSTASY IN XTD

The best dining options in Xīntiāndì.

- Crystal Jade (p165) Join the queue for dim-sum delicacies.
- Din Tai Fung (p164) Glorified street food from the renegade province.
- Kabb (p164) Sandwiches, wraps and salads for a taste of home.
- T8 (p161) A feng-shui fusion masterpiece.
- TMSK (p182) The inexpensive option: set lunches from the bar that redefine weird.
- Xīnjíshì (p165) Home-style Shanghainese in all its sweet and oily glory.
- Yè Shanghai (opposite) 1930s class and delectable Shànghǎi cooking.

sauce (Y98) and their adopted national dish, *couscous royal* (Y118). But it's the desserts which really get the regulars salivating – the apple crumble and chocolate fondant are equally fantastic. You might have to try them both. The house wine is Y48 a glass.

HAIKU Map pp86-7 — Japanese YY
隐泉之语 Yǐnquán Zhī Yǔ
☎ 6445 0021; 28B Taojiang Rd; 桃江路28号乙; maki rolls Y60-98, 2 pieces sushi from Y30; ⏱ 11.30am-2pm, 5.30-10pm; Ⓜ Changshu Rd
Though the name may suggest the minimalist beauty of a butterfly perched upon a temple bell, Haiku is anything but. Rather, it's all about 'let's see how many different things we can fit into a maki roll'. On this count they have definitely succeeded: the Ninja wraps up shrimp and crab with a killer spicy sauce (Y65), while the Philly Roll does cream cheese and salmon (Y75). Can't make up your mind? Pimp My Roll (Y98) may be the one for you – it's loaded with everything. Reserve.

BOXING CAT BREWERY
Map pp86-7 — American YY
拳击猫啤酒屋 Quánjīmāo Píjiǔwū
☎ 6431 2091; www.boxingcatbrewery.com; 82 West Fuxing Rd; 复兴西路82号; pints Y45, pitcher Y100, food Y75-128; ⏱ 5pm-2am Mon-Fri, 11am-2am Sat-Sun; Ⓜ Shanghai Library/Changshu Rd; 🛜
A deservedly popular three-floor microbrewery, helmed by Texan brew master Gary Heine, with a rotating line-up of fresh beers that range from the Standing 8 Pilsner to the Right Hook Helles. But that's not all – Kelley Lee (of Cantina Agave, p167) has paired southern classics (gumbo, Y80), and sandwiches (Cali-Cajun Chicken Club, Y80) to go with the drinks. Come for a pint, stay for dinner. The top floor is equipped with a pool table, foosball and a Wii console.

KABB Map pp86-7 — American YY
凯博西餐厅 Kǎibó Xīcāntīng
☎ 3307 0798; Bldg 5 North Block Xīntiāndì, Lane 181 Taicang Rd; 太仓路181弄新天地北里5号楼; mains Y60-85; ⏱ 7am-midnight; Ⓜ South Huangpi Rd/Xintiandi; 🛜
For those times when the desire to chew becomes overpowering, this smart grill hits the spot, delivering authentic American-portioned comfort food at midrange prices. There's a good selection of main-course

salads, burgers and wraps. The outdoor cafe-style seating is particularly popular for a slower-paced weekend brunch (from Y70), when the menu stretches to French toast with bananas and walnut syrup, and eggs Benedict – all with unlimited coffee.

COCONUT PARADISE Map pp86-7 — Thai YY
椰香天堂 Yēxiāng Tiāntáng
☎ 6248 1998; 38 Fumin Rd; 富民路38号; dishes from Y48; Ⓜ Jing'an Temple
Coconut Paradise is a tropical delight, its lush garden seating and dimly lit interior making for a decidedly romantic venue. Curries (Y68), fish salads and Chiang Mai soup will bring back memories of days spent lazing around in northern Thailand, and by the end of the meal on a good night, you might even forget you're in Shànghǎi. No MSG. Reserve.

DIN TAI FUNG Map pp86-7 — Dumplings YY
鼎泰丰 Dǐng Tài Fēng
☎ 6385 8378; 2nd fl, Bldg 6 (in the mall) South Block Xīntiāndì, Lane 123 Xingye Rd; 兴业路123弄新天地南里6号楼2楼; 10 dumplings from Y56, noodles Y29-50; ⏱ 10am-midnight; Ⓜ South Huangpi Rd/Xintiandi; Ⓥ
Taiwan's Din Tai Fung has clearly hit upon a winning formula: glorified street food in a sanitized environment. Dumpling styles run from Shānxī's crinkled *shāomài* (Y68) to Shànghǎi's steamed *xiǎolóngbāo* (with/without crab Y86/Y58), as well as vegetarian dumplings (Y56), wonton soup (Y45) and various other options. Critics harp that DTF charges outrageous prices (true), but the throngs inside make a convincing riposte: the dumplings here really are that good. Branches in the Old Town (see Dragon Gate Mall, p161) and Pǔdòng's Superbrand Mall (p147). Reserve.

XIAN YUE HIEN Map pp86-7 — Dim Sum YY
申粤轩酒楼 Shēnyuèxuān Jiǔlóu
☎ 6251 1166; 849 Huashan Rd; 华山路849号; dishes from Y28; ⏱ 11am-2.30pm & 5.30pm-midnight; taxi
The Ding Xiang Garden, originally built for the concubine of a Qing dynasty mandarin, is now reserved for retired Communist Party cadres, so the only way you'll get to peek behind the undulating dragon wall is to eat at this serene restaurant. Stroll past the octogenarian officials in wheelchairs reminiscing about the good old days when the Chairman was running things to sample

classic Shanghainese and Cantonese dishes such as lion's head meatballs (Y56). The seafood dishes can get very expensive here, but the real draw is the dim sum, served overlooking the lawn on mornings and afternoons. Picture menu available.

GINGER Map pp86–7   Cafe YY
☎ 6433 9437; 299 West Fuxing Rd; 复兴西路299号; dishes from Y62; ⏱ 9am-11pm; Ⓜ Shanghai Library; 📶

Shades of yellow cloak this secluded chill-out space, which does Asian standards, French cafe fare and gingery desserts with equal panache. Try the quiches (Y62) or skip straight to the sweet stuff (apple crumble with ginger ice cream, Y45) to go with afternoon coffee. Two branches are in the Taikang Road Art Centre (p85): Miss Ginger (Map pp86–7; ☎ 5465 7355; No 47, Lane 248, Taikang Rd; 泰康路248弄47号田子坊; Ⓜ Dapuqiao Rd) and Ginger Indochine (Map pp86–7; No 34, Lane 248; 泰康路248弄34号田子坊), specialising in noodles and curries (Y68).

ORIGIN Map pp86–7   Cafe YY
源于自然 Yuányú Zìrán

☎ 6467 0100; Taikang Rd Art Centre, No 39, Lane 155, Middle Jianguo Rd; 建国中路155弄39号田子坊; mains Y38-68, dinner menu Y138/168; ⏱ 10.30am-11pm; Ⓜ Dapuqiao Rd; 📶 Ⓥ

Serving Shànghǎi's locavores, Origin is an upbeat Italian-run cafe that uses seasonal ingredients to create a clever menu of salads (crispy goose and mango), sandwiches (sweet potato and *chèvre* on focaccia), and, of course, pasta and homemade gelato. Not everything on the menu appears to come from within a 160km radius, but hey, they're trying. Arrive early to stake out seats on the upstairs terrace.

JÍSHÌ JIǓLÓU Map pp86–7   Shanghainese YY
吉士酒楼

☎ 6282 9260; 41 Tianping Rd; 天平路41号; dishes from Y28; ⏱ 11am-2.30pm & 5-10pm; Ⓜ Jiatong University

Jíshì specialises in packing lots of people into tight spaces, so if you tend to gesture wildly when you talk, watch out with those chopsticks. This is Shanghainese home cooking at its best: crab dumplings, Grandma's braised pork and plenty of fish (carp cream soup Y28), drunken shrimp (Y10) and eel. It's easy to miss; the sign outside says 'Jesse's'. There are branches (aka 新

吉士; Xīnjíshì) at Xīntiāndì (Map pp86–7; ☎ 6336 4746; Bldg 9 North Block, 新天地北里9号楼) and in Pǔdōng (Map p108; ☎ 6841 9719; 2nd fl, China Insurance Building, 166 East Lujiazui Rd; 陆家嘴东路166号中国保险大厦2楼). Reserve.

BELLAGIO CAFÉ Map pp86–7   Chinese YY
鹿港小镇 Lùgǎng Xiǎozhèn

☎ 6386 5701; 68 Taicang Rd; 太仓路68号; dishes from Y28; ⏱ 11.30am-4am; Ⓜ South Huangpi Rd

Nope, not another pizza place – this Bellagio has nothing to do with Lake Como (or Las Vegas). It's actually a trendy Taiwanese restaurant popular with the 20-something crowd, where identically coiffed waitresses (sometimes confusing customers) are dressed to match the black-and-white decor. Taiwanese specialities on offer include three-cup chicken (Y46) and pineapple fried rice (Y39), but when the mercury rises it's the shaved-ice desserts and smoothies (from Y26) that bring in the crowds. There are other branches off West Nanjing Rd (Map pp98–9; ☎ 6247 2666; 111 Xikang Rd; 西康路111号; Ⓜ West Nanjing Rd) and in Gǔběi (Map pp128–9; ☎ 6270 6866; 101 South Shuicheng Rd; 水城南路101号; taxi).

LEI GARDEN RESTAURANT
Map pp86–7   Dim Sum YY
利苑酒家 Lìyuànjiǔjiā

☎ 6445 3538; 6th fl, 755 Middle Huaihai Rd; 淮海中路755号新华联大厦(东楼)6楼; dim sum dishes Y12-26; ⏱ 11am-2.30pm, 5-10pm; Ⓜ South Shanxi Rd

This authentic, bustling dim-sum restaurant makes a good lunch spot if you're on the shopping trail in the area. They get through an awful lot of congee here, but there's a wide range of dishes to choose from, such as the delectable steamed shrimp dumplings (Y26). The restaurant is inside the New Hualian Commercial Building, the large office block on the corner of Huaihai Rd and Ruijin No 2 Rd. Enter around the back of the building and take the lift to the 6th floor.

CRYSTAL JADE Map pp86–7   Dim Sum YY
翡翠酒家 Fěicuì Jiǔjiā

☎ 6385 8752; Xīntiāndì South Block, 2nd fl, Bldg 6 (in the mall); 兴业路123弄新天地南里6号2楼; dumplings from Y22; ⏱ 11am-11pm; Ⓜ South Huangpi Rd/Xintiandi

Once Xīntiāndì's most popular Chinese restaurant, Crystal Jade has taken a hit with the opening of neighbouring Din Tai Fung (p164), but it can still draw lines out the door. What distinguishes it from other dim-sum restaurants is the dough: dumpling skins are perfectly tender, steamed buns come out light and airy, and the noodles (from Y30) are plain delicious. Go for lunch, when both Cantonese and Shanghainese dim sum are served. Other branches are in the Westgate Mall (Map pp98–9; ☎ 5288 1133) and the Hong Kong New World Tower (Map pp86–7; ☎ 6335 4188). Reserve.

DĪ SHUǏ DÒNG Map pp86-7 Hunanese YY
滴水洞饭店

☎ 6253 2689; 2nd fl, 56 South Maoming Rd; 茂名南路56号2层; dishes Y20-88; ☒ 10am-12.30am; Ⓜ South Shanxi Rd

It's hard to imagine Mao as a restaurateur, but he may have liked this place with its unpretentious, down-home atmosphere and red-faced diners chatting it up over an increasingly raucous dinner. Along with Guyi Hunan Restaurant (below), Dī Shuǐ Dòng (named after a cave in the Chairman's home village) is the discerning local's choice for spicy Hunanese cooking. The claim to fame is the *zīrán* (cumin) ribs, but there's no excuse not to sample the chicken-and-chilli clay pot or even the classic boiled frog (all Y48). Cool down with plenty of beers (Y12 a bottle) and the crowd-pleasing caramelised bananas for dessert. There's another branch (Map pp86–7; ☎ 6415 9448; 5 Dongping Rd; 东平路5号). Reserve.

GUYI HUNAN RESTAURANT
Map pp86-7 Hunanese YY

古意湘味浓 Gǔyì Xiāngwèinóng
☎ 6249 5628; 87 Fumin Rd; 富民路87号; dishes Y22-68; ☒ 11.30am-midnight; Ⓜ Jing'an Temple/Changshu Rd

Shànghǎi's foodies divide into those who back this place to the hilt and others who prefer the more laid-back charms of Dī Shuǐ Dòng (above). The classy atmosphere is equalled by the comprehensive menu, which includes great *huǒguō* (hotpots; Y48–68) featuring beef, chicken, crab or frog and, once again, those delectable cumin ribs. No reservations; come prepared to wait.

BǍOLUÓ JIǓLÓU
Map pp86-7 Shanghainese YY

保罗酒楼
☎ 6279 2827; 271 Fumin Rd; 富民路271号; dishes Y18-68; ☒ 10.30am-4.30am; Ⓜ Changshu Rd/Jing'an Temple

Gather up a boisterous bunch of friends and join the Shanghainese night owls who queue down the street well into the early hours to get into this amazingly busy venue. Bǎoluó is typically chaotic, cavernous and packed – a great place to get a feel for Shànghǎi's famous buzz. The English menu isn't much help here (the translations are gibberish) so follow your nose and see what other tables are ordering. Try the excellent baked eel (保罗烤鳗; *bǎoluó kǎomán*; Y68), pot-stewed crab and pork (Y42) or lotus-leaf roasted duck (Y38). Reserve or be prepared to wait, especially at weekends.

VEDAS Map pp86-7 Indian YY

☎ 6445 3670/6445 3670; 550 West Jianguo Rd; 建国西路550号; mains from Y60; ☒ 11.30am-2pm & 5.30-11pm; Ⓜ Zhaojiabang Rd

Shànghǎi's best Indian restaurant presents classic northern Indian cuisine, with a smattering of vegetarian dishes from south India, in a soothing atmosphere. You can sample one of the decent cocktails (from Y45) in the separate bar area before heading into the main dining room for your rogan josh or korma. As with all Indian restaurants on the mainland, it would be nice if the curries had a bit more bite, but the flavours are spot on.

1001 NIGHTS Map pp86-7 Middle Eastern YY

一千一夜餐厅 Yìqiānyīyè Cāntīng
☎ 6473 1178; 2nd fl, 4 Hengshan Rd; 衡山路4号2楼; meze Y25-68, mains Y48-98; ☒ 11am-2am; Ⓜ Hengshan Rd

The stars of the show here – apart from the Uighur belly dancers (from 8pm to 11pm) of course – are the meze and salads, with everything from tabouleh to *baba ganoush* (eggplant dip). Heavier fare stretches to grilled meats and couscous, but be sure to leave space for a baklava, Turkish coffee and perhaps a toke on the hookah to round the evening off.

QUÁNJÙDÉ Map pp86-7 Peking Duck YY
全聚德

☎ 5403 7286; 4th fl, 786 Middle Huaihai Rd; 淮海中路786号4层; roasted duck Y138; ☒ 11am-2pm & 5-10pm; Ⓜ South Shanxi Rd

Shànghǎi doesn't usually venture onto the capital's culinary turf, but if you've got a hankering for Peking duck, then try out this old-school but dependable branch of the famous chain. Quánjùdé offers more than 100 dishes made from every conceivable part of a duck's anatomy, but the big draw, of course, is the juicy roasted duck, served with pancakes, scallions, plum sauce and a soup. You can get half a duck with all the trimmings for Y66.

NEPALI KITCHEN Map pp86-7 — Nepalese YY
尼泊尔餐厅 Níbó'ěr Cāntīng

☎ 5404 6281; No 4, Lane 819, Julu Rd; 巨鹿路 819弄4号; mains Y30-65, set lunch Y55-70, set dinner Y100-150; ☯ 11am-2pm & 6-11pm; Ⓜ Jing'an Temple/Changshu Rd; Ⓥ

Reminisce about that Himalayan trek over a plate of Tibetan *momos* (meat or vegetable dumplings) or a *choila* (spicy chicken; Y45) amid prayer flags in this homey, lodgelike place. For a more laid-back meal, take your shoes off and recline on traditional cushions, surrounded by colourful *thangkas* and paper lamps. Prices are higher than the Annapurna Circuit, but then you're not just eating *dhal bhat* (lentils and rice). Both the set lunch and dinner (vegies pay less than meat-eaters) are a good bet, with traditional Nepali dishes such as *sekuwa* (grilled beef) and *sikarni* (yogurt).

SIMPLY THAI Map pp86-7 — Thai YY
天泰餐厅 Tiāntài Cāntīng

☎ 6445 9551; 5c Dongping Rd; 东平路5号C座; dishes from Y48; ☯ 11am-10.30pm; Ⓜ Changshu Rd

Simply Thai serves up reasonably priced classics such as green and red curries (Y55), tom yum soup (Y48) and fiery green papaya salad (Y48). This branch has a tree-shaded patio, perfect for alfresco dining in the warmer months. A less intimate branch is at Xīntiāndì (Map pp86-7; ☎ 6326 2088; North Block, cnr Madang Rd & Xingye Rd; 马当路与兴业路路口) and there's one in Hóngqiáo (Map p132; ☎ 6465 8955; House 28, Lane 3338, Hongmei Entertainment Street; 虹梅路3338弄 虹梅休闲街28号; Ⓜ Longxi Rd).

CANTINA AGAVE Map pp86-7 — Mexican YY

☎ 6170 1310; Unit A2, 291 Fumin Rd; 富民路 291号A2室; burritos from Y55; Ⓜ Changshu Rd/South Shanxi Rd; Ⓥ

It used to be that if you went out for a burrito in Shànghǎi, it would taste like cardboard and you'd pay up the wazoo, but no longer. Kelly Lee's Cantina Agave has come to the rescue, and oh, what a rescue – flavour-filled chicken and salsa verde burritos, vegie or beef *machaca* soft tacos (Y20), an extensive list of margaritas (Y60) and a fresh salsa bar.

BAI'S RESTAURANT
Map pp86-7 — Shanghainese YY

白家餐厅 Báijiā Cāntīng

☎ 6437 6915; No 12, Lane 189, Wanping Rd; 宛 平路189弄12号; dishes Y18-68; ☯ 11-2pm, 5-10pm; Ⓜ Hengshan Rd/Zhaojiabang Rd

Hidden down an alley off Wanping Rd is this family-style restaurant (based out of what appears to be the living room) with tasty, authentic Shanghainese food. The *hǔpí jiānjiāo* (虎皮煎椒; tiger-skin chillies; Y20) are mild and sweet and there are plenty of affordable delicacies like the steamed yellow croaker in soy sauce (Y38). The *suànxiāng bàngbànggǔ* (蒜香棒棒骨; fried pork ribs in garlic; Y20 each) are a house speciality, but a little pricey (Y20 each). It's a reader favourite, but there are only five tables so book ahead.

SOUTHERN BARBARIAN
Map pp86-7 — Yunnanese YY

南蛮子 Nánmánzi

☎ 5157 5510; E7, 2nd fl, Life Art Gallery Space, 56 South Maoming Rd; 茂名南路56号生活艺术 空间2楼E7; dishes Y15-60; ☯ 11am-2.30pm & 5-10.30pm; Ⓜ South Shanxi Rd

Despite the alarming name, there's nothing remotely barbaric about the food here.

top picks

FOREIGN FAVOURITES

Where to go when you don't want to eat Chinese.

- **A Future Perfect** (p163) Never mind the attitude, enjoy the fresh bread and cafe classics.
- **Bali Laguna** (p171) A taste of Indonesia in a setting that's as idyllic as it gets in Shànghǎi.
- **Cantina Agave** (left) Delicious burritos that won't break the bank.
- **Coconut Paradise** (p164) Romantic venue and Chiang Mai curries.
- **el Willy** (p162) The place for clever tapas straight outta Barcelona.
- **Factory** (p174) From the Big BLT (with cod) to the grilled cheese experiment of the day – it's comfort food for the next generation.
- **Haiku** (p164) Wacky maki rolls that live up to the hype.
- **Vedas** (opposite) Upmarket Indian in an atmosphere far removed from your local curry house.
- **Wagas** (p172) Wi-fi-enabled cafe with cheap breakfasts, wraps and sandwiches.

Instead, you get fine, MSG-free Yúnnán cuisine served by friendly staff in a laid-back (though somewhat noisy) atmosphere. It's hard to fault any of the dishes, but the barbecued freshwater snapper with a cumin and peppercorn glaze (Y60) is a sublime explosion of flavours. The stewed beef and mint casserole (Y45) is almost as good, as is the incomparable 'grandmother's mashed potatoes' (Y20). It's essential to make room for the chicken wings (Y25) too, which come covered in a seriously addictive secret sauce. To top it off, they have an impressively long imported beer list (Y35–55). Reserve.

ARUGULA Map pp86-7 — Continental YY

☎ 6433 8577; No 2, Lane 49, West Fuxing Rd; 复兴西路49弄2号; dishes from Y40; ☺ 10am-11pm Sun-Thu, 10am-2am Fri & Sat; Ⓜ Changshu Rd

Located in a garish, orange-coloured three-storey house in an alley off West Fuxing Rd, this restaurant is a cosy place for lunch or to while away an afternoon. The menu mixes Mediterranean flavours – the house special Arugula Canard Salad (Y48) features slices of duck breast with cherry tomatoes and an orange dressing – with more hearty dishes, such as pasta (from Y45), lamb chops and steaks (Y110). There's a strong cocktail menu (from Y45) and it's an excellent spot for long, lazy weekend brunches. Reserve.

INDIAN KITCHEN Map pp86-7 — Indian YY

印度小厨 Yìndù Xiǎochú

☎ 6473 1517; 572 Yongjia Rd; 永嘉路572号; mains Y35-55, set lunch Mon-Fri only Y30-40; ☺ 11.30am-2.30pm & 5.30-11.30pm; Ⓜ Hengshan Rd

One of Shànghǎi's growing number of Indian restaurants, this is a popular place, especially with expat Brits yearning for a taste of their national cuisine. All the classics are on the menu, from kormas to vindaloos and they deliver too. The set lunch, which isn't available at weekends, is a good deal. There's another branch in Hóngqiáo (Map p132; ☎ 6261 0377; House 8, 3911 Hongmei Rd; 虹梅路3911号8号房; Ⓜ Longxi Rd).

NAM 1975 Map pp86-7 — Vietnamese YY

越楼 Yuèlóu

☎ 5386 1975; No 41, Lane 816, Middle Huaihai Rd; 淮海中路816弄41号; dishes Y30-68; Ⓜ South Shanxi Rd

Debates rage over whether Shànghǎi will ever have an authentic Vietnamese restaurant, but unless you're a serious connoisseur, you'll probably find Nam to be a first-rate choice. Large bowls (Y39) of pho (rice noodles) and bun (vermicelli noodles) are the stars, though for an extra Y35, why not sample some of the spring rolls too? It's lost down an alley off Middle Huaihai Rd.

KOMMUNE Map pp86-7 — Cafe Y

公社 Gōngshè

☎ 6466 2416; Taikang Rd Art Centre, The Yard, No 7, Lane 210, Taikang Rd; 泰康路210弄7号田子坊; meals from Y38; ☺ 8am-midnight; Ⓜ Dapuqiao Rd; ☺

The original Taikang Rd cafe, Kommune is a consistently packed hangout with outdoor seating, big breakfasts, sandwiches and barbecue on the menu. Kids under 10 eat free.

SICHUAN CITIZEN Map pp86-7 — Sichuanese Y

龙门阵茶屋 Lóngménzhèn Cháwū

☎ 5404 1235; 30 Donghu Rd; 东湖路30号; dishes Y15-58; Ⓜ South Shanxi Rd

Citizen has opted for the 'rustic chic' look, the wood panelling and whirring ceiling fans conjuring up visions of an old-style Chéngdū teahouse that's been made over for an Elle photo shoot. But the food is the real stuff, prepared by a busy Sìchuān kitchen crew to ensure no Shanghainese sweetness creeps into the peppercorn onslaught. If you're new to Sichuanese, this is a great place to try the classics, including twice-cooked pork (Y22), mapo tofu (Y18), and kung pao shrimp (Y58).

LÁNXĪN CĀNTĪNG

Map pp86-7 — Shanghainese Y

兰心餐厅

130 Jinxian Rd; 进贤路130号; dishes from Y20; ☺ 11am-2pm, 5-9pm; Ⓜ South Shanxi Rd

The best Shanghainese kitchens are the hole-in-the-walls along Jinxian Rd. These aren't design-heavy restaurants started by savvy investors or international superchefs, they're unpretentious and family-run – the last of a dying breed. Dishes to savour include the classic hóngshāo ròu (红烧肉; braised pork; Y30), the delectable gānshāo chāngyú (干烧鲳鱼; quick-fried Pomfret fish; Y50-65) and even the xiǎopái luóbo tāng (小排萝卜汤; spare-rib-and-radish soup; Y20). For total immersion, order a bottle of warm huáng jiǔ (黄酒; traditional Chinese wine; Y30). If the wait is too long, Hǎijīnzī (海金滋; 240 Jinxian Rd) at the western end of the street is a comparable experience. No reservations, no English and cash only.

DŌNGBĚI RÉN Map pp86-7   Manchurian Y
东北人

☎ 5228 8288; 1 South Shaanxi Rd by Middle Yan'an Rd; 陕西南路1号; dishes Y15-50; ⏱ 11am-2pm & 4.30-10pm; Ⓜ South Shanxi Rd
No one would ever call northeastern (*dōngběi*) cuisine refined, but it's just the thing when you're in the mood for some hearty rib-stickin' home cooking. The exuberant waitresses – all smiles, pigtails and bright flower-patterned fabric – occasionally break into folk songs and do their best to make dinner seem like a peasant musical revival. There's an outstanding selection of dumplings (16 for Y8), as well as the delicious 'stir-fried three vegetables' (Y15), cumin lamb (Y32) and all manner of cornbreads.

GRAPE RESTAURANT
Map pp86-7   Shanghainese Y
葡萄园酒家 Pútáoyuán Jiǔjiā

☎ 5404 0486; 55 Xinle Rd; 新乐路55号; dishes Y15-48; ⏱ 9.30am-midnight; Ⓜ South Shanxi Rd
This long-standing expat fave from the 1980s has probably seen better days, but the Grape still serves up reliable and inexpensive Shanghainese in its bright premises beside the old Russian Orthodox church. Try the delicious *yóutiáo chǎoniúròu* (油条炒牛肉; dough sticks with beef; Y22), or any of the crab dishes – you won't find them any cheaper than here.

TSUI WAH
Map pp86-7   Cantonese Y
翠华餐厅 Cuìhuá Cāntīng

☎ 6170 1282; 291 Fumin Rd; 富民路291号; dishes from Y25; ⏱ 11am-1am; Ⓜ Changshu Rd/South Shanxi Rd
The famous Hong Kong tea restaurant has finally set up shop in Shànghǎi, garnering instant acclaim not only among homesick Hong Kongers but pretty much everyone else in the 'hood. Notable dishes include Hainan chicken (Y42) and the Malaysian curries (Y35), but the menu skips from Cantonese to club sandwiches to Italian pasta without missing a beat. And what would a tea restaurant be without milk tea (Y11)?

SĀNGÙ NIÚWĀ Map pp86-7   Sichuanese Y
三顾牛蛙

☎ 6466 6155; 3 Fenyang Rd; 汾阳路3号; frog hotpot Y69; ⏱ 11am-2pm, 5-11pm; Ⓜ South Shanxi Rd

Once you're ready for a slightly more off-the-beaten-track Chinese meal, it's time for some frog hotpot. Of course, there are plenty of places in town to sample the famous 'it tastes just like chicken' (it doesn't really), but Sāngù specialises in it. No English? No worries. Almost everyone here orders the same thing: *gānguō niúwā* (干锅牛蛙; Y69), a peppercorn-and-black-bean-smothered medley of tender frog meat, lotus root and vegetable chips. One serving will feed two to three people.

SHǓ DÌ LÀZI YÚ GUǍN
Map pp86-7   Sichuanese Y
蜀地辣子鱼馆

☎ 5403 7684; 187 Anfu Rd; 安福路187号; dishes from Y12-28; ⏱ 11am-2pm, 5-11pm; Ⓜ Changshu Rd
Most celebrity-owned restaurants in China are temples of style over substance. Not this place, which is the brainchild of a famous Sìchuān actor. Both the prices and decor are decidedly downmarket, but there's nothing cut-rate about the food. An intriguing mix of Sìchuān and northeastern classics with a dash of Shanghainese flavour, they're consistently tasty. Try the fried shredded beef with preserved chillies (Y22), or the spicy fish if you can handle hotter food.

NOODLE BULL
Map pp86-7   Noodles Y
狠牛面 Hěnniú Miàn

☎ 6170 1299; Unit 3B, 291 Fumin Rd (entrance on Changle Rd); 富民路291号1F3B室; noodles Y18-28; Ⓜ Changshu Rd/South Shanxi Rd; Ⓥ
Noodle Bull has all the makings of a cult favourite: it's far cooler than your average street-corner noodle stand (minimalist concrete chic and funky bowls), it's inexpensive, and boy is that broth slurpable. It doesn't matter whether you go vegetarian or for the roasted beef noodles (Y28), it's hard not to find satisfaction. The cherry on the cake? No MSG.

YĪ JIĀ YĪ
Map pp86-7   Chinese Y
伊加伊

145 South Shaanxi Rd; 陕西南路145号; dishes Y10-32; ⏱ 24hr; Ⓜ South Shanxi Rd
One of the most affordable French Concession eateries, Yī Jiā Yī is a round-the-clock diner that covers all the bases – noodles (from Y12), dumplings (six for Y8) and popular standards like *kung pao* chicken.

EATING FRENCH CONCESSION

BÌ FĒNG TÁNG Map pp86-7   Dim Sum Y
避风塘

☎ 6467 0628; 175 Changle Rd; 长乐路175号; dumplings from Y8; ☼ 24hr; Ⓜ South Shanxi Rd

At busy times, this popular wicker-and bamboo-clad dim sum joint resonates to the constant clatter of porcelain dishes and wait staff shouting back and forth to each other. There's a slack period in the late afternoon, but it's still bustling in the early hours as the late-night crowd file, or stagger, in. Winners here include steamed shrimp and chive dumplings, duck noodle soup and barbecued pork buns. Another Bì Fēng Táng branch can be found in Gǔběi (Map pp128–9; ☎ 6208 6388; 37 South Shuicheng Rd; 水城南路37号; Ⓜ Shuicheng Rd).

FĒNGYÙ SHĒNGJIĀN
Map pp86-7   Dumplings Y
丰裕生煎

41 Ruijin No 2 Rd, cnr Nanchang Rd; 瑞金二路41号; 4 dumplings Y3; ☼ 6am-8pm; Ⓜ South Shanxi Rd

Don't let the Stalinist service and lack of English put you off at this nondescript canteen, as it turns out popular *shēngjiān* (生煎; fried dumplings) for a bargain Y3, in addition to a range of cheap noodle dishes (Y6). Pay at the entrance and then join the queue.

JÌNG'ĀN 静安区

Although business lunches and after-dinner drinks are the rule in Jìng'ān, most of the dining options here have long been first-rate, and those on a culinary tour of Shànghǎi should definitely squeeze it on to the itinerary.

FU 1039 Map pp86-7   Shanghainese YYY
福一零三九 Fú Yī Yào Líng Sān Jiǔ

☎ 6288 1179; 1039 Yuyuan Rd; 愚园路1039号; dishes Y40-288; ☼ 11am-2.30pm & 5-11pm; Ⓜ Jiangsu Rd

Set in a three-storey 1913 villa, Fu attains an old-fashioned charm uncommon in design-driven Shànghǎi. Foodies who appreciate sophisticated surroundings and Shanghainese food on par with the decor, take note – Fu is a must. The succulent standards here won't let you down: the smoked fish starter (Y42) and stewed pork in soy sauce (Y68) are recommended, with the sautéed chicken and mango (Y42) and sweet-and-sour Mandarin fish (Y128) coming in close behind. This is still a locals' place; the entrance, down an alley and on

the left, is unmarked and the staff speak little English. Sister restaurant Fu 1088 (Map pp98–9; ☎ 5239 7878; 1088 Zhenning Rd; 镇宁路 1088号) is much more exclusive – it's private dining only, with a minimum charge of Y300 per head. Reserve.

ZEN Map pp98-9   Cantonese YY
采蝶轩酒家 Cǎidiéxuān Jiǔjiā

☎ 6288 1141; 5th fl, Plaza 66, 1266 West Nanjing Rd; 南京西路1266号恒隆广场5楼; dishes Y38-108; ☼ 11am-10pm; Ⓜ West Nanjing Rd

The swish Plaza 66 shopping mall (p146) may give mere mortals the heebie-jeebies, but Zen, arched around the horseshoe-end of the 5th floor, is a delectable surprise. Cantonese favourites include the sautéed chicken with ginger and spring onion in clam sauce (half/whole serve Y55/108) and baked spare ribs (Y58). There's also branches near the Bund in the Hongyi Plaza (Map pp66–7; 7th fl, Hongyi Plaza, 299 East Nanjing Rd; 南京东路299号宏 伊国际广场7楼; Ⓜ West Nanjing Rd) and on the 5th floor of the Grand Gateway mall (p148).

LYNN Map pp98-9   Shanghainese YY
琳怡 Lín Yí

☎ 6247 0101; 99-1 Xikang Rd; 西康路99-1号; dishes Y14-108; ☼ 11.30am-10.30pm; Ⓜ West Nanjing Rd

Another one of the growing number of restaurants pushing the boundaries between Shanghainese and Cantonese cuisine, Lynn offers consistently good, cleverly presented dishes at reasonable prices in plush but unfussy surroundings. The lunch dim-sum menu offers a range of delicate dumplings (from Y16), while for dinner there are more traditional Shanghainese dishes, like eggplant with minced pork in a garlic and chilli sauce (Y38). More adventurous standouts include the sautéed chicken with sesame pockets (Y52) and deep-fried spare ribs with honey and garlic (Y95). Sundays bring an all-you-can-eat brunch menu for Y78. Reserve.

QIMIN ORGANIC HOTPOT
Map pp98-9   Hotpot YY
齐民有机中国火锅 Qímín Yǒujī Zhōngguó Huǒguō

☎ 6258 8777; 407 North Shaanxi Rd; 陕西北路 407号; set menu lunch Mon-Fri Y68/88; set menu lunch & dinner 120/150; ☼ 11am-2pm, 5-9pm; Ⓜ West Nanjing Rd; Ⓥ

Hotpot aficionados may scoff at the idea of healthy *huǒguō* and iced organic vinegar drinks, but if Alice Waters ever comes to Shànghǎi, we recommend she make this one of her first stops. True, the renovated art deco villa, low-fat lamb and local vegies are a long way from what generally passes for hotpot in the rest of the country, but Qimin does make use of a 6th-century treatise on agriculture and food preparation (the *Qímín Yàoshù*), effectively taking an old tradition in a new direction.

BALI LAGUNA Map pp98-9   Indonesian YY
巴厘岛 Bālí Dǎo
☎ 6248 6970; 1649 West Nanjing Rd; 南京西路1649号; mains Y75-110; ☉ 11am-10.30pm; Ⓜ Jing'an Temple
The restaurant's tranquil lakeside setting in Jing'an Park belies its proximity to the roaring Yan'an Rd, while the open long-house interior, decked out in dark wood and rattan, has a genuine tropical feel. Waiters in sarongs serve up excellent dishes, such as seafood curry in a fresh pineapple, *gado gado* (vegetable salad with peanut sauce) and *kalio daging* (beef in coconut milk, lemongrass and curry sauce). The outside terrace is a particularly prized spot and this is one of Shànghǎi's more intimate restaurants. Reserve.

MÉILÓNGZHÈN JIǓJIĀ
Map pp98-9   Chinese YY
梅陇镇酒家
☎ 6253 5353; No 22, Lane 1081, West Nanjing Rd; 南京西路1081弄22号; dishes from Y40; ☉ 11am-2pm, 5-9pm; Ⓜ West Nanjing Rd
Shànghǎi has a host of famous local restaurants, none more so than this fantastic old building, which has been churning out food since the 1930s. The rooms once housed the Shanghai Communist Party headquarters, but are now bedecked in woodcarvings, huge palace lamps and photos of foreign dignitaries. The menu mixes Sìchuān and Shanghainese tastes and ranges from the pricey (crab with tofu, Y120) to the more reasonable, such as the fish slices with tangerine peel (Y45).

LÙLU JIǓJIĀ Map pp98-9   Shanghainese YY
鹭鹭酒家
☎ 6288 1179; 5th fl, Plaza 66, 1266 West Nanjing Rd; 南京西路1266号5楼; dishes Y38-128; ☉ 11am-2.30pm & 5-10pm; Ⓜ West Nanjing Rd

Lùlu is fancy Shanghainese without the overbearing attitude – it's more popular with families and the ladies who lunch crowd than urban hipsters – and the prices are surprisingly reasonable. With over 20 aquariums on display, you'd be foolish not to try at least one of the braised seafood specialities, though steer clear of the fish heads. There are branches behind Jing'an Temple (Map pp98–9; ☎ 6248 6969; 161 Yuyuan Rd; 愚园路161号; Ⓜ Jing'an Temple) and in Pǔdōng (Map p108; ☎ 5882 6679; 2nd fl, China Merchants Tower, 161 East Lujiazui Rd; 陆家嘴东路161号招商大厦2楼). Reserve.

ELEMENT FRESH Map pp98-9   Cafe YY
新元素 Xīnyuánsù
☎ 6279 8682; www.elementfresh.com; Shanghai Centre, 1376 West Nanjing Rd; 南京西路1376号; sandwiches & salads Y39-88, dinner Y118-188; ☉ 7am-11pm Sun-Thu, 7am-midnight Fri & Sat; Ⓜ Jing'an Temple; 🛜 Ⓥ
Perennially popular, Element Fresh hits the spot with its tempting selection of healthy salads, pasta dishes (Western and Asian) and hefty sandwiches. Vegetarians may well faint with excitement at the roasted eggplant on ciabatta bread or the Italian tofu sandwich smothered in pesto.

top picks

EATING ORGANIC

The organic movement in China has only just sprouted, but it has quickly spread its leaves in Shànghǎi. With the quality of produce and manufactured products becoming increasingly dubious, there's been enough negative publicity (in 2009 this included the discovery of bean sprouts being soaked in a banned chemical solution at local markets, glass noodle samples that contained aluminium, mutated eggs that bounced 'like ping-pong balls' and a Greenpeace study that reported high levels of pesticide residue in supermarket produce) that Shanghainese are starting to get interested. Organic farms in the area have gone from five to 30 in just three years. Upscale restaurants (T8, el Willy, Jean Georges) usually use at least some organic produce, while the following restaurants specialise in local organic ingredients:

- Vegetarian Lifestyle (p172)
- Mingtang Organic Dining (p160)
- Qimin Organic Hotpot (opposite)
- Origin (p165)

top picks

PLACES TO SPLURGE

- **Chinoise Story** (p161) A sensuous Shànghǎi beauty.
- **Fu 1039** (p170) Old-fashioned charm and succulent Shanghainese.
- **On 56** (opposite) Savour a night out in the stratosphere.
- **T8** (p161) For celeb-spotting and seduction.
- **Jean Georges** (p157) From Manhattan to Shànghǎi, with a stopover in France.

Then there are the imaginative smoothies (from Y22), big breakfasts (Y38–68), coffee and after-work cocktails. There are other branches in the French Concession (Map pp86–7; 4th fl, K Wah Centre, 1028 Middle Huaihai Rd; 淮海中路1028号嘉华中心4楼), Pǔdōng's Superbrand Mall (p147; ground floor), and Xújiāhuì's Grand Gateway mall (p148; ground floor).

BLUE FROG Map pp98-9   American YY

蓝蛙 **Lánwā**

☎ 6247 0320; 86 Tongren Rd; 铜仁路86号; burgers Y80, beers Y30-55; ⏰ 10am-late; Ⓜ Jing'an Temple; 🛜

There are seven Frogs around Shànghǎi, and their mix of burgers, sports TV and four-hour happy hours (⏰ 4-8pm) mean they're perennially popular. On Tuesday nights drinks are Y25, but if you can down all 100 of the shots they list, then you'll get a free one every day for life and your name on their wall of fame. Other branches are at the Superbrand Mall (p147) and in Hongqiao (☎ 5422 5199; 30 Hongmei Entertainment Street; 虹梅路3338弄虹梅休闲步行街30号).

DA MARCO Map pp86-7   Italian YY

大马可餐厅 **Dàmǎkě Cāntīng**

☎ 6210 4495; 103 Dong Zhu'anbang Rd, inside Metro Park Apartments; 东诸安浜路103号; pasta & pizza Y63-78, mains Y108-158; ⏰ noon-11pm; Ⓜ Jiangsu Rd

This homey spot is one of the best and most popular Italian restaurants in town and remains a steal after a decade in business (which, it should be noted, is an eternity in Shànghǎi). Daily specials such as pear-and-gorgonzola pizza and fettuccine porcini are chalked up on the blackboard.

There's another branch at the Grand Gateway mall (p148). Reserve.

VEGETARIAN LIFESTYLE

Map pp98-9   Chinese, Vegetarian YY

枣子树 **Zǎozishù**

☎ 6215 7566; 258 Fengxian Rd; 奉贤路258号; dishes Y26-42; ⏰ 11am-9pm; Ⓜ West Nanjing Rd; Ⓥ

These folks are surely improving their karma by making organic, vegetarian fare fashionable for the masses. There's a wide range of clever dishes, including soup served in a pumpkin, but best are the sweet Wuxi spareribs (Y36), stuffed with lotus root of course, and the diverse clay pots (from Y26). No MSG is used and cooks go light on the oil. There's another hard-to-find branch in the French Concession (Map pp86–7; ☎ 6384 8000; 77 Songshan Rd; 嵩山路77号) and near Carrefour in Gǔběi (Map pp128–9; ☎ 6275 1798; 848 Huangjincheng Rd; 黄金城道848号).

CITY DINER Map pp98-9   American YY

☎ 6289 3699; 3rd fl, 142 Tongren Rd; 铜仁路142号3楼; breakfast from Y60, sandwiches Y30-60; ⏰ 24hr; Ⓜ Jing'an Temple; 🛜

With vintage posters on the walls, the American-sized portions and a menu full of classics such as southern fried chicken, grilled cheese, and burgers (including a vegie option) from Y50, this place pulls out all the stops in its efforts to re-create the style of a genuine US diner. It's gotten rough around the edges but it mostly works, although the slightly erratic service sometimes spoils things. The hefty all-day breakfasts (from Y60) take some effort to walk off.

WAGAS Map pp98-9   Cafe Y

沃歌斯 **Wògēsī**

☎ 5292 5228; B11A, Citic Square, 1168 West Nanjing Rd; 南京西路1168号中信泰富地下一层11A室; meals from Y48; ⏰ 7am-9.30pm; Ⓜ West Nanjing Rd; 🛜

Breakfasts are 50% off before 10am, the pasta is Y33 after 6pm, and you can hang out here for hours with your laptop and no one will shoo you away – need we say more? Wagas is the best and most dependable of the local cafes, with tantalising wraps, salads and sandwiches, perfect for a quick bite at any time of the day. Locations abound (this one is hidden next to a McDonald's): the French Concession (Map pp86–7;

G107, Hong Kong New World Tower, 300 Middle Huaihai Rd; 淮海中路300号香港新世界大厦G107室), the Bund (Map p71; G116, Hongyi Plaza, 288 Jiujiang Rd; 九江路288号宏伊广场G116室) and Grand Gateway (Map p122; Room 151, 1 Hongqiao Rd; 虹桥路1号港汇广场151室) all have branches.

GŌNGDÉLÍN
Map pp98-9   Chinese, Vegetarian Y

功德林

☎ 63270218; 445 West Nanjing Rd; 南京西路445号; dishes Y14-38, set menu Y125; ⏲ 11am-3pm & 5-10.30pm; Ⓜ People's Square; Ⓥ
Shànghǎi's second-oldest vegetarian restaurant (opened in 1922), Gōngdélín never fails to perplex Western vegetarians – close to everything on the menu is prepared to resemble meat! Don't worry though, the beef with *shacha* sauce and the sesame chicken rolls are actually made of tofu, no matter how convincing they look. The interior is a mix of stone and wood with Venetian blinds, honeycombed lamps and a couple of Buddhist statues thrown in for good fortune.

NEW YORK STYLE PIZZA
Map pp98-9   Pizza Y

比萨 Bǐsà

☎ 6247 2265; J16 Jing'an Temple Plaza, 1699 West Nanjing Rd; 南京西路1699号静安寺广场J16; slices Y15, whole pizza Y108/118; ⏲ 11.30am-9pm; Ⓜ Jing'an Temple (exit No 5)
This isn't some fancy pseudo-Italian wood-burning-oven pie, this is the real deal: gooey, greasy, calorie laden and utterly delicious. Perfect for a lunch on the run. It's located outside exit No 5 of the Jing'an Temple metro station. Another outlet is in Lane 248 at the Taikang Rd Art Centre (Map pp86–7).

ALWAYS CAFÉ
Map pp98-9   Cafe Y

奥维斯咖啡馆 Àowéisī Kāfēiguǎn

☎ 6247 8333; 1528 West Nanjing Rd; 南京西路1528号; set lunch Y20-35; ⏲ 11am-2am; Ⓜ Jing'an Temple; 🛜
What draws the regulars here are the excellent value set-lunch specials with coffee (11am to 5pm), and the buy-one-get-one-free happy hour (5pm to 8pm). The food is a mix of Asian and Western, from Indonesian *nasi goreng* (fried rice) and Shànghǎi-style eel to bacon cheeseburgers and pasta. It's a friendly place with chequered tablecloths and an old parquet floor which, along with the wi-fi access, makes it an easy place to while away an afternoon or evening. Fans of afternoon tea can find it here (Y48 for two).

PǓDŌNG 浦东

While there are few restaurants distinctive to Pǔdōng, you can be assured that wherever you go you'll find something to eat. Most sights have popular citywide chains in the immediate vicinity; malls (of which there are many) are another sure bet. The gargantuan Superbrand Mall (p147) in Lùjiāzuǐ has restaurants spread out across 10 floors. In the Century Avenue area, the plaza outside of the Zendai Museum of Modern Art (p113) has loads of good chains plus a Carrefour supermarket.

ON 56
Map p108   International YYY

意庐 Yìlú

☎ 5047 1234; 54th-56th fl, Grand Hyatt, Jinmao Tower, 88 Century Ave; 世纪大道88号君悦大酒店; meals from Y120; ⏲ 11.30am-2.30pm & 5.30-10.30pm; Ⓜ Lujiazui
The Grand Hyatt in the Jinmao Tower offers a stylish selection of Western and Asian restaurants, all of which owe their superb vistas looking out into the void. Cucina (pizza from Y120) has wonderful Italian dishes from Campania and breads and pizzas fresh from the oven. Grill (mains from Y210) offers fine imported meats and seafood. The Japanese Kobachi (set meals Y290 to Y480) features sushi, sashimi and *yakitori*. Canton (dishes from Y40) is the flagship and features Cantonese food and afternoon dim sum.

On the 54th floor (the hotel lobby) is the Grand Café (⏲ 24 hours) offering stunning panoramas through its glass walls and a good-value lunchtime buffet during the week (Y208), which allows you to choose a main course and have it prepared fresh in the show kitchen. On weekends and in the evening the buffet is Y278. To reserve a table by the window, book well in advance.

SOUTH BEAUTY
Map p108   Sichuanese, Cantonese YY

俏江南 Qiào Jiāngnán

☎ 5047 1817; 10th fl, Superbrand Mall, 168 West Lujiazui Rd; 陆家嘴西路168号10楼; dishes from Y18; ⏲ 11am-10pm; Ⓜ Lujiazui
Views, views and more views – while everyone else is gazing at Pǔdōng's lights, you can stare back at them from this elegant Sìchuān-Cantonese combo. The stuffed

chillies at the entrance hint at what's to come (spicy beef; Y58), but for those who enjoy milder tastes, southern dishes such as the crispy chicken (Y58) will soothe the tastebuds. You'll need to reserve for window seats, but an equally attractive locale is in front of the glass-paned kitchen, where you can watch the 30-plus chefs work the woks. There are several other branches, including in the French Concession (Map pp86–7; ☎ 6445 2581; 28 Taojiang Rd; 桃江路28号).

THAI TASTE

Map p108   Thai Y

泰泰餐厅 **Tàitài Cāntīng**

5th fl, Superbrand Mall, 168 West Lujiazui Rd; 陆家嘴西路168号正大广场5层; dishes from Y16; 🕑 11am-10pm; M Lujiazui

For a cheap meal in the Superbrand Mall, Thai Taste is a step above the rest of the food-court restaurants. Dishes such as *tom kah gai* (coconut, lemongrass and chicken soup) and green curry (Y20) may be small, but they are served with rice and carry enough chilli and lemongrass to bring back memories of sweaty meals in Thailand.

HÓNGKǑU & NORTH SHÀNGHǍI
虹口区、北上海

XĪNDÀLÙ

Map p116   Peking Duck, Zhèjiāng YYY

新大陆

☎ 6393-1234 ext. 6318; 1st fl, Hyatt on the Bund, 199 Huangpu Rd; 黄浦路199号外滩茂悦大酒店1楼; roast duck half/whole Y138/198, dishes from Y48; 🕑 11.30am-2.30pm, 6-11pm; M Tiantong Rd

Shànghǎi's premier *kǎoyā* (roast duck) experience, this upscale hotel restaurant pulls out all the stops, importing all the necessary ingredients (including the chefs and a special brick oven) direct from the capital in order to make your duck as crispy and authentic as possible. In addition to the sleek open kitchen, it's unusually intimate inside – well, that part might not be authentic, but it's not exactly something that most diners are going to complain about. Other first-rate dishes on offer include beggar's chicken (a Hángzhōu speciality), which needs to be ordered at least four hours in advance. Reserve.

FACTORY

Map p116   Fusion YY

意工场 **Yì Gōngchǎng**

☎ 6563 3393; www.factoryshanghai.com; Bldg 4, 29 Shajing Rd; 沙泾路29号4楼; lunch Y27-75, dinner Y55-195; 🕑 8am-midnight; M North Sichuan Rd/Hailun Rd; 🛜

This place is all about creativity, with a recording studio, art exhibition space, digipod and small retail shop selling the wares of designers-in-residence. Oh, and did we mention that it's also a restaurant? Shànghǎi really needs more places like this – it's fun, the food is delicious (and creative), and it's a promising cultural nexus. Dig into a *kung pao* chicken salad (Y35) and grilled shrimp burger (Y55) for lunch or the peppercorn-crusted scallops (Y125) for dinner. Check the website for event listings.

AFANTI RESTAURANT

Map pp62-3   Uighur YY

阿凡提美食城 **Āfántí Měishíchéng**

☎ 6555 9604; 775 Quyang Rd; 曲阳路775号; dishes from Y30; 🕑 11.30am-11.30pm; M Chifeng Rd

Discerning fans of hearty Uighur cuisine can make the trek to the northern boonies for some of the city's best Central Asian food in a friendly and authentic environment. The delicious *dàpánjī* (fried chicken, peppers and potatoes; Y80), *gosh gorma* (fried mutton; *chǎo kǎoròu* in Chinese) and cumin-rubbed lamb are all praiseworthy, and don't forget to try the homemade *suān nǎi* (yogurt). The restaurant is in the basement of the Tianshan Hotel, next to the Silk Rd Hotel. Look for the building with the golden domes.

XÚJIĀHUÌ & SOUTH SHÀNGHǍI
徐家汇、南上海

The Grand Gateway mall (p148) and food courts galore cater to the hardened shoppers of Xújiāhuì, but there are also some good restaurants nearby, particularly on Tianyaoqiao Rd.

SHANGHAI UNCLE

Map p122   Shanghainese YYY

海上阿叔 **Hǎishàng Āshū**

☎ 6464 6430; 211 Tianyaoqiao Rd; 天钥桥路211号; dishes from Y28; 🕑 10am-midnight; M Xujiahui

UIGHUR & MUSLIM FOOD

Most of Shànghǎi's Muslim restaurants are run by Uighurs – Central Asians from Xīnjiāng, China's far northwest. A refreshing alternative to the seafood and sweetness of Shanghainese cuisine, Xinjiang dishes consist of lots of mutton (though chicken and fish dishes are available), peppers, potatoes, cumin and delicious naan bread. Shànghǎi's other main Muslim food is that of the Hui, represented by Lánzhōu-style noodles.

One good reason to try a Uighur restaurant is to check out the conspicuously non-Chinese atmosphere. Recordings of swirling Central Asian lute music complement the Arabic calligraphy on the walls, and meals are washed down with bowls of Central Asian *kok chai* (green tea).

Try *shashlyk* (shish kebabs), *suoman* (delicious fried noodle squares) or *laghman* (pulled noodles). Vegetarians should ask for *gush siz* (without meat). To avoid a mutton overdose, try the generally excellent *chon tashlick tokhor* (*dàpánjī* in Chinese; fried chicken, peppers and potatoes). Fancier places sell fruity Xinjiang wines like Loulan (named after a ruined Silk Rd city).

The best Uighur restaurants are now spread throughout the city, and include the following.

Afanti Restaurant (opposite) Tuck into classic Uighur dishes at this traditional and dependable favourite.

Pamir Restaurant (新疆风味饭店; Xīnjiāng Fēngwèi Fàndiàn; Map pp86–7; 166 Fumin Rd, French Concession; 富民路166号; M Changshu Rd/Jing'an Temple) Below street level, and located by the shouts from Uighur kebab *Meisters*, the Pamir does decent kebabs, naan and more, all washed down with Xinjiang beer.

Uighur Restaurant (维吾尔餐厅; Wéiwú'ěr Cāntīng; Map pp86–7; 1 South Shaanxi Rd, French Concession; 陕西南路1号; M South Shanxi Rd) Not as good as the others, though the *polo* (*zhuāfàn*; rice pilaf; Y15) makes up for it. There's also obligatory dancing to Radio Xinjiang's top 40 hits – sung by the staff.

Xinjiang Fengwei Restaurant (below) The friendliest waiters in town, lots of dancing, and food so good you could be in Xīnjiāng.

This restaurant is what Shànghǎi is all about: brash, bustling and just a little tacky. The owner is the son of a *New York Times* food critic and the dishes mix Western and Asian influences with Shanghainese cooking to surprising and succulent effect. The seafood dishes are particularly good – a steamed Yangzi sole, a gingery-sweet smoked fish (Y36) – but the pine-seed pork ribs in a soy, Worcester and red wine sauce (Y88) and crispy duck with sticky-rice stuffing (Y108) are excellent too. There are branches in the Bund Center (Map pp66–7; ☎ 6339 1977; 222 East Yan'an Rd; 延安东路222号) and Pǔdōng (Map p114; ☎ 5836 7977; 8th fl, Times Square, 500 Zhangyang Rd; 张杨路500号时代广场8楼).

YE OLDE STATION RESTAURANT
Map p122   Shanghainese YY

上海老站 Shànghǎi Lǎozhàn

☎ 6427 2233; 201 North Caoxi Rd; 漕溪北路201号; dishes from Y28; ⏰ 11am-10.30pm; M Xujiahui

With crisp linen and a sharp colonial facade, this restaurant serves meals that are infinitely classier than most of the alternative fare around Xújiāhuì. You can spend a lot here, but the stewed chicken with chestnut (Y45) and the house special of smoked duck with a flavour of tea (Y58)

are reasonable. The name suggests it was a former railway station, but it actually used to be the St Ignatius Convent (there's a chapel upstairs). Not to worry, train buffs, there are two period railway cars outside – one purportedly belonging to the Dragon Lady, Empress Dowager Cixi, herself. Reserve.

DŌNGLÁISHÙN Map p122   Hotpot YY
东来顺

☎ 6474 7797; 235 Guangyuan Rd; 广元路235号; hotpot from Y60; ⏰ 10.30am-2am; M Xujiahui/Jiaotong University

Hotpot king Dōngláishùn enjoys a reputation among locals as highly burnished as its brass hotpots. Perfect for one of those clammy, frigid Shànghǎi winters, but any season will do. There's no English menu so hand gesticulations are in order, or point at the characters in the menu decoder. Look for the green sign across the road from Ajisen (noodle shop).

XINJIANG FENGWEI RESTAURANT
Map p122   Uighur Y

维吾尔餐厅 Wéiwú'ěr Cāntīng

☎ 6468 9198; 280 Yishan Rd; 宜山路280号; dishes from Y15; ⏰ 10am-2am; M Yishan Rd/Xujiahui

Any reservations you might have about the Fengwei's far-flung location will dissolve the minute you walk through the door. 'Hey man, how you doing!' Yup, you've just been teleported to Kashgar. The raucous atmosphere and Uighur vibe reaches a new level once the music and dancing get going later in the night. Try the *dàpánjī* (small/medium/large Y35/50/70) – a spicy stew of chicken, peppers and potatoes – as well as fresh yogurt, *plov* (mutton pilaf; Y15), lamb kebabs (four for Y12), and *naan* (flat bread), and wash it all down with some Xīnjiāng black beer (Y8).

CHÁNGNÍNG, GŮBĚI & HONGQIAO AIRPORT AREA 长宁、古北

The Hongmei Rd Entertainment Street (虹梅路虹梅休闲步行街; Map p132) has a selection of Asian and Western places for the locals and expats who don't want to head into town. There are branches of Big Bamboo (p183) and Simply Thai (p167) here.

1221

Map pp128-9   Shanghainese YY

Yī Èr Èr Yī

☎ 6213 6585; 1221 West Yan'an Rd; 延安西路1221号; dishes from Y22; ⏰ 11am-2pm & 5-11pm; taxi

No one has a bad thing to say about this smart expat favourite and rightly so, as it has never let its standards dip over the years. Meat dishes start at Y42 for the beef and dough strips (*yóutiáo*), and the plentiful eel, shrimp and squid dishes are around twice that. Other tempting fare includes the roast duck (Y108) and braised pork (Y68). The pan-fried sticky rice and sweet bean paste (from the dim-sum menu) makes a good dessert. It's also worth ordering the eight-fragrance tea just to watch it served spectacularly out of 60cm-long spouts. Reserve.

top picks

- **Citizen Café** (p183)
- **Cloud 9** (p184)
- **Cotton's** (p181)
- **New Heights** (p179)
- **LOgO** (p181)

DRINKING

After teahouse culture went out of style in the 20th century, nothing, apart from karaoke, really ever replaced it. Social drinking today is mainly carried out over meals, and for many older Chinese, going out to drink at a bar still evokes an aura of spiritual pollutedness (or at least wasteful spending of money). The new generation is growing up fast though, and the taboos of the past are having a hard time keeping up.

So while bars and pubs toady are frequented predominantly by foreigners, the race is on to capture the domestic market. In Běijīng there's a more populist approach – Y15 Tsingtaos and unpretentious watering holes – but Shànghǎi has stayed true to its roots: it's all about looking flash, sipping glam cocktails and tapping into the insatiable appetite for new trends. As might be expected, new bars pop up and disappear again with impressive rapidity, but the upside to the intense competition is that weekly specials and happy hours (generally from 5pm to 8pm) manage to keep Shànghǎi affordable, at least in relation to cities outside of China.

Cafe culture is the latest rage to sweep Shànghǎi – they're much more popular than the bars – and while you'd be hard pressed to find a decent teahouse within a 20km radius, cappuccinos and sandwiches served at hip wireless hang-outs – some familiar names, some not – are all over the place. Another common sight are the street stalls selling bubble tea (zhēnzhū nǎichá), a strangely addictive Taiwanese milk tea with tapioca balls, and all sorts of related spin-offs, like hot ginger drinks or freshly puréed watermelon smoothies.

On average, expect to spend around Y40 for beer, Y60 for cocktails, Y20 to Y30 for coffee and Y6 to Y20 for tea and juice. For the cheapest caffeine fix in town look for branches of Café 85℃ (p184). To keep up with the latest hotspots, check the expat mags, www.cityweekend.com.cn/shanghai or www.smartshanghai.com.

THE BUND & PEOPLE'S SQUARE
外滩、人民广场

The Bund is home to some of Shànghǎi's premier drinking spots that jump at the weekends. These are places to get dressed up for and the drinks don't come cheap. But a trip to at least one of these bars is obligatory, if only for the stunning night time view of the Huangpu River and the glittering lights of Pǔdōng.

BAR ROUGE Map pp66-7 Bar
☎ 6339 1199; 7th fl, Bund 18, 18 East Zhongshan No 1 Rd; 中山东一路18号7楼; cocktails from Y80; ☾ 6pm-2am Sun-Thu, 6pm-4.30am Fri & Sat; Ⓜ East Nanjing Rd
Bar Rouge attracts a cashed-up party crowd and is good for a one-time trip, but it's hardly a regular's place. The red-curtained booths are reserved for big spenders, and ordinary mortals can sometimes struggle to get served on busy nights. But it remains a late-night Shànghǎi staple – the terrace offers fantastic views and big-name European DJs are frequently flown in to provide the soundtrack. If one of them is on the decks, expect to pay Y300 to get in. Otherwise, it's Y100 on Fridays and Saturdays after 10pm.

BARBAROSSA Map pp66-7 Bar
芭芭露莎会所 Bābālùshā Huìsuǒ
☎ 6318 0220; People's Park, 231 West Nanjing Rd; 南京西路231号人民公园内; beers Y50, cocktails Y70-85, hookah Y100; ☾ 11am-2am; Ⓜ People's Sq
Set back in People's Park alongside a pond, Barbarossa is all about escapism. Forget Shànghǎi, this brash and flash concept bar is like Morocco as imagined by Hollywood set designers. The action gets steadily more intense as you ascend to the roof terrace, via the ground floor dining area and the cushion-strewn 2nd floor, where the hordes puff on fruit-flavoured hookahs. Happy hour is from 5pm to 8pm, when all drinks are half price, and there's a strong music policy and tasty, if expensive, food. At night use the park entrance just east of the Shanghai Art Museum.

CAPTAIN'S BAR Map pp66-7 Bar
船长青年酒吧 Chuánzhǎng Qīngnián Jiǔbā
☎ 6323 7869; 6th fl, 37 Fuzhou Rd; 福州路37号6楼; beer Y40; ☾ 11am-2am; Ⓜ East Nanjing Rd

Don't let the crummy lift up to this bar on the top floor of the Captain Hostel (p206) put you off. This is the only bar in the area that offers both a decent, if slightly restricted, view of Pǔdōng's lights from the outside terrace and drinks that don't cost a bomb. It's also less crowded and far more laidback than the other Bund bars. They serve pizza (Y40) too.

GLAMOUR BAR

Map pp66–7   Bar

魅力酒吧 Mèilì Jiǔbā

☎ 6329 3751; www.m-onthebund.com; 6th fl, 20 Guangdong Rd; 广东路20号6楼; cocktails from Y78; ☷ 5pm-2am Sun-Thu, 5pm-late Fri & Sat; Ⓜ East Nanjing Rd

The Glamour Bar is more than just one of Shànghǎi's most popular watering holes, it's a cultural institution. It hosts film screenings, the annual literary festival, chamber music performances and China-related book launches. Of course, none of that would hold up if the martinis weren't so good. Get here before midnight on weekends or be prepared to queue to get in. Check the website for events listings.

NEW HEIGHTS

Map pp66–7   Bar

新视角 Xīn Shìjiǎo

☎ 6321 0909; 7th fl, Three on the Bund, 3 East Zhongshan No 1 Rd; 中山东一路3号7楼; beer from Y60; ☷ 11am-1.30am; Ⓜ East Nanjing Rd

The most amenable of the big three Bund bars, this splendid roof terrace offers the best views of the Huangpu River and Pǔdōng. It's easy to become mesmerised by the seductive lights across the way, and time tends to lose its meaning here, especially after a few of their properly mixed cocktails (Y75). Inside it's slightly less appealing, but the DJ and fine nibbles are some consolation.

NUMBER 5

Map pp66–7   Bar

外滩五号 Wàitān Wǔhào

☎ 6329 4558; basement, 20 Guangdong Rd; 外滩广东路20号B1; beer from Y30; ☷ 9.30am-2am; Ⓜ East Nanjing Rd; ☷

The only view from this easy-going Bund bar is of people's shoes on the pavement outside. It may sound anticlimactic compared with the rest of the strip, but it's actually one of the nicer places to kick back and relax after a busy day of seeing the sights. There's free pool, foosball, big leather armchairs, live music (Wednesday to Sunday) and a good selection of Asian and Western pub food (from Y48).

BUND 12 CAFÉ

Map pp66–7   Cafe

外滩12号 Wàitān Shí'èrhào

☎ 6329 5896; Room 226, 2nd fl, 12 Zhongshan East No 1 Rd; 中山东一路12号226房间; espresso Y19, sandwiches from Y36; ☷ 8am-7pm; Ⓜ East Nanjing Rd

If you find yourself in need of a caffeine fix while pounding the Bund, then head for

---

SHANG HIGH

Much like Babel, Shànghǎi yearns to reach the heavens, and not in a spiritual sense. With so many towers scattered around town, a high-altitude view of the metropolis is inevitable, so why not choose a spot where you can relax with a drink? Bund bars have fantastic views, of course, but if you want to get really high, you'll need to hit the hotel bars. Don't yawn yet – they're cheaper (coffee from Y55, cocktails from Y70) and often more congenial than the crowded viewing platforms. Smog can obscure daytime views, so time your visit for dusk.

100 Century Avenue (p184) The world's highest bar (for now), 414m above the ground.

789 Nanjing Lu Bar (Map pp66–7; 789南京路酒吧; Qībǎi Bāshíjiǔ Nánjīng Lù Jiǔbā; ☎ 3318 9999; 64-66 fl, Le Royal Meridien, 789 East Nanjing Rd; 南京东路789号64-66楼; cocktails from Y78; ☷ 3pm-1am; Ⓜ People's Sq) Chocolate martinis (Y98) and 360-degree views are the specialities at the apex of this People's Sq skyscraper.

Cloud 9 (p184) No longer the highest bar in the city, but still the coolest in the stratosphere.

Sin Lounge (p191) It's after midnight and you're looking for a glamorous Shànghǎi dance floor overlooking the city. This is your place.

Vue (Map p116; 非常时髦; Fēicháng Shímáo; ☎ 3318 9999; 32nd & 33rd fl, Hyatt on the Bund, 199 Huangpu Rd; 黄浦路199号外滩茂悦大酒店32-33楼; cocktails from Y70; ☷ 6pm-1am; Ⓜ Tiantong Rd) A rooftop terrace with beds and outdoor jacuzzi to accompany bottles of bubbly and Vue martinis (vodka and mango purée).

this cafe located on the second floor of the old HSBC building. Take the aged lift and then traverse the Whitehall-like corridors that have hardly changed since the 1930s. The cafe itself has a charming terrace and is a great spot to recharge.

OLD TOWN 南市

OLD SHANGHAI TEAHOUSE Map p79   Cafe
老上海茶馆 **Lǎo Shànghǎi Cháguǎn**
☎ 5382 1202; 385 Middle Fangbang Rd; 方浜中路385号; tea Y35-Y65; ⏰ 9am-9pm; Ⓜ Yuyuan Garden

If you need a place to put your feet up after a day spent wandering the Old Town, visit this wonderfully decrepit 2nd-floor teahouse, overlooking Old St. It's a shrine to the 1930s, with period typewriters, sewing machines, electric fans and even an ancient fridge.

FRENCH CONCESSION 法租界

Home to the biggest concentration of bars, cafes and teahouses in the whole of Shànghǎi, the French Concession offers drinkers a choice between elegant bars housed in colonial-era villas, the foreign pubs around the north end of Hengshan Rd, the more dubious delights of the Julu Rd strip, as well as a brand new crop of places springing up in the far west section of the Concession.

ABBEY ROAD Map pp86-7   Bar
艾比之路 **Aìbǐ Zhī Lù**
☎ 6431 6787; 45 Yueyang Rd; 岳阳路45号; pints Y30; ⏰ 4pm-late Mon-Fri, 8.30am-late Sat & Sun; Ⓜ Changshu Rd; 📶

The cheap beer–classic rock combination works its stuff again, attracting plenty of regulars to this neighbourhood pub. Once the weather gets nice, the tree-shaded outdoor patio adds the final ingredient to make Abbey Rd an irresistible favourite. There's Swiss pub food too.

ANAR POMEGRANATE LOUNGE
Map pp86-7   Bar
石榴 **Shíliu**
☎ 6280 9326; 137 Xingfu Rd; 幸福路137号; Xinjiang black beer Y20; ⏰ 8pm-3am Sat-Thu, 8pm-8am Fri; Ⓜ Jiaotong University; 📶

This out-of-the-way bar is one of the cooler dives in town, attracting a mix of dressed-down locals and foreigners. The front room is a chill spot for drinks and food (wraps, curries and tapas, from Y35) while from Wednesday to Saturday the back room hosts DJs and occasionally live groups like Magnetic, a trippy band that crosses Xīnjiāng sounds with acid jazz (or something like that).

BLARNEY STONE
Map pp86-7   Bar
上海岩烧 **Shànghǎi Yánshāo**
☎ 6415 7496; 5A Dongping Rd; 东平路5号A座; pints Y65; ⏰ 11am-1.30am; Ⓜ Changshu Rd

More intimate than O'Malley's (p182) and more authentically Irish, the low ceilings, stone floor and wood panelling give the Blarney Stone a genuine pub feel. It's a friendly place that attracts a slightly older expat crowd, who enjoy the fish and chips (Y85) and pints of Guinness and Kilkenny. There's also a small roof terrace, live Irish music every night except Tuesday and lots of sport on the telly.

BRITISH BULLDOG
Map pp86-7   Bar
英国斗牛犬俱乐部 **Yīngguó Dòuniúquǎn Jùlèbù** ☎ 6466 7878; 1 South Wulumuqi Rd; 乌鲁木齐南路1号; pints Y50-90; ⏰ 11am-6am; Ⓜ Hengshan Rd

With its Filipina barmaids and by-the-book English pub styling, this place is not so much British as firmly located in expat land. Nevertheless, it pulls in sports fans when there's a big game on, thanks to the big screen, while the upstairs pool table has a loyal following. The pub food is so-so, but there's McEwan's Ale, Kilkenny and cider on tap. Happy hour is 11am to 7pm Monday to Friday and 6pm to 7pm on the weekend.

CONSTELLATION

Map pp86-7   Bar

酒池星座 Jiǔchí Xīngzuò

☎ 5404 0970; 86 Xinle Rd; 新乐路86号; cocktails from Y60; ⏰ 7pm-2am; Ⓜ South Shanxi Rd

The bow-tied staff at the Japanese-run Constellation (or, as the original name translates, 'Constellations in a pool of liquor') take their drinks seriously – you're not going to get any watered-down cocktails here. A choice selection of whiskies (including a samurai-helmeted Nikka), Van Gogh prints on the walls and overhead black lights make this a classy yet appealingly weird place. Its small size necessitated the opening of Constellation 2 (Map pp86–7; 33 Yongjia Rd; 永嘉路33号).

COTTON'S Map pp86-7   Bar

棉花酒吧 Miánhuā Jiǔbā

☎ 6433 7995; 132 Anting Rd; 安亭路132号; beer Y35-50, cocktails from Y50; ⏰ 11am-2am; Ⓜ Hengshan Rd or Zhaojiabang Rd

This excellent bar is perhaps the most pleasant spot in the Concession for a libation or three. Situated in a converted 1930s villa, the interior has cosy sofas and fireplaces to snuggle around in the winter and a tiny outdoor terrace on the 2nd floor. The real draw, though, is the garden, which is intimate yet still big enough not to feel cramped. The drinks and bar snacks, pizzas, burgers, salads and sandwiches are reasonably priced and the crowd is a good mix of locals and expats. You'll have to get here early on weekends to grab a table outside, or book ahead.

EDDY'S BAR Map pp86-7   Bar

嘉浓休闲 Jiānóng Xiūxián

☎ 6282 0521; 1877 Middle Huaihai Rd (entrance Tianping Rd); 淮海中路1877号(近天平路); beers Y30, cocktails from Y40; ⏰ 8pm-2am Mon-Thu, to 3am Fri-Sun; Ⓜ Jiaotong University

Shànghǎi's longest-running gay bar is a friendly place with a flash, square bar to sit around, as well as a few corners to hide away in. It attracts both locals and expats, but it's mostly for the boys rather than the girls.

ENOTECA Map pp86-7   Bar

依诺甜珑 Yīnuòtiánlóng

☎ 5404 0050; 53-57 Anfu Rd; 安福路53-57号; glass of wine Y38-66; ⏰ 9am-11.30pm; Ⓜ Changshu Rd; 🛜

Wine bars are the latest fad to hit Shànghǎi, but retailers may have been a little too eager to enter the market – most are conspicuously empty throughout the week. Enoteca has proven to be an exception, and while its strategic location across from a gigantic office tower doesn't hurt, the keyword here is affordability – plenty of bottles fall into the Y100 to 200 range, and glasses of smooth, new-world wines go for as little as Y38. A less popular branch (58 Taicang Rd; 太仓路58号; Ⓜ South Huangpi Rd) is near Xīntiāndì.

LITTLE FACE

Map pp86-7   Bar

☎ 6466 4328; 2nd fl, 30 Donghu Rd; 东湖路30号2楼; beer from Y40, cocktails from Y55; ⏰ 5.30pm-1am; Ⓜ South Shanxi Rd

Little Face has the same antique-strewn elegance as its previous incarnation (Face Bar), with a few hidden nooks adding a touch of privacy. It's a stylish place for pre- or postdinner drinks, and the old opium bed retained from its Face Bar days adds to the decadent undertow. Upstairs you'll find the dining area (p163).

LOGO

Map pp86-7   Bar

☎ 2230 2255; 13 Xingfu Rd (by Fahuazhen Rd); 幸福路13号(法华镇路附近); beers from Y20; ⏰ 8.30pm-late; Ⓜ Jiaotong University

Had enough of Shànghǎi poseurs and glam cocktails? Tatty cigarette-burned couches and graffiti-covered walls may have never looked so good. LOgO exudes an alternative vibe, but there are really all sorts of folks that take refuge here, from penniless English teachers and local musicians to aspiring Italian designers working the foosball table. There's music of some sort almost every night of the week, whether it be electro-funk DJs, reggae nights or the sporadic out-of-town indie band.

MANIFESTO

Map pp86-7   Bar

☎ 6289 9108; 748 Julu Rd; 巨鹿路748号; cocktails from Y58; ⏰ 11am-2am; Ⓜ Jing'an Temple

Upstairs from Mesa restaurant is this swish, sophisticated bar. The cocktails are strong, if pricy, but it's the large outside terrace, one of Shànghǎi's best, that make this place. Happy hour is from 4pm to 8pm.

MURAL

Map pp86-7   Bar

摩砚酒吧 Móyàn Jiǔbā

☎ 6433 5023; basement, 697 Yongjia Rd; 永
嘉路697号底层; beer Y35-60; ⏰ 6pm-2am;
Ⓜ Hengshan Rd

If those crazy Buddhist monks ever had a
raging 8th-century party out in Dūnhuáng's
Thousand Buddha Caves, this is probably
what it would have looked like, minus the
funky beats and DJ of course. Mural's big
claim is not really the Silk Rd decor, but
the all-you-can-drink Y100 bar every Friday
night (10pm to 2am). There's a fun reggae
night on Thursday. It's more popular with
locals than expats, which is another reason
to check it out.

O'MALLEY'S

Map pp86-7   Bar

欧玛莉爱尔兰酒吧 Ōumǎlì Ài'ěrlán Jiǔbā

☎ 6474 4533; 42 Taojiang Rd;桃江路42号; pints
Y45-65; ⏰ 11am-1.30am Mon-Sat, 1pm-1am Sun;
Ⓜ Changshu Rd

With an all-you-can-eat barbecue on Tuesday (Y60), an all-you-can-eat European-style
brunch on Sunday (Y85), a Thursday-night
quiz, good (though somewhat expensive)
pub food and nonstop sport on the many
TVs, O'Malley's spares no effort to pack in
the punters. Families like the lawn area and
kids playground. Happy hour is from 5pm
to 8pm, when pints of Guinness and Kilkenny are Y44.

PEOPLE 7 Map pp86-7   Bar

人间荧七 Rénjiān Yíngqī

☎ 5404 0707; 803 Julu Rd; 巨鹿路803号;
Japanese cocktails from Y50; ⏰ 11.30am-2pm,
6pm-midnight; Ⓜ Jing'an Temple/Changshu Rd

Getting into this superstylish bar/restau-
rant is an achievement in itself. That's not
because there's a door policy, rather it's
because the shiny steel doors will only
open if you insert your hand (twice) into
one of the nine holes set into the wall
(we're not saying which one). Once inside,
there's a backlit, long steel bar on which to
rest the oddly shaped glass your cocktail
will arrive in. With white armchairs scattered throughout the darkly lit interior and
bathrooms that are even harder to work
out than the front door, this place could
be oppressively trendy. But it isn't. They do
affordable minimalist fusion food (Y35 to
Y60) too.

SASHA'S Map pp86-7   Bar

萨沙 Sàshā

☎ 6474 6628; 11 Dongping Rd (cnr of Hengshan
Rd); 东平路11号 (近衡山路); cocktails
Y65; ⏰ 11am-1am Sun-Thu, to 2am Fri & Sat;
Ⓜ Changshu Rd/Hengshan Rd; 🛜

Housed in a fine old villa that once belonged to the Soong family, Sasha's large
garden is one of Shànghǎi's most splendid summer spots. Inside there's a vague
French colonial feel with wicker furniture,
wood floors and a cosy bar to perch at.
Upstairs there's an expensive restaurant
offering Western food. Given the prices
here, it's worth checking out the happy
hour, from 5.30pm to 7pm, when all drinks
are half-price.

SHANGHAI STUDIO Map pp86-7   Bar

嘉浓休闲 Jiānóng Xiūxián

☎ 6283 1043; No 4, Lane 1950, Middle Huaihai
Rd; 淮海中路1950弄4号; cocktails from Y40;
⏰ 9pm-2am; Ⓜ Jiaotong University

This hip newcomer to the Shànghǎi gay
scene has transformed the cool depths
of a former bomb shelter into a laid-back
bar, art gallery and men's underwear shop
(MANifesto; open 2pm to 2am). There's a
Y100 open bar on Thursday.

TIME PASSAGE Map pp86-7   Bar

昨天今天明天 Zuótiān Jīntiān Míngtiān

☎ 6240 2588; No 183, Lane 1038, Caojiayan
Rd; 曹家堰路1038弄183号; beers from Y25;
⏰ 2pm-2am; Ⓜ Jiangsu Rd; 🛜

Tucked down a small street, Time Passage is that rare thing in Shànghǎi, a pub
that could be your local back home. With
friendly staff, cheap drinks and a faithful
clientele of local musos, students and expat
teachers, it's a businessman-free zone.
There's live music on Tuesday, Thursday
and Friday, and a daily happy hour from
5.30pm to 7.30pm.

TMSK Map pp86-7   Bar

透明思考 Tòumíng Sīkǎo

☎ 6326 2223; Xintiāndì North Block, Bldg 11;太
仓路181弄新天地北里11号楼; cocktails
from Y60; ⏰ 11.30am-1am; Ⓜ South Huangpi
Rd/Xintiandi

A place to visit as much for the decor as
for the drinks, TMSK is designed to within
an inch of its life. The whole place is full of
glass 'art', or more specifically, pieces of
swirled pastel-coloured glass. There's a cool

water feature too, but the interior design pales into insignificance once the house band gets going with its unholy fusion of techno and traditional Chinese music (Monday to Saturday 9pm to 10pm).

VELVET LOUNGE Map pp86-7 Bar
☎ 5403 2976; 913 Julu Rd; 巨鹿路913号; cocktails from Y55; ⏱ 5pm-3am Sun-Thu, to 5am Fri & Sat; Ⓜ Changshu Rd/Jing'an Temple
An anomaly amongst the girlie bars of Julu Rd, Velvet Lounge is a relaxed night-spot that has become something of a cult favourite among the late-night crowd. There's a circular bar to sit around, sofas to sink into and old-school tunes for the dance floor on weekends. It's notably one of the few places where you can refuel with a delicious pizza (from Y88) after midnight. Oh, and Thursday is Swedish Erotica night.

WINDOWS Map pp86-7 Bar
蕴德诗 Yùndéshī
☎ 5382 7757; 3rd fl, 681 Middle Huaihai Rd; 淮海中路681号3楼; beer from Y15; ⏱ 5pm-3am; Ⓜ South Shanxi Rd
There's nothing particularly special about Windows, but in a city that has few places to get cheap drinks, Y15 Tsingtaos and a pool table are enough to pack 'em in.

YY'S Map pp86-7 Bar
轮回酒吧 Lúnhuí Jiǔbā
☎ 6466 4098; 125 Nanchang Rd; 南昌路125号; cocktails Y35-70; ⏱ 24hr; Ⓜ South Shanxi Rd
Once home to the Shànghǎi underground scene (like, back in the '90s), YY's has suc-cessfully remained on the fringes of the city's consciousness without ever becom-ing too hip. It still attracts an alternative crowd and has its own rough-edged ap-peal, which increases with the onset of the witching hour.

ZAPATA'S Map pp86-7 Bar
☎ 6474 6166; 5 Hengshan Rd; 衡山路5号; pints Y50, margaritas Y70; ⏱ 5.30pm-2am; Ⓜ Changshu Rd/Hengshan Rd; 🛜
One of the city's most popular mainstream bars, Zapata's owes its place in Shànghǎi's nightlife pantheon to its ladies night on Wednesday. But it doesn't matter what day you go – by the time 11pm rolls around, folks have usually had enough to drink to be ready to leave the dance floor behind and start shaking it all on top of the bar.

Soon after free-flow tequila is poured straight into the mouths of the willing… and the party begins. Not exactly classy, but definitely fun.

BOONNA CAFÉ
Map pp86-7 Cafe
布那咖啡 Bùnà Kāfēi
☎ 5404 6676; 88 Xinle Rd; 新乐路88号; coffee Y15-30; ⏱ 8am-1am; Ⓜ South Shanxi Rd; 🛜
Boonna is an excellent boho cafe with changing art exhibitions on the walls, a book exchange and cheap lunch sets (Y35). The coffee is thumbs up, as are the juices and shakes (Y25). A computer is available for use if you don't have a laptop. There's also another outlet (Map pp86–7; ☎ 6433 0835; 1690 Middle Huaihai Rd; 淮海中路1690号; Ⓜ Shang-hai Library).

CITIZEN CAFÉ Map pp86-7 Cafe
天台餐厅 Tiāntái Cāntīng
☎ 6258 1620; 222 Jinxian Rd; 进贤路222号; coffee Y20-30, cocktails Y45-55; ⏱ 11am-12.30am; Ⓜ South Shanxi Rd; 🛜
The perfect place to hide out with a cap-puccino and netbook on a rainy day, Citi-zen's burgundy-and-cream colours, antique ceiling fans and well-worn parquet offer calming respite from the Shànghǎi crush. Recharge with a club sandwich (Y45) or sit back with one of the much-loved ginger cocktails (Y45) while watching street scenes unfold from the 2nd-floor terrace.

JÌNG'ĀN 静安区

Jìng'ān drinking options don't match the diversity of the area's restaurants; it caters almost exclusively to the expat and business crowd. Sports bars and the not-quite red-light strip (which has received official blessing) on Tongren Rd are what to expect.

BIG BAMBOO Map pp98-9 Bar
☎ 6256 2265; 132 Nanyang Rd; 南阳路132号; beers from Y40, cocktails from Y50; ⏱ 11am-2am; Ⓜ Jing'an Temple; 🛜
Popular sports bar on two floors that serves up decent Western food, while offering pool, darts and all the big games on TV. There's another branch in Hóngqiáo (Map p132; ☎ 6405 8720; No 20, Hongmei Rd Entertainment Street, Lane 3338, Hongmei Rd; 虹梅路3338弄虹梅休闲步行街20号; Ⓜ Longxi Rd).

FRANGIPANI

Map pp98-9   Bar

☎ 5375 0084; 399 Dagu Rd; 大沽路399号;
⏱ 6pm-2am; Ⓜ West Nanjing Rd
Not to be confused with the nail salon of
the same name, friendly Frangipani features
Shànghǎi's only girls' hang-out (the lesbian
lounge on the 2nd floor) and a modern
downstairs area with comfy couches and
occasional dancing. Happy hour is from
6pm to 9pm.

I LOVE SHANGHAI

Map pp98-9   Bar

我爱上海 Wǒ Ài Shànghǎi
☎ 5228 6899; 3rd fl, 1788 Xinzha Rd; 新闸
路1788号3楼; beer from Y35; ⏱ 5pm-2am;
Ⓜ Jing'an Temple
Despite the name, this bar has little to do
with Shànghǎi and everything to do with
getting hammered and having fun along
the way. Pitchers of beer (Y85), Strong
Island Tea (Y55) and absinthe shots (Y40)
are all the ammo you'll need. Each night
is a theme night of some sort, the climax
coming with Saturday's open bar (Y100).
It's above the Orchard Restaurant.

KAIBA BELGIAN BEER BAR

Map pp98-9   Bar

☎ 6289 3715; 528 Kangding Rd; 康定路528号;
beer Y40-60; ⏱ 4pm-2am; Ⓜ Changping Rd
Beer-o-philes who have had to suffer
through too many bottles of Shànghǎi's
watery Reeb will be thrilled at the impressive
selection of Trappist brews and other imported micro beers served in a chill setting.

SPOT

Map pp98-9   Bar

☎ 6247 3579; 331 Tongren Rd; 铜仁路331号; beers
from Y30; ⏱ 11am-late; Ⓜ Jing'an Temple; 📶
The latest addition to the Jìng'ān sports bar
scene, the Spot is a laid-back locale with
all-day breakfasts (Y60), salads, burgers
(Y65) and hearty German fare to go with
the draught beer. The beef roulade (Y115)
receives lavish praise.

CAFÉ 85°C Map pp98-9   Cafe

85度C咖啡店 Bāwǔ Dù C Kāfēidiàn
408 North Shaanxi Rd; 陕西北路408号; coffee
Y8, tea Y4; ⏱ 24hr; Ⓜ West Nanjing Rd
This Taiwanese chain serves the cheapest coffee and tea in Shànghǎi – and it's

decent quality too. There are some truly
bizarre pastries (from Y4) sold in the bakery section, if you want to experience a
modern-day Chinese breakfast on the go.
The only sore point here is that seating is
limited. There are over 20 branches in the
city, including one near People's Square (Map
pp66–7; 575 Fuzhou Rd; 福州路575号; Ⓜ People's
Square).

PǓDŌNG 浦东

Pǔdōng is a wasteland when it comes to drinking spots. Most bars are in hotels.

100 CENTURY AVENUE Map p108   Bar

世纪大道100号 Shìjì Dàdào Yìbǎi Hào
☎ 3855 1428; 91st & 92nd fl, Park Hyatt, Shanghai World Financial Center, 100 Century Ave; 世
纪大道100号柏悦酒店91-92楼; coffee Y55,
cocktails Y80; ⏱ bar & restaurant 4.30pm-1am
Mon-Sat, restaurant 4.30pm-10.30pm Sun;
Ⓜ Lujiazui
Pǔdōng continues to maintain its hold on
the title of the highest bar in the world
with 100 Century Avenue, but this place
lacks the ambiance of its cross-street
competitor, Cloud 9 (below). Still, it's pretty
impressive inside (there are six open kitchens in the restaurant area) and is a cheaper
alternative than going up to the viewing
platforms. The restaurant (on the 91st floor)
has better views than the bar (on the 92nd
floor) as you can get up close to the windows. The bar is closed on Sunday. Access
is through the lobby of the Park Hyatt, on
the south side of the building.

CLOUD 9 Map p108   Bar

九重天酒廊 Jiǔchóngtiān Jiǔláng
☎ 5049 1234; 87th fl, Jinmao Tower, 88 Century
Ave; 世纪大道88号金茂大厦87楼; wine
from Y65, cocktails Y90; ⏱ 5pm-1am Mon-Fri,
11am-2am Sat & Sun; Ⓜ Lujiazui
Pǔdōng's coolest bar by a long shot, Cloud
9 is a fantastic place to watch day fade
into night as the neon slowly flickers on
across the curving horizon. Addictive beats
provide the soundtrack for the illuminated
skyline and, after an espresso martini or
two, you'll probably find out what it means
to be *shanghaied* in the best sense of
the word. The occasional appearance of
fortune tellers and magicians adds to the
entertainment. Access is through the lobby
of the Grand Hyatt.

HÓNGKŎU & NORTH SHÀNGHĂI
虹口区、北上海

OLD FILM CAFÉ

Map p116   Cafe

老电影咖啡馆 **Lǎodiànyǐng Kāfēiguǎn**
☎ 5696 4763; 123 Duolun Rd; 多伦路123号;
coffee from Y22, tea from Y35; ☿ 10am-1am;
Ⓜ **Dongbaoxing Rd**

With the golden age of Shànghǎi cinema as its theme, this place makes for a pleasant pit stop if you're touring the Duolun Rd area. Movie buffs will enjoy the photos of the vintage Chinese movie stars and the screenings of classic films from the '30s. There's a wide range of teas available and they serve alcohol, too.

HONGQIAO AIRPORT AREA

With so many expats resident in the Hongqiao Airport area and Gǔběi, the area now has its own bar/restaurant strip, the Hongmei Rd Entertainment Street, for those who don't want to make the trek to the French Concession or Bund. There's an outlet of Blue Frog (Map p132; ☎ 5422 5119; No 30, Hongmei Rd Entertainment Street, Lane 3338, Hongmei Rd) here, as well as various other places that are OK for a local drink.

ENTERTAINMENT

top picks

What's your recommendation? lonelyplanet.com/shanghai

> Perhaps in no other city does so much human energy go into the search for amusement as among the foreign population of Shànghǎi.
>
> Journalist George Sokolsky, 1930s

A night on the town in Shànghǎi leaves many visitors wondering if they really are in China. Certainly, the crowds that pack the growing number of nightclubs are reminiscent of the West and the prices aren't much different either. Of course, it would be an exaggeration to suggest that Shànghǎi can compare to London or New York when it comes to nightlife – the diversity and home-grown performers just aren't there yet. But for a city that offered people little to do back in the '90s besides see a 1930s jazz band in the Peace Hotel or belt out a few karaoke numbers, Shànghǎi has certainly come a long way.

The run-up to the 2010 World Expo was the latest catalyst in ratcheting the entertainment level up a notch. From a new acrobatics troupe and jazz cabarets on the Bund to a smattering of rock clubs and an old-timey burlesque club, the entertainment scene is fermenting with promise. First-time visitors will be most interested in the classic experiences: a night out with the acrobats is the Shànghǎi answer to Běijīng opera, traditional Chinese massages are an inexpensive indulgence and the clubs – regardless of whether you prefer the underground bomb shelter crew or exclusive top-floor glamour – are always a good time. Classical music and Western opera performances featuring international symphonies are always on at a variety of venues while traditional Chinese music is tough, but not impossible, to find.

There are also plenty of festivals taking place throughout the year that are worth catching if you happen to be in town at the right time. In June the city boasts the biggest and best film festival, the SIFF (p18) in China, when Asian and Hollywood stars arrive to promote their movies (director Danny Boyle chaired the 2009 jury). The Asia Pacific Contemporary Art Fair (www.shcontemporary .info; September), which is Asia's biggest art event, takes place at the Shanghai Exhibition Centre. The China International Arts Festival (www .artsbird.com; October & November; p19) features traditional Chinese and classical music. Also worth checking out is the Shanghai Biennale (www.shanghai biennale.org; Sep-Nov 2010; p19), which takes place at the Shanghai Art Museum and presents a mixed bag of local and international artists.

Racing fanatics from all over the world jet in for the Formula One Grand Prix (p18), and Shànghǎi is now also an established stop on the golf and tennis pro tours. For details of the many parties and events that take place, check the local listings mags such as *That's Shanghai* or go to www.smart shanghai.com.

NIGHTLIFE & THE ARTS
ACROBATICS
The Shànghǎi troupes are among the best in the world and spending a night watching them spinning plates on poles and contorting themselves into unfeasible anatomical positions never fails to entertain.

SHANGHAI CENTRE THEATRE
Map pp98-9
上海商城剧院 Shànghǎi Shāngchéng Jùyuàn
☎ 6279 8948; 1376 West Nanjing Rd, Jìng'ān; 南京西路1376号; tickets Y100-280; Ⓜ Jing'an Temple
The Shanghai Acrobatics Troupe (Shànghǎi Zájì Tuán) has popular performances here most nights at 7.30pm. It's a short but fun show and is high on the to-do list of most first-time visitors. Buy tickets a couple of days in advance from the ticket office on the right-hand side at the entrance to the Shanghai Centre.

SHANGHAI CIRCUS WORLD
Map pp62-3
上海马戏城 Shànghǎi Mǎxì Chéng
☎ 6652 5468; www.era-shanghai.com; 2266 Gonghexin Rd, Zhabei; 闸北区共和新路2266号; tickets Y80-580; Ⓜ Shanghai Circus World
Out on the far northern outskirts of town is this impressive complex. The shows combine awesome acrobatics with new-fangled multimedia elements. Shows start at 7.30pm. Tickets are available at the door, but booking ahead is advised.

SHANGHAI FANTASIA Map pp86-7

梦上海 Mèng Shànghǎi

☎ 6248 2340; Children's Art Theatre, 643 Huashan Rd, French Concession; 华山路643号 儿童艺术剧院; tickets Y150-280; taxi

The newest acrobatics show to hit Shànghǎi, with daily shows at 7.30pm. It's a mixture of traditional displays of contortionism and amazing dexterity, enhanced by modern effects and choreography. Call for tickets or order online through www.smartshanghai.com.

CHINESE OPERA

The shrill falsetto, crashing cymbals, expressive masks and painted faces of Běijīng opera are what most people have in mind when they think of Chinese opera, though the art form actually has a number of different styles. A local predecessor to Běijīng opera is the melodic *Kūnjù* or *Kūnqǔ* (Kun opera, from nearby Kūnshān), one of the oldest existing forms of Chinese opera, and best known for its adaptation of the 16th-century erotic-love ghost story *The Peony Pavilion*. One of the only Kun opera troupes in the country is based in Shànghǎi.

The main problem with going to see a traditional opera in Shànghǎi is that there are no English subtitles. But the plotlines are relatively simple, which makes following the action not impossible. Before snatching up tickets for *A Dream of Red Mansions* at the Shanghai Grand Theatre, try the Běijīng opera highlights show in Yifu Theatre (below) first.

KUN OPERA HOUSE Map p62-3

上海昆剧团 Shànghǎi Kūnjù Tuán

☎ 6437 7756; 295 No 2 South Zhongshan Rd, South Shànghǎi; 中山南二路295号; Ⓜ Damuqiao Rd

Shànghǎi's Kun opera troupe has moved to a new home south of the city. There are usually monthly performances, but you'll have to call ahead for the schedule. No English.

YIFU THEATRE Map pp66-7

逸夫舞台 Yìfū Wǔtái

☎ 6322 5294; www.tianchan.com; 701 Fuzhou Rd, People's Square; 人民广场福州路701号; tickets Y30-380; Ⓜ People's Sq

One block east of People's Square, this is the main opera theatre in town and recog-

nisable by the huge opera mask above the entrance. The theatre presents a popular programme of Beijing, Kun and Yue (Shaoxing) opera. A Beijing opera highlights show is performed several times a week at 1.30pm and 7.15pm; pick up a brochure at the ticket office or check the website (click on 英语 in the menu bar for English) for exact dates. A shop in the foyer sells CDs.

CINEMAS

Běijīng allows in about 30 foreign (read Hollywood) movies per year, after they pass the censors' scissors of course. See the boxed text, p190, for a list of cinemas showing undubbed foreign films.

Over 150 films are screened at the annual Shanghai International Film Festival (www.siff.com; p18) in June, though Cannes doesn't need to worry about the competition quite yet. For art-house cinema year round, sign up with Maria's Choice (mariaschoice-subscribe@topica.com), a private film club that arranges screenings of independent Chinese films with English subtitles at Kodak Cinema World (see the boxed text, p190) and the Glamour Bar (p179). Image Tunnel (影像隧道; Yǐngxiàng Suìdào; Map pp98-9; ☎ 2813 0548; M50, 50 Moganshan Rd, Bldg 19, 2nd fl; admission Y30) shows slideshows (2pm) and independent Chinese films (7pm) on Saturdays, and the Vienna Café (Map pp86-7; ☎ 6445 2131; 25 Shaoxing Rd; 绍兴路25号) also shows weekly art-house films on Thursdays. The Shanghai Science & Technology Museum (p113) has four theatres, including two IMAX shows.

CLUBBING

Shànghǎi's clubs are mostly big, glossy places devoted to playing mainstream house, techno and hip-hop. A number of big-name DJs are flying in these days, which has helped boost interest among the locals, although the crowds are still predominantly made up of the upper class, Hong Kong and Taiwanese expats and Westerners. Check www.smartshangai.com and local listing mags for up-to-date information.

BABYFACE Map pp86-7

☎ 6375 6667; Unit 101, Shanghai Sq, 138 Middle Huaihai Rd, French Concession; 淮海中路138号101室; beer Y50; ☑ 9pm-2am; Ⓜ South Huangpi Rd

Babyface may be a nationwide chain, but it's still one of the longest-running and least exclusive clubs in the city. While slightly soulless, there is a steady stream of top-name house DJs, and it's always busy with the local crowd. Cover on weekends is Y50.

D2 Map p79

☎ 6152 6543; Cool Docks, 505 South Zhongshan Rd, Old Town; 中山南路505号老码头南里; ☑ 8.30pm-late Wed-Sun; Ⓜ Xiaonanmen

Shanghai's only gay disco at the time of write-up, D2 occupies a large space at the Cool Docks (p82) There's a cruzy room (a mezzanine that looks down on the dance floor), a lazy room (with beds) and a crazy room (the main dance floor). Thursdays is the open bar night (Y100 for all you can drink).

DRAGON CLUB Map pp86-7

木易龙 Mùyìlóng

☎ 6433 2187; 156 Fenyang Rd, French Concession; 汾阳路156号; drinks from Y60; ☑ 10pm-4am Wed & Thu, 10pm-8am Fri & Sat; Ⓜ Changshu Rd

More of an after-hours place than a genuine club, the Dragon is a good spot to head to when you don't want the night to end. It's usually free to get in.

GUANDII Map pp86-7

官邸 Guāndǐ

☎ 5383 6020; Fuxing Park, 2 Gaolan Rd, French Concession; 皋兰路2号, 复兴公园内; beer from Y40; ☑ 9pm-5am Wed-Sat; Ⓜ South Shanxi Rd

Recently redone, this Taiwanese nightclub pulls in a 20-something crowd with late nights and (relatively) cheap drinks. There are two rooms, West Coast hip-hop and house. Look out for open bar nights.

MOVIE SCREENINGS FOR FOREIGNERS

The following cinemas have Western movies in the original language (原版; yuán bǎn). Ticket prices range from Y30 to Y100; matinées are usually Y20 cheaper.

Cathay Theatre (国泰电影院; Guótài Diànyǐngyuàn; Map pp86-7; ☎ 5404 2095; 870 Middle Huaihai Rd, French Concession; 淮海中路870号; Ⓜ South Shanxi Rd)

Kodak Cinema World (柯达电影世界; Kēdá Diànyǐng Shìjiè; Map p122; ☎ 6426 8181; 5th fl, Metro City, 1111 Zhaojiabang Rd, Xújiāhuì; 肇嘉浜路1111号5楼; tickets Y45-90; Ⓜ Xujiahui)

Peace Cinema (和平影都; Hépíng Yìngdū; Map pp66-7; ☎ 6322 5252; 290 Middle Xizang Rd, People's Sq; 西藏中路290号; Ⓜ People's Sq) Central location with an attached IMAX theatre (巨幕影院; Jùmùyǐngyuàn).

Shanghai Film Art Centre (上海影城; Shànghǎi Yǐngchéng; Map pp128-9; ☎ 6280 4088; 160 Xinhua Rd, French Concession; 新华路160号; taxi) The main venue for the Shanghai International Film Festival.

Stellar Cinema City (星美正大影城; Xīngměi Zhèngdà Yǐngchéng; Map p108; ☎ 5047 8022; 8th fl, Superbrand Mall, 168 West Lujiazui Rd, Pǔdōng; 浦东陆家嘴西路168号8楼; Ⓜ Lujiazui)

Studio City (环艺电影城; Huányì Diànyǐngchéng; Map pp98-9; ☎ 6218 2173; 10th fl, Westgate Mall, 1038 West Nanjing Rd, Jìng'ān; 静安南京西路1038号10楼; Ⓜ West Nanjing Rd)

UME International Cineplex (国际影城; Guójì Yǐngchéng; Map pp86-7; ☎ 6373 3333; Xīntiāndì South Block, Bldg 6, 5th fl; 新天地南里6号楼5楼; Ⓜ South Huangpi Rd)

Screenings of foreign films are also held at the Alliance Française (法语培训中心; Fǎyǔ Péixùn Zhōngxīn; Map p116; ☎ 6357 5388; www.alliancefrancaise.org.cn; 6th fl, 297 Wusong Rd; 吴淞路297号6楼), which shows French films (with Chinese subtitles) for free, and the Goethe Institute (歌德学院; Gēdé Xuéyuàn; Map pp66-7; ☎ 6391 2068 ext 602; 102A Cross Tower, 318 Fuzhou Rd; 福州路318号102A室), which screens films in German. Call for times.

GAY & LESBIAN SHÀNGHǍI

Shànghǎi is well ahead of the rest of the country in terms of general acceptance of gays and lesbians, though essentially that just means that gay bars and clubs are tolerated. Most locals choose to stay in the closet – many are married – and this isn't the place for public displays of affection. But there are tentative signs that attitudes to homosexuality in China are changing, at least in the big cities. There's more discussion of gay issues in the media, partly prompted by rising rates of HIV, and Shànghǎi even hosted China's first gay-pride festival in June 2009.

For visitors, Eddy's Bar (p181), Frangipani (p184), Shanghai Studio (p182), and D2 (opposite) are the best introduction to gay Shànghǎi. The Utopia website (www.utopia-asia.com/chinshan.htm) has up-to-date listings and a forum.

MAO Map pp86-7

☎ 139 0185 3963; 46 Yueyang Rd, French Concession; 岳阳路46号; ⏰ 9pm-3am Tues-Sat; cover Y100 weekends; Ⓜ Changshu Rd

Don't arrive here too early (before midnight) unless you want to stake out your spot on the designer Italian sofas. MAO gets going late, sometimes stays open till dawn and has an outdoor garden going for it – it's more for fashionable imbibing than dancing, though. It's one of the more high-end clubs in the city.

M1NT Map pp66-7

☎ 6391 2811; 24th fl, 318 Fuzhou Rd; 福州路318号24楼; ⏰ lounge 11.30am-late daily, club 10pm-late Fri-Sat; Ⓜ East Nanjing Rd

Exclusive penthouse-style club with knockout views, snazzy food and not a lot of dance space. Dress to impress or you'll get thrown into the shark tank.

MUSE
Map pp98-9

☎ 5213 5228; www.museshanghai.cn; New Factories, 68 Yuyao Rd, Jìng'ān; 余姚路68号同乐坊; drinks Y60; ⏰ 8.30pm-4.30am; Ⓜ Changping Rd

If a tumbleweed were to blow through the New Factories complex on a Saturday night you probably wouldn't be surprised, yet somehow Muse has managed to turn itself into one of the city's hottest clubs while most of its neighbours flounder in nonrecognition. There are two floors here, with house downstairs and hip-hop upstairs. Don't go looking for a dance floor on either level (there isn't one); just squeeze into the crowd and jump up on a private table (Y3000 per night). There are two more exclusive branches, M2 (Map pp98-9; 5th fl, Plaza 66, 1266 West Nanjing Rd; 南京西路1266号恒隆广场5楼) and Muse at Park 97 (Map pp86-7; inside Fuxing Park, 2 Gaolan Rd; 皋兰路2号复兴公园内).

SHELTER Map pp86-7

☎ 6437 0400; 5 Yongfu Rd, French Concession; 永福路5号; beer from Y20; ⏰ 9pm-4am Wed-Sun; Ⓜ Shanghai Library

The darling of the underground crowd, Shelter is a reconverted bomb shelter where you can count on great music, cheap drinks and a nonexistent dress code. They bring in a fantastic lineup of international DJs and hip-hop artists; the large barely lit dance area is the place to be. Cover for big shows is usually around Y30.

SIN LOUNGE Map pp98-9

☎ 6267 7779; 23rd fl, Want Want Bldg, 211 Shimen No 1 Rd, Jìng'ān; 石门一路1号旺旺大厦23楼; admission Y100 weekends; ⏰ 9pm-2am Sun-Thu, to 5am Fri-Sat; Ⓜ West Nanjing Rd

Cool views, slick design and a large dance space are the temptations in this glamorous hotspot. Big-names regularly man the turntables here; watch the cars fly by in the night as the electro-house heats up the dance floor.

SOHO
Map pp86-7

苏荷 Sūhé

☎ 5469 9898; 4 Hengshan Rd, French Concession; 衡山路4号; cocktails from Y50; ⏰ 8.30pm-3.30am; Ⓜ Hengshan Rd

The bizarre Taoist fairyland meets Alice in Wonderland decor makes for a rather brightly lit nightclub, but no one seems to care. It can get absolutely packed in here with dancers bumpin' to a mostly hip-hop soundtrack.

KARAOKE

Karaoke is by far China's favourite leisure activity and karaoke places, ranging from the seedy to upmarket, outnumber the bars and clubs in town. If you're up for crooning a few Mandopop tunes, or you need to close out a business deal, why not start the night at Partyworld?

PARTYWORLD Map pp86-7
钱柜 Qián Guì
☎ 6374 1111; 109 Yandang Rd, French Concession; 雁荡路109号, 复兴公园内; ⏰ 8am-2am; Ⓜ South Huangpi Rd

Partyworld is the nation's leading karaoke chain and this monster branch gets going early in the morning for those who just can't wait to belt out a tune or two. There are plenty of English-language songs to choose from. Prices go from Y19 to Y265, depending on the number of people, size of the room you want and the time of day.

MUSIC
Rock & Pop

Shànghǎi's live-music scene has greatly improved over the past few years, but it's still got a ways to go. There are a number of local bands, playing everything from Britpop to punk, although up until recently they have struggled to find suitable venues to play or audiences prepared to listen. But a sudden burst of interest in underground rock has perhaps begun to change all that, and some promising new nightspots have recently opened up. In addition to venues listed below, check out Anar Pomegranate Lounge (p180) and L0g0 (p181) which sometimes have live music (and definitely DJs). Visit www.smartshanghai.com and www.shanghaiist.com for news of when and where bands are playing.

BANDU CABIN Map pp98-9
半度音乐 Bàndù Yīnyuè
☎ 6276 8267; Bldg 11, 50 Moganshan Rd, Jìng'ān; 莫干山路50号11号楼; ⏰ 10am-6.30pm Sun-Fri, 10am-10pm Sat; Ⓜ Shanghai Train Station

Tucked away in M50 (p97), this laid-back cafe-cum-record label hosts traditional Chinese music concerts on Saturday at 8pm. Phone ahead on Friday to reserve seats. It also sells a quality selection of Chinese folk music compact discs.

MELTING POT Map pp86-7
☎ 6467 9900; No 288 Taikang Rd, French Concession; 泰康路288号; draught beer Y40, pitcher Y100; ⏰ 5.30pm-1am; Ⓜ Dapuqiao

The Melting Pot has an eclectic lineup of local musicians – some good, some bad – every night of the week. Jam sessions are on Mondays, and Thursdays feature(d) the

gǔzhēng (seven-stringed zither). The crowd is friendly and the Taikang Rd locale means it's often packed. There's another French Concession venue (Map pp86–7; 10 Hengshan Rd; 衡山路10号; Ⓜ Hengshan Rd) with a funky jazz combo in residence.

YÙYĪNTÁNG Map pp128-9
育音堂
☎ 5237 8662; www.yuyintang.org; 1731 West Yan'an Rd, 延安西路1731号; cover Y40, beer Y20; ⏰ 8pm-midnight Thu-Sun; Ⓜ West Yan'an Rd

Small enough to feel intimate, but big enough for a sometimes pulsating atmosphere, Yùyīntáng has long been the place in the city to see live music. Any Shànghǎi rock band worth its amps plays here, but you can also catch groups on tour from other cities in China and beyond. Rock is the staple diet, but anything goes, from hard punk to gypsy jazz. The entrance is on Kaixuan Rd (凯旋路), near the metro stop.

ZHIJIANG DREAM FACTORY
Map pp98-9
芷江梦工场 Zhǐjiāng Mèng Gōngchǎng
☎ 5213 5086; New Factories, 4th fl, Bldg B, 28 Yuyao Rd, Jìng'ān; 余姚路28号B座4楼同乐坊; ⏰ 8pm-1am; Ⓜ Changping Rd

A reconverted factory space, this is one of the best places in town, together with Yùyīntáng (above), to catch live shows. It's only open for large concerts; check entertainment websites for the schedule.

Jazz & Blues

Shànghǎi had a brief heyday in the jazz spotlight, back in the 1920s and '30s when big band swing was the entertainment of choice. In Shànghǎi, the music was adapted for local audiences and a number of Chinese songs were jazzed up by groups like Jimmy King's, creating a new genre which kept dance halls like the Paramount (p103) busy. There's little in the way of swing music today, but you can catch some surprisingly good musicians here. Most won't be household names, but jazz and R&B fans now have enough choices that they should be able to get a shot of soul on any given night.

The Bund has tried to step onto the stage with the addition of high-end nightspots Cabaret (Map pp66–7; Bund 6) and Lounge 18 (Map pp66–7; Bund 18), but performances here are hit or miss and can even wind up deserted on a Friday night.

The Peace Hotel (p204) had the city's most famous tourist show before undergoing renovation – the original 1930s jazz band – though at press time there was no news as to whether or not they'd be back after reopening. September sees the annual JZ Shanghai Jazz Festival (www.jzfestival.com), which is generally held in parks and theatres around town.

BROWN SUGAR Map pp86-7
红糖爵士餐厅 Hóngtáng Juéshì Cāntīng
☎ 5382 8998; Bldg 15 North Block Xīntiāndì,181 Lane,Taicang Rd; 太仓路181弄新天地北里15号楼; beer Y48-68, cocktails Y68-88; ☯ 6pm-2am; Ⓜ South Huangpi Rd

One of the newest faces in town, Brown Sugar is an upscale jazz-and-blues establishment set in the heart of Xīntiāndì. The focus here is on female vocalists (eg Aretha Franklin and Ella Fitzgerald covers), but there's also a salsa band on Sundays.

CHINATOWN Map p116
☎ 6258 2078; www.chinatownshanghai.com; 471 Zhapu Rd, Hóngkǒu; 乍浦路471号; ☯ 8pm-2am Wed-Sat; Ⓜ North Sichuan Rd

Opened in October 2009, Gosney and Kallman's three-floor cabaret was once a former Buddhist temple; now, appropriately enough, it's home to the blush-inducing Chinatown Dolls, gents in top hats, as well as a variety of other acts, ranging from live jazz to acrobatics. As good a fit as it is to the Shànghǎi mystique, it's guaranteed that there's nothing else in the city quite like it.

COTTON CLUB Map pp86-7
棉花俱乐部 Miánhuā Jùlèbù
☎ 6437 7110; 8 West Fuxing Rd, French Concession; 复兴西路8号; ☯ 7.30pm-2am Tue-Sun; Ⓜ Changshu Rd

Harlem it ain't, but this is still the best and longest-running bar for live jazz in Shànghǎi and features blues and jazz groups throughout the week. Wynton Marsalis once stepped in to jam, forever sealing the Cotton Club's reputation as the best live-music haunt in town. The crowd here is younger and the drinks are reasonably priced. The music gets going at 9pm.

HOUSE OF BLUES & JAZZ Map pp66-7
布鲁斯乐爵士之屋 Bùlǔsī Yuè Juéshì Zhīwū
☎ 6323 2779; 60 Fuzhou Rd, The Bund; 福州路60号; ☯ 4.30pm-2am; Ⓜ East Nanjing Rd

This is a classy restaurant and bar for music lovers. The owner, a Chinese TV celebrity, has plastered the walls with old photos of jazz legends, and the in-house band (which changes regularly) delivers live music from 9.30pm to 1am. Sunday night is a free-for-all jam.

JZ CLUB Map pp86-7
☎ 6431 0269; www.jzclub.cn; 46 West Fuxing Rd, French Concession; 复兴西路46号; ☯ 9pm-2am; Ⓜ Changshu Rd

Together with the Cotton Club, JZ is one of the best places in town for serious music lovers. The schedule rotates local and international groups, with sounds ranging from fusion, Latin and R&B to Chinese folk-jazz; music generally gets going around 10pm. Shànghǎi legend Coco also occasionally performs here. They organize the annual JZ Shanghai Jazz Festival.

Classical Music

Local orchestras perform regularly, in addition to a growing number of international guests. For traditional Chinese music, check out the programs at the Oriental Art Centre or Shanghai Grand Theatre.

ORIENTAL ART CENTER Map p114
上海东方艺术中心 Shànghǎi Dōngfāng Yìshù Zhōngxīn
☎ 6854 1234; www.shoac.com.cn; 425 Dingxiang Rd, Pǔdōng; 浦东丁香路425号; tickets Y30-680; Ⓜ Science & Technology Museum

Home of the Shanghai Symphonic Orchestra, the Oriental Art Center was designed to resemble five petals of a butterfly orchid. There are three main halls that host classical, jazz, dance and Chinese and Western opera performances. Saturday brunch concerts (10am) are Y30 to Y80 and in 2009 they ran a traditional Chinese music concert series on Saturday nights (Y40 to Y300).

SHANGHAI CONCERT HALL Map pp66-7
上海音乐厅 Shànghǎi Yīnyuè Tīng
☎ 6386 2836; 523 East Yan'an Rd, People's Square; 人民广场延安东路523号; tickets Y50-680; Ⓜ People's Sq/Dashijie

In 2003 the government moved this classic 1930s building (all 5650 tons of it) 66m away from busy East Yan'an Rd to a quieter park-side setting, a relocation that actually cost more than building a brand-new concert hall. It features smaller-scale concerts and local and international soloists.

SHANGHAI CONSERVATORY OF MUSIC Map pp86-7

上海音乐学院 **Shànghǎi Yīnyuè Xuéyuàn**
☎ 6431 1792; www.shcmusic.edu.cn; 20 Fenyang Rd, French Concession; 法租界汾阳路20号; tickets Y60-480; Ⓜ South Shanxi Rd
The auditorium here holds classical music performances (Chinese and Western) daily at 7.15pm and the musicians are often the stars of the future. The ticket office (售票处; *shòupiàochù*; 🕑 9am-5pm) is in the southern part of the campus. Ask for directions once you're at the school.

SHANGHAI GRAND THEATRE Map pp66-7

上海大剧院 **Shànghǎi Dàjùyuàn**
☎ 6372 8702; www.shgtheatre.com; 300 Renmin Ave, People's Square; 人民广场人民大道 300号; tickets Y50-2280; Ⓜ People's Sq
Shànghǎi's state-of-the-art concert venue hosts everything from Broadway musicals to symphonies, ballets, operas and performances by internationally acclaimed classical soloists. There are also traditional Chinese music performances here. Pick up a schedule at the ticket office.

THEATRE

The Shanghai Grand Theatre (above) and Shanghai Centre Theatre (p188) are the premier venues for local and international opera, ballet and drama productions. Several smaller theatres stage interesting performances, normally in Chinese only but sometimes with English subtitles.

SHANGHAI DRAMATIC ARTS CENTER Map pp86-7

上海话剧艺术中心 **Shànghǎi Huàjù Yìshù Zhōngxīn**
☎ 6473 4567, 6433 4546 for English; www.china-drama.com; 288 Anfu Rd; 法租界安富路 288号; tickets Y100-800; Ⓜ Changshu Rd
The best place in Shànghǎi to catch English-language plays, or Chinese adaptations of Western classics with English subtitles, this theatre has a reputation for pushing the buttons of the censors. Recent productions

include *The Heidi Chronicles* and *The Tempest*. Some of China's finest thespians, such as Ge You, have trodden the boards here.

SPORTS & ACTIVITIES

There are gyms galore in Shànghǎi, and if team sports are your thing there's no shortage of expat clubs, ranging from softball to football (soccer), basketball and even ultimate frisbee. See local listings magazines for contact details, or check the sports forum on www.shanghaiexpat.com. Even those who eschew exercise can keep mind and body unified in one of the city's dozens of massage centres (p196) – a definite Shànghǎi treat.

DANCE

JAZZ DU FUNK Map pp98-9

☎ 5239 9922; www.jazzdufunk.com; Bldg C, UDC Innovative Plaza, 125 North Jiangsu Rd; 江苏北 路125号C楼; Ⓜ Zhongshan Park
Lessons in everything from ballet to tap, via belly dancing, flamenco and salsa, are available here at beginner, intermediate or advanced levels. The teachers are professional and speak English. A course of 20 classes is Y1600. Children's classes are Y650 for eight sessions. There is another studio (Map pp86–7; ☎ 5403 9387; 5th fl, No 2, Lane 113, Changshu Rd; 常熟路113弄2号5楼).

FOOTBALL

There's no shortage of amateur football/soccer teams in Shànghǎi, ranging from those that take the game very seriously, and compete in the grandly named Shanghai International Football League, to more socially orientated teams. Check local listing mags for further details, or ask at Big Bamboo (p183) or O'Malley's (p182), which both run teams.

GYMS

Most top-end hotels provide gyms free for their guests, with steep membership for everyone else. But there are gyms all over town now, offering everything from Pilates to yoga and taichi, as well as all the usual workout facilities.

CALIFORNIA FITNESS Map pp86-7

加州健身 **Jiāzhōu Jiànshēn**
☎ 1008 100 988; 6th fl, Infiniti Shopping Mall, 138 Middle Huaihai Rd, French Concession; 淮

海中路138号无限度广场6楼; ⏰ 6am-midnight Mon-Fri, 8am-10pm Sat-Sun; Ⓜ South Huangpi Rd
American chain featuring top-notch facilities and classes, including yoga, taichi sword and dance. A day here costs Y180; a 12-month membership is Y9888.

KERRY GYM
Map pp98-9
嘉里健身中心 Jiālǐ Jiànshēn Zhōngxīn
☎ 6279 4625; 2nd fl, Kerry Centre, 1515 West Nanjing Rd, Jìng'ān; 静安区南京西路1515号嘉里中心2楼; ⏰ 6am-11pm; Ⓜ Jing'an Temple
Facilities here include an indoor swimming pool, outdoor tennis courts and aerobics and taichi classes. A month-long membership is Y2500, or it's Y13,000 for a year.

MEGAFIT
Map pp86-7
美格菲健身中心 Měigéfēi Jiànshēn Zhōngxīn
☎ 5383 6633; B3, Hong Kong New World Tower, 300 Middle Huaihai Rd, French Concession; 法租界淮海中路300号香港新世界; ⏰ 6.30am-11pm Mon-Fri, 9am-9pm Sat & Sun; Ⓜ South Huangpi Rd
This gym in the basement of the Hong Kong New World Building is the cheapest place for visitors, with a day rate of Y100 and Y500 for one month. A year-long membership is a very reasonable Y1400. Top-end equipment in the gym, and lots of group classes including taichi, yoga and Pilates.

ONE WELLNESS Map pp98-9
咪猫健身 Mīmāo Jiànshēn
☎ 6267 1550; www.onewellness.com.cn; 2nd fl, 98 Yanping Rd, Jìng'ān; 静安区延平路98号2楼; ⏰ 6am-11pm; Ⓜ Jing'an Temple
A boutique fitness club located in a renovated factory, One Wellness has a gourmet cafe on the premises and in-house massage therapy. Classes range from yoga and taichi to bodypump and aerobics, and the equipment is all state-of-the art. It also boasts the claim of being China's first carbon-neutral gym. The day rate is Y300; a month-long membership starts at Y1588.

MARTIAL ARTS
Early morning taichi (tàijí quán; 太极拳) on the Bund is one of the classic images of Shànghǎi. If you're interested in learning ei-

ther taichi or one of the harder martial arts (wǔshù; 武术) styles, there are a number of schools around town offering a range of classes for everyone from kids to adults. There are also aikido, karate and tae kwon do groups.

Serious students of the more esoteric Chinese martial arts will have to network to find a genuine teacher who will accept a foreigner as their student. You can also try showing up on early mornings in the local park and following alongside a group of practitioners (ask first), though it helps if you can speak some Chinese.

LONGWU KUNG FU CENTER
Map pp86-7
龙武功夫馆 Lóngwǔ Gōngfu Guǎn
☎ 6287 1528; www.longwukungfu.com; 1 South Maoming Rd, French Concession; 法租界茂名南路1号; Ⓜ South Shanxi Rd
Coaches from Shànghǎi's martial arts teams give classes in Chinese, Japanese and Korean martial arts. The largest centre in the city, it also offers children's classes on weekend mornings and lessons in English. Prices are Y1500/2600/4800 for 3/6/12 months. Kids classes are Y600 for three months.

MINGWU INTERNATIONAL KUNGFU CLUB Map p132
明武国际功夫馆 Míngwǔ Guójì Gōngfu Guǎn
☎ 6465 9806; www.mingwukungfu.com; 3rd fl, 359 Hongzhong Rd, Hongqiao Airport Area; 虹中路359号1号楼3楼
This versatile gym offers bilingual classes in a wide range of martial arts, from taichi and qigong to wǔshù and karate, for both children and adults. There's also a shop on site, selling clothing and weapons. A three-month membership is Y1000.

OZ BODY FIT Map pp98-9
☎ 6288 5278; www.ozbodyfit.com; 528 Kangding Rd, Jìng'ān; 静安区康定路528号; Ⓜ Changping Rd
Popular kickboxing and aerobics workouts, for those who want to keep fit using martial-arts training. Yoga is also offered. Ten classes for Y1000, or one- (Y1000), three- (Y2800) or six-month (Y5400) memberships.

WUYI CHINESE KUNGFU CENTRE

Map pp86–7

武懿国术馆 **Wǔyì Guóshù Guǎn**

☎ 137 0168 5893; Room 311, 3rd fl, International Artists' Factory, No 3, Lane 210, Taikang Rd, French Concession; 法租界泰康路210弄3号3楼311; Ⓜ Dapuqiao

English-language taichi classes on Thursday and Sunday and *wǔshù* classes on Wednesday and Sunday for adults and kids. It all costs Y600 per month.

MASSAGE & SPAS

In the 17th and 18th centuries, Qing dynasty barbers developed the current form of Chinese massage, known as *tuīná* (推拿; literally push-grab). In addition to cutting hair, skilled barbers learned to use acupressure points to treat different ailments and the practice, which was cheaper, less painful and safer than acupuncture, soon became quite popular – even late Qing emperors employed *tuīná* masseurs. In 1822, Emperor Daoguang decried acupuncture as unsafe and banned the practice, helping *tuīná* to secure its position as an integral part of Chinese medical treatment.

The general idea behind Chinese massage is that it stimulates your *qì* (vital energy that flows along different pathways or meridians, each of which is connected to a major organ) and removes energy blockages, though of course it is often used to treat specific ailments, from muscular and joint pain to the common cold.

Interestingly, the hairdresser-massage association is still quite common in China, though the roles have again changed: many businesses that advertise themselves as hairdressers are now nothing more than brothels, with rows of young girls seated beneath lurid pink lighting waiting to provide 'massage services' to their clients. This doesn't mean that *tuīná* has disappeared, though – getting a real massage or reflexology treatment (foot massage) has never been easier, and in Shànghǎi, they come at a fraction of the price that you'd pay at home. Just remember, traditional massage is not necessarily gentle, so if it's relaxation you're after, head to one of the midrange places, which offer a wider range of choices. For details, see the boxed text (opposite). If you're interested in treating a specific ailment, see the list of Chinese medicine clinics in the Directory (p262).

MOTOR RACING

The regular Chinese roads can sometimes resemble racetracks, but the real thing is now available too.

FORMULA ONE GRAND PRIX

off Map pp62–3

上海国际赛车场 **Shànghǎi Guójì Sàichē Chǎng**

☎ 6956 9999; www.formula1.com; Shanghai International Circuit, Anting Town, Jiādìng District; 嘉定区安亭镇; Ⓜ Shanghai International Circuit (Line 11)

The Formula One circus roars into town every year at this impressive, state-of-the-art circuit, which is 40 minutes northwest of the city centre. It's one of the most glamorous events on the Shànghǎi calendar, and tickets, costing Y380 to Y3980, get snapped up quickly. Book ahead through the website, check www.smartshanghai.com or visit a friendly ticket tout.

OUTDOOR ACTIVITIES

There are a surprising number of adventure sports on offer in and around the city. Cycling through rush-hour traffic is the easiest and cheapest way to get a few thrills, but there are other options too, including rock climbing and sailing, that may not be so life-threatening.

Cycling

Shànghǎi's mad traffic can make cycling the city's most stressful, if not potentially lethal, activity. However, the French Concession offers some charming areas for biking and weekends are perfect for popular longer excursions out of the city and into the countryside. The following companies all rent bikes by the day; some also rent out children's bikes and baby seats.

BOHDI ADVENTURES

Map pp62–3

☎ 5266 9013; www.bohdi.com.cn; Rm 2308, 3rd fl, Bldg 2, 2918 North Zhongshan Rd; 中山北路2918号2号楼2308室; Ⓜ Caoyang Rd

BOHDI got its start as a cycling club, but it now organises all manner of adventure sports, from climbing to hiking. The out-of-town bike tours are still the best, though. Check their website for trip details. They also hold night-time bike tours of Shànghǎi every Tuesday and Thursday (Y150).

CHINA CYCLE TOURS

☎ 137 6111 5050; www.chinacycletours.com

Joint Sūzhōu–Shànghǎi cycling group with tours of both cities as well as the surrounding countryside. Family friendly.

SISU CYCLING CLUB

Map pp62-3

☎ 5059 6071; www.sisucycling.com; 395 Dujuan Rd, Pǔdōng; 浦东杜鹃路395号; Ⓜ Longyang Rd

SISU is based in Pǔdōng and offers organized tours in and around the city for all levels; rides are also available for families. They offer night-time rides through Pǔdōng every Wednesday (Y150).

Golf

Golf in China is the preserve of business-people, the nouveaux riches and expats. You can actually pick up a basic set of clubs at one of the many golf shops around town for about the same price as a day's green fees. The clubs listed below are also open to nonmembers.

PUSH, PULL...PEACE

Blind Massage Parlours

The most inexpensive massages are given by the blind at no-frills massage parlours. Don't come expecting any candles, soft lighting or gurgling water displays in the background, but you can count on getting an experienced masseuse.

Lulu Massage (璐潞盲人按摩中心; Lùlu Mángrén Ànmó Zhōngxīn; Map pp86–7; ☎ 6473 2634; 597 Middle Fuxing Rd, French Concession; 法租界复兴中路597号; ⏱ noon-1am; Ⓜ South Shanxi Rd) This is a typical blind massage parlour, offering 45-minute full-body massages for Y40, seventy-minute full-body massages for Y60, and one-hour foot massages for Y45. Regulars can purchase discount cards.

Deluxe Massage Centres

To achieve a greater sense of inner peace, book a session at one of the more deluxe massage centres. Most follow a similar formula of serene, candlelit rooms, and you may get your own set of PJs. Reserve well in advance.

Apsara Spa (馨园水疗; Xīnyuán Shuǐliáo; Map pp98–9; ☎ 6258 5580; 457 North Shaanxi Rd; 陕西北路 457号; ⏱ 10am-10pm; Ⓜ West Nanjing Rd) Angkor-style massage therapy with treatments such as a 60-minute qì reenergizing massage (Y190), facials (Tibetan black mud purification, Y440), body wraps, manicures and Cambodian coconut scrubs (Y280).

Dragonfly (悠庭保健会所; Yōutíng Bǎojiàn Huìsuǒ; www.dragonfly.net.cn; ⏱ 10am-2am) Dragonfly offers hour-long Chinese body massage (Y135), Japanese-style shiatsu (Y135) and aroma oil massage (Y225) in soothing surroundings. There are French Concession branches at 20 Donghu Rd (Map pp86–7; ☎ 5405 0008; 东湖 路20号; Ⓜ South Shanxi Rd), 206 Xinle Rd (Map pp86–7; ☎ 5403 9982; 新乐路206号; Ⓜ South Shanxi Rd), 84 Nanchang Rd (Map pp86–7; ☎ 5386 0060; 南昌路84号; Ⓜ South Huangpi Rd) and elsewhere around town.

Green Massage (青专业按摩; Qīng Zhuānyè Ànmó; Map pp86–7; ☎ 5386 0222; www.greenmassage.com. cn; 58 Taicang Rd; 太仓路58号; ⏱ 10.30am-2am; Ⓜ South Huangpi Rd) Forty-five minute tuīná and shiatsu massages (Y98) with Chinese cupping (Y10) and hour-long foot massages (Y98).

Luxury Spas

For those who love to pamper themselves, you can't skip the luxury spas. From seaweed body masks to a G5 massage designed to break down fatty deposits, the following offer the most privileged treatments in town.

Banyan Tree (悦榕庄; Yuèróng Zhuāng; Map pp66–7; ☎ 6335 1888; 3rd fl, Westin Shanghai, 88 Middle Henan Rd, the Bund; 外滩河南中路88号威斯汀酒店3楼; ⏱ 10am-midnight; Ⓜ East Nanjing Rd) Banyan Tree offers a range of two- to three-hour Thai and Balinese massage sessions from Y1100. Try the lemongrass and cucumber balm, followed by a Thai acupressure session and a ginseng bath. A 90-minute massage is Y820, plus 15% service charge.

Mandara Spa (蔓达梦; Màndá Mèng; Map pp66–7; ☎ 5359 4969; 6th fl, JW Marriot Tomorrow Sq, 399 West Nanjing Rd; 南京西路399号6楼; ⏱ 10am-10pm; Ⓜ People's Sq) Thai spa with shíkùmén (stone-gate house) interior offering facials, aromatherapy, hot-stone and Chinese massages (from Y620). You can also invigorate yourself with the three-hour 'perfect spa experience' (Y1620). 15% service charge.

Binhai Golf Club (滨海高尔夫俱乐部; Bīnhǎi Gāo'ěrfū Jùlèbù; ☎ 3800 1888; www.binhaigolf.com; Binhai Resort, Baiyulan Dadao, Pǔdōng; 浦东南汇滨海东大公路东首; Y980 Mon-Fri, 18 holes Y1780 Sat & Sun; ☼ 5.30am-8pm)

Shanghai International Golf & Country Club (上海国际高尔夫俱乐部; Shànghǎi Guójì Gāo'ěrfū Jùlèbù; ☎ 5972 8111; sigc@sh163.net.cn; Xinyang village, Zhūjiājiǎo, Qīngpǔ County; 青浦区朱家角盈朱路61号; 18 holes Y680 Mon-Fri, Y1110 Sat & Sun; ☼ 7am-7pm Mon-Fri, 6am-7pm Sat-Sun)

Hiking

Shànghǎi is as flat and concrete as they come, but there are a number of decent hiking spots within a few hours' drive if you know where to look. Destinations such as Wùyuán in Jiāngxī and Huáng Shān in Ānhuī are doable in a long weekend (see *Lonely Planet China* for more information). The YANA Outdoors Club (☎ 6248 3494; www.withyana.com) and BOHDI Adventures (p196) organise some interesting weekend trips as well as longer excursions throughout China. Check their websites for details.

Rock Climbing

Crags are in short supply in Shànghǎi, but the odd climbing wall around town will at least keep climbers' forearms in shape.

MASTERHAND CLIMBING CLUB
Map p116

攀岩俱乐部 Pānyán Jùlèbù

☎ 5696 6657; Hongkou Stadium, 21 Upper Stand, 444 Dongjiangwan Rd, Hóngkǒu; 虹口东江弯路444号; ☼ 10am-10pm; Ⓜ Hongkou Football Stadium

There are five walls here with marked routes, as well as some bouldering workouts. Fees are Y55 without time limit and harnesses are provided. A year-long membership costs Y1200. It's on the 2nd level at gate 21.

Running

Eccentric expat organisation Hash House Harriers ('drinkers with a running problem') originated in Malaysia. The Shànghǎi chapter organises runs on Sundays, at 3pm in winter and 4pm in summer, followed by a meal. Check the website www.shanghai-hhh.com.

RUGBY

Local heroes, the Shanghai Hairy Crabs, take on expat rivals such as the Beijing Devils. Practice is held every Saturday afternoon at the Shanghai Football Club ground opposite Carrefour in Pǔdōng's Jīnqiáo district. Check www.shanghaifootballclub.com for contact details.

SPECTATOR SPORTS

Shanghai Stadium (上海体育场; Shànghǎi Tǐyùchǎng; Map p122; Ⓜ Shanghai Stadium) seats 80,000 spectators for major sports events and occasional soft-rock concerts.

Shanghai Shenhua is the city's top football team and local matches are played in Hongkou Stadium (虹口足球场; Hóngkǒu Zúqiúchǎng; Map p116; Ⓜ Hongkou Football Stadium) in north Shànghǎi. The local basketball team is the Shanghai Sharks, who haven't been the same since Yao Ming departed for the Houston Rockets in 2002. They play at Luwan Stadium (卢湾体育场; Lúwān Tǐyùchǎng; Map pp86–7; ☎ 6467 5358; 128 Zhaojiabang Rd; 肇嘉浜路128号).

Other big draws include the annual Shanghai Open tennis tournament in October, and the Volvo China Open golf tournament in April.

SQUASH

The squash (壁球; bì qiú) courts at Hotel Equatorial (国际贵都大酒店; Guójì Guìdū Dàjiǔdiàn; Map pp86–7; ☎ 6248 1688; www.equatorial.com/sha; 65 West Yan'an Rd, French Concession; 法租界延安西路65号; Ⓜ Jing'an Temple) can be rented for Y120 per hour, plus the Y15 per person entrance fee as well as Y30 for a racquet. For a cheaper hit, there are also courts at Hongkou Stadium (Map p116; Ⓜ Hongkou Football Stadium), on the 5th floor opposite the main entrance. Charges are Y35 per hour, plus Y10 for a racquet and Y3 for balls.

SWIMMING

All top-end hotels have pools; however, if swimming is your thing and you're coming in winter, make sure your hotel has an indoor pool.

MANDARINE CITY
Map pp128-9

明都城游泳池 Míngdūchéng Yóuyǒng Chí

☎ 6405 8814; 788 Hongxu Rd, entrance at cnr Guyang & Shuicheng Rds, Hongqiao; 虹桥虹许路788号; ☼ 8am-7pm Jun-Oct; Ⓜ Shuicheng Rd

This outdoor pool is particularly popular with expats – possibly more for pool-side lounging (got to work on that tan) than actual swimming. It's Y80 for adults and Y50 for kids.

ORIENTAL RIVERSIDE HOTEL
Map p108

东方滨江大酒店 **Dōngfāng Bīnjiāng Dàjiǔdiàn**
☎ 5037 0000; 2727 Riverside Ave, Pǔdōng; 浦东滨江大道2727号; ⏰ 6.30am-11.30pm; Ⓜ Lujiazui
Head over to Pǔdōng to check out this great circular pool, enclosed in a glass dome with views of the Bund. Entry is Y80.

SHANGHAI SWIMMING POOL
Map p122

上海游泳池 **Shànghǎi Yóuyǒng Chí**
☎ 6438 2372; South Zhongshan No 2 Rd, Xujiahui; 徐家汇中山南二路; ⏰ 7am-10pm; Ⓜ Shanghai Stadium
Public swimming pools in China may not be a first choice for serious swimmers, although they are considerably cheaper than hotel pools. A shop next door sells swimming gear. Tickets are Y25 before 5.30pm, Y30 after. Kids below 1.2m get in for half price. It's just near Shanghai Stadium.

TENNIS

There are several places to play tennis (网球; *wǎng qiú*). Reserve courts in advance, especially at the weekend.

CHANGNING TENNIS CLUB
Map pp86-7

长宁网球俱乐部 **Chángníng Wǎngqiú Jùlèbù**
☎ 6252 4436; Lane 1038, Caojiayan Rd, French Concession; 法租界曹家沿路1038弄; ⏰ 8am-10pm; Ⓜ Jiangsu Rd
These hard courts are fairly central, in the French Concession off Huashan Rd, next to Time Passage (p182). It's Y30 per hour during day, Y70 in the evening. There's also a small shop selling tennis equipment.

XIANXIA TENNIS CENTRE
Map pp128-9

仙霞网球中心 **Xiānxiá Wǎngqiú Zhōngxīn**
☎ 6262 8327; 1885 Hongqiao Rd; 虹桥路1885号; ⏰ 7am-10pm; Ⓜ Longxi Rd
This is a premier site. Weekdays cost Y40 per hour for daytime play and Y80 for the evening (Y60/100 on weekends), with Y30 racquet hire. Reception is in the north side of the tennis stadium.

WATER SPORTS

For a city by the sea, there's surprisingly little water-borne sports activity in Shànghǎi. What there is mostly takes place inland on Dianshan Lake.

SHANGHAI BOAT AND YACHT CLUB
www.shanghaibyc.org
SBYC organises outings and races at the Shanghai Water Sports Centre on Dianshan Lake, about 50 minutes' drive from Shànghǎi. Sailing classes are also offered. Nonmembers can tag along on designated open days; see website for details.

SHANLONG DRAGONBOAT TEAM
dragonboatsh@yahoo.com
For something more physical, try competitive dragon-boat racing held at Dianshan Lake (Y50). The Shanlong Dragonboat team meets Sunday mornings at the Portman Ritz-Carlton (p211).

YOGA

Popular with both well-heeled locals and expats, yoga classes aren't cheap, but there are plenty of options to choose from.

HATHA YOGA CENTER
Map pp86-7

哈达瑜伽会所 **Hādá Yújiā Huìsuǒ**
☎ 6427 3923; 1 South Maoming Rd, French Concession; 法租界茂名路1号; Ⓜ South Shanxi Rd
A new yoga space attached to the Longwu Kung Fu Center (p195). Classes (Hatha, Flow, Pilates) here are cheaper than elsewhere: a six-month membership (including classes) is Y1850; one year is Y2680.

Y+ Map pp86-7

Y+瑜伽会馆 **Yújiā Huìguǎn**
☎ 6433 4330; www.yplus.com.cn; 299-2 West Fuxing Rd, French Concession; 法租界复兴西路299-2号; taxi
Shànghǎi's poshest and most popular yoga centre offers a full range of classes in Ashtanga yoga, along with hot (Bikram) yoga, which takes place in a heated room to aid stretching and toning. Classes run daily from 6.30am to 8.45pm. One class is Y200; otherwise a year membership (50 classes) is Y6800. Another branch is located near Xīntiāndì (☎ 6340 6161; 2nd fl, 2 Corporate Avenue, 202 Hubin Rd; 湖滨路202号企业天地2号楼2楼).

lonely planet Hotels & Hostels

Want more sleeping recommendations than we could ever pack into this little ol' book? Craving more detail — including extended reviews and photographs? Want to read reviews by other travellers and be able to post your own? Just make your way over to **lonelyplanet.com/hotels** and check out our thorough list of independent reviews, then reserve your room simply and securely.

SLEEPING

top picks

- Mansion Hotel (p207)
- Le Tour Traveler's Rest (p212)
- Astor House Hotel (p214)
- Urbn (p211)
- Old House Inn (p210)
- The Nine (p209)
- Park Hyatt (p213)

SLEEPING

For a long time there has been a dazzling choice of top-end accommodation in moneyed Shànghǎi, but a recent boom in youth hostels, as well as the emergence of some ultrachic boutique hotels, has spiced up the city's previously one-dimensional hotel market, meaning there's never been a better time to stay here. From slick five-star hotels housed in glimmering skyscrapers to down-to-earth backpacker haunts with dirt-cheap dorm beds, the range of accommodation here is, at last, close to what you'd expect from a city of this standing.

Top-end stays tend to fall into two categories: historic hotels where guests can swathe themselves in nostalgia, and the stylish new breed of modern hotel, bursting with the latest amenities and sparkling with highly polished service.

The midrange market, which includes some handy chain hotels, has been bolstered by some wonderful boutique offerings. Some are almost painfully trendy. Others have more class and offer glimpses of Shànghǎi's charming past.

Those on a budget can breathe a collective sigh of relief as, finally, Shànghǎi can be said to boast a decent choice of youth hostels. Almost universally staffed by competent English speakers, they offer well-priced dorm beds and private rooms as well as a host of familiar facilities such as wi-fi, communal internet terminals, bike rental, kitchen and laundry rooms and even the odd table tennis or pool table. Most have small bar-cafe-restaurant areas which are among the cheapest places in town to get a beer. Neat, comfortable, but largely soulless express hotels are another decent budget option, offering bigger rooms than hostels, but without the Western-friendly facilities or language skills.

Except at youth hostels and the very best hotels, English-language skills can be rudimentary. Rack rates are listed here, but are seldom used so we also list the possible discount rate. There is, of course, no guarantee you will get this.

Almost all the hotels we've listed have air-conditioning and either broadband, albeit sometimes at extortionate daily rates, or wi-fi. If a hotel doesn't have internet access, we say so.

Most midrange and top-end hotels will change money for guests and very few don't accept credit cards these days. All hotel rooms are subject to a 10% or 15% service charge, but many cheaper hotels don't bother to charge this.

When you check into a hotel you will have to fill in a registration form (sometimes hotels simply scan your passport instead), a copy of which will be sent to the local Public Security Bureau (PSB; 公安局; Gōng'ānjú) office. Frustratingly, some very cheap Chinese hotels still refuse to take foreigners, citing the hassles involved with this registration as the reason.

For hotel bookings, the online agency CTrip (☎ 3406 4880, 800-820 6666; http://english.ctrip.com) is a good choice.

LONGER-TERM RENTALS

There are several types of longer-term accommodation in Shànghǎi. One thing common to all is the need to register with the local PSB within 24 hours of moving in.

The cheapest way to stay in Shànghǎi is to share a flat or rent local accommodation from a Chinese landlord. Classified ads in listings magazines such as *City Weekend* (www.cityweekend.com.cn/shanghai) are a good place to start. Other useful websites include enjoyclassifieds.com, shanghai.craigslist.com.cn and classifieds.urbanatomy.com. The city is also stuffed with *dìchǎn gōngsī* (real-estate agents), although English skills are limited to a few of the more expensive ones.

Expect to pay at least Y1500 per month for a flat share that's anything like central. A two-bedroom Chinese apartment in a French Concession low-rise, with no lift will cost from Y4000 per month. You'll pay more for a newer high-rise with lifts, and anything between Y10,000 and Y40,000 for a fully serviced apartment in a modern high-rise with hotel-style facilities such as a maid and a gym.

It is also worth considering living in an old-style Shànghǎi house, such as the three-floor apartment houses of the French Concession. What you gain in style, however, you often lose in suspect electricity and plumbing, poor heating and a continual need for renovations. Kitchen facilities are traditionally located in the landing and shared by all residents on the same floor. Prices here start from Y3000 for a one-bed place, but can rise significantly depending on the level of renovations.

Expect the above prices to double or even treble if you want to rent places or rooms for just one month at a time.

If you want to actually buy a place you will need a property agent to help you through the legal minefield.

ROOM RATES

Dorm beds go for around Y40 or Y50, but double rooms under Y200 can be hard to find. Expect to pay at least Y500 for a midrange room. The fancier boutique hotels will charge more. A standard room in a top-end place will almost certainly be over Y1000, even after discount. Many of the better hotels, especially those aimed at business travellers, have cheaper weekend rates.

Apart from youth hostels and express hotels, almost no hotel in Shànghǎi actually charges the full rack rate, the exceptions being during peak holiday times and Formula One grand prix weekend. So always ask for discounts (折扣; zhékòu). It's not uncommon for this to be as much as 50%. Booking online will often get you a similar discount. We've noted hotel websites where applicable.

For an explanation of the symbols used in this chapter to describe room types, see the Quick Reference page on the inside front cover.

THE BUND & PEOPLE'S SQUARE
外滩、人民广场

This is the natural centre of gravity for tourists. It's close to the historic highlights of the Bund – with its lavish views of Pǔdōng – and the excellent transport links at People's Square, and is jam-packed with hotels. At the time of research the finishing touches were being applied to the Bund's latest five-star offering: Peninsula Shanghai (半岛酒店; Bàndǎo Jiǔdiàn; Map pp66–7; ☎ 2327 2888; www.peninsula.com; 32 East Zhongshan No 1 Rd; 中山东一路32号; r from Y3200; ⓔ East Nanjing Rd). It

PRICE RANGE FOR HOTELS	
YYY	more than Y1300 a night
YY	Y500-1300 a night
Y	less than Y500 a night

looked like being an absolute corker and should be open by the time you read this.

WESTIN SHANGHAI Map pp66-7 Hotel YYY
威斯汀大饭店 Wēisītīng Dàfàndiàn
☎ 6335 1888; www.westin.com/shanghai; 88 Middle Henan Rd; 河南中路88号; d Y3600-3800; 🍴 🖥 🛜 🛗 ; Ⓜ East Nanjing Rd
Partly housed inside one of the most instantly recognisable buildings in Pǔxī – the crown-topped Bund Centre – this top quality five-star hotel puts others in this neck of the woods to shame. Announced by a hugely impressive grand lobby, home to one of the three restaurants here, the Westin boasts more than 500 top-notch rooms. The cheapest – deluxe doubles – are a bit smaller than you'd expect for the price, but are as beautifully decorated as the rest. Crown and grand deluxe rooms are both semisuite, although the living area is more office-like than homely with leather trim desk, chair and sofa laid out in front of the TV. The beds are heavenly, though, and the bathtubs – some with city views – are nice and deep. There's a gym, a pool and the Thai-style spa, Banyan Tree (p197). Expect at least 50% discounts.

SOFITEL HYLAND HOTEL
Map pp66-7 Hotel YYY
海仑宾馆 Hǎilún Bīnguǎn
☎ 6351 5888; 505 East Nanjing Rd; 南京东路505号; r from Y2000; 🍴 🖥 🛜 ; Ⓜ East Nanjing Rd
Standard doubles (Y1100 after discounts) in this well-run hotel are a bit dated – way too much beige – and small for this price, but the executive rooms (Y1700 after discount) are much more modern with chunky wood furnishings, better artwork, and widescreen TV. Like the standard rooms, they also come with mouse-size bathtubs, but do at least have separate shower cubicles. Facilities include a spa, two restaurants, a bar and a French bakery. The all-round service is excellent and the location is spot on.

JW MARRIOTT TOMORROW SQUARE
Map pp66-7 Hotel YYY
明天广场JW万怡酒店 Míngtiān Guǎngchǎng JW Wànyí Jiǔdiàn
☎ 5359 4969, toll-free 10 800-260 0660; www.marriotthotels.com/shajw; 399 West Nanjing Rd; d Y1800; 南京西路399号; 🍴 🖥 🛜 🛗 ; Ⓜ People's Sq
Housed in the breathtaking Tomorrow's Square tower, this branch of JW Marriott,

with its fabulous city views, is one of Shànghǎi's best hotels. Service is unquestionably five star and even standard rooms are immaculate with nice touches such as a coffee percolator and separate bathtub and shower. Facilities are top class – spa, gym, indoor and outdoor pools and a range of restaurants – but with rooms located from the 41st floor up, the star attraction is the stellar views. Discounts are rare, although weekend rates are around 20% cheaper. Broadband costs Y120 a day.

PEACE HOTEL Map pp66-7   Historic Hotel YYY
和平饭店 **Hépíng Fàndiàn**
☎ 6321 6888; www.peacehotel.com.cn; 20 East Nanjing Rd; 南京东路20号; ❒ 🖳 🛜 ; Ⓜ East Nanjing Rd

Shànghǎi's most iconic hotel, where the distinctive pyramid-shaped rooftop penthouse was the former eyrie of tycoon Sir Victor Sassoon, was still closed for extensive refurbishment at the time of research. The owners had promised to maintain the art deco features and styling that gave the place its unique character. The national suites, the only rooms which overlook the Bund, were deservedly famous for being laid out in the style of different countries. In the past, the hotel coasted on its reputation and both the facilities and service didn't match the prices charged, although nostalgia buffs will be hoping that the septuagenarian jazz band will once again be on duty every night in the bar. As part of the new look, the separate, red-and-white-brick south wing of the hotel, on the other side of East Nanjing Rd, will become an art centre.

PACIFIC HOTEL Map pp66-7   Historic Hotel YYY
金门大酒店 **Jīnmén Dàjiǔdiàn**
☎ 6327 6226; fax 6372 3634; 108 West Nanjing Rd; 南京西路108号; s Y1000, d Y988-1988; ❒ 🖳 ; Ⓜ People's Sq

Capped by a distinctive clock tower, this historic hotel built in 1926 is strong on both character and style. The Greek temple–like entrance leads to a marble lobby with attractive ceiling artwork and in turn to wood-trimmed corridors with deep-red carpets. The cheaper rooms at the back of the hotel are distinctly ordinary, but ones at the front, overlooking People's Park, come with free broadband, period furniture and much more

space. All the bathrooms are tiny, though. 40% discounts are common.

PARK HOTEL
Map pp66-7   Historic Hotel YYY
国际饭店 **Guójì Fàndiàn**
☎ 6327 5225; www.parkhotel.com.cn; 170 West Nanjing Rd; 南京西路170号; s Y910 d Y1245-1850; ❒ 🖳 ; Ⓜ People's Sq

Despite the wonderful art deco–style building, constructed in 1934 and until the 1980s the tallest building in Shànghǎi, the rooms here have less character than the nearby Pacific Hotel. Decor is plain and bathrooms are more akin to a standard three-star Chinese hotel than a historic four-star one. Old lifts add charm but are annoyingly slow. Staff members are very friendly, though, and 40% discounts are common. There's broadband, but it's not cheap (Y100 per day). For more information on this historic hotel see p76.

VILLAS HOTEL Map pp66-7   Hotel YY
维拉斯酒店 **Wéilāsī Jiǔdiàn**
☎ 5158 8666; 306 Guangdong Rd; 广东路306号; s/d/tw Y980/1080/1180; ❒ 🖳 ; Ⓜ East Nanjing Rd

Don't be put off by the rack rates. The discounts at this excellent hotel are staggering – doubles and twins were going for Y480 when we were here. Rooms are a little compact, but beautifully decorated with tasteful artwork, luxurious bedding and dark-wood furniture. They come with the usual kettle, TV and broadband as well as nice touches such as a coffee percolator and a funky bathroom mirror.

MANHATTAN BUSINESS HOTEL
Map pp66-7   Hotel YY
曼哈顿商务酒店 **Mànhādùn Shāngwù Jiǔdiàn**
☎ 6888 8123; www.manhattanhotel.com.cn; 81-85 Dianchi Rd; 滇池路81-85号; d from Y588; ❒ 🖳 ; Ⓜ East Nanjing Rd

This charming 1930s building, in a narrow street leading down to the Bund, is fronted by neoclassical-style pillars and burgundy awnings, but once inside it's art deco all the way, from the lifts in the lobby to the mirrors in the bedrooms. Rooms are pokey, but have character, with retro furniture and antique-style telephones, and also come with smart wall-mounted satellite TV. The cheapest have no windows. 30% discounts are the norm.

SHANGHAI RAILWAY HOTEL

Map pp66–7   Hotel Y

上海铁道宾馆 **Shànghǎi Tiědào Bīnguǎn**
☎ 550 8777; www.shtdhotel.com; 160 Guizhou
Rd; 贵州路160号; s Y280-400, d Y360-480;
❌ 🖳 ; Ⓜ People's Sq

Built in 1930 as the China Hotel, and in
1937 used by Zhou Enlai to address an
underground meeting of the Chinese
Communist Party, this historic hotel is a
short hop from East Nanjing Road and
People's Square and makes a solid budget
choice. The A-category rooms are spacious and bright with wide windows,
good lighting and clean white-tiled bathrooms. They come with built-in wardrobe,
TV, kettle, free broadband and a computer (per day Y35). B-category rooms,
which are Y120 cheaper, are kitted out
the same (minus the computer) but are
slightly smaller and gloomier. Discounts
here are rare.

SHANGFU HOLIDAY HOTEL

Map pp66–7   Hotel Y

上服假日酒店 **Shàngfú Jiàrì Jiǔdiàn**
☎ 6352 0808; 67 Guizhou Rd; 贵州路67号; s/d/
tw/t Y288/308/360/398; ❌ 🖳 ; Ⓜ People's Sq

Considering the location, so close to
People's Square, this charming old-school
hotel is fabulous value. Corridors abound
with dark wood-panelling and have nice
touches such as leather sofas to sit on while
waiting for the lift. Standard rooms are
nothing special but some of the doubles
overlooking East Nanjing Rd are more kitsch
with unusual floor plans, gold wallpaper and
pine-panelled shower cubicles. 10% to 15%
discounts are available.

JINJIANG INN Map pp66–7   Hotel Y

锦江之星旅馆 **Jinjiāng Zhīxīng Lǚguǎn.**
☎ 6326 0505; fax 6355 5180; 33 South Fujian Rd;
福建南路33号; s/d Y229/289, tw Y269-289;
❌ 🖳 ; Ⓜ Dashijie

This central hotel, which looks like it
may have struck a deal with IKEA (think
cream bedding, pine-coloured furniture
and laminated wood flooring), has bright,
spacious, functional rooms with TV, kettle,
broadband and clean shower rooms. There
are a few doubles, a handful of singles but
most rooms are twins. Note, the ones at
the back of the hotel are Y20 cheaper than
the ones overlooking the park despite
having an extra dressing-room area. For

discounts you need to buy a Y158 two-
year members card (会员卡; huìyuán kǎ),
which will get you 10% off at all branches
nationwide.

MOTEL 268 Map pp66–7   Hotel Y

莫泰连锁旅馆 **Mòtài Liánsuǒ Lǚguǎn**
☎ 5179 3333; 50 Ningbo Rd; 宁波路50号; s
Y198, d Y268-318; ❌ 🖳 ; Ⓜ East Nanjing Rd

Originally a Motel 168 (with rooms from
Y168) this place has been refurbished and
rebranded so that its name matches the
price of its new, improved standard doubles (Y268). It's still good value for this
location with modern doubles coming
with huge beds, wood-trimmed furnishings and smartly tiled chrome and glass
bathrooms. There's the usual kettle and
TV. And for an extra Y50 you get a room
with its own PC. For discounts at any of
this chain's branches, buy a Y50 lifetime
members card (会员卡; huìyuán kǎ) which
gives you Y20 off each night's stay. The
only quibble; wafer-thin walls means you
need to be lucky with the neighbours you
get.

HOME INN Map pp66–7   Hotel Y

如家酒店 **Rújiā Jiǔdiàn**
☎ 6323 9966; Lane 26, Sijing Rd; 泗泾路26弄;
d Y239-269; ❌ 🖳 ; Ⓜ East Nanjing Rd

Housed in a delightful *lòngtáng* (lane)
which is accessed from Sijing Rd, this is
one of the better branches of the dependable Home Inn chain. The pastel interior
may leave you feeling queasy but it means
clean, functional rooms are nice and bright.
All come with free broadband, TV, kettle
and pretty much spotless bathrooms. No
discounts.

HAO JIANG MOTEL

Map pp66–7   Historic Hotel Y

皓江旅馆 **Hàojiāng Lǚguǎn**
☎ 3313 0878; Lane 126, 5 Middle Sichuan Rd;
四川中路126弄5号; s/d/tr Y200/228/258; ❌ ;
Ⓜ East Nanjing Rd

If you don't mind your rooms being a little
on the shabby side, this place, housed in
a 100-year-old colonial building and just
a stone's throw from the Bund, isn't a bad
deal. Originally the Shanghai-Nanking
Railway Administration Offices, the red-brick
building, set back slightly from the main
road, dates from 1911. No-nonsense rooms
come with TV, kettle and a small shower

room. Some rooms have arched windows, some have none at all, but all lack natural light because of the tall building next door. Staff members don't speak English, but are reasonably welcoming and happy to throw in discounts of around 30%. No internet.

HOTEL TONGFU Map pp66-7   Hotel Y
桐福旅馆 **Tóngfú Lǚguǎn**
☎ 5152 6189; 266 Fuzhou Rd; 福州路266号;
s without/with bath Y100/150, d without/with bath
Y220/240; ✖ ; Ⓜ East Nanjing Rd
Housed in a tiny block of red brick-fronted *shíkùmén* (stone-gate house), this hotel has more character outside than in. Rooms are basic, especially the ones without private bathrooms, although some come with cute, wood-framed windows overlooking Fuzhou Rd. Private bathrooms are OK but the communal ones, without shower cubicles, aren't for the shy. Expect discounts of around 20%. Don't expect much English. No internet.

CAPTAIN HOSTEL Map pp66-7   Hotel Y
船长青年酒店 **Chuánzhǎng Qīngnián Jiǔdiàn**
☎ 6323 5053; www.captainhostel.com.cn; 37
Fuzhou Rd; 福州路37号; dm Y55, r Y300-400;
✖ 🖳 🛜 ; Ⓜ East Nanjing Rd
Despite being hands down the least friendly youth hostel in Shànghǎi, this naval-themed backpackers favourite still reels in punters by the boat load with its fantastic location, and fine roof-top bar. Hallways dotted with portholes lead to ship-shape, pine-bed dorms (note, those on the ground floor are inconveniently separated from the communal bathroom by the dining room), private 'cabins', with more pine furniture and clean shower rooms, and one 'luxury' suite (Y1200). There's internet, a microwave and a washing machine, but the Captain's pride is the top-floor balcony bar (coffee from Y30, beer from Y40, pizza from Y45) with pleasant decking and good views of Pǔdōng.

MING TOWN E-TOUR YOUTH HOSTEL
Map pp66-7   Hostel Y
明堂青年旅舍 **Míng Táng Qīngnián Lǚshè**
☎ 6327 7766; 57 Jiangyin Rd; 江阴路57号;
dm Y55, d & tw without/with bathroom Y160/260;
✖ 🖳 🛜 ; Ⓜ People's Sq
One of Shànghǎi's best youth hostels, E-tour has a historic setting – in among the alleys just west of People's Park – and pleasant rooms, many with reproduction

antique furniture. But it's the tranquil courtyard with fish pond, water feature and split-level bar-restaurant that really sells this one. A superb communal area, it comes with computers (free for one hour), a projector-screen DVD player, free pool table and plenty of outdoor seating on wooden decking. There are also women-only, as well as mixed dorms. Booking ahead is advisable.

MING TOWN HIKER YOUTH HOSTEL
Map pp66-7   Hostel Y
明堂上海旅行者青年旅馆 **Míngtáng Shànghǎi Lǚxíngzhě Qīngnián Lǚguǎn**
☎ 6329 7889; 450 Middle Jiangxi Rd; 江西中路
450号; dm without/with window Y45/55; s/tw/d
Y140/180/250; ✖ 🖳 🛜 ; Ⓜ East Nanjing Rd
Far friendlier than its main Bund rival – Captain Hostel – this justifiably popular hostel is also just a short stroll from the famous esplanade, on the southern corner of the grand old Hengfeng Building. It offers tidy four- and six-bed dorms with pine bunk beds and clean communal shower facilities as well as a range of decent private rooms including some cheaper ones (Y160) with shared bathrooms. The bar/restaurant sells beer (from Y6), coffee (from Y10) and well-priced Western and Chinese food. There's a free pool table, free internet, and free movies as well as a useful noticeboard in the lobby.

Y35 YOUTH HOSTEL Map pp66-7   Hostel Y
上海迎泽旅舍 **Shànghǎi Yíngzé Lǚshè**
☎ 6328 7511; 35 Yongshou Rd; 永寿路35号;
dm/d Y40/160; ✖ 🖳 🛜 ; Ⓜ Dashijie
Basic, but well turned-out private rooms are among the cheapest you'll find anywhere in central Shànghǎi. Dorms are also good value and there's a decent bar-restaurant area (beer and coffee Y10, pizza Y25) with a pool table, giant-screen DVD player and flop-into sofas. The internet connection is annoyingly temperamental.

OLD TOWN 南市
There's a dearth of hotels in this part of town and even when you do find one it often isn't set up to be able to register non-Chinese guests. The two listed below welcome foreigners, though, and are convenient bases from which to explore Shànghǎi's grainier textures.

SHANGHAI CLASSIC HOTEL

Map p79   Hotel YY

上海老饭店 **Shànghǎi Lǎo Fàndiàn**

☎ 6311 1777; 5th fl, 242 Fuyou Rd; 福佑路242号 5层; d Y480-580; ✕ 🖳; Ⓜ Yuyuan Garden

This smart three-star hotel, right in the thick of the Old Town action, has comfortable carpeted rooms with TV, kettle, free broadband and clean bathrooms. Room rates include breakfast for one person and 30% discounts are common. Not too much English, but staff members are welcoming all the same. Accessed from Jiujiaochang Rd.

MINOR WORLD CONVENTION HOTEL

Map p79   Hotel Y

小世界商务酒店 **Xiǎoshìjiè Shāngwù Jiǔdiàn**

☎ 5108 2588; 64-68 Xueqian St; 学前街64-68号; s/d Y298/358. tw Y360-390; ✕ 🖳; Ⓜ Laoximen

A stone's throw from the Confucian Temple and not much further from the enchanting *shíkùmén* found around Zhuangjia St, this clean, modern hotel may be a bit of a trek from the main Shànghǎi sights but it's handy for exploring the Old Town. Rooms are smart and functional with laminated wood flooring, firm armchairs, a desk and TV, while nicely-tiled bathrooms are spotless. Staff members do their best with very limited English. Expect 20% discounts.

FRENCH CONCESSION
法租界

Leafy, tree-lined streets, excellent restaurants, good shopping and a number of hotels with strong historic ties make this the most aesthetically pleasing district in which to be based.

88 XĪNTIĀNDÌ Map pp86-7   Hotel YYY

88 新天地

☎ 5383 8833; www.88xintiandi.com; 380 South Huangpi Rd; 黄陂南路380号; r from Y3300; ✕ 🖳 🛜 🖳; Ⓜ Xintiandi

Given that the best discounts you'll receive are likely to be no better than 20% the prices here are extraordinary. That said, this is a charming hotel. Huge rooms feature sleeping areas that are raised slightly on a wooden platform and enclosed with delicate lace curtains. Large beds come with an unusual wicker roll pillow, tasteful wicker headboard and luxury cushions, while all rooms have TV units with satellite channels, DVD player and music system. There's also free broadband.

Kitchen facilities such as a microwave, kettle and coffee percolator also come as standard. The small bathrooms, though, are frustrating to use. There's a small health club with pool, gym and spa and a rooftop restaurant serving breakfast only.

MANSION HOTEL

Map pp86-7   Historic Hotel YYY

首席公馆酒店 **Shǒuxí Gōngguǎn Jiǔdiàn**

☎ 5403 9888; www.chinamansionhotel.com; 82 Xinle Rd; 新乐路82号; tw Y2888, d Y2888-5288; ✕ 🖳 🛜; Ⓜ South Shanxi Rd

Combining historic charm and modern luxury like no other hotel in Shànghǎi, this exceptional place could be the highlight of your stay. Mansion's beautiful 1930s building was originally the residence of Sun Tingsun, a business partner of Huang Jinrong and Du Yueshang, two of Shànghǎi's most powerful gangsters (see the box text on p28). It was used as offices for the trio's business dealings and as a venue for extravagant parties. And stepping inside is like stepping back in time to the city's glorious, notorious past. There are antiques everywhere, but it's more than a museum – there's exquisite luxury, too. Your feet sink into the carpet as you enter the rooms, which are all huge and come with beautifully upholstered wood furniture, big-screen satellite TVs, double-sized showers and, in all but the twin rooms, Jacuzzis big enough for two. Expect discounts of around 40%. At the time of research

top picks

BUDGET

- Le Tour Traveler's Rest (p212) Fabulous youth hostel facilities combined with old Shànghǎi textures in this former towel factory.
- Ming Town E-Tour Youth Hostel (opposite) Tucked away down an alley, but a stone's throw from People's Square. Cool courtyard.
- Shangfu Holiday Hotel (p205) Good for those with an aversion to youth hostels. Basic, but slightly eccentric and oh so central.
- Sleeping Dragon Hostel (p215) Three-storey *shíkùmén* (stone-gate house) with wooden floorboards, huge rooms and a fabulous back door stone gateway.

another branch – Garden Mansion Hotel – was soon to be opened on Nanyang Rd.

JINJIANG HOTEL

Map pp86-7   Historic Hotel YYY

锦江饭店 Jǐnjiāng Fàndiàn

☎ 3218 9888; 59 South Maoming Rd; 茂名南路 59号; r from Y2500; ⊠ 🖳 ; Ⓜ South Shanxi Rd

This historic 1931 complex consists of two main buildings – the red-brick Georgian-style Cathay Building which houses the doubles, and the art deco–style Grosvenor Villa (Guìbīn Lóu) which has the suites (Y8000 to Y25000). Cathay has huge rooms with large beds, but a dated cream and brown colour scheme. The bathrooms are more modern with sparkling showers and deep tubs, albeit plastic ones. All rooms have a TV, a safe and ironing board. Internet, though, is an extra Y90 per day. Expect 40% discounts.

OKURA GARDEN HOTEL SHANGHAI

Map pp86-7   Hotel YYY

花园饭店上海 Huāyuán Fàndiàn

☎ 6415 1111; www.gardenhotelshanghai.com; 58 South Maoming Rd; 茂名南路58号; s/d/tw from Y2100/2600/2500; ⊠ 🗶 🖳 🛜 🐾 ; Ⓜ South Shanxi Rd

The elegant Japanese-run five-star Okura Garden boasts beautiful grounds, on the site of the old French Club, and an excellent location, near the shops on Middle Huaihai Rd. Popular with Japanese visitors, it has an indoor pool, a gym, five restaurants and three bars. Rooms are decorated tastefully in natural colours and come with

top picks

HISTORIC HOTELS

- Mansion Hotel (p207) Lap up the luxury like a 1930s bad boy in this one-time business base for Shànghǎi's gangland bosses.
- Broadway Mansions (p214) Art-deco-tastic Orwellian-like brick pile of a building filled with class, and fine river views.
- Astor House Hotel (p214) Bags of old-world charm and the ghosts of celebrities past.
- Ruijin Hotel (opposite) All about Building No 1, here, with its gorgeous garden setting, exquisite furniture and distinguished former guests.

broadband, although it costs Y120 per day in the standard rooms. Modern bathrooms have the automatic flush and seat-warming toilets that seem all the rage in Shànghǎi's top-notch hotels. The service here is first-class. Blue dots on the employees' uniforms reveal their language ability, with three dots being the best. Discounts are around 40%.

PUDI BOUTIQUE HOTEL

Map pp86-7   Boutique Hotel YYY

璞邸精品酒店 Púdǐ Jīngpǐn Jiǔdiàn

☎ 5158 5888; www.boutiquehotel.cc; 99 Yandang Rd; 雁荡路99号; r from Y1600; ⊠ 🖳 🛜 ; Ⓜ Xintiandi

This trendy, ultramodern hotel tries so hard to be cool that it sometimes borders on tacky. Unusual flat fish tanks in the dark corridors are neon-lit (poor fish). Freestanding wooden cabinet with large-screen TV, DVD player and music system revolve to reveal a gaudy minibar, and the digital clocks by the bed use a laser to throw a time display on the ceiling. There is some genuine class, though. The modern artwork above each bed is edgy but dead cool and comes on huge canvasses, guests are given a pillow menu when they arrive so they can choose from a list of scented pillow fillings, and bathrooms which, like the rooms themselves, are enormous, are beautifully designed and come with a rainforest shower head as well as a deep bathtub with Jacuzzi jets. All rooms have internet connection, fax machine with scanner and printer, and a 24-hour personal butler service. If your own Jacuzzi isn't enough there's an outdoor one on the roof where there's a bar-restaurant and a small gym. There's also a pet hospitality service for those who can't bear to leave their best friend at home. Prices include breakfast. Discounts of 20% are the best you'll get. You must book.

HILTON HOTEL Map pp86-7   Hotel YYY

静安希尔顿饭店 Jìng'ān Xī'ěrdùn Fàndiàn

☎ 6248 0000; www.hilton.com; 250 Huashan Rd; 华山路250号; r from Y1500; ⊠ 🗶 🖳 🛜 🐾 ; Ⓜ Jing'an Temple

A favourite with airline crews (who should know a thing or two about hotels), the Hilton's standard rooms are a bit old fashioned, but the deluxe versions – only Y100 to Y200 more – have had a modern refit, meaning more style (slick furniture, rainforest showers), more comfort (thick carpets, big beds) and better views. All rooms have broadband, while the usual five-star facilities abound. Discounts of 15% are the norm.

HENGSHAN MOLLER VILLA

Map pp86-7   Historic Hotel YYY

衡山马勒别墅饭店 Héngshān Mǎlè Biéshù Fàndiàn

☎ 6247 8881; www.mollervilla.com; 30 South Shanxi Rd; 陕西南路30号; r from Y1500; ✷ 🖵 ; Ⓜ South Shanxi Rd

This fairy-tale castle lookalike, built by Swedish businessman and horse-racing fanatic Eric Moller was a family home until 1949 when the Communist Youth League took it over. Rooms, with old Shànghǎi artwork on the walls, are well turned out with sumptuous bedding and a large-screen TV that doubles as a computer. The gaudy, two-tone brick building, with outrageous roof design, is set in a landscaped garden dotted with statues, including a bronze horse, said to be standing over the spot where Moller buried his favourite nag. Expect 20% discounts.

LAPIS CASA Map pp86-7   Boutique Hotel YYY

☎ 5382 1600; www.lapiscasahotel.com; 68 Taicang Rd; 太仓路68号; d/tw Y1500/1800; ✷ 🖵 ; Ⓜ South Huangpi Rd

Natural textures are a feature of this small but charming boutique hotel beside Huaihai Park. The paving-stone corridor on the ground floor leads to rooms with beautiful traditional wooden furniture and granite-tiled bathrooms. Showers are double-sized. There's a Japanese and a Taiwanese restaurant but no separate bar. Discounts of 40% aren't unheard of.

RUIJIN HOTEL Map pp86-7   Historic Hotel YYY

瑞金宾馆 Ruìjīn Bīnguǎn

☎ 6472 5222; www.ruijinhotelsh.com; 118 Ruijin No 2 Rd; 瑞金二路118号; d standard/executive Y1300/2300; ✷ 🖵 ; Ⓜ South Shanxi Rd

There are four buildings in this lovely garden estate, housing a range of rooms, but the one you want is Building No 1, a 1919 red-brick mansion and the former residence of Benjamin Morris, one-time owner of *North China Daily News*. Dark wood panelled corridors and a gorgeous staircase lead to a series of enormous, executive-class rooms that have attracted guests such as Mao Zedong and President Nixon. The furniture is exquisite – redwood

double bed, antique desk and chair – and they come with TV, computer, DVD player and bathrooms with deep tubs. Buildings 2, 3 and 4 are more modern and house a mixture of nothing-special standard and executive rooms. Check the website for discounts.

ANTING VILLA HOTEL

Map pp86-7   Historic Hotel YYY

安亭别墅花园酒店 Āntíng Biéshù Huāyuán Jiǔdiàn

☎ 6433 1188; 46 Anting Rd; 安亭路46号; r from Y1180; ✷ 🖵 ; Ⓜ Hengshan Rd

On a quiet tree-lined street, this pleasant hotel shares its grounds with a 1936 colonial Spanish-style villa. It offers bright, comfortable rooms, with broadband and quality furniture including a chaise longue by the window. Some have fine views over the garden which is a popular spot for weddings at weekends. There's a restaurant and a bar, and discounts of up to 40% are available.

DONGHU HOTEL Map pp86-7   Historic Hotel YY

东湖宾馆 Dōnghú Bīnguǎn

☎ 6415 8158; www.donghuhotel.com; 70 Donghu Rd; 东湖路70号; s US$100, d US$150-330; ✷ 🖵 ; Ⓜ South Shanxi Rd

Once the home of feared Shànghǎi gangster Du Yuesheng (see the boxed text, p28), the historic Donghu is divided into several areas and buildings, although only two of them house ordinary guest rooms. The first, an austere 1934 white concrete building, houses the better rooms, although their colour schemes – burgundy with orange – leave little to be desired. The second, newer building is an ugly white-tiled affair across the road and has overpriced rooms with cheap carpets and tatty furnishings. There are massive discounts to be had here (at least 50%) and all rooms have broadband.

THE NINE Map pp86-7   Boutique Hotel YY

☎ 6471 9950; 355 West Jianguo Rd; 建国西路355号; rooms Y800-1500; ✷ 🖵 ; Ⓜ Jiashan Rd

No website, no sign and hidden away down a small alleyway, this is about as exclusive as it gets. Walk-in guests will be turned away so you must phone ahead. But it's worth the hassle. Once booked, scout around for Lane 355, walk to the end, turn left and ring the bell by the large wooden gateway marked only with the number

top picks

BOUTIQUE HOTELS

- **Urbn** (opposite) Open-plan spaciousness and bedside bathtubs in China's first carbon-neutral hotel.
- **The Nine** (p209) Beautiful old garden villa with no sign, no website and no walk-in guests. As exclusive as it gets.
- **Lapis Casa** (p209) Cute, quaint and much more welcoming than its trendier peers.
- **Pudi Boutique Hotel** (p208) Jacuzzis, neon-lit fish tanks and TVs that spin round to reveal a drinks cabinet. Got to love it.

9. Inside is a small, tranquil garden housing an old colonial building with antique tables, unusual statues and six delicious double rooms, all different and all decorated exquisitely. Rates include breakfast and there's a small bar-cafe.

QUINTET Map pp86-7 Boutique Hotel YY

☎ 6249 9088; www.quintet-shanghai.com; 808 Changle Rd; 长乐路808号; d Y800-1100; ✖ ✖ ▯ 🛜; Ⓜ Changshu Rd

This chic B&B has five beautiful double rooms in a 1930s town house not short on character. Some of the rooms are on the small side, but each is decorated with style, incorporating modern luxuries such as large-screen satellite TV, and laptop-sized safes with more classic touches such as wood-stripped floorboards and deep porcelain bathtubs. Staff members sometimes get a BBQ going on the roof terrace – the only place, incidentally, where you're allowed to smoke – but there's an excellent restaurant on the ground floor in any case. No sign – just buzz on the gate marked 808 and wait to be let in. No discounts.

OLD HOUSE INN

Map pp86-7 Boutique Hotel YY

老时光酒店 Lǎoshíguāng Jiǔdiàn

☎ 6248 6118; www.oldhouse.cn; Lane 351, No 16 Huashan Rd; 华山路351弄16号; s Y640, tw Y880, d Y880-1250; ✖ ▯ 🛜; Ⓜ Changshu Rd

This 1930s red-brick building has been lovingly restored to create an exclusive, yet affordable place to stay. All 12 rooms are decorated with care and attention and come with wooden floorboards, traditional

Chinese furniture, stylish artwork, and a few antiques. No discounts, but rates include breakfast at A Future Perfect (p163), the funky bar-restaurant on the ground floor.

YUEYANG HOTEL Map pp86-7 Hotel Y

悦阳商务酒店 Yuèyáng Shāngwù Jiǔdiàn

☎ 6466 7000; 58 Yueyang Rd; 岳阳路58号; d & tw Y218-388; ✖ ▯; Ⓜ Hengshan Rd

One of the best budget options in the French Concession that's within easy walking distance of a metro station, Yueyang has smart, spacious rooms with big double beds, desk and chair, TV, kettle and free broadband. Shower rooms are clean and modern, although, annoyingly, the hot water isn't always piping hot. Also annoying is the fact that foreigners aren't allowed to stay in the cheapest rooms (A-category, Y178) which, like the B-category rooms (Y218), come with laminated wood flooring rather than carpets. Expect only small discounts, if any.

MOTEL 268 SUPER Map pp86-7 Hotel Y

莫泰连锁旅店 Mòtài Liánsuǒ Lǚdiàn

☎ 5170 3333; www.motel168.com; 113 Sinan Rd; 思南路113号; r from Y198; ✖ ▯; Ⓜ Dapuqiao

This dependable chain on leafy Sinan Rd is ideally located for those wanting to explore the maze of charming alleyways that houses the Taikang Rd Art Centre (p85), also known as Tiánzífáng (田子房). Rooms are business-like with a large desk, comfy chair and free broadband as well as wardrobe, TV and kettle, while the showers are invigoratingly powerful. Some rooms are windowless so gloomier than others. English is limited. You get a discount of Y20 per night if you buy a lifetime members card (Y50; 会员卡; huìyuán kǎ).

BLUE MOUNTAIN YOUTH HOSTEL

Map pp86-7 Hostel Y

蓝山国际青年旅舍 Lánshān Guójì Qīngnián Lǚshě

☎ 6304 3938; www.bmhostel.com; 2nd fl, Building 1, 1072 Quxi Rd; 瞿溪路1072号1号甲2楼; dm Y45-55, d without/with private bath Y130/180, tw Y180, t Y250; ✖ ▯ 🛜; Ⓜ Luban Rd

A fabulous hostel, which, although slightly out of the way, is practically next door to Luban Rd metro station so it shouldn't leave you feeling too isolated. Rooms are simple but clean with pine furniture and flooring, TV and kettle. There are women-only, men-only and mixed dorms, and the communal facilities are excellent – a wi-fi-enabled bar-restaurant area with free pool table, free internet and free movie screenings, a kitchen with microwave, washing machines (Y15 per cycle) and even hairdryers and irons that you can borrow. Staff members speak good English and are very friendly.

JÌNG'ĀN 静安

This diverse district – with its gritty art scene, half-decent bars and top-end designer-label shopping – has now thrown chic boutique hotels and funky little youth hostels into the mix to make it one of the more attractive places to stay in Shànghǎi. It also offers a couple of hotels within handy striking distance of the main train station.

PORTMAN RITZ-CARLTON

Map pp98-9   Hotel YYY

波特曼丽嘉酒店 Bōtèmàn Lìjiā Jiǔdiàn
☎ 6279 8888; www.ritzcarlton.com; 1376 West Nanjing Rd; 南京西路1376号; r from Y4000; 🖾 🖳 🛜 🖳 ; M Jing'an Temple

Impeccable service, excellent facilities and a decent location make this one of the best business hotels this side of the Huangpu River. Rooms are smart and spacious with DVD player, radio alarm clock, internet (per day Y96), two telephone lines, an ironing board, safe and fridge as standard, and have good-sized bathrooms. There are two pools – indoor and out – squash and tennis courts, a gym and four top restaurants. The hotel is part of the Shanghai Centre, with a medical clinic, supermarket, cafes and more. Discounts sometimes exceed 50%. Good job, because the rack rates are frightening.

JIA SHANGHAI Map pp98-9   Boutique Hotel YYY
☎ 6217 9000; www.jiashanghai.com; 931 West Nanjing Rd; 南京西路931号; r from Y2500; 🖾 🖳 🛜 ; M West Nanjing Rd

A bit like nearby Urbn (right), this undeniably stylish boutique hotel, housed in a charming 1920s building with cute balconies, is perhaps just a little too cool for its own good. Staff members seem to look down on walk-in guests, so try to book ahead if at all possible. Once you're in, though, you'll be treated to slick, sassy, open-plan rooms with funky furniture and extras such as DVD player and heated towel racks. There's also a swish Italian restaurant. Booking online will get you the best discounts, with

standard rooms plummeting to around Y1000. Prices include breakfast as well as afternoon cakes and wine. The hotel entrance is on Taixing Rd.

URBN

Map pp98-9   Boutique Hotel YYY
☎ 5153 4600; www.urbnhotels.com; 183 Jiaozhou Rd; 胶州路183号; r from Y1600; 🖾 🖳 🛜 ; M Changping Rd

Snooty staff and a general air of superiority is a small price to pay for staying in China's first carbon-neutral hotel. Not only are recyclable materials and low-energy products used where possible, Urbn also calculates its complete carbon footprint – including staff commutes and delivery journeys – then offsets it by donating money to environmentally friendly projects. Open-plan rooms are beautifully designed with low furniture and sunken living areas exuding space. Bathtubs in the bedroom rather than in the bathroom (and sometimes right next to the bed!) are an unusual feature, while grey slate tiling gives this luxury boutique hotel its urban vibe. Discounts are a measly 10%. Walk-in guests are generally not welcomed, so call ahead.

IVY SHANGHAI

Map pp98-9   Boutique Hotel YYY
☎ 3221 2600; www.ivyshanghai.com; 709 Jiaozhou Rd; 胶州路709号; r Y1288; 🖾 🖳 🛜 ; M Changping Rd

This off-the-wall boutique hotel, with its horrendous army-camouflage exterior, and bizarre inner atrium with cotton-wool clouds suspended from the ceiling, used to be a cinema. If you can take your eyes off the vomit-inducing pink and green carpets in the corridors, you'll notice quotes from famous films plastered across the walls, while there's a cinema screen in the lobby which shows films on demand every evening. Rooms are funky and come with wall-mounted wide-screen TV, broadband and a small dining table and chairs. Bathrooms are small, but ultramodern and some have lovely deep bathtubs. Discounts can be as much as 50%.

HOLIDAY INN DOWNTOWN

Map pp98-9   Hotel YY
上海广场长城假日酒店 Shànghǎi Guǎngchǎng Chángchéng Jiàrì Jiǔdiàn
☎ 6353 8008; www.holidayinn.com; 285 West

Tianmu Rd & 585 Hengfeng Rd; 天目西路 285号、恒丰路585号; d from Y988; ✗ 🖳; Ⓜ Shanghai Train Station
Easy to spot as you come out of the train station, the four-star Holiday Inn is made up of two buildings separated by a small pedestrianised street. The Great Wall Wing (上海长城假日酒店) is accessed from Hengfeng Rd, while the Plaza Wing (上海广场假日酒店) is accessed from West Tianmu Rd. Prices are the same in both, as are the modern, tastefully decorated rooms which come with TV, broadband (per day Y115), a safe, fridge and ironing board. Bathrooms are smart but small. Expect 40% discounts.

FAR EAST HOTEL Map pp98-9   Hotel YY
机电大厦远东大酒店 Jīdiàn Dàshà Yuǎndōng Dàjiǔdiàn
☎ 6317 8900; 600 Hengfeng Rd; 恒丰路600号; d from Y560; ✗ 🖳; Ⓜ Shanghai Train Station
A stone's throw from the train station, this three-star concrete tower is just across the road from the Holiday Inn, but has much cheaper rooms that are still neat and tidy with small, but clean bathrooms. All have TV, kettle and broadband (per day Y30). 50% discounts are common.

LE TOUR TRAVELER'S REST
Map pp98-9   Hostel Y
乐途静安国际青年旅舍 Lètú Jìng'ān Guójì Qīngnián Liǔshè
☎ 6267 1912; www.letourshanghai.com; 319 Jiaozhou Rd; 胶州路319号; dm Y65, d/tw/tr Y200/210/270; ✗ 🖳 📶; Ⓜ Changping Rd
Housed in a former towel factory, this fabulous youth hostel leaves most others out to dry. You'll pass a row of splendid *shíkùmén* on your way down the alley to get here, and the old-Shànghǎi textures continue once inside, with red-brick interior walls and reproduced stone gateways above doorways to rooms which are simple, but smart and have broadband and clean shower rooms. The ground floor has a table tennis table, a pool table and wi-fi, all of which are free to use, while there's a fine rooftop bar-restaurant with outdoor seating. Bicycles can also be rented (per 12 hours, Y30). Its sister hostel, Le Tour Shanghai Youth Hostel (Map pp62–3; ☎ 5251 0808; www .letourshanghai.com; 136 Bailan Rd; 白兰路319号; dm Y60, d & tw without/with bathroom Y150/190, tr Y195), near Caoyang Rd metro station, is cheaper but further out of town.

SHANGHAI CITY CENTRAL INTERNATIONAL YOUTH HOSTEL
Map pp62-3   Hostel Y
上海万里路国际青年酒店 Shànghǎi Wànlǐlù Guójì Qīngnián Jiǔdiàn
☎ 5290 5577; www.hostelshanghai.cn; 300 Wuning Rd; 武宁路300号; dm Y60, tw/d Y198/218; ✗ 🖳 📶; Ⓜ Caoyang Rd
One for those travellers looking for the nontouristy side of Shànghǎi, this out-of-the-way hostel, set back off the main road in a residential block, has an engaging atmosphere, thanks largely to its huge bar-restaurant area, with sports-screening TVs and pool table. There's a small seating area out the front with an outdoor table-tennis table, while the lobby has free-to-use computers and a good selection of books. Standard rooms and dorms are painted a cold blue and are very basic, but clean. A free shuttle bus runs into town every day, but it's very close to Caoyang Rd metro station. Prices include an all-you-can-eat breakfast. Small discounts are sometimes available.

PŬDŌNG 浦东

Despite good metro links, and some standout five-star hotels, it's hard not to feel isolated on this side of the river.

GRAND HYATT
Map p108   Hotel YYY
金茂君悦大酒店 Jīnmào Jūnyuè Dàjiǔdiàn
☎ 5049 1234; www.shanghai.grand.hyatt .com; Jin Mao Tower, 88 Century Ave; 世纪大道88号金茂大厦; d from Y3500; ✗ 🖳 📶 🖵; Ⓜ Lujiazui
Before being superseded by its even taller, even grander next-door neighbour (the Park Hyatt), this classy joint, spanning the top 34 floors of the majestic Jinmao Tower (p109), was *the* place to stay in Shànghǎi. It's still pretty swanky with big, comfortable beds and huge windows affording fabulous city views, especially in the deluxe rooms, and the service is still five-star. The half-carpeted, half marble-floored interiors are looking a bit dated these days, though, as is the geeky-looking light-brown furniture. Wi-fi comes at a cost (per day Y120) and the safes are a bit small for laptops, but 50% discounts aren't uncommon. Accessed from the south side of the tower.

PARK HYATT Map p108 Hotel YYY

柏悦酒店 Bóyuè jiǔdiàn

☎ 68881234; www.parkhyattshanghai
.com; Shanghai World Financial Center, 100 Century
Ave; 世纪大道100号世界金融中心; d from
Y2800; ✖ 🖳 🛜 📺 ; Ⓜ Lujiazui

Spanning the 79th to 93rd floors of the
towering Shanghai World Financial Center
(p107), this jaw-dropper is the world's highest hotel above ground level and could
easily lay claim to being the coolest hotel
in China, never mind Shànghǎi. Service is
impeccable, facilities are top-notch and
its funky interior design is almost art gallery–like. High-walled corridors with brown-
fabric and grey-stone textures lead to
luxurious rooms with quirky features such
as a mist-free bathroom mirror containing
a small TV screen, a rainforest shower in
the bathroom ceiling, a plug socket in the
safe for your laptop and a toilet seat that
opens automatically as you approach it. All
rooms come with huge TV, free wi-fi, free
fresh coffee, deep bath tubs, leather chaise
lounges, sumptuous beds and, as you'd
expect, outrageously good views. Don't
expect much of a discount. Accessed from
the south side of the tower.

PUDONG SHANGRI-LA Map p108 Hotel YYY

浦东香格里拉大酒店 Pǔdōng Xiānggélǐlā
Dàjiǔdiàn

☎ 6882 8888; www.shangri-la.com; 33 Fucheng
Rd; 富城路33号; r from Y2650; ✖ 🖳 🛜 📺 ;
Ⓜ Lujiazui

They don't look much from the outside,
but the Shangri-La's two towers – one
neoclassical in design, the other much more
modern – house an elegance found at few
other five-star hotels in Shànghǎi. The lobby,
corridors, restaurants and rooms are tastefully decorated in natural colours, the beds
are sumptuous with pillows galore and the
marble bathrooms are exquisite. All rooms
have wi-fi and those in the new tower also
have fax machines and DVD players as well
as ceiling-to-floor windows. Discounts bring
the standard rooms down to around Y1800
in the old tower and Y2000 in the new tower.

BEEHOME HOSTEL Map p108 Hostel Y

宾家国际青年旅舍 Bīnjiā Guójì Qīngnián Lǚshè

☎ 5887 9801; www.beehome-hostel.com; Lane
490, No 210 Dongchang Rd; 东昌路490弄
210号; dm Y69-79, tw/tr Y189/230, d Y250-360;
✖ 🖳 🛜 ; Ⓜ Dongchang Rd

top picks

FIVE-STAR

- Park Hyatt (left) Funky, luxurious and, for now at
  least, the world's tallest hotel.
- Grand Hyatt (opposite) Spectacular inner atrium,
  fabulous views and, for now at least, the world's
  second-tallest hotel.
- St Regis Shanghai (below) The preferred choice of
  the Ferrari Formula One team, with more class than
  its eye-catching rivals.
- JW Marriott Tomorrow's Square (p203) Striking
  building, delicious rooms and not in Pǔdōng!

Part of the Captain Hostel group, but far
friendlier than the other Shànghǎi branches,
this fine hostel with a small courtyard garden
is a leafy oasis in an otherwise innocuous
Pǔdōng housing estate. It offers basic but
clean rooms, all with private bathrooms (even
the dorms), and excellent communal areas –
a bar-restaurant (beer from Y15, coffee from
Y10, pizza from Y20) with funky artwork, a
balcony seating area and a cute, tree-shaded
courtyard garden. There's wi-fi throughout,
one free-to-use PC and free foosball. The
hostel is set back off the main road through
a wooden gateway marked 东园新村
(Dōngyuán Xīncūn). There's a small sign for
the hostel by the gate.

CENTURY AVENUE AREA

ST REGIS SHANGHAI Map p114 Hotel YYY

瑞吉红塔大酒店 Ruìjí Hóngtǎ Dàjiǔdiàn

☎ 5050 4567; www.stregis.com/shanghai;
889 Dongfang Rd; 东方路889号; s/d from
Y3290/3390; ✖ 🖳 🛜 📺 ; Ⓜ Pudian Rd

It's not as hip as the Park Hyatt or as elegant
as the Shangri-La, but many visitors to
Shànghǎi – including the Ferrari Formula
One team – rank this as the classiest joint
in town. Service is as good as it gets, rooms
are huge and tastefully decorated and the
bathrooms, accessed via swish sliding doors,
have rainforest showers as well as bathtubs
with the taps thoughtfully lined along the
side. Broadband comes free, women can
check into the Ladies Only floors if they
prefer and there's a pool, gym, sauna and
snooker room. The huge Imperial Suite
(room number 8888), spanning two floors, is
where Michael Schumacher stays whenever

he comes to watch the Shanghai Grand Prix and can be yours for a mere Y37,260! Fear not, discounts of 60% – and even more for the suites – are not uncommon.

HOLIDAY INN PUDONG Map p114 Hotel YYY

浦东假日酒店 Pǔdōng Jiàrì Jiǔdiàn
☎ 5830 6666; www.holiday-inn.com; 899 Dongfang Rd; 东方路899号; d from Y998; ✕ 🖳 🖵 ; 🅜 Pudian Rd

This busy four-star hotel is very popular with tour groups – both domestic and international – so it can feel overcrowded at times. Rooms are comfortable, though, with thick carpets and puffy duvets, and come with a safe, TV and broadband (per day Y80). Executive rooms have an unusual square-shaped bathtub which is big enough for two. Otherwise, there's a pool. Rates often halve at weekends.

NOVOTEL ATLANTIS Map p114 Hotel YY

海神诺富特大酒店 Hǎishén Nuòfùtè Dàjiǔdiàn
☎ 5036 6666; www.novotel.com; 728 Pudong Ave; 浦东大道728号; d Y1000-2000; ✕ 🖳 🖵 ; 🅜 Pudong Av

Functional, no-frills business hotel with fabulous views of Pǔdōng. Rooms have free broadband and there's a pool, a gym, some no-smoking floors and a top-floor revolving restaurant. Executive rooms are the same as standard ones, only on higher floors and with use of the club lounge. Discounts of 50% are common if it's quiet.

ZHONGDIAN HOTEL Map p114 Hotel YY

中电大酒店 Zhōngdiàn Dàjiǔdiàn
☎ 5879 8798; 1029 Nan Quan Rd; 南泉路1029号; d Y680-880; ✕ 🖳 ; 🅜 Century Ave

Smart wooden furniture with leather upholstery, TV, free internet, a safe in every room and small but spotless bathrooms make this a decent choice after the 30% discounts. Some of the smaller doubles sometimes go for a discounted price of around Y350. Ask for 'tèjià' (特价; special price).

HIDDEN GARDEN YOUTH HOSTEL

Map p114 Hostel Y
大隐国际青年旅舍; Dàyǐn Guójì Qīngnián Lǚshè; ☎ 5831 2330; Lane 834, No 840A Pudong Ave; 浦东大道834弄840A号; dm Y50, r Y148-Y168; ✕ 🖳 🛜 ; 🅜 Pudong Ave

Hidden, yes, but in the suburbs rather than in a garden, this very basic hostel does, nonetheless, give you a chance to see what

Pǔdōng looks like without its suit and tie. Twins are bright and clean, but singles are a bit cramped and dorms can be smoky. All rooms have TV but, unusually, no kettle. There's a small bar-restaurant area, free internet, wi-fi on the ground floor and use of a big kitchen, while young, welcoming staff do their absolute best with limited English. Look for the Hostelling International sign at the end of Lane 834. YHA members get Y20 discounts.

HÓNGKǑU & NORTH SHÀNGHǍI
虹口区、北上海

With two of Shànghǎi's best-loved historic hotels and a trio of tip-top youth hostels to choose from, staying slightly north of the action may not be such a bad choice after all.

BROADWAY MANSIONS

Map p116 Historic Hotel YYY
上海大厦 Shànghǎi Dàshà
☎ 6324 6260; www.broadwaymansions.com; 20 North Suzhou Rd; 苏州北路20号; d Y2200-3600; ✕ 🖳 ; 🅜 Tiantong Rd

Whether you love or hate the design of this classic Orwellian brick pile that looms over Suzhou Creek there's no doubting the luxury on offer inside. Built to great fanfare in 1934 as an apartment block, it was later used to house American officers after WWII. These days, though, its rooms ooze class with thick carpets, tasteful furnishings and modern bathrooms, all with bathtubs. Considering the shockingly good discounts (more than 50% is not uncommon) it's well worth paying slightly more for the Bund-facing rooms which have wonderful views over the northern part of the Bund, the Huangpu River and Pǔdōng. All rooms have broadband, although it's pricey (per day Y110). Like nearby Astor House (above), Broadway Mansions is a short stroll from the Bund despite being located on the north side of Suzhou Creek.

ASTOR HOUSE HOTEL

Map p116 Historic Hotel YYY
浦江饭店 Pǔjiāng Fàndiàn
☎ 6324 6388; fax 6324 3179; www.astorhousehotel.com; 15 Huangpu Rd; 黄浦路15号; d Y1280-1680; ✕ 🖳 ; 🅜 Tiantong Rd

Originally the Richards Hotel, this distinguished old gentleman was built in the latter part of the Qīng dynasty in 1846, and was Shànghǎi's first hotel. More than 160 years on, there remains a distinct air of elegance, with the hotel's original wooden flooring still covering some of the halls and corridors. Rooms are huge, with sofas, good sized beds and TVs that double-up as computers, while some on the higher floors have river views. For an extra Y400 you can stay in rooms once occupied by guests as esteemed as Albert Einstein, Bertrand Russell and Charlie Chaplin. Discounts of 40% are the norm.

NANXINYUAN HOTEL Map p116 Hotel Y
南馨园酒店 Nánxīnyuán Jiǔdiàn
☎ 5696 1178; 277 Shanyin Rd; 山阴路277号; r Y280; ✗ ⬜ ; Ⓜ Hongkou Stadium
Situated on charming Shanyin Rd, this stylish three-star hotel is a roomier alternative to the excellent youth hostels in the area. A spiral staircase leads to clean, very spacious doubles with comfortable, quality furniture, TV, kettle, a coffee percolator (Y15) and broadband (per day Y20). Standard rooms slide down to Y238 after discounts.

KOALA GARDEN HOUSE Map p116 Hostel Y
考拉花园旅舍 Kǎolā Huāyuán Lǚshè
☎ 5671 1038; www.koalahouse.cn; 240 Duolun Rd; 多伦路240号; dm Y50, d without bath Y160, d with bath Y180-580; ✗ ⬜ 🛜 ; Ⓜ Dongbaoxing Rd
Youth hostels don't come much more charming than this one. Even the lobby (which doubles up as a chic wi-fi cafe), with its high ceilings and brightly painted walls, is a joy to be in. But it's the rooms, all slightly different, that really stand out. Although on the small side, all are beautifully decorated with cosy furniture, flower-patterned wallpaper and gathered-up curtains, and all come with wall-mounted flat-screen TV and a funky little bathroom. The two most expensive – Tulip and Rose – have private balconies overlooking pleasant Duolun Rd. Dorms are small, but neat and clean. Internet is free.

NAZA INTERNATIONAL YOUTH HOSTEL Map p116 Hostel Y
那宅青年旅舍 Nàzhái Qīngnián Lǚshè
☎ 65417062; 318 Baoding Rd; 保定路318号; dm without/with bathroom Y45/65, s/d/tw Y159/199/219; ✗ ⬜ 🛜 ; Ⓜ Dalian Rd
Another decent Hóngkǒu youth hostel, Naza comes with some fine communal

spaces including a nice bar area with free pool table and a cute cafe. Rooms are a bit sterile with all-white walls – surprising for a hostel housed in a former paint factory – and basic furniture, but all (apart from some dorms) have TV and ensuite bathroom. There are more expensive rooms with reproduction antique furniture, including one with a four-poster bed (Y319). Internet is free and the ground floor has wi-fi.

SLEEPING DRAGON HOSTEL
歇龙青年旅舍 Xiēlóng Qīngnián Lǚshè Hostel Y
☎ 6535 1562; www.zzzdragon.com; 394 Zhoushan Rd; 舟山路394号; dm Y45, s without/with bath Y100/160, d Y180; ✗ ⬜ 🛜 ; Ⓜ Linping Rd
Housed in a fabulous three-storey 1924 shíkùmén, with original wooden floorboards and staircases and a gorgeous stone gateway over the back door, this hostel is another great choice. The 10- and 12-bed dorms are huge, as are all the rooms in the older half of the building. In the newly refurbished half, rooms are a bit ordinary and much smaller. There's free use of a kitchen, free internet, wi-fi on the ground floor, bicycles to rent (Y30) and very friendly staff. It's also a stone's throw from the shíkùmén on Dongyuhang Rd, which at weekends becomes a bustling street market.

XÚJIĀHUÌ & SOUTH SHÀNGHǍI
徐家汇、南上海

JIANGUO HOTEL Map p122 Hotel YYY
建国宾馆 Jiànguó Bīnguǎn
☎ 6439 9299; www.jianguo.com; 439 North Caoxi Rd; 漕溪北路439号; r from Y1850; ✗ ⬜ 🖳 ; Ⓜ Xujiahui
Don't be put off by the extortionate rack rates at this four-star business hotel. When we were here, discounts were more than 60%, making this a reasonable choice for those who want to explore the Jesuit charms of Xújiāhuì. Comfortable rooms have broadband (Y100), TV and kettle, but bathrooms are pretty small and have those annoyingly tiny bathtubs that hotels still seem to love in this part of town. There's a pool, gym, snooker room and four good restaurants.

ASSET HOTEL

Map p122   Hotel Y

雅舍宾馆 **Yǎshè Bīnguǎn**
☎ 6438 9900; www.asset-hotel.com; 590 South Wanping Rd; 宛平南路590号; r from Y420; 💬 💻 ; 🅼 Shanghai Stadium

Housed in a charming yellow and white building hidden from the main road by apartments, this higher-end budget option has smart, clean rooms with free broadband, complimentary mineral water, a fridge, TV and kettle. Rates include breakfast, and discounts can be 45%.

QIXIANG HOTEL (METEOROLOGICAL HOTEL)

Map p122   Hotel Y

气象宾馆 **Qixiàng Bīnguǎn**
☎ 5489 6900; 166 Puxi Rd; 蒲西路166号; d/tw Y288; 💬 💻 ; 🅼 Xujiahui

The Qixiang may not be much to look at but the wonderful location (practically shoulder-to-shoulder with the St Ignatius Cathedral and on the corner of a pleasant square) makes this a fine budget option. This is a typical Chinese three-star hotel, with female assistants *(fúwùyuán)* on every floor, little English spoken and no English signs, but it's quiet, and the rooms (which have dial-up internet connection, TV and kettle) and shower rooms are clean. It's on the fifth floor above a restaurant. Don't expect more than 10% discounts, but hey, it's already cheap.

CHÁNGNÍNG & GŬBĚI
长宁、古北

HONGQIAO STATE GUEST HOUSE

Map pp128-9   Hotel YYY

虹桥迎宾馆 **Hóngqiáo Yíngbīnguǎn**
☎ 6219 8855; www.hqstateguesthotel.com; 1591 Hongqiao Rd; 虹桥路1591号; d from Y1660; 💬 💻 🚻 ; 🅼 Yili Rd

Housed in very pleasant garden grounds, rooms here have a homey feel, decorated in warm colours and benefiting from floor-to-ceiling windows. All come with broadband and ok bathrooms with tubs. The executive rooms, which are far classier and come with cute little balconies as well as much more modern bathrooms, are in a more impressive building nearby with a beautiful marble lobby and antiques in the corridors. Facilities include the excellent

Clark Hatch Fitness Centre. Discounts of 40% are common.

HOTEL CAROLINA

Map pp128-9   Hotel YY

美卡商务酒店 **Měikǎ Shāngwù Jiǔdiàn**
☎ 5258 2000; www.hotelcarolina.cn; 643 Xinhua Rd; 新华路643号; d from Y738; 💬 💻 ; 🅼 West Yan'an Rd

Set back slightly from leafy, historic Xinhua Rd, this smart, well-run business hotel has neat, well-equipped rooms with TV, broadband, safe, fridge and rainforest showers as well as elegant touches such as silk bedrunners. Discounts bring standard doubles down to below Y400.

HONGQIAO AIRPORT AREA

MARRIOTT HOTEL HONGQIAO

Map p132   Hotel YYY

万豪虹桥大酒店 **Wànháo Hóngqiáo Dàjiǔdiàn**
☎ 6237 6000; www.marriott.com; 2270 Hongqiao Rd; 虹桥路2270号; r from Y2500; 💬 💻 📶 📺 ; 🅼 Longxi Rd

A grand lobby introduces guests to good all-round quality and facilities that include a bright, semicircular swimming pool, tennis court, bar and a number of top restaurants. Rooms are a bit on the basic side and broadband in the standard 'deluxe' rooms costs extra (Y120 per day). Bathrooms are small and have showers placed above old-fashioned plastic bathtubs. But discounts are sometimes as much as 50%.

XIJIAO STATE GUEST HOUSE

Map p132   Hotel YY

西郊宾馆 **Xijiāo Bīnguǎn**
☎ 6219 8800; www.hotelxijiao.com; 1921 Hongqiao Rd; 虹桥路1921号; r from Y996; 💬 💻 📺 ; 🅼 Longxi Rd

This quiet, sleepy hotel, which has hosted guests as esteemed as Queen Elizabeth II and Mao Zedong, claims to be the largest garden hotel in Shànghǎi. Its 80 hectares include huge lawns, streams, mature trees and a large lake. Standard rooms are nothing special, but comfortable enough and come with free broadband. Facilities include indoor and outdoor tennis courts, a delightful indoor pool and a gym. Discounts can be as much as 40%.

EASE HOTEL

Map pp128-9   Hotel Y

驿居酒店 **Yìjū Jiǔdiàn**

☎ 5153 8888; www.ease-hotel.com; 38 Huqingping Hwy; 沪青平公路38号; r from Y218;
❌ 🖳 ; Ⓜ Shanghai Zoo

Circular-shaped double beds, podlike
shower cubicles and funky curved furniture
are all features of this well-rounded budget
option. All rooms have broadband and
there's a free shuttle bus service to Hongqiao Airport. If rooms here are full, next
door there's a branch of the dependable,
and even cheaper Motel 168 (☎ 5153 8888; www
.motel168.com; d/tw from Y168/188), owned by the
same company.

EXCURSIONS

contents

Shànghǎi certainly has its own unique tale to tell, but within range of town are other enthralling destinations offering a completely different take on China. Bamboo-forested mountain retreats, ancient water villages, willow-tree-lined lakes and even a sacred island (with beaches!) are all just a few hours from Shànghǎi's urban jungle, and can make perfect day trips or weekend jaunts.

The big centres of trade in this region's dynastic history were Hángzhōu (below) and Sūzhōu (p229). The former was the southern terminus of the astonishing 7th-century engineering feat known as the Grand Canal (which at 1800km long is still the longest canal in the world), linking the Yang and Yellow River basins. Hángzhōu is steeped in history, but its real drawcard is the wonderfully romantic West Lake which, with its wispy willow trees and early morning mist, is the epitome of a traditional Chinese landscape. The city lies on one side of the lake, but the other is overlooked by rolling hills of tea plantations and forests, making for good hiking or cycling.

Sūzhōu also goes way back, and is famed throughout the country for its traditional Chinese gardens as well as silk production. You'll also find a few quaint canals here, left over from times gone by. But if it's cute waterways you're after, skip Sūzhōu and head straight to one of the Yangzi River Delta's wonderful ancient canal towns (p235). These tiny whitewashed water villages have remained pretty much unchanged over the centuries and make fascinating day trips or overnight stays.

Further afield, tiny Lǐzhāng (p240) will give you a much more rural take on Chinese village life, while Mògānshān (p237), with its European-style stone-walled villas, offers some great mountain walks among bamboo forests. For something more spiritual, hop on an overnight ferry and cruise your way to the lush, Buddhist island of Pǔtuóshān (p238), where you'll find temples, tranquillity and even a couple of decent beaches.

HÁNGZHŌU 杭州

An otherwise underwhelming Chinese city, Hángzhōu is transformed into one of China's very best tourist destinations by the simply gorgeous West Lake and its fabulous green environs.

The Chinese tourist brochure hyperbole surrounding West Lake is – perhaps for the very first time – almost justified in its shrill accolades. The very definition of classical beauty in China, West Lake continues to mesmerise while methodical prettification over the past decade has worked its cunning magic. Hazy hills rise above the willow-lined banks, forming crinkled silhouettes punctuated by solitary pagodas, while tiny boats lazily float by. The landscapes are quintessentially Chinese, and there's more than enough walking, cycling and (take a deep breath) green spaces to keep everyone leisurely occupied. You'll need about three days to fully savour what's on view but the inclination is to take root – like one of the lilting West Lake willows – and stay put.

Be warned, though. Hángzhōu is one of the country's most famous tourist attractions. Droves descend from all over China to digitally capture West Lake – especially on holidays and weekends – resulting in a blight of overpriced, fully booked hotels and chattering tour groups. But don't despair, the West Lake area is large enough to absorb the tourist swell and still leave pockets of tranquillity and unspoiled beauty.

Hángzhōu has been in existence since at least the start of the Qin dynasty (221 BC). When Marco Polo passed through here in the 13th century he described it as one of the finest and most splendid cities in the world. Calling the city Kinsai, the Italian traveller noted in amazement that Hángzhōu had a circumference of 100 miles while its waters were vaulted by 12,000 bridges.

Although Hángzhōu prospered greatly after it was linked with the Grand Canal in 610 (the canal ferried the region's grain and silk tribute up to Běijīng), it really came into its own after the Song dynasty (based at Kāifēng) was

USEFUL WEBSITES

Hángzhōu www.hangzhou.com.cn/english, www.gotohz.com, www.morehangzhou.com

Sūzhōu www.visitsz.com, www.moresuzhou.com

overthrown by the invading Jurchen in 1126. The Song court fled south and finally settled in Hángzhōu, establishing it as the capital of the Southern Song dynasty.

While the north of China remained firmly in the hands of the invaders, Hángzhōu, in the south, became the central hub of the Chinese state. The court, civil officials, artists and merchants all congregated in Hángzhōu, where the population rose from half a million to around 1.75 million by 1275. The city's burgeoning population and its good links to the ocean promoted the growth of river and sea trade, ship building and other naval industries, although it was downgraded from capital when the Mongols conquered China. Hángzhōu's wooden buildings made fire a perennial hazard; among major conflagrations, the great fire of 1237 reduced some 30,000 residences to piles of smoking carbon.

Hángzhōu took a hammering during the Taiping Rebellion. In 1861 the Taiping laid siege to the city and captured it, but two years later the imperial armies reclaimed it. These campaigns left almost the entire city in ashes, led to the deaths of more than half a million of its residents through disease, starvation and warfare, and finally ended Hángzhōu's significance as a commercial and trading centre.

Few monuments survived the devastation, and most of those that did became victims of the Red Guards, 100 years later during the destructive Cultural Revolution. Much of what may be seen in Hángzhōu today is of fairly recent construction.

West Lake 西湖

There are 36 lakes in China called West Lake (Xī Hú), but this is *the* West Lake that all others are christened after. Originally a lagoon adjoining the Qiantang River, the

TRANSPORT: HÁNGZHŌU

Distance from Shànghǎi 170km

Direction Southwest

Bus Frequent buses to Hángzhōu's East Bus Station (Y65 to Y68, 2½ hours, 6.30am to 7.30pm) leave from Shanghai South Long-Distance Bus Station (Map pp62–3), Shànghǎi's Hengfeng Rd Bus Station (Map pp98–9) and the main Shanghai Long-Distance Bus Station (Map pp98–9), just north of Shanghai Train Station. Hourly buses (Y85, two hours) to Hángzhōu also run from Hongqiao Airport, and six daily buses (Y100, three hours) go from Pudong International Airport. Return buses to Shànghǎi run every 10 minutes (Y65, 6.30am to 7.50pm).

Train Eleven fast trains (Y54, 1¼ to 1½ hours) run daily to Hángzhōu from Shanghai South Train Station (Map pp62–3), leaving at 7.20am, 7.44am, 9.30am, 11.45am, 1.07pm, 1.12pm, 3.04pm, 4.40pm, 5.47pm, 7.03pm and 8.03pm. There are a number of slower trains (two to 2½ hours), the last leaving at 11.50pm. The last train back to Shanghai South Train Station is at 8.40pm (fast) or 9.08pm (slow). Book weekend tickets as far in advance as possible. You can buy them up to 10 days in advance.

Getting Around

Airport Bus Services (Y20, one hour) run from the Civil Aviation Administration of China (CAAC; Zhōngguó Mínháng) office in town to Hángzhōu airport every 30 minutes from 5.30am to 9pm. A taxi is about Y100.

Bicycle Cycling is a brilliant way to see Hángzhōu. Youth hostels rent bikes, but why not use the city's wonderful public bicycle scheme (see box text p226)?

Boat Pleasure boats aplenty ply the shores of West Lake, especially by the causeways. See p225.

Bus Useful buses include Y1 and Y2 which do circuits of West Lake, taking in Lingyin Temple. Y2 also goes by the train station. Bus Y3 runs from Yan'an Lu, past Beishan Lu and on to Longjing Tea Village. Bus 7 goes from Lingyin Temple, past Beishan Lu and Hubin Lu and on to Xihu Dadao. Bus Y8 goes from the south end of Yan'an Lu to the CAAC office for the airport shuttle bus. Bus 518 connects the train station with the East Bus Station. Bus 188 connects it with the North Bus Station. Minibuses (Y4) connect the East and North Bus Stations.

Electric carts These run around the lake, including the Su Causeway, for around Y10 per short trip.

Metro The first line of Hángzhōu's new metro system is due to open in 2012, but although it connects the train station it will be of limited use to tourists as it only skirts the northeast corner of West Lake.

Taxi Taxis start at Y10.

lake didn't come into existence until the 8th century, when the governor of Hángzhōu had the marshy expanse dredged. As time passed, the lake's splendour was gradually cultivated. Gardens were planted, pagodas were built, and causeways and islands were constructed from dredged silt. The poet Su Dongpo famously personified West Lake as a young woman whose beauty was enhanced by her elegant dress.

Su himself had a hand in the lake's development, constructing the Su Causeway (苏堤; Sūdī) during his tenure as local governor in the 11th century. It wasn't an original idea – the poet-governor Bai Juyi had already constructed the Bai Causeway (白堤; Báidī) some 200 years earlier. Lined by willow, plum and peach trees, today the traffic-free causeways with their half-moon bridges make for excellent outings, particularly by bike.

Since none of the sights around the lake are a must see, the best way to tour is to take off in one direction and stop at places when the fancy strikes you. Dawn and dusk are particularly good times to visit, especially when the lake is covered in mist.

Connected to West Lake's northern shores by the Bai Causeway is Gushan Island (孤山; Gū Shān), the lake's largest island. It's the site of the modest Zhejiang Provincial Museum (Zhèjiāng Shěng Bówùguǎn; 25 Gushan Lu; 孤山路25号; admission free, audio guide Y20; ☷ 9am-5pm Tue-Sun, noon-5pm Mon), which introduces visitors to the region's prehistory and history, and Zhongshan Park (Zhōngshān Gōngyuán). You'll also find the intriguing Seal Engravers' Society (Xīlíng Yìnshè; admission free; ☷ 9am-5.30pm) here, dedicated to the ancient art of carving the name seals (or chops) that serve as personal signatures. It's housed in beautiful, shaded gardens on the slope of a hill. There's an old teahouse at the top (pots of tea from Y20). In the northwest of the lake is the lovely Quyuan Garden (Qūyuàn Fēnghé), a collection of gardens spread out over numerous islets and renowned for its fragrant spring lotus blossoms.

Across from the entrance to the 3km-long Su Causeway is Yue Fei Temple (Yuè Miào; Beishan Lu; admission Y25; ☷ 7am-6pm), bounded by a red-brick wall and dedicated to General Yue Fei (1103–41) whose tomb is here. Commander of the Song armies, Yue was executed after being deceived by Qin Hui, a treacherous court official. More than 20 years later, Song emperor Gao Zong exonerated Yue and had his corpse reburied at the present site.

At the other end of the Su Causeway is Red Carp Pond (Huāgǎng Guānyú), another collection of gardens on the southern shore that is home to a few thousand red carp. East along the shore is the eye-catching Leifeng Pagoda (Léifēng Tǎ, Thunder Peak Pagoda; admission Y40; ☷ 7.30am-9pm mid-Mar–mid-Nov, 8am-5.30pm mid-Nov–mid-Mar). Topped with a golden spire, it's climbable for fine views of the lake. The original pagoda, built in 977, collapsed in 1924. Set against the hillside across the road is the peaceful Jingci Zen Monastery (Jìngcí Sì; Nanshan Lu; admission Y10; ☷ 6am-5.15pm summer, 6.30am-4.45pm winter); check out the vast effigy of Sakyamuni in the main hall and the magnificent 1000-arm statue of Guanyin (Buddhist goddess) in the Guanyin Hall (观音殿; Guānyīn Diàn).

On the eastern shore, housed in the Chinese Academy of Art (中国美术学院; Zhōngguó Měishùxuéyuàn) is an excellent art gallery (美术馆; měishùguǎn; ☷ 9.30am-4.20pm Tue-Thu).

WALKS

The West Lake area is littered with fine walks – just follow the views. For a splendid trek into the forested hills above the lake, however, walk up a lane called Xixialing, immediately west of the Yue Fei Temple.

Stone map inscriptions and some signs can help you find the way if you get lost, but they are mostly in Chinese, so refer to the characters given here and in our map key. The road initially runs past the west wall of the temple and then enters the shade of towering trees, with stone steps leading you up. At Ziyun Cave (Zǐyún Dòng) the road forks; take the right-hand fork in the direction of the Baopu Taoist Temple, 1km further, and the Baochu Pagoda.

At the top of the steps turn left and, passing the Sunrise Terrace (Chūyáng Tái), again bear left. Down the steps, look out for the tiled roofs and yellow walls of the striking Baopu Taoist Temple (Bàopù Dàoyuàn; admission Y5; ☷ 6am-5pm) below you to your right; head right along a path to reach it. The temple's first hall contains a statue of Guanyin in front of a Yin and Yang diagram; an effigy of Gehong (葛洪) – who once smelted cinnabar here – resides in the next hall, behind a fabulously carved altar decorated with figures.

Come out of the temple's back entrance and turn left towards the Baochu Pagoda (Bǎochù Tǎ) and, after hitting a confluence of three paths, take the middle track. Squeeze through a gap between some huge boulders (some of which

HĂNGZHŌU

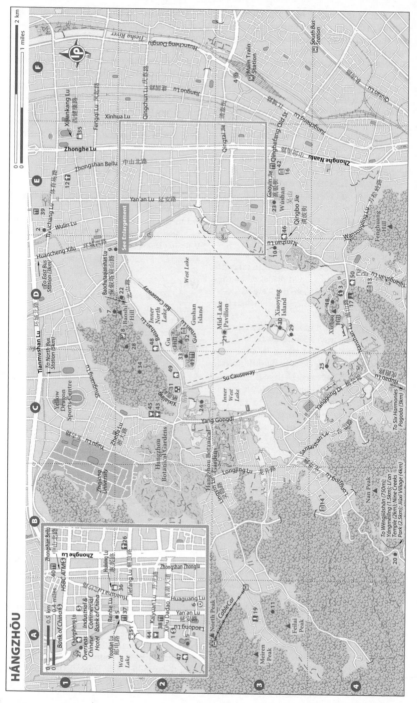

can be climbed for lake views) and you will see the Baochu Pagoda rising up ahead. Restored many times, the seven-storey brick pagoda was last rebuilt in 1933, although its spire tumbled off in the 1990s.

Continue on down and pass through a páilou (牌楼) – or decorative arch – erected during the Republic (with some of its characters scratched off) to a series of stone-carved Ming dynasty effigies, all of which were vandalised in the tumultuous 1960s, apart from two effigies on the right. Residents in a couple of the old courtyard homes here sell cheap food to weary walkers. Bear right and head down to Beishan Lu, emerging from Baochutaqianshan Lu.

BOAT TRIPS

Wooden cruise boats (游船; yóu chuán; 1½hr; adult/child incl entry to Three Pools Y45/22.5; ☻ 7am-4.45pm) shuttle every 20 minutes from a number of points (including Gushan Island, Yue Fei Temple, Red Carp Pond and the south end of Hubin Lu) to the Mid-Lake Pavilion (湖心亭; Húxīn Tíng) and Xiaoying Island (小瀛洲; Xiǎoyíng Zhōu),

which has a fine central pavilion and 'nine-turn' causeway. From the island you can look over at the Three Pools Mirroring the Moon (Sāntán Yìnyuè), a string of three small towers in the water, each of which has five holes that release shafts of candlelight on the night of the Mooncake Festival in midautumn.

If you want to contemplate the moon at a slower pace, hire one of the smaller six-person boats (小船; xiǎo chuán; about 1hr; per boat Y160) rowed by a boatman. Look for them across from the Overseas Chinese Hotel or along the causeways. You can also hire your own electric boat (电船; diàn chuán; Y40 per hr, Y200 deposit) at a number of points on the Bai Causeway.

BIKE TOURS

There are numerous possibilities for cycling around Hángzhōu. This wonderful circuit loops through the tea plantations and forested hills south of West Lake. It takes about two hours without stopping, but take your time; all the villages you pass have places where you can buy food and, of course, a cup of tea, and there are some fabulous picnic spots. The initial climb gets quite tough, so be prepared and don't forget to bring plenty of water.

Begin by heading south from the lake on Longjing Lu (龙井路). It's a gradual ascent into the hills, past the China Tea Museum (opposite) and fields of tea plantations. From here the gradient becomes significantly steeper. When you approach Longjing Village (龙井村; Lóngjǐng Cūn), the road will fork; put in the extra effort, go left and keep on heading up the mountain on Manjiaolong Lu (满觉陇路).

Skip the tacky tea park, which is just before the pass. At the top of the pass, is the small tea village of Wēngjiāshān (翁家山). Enjoy the downhill into the forest, but don't go too fast, or you'll miss the turnoff for Yángméilǐng (杨梅岭). The small road on your right leads down through another village and out onto the forest floor, following a small stream past Li'an Temple (理安寺; Lǐ'ān Sì).

Not far after this is Nine Creeks Park (九溪烟树; Jiǔxī Yānshù), with a lovely pool fed by a waterfall. From here you'll be winding your way through scenic countryside, until you reach Jiǔxī Village (九溪村) at the highway.

Turn left on the highway, and follow Qiantang River until you reach Six Harmonies Pagoda (opposite). Fork left, go under the bridge, and head north on Hupao Lu (虎跑路), from where it's a 15-minute ride back to the lake.

Lingyin Temple 灵隐寺

Lingyin Temple (Língyǐn Sì; Lingyin Lu; 灵隐路; grounds Y35, grounds & temple Y65; 7am-5pm) is Hángzhōu's principle Buddhist temple. It was built in 328, and due to war and other calamities it has been destroyed and restored no fewer than 16 times.

The main temple buildings are restorations of Qing dynasty structures. The Great Hall envelops a magnificent 20m-high statue of Siddhartha Gautama (the historical Buddha), sculpted from 24 blocks of camphor wood in 1956. Behind the giant statue is a startling montage of 150 small figures, which charts the journey of 53 children on the road to buddhahood.

The large grounds house other temples too and are also home to Feilai Peak (飞来峰; Fēilái Fēng; Peak Flying from Afar) – magically transported here from India, according to myth – and a stunning series of 470 Buddhist carvings, dating from the 10th to 14th centuries. To get a close-up view of the best carvings, including the famous 'laughing' Maitreya Buddha, follow the paths along the far (east) side of the stream.

Behind the Lingyin Temple is North Peak (北高峰; Běi Gāofēng), which can be scaled via a cable car (suǒdào; up/return Y30/Y40) or on foot. From the summit are sweeping views across the lake and city.

To get to Lingyin Temple, take bus K7 from Beishan Lu, or bus Y1 or Y2 from Nanshan Lu.

FREE BIKES

Sounds too good to be true but, thanks to the city's fabulous public bicycle scheme, that's essentially what you get in Hángzhōu – free cycling!

Bike-rental kiosks, with rows of bright red bicycles, are all over the city. Once you've obtained a swipe card, you can pick up a bike from any one of these kiosks and return it to any other. The first hour is free, as long as you remember to keep switching bikes every hour, you don't pay a thing. Note, only a few of the kiosks have facilities to hand out and take back swipe cards. We've marked two of them on our map. Also note, you cannot return a bike after the kiosks are closed – the swipe units become inactive, and you will end up having to pay a full night's bike rental. Kiosk opening hours are 6am to 9pm April to October and 6.30am to 8pm November to March.

Rental costs at a glance

- First/second/third hour – free/Y1/Y2
- Every hour thereafter – Y3 per hr
- Swipe card deposit – Y200
- Minimum credit on swipe card – Y100

You must show your passport when obtaining a swipe card. Your deposit and any unused credit is fully refunded upon return of swipe card.

HÁNGZHŌU'S INCREDIBLE GIANT WAVE

An often spectacular natural phenomenon occurs every month on Hángzhōu's Qiantang River when the highest tides of the lunar cycle cause a wall of water – sometimes almost 9m high – to thunder up the narrow mouth of the river from Hangzhou Bay at speeds of up to 40km per hour.

This awesome tidal bore (钱塘江潮; qiántáng jiāngcháo) is the world's largest and can be viewed from the riverbank in Hángzhōu, but one of the best places to witness it is on the north side of the river at Yánguān (盐官), a delightful ancient town about 38km northeast of Hánghzhōu. The most popular viewing time is during Mid-Autumn Festival, which falls in September or October, on the 18th day of the eighth month of the lunar calendar, when the International Qiantang River Tide Observing Festival takes place. However, you can see it throughout the year when the highest tide occurs at the beginning and middle of each lunar month. The Hangzhou Tourist Information Centre (p228) can give you upcoming tide times.

To get to Yánguān, take a bus from Hángzhōu's East Bus Station to Guōdiàn (郭店; Y14, one hour, 7am to 5.25pm) then take local bus 109 (25 minutes).

South of West Lake

The hills southwest of West Lake are Hángzhōu's least developed area and are a prime spot for walkers, cyclists and green-tea connoisseurs. Not far into the hills, you'll begin to see fields of tea bushes planted in undulating rows, the setting for the China Tea Museum (Zhōngguó Cháyè Bówùguǎn; Longjing Lu; 8.30am-4.30pm Tue-Sun) – 3.7 hectares of land dedicated to the art, cultivation and tasting of tea. Further up are several tea-producing villages, all of which harvest China's most famous variety of green tea, *lóngjǐng chá* (龙井茶; dragon well tea). Longjing Village (Lóngjǐng Cūn) itself is up near the first pass. Everyone will want to sell you tea, but if you do buy some, do it for the novelty, because prices aren't cheap. Buses 27 and Y3 run to the village from Beishan Lu and Nanshan Lu respectively.

Three kilometres southwest of the lake stands an enormous rail-and-road bridge, which spans Qiantang River. Close by is the 60m-high octagonal Six Harmonies Pagoda (六和塔; Liùhé Tǎ; 16 Zhijiang Lu; 之江路16号; grounds Y20, grounds & pagoda Y30; 6am-6.30pm), first built in 960 and named after the six codes of Buddhism. The pagoda also served as a lighthouse, and was supposed to have magical power to halt the tidal bore which thunders up Qiantang River twice a month (see box text, above). To get to the pagoda, take bus 504 or K4 from Nanshan Lu. Behind the pagoda stretches a charming walk, through terraces dotted with sculptures, bells, shrines and inscriptions. Serious hikers can also do a number of long walks from here, but finding maps with walking trails is tricky – ask at your hotel – and you will need to take food and water.

Just south of the lake, the China Silk Museum (Zhōngguó Sīchóu Bówùguǎn; 8706 2079; 73-1 Yuhuangshan Lu; 玉皇山路73-1号; admission free, audio guide deposit Y100; 8.30am-4.30pm) has good displays of silk samples, and explains the history and processes of silk production. take bus 12 or Y3.

Qinghefang Old Street 清河坊历史文化街

Although pretty touristy, Qinghefang Old Street (Qīnghéfǎng Lìshǐ Wénhuà Jiē) houses a host of attractive buildings, some of genuine antiquity, and can make for a fun wander. Join the crowds enjoying souvenir stalls, teahouses and makeshift puppet theatres, chomp on a chewy pink-coloured Southern Song Dingsheng Cake (南宋定胜糕; Nánsòng Dìngshèng Gāo; Y1.50) or pick up some Longjing tea (龙井茶; Lóngjǐng chá; Y10 for a 50g box) or a box of delicious nutty-flavoured Dragon Whiskers Sweets (龙须糖; Lóngxūtáng; Y10 a box). There are several pungent traditional Chinese medicine shops on the side streets. One, Húqìngyú Táng (胡庆余堂; since 1874), is home to the Chinese Medicine Museum (Zhōngyào Bówùguǎn; 95 Dajing Xiang大井巷95号; admission Y10; 8.30am-5pm), housed in a fabulous wooden courtyard building.

Other Sights

Hidden away behind sheet-metal gates, the blue-and-white Catholic Church (Tiānzhǔ Táng; 415 Zhongshan Beilu; 中山北路415号; English mass 6pm Sat, Chinese mass 9am Sun) is a lovely building, with an effigy of a compassionate Mary above the door. The brick Protestant Si-Cheng Church (Sīchéng Táng; 132 Jiefang Lu; 解放路132号) is more Chinese in style.

INFORMATION

ATMs ATMs accepting foreign cards are marked on the map.

Bank of China (Zhōngguó Yínháng; 177 Laodong Lu; 劳动路177号; ☿ 9am-5pm) Money-changing facilities and a 24-hour ATM.

Civil Aviation Administration of China (CAAC; Zhōngguó Mínháng; ☎ 8666 6666; 390 Tiyuchang Lu; 体育场路390号; ☿ 7.30am-8pm)

Hangzhou Tourist Information Center (Hángzhōu Lǚyóu Zīxún Fúwù Zhōngxīn) At the train station, near Leifeng Pagoda and at other locations.

Internet cafes (wǎngbā; per hr Y3; ☿ 24hr) There are a couple of 2nd-floor internet cafes on your right as you exit the train station.

Kodak Express (Kēdá; Youdian Lu; 邮电路; ☿ 8.30am-9pm) CD burning; Y20 per disc.

Public Security Bureau (PSB; Gōngānjú; ☎ 8728 0600; 35 Huaguang Lu; 华光路35号; ☿ 8.30am-noon & 2-5pm Mon-Fri) Can extend visas.

SHOPPING

Qinghefang Old Street (p227) Offers bundles of souvenir and gift possibilities from Chinese tiger pillows to taichi swords.

Wushan Lu Night Market (Wúshān Lù Yèshì; ☿ 6-11pm) Relocated to Huixing Lu (惠兴路) between Youdian Lu (邮电路) and Renhe Lu (仁和路), this bustling evening street market sells clothing and souvenirs.

Silk Market (Sīchóu Shìchǎng; ☿ 8am-5.30pm) Contains a string of silk shops and clothing stores on and around Xijiankang Lu (西健康路), just north of Fengqi Lu (凤起路).

EATING & DRINKING

The top restaurant strip in town is Gaoyin Jie, parallel to and immediately north of Qinghefang Old St. For a rundown on Hángzhōu cuisine see the boxed text, opposite.

Shuguang Lu (曙光路), northwest of West Lake, is the main place for beers. There are also some bars near Ming Town Youth Hostel (opposite). For a good introduction to what's on and where, grab a copy of *More – Hangzhou Entertainment Guide* (www.morehangzhou.com) available at some bars and hotels.

Lóuwàilóu (30 Gushan Lu; 孤山路30号; mains Y20-200; ☿ 10.30am-3.30pm & 4.30-8.45pm) With a choice location on Bai Causeway, and fine lakeside views, the city's most famous restaurant has been going since 1848. It serves up expensive but delicious Hángzhōu favourites such as Longjing shrimp (龙井虾仁; *Lóngjǐng xiārén*; Y198) and braised pork (东坡肉; *dōngpō ròu*; Y14 per chunk), as well as reasonably priced standard Chinese dishes (Y20 to Y50). English menu.

Grandma's Kitchen (Wàipójiā; fl 8, Bldg B, Hangzhou Tower, Huancheng Beilu; 环城北路杭州大厦B座八楼; mains Y6-55; ☿ 10.30am-2pm & 4-9pm) With all the Hángzhōu classics and more at unbeatable prices, this superb restaurant chain is a huge favourite with the locals. There's an English menu with photos of every dish, but if you can't decide for yourself, the braised pork (红烧东坡肉; *hóngshāo dōngpō ròu*; Y12) and chicken in Longjing tea (龙井茶香鸡; *lóngjǐng cháxiāng jī*; Y45) are divine. The Zhongshan Beilu branch, which is slightly closer to West Lake, has the same menu but a stuffier atmosphere. There's also a branch at the train station.

Oriental Restaurant (Dōngyīshùn; 101 Gaoyin Jie; 高银街101号; mains Y12-50; ☿ 11am-9pm) Specialising in food from China's Muslim Hui minority, this is much more than the average Xīnjiāng restaurant you find all over China. It has lamb kebabs (羊肉串; *yáng ròu chuàn*; Y2), lamb on naan bread (囊包肉; *nángbāo ròu*; Y50) and fried noodle pieces (炒片; *chǎo piàn*; Y12) like all the others, but you'll also find hummus dishes, doner kebabs and even felafel (Y20). English menu.

Ajisen (Wèiqiān Lāmiàn; 10 Hubin Lu; 湖滨路10号; dishes Y15-30; ☿ 10am-11pm) An array of eye-wateringly spicy noodle dishes and huge fried rice servings make this affordable Japanese chain a popular choice. English picture menu and free tea. Pay up front.

Carrefour (Jiālèfú; 135 Yan'an Lu; 延安路135号; ☿ 9am-9pm) Huge supermarket, perfect for picnic supplies.

1944 Bar (Yījiǔ Sìsì Jiǔbā; 119 Shuguang Lu; 曙光路119号; beer Y20; ☿ 8pm-2am) Loud, brash and popular with locals as well as expats, this small place is often the busiest of the Shuguang Lu bars.

Old Shanghai Bar (Lǎo Shànghǎi Yīnyuèbā; 113 Shuguang Lu; 曙光路113号; beer Y25; ☿ 8pm-2am) Cosy atmosphere, friendly staff and occasional live acts singing Shànghǎi classics.

House 79 (Hàoshì; 89 Kaiyuan Lu; 开元路89号; beer Y10; ☿ 7pm-2am) A good, cheaper alternative to Shuguang Lu, this low-lit funky little bar has been pulling in the beer-necking, dice-shaking locals for more than 10 years.

HÁNGZHŌU CUISINE

Part of the so-called 'Eastern School', Hángzhōu cuisine is sometimes described as southern food cooked in a northern style and has noticeably less oil than Shanghainese cuisine. There's a predominance of fish, shrimp and green vegetables, in fresh and subtle sauces. *Lóngjǐng xiārén* (龙井虾仁; Longjing shrimp) are soaked with Hángzhōu's famous *lóngjǐng* tea. *Xīhú chúncài tāng* (西湖莼菜汤; West Lake soup) is made with water shield, a green plant that grows in West Lake. *Xīhú tángcù yú* (西湖糖醋鱼; sweet-and-sour West Lake fish) is another popular dish.

Look out for the mouth-watering *dōngpō ròu* (东坡肉; braised pork chunks), named after the Song dynasty poet Su Dongpo. Flavoured with Shàoxīng wine, and cooked and served in a pot, the pork is often quite fatty.

Another local delicacy, apparently a firm favourite with Emperor Qianlong, is *shāguō yútóu dòufu* (沙锅鱼头豆腐; earthenware pot fish-head tofu).

Jiàohuā jī (叫花鸡; beggar's chicken) was supposedly created by a pauper who stole a chicken but had no pot to cook it in. So he plucked it, covered it with clay and put it on the fire. These days, the bird is stuffed with mushrooms, pickled Chinese cabbage, herbs and onions, wrapped in lotus leaves, sealed in clay and baked all day in hot ashes, ending up deliciously crispy.

SLEEPING

If you don't stay in a hotel within walking distance of the lake, you'll be kicking yourself afterwards. If calling ahead to book, note that the area code for Hángzhōu is 0571.

Shangri-La (Xiānggélǐlā Fàndiàn; ☎ 8797 7951; www.shangri-la.com; 78 Beishan Lu; 北山路78号; d from Y1900) Amid spacious forested grounds on the northern lakeshore, this is the most refined and romantic of Hángzhōu's five-star hotels. View rooms first, as quality varies. Discounts of 30% are common.

New Hotel (Hángzhōu Xīnxīn Fàndiàn ☎ 8766 0008; 58 Beishan Lu; 北山路58号; d from Y980) Despite the name, this place goes back almost 100 years and is housed in three attractive European-style buildings. Standard rooms are nothing special, but there are some nice lake-view options and discounts can be excellent (at least 40%).

Crystal Orange Hotel (Júzi Shuǐjīng Jiǔdiàn; ☎ 2887 8988; www.orangehotel.com; 122 Qingbo Jie; 清波街122号; r from Y788) Andy Warhol prints in the lobby, a glass lift, crisp rooms with flat-screen TV, wi-fi and Kohler-branded bathroom amenities, and discounts of up to 50% make this trendy business hotel, housed in a cool colonial-style building with cute balconies, a smart choice. It's very popular so book ahead.

West Lake Youth Hostel (Hángzhōu Guòkè Qīngnián Lǚshè; ☎ 8702 7027; www.westlakehostel.com; 62-3 Nanshan Lu; 南山路62-3号; dm Y45-50, s Y160, d Y200-210) South of the action so quieter than Ming Town. Has pleasant rooms and a cosy lounge area. Book ahead.

Ming Town Youth Hostel (Míngtáng Hángzhōu Guójì Qīngnián Lǚshè; ☎ 8791 8948; 101-11 Nanshan Lu; 南山路101-11号; dm Y45, d Y120-230) Fab hostel. Fab location. Make sure you call ahead.

SŪZHŌU 苏州

Famed far and wide for its gardens, canals and silk production, Sūzhōu is another major stop on the domestic tourism trail. That means more megaphone-wielding tour groups and less tranquillity than perhaps you would like. Nevertheless, if you time your visit well (avoid weekends and get to the main sights nice and early) this small, manageable city can be an extremely rewarding break. You won't fall for its 'Venice-of-the-East' claims, but Sūzhōu still offers pockets of canal-side charm and is only a short hop from some of the area's gorgeous, smaller canal towns such as Tónglǐ (p236) and Nánxún (p236).

Dating back some 2500 years, Sūzhōu is one of the oldest towns in the Yangzi Basin. With the completion of the Grand Canal in the Sui dynasty, it found itself strategically located on a major trading route, and the city's fortunes and size grew rapidly.

By the 12th century the town had attained its present dimensions. The city walls, a rectangle enclosed by moats, were pierced by six gates (north, south, two in the east and two in the west). Crisscrossing the city were six canals running north to south and 14 canals running east to west. Although the walls have largely disappeared and a fair proportion of the canals have been plugged, central Sūzhōu, particularly the eastern side, retains some of its 'Renaissance' character.

By the 14th century, Sūzhōu had established itself as China's leading silk-producing city, and at the height of Sūzhōu's development in the 16th century, its gardens numbered over 100.

In 1860 Taiping troops took the town without a blow, and in 1896 Sūzhōu was opened to foreign trade, with Japanese and other international concessions.

Gardens 园林

Sūzhōu's delightful gardens (*yuánlín*; see boxed text, p232) were generally small, private compounds attached to family residences and, in principal at least, they were designed to help achieve the intellectual ideal of balancing Confucian social duties (in the city) with Taoism's worldly retreat (in nature).

Unless stated otherwise, the gardens listed here are open from 7.30am to 5.30pm during high season (March to mid-November) but close at 5pm in winter. Peak prices are from mid-April to October.

Accessed via a cute cobbled lane that links Shiquan Jie (十全街) and Daichengqiao Lu (带城桥路), the smallest garden of all, the **Garden of the Master of the Nets** (Wǎngshī Yuán; off-peak/peak Y20/30) is also widely considered the best,

with a striking use of space. Originally laid out in the 12th century, it was later restored in the 18th century as part of the home of a retired official turned fisherman (hence the name). Architecturally heavy – with residence halls, viewing pavilions and walkways – the garden relies on select landscape arrangements set against whitewashed walls, which are like the blank space of a Chinese ink painting.

In contrast, the luxuriant five-hectare **Humble Administrator's Garden** (Zhuózhèng Yuán; 178 Dongbei Jie; 东北街178号; off-peak/peak Y50/70; audio guide free, deposit Y200), dating to 1509, is large enough to be a park. There's also a bonsai (*pénjǐng*) garden, a teahouse and a small museum that explains Chinese gardening concepts.

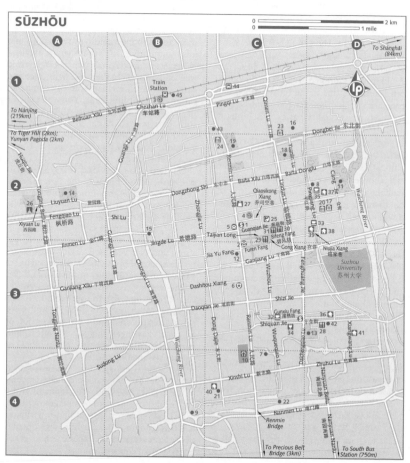

Around the corner is the one-hectare Lions' Grove (Shīzi Lín; 23 Yuanlin Lu; 园林路23号; off-peak/peak Y20/30), constructed in 1350 by the monk Tian Ru and famed for its strangely shaped rocks, meant to resemble lions, protectors of the Buddhist faith.

A bit on the wild side, with winding creeks and corridors of bamboo, Blue Wave Pavilion (Cānglàng Tíng; Renmin Lu; 人民路; off-peak/peak Y15/20) is one of the oldest gardens in Sūzhōu, originally dating from the 11th century. Lacking a northern wall, the one-hectare garden creates an illusion of space by borrowing scenes from the outside, incorporating the adjacent canal and distant hills.

The three-hectare Garden to Linger In (Liú Yuán; Liuyuan Lu; 留园路; off-peak/peak Y30/40), dates from the Ming dynasty and was built by a doctor as a place of relaxation for his recovering patients. Ornamental doorways and windows open onto wisteria-draped rockeries, ivy-covered tiled roofs and overgrown fairyland landscapes.

The less visited Couple's Garden (Ǒu Yuán; Cang Jie; 仓街; admission Y15; 8am-4.30pm) is in a delightful part of town and has a lovely pond and courtyards.

Also less visited than others is the small Qing dynasty Garden of Harmony (Yí Yuán; Renmin Lu; 人民路; admission Y15), which has assimilated many of the features of older gardens and delicately blended them into a style of its own.

Other Sights

The highly recommended Suzhou Silk Museum (Sūzhōu Sīchóu Bówùguǎn; ☎ 6753 6538; 2001 Renmin Lu; 人民路2001号; admission Y15; 9am-5pm) houses live silk worms as well as fascinating exhibitions providing a thorough history of Sūzhōu's silk industry over the past 4000 years.

The new IM Pei–designed Suzhou Museum (Sūzhōu Bówùguǎn; 204 Dongbei Jie; 东北街204号; admission free; 9am-5pm, last entry 4pm) – which stands beside its former building, once the residence of Taiping leader Li Xiucheng – houses jade, ceramics, textiles and other displays in an eye-catching, modern interpretation of a Sūzhōu garden, but loses points for its no thongs (flip-flops) policy.

By the southwest corner of the outer moat (but entered from Dong Dajie), and part of one of Sūzhōu's few remaining stretches of city wall, Coiled Gate (Pán Mén; 1 Dong Dajie; 东大街1号; admission Y25, incl Ruiguang Pagoda Y31, boat rides Y12; 7.30am-6pm) is thought to be China's last remaining land-and-water-gate, and dates from 1355. Inside the

GARDENS TO LINGER IN

Classical Chinese gardens can be hard to come to grips with: there are no lawns, few flowering plants, and misshapen, huge rocks everywhere. Yet a stroll through one of Sūzhōu's gardens is a walk through many different facets of Chinese civilisation, and this is what makes them so unique. Architecture, philosophy, art and literature all converge, and a background in some basics of Chinese culture helps to fully appreciate garden design.

The Chinese for 'landscape' is shānshuǐ (山水), literally 'mountain-water'. Mountains and rivers constitute a large part of China's geography, and are fundamental to Chinese life, philosophy, religion and art. So the central part of any garden landscape is a pond surrounded by rock formations.

This also reflects the influence of Taoist thought. Contrary to geometrically designed formal European gardens, where man saw himself as master, Chinese gardens seek to create a microcosm of the natural world through an asymmetrical layout of streams, hills, plants and pavilions (they symbolise man's place in the universe – never in the centre, just a part of the whole).

Symbolism works on every level. Plants are chosen as much for their symbolic meaning as their beauty (the pine for longevity, the peony for nobility), the billowy rocks call to mind not only mountains, but also the changing, indefinable nature of the Tao (the underlying principle of the universe in Taoist thought), and the names of gardens and halls are often literary allusions to ideals expressed in classical poetry. Painting, too, goes hand in hand with gardening, its aesthetics reproduced in gardens through the use of carefully placed windows and doors that frame a particular view.

Finally, it's worth remembering that gardens in China have always been lived in. Generally part of a residence, they weren't so much contemplative (as in Japan) as they were a backdrop for everyday life: family gatherings, late-night drinking parties, discussions of philosophy, art and politics – it's the people who spent their leisure hours there that ultimately gave the gardens their unique spirit.

same grounds, Ruiguang Pagoda (Ruìguāng Tǎ) dates from the 3rd century and can be climbed. Further north, Gold Gate (Jīn Mén), just inside the western stretch of the city moat, is a plain but charming, unrestored city gate.

At the heart of what was once Suzhou Bazaar, the Taoist Temple of Mystery (Xuánmiào Guàn; Guanqian Jie; 观前街; admission Y10; 7.30am-5pm) was originally laid out between AD 275 and 279, with many later additions. Its enormous Three Purities Hall (Sānqīng Diàn), supported by 60 pillars and capped by a double roof with upturned eaves, dates from 1181, and is the only surviving example of Song-era architecture in Sūzhōu.

The North Temple Pagoda (Běisì Tǎ; 1918 Renmin Lu; 人民路1918号; admission Y25; summer 7.45am-6pm, winter to 5.30pm) is the tallest pagoda south of the Yangzi River. At nine storeys high it dominates the northern end of Renmin Lu and can be climbed for city views.

In amongst the delightful cobblestone, canal-side alleyways in the east of town is the pretty Kunqu Opera Museum (Kūnqǔ Bówùguǎn; 14 Zhongzhangjia Xiang; 中张家巷14号; admission free; 8.30am-4.30pm), housing a beautiful old stage, musical instruments, costumes and photos. Just before the opera museum is the Pingtan Museum (Píngtán Bówùguǎn; 3 Zhongzhangjia Xiang; 中张家巷3号; admission Y4) where two-hour storytelling performances (说书; shuō shū), with free tea flowing throughout, are held every day at 1.30pm. Sadly, when we last visited,

the more musical versions, known as píngtán (p43), had stopped running.

About 500m west of the Garden to Linger In, which it once belonged to, West Garden Temple (Xiyuán Si; Xiyuan Lu; 西园路; admission Y25; 8am-5.30pm) was built on a garden donated to the Buddhist community in the 17th century. Greeting you upon entering the simply magnificent Arhat Hall (罗汉堂; Luóhàn Táng) is a stunning four-faced and thousand-armed statue of Guanyin, leading to mesmerising and slightly unnerving rows of glittering statues of luóhàn (Buddhist monks who have achieved enlightenment), each one unique. The Ming dynasty hall was torched by Taiping rebels in 1860, and rebuilt.

At the southern end of Renmin Lu is the old Confucius Temple (Wén Miào; Renmin Lu; 人民路; admission free; 8.30-11am & 12.30-4.30pm), which these days holds a souvenir market.

Boat Tours

Hour-long evening boat tours (Y100 per person) do half-circuit return trips along the outer moat. Boats leave every half hour between 6.30pm and 8.30pm. Buy tickets from the Suzhou Wharf (Sūzhōu Mǎtóu; 苏州码; 6520 8484; near Renmin Bridge; 人民桥附近). At the time of writing, plans were in place to make possible a complete circuit of the moat. Eight-person row boats (per boat Y150) ply the canals by Pingjiang Lu where, towards the northern end of the lane, you'll find a ticket office

Out of Town

In the far northwest of town, Tiger Hill (虎丘山; Hǔqiū Shān; ☎ 6723 2305; Huqiu Lu; 虎丘路; winter/sunmer Y40/60; ☯ summer 7.30am-6pm, winter to 5pm; bus 46 from cnr Renmin Lu & Guanqian Jie) is topped by the impressive, leaning Yunyan Pagoda (云岩塔; Yúnyán Tǎ), built in the 10th century. Take bus游1 (not bus 1) from the Renmin Lu end of Jingde Lu. It passes close to the Garden to Linger In and West Garden Temple. Alternatively, it's an interesting cycle along Dongzhong Shi and Fengqiao Lu, passing attractive canal bridges.

The Grand Canal (大运河; Dà Yùnhé) passes to the west and south of Sūzhōu, within a 10km range of the town. Suburban buses 13, 14, 15 and 16 will get you there. In the northwest, bus 11 follows the canal for a fair distance, taking you on a tour of the surrounding countryside.

Straddling the Grand Canal southeast of Sūzhōu, and boasting 53 arches, the highly impressive Precious Belt Bridge (宝带桥; Bǎodài Qiáo) is thought to be a Tang-dynasty construction. It's a 40-minute bike ride. Head south on Renmin Lu, past the south moat, then left at the TV towers, and the bridge will be on your right. If you're heading to Tónglǐ (p236), you'll see the bridge on your right.

INFORMATION

ATM The ATMs on the lobby level at the Sheraton Suzhou (p234) take international cards.

Bank of China (Zhōngguó Yínháng; 1450 Renmin Lu; 人民路1450号; ☯ 8.15am-5.15pm) Has a 24-hour ATM, and changes cash and travellers cheques Monday to Friday.

China Telecom (Zhōngguó Diànxìn; 1296 Renmin Lu; 人民路1296号; ☯ 9am-8pm)

Liánsuǒ Internet (Liánsuǒ Wǎngbā; 28-30 Qiaosikong Xiang; 乔司空巷28-30号; per hr Y3; ☯ 24hr) On the second floor. There is also a 24-hour internet cafe beside the train station.

Post office (Zhōngguó Yóuzhèng; cnr Renmin Lu & Jingde Lu; 人民路, 景德路交叉口; ☯ 8am-8pm)

PSB (Gōngānjú; ☎ 6522 5661; 1109 Renmin Lu; 人民路1109号)

SHOPPING

Wherever you look you will be bombarded with Sūzhōu-style embroidery, calligraphy, paintings, sandalwood fans, writing brushes, silk underclothes and freshwater pearls from Lake Tai (Tàihú).

There is a row of silk shops halfway along Renmin Lu where an old silk factory used to operate. Otherwise, head to the excellent Silk Road Centre (Sūzhōu Sīchóu Bówùguǎn Chóudiàn; ☯ 9am-5pm), attached to the silk museum (p231). You can access the shop without entering the museum, although the museum is well worth visiting.

EATING

Sūzhōu's most celebrated restaurants are in and around the pedestrianised shopping street of Guanqian Jie (观前街), while there's a load of cheap restaurants at the eastern end of Shizi Jie (十梓街), immediately south of the university.

Déyuèlóu (☎ 6523 8940; 43 Taijian Long; 太监弄; dishes Y20-180; ☯ 10.30am-2pm & 4.30-9pm) For local specialities such as squirrel-shaped mandarin

---

TRANSPORT: SŪZHŌU

Distance from Shànghǎi 85km

Direction West

Bicycle You can rent bikes at 371 Shiquan Jie (per day Y20, deposit Y300, ☯ 8am-10pm) or down a little alley beside 2061 Renmin Lu (per day Y20, deposit Y200, ☯ 6.30am-7pm).

Bus Services from Shànghǎi to Sūzhōu leave regularly from Shànghǎi's Hengfeng Rd Bus Station (1½ to two hours; Y30; 9.20am to 6.30pm), the long-distance bus station north of Shanghai Train Station (Y38; 7am to 7.40pm), Shanghai South Train Station (Y38; 6.27am to 8pm), Hongqiao Airport (Y53; 10am to 9pm) and Pudong International Airport (three hours; Y84). Most buses arrive and depart from Sūzhōu's hectic north bus station (☎ 6577 6577), east of the train station, although the south bus station is far better organised and easier to use. City bus 1 runs the length of Renmin Lu from the train station. Bus 101 links the two bus stations and the train station.

Train Express trains run regularly from Shànghǎi's main station to Sūzhōu (40 minutes, 5.35am to 7.58pm, Y15 to Y26), although slower trains (1 to 2 hours) run until almost midnight. Fast trains back to Shànghǎi run from 6.47am to 8.43pm.

fish (Y140) and Sūzhōu-style fried fish (Y25), try this long-standing restaurant near the Temple of Mystery. English menu.

Bǎochén Fàndiàn (519 Shiquan Jie; 十全街519号; dishes Y12-58; ☺ 24hr) If you're fed up with all the restaurants around here closing before you're even hungry, this one's open all night. It specialises in dishes from Yúnnán province. English menu.

Zhūhóngxīng (Gong Xiang; 宫巷; dishes Y10-42; ☺ 7am-9pm) One of Sūzhōu's most popular noodle joints, this canteen-style place was founded in 1934 and moved here in 2000. If you can't decipher the badly translated English menu, try; 'braise the meat noodles' (焖蹄浇面; *mèntí jiāomiàn*; Y15) – noodles with pig trotters – or; 'burst the and braise the meat noodles' (虾仁煲鳝面; *xiārén bāoshànmiàn*; Y35) – which is actually the restaurant's speciality seafood noodle dish with prawn and eel.

Lǚyáng Húntúndiàn (88 Bifeng Fang; 碧风坊88号; dishes Y8-15; ☺ 6.40am-8.30pm) Founded in 1802, Lǚyáng moved here in 1999 and continues to satisfy ever-hungry local appetites with wonton dumplings (馄饨, *húntun*, Y8 to Y15), fried rice dishes (炒饭, *chǎofàn*, Y12 to Y15) and soups (汤, *tāng*, Y8 to Y12). No English menu, but try *yínyú húntun* (银鱼馄饨, whitebait wonton soup, Y15), *gālí jīdīng chǎofàn* (咖喱鸡丁炒饭, curry-flavoured chicken fried rice, Y15) or *yāxuè fěnsī tāng* (鸭血粉丝汤, duck's blood soup, Y8). They also do delicious steamed dumplings (小笼包, *xiǎolóngbāo*, Y8 for four dumplings). Pay first at the counter, then hand your slip to a waitress.

DRINKING

For cute canal-side cafes and traditional(ish) tea houses, head to the charming cobble-stone street of Pingjiang Lu (平江路). For brash, late-night bars and more wi-fi cafes, Shiquan Jie (十全街) is your best bet.

Jane's Pub Bar (621 Shiquan Jie; 十全街621号; beer from Y15; ☺ 7pm-3am) One of the bars on Shiquan Jie that doesn't have scantily dressed girls beckoning you inside as you walk past, Jane's has Guinness on tap (Y55), pie and chips (Y50), a pool table and sports TVs.

Bǐ'àn (36 Pingjiang Lu; 平江路36号; coffee from Y20; ☺ 10am-midnight) Housed in a gorgeous wooden building that juts out slightly over the water, Bǐ'àn is the cutest of a bunch of canal-side cafes along Pingjiang Lu. There's beer (from Y18) and a huge selection of tea. Has wi-fi.

Bookworm (Lǎoshūchóng; 77 Gunxiu Fang; 滚绣坊77号; www.suzhoubookworm.com; coffee from Y10; ☺ 9am-1am) Set back from Shiquan Jie, over the other side of the canal, and housed in an attractive white-washed, two-storey building, Bookworm makes a smart choice for a coffee stop. Like its popular Běijīng branch, this one also has a fantastic range of English-language books, some of which are for sale, and hosts occasional cultural events (check the website for details). The Western-friendly food is pricy. Has wi-fi.

Shūxiāng Guǎn (16 Pingjiang Lu; 平江路16号; tea from Y5, beer from Y12; ☺ 7am-11pm) Tea house by day, quiet bar by night, this place sometimes has free performances of *píngtán* during the afternoons.

SLEEPING

The area code for Sūzhōu is ☎ 0512.

Sheraton Suzhou (Wúgōng Xǐláidēng Dàjiǔdiàn; ☎ 6510 3388; www.sheraton-suzhou.com; 259 Xinshi Lu; 新市路259号; r from Y1880) Despite the hideous mock-castle appearance, this is undoubtedly the top stay in town. Fabulous facilities, including indoor and outdoor pools, tastefully decorated rooms and five-star service. And when we were last here, standard rooms were going for Y568 – an absolute steal.

Pingjiang Lodge (Píngjiāng Kèzhàn; ☎ 6523 3888; www.the-silk-road.com; 33 Niujia Xiang; 纽家巷33号; r from Y1000) A 400-year-old former residence with quiet courtyards, well-kept gardens and 51 delightful rooms, all with broadband and traditional Chinese furniture. Some travellers have complained about indifferent service. Discounts of 50% are common.

Joya Youth Hostel (Sūzhōu Xiǎoyǎ Guójì Qīngnián Lǚshè; ☎ 6755 1752; www.joyahostel.com; 1/21 Daxinqiao Xiang; 大新桥巷1/21号; dm Y50-60, tw & d with/without bathroom Y180/130) Another wonderful former residence, this one was built in 1883 and is bursting with Qing-dynasty charm, with floral lattice windows and many original wooden beams. Rooms are small, but have high ceilings and open out onto courtyards. There's wi-fi, bike rental, peace and tranquillity.

Ming Town Youth Hostel (Sūzhōu Míngtáng Qīngnián Lǚshè; ☎ 6581 6869; mingtown@foxmail.com; 28 Pingjiang Lu; 平江路28号; dm Y40, tw without bathroom Y120, s Y140, tw & d Y160) Ming Town's winning formula is transported to the charming canal-side lane of Pingjiang Lu. Decent rooms (although some are slightly musty) are housed in two equally attractive buildings with a smart cafe next door. There's wi-fi, bike rental and a pool table.

Suzhou Youth Hostel (Sūzhōu Guójì Qīngnián Lǔshè; ☎ 6510 9418; www.yhasuzhou.com; 178 Xiangwang Lu; 相王路178号; dm/tw/tr Y40/90/120) Sūzhōu's first youth hostel is a bit behind the game these days, but offers a solid alternative if others are full. It has the usual hostel facilities, but there's no historical architecture to gawp at here. It also has four cute little rooms (s/d Y110/150), with a shared bathroom, above nearby Fisher Coffee (Fēishè Kāfēi).

CANAL TOWNS

It should come as no surprise to anyone that the Yangzi Delta, bounded by the Yangzi River to the north, Lake Tai to the west and Hangzhou Bay to the east and south, is inundated with water. Many of the villages in this region are picturesque canal towns, with original Ming and Qing architecture, cobbled lanes, humpbacked bridges and, of course, interlocking canals. Some of them date back to the Tang dynasty and, as nearly all had access to the Grand Canal, they were traditionally fairly prosperous places. Analogies with Venice stuff the local tourist literature; suffice to say this is rubbish, but the towns are certainly picturesque and a welcome counterpoint to Shànghǎi's brash urban frenzy.

Here's the bad news though: the canal towns are tiny and are often overrun with visitors. Try to either visit during the week, or stay overnight so you can enjoy the peaceful early mornings before the tour groups roll in.

The easiest way to reach the canal towns from Shànghǎi is via the well organised sightseeing buses on a day trip. Alternatively, take public buses from Sūzhōu or Hángzhōu. As well as the three canal towns featured here, Mùdú (木渎), Lùzhí (角直), Xītáng (西塘) and Wūzhèn (乌镇) can also make rewarding day trips and can also be reached using Shànghǎi's sightseeing bus system.

ZHŪJIĀJIǍO朱家角

Zhūjiājiǎo is both easy to reach from Shànghǎi and truly delightful, although at weekends and during public holidays it's packed to the rafters. Admission including entry to four/eight/10 of the main sights is Y30/60/80.

Chinese guidebooks vaguely identify human activity in these parts 5000 years ago and a settlement here during the Three Kingdoms period 1700 years ago. It was during the Ming dynasty, however, that a commercial centre built on its network of waterways had truly developed. What survives today is a charming tableau of Ming and Qing dynasty alleys, bridges and old town (古镇; gǔzhèn) architecture.

The riverside settlement is small enough to wander completely in three hours. You'll receive a handy map with your entrance ticket, although it's tough to get lost here.

Sights worth checking out include the City God Temple (城隍庙; Chénghuáng Miào; Caohe Jie; 漕河街; admission Y5; ⏰ 7.30am-4pm), moved here in 1769 from its original location in Xuějiābāng; the Yuanjin Buddhist Temple (圆津禅寺; Yuánjin Chánsì; Caohe Jie; 漕河街; admission Y5; ⏰ 8am-4pm) – near the distinctive Tai'an Bridge (泰安桥; Tài'ān Qiáo) – which contains the Qinghua Pavilion (清华阁; Qīnghuá Gé); a towering hall visible from many parts of town; and the charming Zhujiajiao Catholic Church of Ascension (朱家角耶稣升天堂; Zhūjiājiǎo Yēsū Shēngtiāntáng; 27 Caohe Jie, No 317 Alley; 漕河街27号317弄), built in 1863.

Of Zhūjiājiǎo's quaint band of ancient bridges, the standout must be the graceful, 72m-long, five-arched Fangsheng Bridge (放生桥; Fàngshēng Qiáo), first built in 1571 with proceeds from a monk's 15 years of alms-gathering.

At various points including Fangsheng Bridge, you can jump on six-person row boats (15 or 30mins; per boat 15/30mins Y60/120) for waterborne tours of the town.

You'll be tripping over souvenir shops and their vocal vendors, and you can buy anything from a pair of children's tiger shoes to 'antique' Chinese eyeglasses.

TRANSPORT: ZHŪJIĀJIǍO

Distance from Shànghǎi 30km

Direction West

Bus from Shànghǎi Day-trip buses (one hour, Y85 return) depart daily from the Shanghai Sightseeing Bus Centre (Map p122) every half hour between 9am and noon. Tickets include admission to the town and its sights; last bus back to Shànghǎi is at 4.45pm.

Bus from Tónglǐ Nine daily buses (one hour, 8.25am to 4.15pm, Y15.50) run between Tónglǐ bus station and Zhūjiājiǎo, although they drop you on the main road, a 10-minute walk from the old town (古镇; gǔzhèn).

The tight streets are stuffed with restaurants overlooking the water. For great snacks, look out for *zòngzi* (粽子; leaf-wrapped bundles of fragrant sticky rice; Y2 to Y3) and the town's mouth-watering speciality *zhāròu* (扎肉; leaf-wrapped chunks of braised pork; Y2 to Y3).

Overnighting is highly recommended. Try the delightful Uma Hostel (☎ 021 5924 0487; umahostel@gmail.com; 103 Xijing Jie; 西井街103号; dm/s/d Y50/120/200), by Kezhi Garden (课植园; Kèzhí Yuán), with its high ceilings, wooden furniture and Bohemian feel. There's wi-fi and breakfast, but not many rooms, so book. Otherwise, look out for signs reading '客房' (*kèfáng*; guestrooms).

TÓNGLǏ 同里

Its sights neatly parcelled together in a more picturesque and easily navigable setting than Sūzhōu, the charming canal town of Tónglǐ is a marvellous day out.

With its whitewashed houses, laundry hanging out to dry and unhurried canal scenes, the old town (古镇; gǔzhèn; admission Y80; ☾ ticket office 7.30am-5.30pm) is best explored in a lazy meandering loop; bilingual signs guide the way, and maps (地图; *dìtú*) are available at the ticket office, but getting lost is half the fun.

There are three old residences that you'll pass at some point during your wander (unless you're really lost), the best of which is the Gēnglè Táng (耕乐堂), a vast Ming dynasty country estate with 41 rooms and courtyards in the west of town.

In the north of Tónglǐ is the Pearl Pagoda (珍珠塔; Zhēnzhū Tǎ), originally the home of a Ming dynasty official, containing a large residential compound, an ancestral hall, a garden and even an opera stage.

In the east of the old town you'll find Tuisi Garden (退思园; Tuìsī Yuán), a gorgeous 19th-century garden that delightfully translates as the 'Withdraw and Reflect Garden'. The Tower of Fanning Delight served as the living quarters while the garden itself is a lovely portrait of pond water churning with outsized goldfish (fish food Y2 a pack), rockeries and pavilions, caressed by traditional Chinese music. It's a lovely place to find a perch and drift into a reverie, unless you are outflanked by one of the marauding tour groups.

It's definitely not for infant Tónglǐ-visitors, but the highly recommended Chinese Sex Museum (中华性文化博物馆; Zhōnghuá Xingwénhuà Bówùguǎn; admission Y20) is Tónglǐ's most famous sight and displays ritual sex objects, ancient sex toys and erotic carvings from as far back as 3000 BC.

Slow-moving six-person boats ply the waters of Tónglǐ's canal system (Y70, 25 minutes).

Restaurants are everywhere and guesthouses (客栈; *kèzhàn*) are similarly in abundance. Try Zhèngfú Cǎotáng (正福草堂; ☎ 0512-6332 0576; www.zfct.net; 14 Mingqing Jie; 明清街14号; d Y180-380), a beautifully restored courtyard hotel. All rooms have private bathrooms, but there are only four of them, so book ahead. For something more basic, try Zhōuzhuāng Dàjiǔdiàn (周庄大酒店; ☎ 0512-5720 5153; Zhongchuanbei Lu; 中川北路; d Y120), on the left just over the first bridge past the ticket office.

NÁNXÚN 南浔

Accessed easily from Hángzhōu, the pretty canal town of Nánxún became prosperous on the back of the silk trade during the Southern Song dynasty. A typical ancient waterside Jiāngnán town with arched bridges, historic

TRANSPORT: TÓNGLǏ

Distance from Shànghǎi 80km

Direction West

Buses from Shànghǎi Day-trip buses (1¾ hours; Y130 return) depart daily from the Shanghai Sightseeing Bus Centre (Map p122) at 8.30am, returning from Tónglǐ at 4.30pm. Tickets include admission to the old town (古镇; *gǔzhèn*). You will be dropped off 2km from town at Tongli Lake, from where there's a shuttle (Y4) to the gate. The boat trip on Tongli Lake is free, though of no particular interest. Half-hourly public buses (Y31, 6.25am to 3.10pm) leave Tongli Bus Station for Shànghǎi, dropping you near the main train station.

Buses from Sūzhōu Regular buses (50 minutes; 7.40am to 5.20pm; Y8) run to Tongli Bus Station from Sūzhōu's South Bus Station. Return buses run from 6.30am to 5pm. Frequent buses also run to Sūzhōu train station (6.15am to 7pm). Tongli Bus Station is a five-minute walk from the old town (古镇; *gǔzhèn*).

TRANSPORT: NÁNXÚN

Distance from Shànghǎi 140km

Direction West

Buses from Shànghǎi One daily bus (three hours; 9am; Y150) leaves for Nánxún from the Shanghai Sightseeing Bus Centre (Map p122), returning at 4.30pm. Return tickets include entrance. Six daily public buses leave Nánxún bus station for Shànghǎi South Bus Station (two hours; 7.50am to 4.55pm; Y43).

Buses from Hángzhōu Regular buses (two hours; 7.30am to 5.40pm; Y39) leave Hángzhōu's North Bus Station. The last bus back leaves at 5pm.

Buses from Sūzhōu Buses (one hour; 6.55am to 5.55pm; Y21) leave regularly for Nánxún from Sūzhōu's South Bus Station.

residences and pinched alleys, Nánxún is becoming increasingly popular as a destination, but plentiful charm and pockets of tranquillity make it a desirable spot for a trip back in time.

You can see everything in a few hours. Once again, meandering around the streets is the best way to appreciate the stone bridges and historic residences that typify the old town.

From the bus station, cross the bridge over the Grand Canal and the old town (古镇; gǔzhèn; admission Y100 incl entry to sights) is down the first small canal-side lane on your left. Everything of interest will then be in front of you and to your right. There are large wooden maps around town to keep you on track, but just follow the canals.

Sights worth seeking out include the pretty gardens of Little Lotus Villa (小莲庄; Xiǎolián Zhuāng), note the fabulous highly decorative carved stone gates; the 100 Room Pavilion (百间楼; Bǎijiān Lóu), a Ming dynasty structure; and the Jiaye Library (嘉业堂藏书楼; Jiāyètáng Cángshūlóu), which dates from 1920 and is set within a scenic courtyard with a lotus pond. With its blend of European and Chinese architectural motifs, the Zhang Family Compound (张氏铭旧宅; Zhāngshìmíng Jiùzhái) is an elaborate old residence once owned by a prosperous silk merchant. Among the historic bridges, look out for Guanghui Bridge (广惠侨; Guǎnghuì Qiáo), Tongjin Bridge (通津桥; Tōngjīn Qiáo) and Hongji Bridge (洪济桥; Hóngjí Qiáo).

MÒGĀNSHĀN 莫干山

Forested with feathery bamboo, pine and juniper, the mist-shrouded mountains of Mògānshān (admission Y80) have long been a popular retreat – on summer days it can be a whole seven degrees cooler than in Shànghǎi.

Legend has it that during the Spring and Autumn Period (722–481 BC), Gan Jiang, the best swordsman in the land, came here to forge two special swords in the crystal-clear mountain streams. Gan's wife was surnamed Mo, and from then on the mountain went by the name Mògānshān, *shān* (山) meaning mountain.

It wasn't until the turn of the 20th century, though, that Mògānshān was turned into a resort by taipans and missionaries. Later still it became a fashionable retreat for Shànghǎi gangsters (such as 'Big-Eared' Du Yuesheng; see boxed text, p28) and politicians (such as

TRANSPORT: MÒGĀNSHĀN

Distance from Shànghǎi 190km

Direction West

Buses from Hángzhōu Buses leave the North Bus Station (汽车北站; qìchē běizhàn) for Wǔkāng (武康) every 20 minutes from 7.20am to 7pm (Y15, 50 minutes). From Wǔkāng, minibuses (at least Y60) run to the top of Mògānshān. Bargain hard. Alternatively, get off the Hángzhōu–Wǔkāng bus at the Jíxiáng Jiēkǒu (吉祥街口) bus stop then take a cycle rickshaw (Y4) to the Mògānshān bus stand (莫干山小车站; Mògānshān Xiǎochēzhàn) from where local buses (Y3.50, until 5.45pm) run to the foot of the mountain. It's then an hour's walk to the main hotel strip near the top, or Y20 to Y30 in a minibus.

Buses from Shànghǎi Buses from the Shanghai Sightseeing Bus Station (Map p122) run to Mògānshān (8am and 2pm, Y408) in July and August only. Return tickets include three-star accommodation, but not entrance to the mountain. There are three public buses that go from Shànghǎi to Déqìng (德清; four hours; 6.50am, 11.50am and 12.40pm; Y62) from where you can catch minibuses (Y100) to the top of Mògānshān. They leave Shànghǎi from the small bus station at 80 Gongxing Lu (公兴路80号) (Map p116) near Baoshan Lu metro station.

Chiang Kaishek and Mao Zedong) before becoming a military garrison in the 1960s. If you aren't staying overnight, you will need to leave the area by 6pm.

Today Mògānshān has reverted to the people and is refreshingly rural. The villagers have taken over the stately granite villas that are scattered across the hillside, and those that aren't tied up with the area's growing tourism trade spend their time tending their gardens, raising chickens and harvesting wild herbs. There's not an awful lot to do here, but that's kind of the point. Sitting on a terrace with a beer and book suffices for most visitors. If that's not enough for you, hike on over to the other side of the mountain to watch the sun set.

Yinshan Street (荫山街), towards the top of the mountain, is the main strip where you'll find a cluster of hotels and restaurants (including one that does steaming breakfast *bāozi* –包子, dumplings) as well as a small post office and a market selling dried fruit, wild herbs, tea and the like.

SLEEPING

There are more than 20 hotels up here now, so you'll always find a room, but it's definitely worth calling ahead on summer weekends.

Léidísēn Mògānshān Jiǔdiàn (雷迪森莫干山酒店; ☎ 0572-803 3601; d from Y1050) This is gangster Du Yuesheng's old villa, and is now owned by the Radisson group. It's one of the first hotels you reach on your way up the mountain, and yet it has the best views of all. There's wi-fi, and weekday discounts are decent.

Xīnlóng Shānzhuāng (鑫龙山庄; ☎ 0572-803 3439; 256 Gangtouyun Lu; 岗头云路256号; d/tr Y480/880) At the brow of a hill up the slip road just past the main strip on Yinshan St, this hotel has four attractive villas with a variety of well-kept rooms. Views from the tea terrace by reception are wonderful. Expect 50% discounts during the week.

Yinshān Fàndiàn (荫山饭店; ☎ 0572-803 3181; Yinshan Jie; 荫山街; s Y50, d with/without bathroom Y90/240) This slightly run-down place offers extremely basic rooms right on the main street. Shared balconies overlook the main strip. Hot water is evenings only.

PǓTUÓSHĀN 普陀山

With its clean beaches, fresh air, thick forests and, of course, many temples, the lush Buddhist island of Pǔtuóshān (entrance summer/winter Y160/140) seems a world away from Shànghǎi and can make a thoroughly rewarding two- or three-day trip.

The 10km-long island, regarded as one of China's four sacred Buddhist mountains, is the enchanting abode of Guanyin, the eternally compassionate Goddess of Mercy. Devotees come here from afar to worship her, and a distinct spiritual aura permeates parts of the island, despite the naff recorded music coming from speakers camouflaged as rocks.

Buses from the ferry terminal (Y4 to Y10; 6am to 5pm) go to all the main sights, but most sights are within a 30-minute walk from where the ferry drops you off. The road from the ferry terminal leads both east (right) and west (left). Walking in either direction, it takes about 30 minutes to loop round the hill in

---

LOCAL VOICES: MY PERFECT SHÀNGHǍI RETREAT

Brought up in Wǔkāng, 28-year-old Yang Yuli, an executive assistant for Intel China, fell in love with Mògānshān when she was a child, and continued to make regular trips there when she was working in Shànghǎi.

When did you first visit Mògānshān? When I was eight years old, still in primary school.

How often do you visit these days? When I was still working in Shànghǎi, before I relocated to Běijīng, I used to go there every summer with my work colleagues.

Why do you think Mògānshān makes such a good retreat from Shànghǎi? First of all, it's only three hours driving distance from Shànghǎi, which is very convenient for a weekend trip. Second, it has a really interesting history going all the way back to Gan Jiang and then in the 1900s when expats used to go to escape the summer heat. Also, several famous people have spent summers there, like Mao Zedong and Chiang Kaishek.

What's the best thing about Mògānshān? I like renting one of the old villas there with my friends in the summer, and just playing cards, drinking tea and generally having a relaxing time.

Has it changed much since you first went there? It became more and more well facilitated – like the Radisson hotel that's there now – and more and more modern. But personally I still like the old villas that were built there in the 1930s.

TRANSPORT: PŬTUÓSHĀN

Distance from Shànghǎi 160km

Direction Southeast

Overnight ferry from Shànghǎi One daily evening ferry (12½ hours; 8pm; Y109 to Y499) leaves for Pŭtuóshān from the Wusong Wharf (吴淞码头; Wúsōng Mǎtóu), although there are two extra services on Fridays (7.20pm and 8.40pm). The return ferry leaves Pŭtuóshān at 4.40pm. Beds range from 40-bunk dorms to private cabins. All are quite cramped, but passengers are free to walk around the ferry, including on parts of the deck. There's a small cafeteria and a shop selling snacks and beer. To get to Wusong Wharf, take metro line 3 to Songbin Lu from where it's a 15-minute walk. Cross the eight-lane highway and keep going straight, following the signs. The trip takes about 1½ hours from People's Square.

Bus/high-speed ferry Faster ferries (four hours, including a two-hour bus trip; Y258) leave twice daily from Lúcháogǎng (芦潮港), south of Shànghǎi. Shuttle buses leave Shànghǎi at 7.40am and 8am from Nanpu Bridge (Map p79, near the ferry ticket office) to connect with them. Tickets for both overnight ferry and bus/ferry services should be bought at the Shanghai Port Wusong Passenger Transport Centre Ticket Office (上海港吴淞客运中心售票处; Shànghǎi Gǎng Wúsōng Kèyùn Zhōngxīn Shòupiàochù; Map pp66–7; ☎ 5657 5500; 59 East Jinling Lu; 金陵东路59号; open 7am to 5.30pm). Half-hourly ferries also go from Pŭtuóshān to Níngbō (宁波; 2½ hours including shuttle bus into Níngbō; 7.30am to 5.50pm; Y83) from where you can catch trains to Hángzhōu (two hours) or Shànghǎi (3½ hours).

front of the ferry terminal and reach Puji Temple (普济寺; Pǔjì Sì; admission Y5; ⏰ 5.30am-6pm), a beautiful 17th-century building in a tree-covered square which is the focal point of the island. Island maps (地图; dìtú; Chinese only) cost Y2 at the ferry terminal.

The west route from the ferry terminal leads to Xīshān Xīncūn (西山新村), a modern village with some cheap hotels (see p240). Continuing along the main road you'll reach a string of banks, some with ATMs that take foreign cards, Puji Hospital and the post office before a signposted pathway leads right to Puji Temple. Just northeast of the temple, still around the main square, is the five-storey, white-stone Duobao Pagoda (多宝塔; Duōbǎo Tǎ; admission Y15), built in 1345.

The east route from the ferry terminal takes you past the 100-year-old Duangu Dock (短姑胜迹; Duǎngū Shèngjì) and the island's Coastal Memorial Arch. (海岸牌坊; Hǎi'àn Páifāng), of similar age, before, on your left, you reach the charming Ming-dynasty village of Sānshèngtáng (三圣堂), the oldest surviving village on the island. The path leading up through the village carries on into the forest to Puji Temple. If you stay on the main road, though, and don't turn into the old village, you'll soon reach a signposted path on your right which takes you through the more modern village of Lóngwān Xīncūn (龙湾新村) – where you'll find more cheap places to sleep and eat – and on to Nánhǎi Guānyin (南海观音), the 33m-tall golden statue of Guanyin which dominates

the southeast tip of the island. Note, it's at least a 45-minute walk to the statue from the ferry terminal.

The island's two best beaches – One Hundred Step Beach (百白步沙; Bǎibùshā) and One Thousand Step Beach (千步沙; Qiānbùshā) – are both just north of the Puji Temple, past Duobao Pagoda. One Hundred Step Beach is reached first, and is the busier of the two, with pedal boats and the like for rent. Beyond it, the longer One Thousand Step Beach remains less spoilt. It takes about an hour to walk to One Thousand Step Beach from the ferry terminal (Y6 by bus). Swimming is only allowed from May to August.

Inland from One Thousand Step Beach is the impressive Fayu Temple (法雨禅寺; Fǎyǔ Chánsì; admission Y5), which can also be reached by bus (Y6). From here, it's a steep but beautifully shaded half-hour climb to Huiji Temple (惠济禅寺; Huìjì Chánsì; admission Y5), one of the highest points on the island. Watch pilgrims stop every three steps to either bow or kneel in supplication. The less devout can take a cable car (索道; suǒdào, 1-way/return Y30/50; ⏰ 6.40am-5pm) from the north side of the mountain. It's Y10 in a bus from the ferry terminal to the cable car.

SLEEPING & EATING

Food is pricy on Pŭtuóshān as most of it has to be shipped in from the mainland, but restaurants are plentiful and there's a great choice of

TRANSPORT: LĬZHĀNG

Distance from Shànghǎi 270km

Direction Southwest

Train and bus from Shànghǎi Five fast trains (2¼ hours; Y97) leave from Shanghai South Train Station at 7.20am, 7.44am, 1.12pm, 3.27pm and 3.35pm to Yiwū (义乌). There are plenty more slow trains (three to four hours; Y47). From Yiwū, a taxi (Y70) takes 45 minutes. Make sure you take one with a number plate prefixed with the character-letter combination '浙GH'. These come from the area Lĭzhāng lies in so are cheaper and more likely to be driven by someone who's heard of the village. Alternatively, from the main road outside Yiwū train station, wave down a bus to Pǔjiāng (浦江; 30 minutes; Y8; last bus around 6pm), then take local bus 1 or 6 (Y1; 10 minutes) from Pǔjiāng's main bus station (汽运中心; qìyùnzhōngxīn) to Pǔjiāng's west bus station (西站; xīzhàn) to catch one of the two daily buses to Lĭzhāng (30 minutes; 10.10am and 2.30pm; Y3). Buses leave Lĭzhāng for Pǔjiāng at 7am and 11am. Fast trains returning to Shànghǎi leave Yiwū at 10am, 11.28am and 12.27pm.

Train from Hángzhōu Six fast trains to Yiwū (50 minutes; Y43) leave Hángzhōu at 7.22am, 8.45am, 9.14am, 12.34pm, 2.37pm and 4.58pm. Fast trains return at 10am, 11.12am, 11.28am and 12.27pm.

seafood, as you'd expect. One handy cheapy, right opposite Putuoshan Hotel, is Āxiáng Kuàicān (阿祥快餐; Meicen Lu; meals Y20; ⏱ 5am-8pm), a small cafeteria-style restaurant.

In Xīshān Xīncūn you'll find the island's cheapest hotels, as well as some home stays. Look for signs reading 住宿 (zhùsù; lodgings), but be aware that many locals won't take in foreigners because of registration hassles. You may have more luck if you speak some Chinese.

Putuoshan Hotel (普陀山大酒店; Pǔtuóshān Dàjiǔdiàn; ☎ 0580-609 2828; 93 Meicen Lu; 梅岑路93号; d Y1188) West of the ferry terminal, beyond Xīshān Xīncūn and the string of banks, this spacious four-star outfit is the island's best hotel. Discounts see rooms drop to Y950/580 (weekend/weekday).

Haitong Hotel (海通宾馆; Hǎitōng Bīnguǎn; ☎ 0580-609 2569; 2 Meicen Lu; 梅岑路2号; d Y880) A solid choice, right opposite the ferry terminal. Discounts see doubles go as low as Y580/Y200 (weekend/weekday).

LĬZHĀNG礼张

Welcome to rural Zhèjiāng. No tour groups, no souvenir stalls, no bars, one restaurant, one guesthouse and a shop. A trip to Lĭzhāng is a glimpse of pure, unadulterated village life and there's pretty much nothing to do here

except walk around the countryside, listening to frogs croak and birds chirp whilst breathing in lung-fulls of fresh air.

Villagers spend much of their time tending to crops or washing clothes in the river, but they are also extremely keen calligraphers. It is said that at least one person in every household here has mastered the ancient art, and there's a small calligraphy exhibition hall (书画陈列馆; Shūhuà Chénlièguǎn) showcasing some of their work, although you'll need to ask a villager to open it for you, as it doesn't get too many visitors.

Facilities in Lĭzhāng are distinctly no-frills. However, a French woman and her family have renovated a beautiful courtyard building and transformed it into the first-class Lizhang Guesthouse (☎ 0579-8422 5290/139-0169 2820 lizhang.house@gmail.com; r Mon-Fri/Sat & Sun from Y450/550). It has delightful rooms with traditional wooden furniture, modern bathrooms and wi-fi. Rates include three meals a day. For something cheaper, and much more basic, your only other option is the village's only restaurant, Dānqīng Shítáng (丹青食堂; ☎ 131-7493 7848/130-6596 3988), which has a handful of double rooms going for around Y100. There's no hot water, or English spoken. It's in a three-storey, white-tiled guesthouse down the first lane on your right as you enter the village.

TRANSPORT

Shànghǎi is simple to get to. It is China's second-largest international air hub (third-largest if you count Hong Kong) and if you can't fly direct, you can go via Běijīng or Hong Kong. With rail and air connections to places all over China, and buses to destinations in adjoining provinces and beyond, Shànghǎi is also a handy springboard to the rest of China.

Flights and tours can be booked online at www.lonelyplanet.com/travel_services.

Shànghǎi itself is not very easy to navigate. Although it's fascinating to stroll around certain areas, Shànghǎi's sheer size and staggering sprawl makes foot-slogging useful only for brief trips.

The best way to get around town is either by taxi or on the metro. The rapidly expanding metro and light railway system works like a dream; it's fast, efficient and inexpensive. Rush hour on the metro operates at overcapacity, however, and you get to savour the full meaning of the big squeeze. Taxis are ubiquitous and cheap, but flagging one down during rush hour or during a rainstorm requires staying power of a high order. With a wide-ranging web of routes, buses may sound tempting, but that's before you try to decipher routes and stops or attempt to squeeze aboard during the crush hour. Buses also have to contend with the increasing solidity of Shànghǎi's traffic, which can slow movement to an agonising crawl.

Shànghǎi is hurling money into transport infrastructure like a city possessed, but with everyone and his dog wanting a car, vehicle ownership is undergoing parabolic growth. It's a war of attrition between road builders and gridlock, with minor victories for the transport department swiftly wrested back by the expanding mass of vehicles. The metro is spearheading Shànghǎi's best offensive against the transport quagmire. Plans to extend the celebrated MagLev line – bringing Pǔdōng's blindingly fast hover train rocketing into central Shànghǎi – may one day get off the drawing board, but don't hold your breath.

To the untrained Western eye, the traffic in Shànghǎi can seem totally anarchic. The roads can be lethal (especially to pedestrians), with unpredictable swerving, sudden lunges and weaving manoeuvres. Every square metre of tarmac is fought for, tooth and nail. Take a cab and see how often the driver hits the brakes.

THINGS CHANGE...

The information in this chapter is particularly vulnerable to change. Check directly with the airline or a travel agent to make sure you understand how a fare (and ticket you may buy) works and be aware of the security requirements for international travel. Shop carefully. The details given in this chapter should be regarded as pointers and are not a substitute for your own careful, up-to-date research.

It's also worth noting that drivers travel more slowly than their Western counterparts, as other vehicles are driven erratically. Traffic rules are, however, widely ignored. Indicators are often shunned in favour of the sudden and unexpected manoeuvre.

Unpopular and unloved, Shànghǎi's 8000 whistle-blowing crossing guards man intersections across the city, preventing pedestrians from crossing into oncoming traffic. Wearing ill-fitting uniforms and armed with no more than a whistle, crossing guards do their best to keep Shànghǎi's increasingly gridlocked roads open.

Come rush hour (from around 7am to 9.30am and 4pm to 6.30pm) it's every frail old man for himself. Cool aggression and elusive speed, along with a friendly smile, keep things from getting ugly.

AIR

China Eastern Airlines operates out of Shànghǎi; Shanghai Airlines is a smaller airline, with limited international routes.

For domestic and international flights on Chinese airlines, the baggage allowance for an adult passenger is 20kg in economy class and 30kg in 1st class. You are also allowed 5kg of hand luggage, though this is rarely weighed. The charge for excess baggage is 1% of the full fare for each kilogram over the allowance.

Airline information in Chinese is available at ☎ 6247 5953 (domestic) and ☎ 6247 2255 (international). Departure tax is now included in the air ticket price.

Domestic air travellers can conveniently check in baggage at the airport city terminal (Shànghǎi Jīchǎng Chéngshì Hángzhàn Lóu; Map pp98–9; ☎ 3214 4600; 1600 West Nanjing Rd; Ⓜ Jing'an Temple) just east of Jing'an Temple, before proceeding to Hongqiao Airport by bus (from the terminal basement) or the nearby metro.

Daily (usually several times a day) domestic flights connect Shànghǎi to every major city in China. Minor cities are less likely to have daily flights, but chances are there will be at least one flight a week, probably more, to Shànghǎi. Domestic flights are from Hongqiao Airport and Pudong International Airport, so check when you buy your ticket as it is generally more convenient to fly from Hongqiao Airport, which is closer to downtown. You can buy tickets from hundreds of airline offices and travel agencies (including hotel travel agents) around town (few take credit cards); try to book several days in advance of your flight. Tickets are typically substantially discounted so shop around. Prices quoted in this book are the full fare. Discounts can be harder to come by during the main holiday seasons (Chinese New Year, first week of May and October) and on weekends.

Business-class tickets cost 25% over economy class, and 1st-class tickets cost an extra 60%. Babies pay 10% of the adult fare; children aged two to 12 are charged 50% of the adult fare; those over 12 pay the adult fare.

DOMESTIC AIRFARES FROM SHÀNGHǍI

Destination	One-way fare (¥)
Běijīng 北京	1180
Chéngdū 成都	1660
Chóngqìng 重庆	1540
Fúzhōu 福州	830
Guǎngzhōu 广州	1330
Guìlín 桂林	1350
Hǎikǒu 海口	1710
Huángshān 黄山市 (Túnxī)	550
Kūnmíng 昆明	1950
Níngbō 宁波	470
Qīngdǎo 青岛	790
Shēnzhèn 深圳	1320
Tiānjīn 天津	1080
Xiàmén 厦门	1010
Xī'ān 西安	1310

Prices are approximate; check current fares with the relevant airlines. Note that there are direct buses to Kowloon from the Shēnzhèn airport, which is a cheaper option than flying direct to Hong Kong. Also note that there are now direct flights from Shànghǎi to Taipei (roughly ¥3000).

Cancellation fees depend on how long before departure you cancel. On domestic flights, if you cancel 24 to 48 hours before departure you lose 10% of the fare; if you cancel between two and 24 hours before the flight you lose 20%; and if you cancel less than two hours before the flight you lose 30%. If you don't show up for a domestic flight, you are entitled to a refund of 50%.

Airlines

China Eastern Airlines has many sales offices, as well as ticket sales counters at most major hotels.

Air China (Zhōngguó Guójì Hángkōng; Map pp98–9; ☎ 400 810 0999; www.airchina.com.cn; Room 307, Kerry Centre, 1515 West Nanjing Rd; 南京西路1515号307室)

China Eastern Airlines (Dōngháng; Map pp98–9; ☎ 95808; www.ce-air.com; 258 Weihai Rd; 威海路258号; ☺ 24hr) There is also a branch at the Shanghai Train Station (Map pp98–9).

Shanghai Airlines (Shànghǎi Hángkōng; ☎ 1010 5858; www.shanghai-air.com) French Concession (Map pp86–7; 90 South Shaanxi Rd; 陕西南路90号); Jing'ān (Map pp98–9; 212 Jiangning Rd)

Spring Airlines (Chūnqiū Hángkōng; Map pp128–9; ☎ 400 820 6222; www.chinaspringtour.com; 1558 Dingxi Rd; 定西路1558号)

International airlines in Shànghǎi include the following:

Air Canada (Jiānádà Hángkōng; Map pp98–9; ☎ 6279 2999; www.aircanada.cn; Room 3901, United Plaza, 1468 West Nanjing Rd; 南京西路1468号3901室)

Air France (Fǎguó Hángkōng; Map pp66–7; ☎ 400 880 8808; www.airfrance.com.cn; Room 3901, Ciro's Plaza, 388 West Nanjing Rd; 南京西路388号3901室)

Air Macau (Àomén Hángkōng; Map pp86–7; ☎ 6248 1110; www.en.airmacau.com.mo; Room 302, Hotel Equatorial, 65 West Yan'an Rd; 延安西路65号302室)

British Airways (Yīngguó Hángkōng; Map pp66–7; ☎ 800 810 8012; www.ba.com; Room 703, Central Plaza, 227 North Huangpi Rd; 黄陂北路227号703室)

Cathay Pacific/Dragonair (Guótài Hángkōng; Map pp86–7; ☎ 6375 6375; www.dragonair.com; Room 2101-2104, Shanghai Plaza, 138 Middle Huaihai Rd; 淮海中路138号2101-2104室)

Lufthansa (Hànshā Hángkōng Gōngsì; Map pp86–7; ☎ 5352 4999; www.lufthansa.com.cn; 3rd fl, Bldg 1, Corporate Ave, 222 Hubin Rd; 湖滨路222号1号楼3层)

CLIMATE CHANGE & TRAVEL

Climate change is a serious threat to the ecosystems that humans rely upon, and air travel is the fastest-growing contributor to the problem. Lonely Planet regards travel, overall, as a global benefit, but believes we all have a responsibility to limit our personal impact on global warming.

Flying & Climate Change

Pretty much every form of motor transport generates CO_2 (the main cause of human-induced climate change) but planes are far and away the worst offenders, not just because of the sheer distances they allow us to travel, but because they release greenhouse gases high into the atmosphere. The statistics are frightening: two people taking a return flight between Europe and the US will contribute as much to climate change as an average household's gas and electricity consumption over a whole year.

Carbon Offset Schemes

Climatecare.org and other websites use 'carbon calculators' that allow jetsetters to offset the greenhouse gases they are responsible for with contributions to energy-saving projects and other climate-friendly initiatives in the developing world – including projects in India, Honduras, Kazakhstan and Uganda.

Lonely Planet, together with Rough Guides and other concerned partners in the travel industry, supports the carbon offset scheme run by climatecare.org. Lonely Planet offsets all of its staff and author travel.

For more information check out our website: www.lonelyplanet.com.

Northwest Airlines (Xīběi Hángkōng Gōngsì; Map pp98–9; ☎ 400 814 0081; www.nwa.com; Room 1007, Kerry Centre, 1515 West Nanjing Rd; 南京西路1515号 1007室)

Qantas (Àozhōu Hángkōng Gōngsì; Map pp86–7; ☎ 800 819 0089; www.qantas.com.au; Room 3202, K Wah Center, 1010 Middle Huaihai Rd; 淮海中路1010号 3202室)

Singapore Airlines (Xīnjiāpō Hángkōng; Map pp98–9; ☎ 6288 7999; www.singaporeair.com; Room 1106-1110, Plaza 66, 1266 West Nanjing Rd; 南京西路1266号 1106-1110室)

United Airlines (Liánhé Hángkōng; Map pp86–7; ☎ 3311 4567; www.united.com; 33rd fl, Shanghai Central Plaza, 381 Middle Huaihai Rd; 淮海中路381号33层)

Virgin Atlantic (Wéizhēn Hángkōng; Map pp66–7; ☎ 5353 4600; www.virgin-atlantic.com; Room 217, 12 East Zhongshan No 1 Rd; 中山东一路12号217室)

Airports

All international flights (and a few domestic flights) operate out of Pudong International Airport, with most (but not all) domestic flights operating out of Hongqiao Airport on Shànghǎi's western outskirts. If you're making an onward domestic connection from Pudong it's essential that you find out whether the domestic flight leaves from Pudong or Hongqiao, as it will take *at least* an hour to cross the city. Your ticket should indicate which airport you are flying to or from; Pudong's airport code is PVG, Hongqiao's is SHA. If you do

have to transfer, taxis, a regular shuttle bus (see the boxed text, p244) and metro line 2 link the two airports. Getting a taxi from Pudong International Airport is simple, but can be far more fraught at Hongqiao Airport.

PUDONG INTERNATIONAL AIRPORT
浦东国际机场

Pudong International Airport (Pǔdōng Guójì Jīchǎng; Map p221; ☎ 6834 1000, flight information 96990; www.shairport .com) is located 30km southeast of Shànghǎi, near the East China Sea.

The well-designed and impressive airport is simple to navigate. There are currently two main passenger terminals, with a third terminal that may already be open by the time you read this. Departures are on the upper level and arrivals on the lower level, where you can find a tourist information counter. Between terminals 1 and 2 is the MagLev train; terminal 3 will also be connected. Shuttle buses connect the terminals, stopping at doors 1 and 8 (terminal 1) and doors 23 and 27 (terminal 2). Try to dine beforehand as the airport restaurants are uniformly bad and overpriced.

Banks and ATMs are easily located throughout the airport, on both sides of customs. The Shanghai Pudong Development Bank, at the international end of the lower level, will cash travellers cheques and give Visa credit-card cash advances.

Post offices and baggage storage (1hr Y20, full day Y30; ⏱ 6am-9.30pm) are located in the arrival and departure halls. You can get online at

GETTING INTO TOWN

Most top-end and some midrange hotels operate shuttle buses to and from their hotels at fixed times (Y40 to Pudong International Airport, free to Hongqiao Airport). Enquire at the rows of hotel desks at the airports.

Pudong International Airport

The warp-speed MagLev (☎ 2890 7777; economy single/return Y50/80, with same-day air ticket Y40, VIP single/return Y100/160, children under/over 1.2m free/half-price) runs from Pudong International Airport to Longyang Rd metro stop on metro line 2; see the boxed text, p246, for further details. It runs every 15 minutes in both directions; from Longyang Rd to the airport between 6.45am and 9.32pm, and from the airport to Longyang Rd between 7am and 9.32pm. An extension of metro line 2 from Hongqiao Airport to Pudong International Airport (via People's Square) should be complete by the time this book is in print.

Pudong International Airport operates numerous airport bus routes (☎ 6834 1000). They drop off at all departures halls and pick up outside arrivals, at both terminals 1 and 2. The journey into Pǔxī (浦西) takes between 60 and 90 minutes, with buses leaving the airport every 15 to 30 minutes from 7am to 11pm. A midnight line operates from 11pm to the last arrival. The hours of buses running to the airport are more erratic; see below. The bus routes are as follows:

Bus 1 (Y30; ⊙ 6am-9.30pm) Pudong International Airport (浦东国际机场) to/from Hongqiao Airport (虹桥机场).

Bus 2 (Y22; ⊙ 5.30am-9.30pm) Pudong International Airport to/from Airport City Terminal (城市航站楼) on West Nanjing Rd (just east of Jing'an Temple).

Bus 3 (Y16-24; ⊙ 5.30am-8pm) Pudong International Airport to/from Galaxy Hotel in Xújiāhuì (徐家汇) via Longyang Rd metro station (龙阳路地铁站) in Pǔdōng.

Bus 4 (Y16-22; ⊙ 5.40am-9pm) Pudong International Airport to/from Lu Xun Park (鲁迅公园) via Wujiaochang (五角场) and Yunguang Village (运光新村).

Bus 5 (Y16-22; ⊙ 5.30am-9pm) Pudong International Airport to/from Shanghai Train Station (上海火车站), via Dongfang (East) Hospital (东方医院) in Pǔdōng and the intersection of North Chengdu Rd and Central Yan'an Rd behind People's Square.

Bus 6 (Y14-24; ⊙ 6am-8pm) Pudong International Airport to Zhongshan Park (中山公园), via Shimen No 1 Rd (石门一路) and Huashan Rd (华山路).

Bus 7 (Y20; ⊙ 6.50am-11pm) Pudong International Airport to Shanghai South Train Station (上海南站).

Midnight Line (Y16-30) Pudong International Airport to Hongqiao Airport via Longyang Rd metro station (龙阳路地铁站) in Pǔdōng, Shimen No 1 Rd (石门一路) and Huashan Rd (华山路).

the China Telecom office in the international terminal; wi-fi is available, but you need to purchase time.

The Merry Lin Air Terminal Hotel (大众美林阁空港宾馆; Dàzhòng Měilín Gékōng Gǎng Bīnguǎn; ☎ 3879 9999; 6hr from Y198; 24hr from Y298), part of the Motel 168 chain, is located between terminals 1 and 2, just in front of the MagLev ticket office.

Buses to Hángzhōu and Sūzhōu leave from the airport.

HONGQIAO AIRPORT 虹桥机场

Hongqiao Airport (Hóngqiáo Jīchǎng; Map p132; ☎ 6268 8899; flight information 5260 4620; www.shairport.com) has two terminals, the older east terminal (halls A and B) and the new west terminal, due to be completed in 2010. Most traffic will be routed through the west terminal once it begins operation. Avoid the hotel and taxi touts. Buses to Sūzhōu and Hángzhōu depart from the long-distance bus station west of McDonald's.

The information counters (⊙ 5.30am-11pm) are useful, booking discounted accommodation, providing free maps, offering advice on transportation into town and writing the Chinese script for a taxi. Note that they were located upstairs in the departure halls at the time of writing. A post office is also located in the departure halls. Public telephones take phonecards, for sale (Y100 value only) at the information counters. ATMs taking international cards are located at most exits.

Luggage storage (⊙ 7am-8.30pm) is available in the departure halls and also in Hall A of arrivals.

During the day, a taxi (出租汽车) ride into central Shànghǎi will cost around Y150 and will take about an hour. A taxi to Hongqiao Airport costs around Y160. Most taxi drivers in Shànghǎi are honest, though make sure they use the meter; avoid monstrous overcharging by steering clear of taxi sharks in the arrivals hall and locate the regular taxi rank outside the arrivals hall instead. There are also regular buses to Sùzhōu (苏州; Y84, three hours, 17 per day) and Hángzhōu (杭州; Y100, three hours, six per day).

Hongqiao Airport

Hongqiao Airport is 18km from the Bund; getting there takes about 30 minutes if you're lucky, and more than an hour if you're not. Metro line 2 should connect Hongqiao Airport with Pudong International Airport (via People's Square) by the time this book is in print.

The following bus routes are useful:

Airport Bus 1 (机场一线; Jīchǎng Yīxiàn; Y30; ☯ every 20-30min 6am-11pm) To Pudong International Airport.

Airport Shuttle Bus (机场专线; Jīchǎng Zhuānxiàn; Y4; ☯ every 15min 7.50am-11pm) Direct to the Airport City Terminal east of Jing'an Temple.

Bus 925 (Y4; ☯ 6.40am-9.25pm) To People's Sq (人民广场) via Hongmei Rd (虹梅路), Huashan Rd (华山路) and Shimen No1 Rd (石门一路).

Bus 941 (Y4; ☯ 6am-8.30pm) To Shanghai Train Station (上海火车站) via Zhongshan Park (中山公园) and Jiangsu Rd (江苏路).

Bus 806 (Y5; ☯ 6am-11pm) To Lupu Bridge (卢浦大桥) via Jiaotong University (交通大学) and Huashan Rd (华山路).

Bus 938 (Y7; ☯ 6am-midnight) Runs to Yángjiādù (杨家渡) in Pǔdōng via Hongxu Rd (虹许路), North Caoxi Rd (曹溪北路) and South Xizang Rd (西藏南路). Stops near the Shanghai Indoor Stadium metro station in Xújiāhuì.

A taxi (出租汽车) to the Bund (外滩) will cost around Y60; to Pudong International Airport should cost around Y160. Unlike at Pudong International Airport, the taxi queue at Hongqiao is sometimes astonishing and waits of an hour or more are common. If you don't have too much baggage and you're in a rush, jump on a bus to escape the airport and then grab a cab. Avoid the taxi sharks loitering in the arrivals hall unless the taxi queue outside is a serious chánglóng (long dragon), as the Chinese say, but ensure you don't pay over the odds. They should be able to drive you to People's Square for around Y100.

Frequent buses run from 10am to 9pm to Sùzhōu (Y53, 90 minutes, 20 per day) and Hángzhōu (Y85, two hours, 10 per day) from the Hongqiao Airport Long Distance Bus Station, west of McDonald's.

Bags must be locked and a passport or ID is required. Wi-fi is available; however, you'll need to ask for the password at an information counter.

BICYCLE

If you can handle the fumes and menace of Shànghǎi's vicious traffic, biking is an excellent way to get around town, especially if you occasionally link it in with public transport. Despite being shunted down the transport ladder by the mushrooming number of cars, 9 million bicycles whisk their owners about town. Come sunny summer, cyclists sport a wide array of sun shields, from wide-brimmed hats resembling lampshades to vast sun visors that could pass for welding masks.

Bikes have been banned from major roads for several years now, so you may have to join cyclists surging pell-mell down the footpaths (sidewalks) of busy streets. Remember you will be on the lowliest transportation device in town, and buses, trucks, taxis, cars and scooters will ceaselessly honk at you, in that pecking order (just ignore them). Cars will give you little room and will turn into your bike without a second thought; if you're new to the roads of Shànghǎi, allow a few days to adjust to the swing of things. Note that cyclists never use lights at night and Chinese pedestrians favour dark clothing, so eat a lot of carrots and ride carefully. Helmets are also a rarity. In a sign of the resurgent love affair with the bike, bicycle lanes are due to

OFF THE RAILS

If you need to reach or exit Pudong International Airport chop-chop, Shànghǎi's futuristic MagLev train (磁浮列车) comes with a top speed of 430km/hr. It's the world's sole MagLev (magnetic levitation) train in commercial operation; in place of conventional wheels, the Sino-German train's carriages are supported above the tracks by a magnetic field. With ample legroom, carriages have simple interiors and, perhaps tellingly, no seatbelts. LED meters notch up the rapidly escalating velocity, although the train starts to decelerate around five minutes into its eight-minute cruise, in preparation for arrival. Despite a slight wobble it's a smooth ride, although rumours abound that the track is slowly sinking into marshy Pǔdōng. Launched in 2003, the MagLev train may be a wonder of the modern world but it's of limited use in getting into central Shànghǎi, as the train only takes you as far as the terminus at Longyang Rd station (Map pp62–3) in Pǔdōng, from where you'll have to lug your luggage a few hundred metres to the metro station of the same name to continue your journey. Nonetheless, a trip on the train is thrilling and a return trip to the airport is a fun outing for the family. A planned extension to the route, whisking the train through the 2010 World Expo site (and possibly on to Hongqiao Airport in the west of town), awaits final approval. The MagLev, however, needs to brace itself for fierce competition from metro line 2, which should connect the two airports by the time this book is in print. The planned Shànghǎi–Hángzhōu MagLev will run between the two cities at 450km/hr, reducing the 200km journey to 27 minutes, although there is no word on when the project will be given the green light.

be massively expanded by 180km over the coming years.

Purchase is straightforward and you can pick up a trashy mountain bike for as little as Y250 at supermarkets and hypermarkets such as Carrefour. Bikes need to be taxed, with a disc (obtainable at bike shops) displayed. At the Shanghai Stadium, Giant (Jiéāntè; Map p122; ☎ 6426 5119; 666 Tianyaoqiao Rd; ☺ 9am-8pm) has a good collection of bikes. For fold-up bicycles, Oyama (Ōuyámǎ Zhédiéchē; Map p122; ☎ 6426 5218; 666 Tianyaoqiao Rd; ☺ 10am-8pm) next door has lightweight bikes starting from Y678 and kicking off from around 8.5kg. BOHDI (p196) and SISU (p197) also sell and rent quality bikes. Bicycle repairmen litter the side streets of Shànghǎi, charging around Y1 to pump up your tyres.

Around 130 bikes are stolen every day in Shànghǎi so make sure that you have your own bicycle cable lock. It's a good idea to leave your bike at bike parks (available at most shopping areas and subway stations for Y0.50), as an attendant will keep an eye on your wheels.

Several hostels around town, including the Captain Hostel (p206), can rent you bikes.

BOAT

The new Shanghai Port International Cruise Terminal (Shànghǎi Gǎng Guójì Kèyùn Zhōngxīn; Map p116; Gaoyang Rd; 高阳路) is located north of the Bund and mostly serves cruise ships. There are few regular passenger routes that serve Shànghǎi.

The China-Japan International Ferry Company (Zhōngrì Guójì Lúndù; Map p116; ☎ 6325 7642; www.xinjianzhen.com; 18th fl, Jin'an Tower, 908 Dongdaming Rd; 东大名路908号

金岸大厦18楼) runs boats to and from Japan once a week (depart Saturday 1pm, arrive Monday 9.30am; tickets 2nd class/1st class/private Y1300/1600/2600). They leave from the nearby International Cruise Terminal, alternating the destination (Osaka or Kobe) weekly.

For details on the ferry to Pǔtuóshān, see p239.

BUS

The closest thing to revolutionary fervour in Shànghǎi today is the rush-hour bus ambush. During rush hour and on the weekend, the scrum of passengers fighting to board the same bus resembles a world record challenge.

Despite impressively running over 1000 routes, the bus system repels many foreigners as it is torturous for non-Chinese passengers to use and is often a traumatic way of getting from A to B. Bus-stop signs and routes are in Chinese only and drivers and conductors speak little if any English, although on-board announcements in English will alert you to when to get off. The conductor will also tell you when your stop is arriving, if you ask. Added confusion can occur when you want to get off. Bus stops are widely spaced and your bus can race past your destination and on to the next stop up to a kilometre away. In general try to get on at the terminus (thus guaranteeing you a seat), avoid rush hours, and stick to a few tried-and-tested routes. Be alert to pickpockets, especially during the rush-hour squeeze.

Air-con buses (with a snowflake motif and the characters 空调 alongside the bus number) cost Y2 to Y3 and are a godsend in summer.

TRANSPORT BOAT

Older buses have no air-con and cost Y1, though there are few remaining. The swipeable Transport Card (see boxed text, p248) works on many but not all bus routes. Private minibuses (Y2) serve some routes on the edges of town. Passengers over 180cm (6ft) tall may have to stand in the stairwell of double-decker buses as the ceilings are painfully low.

Suburban and long-distance buses don't carry numbers – the destination is in characters. Buses generally operate from 5am to 11pm, except for 300-series buses, which operate all night.

See p264 for details about sightseeing buses in Shànghǎi.

Travelling by bus is not a very useful way to leave or enter Shànghǎi. Buses to Běijīng take between 14 and 16 hours, and it is faster and more comfortable to take the 10-hour express trains to the capital.

The huge Shanghai Long-Distance Bus Station (Shànghǎi Chángtú Qìchē Kèyùn Zǒngzhàn; Map pp98–9; ☎ 6605 0000; 1666 Zhongxing Rd; 中兴路1666号) north of Shanghai Train Station has buses to destinations as far away as Gānsù province and Inner Mongolia. Twenty buses per day run to Sūzhōu (苏州; 7am to 7.40pm) and 24 buses per day run to Hángzhōu (杭州; 6am to 8.30pm). Buses also run to Zhōuzhuāng (周庄; six per day), Nánjīng (南京; five per day) and Běijīng (北京; one per day, 4pm).

Another long-distance bus station is the Hengfeng Road Bus Station (Héngfēng Lù Kèyùnzhàn; Map pp98–9; ☎ 962 168; 258 Hengfeng Rd; 恒丰路258号), near the Hanzhong Rd metro station. Catch buses here to Sūzhōu (苏州; five daily) and Hángzhōu (杭州; eight daily).

The huge Shanghai South Long-Distance Bus Station (Shànghǎi Chángtú Kèyùn Nánzhàn; Map pp62–3; ☎ 5435 3535; 666 Shilong Rd; 石龙路666号) has buses largely to destinations in south China. Destinations include Sūzhōu (苏州; 40 per day, 6.27am to 8pm), Nánjīng (南京; four per day, 9.27am to 4.50pm), Wūzhèn (乌镇; 9.40am and 3.10pm), Hángzhōu (杭州; 39 per day, 6.40am to 8.50pm) and Níngbō (宁波; 39 per day, 6.20am to 8.30pm).

Buses also depart for Hángzhōu and Sūzhōu from Hongqiao Airport and Pudong International Airport.

From the Shanghai Sightseeing Bus Centre (Shànghǎi Lǚyóu Jísàn Zhōngxīn; Map p122) at Shanghai Stadium, you can join tours to Sūzhōu, Hángzhōu, Tónglǐ, Mùdú, Zhūjiājiǎo, Nánxún, Lùzhí, Mògānshān and other destinations around Shànghǎi; see the Excursions chapter (p220) for details.

CAR

As you need a residency permit to drive in Shànghǎi, short-stay tourists are effectively barred from hiring cars in the city. This is not as tragic as it sounds, as Shànghǎi's roads can be lethal for novices. To drive in Shànghǎi, you will need a Chinese driving licence and a residency permit. Residents can apply for a Chinese license at their local Public Security Bureau or Shanghai Transport Bureau (www .jt.sh.cn). You will also need to take along your passport, international driving licence and health certificate, have your driving licence translated into Chinese and sit a written test. For most visitors, it is more advisable to hire a car and a driver. A Volkswagen Santana with driver and petrol starts at around Y600 per day. Ask for more information at your hotel.

Car hire (for residents) is available at Hertz (☎ 800 988 1336; www.hertz.net.cn). Other car-hire agencies include Avis (☎ 6229 1119; www.avischina .com) and Shanghai ASD (☎ 5465 7659; www.carrenting .com.cn). Prices start at Y300 a day for a Santana and Y900 for an Audi, without a driver.

Foreigner residents are technically allowed to drive in Shànghǎi municipality only, though expats report few problems driving into neighbouring Jiāngsū and Zhèjiāng provinces.

FERRY

Several ferries cross the Huangpu River between Pǔxī and Pǔdōng, and 12 new docks were expected to be added for the 2010 World Expo (remaining in operation afterward), though the new routes were not yet public at press time. The most useful ferry operates between the southern end of the Bund and Pǔdōng from the Jinling Donglu Dukou (Jīnlíng Dōnglù Dùkǒu; Map pp66–7; ☎ 6326 2135; 127 East Zhongshan No 2 Rd; 中山东二路127号), running every 15 minutes from 7am to 10pm for the six-minute trip (Y2). Tickets are sold at the kiosks on the pavement out front.

METRO

The city's metro trains are easily the best way to get around Shànghǎi. They are fast, cheap, clean and easy, though it's hard to get a seat at the best of times. With well over three million daily users, the opening of the metro doors serves as a signal for an indecorous scramble for seats and the rush hour sees carriages filled to overcapacity, but trains are frequent

TRANSPORT CARD 交通卡

If you are making more than a fleeting trip to Shànghǎi, it's worth getting a transport card *(jiāotōng kǎ)*. Available at metro stations and some convenience stores, cards can be topped up with credits and can be used on the metro, on some buses and ferries, and in taxis. Credits are electronically deducted from the card as you swipe it over the sensor, equipped at metro turnstiles and near the door on buses; when paying your taxi fare, hand it to the taxi driver who will swipe it for you. Credits are automatically deducted. They don't save you money, but they are much more convenient than fishing through your pockets for change every time you want to go somewhere. A deposit of Y20 is required; refunds are available at the East Nanjing Rd metro station.

Tourist passes, which would offer unlimited travel on the metro for one day (Y25), may be introduced by the time this book is in print.

and the system is being rapidly expanded to envelop more and more of the city.

At the beginning of 2003 there were only three lines in operation, at the time of writing this guide there were eight lines in operation, and by the time you read this there will be a total 11 lines in operation, barring any unforeseen setbacks! We've included the stations for the new lines 7, 10 and 11 throughout the book. The year 2012 is the next target for expansion (two new lines and three extensions); we have not covered these new stations here.

The most useful lines for travellers are 1, 2 and 10. Line 1 runs from Fujin Rd in the north, through Shanghai Train Station and People's Square, along Middle Huaihai Rd, through Xújiāhuì and Shanghai South Train Station to Xinzhuang in the southern suburbs.

Line 2 runs from Hongqiao Airport in the west to the Pudong International Airport in the east (not yet complete at press time). It passes through Jing'ān, East Nanjing Rd (and the Bund district) in the centre of town and Longyang Rd, the site of the MagLev terminus. Lines 1 and 2 connect at People's Square interchange, the busiest of all stations.

Line 10 will run from Hongqiao Airport in the west through the French Concession, the Old Town, the Bund area and Hóngkǒu before terminating far to the north of Fudan University.

Tickets range between Y3 and Y7 depending on the distance. They are only sold from the automated machines (except in rare cases). Service counters will provide you with change if your bills are not accepted. Keep your ticket until you exit. When entering the metro, swipe your card across the turnstile sensor for access; when exiting, enter it into the slot where it will be retained.

The rechargeable Transport Card (see the boxed text, above) can be used on the metro, some buses, ferries and all taxis.

There's one main shortcoming to the metro system, and that's that it stops running relatively early in the night. Most lines make begin their final run between 10pm and 10.30pm (some earlier), so anyone out later than 11pm will need to catch a cab home.

The metro station exits can be very complicated so look for a street map (usually easy to find) before exiting. To find a metro station look for the red M.

TAXI

Shànghǎi has around 45,000 taxis. Most are Volkswagen Santanas, though some are Volkswagen Passats and there's a fleet of Mercedes-Benz taxis.

Shànghǎi's taxis are reasonably cheap, hassle-free and easy to flag down outside rush hour, although finding a cab during a rainstorm is impossible. Few taxis come with rear seatbelts, so sit up front. On many taxis the rear left-hand door is locked, so board by the doors on the right side. Flag fall is Y11 for the first 3km, and Y2 per kilometre thereafter; there is no need to tip. A night rate operates from 11pm to 5am, when the flag fall is Y14, then Y2.60 per kilometre. Note that taxis can't take the tunnel to Lùjiāzuǐ in Pǔdōng from 8am to 9.30am and 5pm to 6.30pm.

Most taxi drivers (mostly male) are surprisingly honest, though you should always go by the meter. Pay by cash *(xiànjīn)* or use a Transport Card (see the boxed text, above). At night you can tell if a taxi is empty by the red 'for hire' sign on the dashboard of the passenger side. The driver should push this down to start the meter when you get in the cab. It's always worth asking for a printed receipt, as this gives not only the fare but also the driver and car number, the distance driven, waiting time and the number to call if there are any problems or if you left something in the taxi.

Many drivers are immigrants and are sometimes inept at finding their way around, even to the most obvious of places. Some stick to the main roads and have little grasp of shortcuts. To avoid total novices, examine (if you have a choice between taxis) the number of stars below the driver's photo affixed to the dashboard; stars range from one to five in order of expertise (and English-language skills). If you don't speak Chinese, take a Chinese character map or have your destination written down in characters or pack a business card for your destination. Alternatively, use your mobile to phone your local contact (or the 24-hour tourist hotline – ☎ 962288) in Shànghǎi and ask him or her to give instructions to the driver. It also helps if you have your own directions and sit in the front with a map, looking knowledgeable (to deter circuitous, looping detours).

Shànghǎi's main taxi companies include turquoise-coloured Dazhong Taxi (☎ 96822), Qiangsheng (☎ 6258 0000) and Bashi (☎ 96840). For taxi complaints, phone ☎ 962000.

Motorcycle taxis wait at some intersections and metro stations to whisk travellers off to nearby destinations. Most trips cost less than Y10.

TRAIN

China's rail service is gargantuan, excellent and more than a little mind-boggling. The Chinese have travelled by train for decades like total naturals, but the contemporary passion for trains wasn't love at first sight. Railways were strongly resisted in the 19th century, as people feared they would disturb ancestors' graves and obstruct feng shui. Běijīng was also concerned that railroads would accelerate the military domination of China by foreign powers. China's first railway (1875) ran from Shànghǎi to Wúsōng at the mouth of the Yangzi River, operating for a few brief years before it encountered stiff local resistance and was torn up and shipped to Taiwan. No such qualms exist these days, as passenger trains trundle through every province except Hǎinán Island; even the high-altitude bastion of Tibet has been finally breached by rail engineers. If any nationality travels by train, it's surely the Chinese, with up to 155 million souls taking to the railways during the Chinese New Year. Chinese train travel is a marvellous subculture and if you have time to travel around China after a visit to Shànghǎi you should try to incorporate at least one train journey into your itinerary.

The city has two principal stations: the main Shanghai Train Station (Shànghǎi Huǒchē Zhàn; Map pp88–9; ☎ 6317 9090; 385 Meiyuan Rd) and the Shanghai South Train Station (Shànghǎi Huǒchē Zhàn; Map pp62–3; ☎ 9510 5123; 200 Zhaofeng Rd). Most trains depart from the main station, though some southern destinations, like Hángzhōu, leave primarily from Shanghai South. A few trains may also leave from the renovated West Station (上海西站; Shànghǎi Xīzhàn; due to reopen in 2010), however, it's less convenient. A new station, the Hongqiao train station (west of Hongqiao Airport and part of the Hongqiao Transport Hub), will serve as the terminus for the new high-speed rail link between Shànghǎi and Běijīng. The express line will cut travel time in half to a mere five hours, with a completion date of 2014. The Shànghǎi–Nánjīng section will probably be in operation earlier.

Buying Tickets

Although procuring tickets for nearby destinations (Sūzhōu, Hángzhōu etc) is reasonably straightforward, never assume you can

---

TRAVEL AGENCIES

The following agencies can help with travel bookings.

CTrip (☎ 400 619 9999; http://english.ctrip.com) An excellent online agency, good for hotel and flight bookings.

Huochepiao.com (www.huochepiao.com, in Chinese) An up-to-date and comprehensive train schedule with prices and detailed information. Unfortunately, it's Chinese only.

Jinjiang Tours (Jīnjiāng Lǚxíngshè; www.chinacityex.com) Changle Rd (Map pp86–7; ☎ 6445 9525; 191 Changle Rd; 长乐路191号); West Beijing Rd (Map pp98–9; ☎ 6289 4510, 1277 West Beijing Rd, inside CITS Bldg; 北京西路1277号) The Changle Rd branch is just near the Garden Hotel and is good for bus tours of Shànghǎi.

Shanghai Spring International Travel Service (Chūnqiū Hángkōng Lǚxíngshè; www.chinaspringtour.com) Middle Xizang Rd (Map pp66–7; ☎ 6351 6666; 347 Middle Xizang Rd; 西藏中路347号); Dingxi Rd (Map pp128–9; ☎ 800 820 6222; 1558 Dingxi Rd)

casually stroll to the train station and hand over your credit card for a hard-sleeper ticket for a same-day departure, or expect an English-capable automated machine to spit out your ticket with minimum fuss. For most long-haul trips, you will need to pre-purchase your ticket at least 24 hours or, if possible, a few days before your departure date. Reservations for Z-class express trains can be made up to 20 days in advance, and most other types of train tickets can be reserved up to 10 days ahead of departure (as long as the train begins its journey in Shànghǎi). Book tickets for Běijīng as soon as you possibly can.

There are several options for getting hold of train tickets in Shànghǎi. There's the Chinese way – joining the surging masses at the train station ticket office – but prepare for battles with uncomprehending staff and queue barging; stress can take on a whole new meaning. There are two ticket halls (售票厅; shòupiàotīng) at the Shanghai Train Station, one in the main building (same-day tickets) and another on the east side of the square (advance tickets). One counter will claim to have English-speakers. There is also a useful soft-sleeper/seat ticket office with short queues near the west end of Shanghai Train Station. Bilingual automated machines just east of the same-day ticket hall sell soft-seat tickets to Nánjīng, Hángzhōu and Shàoxīng.

Alternatively, your hotel will be able to obtain a ticket for you, albeit sometimes for a hefty surcharge. Tickets can also be purchased for a small surcharge from travel agencies (see the boxed text, p249).

Hard-seat and hard-sleeper train tickets can also be purchased from the Train Ticket Office (Huǒchēpiào Yùshòuchù; Map pp66–7; 230 East Beijing Rd; ⏰ 8am-5pm). Soft-seat or soft-sleeper tickets can be bought at one of the numerous other small train-ticket offices throughout town, such as in Jìng'ān (Map pp98–9; 77 Wanhangdu Rd; 万航渡路77号; ⏰ 8am-5pm), Chángníng (Map pp128–9; 417 Xinhua Rd; 新华路417号; ⏰ 8am-8pm) and Pǔdōng (Map p108; 1396 Lujiazui Ring Rd; 陆家嘴环路1396号; ⏰ 8am-7pm). Train information is available over the phone in Chinese only (☎ 800 820 7890).

Buying train tickets is very difficult during the set holiday periods (particularly Chinese New Year). Try not to make any travel plans at this time.

Classes

In socialist China there are no classes; instead you have hard seat (硬座; yìngzuò), hard sleeper (硬卧; yìngwò), soft seat (软座; ruǎnzuò) and soft sleeper (软卧; ruǎnwò).

The most comfortable way to get to destinations around Shànghǎi (such as Sūzhōu and Hángzhōu) is by soft seat. Soft seats are numbered and are more comfortable than hard seats. Hard-seat carriages – the lowliest form of train travel – can be dirtier and packed to the gills on longer trips.

For overnight trips, hard sleepers are easily comfortable enough, with only a fixed number of people allowed in the sleeper carriage. The carriage consists of doorless compartments with half a dozen bunks in three tiers and foldaway seats by the windows. Sheets, pillows and blankets are provided. Carriages are nonsmoking, although smokers congregate between carriages. Competition for hard sleepers is keen, so reserve early (see p249). Prices vary according to which berth you get: upper, middle or lower berth. The lower berth (下铺; xiàpù) is pricier as you get to sit and have more space but it is often invaded by all and sundry who use it as a seat during the day. The top berths (上铺; shàngpù) are cheapest as you get the least room. The middle berth (中铺; zhōngpù) is a goodie as it's spacious and all yours.

Soft sleepers are expensive (about twice the hard-sleeper price), with four comfortable bunks in a closed, carpeted compartment. Express Z-class trains (such as Shànghǎi–Běijīng) are the most modern, with mobile-phone charging points, free meals (on some routes) and well-made bunks (four to a compartment). Z-class deluxe soft sleepers are two to a compartment, with their own toilet and wardrobe.

Services

Most trains depart and arrive from the main Shanghai Train Station (Map pp98–9) or Shanghai South Train Station (Map pp62–3), though some may use the Shanghai West Train Station (Map pp62–3). Be sure to find out beforehand which one you should leave from. Trains for Běijīng, Sūzhōu and Hong Kong (T99B, departs 6:24pm, 18½ hours, hard/soft sleeper Y395/701) depart from Shanghai Train Station. Trains for Hángzhōu depart from Shanghai South Train Station, although some depart from Shanghai Train Station. For details about train times and ticket prices for trains to Sūzhōu and Hángzhōu, see p233 and p222, respectively. Left-luggage facilities exist at all train stations.

Very comfortable overnight express D-trains to Běijīng do the trip in 10 hours. Trains leave daily at 9.13pm, 9.18pm, 9.23pm, 9.28pm and 9.38pm from Shanghai Train Station (soft seat Y409; soft-sleeper Y655 to Y730); departure times change yearly, so check for an update. Alternatively, fast T-trains depart Shànghǎi around 10pm, arriving in Běijīng around 11.30am the next day (hard/soft sleeper Y317/499). Berths go very quickly so book as early as you possibly can. Trains from Běijīng to Shànghǎi depart at roughly the same time.

DIRECTORY

BUSINESS

As its fanfare coverage in the world media reaches a frenzied crescendo, the Shànghǎi gold rush shows little sign of flagging. If ever there was a time to do business with China, it is now.

The sheer size of the Chinese market, however, generates a fascination that has led many foreign businesses onto the rocks. Vigilance and common-sense caution can go to the wind as companies rush to grab a slice of the pie. Seemingly watertight business plans can be holed by misunderstanding the market and China's highly idiosyncratic business culture.

As with all emerging markets, it is essential to consider a few basic pointers before rushing in. Ascertaining the risks and identifying chief threats, examining the market carefully and working out what your business requirements will be are sound strategies for making a balanced assessment. There is no substitute for knowing how your industry performs in China.

Big slip-ups can lurk at the very outset. Brand-name blunders can be fatal for a product launch. Pepsi originally stumbled into the China market with a name 'Qishang' for its 7-Up carbonated drink, which unfortunately forms the first two syllables of a Chinese idiom meaning 'to be agitated'. The soft drink was belatedly renamed 'Qixi' (Seven Happiness) – the name used today. Pepsi famously did it again with the hip line 'Come alive with the Pepsi generation' which mutated into Chinese as 'Pepsi brings your ancestors back from the grave'. China has big problems with brand naming as well: SOD cleansing milk – heavily marketed in Shànghǎi and throughout China – is a dead duck if it ever goes West without re-branding.

Products that sell well overseas may not sell well in Shànghǎi or China. The 2.6 billion armpits scenario – all joyfully awaiting deodorisation – is a case in point (deodorant sales in China are small as the Chinese have minimal BO). For a horrifying personal account of how to lose a lot of money in China, pick up a copy of Tom Clissold's *Mr China: A Memoir*.

If doing business in China, it is important to develop a strong understanding of Chinese culture, have patience, a sense of humour, cultural adaptability and a tolerance for smoky rooms. Sound business deals can founder on the simplest of cultural misunderstandings.

Steer well clear of political discussions. The Chinese businessman you are chatting to may agree that the CCP is a bunch of good-for-nothings, but they won't want to share that publicly.

It's also a good idea to get karaoke-friendly. The Chinese business set falls over itself to grasp the golden microphone and fully unwind, so learn a few notes and join in.

Last but not least, don't assume that cultural blunders – food shooting from your chopsticks, nonsense Mandarin issuing from your mouth – will scupper a business deal. The Chinese are used to foreigners getting snagged and tend to find mistakes less as improprieties than as opportunities for amusement.

Business Cards

Business name cards are absolutely essential, even if you don't do business – exchanging name cards with someone you've just met goes down extremely well. You could be left high and dry if name cards are being handed around and you are empty-handed. Try to get your name translated into (simplified) Chinese and have it printed on the reverse of the card. You can get name cards made cheaply in Shànghǎi at local printers, but it's better to have some in advance of your arrival. Remember that the Chinese pay particular attention to the quality of business

---

GUANXI

If you want to locate or contact a tourist, entertainment, shopping or business venue in Shànghǎi and have a mobile phone, then text message the name of the venue to the wireless search engine GuanXi on ☎ 1066 9588 2929. The full name, address and telephone number will be immediately returned to you by SMS (Y1 to Y2 per enquiry). The information can also be relayed in Chinese, as long as your mobile phone can support Chinese text. Unfortunately, the number has changed often over the years, so check to see if it is still accurate at www.minfo.com/guanxi/en/product/product.aspx.

cards so aim for a good finish if you want to impress. When proffering and receiving business cards, emulate the Chinese method of respectfully using the thumb and forefinger of both hands.

Exhibitions & Conventions

Apart from the monster venues listed in this section, all the top-end hotels provide conference facilities (see individual entries in the Sleeping chapter).

Shanghai Everbright International Convention & Exhibition Centre (Shànghǎi Guāngdà Huìzhǎn Zhōngxīn; Map p122; ☎ 6475 3288; www.secec.com; 5th fl, 68 Caobao Rd; 漕宝路68号5楼) Has an attached four-star hotel.

Shanghai Exhibition Centre (Shànghǎi Zhǎnlǎn Zhōngxīn; Map pp98–9; ☎ 2216 2216; www.shzlzx.com.cn; 1000 Middle Yan'an Rd; 延安中路1000号) Exhibition hall space of 22,000 sq m, plus a theatre, restaurants and cafes. See also p104.

Shanghai International Convention Centre (Shànghǎi Guójì Huìyì Zhōngxīn; Map p108; ☎ 5037 0000; www.shicc.net; 2727 Riverside Ave; 滨江大道2727号) This centre offers a 3000-seat ballroom, an 800-seat conference room and a hotel (Oriental Riverside Hotel, p199).

Shanghai International Exhibition Centre (INTEX; Shànghǎi Guójì Zhǎnlǎn Zhōngxīn; Map pp128–9; ☎ 6275 5800; intex@public.sta.net.cn; 88 Loushanguan Rd; 娄山关路88号)

Shanghai New International Expo Centre (上海新国际博览中心; Shànghǎi Xīn Guójì Bólǎn Zhōngxīn; off Map pp62–3; ☎ 2890 6857; 2345 Longyang Rd; 龙阳路2345号)

Shanghai Worldfield Convention Centre & Hotel (Shànghǎi Shìbó Huìyì Dàjiǔdiàn; Map p132; ☎ 6270 3388; www.conventhotel.com; 2106 Hongqiao Rd; 虹桥路2106号)

Shanghaimart (Shànghǎi Shìmào Shāngchéng; Map pp128–9; ☎ 2325 5320; www.shanghaimart.com; 2299 West Yan'an Rd; 延安西路2299号)

Useful Organisations

American Chamber of Commerce (AmCham, Shànghǎi Měiguó Shānghuì; Map pp98–9; ☎ 6279 7119; room 568, Shanghai Centre, 1376 West Nanjing Rd; 南京西路1376号568室) This office only helps members.

Australian Chamber of Commerce (AustCham Shanghai; Map pp98–9; ☎ 6248 8301; www.austchamshanghai.com; suite 6709, Apollo Bldg, 1440 Middle Yan'an Rd; 延安中路1440号6709室)

British Chamber of Commerce (BritCham, Shànghǎi Yīngguó Shānghuì; Map pp98–9; ☎ 6218 5022; www.sha.britcham.org; 5th fl, 863 West Nanjing Rd; 南京西路863号5楼) Inside the Marks & Spencer building.

China Britain Business Council (Yīngzhōng Màoyì Xiéhuì; Map pp98–9; ☎ 6218 5183; www.cbbc.org; room 1701-1702, Westgate Tower, 1038 West Nanjing Rd; 南京西路1038号1701-1702室)

European Union Chamber of Commerce in China (Zhōngguó Ōuméng Shānghuì; Map pp86–7; ☎ 6385 2023; www.euccc.com.cn; room 2204, Shui on Plaza, 333 Middle Huaihai Rd; 淮海中路333号2204室)

US Commercial Center (Map pp98–9; ☎ 6279 7640; room 631, Shanghai Centre, 1376 West Nanjing Rd; 南京西路1376号631室) This is the overseas office of the US Department of Commerce and can assist US businesses with finding Chinese business partners.

US-China Business Council (Map pp98–9; ☎ 6288 3840; www.uschina.org; room 1301, 1701 West Beijing Rd; 北京西路1701号1301室)

Business Hours

Banks, offices and government departments are normally open Monday to Friday from 9am to noon and about 2pm to 4.30pm. Most major post offices open daily from 8.30am to 6pm, sometimes until 10pm. Central telecom offices are open 24 hours. Local post offices are closed on the weekend. Bank of China branches are normally open weekdays from 9.30am to 11.30am and 1.30pm to 4.30pm, and most now have 24-hour ATMs. Some branches also open on Saturday mornings. Shopping malls and department stores are generally open until 10pm, especially on weekends.

Restaurants are open from 11am to 10pm or later, but some open from 10am to 2.30pm, with an afternoon break before opening again from 5pm to 11pm or later. Some bars open in the morning, others are open from around 5pm to 2am.

Most museums are open on the weekend; a few close on Monday. They usually stop selling tickets 30 minutes before they close.

Note that businesses in China close for the week-long Chinese New Year (usually in February) and National Day (beginning October 1). Shànghǎi's entertainment industry pulses round the clock, with several restaurants, bars and hotel coffee shops open 24 hours. Internet-gaming dens often operate 24/7.

CHILDREN

A subject worthy of a book in itself, China's one-child policy has spawned a generation of spoiled, demanding and often overweight 'Little Emperors'. This also means that the Shànghǎi Chinese have devised plenty of ways to keep their children regally occupied and entertained.

Of course, there are more than enough cranes, diggers and bulldozers to get any two-year-old boy's heart racing, but what about the rest of the family? Plenty of sights in town can keep young animal-watchers wide-eyed. With its huge and inviting lawns, Shanghai Zoo (p132) is an excellent day out for families; there is even a small children's zoo aimed specifically at tots. At the other end of the animal-kingdom food chain, the creepy crawlies at the Natural Wild Insect Kingdom (p111) will get young eyes on stalks. Young marine biologists can be dazzled by the Shanghai Ocean Aquarium (p111), also in Pǔdōng.

Shànghǎi's parks tend towards hard-edged sculpted concrete and synthetic add-ons, but Century Park (p113) has bundles of activities for kids, from bicycle hire to rides in its crisp, new amusement park. Fundazzle (p130) in Zhongshan Park is a favourite, and Gongqing Forest Park (p119) has a crop of fun attractions and activities, including a rollercoaster and horse riding. Fuxing Park (p92) also has a children's playground and rides. At the Shanghai Botanical Gardens (p124) there is a fun children's park with small funfair attractions.

Tom's World (Tāngmǔ Xióng; Map pp66–7; basement, 673 East Nanjing Rd; 南京东路673号; 9.30am-10pm) is a noisy arcade not far from the Bund, jam-packed with bleeping games and rowdy kids. There is another location in Pǔdōng's Superbrand Mall (p147; 6th fl). Amusement and water parks such as Dino Beach (p124) and Happy Valley (p131) are favourites, and a blessing in summer when temperatures are uncomfortably high.

Numerous McDonald's restaurants offer play areas for young children (remember to take their shoes off), and balloons are regularly handed out.

Acrobatics and Shaolin kung fu are fascinating evening events for older children. The Community Church (p94) has a variety of classes for children and a small nursery (crèche) on Sundays.

For children's books, the 4th floor of the Foreign Languages Bookstore (p138) is well stocked with juvenile literature, and Chaterhouse (p142) also has a good range.

There are several kids' stores for toys and clothing around town, including Bao Da Xiang (Map pp66–7; ☎ 6322 5122; 685 East Nanjing Rd; 南京东路685号; 9.30am-10pm; M East Nanjing Rd) and the Orient Shopping Centre (Dōngfāng Shāngshà; Map p122; ☎ 6487 0000; 8 North Caoxi Rd; 曹溪北路8号; M Xujiahui).

Popular children's films tend to make it to the silver screen in Shànghǎi, so check with cinemas (see p189) to see what's on, and check the film is the English version (英文版; yīngwénbǎn). A trip on the world's first MagLev train (see boxed text, p246) could set little hearts racing.

Active Kidz Shanghai (Map p132; ☎ 6406 6757; www.activekidz.org; Nice Year Villas, AKS Office, Bldg A1-0, 3333 Hongmei Rd; 虹梅路3333号A1-0楼) is a nonprofit initiative aimed at prising expat kids away from the TV screen by providing sports and recreational activities, including after-school sports and summer camps, Saturday baseball and Sunday football.

In general 1.4m is the cut-off height for children's cheaper fares or entry tickets. Children under 0.8m normally get in for free.

For health problems, try the Children's Hospital of Fudan University (Fùdàn Dàxué Fùshǔ Értóng Yīyuàn; Map pp62–3; ☎ 6493 1507; www.ch.shmu.edu.cn; 399 Wanyuan Rd; 万源路399号), which has a foreign-expatriate ward.

For advice on travelling with children, pick up the latest edition of Lonely Planet's *Travel with Children*.

CLIMATE

For detailed information on climate in Shànghǎi, see p53.

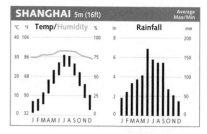

COURSES
Cooking

The Chinese Cooking Workshop (Zhōnghuá Liàolǐ Jiàoshì; Map pp98–9; www.chinesecookingworkshop.com; room 307, 696 Weihai Rd; 威海路696号307室) and the Kitchen...at Huaihai (Map pp86–7; ☎ 6433 2700; www

.thekitchenat.com; No 40, Lane 1487, Middle Huaihai Rd; 淮海中路1487弄40号) hold regular classes teaching everything from Sichuanese to Thai cuisines.

Language

Countless language schools have been set up to feed the throng of eager expats aiming to master Mandarin. It's advisable to talk to students first to gauge their satisfaction with a school's teaching methods. The following language schools are reputable and offer group or private tuition.

iMandarin (Map pp98–9; ☎ 3222 1028; www.imandarin .net; suite 721, Shanghai Centre, 1376 West Nanjing Rd; 南京西路1376号721室) With six branches, new classes start each week; from beginners to advanced, children's courses, summer camps, business Mandarin. Cantonese classes also offered.

Mandarin Center (Wénhuà Yánxí Zhōngxīn; Map pp86–7; ☎ 6270 7665; www.mandarin-center.com; No 2, Lane 113, Changshu Rd; 常熟路113弄2号) Part-run by the humanities department of Fudan University, with evening and weekend Mandarin classes, as well as instruction in Shanghainese dialect. Another branch in Pǔdōng.

Mandarin House (Měihé Hànyǔ; Map pp98–9; ☎ 6288 2308; www.mandarinhouse.cn; room 1901-1903 Plaza 66, 1266 West Nanjing Rd; 南京西路1266号1901-1903室) With four branches around town, new classes start each week. Courses at all levels, with an average of four to six students per class.

CULTURAL CENTRES

The following are useful places to keep you culturally connected to your home country and fellow expats, and are also a good place to meet some internationally minded Shanghainese.

Alliance Française (Shànghǎi Fǎyǔ Péixùn Zhōngxīn; Map p116; ☎ 6357 5388; www.afshanghai.org; 5th & 6th fl, 297 Wusong Rd; 吴淞路297号5 & 6楼) There's fantastic French cinema at the ciné-club on the last Friday of each month at 6.30pm; admission is free. Also at hand is a large French library with magazines, newspapers, DVDs and music CDs; plus exhibitions, music concerts and literary events are held. The centre also offers French language courses and internet access. Another branch (Map pp128–9; ☎ 6226 4005; 2nd fl, 155 Wuyi Rd) can be found in the west of town.

British Council (Yīngguó Wénhuà Jiàoyùchù; Map pp66–7; ☎ 6391 2626; www.britishcouncil.org.cn; Cross Tower, 318 Fuzhou Rd; 福州路318号; ⊙ 9am-5.30pm Mon-Fri) Of interest mainly to Chinese wishing to study in the UK, but it does have recent British newspapers and music magazines such as Q and NME.

Goethe Institute (Gēdé Xuéyuàn; Map pp66–7; ☎ 6391 2068; www.goethe.de/china; Rm 102A, Cross Tower, 318 Fuzhou Rd; 福州路318号102A室) There's a useful library, film screenings, internet access and German courses.

US Consulate Bureau of Public Affairs (Map pp98–9; ☎ 6279 7662; room 532, Shanghai Centre, 1376 West Nanjing Rd; 南京西路1376号532室) This has a reading room with American newspapers and periodicals.

CUSTOMS REGULATIONS

Chinese customs generally pay tourists little attention. There are clearly marked green channels and red channels.

Duty-free, you're allowed to import up to 400 cigarettes (or 100 cigars or 500g of tobacco), 1.5 litres of alcoholic drink and 50g of gold or silver. Importation of fresh fruit or cold cuts is prohibited. Each person is allowed to enter China with one camera, one video camera and a single laptop. Passengers under the age of 16 are not allowed to carry cigarettes or alcohol.

You can legally bring in or take out only Y6000 in Chinese currency. There are no restrictions on foreign currency; however, you should declare any cash that exceeds US$5000 (or its equivalent in another currency).

It's illegal to import into China printed material, film, tapes etc that are 'detrimental to China's politics, economy, culture and ethics'. But don't be too concerned about what you take to read. Pirated DVDs and CDs are illegal exports from China as well as illegal imports into most other countries. If they are found they will be confiscated.

Antiques over 200 years old may be prohibited from export. To be on the safe side, make sure that you have a receipt and business card from the dealer for anything that you purchase. See p137 for more details.

ELECTRICITY

Electricity is 220V, 50 cycles AC. Plugs come in at least four designs: three-pronged angled pins (as in Australia), three-pronged round pins (as in Hong Kong), two flat pins (US-style but without the ground wire), and two narrow round pins (European style).

Conversion plugs and voltage converters are easily found if you need to convert from a Chinese to foreign system but are a pain to track down the other way round. Bring all your converters with you.

EMBASSIES & CONSULATES

Most consulates defer to their embassies in Běijīng; the offices listed below are consulates-general. Most consulates have efficient websites with useful information, from doing business in Shànghǎi to cultural relations, events and downloadable maps of town.

Consulates often have useful information packs for long-term residents, covering things like estate agents, lawyers and hospitals. The US embassy produces a brochure entitled 'Tips for Travellers to the People's Republic of China', which you can get before you travel.

If you are planning a trip to Southeast Asia you'll have to go to Běijīng or Hong Kong for a visa for Vietnam, Laos or Myanmar. There is a Vietnamese consulate in Guǎngzhōu, and Thai, Lao and Myanmar embassies in Kūnmíng.

Australia (Àodàlìyà Lǐngshìguǎn; Map pp98–9; ☎ 5292 5500; www.shanghai.china.embassy.gov.au; 22nd fl, Citic Sq, 1168 West Nanjing Rd; 南京西路1168号 22楼; visa office (Map pp98–9; ☎ 6279 8098; fax 6279 8022; suite 401, Shanghai Centre, 1376 West Nanjing Rd; ☖ 8.30am-noon & 1.30-3.30pm Mon-Fri)

Canada (Jiānádà Lǐngshìguǎn; Map pp98–9; ☎ 3279 2800; www.shanghai.gc.ca; suite 604, Shanghai Centre, 1376 West Nanjing Rd; 南京西路1376号604室); visa office (Map pp98–9; ☎ 3279 2844; suite 668, East Tower, Shanghai Centre; ☖ 8.45-11am & 1.30-4pm Mon-Thu)

France (Fǎguó Lǐngshìguǎn; Map pp66–7; ☎ 6103 2200; room 201, 2nd fl, Hai Tong Securities Bldg, 689 Guangdong Rd; 广东路689号2楼201室)

Germany (Déguó Lǐngshìguǎn; Map pp86–7; ☎ 3401 0106; www.shanghai.diplo.de; 181 Yongfu Rd; 永福路 181号)

Ireland (Ài'ěrlán Lǐngshìguǎn; Map pp98–9; ☎ 6279 8729; www.embassyofireland.cn/ireland/consulate.htm; suite 700A, West Tower, Shanghai Centre, 1376 West Nanjing Rd; 南京西路1376号700A室; ☖ 9.30am-12.30pm & 2-5.30pm)

Japan (Rìběn Lǐngshìguǎn; Map pp128–9; ☎ 5257 4766; fax 6278 8988; 8 Wanshan Rd; 万山路8号)

Netherlands (Hélán Lǐngshìguǎn; Map pp128–9; ☎ 2208 7288; www.hollandinchina.org; 10th fl, East Tower, Dawning Center, 500 Hongbaoshi Rd; 红宝石路500号东银中心东塔10楼; ☖ 9am-noon & 1-5pm Mon-Fri)

New Zealand (Xīnxīlán Lǐngshìguǎn; Map pp86–7; ☎ 5407 5858; www.nzembassy.com; room 1605-1607A, The Centre, 989 Changle Rd; 长乐路989号1605-

1607A室; ☖ 8.30am-5pm Mon-Fri); visa office (Map pp98–9; ☎ 6279 7368; suite 507, Shanghai Centre, 1376 West Nanjing Rd; 南京西路1376号507室)

Russia (Éluósī Lǐngshìguǎn; Map p116; ☎ 6324 2682; fax 6306 9982; 20 Huangpu Rd; 黄浦路20号; ☖ 9.30am-noon Mon, Wed & Fri)

Singapore (Xīnjiāpō Lǐngshìguǎn; Map pp128–9; ☎ 6278 5566; www.mfa.gov.sg/shanghai/; 89 Wanshan Rd; 万山路89号)

Thailand (Tàiwángguó Lǐngshìguǎn; Map pp98–9; ☎ 6288 3030; www.thaishanghai.com; 15th fl, 567 Weihai Rd; 威海路567号15楼; visa office ☖ 9.30-11.30am Mon-Fri)

UK (Yīngguó Lǐngshìguǎn; Map pp98–9; ☎ 3279 2000, visa office ☎ 6279 8130; www.uk.cn; room 301, Shanghai Centre, 1376 West Nanjing Rd; 南京西路1376号 301室)

USA (Měiguó Lǐngshìguǎn; Map pp86–7; www.usembassy-china.org.cn/shanghai; 1469 Middle Huaihai Rd, entrance on Wulumuqi Rd; 淮海中路1469号乌鲁木齐路); US Citizen Services & Visas (Map pp98–9; ☎ 3217 4650, after-hours emergency for US citizens 6433 3936; 8th fl, Westgate Tower, 1038 West Nanjing Rd; 南京西路1038号8楼)

EMERGENCY

Ambulance (☎ 120)

Fire (☎ 119)

Police (☎ 110)

GAY & LESBIAN TRAVELLERS

Local law is ambiguous on this issue, but generally the authorities take a dim view of gays and lesbians. A growing scene exists in Shànghǎi, however, as proven by several gay bars (such as p181, p182 and p184) and China's first gay-pride week in 2009. Chinese men sometimes hold hands; this carries no sexual overtones in China.

For up-to-date information on the latest gay and lesbian hot spots in Shànghǎi and elsewhere throughout China try the Utopia website (www.utopia-asia.com/chinshan.htm). *City Weekend* also runs a bimonthly gay and lesbian column.

HEALTH

Health concerns for travellers to Shànghǎi include pollution, traveller's diarrhoea and winter influenza. Health facilities have improved enormously over the last 10 years and you can find a more than adequate standard of medical care here, providing you have good travel insurance.

If you have arrived from South America or Central Africa you are required to show proof of a yellow-fever vaccination within the last 10 years.

It's a good idea to consult your own government's official travel-health website before departure.

Australia (www.smartraveller.com.au)

Canada (www.hc-sc.gc.ca)

New Zealand (www.mfat.govt.nz/travel)

UK (www.doh.gov.uk)

US (www.cdc.gov/travel)

Recommended Vaccinations

You should see your doctor at least three months before your trip in order to get your vaccinations in time. The following immunisations are recommended for Shànghǎi.

Diphtheria & tetanus (DT) Booster of 0.5ml every 10 years. It will cause a sore arm and redness at the injection site.

Hepatitis A & B (combined in Twinrix) 1ml at day one, day 30 and six months. Minimal soreness at injection site. You are not immune until after the final shot. If you don't have time for the six-month booster you will be fully immune for one year for hepatitis A after the second shot and have some immunity for hepatitis B. You may be able to get the third shot at an international medical clinic while travelling.

Influenza Dose of 0.5ml is recommended if you are travelling in the winter months and especially if you are over 60 years of age or have a chronic illness. It should not be given if you are allergic to eggs. Immunity lasts for one year.

Japanese encephalitis A series of three shots over one month only if you plan on being in rural areas for longer than a month. Immunity will last for three years. As there is a risk of an allergic reaction to the second and third shots you must remain close to medical care after you receive these.

Polio Dose of 0.5ml syrup orally every 10 years. There are no side effects.

Typhoid Booster of 0.5ml every three years. Minimal soreness at the injection site.

Do not have any of these immunisations if you are pregnant or breastfeeding. It is possible to have a shot of gammaglobulin in pregnancy, which gives short-term (four to five months) protection against hepatitis and other viral infections. It is not a common thing to do because it is derived from blood products.

Diseases
AIDS & SEXUALLY TRANSMITTED DISEASES
AIDS is rapidly increasing in China. Always wear a condom if you have sex with a stranger and never share needles.

AVIAN INFLUENZA
Avian influenza, or 'bird flu', presents only a very remote risk to travellers at this time. From 2004 the avian H5N1 virus caused illness in domestic birds around the world. The virus is passed from healthy migratory birds to domestic birds such as chickens and ducks, which then may become sick and die. Transmission has occurred from domestic birds to humans, however it is rare and requires close contact with an infected bird or its droppings. By early 2006 a total of 166 human cases had been confirmed by the World Health Organization (WHO) and 88 people had died. These human cases occurred in Indonesia, Thailand, Vietnam, Cambodia, Turkey, Iraq and China. At the time of writing, China had reported 38 human cases and 25 deaths.

The WHO recommends the following precautions for travellers to affected countries: avoid live poultry markets, avoid eating raw or undercooked poultry or eggs, wash hands frequently, and seek medical attention if you develop a fever and respiratory symptoms (cough, shortness of breath etc).

You can keep up to date on the current situation by visiting the World Health Organization website (www.who.int).

CHOLERA
This bacterial infection comes in epidemics and is spread from sewage contamination in poverty-stricken areas. It causes profound vomiting and diarrhoea. The WHO stopped recommending the cholera vaccine because it is ineffective. Prevent cholera by avoiding local seafood restaurants, local water and street stalls with substandard hygiene.

GIARDIASIS
This parasite often jumps on board when you have diarrhoea. It then causes a more prolonged illness with intermittent diarrhoea or looseness, bloating, fatigue and some nausea. There may be a metallic taste in the mouth. You can prevent giardiasis by avoiding potentially contaminated foods and always washing your hands before eating. Treatment is with Fasigyn or Flagyl.

HEPATITIS A

This virus is common in Shànghǎi and is transmitted through contaminated water and shellfish. It is most commonly caught at local seafood restaurants. Immunisation and avoiding suspicious restaurants will help prevent it. If you do get hepatitis A it means six to eight weeks of illness and future intolerance to alcohol.

HEPATITIS B

While this is common in the area, it is transmitted only by unprotected sex, sharing needles, treading on a discarded needle, or receiving contaminated blood. You should always use a condom, never share needles, and always protect your feet on commonly used beaches. Vaccination against hepatitis B before you travel is a wise option as it can be a chronic, debilitating illness.

INFLUENZA

Shànghǎi has a bad flu season over the cold winter months from December to March. The flu is essentially a cold but with a high fever and aches and pains. You should wash your hands frequently, avoid anybody you know who has the flu, and think about having a flu shot before you travel. Secondary bronchitis is the most common complication of the flu and may require antibiotics.

JAPANESE ENCEPHALITIS

Mosquitoes that feed on birds carry this potentially fatal virus, hence it is limited to rural areas of China, particularly near rice fields. It is most common in summer and autumn. If you avoid mosquito bites you will not get this! Vaccination is recommended if you are travelling in rural areas for longer than one month.

MALARIA

Prophylactic tablets are required only if you are travelling to remote rural communities below 1500m of the following latitudes: from July to November north of latitude 33°N, from May to December between 33°N and 25°N, and throughout the year south of 25°N. For day trips out of Shànghǎi you do not need tablets, though you should take precautions against bites. Mosquitoes that bite between dusk and dawn transmit malaria, so use your DEET insect repellent often.

TRAVELLER'S DIARRHOEA

This is the most common disease that a traveller will encounter throughout Asia. Many different types of organisms, usually bacteria (eg E. coli, salmonella) are responsible and the result is sudden diarrhoea and vomiting or both, with or without fever. It is caught from contaminated food or water. Most locals become immune to the bugs after living in an area for a while so travellers are more at risk, and it usually occurs within the first week of exposure.

TUBERCULOSIS (TB)

The risk of this bacterial infection for travellers is low as it requires prolonged exposure of a weakened immune system to catch it. However, children should have the BCG inoculation if you are going to live in China for longer than six months. Adults should never receive the BCG as it is ineffective against the strains of TB that they are more susceptible to, and can cause a nasty reaction at the injection site.

TYPHOID FEVER

Otherwise known as salmonella, typhoid fever is common throughout China and is caught from faecally contaminated food, milk and water. It manifests as fever, headache, cough, malaise and constipation or diarrhoea. Treatment is with quinoline antibiotics, and a vaccine is recommended before you travel.

Environmental Hazards
POLLUTION

The air quality in Shànghǎi is dreadful, especially on still days. If you suffer from asthma or other allergies you may anticipate a worsening of your symptoms here and you may need to increase your medication. Eye drops may be a useful addition to your travel kit, and contact-lens wearers may have more discomfort here.

WATER

Don't drink tap water or eat ice. Bottled water is readily available. Boiled water is OK.

Online Resources

There is a wealth of travel-health advice on the internet. The Lonely Planet website (www.lonelyplanet.com) is a good place to start. The WHO publishes a book called *International Travel and Health,* which is revised annually and is available online at no cost at www.who.int/publications/en.

HOLIDAYS

Many of the entries below are nominal holidays and do not qualify for a day off work.

New Year's Day (Yuándàn) 1 January

Spring Festival (Chūn Jié) 3 February 2011; 23 January 2012. Also known as Chinese New Year. Officially three days, but it's generally a week-long break.

Tomb Sweeping Day (Qīngmíng Jié) First weekend in April. A three-day weekend.

International Labour Day (Láodòng Jié) 1 May. The closest thing communists have to a nationwide religious holiday.

Dragon Boat Festival (Duānwǔ Jié) 16 June 2010, 6 June 2011

Mid-Autumn Festival (Zhōngqiū Jié) 22 September 2010, 12 September 2011

National Day (Guóqìng Jié) 1 October. Officially three days, but often morphs into a week-long vacation. Celebrates the founding of the PRC in 1949.

For more holidays and festivals, see p16.

INSURANCE

It's very likely that a health-insurance policy you contribute to in your home country will *not* cover you in China – if unsure, ask your insurance company. If you're not covered, it would be prudent to purchase travel insurance.

The best policies will reimburse you for a variety of mishaps such as accidents, illness, theft and even the purchase of an emergency ticket home. Paying for your air ticket with a credit card often provides limited travel-accident insurance. Ask your credit-card company exactly what it covers.

Some backpacker policies offer a cheaper option, that provides only medical cover and not baggage loss, which might be worthwhile if you are not carrying any valuables. Many policies require you to pay the first US$100 or so anyway and will only cover valuables up to a set limit, so if you lose a US$1000 camera you might find yourself only covered for US$350 and having to pay the first US$100.

To make a claim for compensation, you will need proper documentation (hopefully in English). This can include medical reports, police reports and baggage receipts from airlines. You may prefer a policy that pays hospitals directly rather than you having to pay on the spot (often before you receive treatment) and claiming later. Check that the policy covers repatriation and an emergency flight home.

Insurance policies can normally be extended once you are in Shànghǎi by a phone call or online. Make sure you do this *before* the policy expires or you may have to pay a higher premium.

INTERNET ACCESS

China has the world's largest online population, with almost 300 million internet users in 2009. The authorities are keenly aware of the critical role the internet plays in economic prosperity, but they remain highly mistrustful of the technology. As a sophisticated tool for accessing and disseminating information, the internet is regarded as an electronic nemesis by Běijīng's Orwellian censors. It's also blamed for a host of social ills, from teenage delinquency to crime and violence. Internet censorship – known as the Great Firewall of China – is draconian, with an army of 30,000 censors working nonstop to stem the tide of undesirable electronic data from corrupting Chinese minds. The authorities block around 10% of websites and sites like Google or YouTube will sporadically go down, but most online newspapers can be read. Internet monitors are employed by the state to discreetly usher online chat-room discussions on topical and sensitive issues in authorised directions. To get around a blocked website in China, use a proxy like g-proxy.com or download an add-on such as Gladder (for Firefox browsers). The latest addition to the filtering measures is the Green Dam software that will allegedly be used to block pornography, but which most think is in fact government spyware used to collect individual user information. China originally wanted to make installation mandatory on all computers sold in the PRC, however, for the time being, it remains optional.

Most travellers make constant use of internet cafes and free web-based email accounts. Occasionally – as happened in June 2009 – email providers (in this case, Gmail) can go down, so having a backup email address is advised.

The majority of hostels and hotels have internet access; avoid going online in hotel business centres as rates are stratospheric. Most midrange and top-end hotels provide broadband internet, for which there may be a charge. A growing number of hotels, restaurants and cafes provide wireless internet access, so getting online with a laptop is a breeze. Remember that wi-fi is generally unsecured, so take care what kind of information you enter if you're using a wireless connection.

Email Centres & Internet Cafes

Internet cafes in Shànghǎi – mostly gaming dens stuffed with chain-smoking adolescents – are reasonably plentiful although licences are strictly controlled. Hourly rates at internet cafes start at around Y3 per hour. Internet cafes are typically either open 24 hours or from 8am to midnight. You will need some form of ID to register; take your passport. Connections range from reasonably fast to maddeningly slow. Besides the places listed below, many bars and cafes have consoles or wi-fi access where you can get online. The easiest way to find the nearest internet cafe is to ask someone if there is a *wǎngbā* (网吧) nearby.

China Telecom (Zhōngguó Diànxìn; Map pp66–7; 30 East Nanjing Rd; 南京东路30号; per hr Y10; ⏰ 7am-10.30pm)

Eastday B@r (Dōngfāng Wǎngdiàn; Map pp86–7; 24 Ruijin No 2 Rd; 瑞金东二路24号; per hr Y3; ⏰ 8am-2am)

Highland Internet Café (Zhìgāodiǎn Wǎngbā; Map pp66–7; 4th fl, Mànkèdùn Guǎngchǎng, East Nanjing Rd; 南京东路曼克顿广场4楼; per hr Y3; ⏰ 24hr)

Huiyuan Internet Café (Huìyuán Wǎngbā; Map p122; 2nd fl, 1887 Huashan Rd; 华山路1887号2楼; per hr Y4; ⏰ 24hr)

Jidu Kongjian Internet Café (Jídù Kōngjiān Wǎngbā; Map pp86–7; cnr North Xiangyang Rd & Changle Rd; 襄阳北路、长乐路交叉口; per hr Y3; ⏰ 24hr) Game den.

Shanghai Library (Shànghǎi Túshūguǎn; Map pp86–7; 1555 Middle Huaihai Rd; 淮海中路1555号; per hr Y4; ⏰ 8.30am-8.30pm) Has an internet room (open from 9am to 8.30pm) and is the cheapest and most pleasant place in the city for internet use (minimum one hour). Bring your passport or ID if you have no library card. Connections are generally pretty fast. Wi-fi access is available from 3.30pm to 8.30pm.

Tourist Information and Service Centre (Lǚyóu Zīxún Fúwù Zhōngxīn; Map pp86–7; 138 South Chengdu Rd; 成都南路138号; ⏰ 9am-8.30pm) Get online here for 30 minutes (one terminal only; Y5).

Xuandong Internet Café (Xuàndòng Wǎngbā; Map pp98–9; 4th fl, West Nanjing Rd; 南京西路; per hr Y3; ⏰ 24hr) Opposite Children's Palace, and next to a noisy amusement arcade.

LEGAL MATTERS

China does not officially recognise dual nationality or the foreign citizenship of children born in China if one of the parents is a PRC national. If you have Chinese and another nationality you may, in theory, not be allowed to visit China on your foreign passport. In practice, Chinese authorities are not switched on enough to know if you own two passports, and will accept you on a foreign passport. Dual-nationality citizens who enter China on a Chinese passport are subject to Chinese laws and are legally not allowed consular help.

Women over 20 and men over the age of 22 can legally marry. The minimum legal age for obtaining a driving licence is 18. There is no minimum legal age for drinking.

China takes a particularly dim view of opium and all its derivatives. Shànghǎi's foreign concessions owe their entire existence to the 1842 Opium War and many a foreign fortune (including those of some of Hong Kong's largest companies) was made through the opium trade. Today Shànghǎi has a growing drug problem, this time in heroin.

Foreign-passport holders have been executed in China for drug offences, and one US citizen convicted on drug-related charges received a 15-year prison sentence. Trafficking in more than 50g of heroin can lead to the death penalty. Many Uighurs deal quite openly in marijuana (*dàmá*) in Shànghǎi.

The Chinese criminal justice system does not ensure a fair trial and defendants are not presumed innocent until proven guilty. China conducts more judicial executions than the rest of the world combined, up to 10,000 per year according to some reports. If arrested, most foreign citizens have the right to contact their embassy.

LIBRARIES

Shanghai Library (Shànghǎi Túshūguǎn; Map pp86–7; ☎ 6445 5555; www.library.sh.cn/; 1555 Middle Huaihai Rd; 淮海中路1555号; ⏰ 8.30am-8.30pm) is China's largest public library, with a copy of Rodin's *The Thinker* plonked outside. For a postmodern white-tile building, it is actually quite impressive. Y25 gets you a reading card valid for a year, which allows you to read but not borrow foreign publications. The same card for books in Chinese costs Y10. A card to borrow Chinese-language books is Y15 per year, with a deposit of Y100; to borrow foreign-language publications, the card costs Y50 per year, with a deposit of Y1000 (residency permit required). A temporary library card, valid for one month, costs Y10. The 3rd floor has a wealth of foreign magazines and newspapers such as *Newsweek* and *National Geographic*. For English books published within the last four years, head to the 4th-floor Foreign Language Reading Room, otherwise you have to track books down on the computer system then order them through the stacks. The library has a useful internet room (opposite). The stupendous antiquarian collection of the former Jesuit Bibliotheca Zi-Ka-Wei (p123) can be visited between 2pm and 4pm on Saturday.

MAPS

The most convenient place to pick up free tourist maps of Shànghǎi is at Pudong International Airport after luggage collection. Decent English-language maps of Shànghǎi are also available from English-language bookshops such as Chaterhouse (p142) and most top-end hotels.

Geocenter's *Shanghai* has a detailed map of central Shànghǎi, with a street index on the back; the index is particularly useful if you are searching for an address. Periplus is another good choice, with a clear, bilingual 1:15,000 map of Shànghǎi, an additional 1:85,000 map of Pǔdōng and inserts of Sūzhōu, Hángzhōu and the surrounding provinces. Insight also publishes a good map of Shànghǎi.

Locally made English maps of Shànghǎi are available from most bookshops. The best two are the *Shanghai Tourist Map* (with a useful street index, blow-ups of the main areas, and insert maps of Hángzhōu and Sūzhōu) and the *Shanghai Official Tourist Map* (which has details of Shànghǎi's main shopping streets). The 'English maps' offered by hawkers on the Bund are often just a maze of characters.

Quality online maps are available through Google at www.maps.google.com (English) or www.ditu.google.cn (Chinese).

MEDICAL SERVICES
Clinics

Shànghǎi is credited with the best medical facilities and most advanced medical knowledge in mainland China. The main foreign embassies keep lists of the English-speaking doctors, dentists and hospitals that accept foreigners. The children's hospital is listed on p254.

Huashan Hospital (Huáshān Yīyuàn; Map pp86–7; ☎ 5288 9998; www.sh-hwmc.com.cn; 12 Middle Wulumuqi Rd; 乌鲁木齐中路12号) Hospital treatment and outpatient consultations are available at the

8th-floor foreigners' clinic (open 8am to 10pm daily), with 24-hour emergency treatment on the 15th floor in Building 6.

Parkway Health (以极佳医疗保健服务; ☎ 24hr hotline 6445 5999; www.parkwayhealth.cn); Jìng'ān (Map pp98–9; suite 203, Shanghai Centre, 1376 West Nanjing Rd; 南京西路1376号203室), Hóngqiáo (Map pp128–9; unit 30, Mandarine City, 788 Hongxu Rd; 虹许路788号30室). There are six locations around town. Offers comprehensive private medical care from internationally trained physicians and dentists. Consultation fees are around Y800 to Y1800. Members can access after-hours services and an emergency hotline.

Shanghai First People's Hospital/International Medical Care Centre (IMCC) (Shànghǎi Shì Dìyī Rénmín Yīyuàn; Map p116; ☎ 6306 9480, 6324 0090 ext 2101; 585 Jiulong Rd; 九龙路585号)

Shanghai United Family Hospital (Shànghǎi Hémùjiā Yīyuàn; Map pp62–3; ☎ 2216 3900, 24hr emergency 2216 1999; www.unitedfamilyhospitals.com; 1139 Xianxia Rd; 仙霞路1139号) This Western-owned and -managed hospital is a complete private hospital, staffed by doctors trained in the West. Medical facilities run to inpatient rooms, operating rooms, an intensive-care unit and birthing suites.

Other contacts for medical assistance include the following:

Huadong Hospital (Huádōng Yīyuàn Wàibīn Ménzhěn; Map pp86–7; ☎ 6248 3180, ext 63208; 2nd fl, Bldg 3, 221 West Yan'an Rd, Foreigners Clinic; 延安西路221号3号楼2层; ☻ 24hr emergency)

International Peace Maternity Hospital (Guójì Fùyòu Bǎojiànyuàn; Map p122; ☎ 6407 0434; 910 Hengshan Rd; 衡山路910号)

Ruijin Hospital (Ruìjīn Yīyuàn; Map pp86–7; ☎ 6437 0045; 197 Ruijin No 2 Rd; 瑞金二路197号)

Shanghai Chiropractic & Osteopathic Clinic (Shànghǎi Jǐzhuī Yīliáo Zhōngxīn; Map pp86–7; ☎ 5213 0008; www.spine.sh.cn; 7th fl, 937 West Yan'an Rd, cnr Jiangsu Rd; 延安西路937号7层)

Dental Services

Arrail Dental (Ruì'ěr Chǐkē; Map pp86–7; ☎ 5396 6539; www.arrail-dental.com; 2nd fl, 2 Corporate Avenue, 202 Hubin Rd; 湖滨路202号企业天地商业中心2号楼2楼)

Dr Harriet Jin's Dental Surgery (Jīn Yīshēng Kǒuqiāng Zhěnsuǒ; Map p122; ☎ 6448 0882; room 1904, South Bldg, Huiyin Plaza, 2088 Huashan Rd; 华山路2088号汇银广场南楼1904室)

Shanghai Dental Medical Centre (Shànghǎi Kǒuqiāng Yīliáo Zhōngxīn; Map p79; ☎ 6445 5999; 7th fl, 9th People's Hospital, 639 Zhizaoju Rd; 制造局路639号 第 九人民医院7层)

Shanghai United Family Hospital (Shànghǎi Hémùjiā Yīyuàn; Map pp62–3; ☎ 2216 3999; www.unitedfamily hospitals.com; 1139 Xianxia Rd; 仙霞路1139号)

Shenda Dental Clinic (Shēndà Chǐkē; Map p122; ☎ 6437 7987; 8th fl, 807 Zhaojiabang Rd; 肇嘉浜路807号8楼)

Medical Testing

Foreigners planning to live in Shànghǎi for six months or more are required to undergo an AIDS test. You can do the test outside China and present the results to obtain the required certificate, but there is a chance that you may still have to take a local test.

For inquiries and medical tests contact the Shanghai Health & Quarantine Bureau (Shànghǎi Guójì Wèishēng Lǚxíng Bǎojiàn Zhōngxīn; Map p132; ☎ 6268 8851; www.sithc.com; 15 Jinbang Rd; 金浜路15号; ⊗ 8am-noon & 1-4pm Mon-Fri). If you need to undertake a test here, try to get an early-morning slot as it gets busy later on. Full medical tests for the purposes of securing a residence permit (p268) cost Y702 (Y376 for students) – you will also need to take along three photos, your passport, photocopies of your passport information and visa pages, and a copy of your company business licence.

Pharmacies

The Hong Kong store Watson's (Qūchénshì; Map pp86–7; ☎ 6474 4775; 787 Middle Huaihai Rd; 淮海中路787号) can be found in the basements of malls all over town (there's a branch in Westgate Mall; Map pp98–9), mainly selling imported toiletries and a limited range of simple over-the-counter pharmaceuticals.

For harder-to-find foreign medicines try any pharmacy (药房; yàofáng), easily identified by a green cross outside. Nearly all pharmacies stock both Chinese and Western medicines. Take along the chemical/pharmaceutical as well as the brand name of your medicine, in case it is sold under a different name in China. Some pharmacy medicines are sold over the counter in Shànghǎi, so you won't necessarily need a prescription, but check.

The following pharmacies have a large range of medicines:

Huashi Pharmacy (Huáshì Yàofáng; Map pp86–7; ⊗ 24hr) Outside Huashan Hospital on Middle Wulumuqi Rd.

Shanghai No 1 Pharmacy (Dìyī Yīyào Shāngdiàn; ☎ 6322 4567; Map pp66–7; 616 East Nanjing Rd; 南京东路616号)

Wuyao Pharmacy (Wǔyào Dàyàofáng; Map pp86–7; 619 Fanyu Rd; 番禺路619号; ⊗ 24hr)

One of Shànghǎi's most famous Chinese herbal-medicine stores is Cai Tong De (Map pp66–7; 450 East Nanjing Rd; 南京东路450号). You can find a branch of Běijīng's celebrated pharmacy Tong Ren Tang (Map pp128–9; 1672 West Yan'an Rd, cnr Fahuazhen Rd; 延安西路1672号; ⊗ 8.30am-8pm) in Chángníng.

Traditional Chinese Medicine

Traditional Chinese medicine (TCM) is extremely popular in Shànghǎi, both for prevention and cure. There are many Chinese medicine shops, but English is not widely spoken. Chiropractic care, reflexology and acupuncture are popular, but check that disposable needles are used.

Body and Soul TCM Clinic (Map p79; ☎ 5101 9262; www.bodyandsoul.com.cn; suite 5, 14th fl, Anji Plaza, 760 South Xizang Rd; 西藏南路760号安基大厦14层 5室) International staff integrating TCM and Western medical practices. Acupuncture available.

Dr Li Jie's Chinese Medical Clinic (Lǐjié Zhōngyī Zhěnsuǒ; Map p122; ☎ 3424 1989; www.ljtcm.com.cn; 5C, No 28, Lane 18, Hongqiao Rd; 虹桥路18弄28号5C)

Longhua Hospital (Lónghuá Zhōngyīyuàn; Map p122; ☎ 6438 5700; 725 South Wanping Rd; 零陵路725号) A kilomete northeast of Shanghai Stadium.

Shanghai Qigong Institute (Shànghǎi Qìgōng Yánjiūsuǒ; Map pp86–7; ☎ 6387 5180 ext 220; top fl, 218 Nanchang Rd; 法租界南昌路218号; ⊗ 8am-4.30pm) Part of Shànghǎi's TCM school, the Qigong Institute offers qigong (qì-energy development) treatments and massage (Y280), as well as acupuncture sessions (Y280). No English is spoken; call for an appointment.

Shuguang Hospital (Map pp86–7; ☎ 6385 5617; 185 Pu'an Rd; 普安路185号) Next to Huaihai Park.

MONEY

The Chinese currency is known as Renminbi (RMB), or 'people's money'. Officially, the basic unit of RMB is the yuán (Y), which is divided into 10 jiǎo, which again is divided into 10 fēn. In spoken Chinese the yuán is referred to as kuài and jiǎo as máo. The fēn has so little value that it is rarely used these days.

The Bank of China issues RMB bills in denominations of one, two, five, 10, 20, 50 and 100 *yuán.* Coins come in denominations of one *yuán,* five and one *jiǎo,* and one, two and five *fēn* (the last are rare). There are still paper versions of the coins floating around, but these will gradually disappear.

For information regarding exchange rates see the inside front cover. Check p20 for some idea of the costs you are likely to incur during your stay in Shànghǎi.

ATMs

ATMs that take foreign cards are plentiful, but it's generally safest to use Bank of China (中国银行), the Industrial and Commercial Bank of China (工商银行; ICBC) and HSBC (汇丰银行) ATMs, many of which are 24-hour. Many top-end hotels also have ATMs, as do malls and department stores.

A useful 24-hour Citibank ATM (Map pp66–7) is next door to the Peace Hotel on the Bund. The Shanghai Centre (Map pp98–9) has Hongkong and Shanghai Banking Corporation (HSBC), Bank of China, and Industrial and Commercial Bank of China (ICBC) ATMs. Useful 24-hour HSBC ATMs can also be found on the Bund in various locations, at Hong Kong Plaza (Map pp86–7; 282 Middle Huaihai Rd 淮海中路282号) and next to the Regal International East Asia Hotel (Map pp86–7; Hengshan Rd 衡山路).

Changing Money

You can change foreign currency and travellers cheques at money-changing counters at almost every hotel and at many shops, department stores and large banks such as the Bank of China and HSBC, as long as you have your passport. Some top-end hotels will change money only for their guests. Exchange rates in China are uniform wherever you change money, so there's little need to shop around. The Bank of China charges a 0.75% commission to change cash and travellers cheques.

Whenever you change foreign currency into Chinese currency you will be given a money-exchange voucher recording the transaction. You need to show this to change your *yuán* back into any foreign currency. Changing Chinese currency outside China is a problem, though it's quite easily done in Hong Kong.

There's a branch of American Express (Měiguó Yùntōng Gōngsī; Map pp98–9; ☎ 6279 8082; room 455, Shanghai Centre, 1376 West Nanjing Rd; 南京西路1376号455室; ☼ 9am-noon & 1-5.30pm Mon-Fri), but Amex cardholders can also cash personal cheques with their card at branches of the Bank of China, China International Trust & Investment Corporation (Citic), the Bank of Communications or ICBC.

Counterfeit Bills

Counterfeit notes are a problem in China. Very few Chinese will accept a Y50 or Y100 note without first checking to see if it's a fake. Many shopkeepers will run notes under an ultraviolet light looking for signs of counterfeiting; visually checking for forged notes is hard unless you are very familiar with bills, but be aware that street vendors may try and dump forged notes on you in large-denomination change.

Credit Cards

Credit cards are more readily accepted in Shànghǎi than in other parts of China. Most tourist hotels will accept major credit cards (with a 4% processing charge) such as Visa, Amex, MasterCard, Diners and JCB, as will banks, upper-end restaurants and tourist-related shops. Credit hasn't caught on among most Chinese, and most local credit cards are in fact debit cards.

The following are emergency contact numbers in case you lose your card.

American Express (☎ 6279 8082; ☼ 9am-noon & 1-5.30pm) Out of business hours call the 24-hour refund line in Hong Kong (☎ 852-2811 6122).

MasterCard (☎ 108-00-110 7309)

Visa (☎ 108-00-110 2911)

Tipping

Tipping is generally not expected and is even discouraged by the authorities. However, Shànghǎi has always been open to Western ideas and keen to make a buck, so staff are becoming used to it in fancy restaurants, where most people round up the bill. In general there is no need to tip if a service charge has already been added. Hotel porters may expect a tip, but taxi drivers do not.

Travellers Cheques

Besides the advantage of security, travellers cheques are useful in Shànghǎi as the exchange rate is actually more favourable than what you get for cash. You can even cash US-dollars travellers cheques into US-dollars cash for the standard 0.75% commission. Stick to the major companies such as Thomas Cook, American Express and Citibank.

NEWSPAPERS & MAGAZINES

If you want to know what's going on in Shànghǎi, the English-language expat magazines and their associated websites are your best sources of information. They're free and available in most Western-style bars, restaurants and cafes, and in some hotels and art galleries. The classified sections are good places to find accommodation, language teachers and even jobs.

The most comprehensive are the glossy bimonthly *City Weekend* (www.cityweekend .com.cn) and the monthly *That's Shanghai* (www.urbanatomy.com), both packed with cultural info and entertainment listings.

Shànghǎi's other English-language papers and periodicals are anaemic by comparison, but they have national and world news. The Y2 *Shanghai Daily* (www.shanghaidaily.com) is a better read than the insipid national *China Daily* (www.chinadaily.com.cn, Y1), which is often a day out of date. The *Shanghai Daily* has thorough international coverage, albeit largely from wires, and 'Scope', *Shanghai Daily*'s cultural section, has some absorbing articles.

Foreign magazines and newspapers, including the *International Herald Tribune*, the *Financial Times*, the *Asian Wall Street Journal*, *Time*, *Newsweek* and the *Economist* are available in top-end hotels.

ORGANISED TOURS

There are some intriguing tours on offer in Shànghǎi, including the unusual Shanghai Sideways (www.shanghaisideways.com), which provides motorcycle sidecar tours of the city. Night-time cycling tours of the city are available via BOHDI (p196) on Tuesday and Thursday and SISU (p197) on Wednesdays for Y150. Audio tours are available for download from www.tourcaster.com (US$9.95). Jinjiang Tours (Jǐnjiāng Lǚxíngshè; Map pp86–7; ☎ 6445 9525; 191 Changle Rd; 长乐路191号) have one-day (Y4000), half-day (Y250) and night (Y400) English-speaking bus tours that depart from its office on Changle Rd.

PASSPORTS

You must have a passport with you at all times; it is the most basic travel document (all hotels will insist on seeing it). The Chinese government requires that your passport be valid for at least six months after the expiry date of your visa. You'll need at least one entire blank page in your passport for the visa.

Have an ID card with your photo in case you lose your passport, or make photocopies of your passport – your embassy may need these before issuing a new one (a process that can take weeks). Also report the loss to the local Public Security Bureau (PSB; Gōng'ānjú; 公安局). Long-stay visitors should register their passport with their embassy.

PHOTOGRAPHY

Branches of Kodak Express are widespread, and you can burn images to CD there for Y15 to Y20.

POST

The larger tourist hotels and business towers have post offices from where you can mail letters and small packages, and this is by far the most convenient mail option.

Shànghǎi's main post office (Map p116; ☎ 6393 6666; 276 North Suzhou Rd; 苏州北路276号; ⊗ 7am-10pm) is just north of Suzhou Creek in Hóngkǒu.

Useful post offices include the branch across the way from the Site of the 1st National Congress of the CCP in Xīntiāndì (Map pp86–7) and the Shanghai Centre branch (Map pp98–9; 1376 West Nanjing Rd). Post offices and post boxes are green.

Letters and parcels take about a week to reach most overseas destinations; Express Mail Service (EMS) cuts this down to three or four days. Courier companies can take as little as two days. Ubiquitous same-day courier companies (快递; *kuàidì*) can express items within Shànghǎi from Y6 within the same district.

Courier Companies

Several foreign courier companies operate in China with fairly standard prices. The following companies offer door-to-door pick-up and delivery (cash only).

DHL-Sinotrans (Dūnháo Kuàisù; Map pp128–9; ☎ 6275 3543, 800-810 8000; www.dhl.com; Shanghai International Trade Centre, 2201 West Yan'an Rd; 延安西路 2201号) Offices also in Hángzhōu and Sūzhōu.

FedEx Kinko's (Map pp98–9; ☎ 6218 3311; www .fedexkinkos.com.cn; 288 Fengxian Rd; 奉贤路288号; ⊗ 24)

UPS (Yóubìsòng; Map pp86–7; ☎ 6326 6691; www .ups.com; 200 Taicang Rd; 太仓路200号)

RADIO

The BBC World Service can be picked up on 17760, 15278, 21660, 12010 and 9740 kHz. Voice of America (VOA) is often a little clearer at 17820, 15425, 21840, 15250, 9760, 5880 and 6125 kHz. You can find tuning information for the BBC online at www.bbc .co.uk/worldservice/tuning, for Radio Australia at www.abc.net.au/ra, and for VOA at www.voa.gov. Crystal-clear programs from the BBC World Service (www.bbc.co.uk/ worldservice), National Public Radio (www .npr.org) and Radio Australia (www.abc.net .au/ra) can also be heard online.

RELOCATING

The following moving companies can box it up, ship it over, deal with customs officers, and deliver to your new home, though officially only if you have local residency. Prices vary from around US$275 to US$500 per cubic metre, depending on the destination and how much you have to ship. The website www.shanghaiexpat.com has forums and useful info for those planning on moving to Shànghǎi.

Asian Express International Movers (☎ 6258 2244; www.aemovers.com.hk; room 1105, Huasheng Tower, 399 Jiujiang Rd)

Sino Santa Fe (☎ 6233 9700; www.santaferelo.com; 5th fl, Tianhong Bldg, 80 Xianxia Rd)

SAFETY

Shànghǎi feels very safe, and crimes against foreigners are rare; even taxi drivers don't try to rip you off. The virtual absence of sirens or speeding police cars on Shànghǎi's streets creates either a reassuring or worrying picture of crime overall in the city. Don't, however, end up in an ambulance; Shànghǎi drivers don't give way.

If you do get something stolen you need to report the crime at the district PSB office and obtain a police report.

Crossing the road is probably the greatest danger: develop avian vision and a sixth sense to combat the shocking traffic. China's roads kill without mercy; they're the major cause of death for people aged between 15 and 45, with an estimated 600 traffic deaths per day (WHO figures). Older taxis only have seatbelts in the front passenger seat.

Crossing only when it is safe to do so could perch you at the side of the road in perpetuity, but don't imitate the local tendency to cross without looking. The green man at traffic lights does not mean it is safe to cross. Instead, it means it is *slightly safer* to cross, but you can still be run down by traffic allowed to turn on red lights. Bicycles and scooters regularly flout all traffic rules, as do many cars. Bicycles, scooters, mopeds and motorbikes freely take to the footpaths (sidewalks), as occasionally do cars.

Other streets hazards include spent neon-light tubes poking from litter bins, open manholes with plunging drops and welders showering pavements with burning sparks. Side streets off the main drag are sometimes devoid of street lights at night, and pavements can be crumbling and uneven. Also prepare for slippery marbled paving slabs in pedestrian areas (eg on East Nanjing Rd) after rain.

Scams

See the box on p65 for detailed info on Shànghǎi's most common scam.

Watch out for taxi scams, especially at Pudong International Airport and outside the MagLev terminal at Longyang Rd metro station. A registered taxi should always run on a meter and have a licence displayed on the dashboard.

TAXES

All four- and five-star hotels and some top-end restaurants add a service charge of 10% or 15%, which extends to the room and food; all other consumer taxes are included in the price tag.

TELEPHONE

Long-distance phone calls can be placed from hotel rooms, though this is expensive without an internet phonecard (p266). You may need a dial-out number for a direct line. Local calls should be free. For information on using mobile phones in Shànghǎi, see p266.

Apart from streetside card phones, phones are also often attached to magazine kiosks or small shops. Just pick up the phone, make your call, and then pay the attendant (usually five *máo* for a local call). If dialling long-distance within China from Shànghǎi, prefix the number with 17909 for cheaper rates.

Long-distance calls can also be made from any China Telecom (中国电信; Zhōngguó Diànxìn) office. Shànghǎi has hordes of

24-hour phone bars (话吧; *huàbā*), where international calls can be made at cheap rates.

Most international calls cost Y8.20 per minute or Y2.20 to Hong Kong. You are generally required to leave a Y200 deposit for international calls.

Note the following country and city codes:

Běijīng (☎ 010)

People's Republic of China (☎ 00 86)

Shànghǎi (☎ 021)

If calling Shànghǎi or Běijīng from abroad, drop the first zero.

The English-language Shanghai Yellow Pages is available at most business centres or online at http://en.yellowpage.com.cn.

The following numbers are useful:

Enquiry about international calls (☎ 106)

Local directory enquiries (☎ 114)

Weather (☎ 12121)

Mobile Phones

You can certainly take your mobile phone to China, but ensure it is unlocked, which means you can use another network's SIM card in your phone. Alternatively, global SIM cards are available from airports but you might as well wait until you get to China and visit a branch of China Mobile (Zhōngguó Yídòng; 中国移动), which is far cheaper.

Mobile-phone shops (*shǒujīdiàn;* 手机店) can sell you a SIM card, which will cost from Y60 to Y100 and will include Y50 of credit. SIM cards are also available from newspaper kiosks (报刊亭; *bàokāntíng*). When this runs out, you can top up the number by buying a credit-charging card (充值卡; *chōngzhí kǎ*) for Y50 or Y100 worth of credits.

The Chinese avoid the number four (*sì*, (which sounds like but has a different tone from the word for death – *sǐ*) and love the number eight (*bā*). Consequently, the cheapest numbers tend to contain numerous fours and the priciest have strings of eights.

You can rent a mobile phone (Y40 per day, Y200 per week) at Pudong International Airport, but you'll still need to get a SIM card. The deposit is Y800.

Phonecards

Telephone cards (Integrated Circuit – IC; IC卡), available from any China Telecom office, can be used for local and international calls in public phones along the main streets, in telecom offices and in most hotels. Cards come in denominations of Y20, Y30, Y50 and Y100, and there are two kinds: one for use only in Shànghǎi, the other nationwide. Make sure you know which type you are buying.

The internet phonecard (IP card; IP;卡) connects via the internet and is much cheaper than dialling direct. You can use any home phone, some hotel and some public phones (but not card phones) to dial a special telephone number and follow the instructions. Cards can be bought at newspaper kiosks citywide. Cards come in denominations of Y50, Y100, Y200 and Y500 – but they are always discounted, with a Y100 card costing in the region of Y35 to Y40. Again, check that you are buying the right card. Some are for use in Shànghǎi only, while others can be used around the country. Check that the country you wish to call can be called on the card. Generally a safe bet is the CNC *guójì shíguókǎ* (10-country card; 国际十国卡), which can be used for calls to the USA, Canada, Australia, New Zealand, Hong Kong and Macau, Taiwan, England, France, Germany and some East Asian countries. Check the expiry date.

TELEVISION

Expats and travellers staying in midrange and top-end hotels can get their fix of CNN, ESPN, BBC World, HBO, Cinemax and MTV. For the rest, it's slim pickings.

CCTV9 is an English-language cable channel, with stodgy programs on Chinese culture, and hourly news and business reports, all with the usual pro-China bias and censorship.

Around 90% of satellite TV for individual users is the pirated version, which costs around Y1600 for one-off installation (with no subsequent charge)

TIME

Time throughout China is set to Běijīng local time, which is eight hours ahead of GMT/ UTC. There is no daylight-saving time. When it's noon in Shànghǎi, it's 8pm (the day before) in Los Angeles, 11pm (the day before) in Montreal and New York, 4am (the same day) in London, 5am in Frankfurt, Paris and Rome, noon in Hong Kong, 2pm in Melbourne and 4pm in Wellington. Add one hour to these times during the summer.

TOILETS

Shànghǎi has plenty of public toilets. Normally marked by English signs and often charging a small fee, they run the gamut from communal ditches to coin-operated portaloos. The best bet is to head for a top-end hotel, where someone will hand you a towel, pour you some aftershave or exotic hand lotion and wish you a nice day. Fast-food restaurants can be lifesavers. Growing numbers of metro stations have coin-operated toilets.

The golden rule is always carry an emergency stash of toilet paper – you never know when you'll need it and many toilets are devoid of such essentials.

Toilets in hotels are generally sitters, but expect to find squatters in many public toilets. In all but the cheapest hotels it's safe to flush toilet paper down the toilet. If you see a small wastepaper basket in the corner of the toilet, that is where you should throw the toilet paper. Tampons always go in the basket.

Remember, the Chinese characters for men and women are 男 (men) and 女 (women).

TOURIST INFORMATION

There are about a dozen or so Tourist Information and Service Centres (旅游咨询服务中心; Lǚyóu Zīxún Fúwù Zhōngxīn; http://lyw.sh.gov.cn) sprinkled throughout Shànghǎi. The level of information and standard of English spoken by staff varies from passable to nonexistent, and the centres primarily function to book hotel rooms, put you on a tour and sell you souvenirs, but you can get free maps and (sometimes) information from them. For more competent English-language help, call the Shanghai Call Centre (☎ 962 288), a free 24-hour English-language hotline that can respond to cultural, entertainment or transport enquiries (even providing directions for your cab driver).

Tourist Centres include the following:

French Concession (Map pp86–7; ☎ 5386 1882; 138 South Chengdu Rd, just off Middle Huaihai Rd; 成都南路138号; ⏱ 9am-8.30pm)

Huángpǔ (Map pp66–7; ☎ 6357 3718; 518 Jiujiang Rd; 九江路518号; ⏱ 9.30am-8pm)

Jìng'ān (Map pp98–9; ☎ 6248 3259; 1699 West Nanjing Rd; 南京西路1699号; ⏱ 9am-5pm)

Pǔdōng (Map p108; ☎ 3878 0202; 1st fl, Superbrand Mall, 168 Lujiazui Rd; 陆家嘴路168号1楼; ⏱ 9am-6pm)

Yuyuan Gardens (Map p79; ☎ 6355 5032; 149 Jiujiaochang Rd; 旧校场路149号; ⏱ 9am-7pm) Southwest of Yuyuan Gardens.

There is also the useful Shanghai Information Centre for International Visitors (Map pp86–7; ☎ 6384 9366; Xīntiāndì South Block, Bldg 2, Xingye Rd; ⏱ 10am-10pm), where you can pick up a detailed map of Xīntiāndì.

The tourist hotline (☎ 6252 0000; ⏱ 9am-8.30pm) offers a limited English-language service. Your hotel should be able to provide you with most of the tourist information you require and the concierge should have a map of Shànghǎi.

TRAVELLERS WITH DISABILITIES

Shànghǎi's traffic, the city's overpasses and underpasses, and widespread indifference to the plight of the wheelchair-bound are the greatest challenges to disabled travellers. Shànghǎi may have 500,000 wheelchair users, but metro-system escalators only go up to the exit, and not down. Pavements on lesser roads are typically cluttered with bikes, cracked paving slabs, parked cars and other obstacles. Some crossing points, for example at the Xújiāhuì intersection, are impossible to undertake in a wheelchair.

That said, an increasing number of modern buildings, museums, stadiums and most new hotels display the white symbol of a wheelchair, showing that they are wheelchair accessible. It is recommended that you take a lightweight chair for navigating around obstacles and so you can collapse it easily for loading into the back of taxis. Bashi taxis (☎ 6431 2788) has minivan taxis that are wheelchair accessible. All the top-end hotels have wheelchair-accessible rooms. Disabled travellers are advised to travel with at least one able-bodied companion.

China's sign language has regional variations, as well as some elements of American Sign Language (ASL), so foreign signers may have some problems communicating in sign language.

VISAS

For everyone apart from citizens of Japan, Singapore and Brunei, a visa is required for visits to the People's Republic of China. Visas are easily obtainable from Chinese embassies and consulates. Most tourists are issued with a single-entry visa for a 30-day stay, valid for

267

three months from the date of issue. Getting a visa in Hong Kong is also an option.

The Chinese government requires that your passport be valid for at least six months after the expiry date of your visa. You'll need at least one entire blank page in your passport for the visa.

On the visa application you must identify an itinerary and entry and exit dates and points, though nobody will hold you to them once you're in the country. Two passport-sized photos of the applicant are required.

Processing times and fees depend on where you're applying. In the UK single-entry visas cost £30 (plus a £34.50 application fee) and can be issued in three days (express service). In the US all visas cost US$130 (reciprocity for increased visa fees for entry to the US) and are issued in four days. Visas for citizens of other countries usually cost between US$30 to US$50.

Normally visas take a minimum three working days to be processed. Fees are paid in cash either at the time of application or when you collect your passport. With China becoming increasingly popular as a travel and business destination, queues at Chinese embassies and consulates are getting longer. A growing number of visa-arranging agents can do the legwork and deliver your visa-complete passport to you.

A 30-day visa is activated on the date you enter China, and must be used within three months of the date of issue. Longer-stay visas are also activated upon entry into China. Officials in China are sometimes confused over the validity of the visa and look at the 'valid until' date. On most 30-day visas, however, this is actually the date by which you must have *entered* the country, not left.

Although a 30-day length of stay is standard for tourist visas, 6-month and 12-month multiple-entry visas are also available. If you have trouble getting more than 30 days or a multiple-entry visa, try a local visa-arranging service or a travel agency in Hong Kong.

Note that if you go to China, on to Hong Kong and then to Shànghǎi, you will need a double-entry visa to get 'back' into China from Hong Kong or you will need to reapply for a fresh visa in Hong Kong.

A business visa is multiple-entry and valid for three to six months from the date of issue, depending on how much you paid for it.

When you check into a hotel, there is usually a question on the registration form asking what type of visa you have. The letter specifying your visa category is usually stamped on the visa itself. There are eight categories of ordinary visas, as follows:

Type	Description	Chinese name
L	travel	lǚxíng
F	business or student (less than 6 months)	fǎngwèn
D	resident	dìngjū
G	transit	guòjìng
X	long-term student	liúxué
Z	working	rènzhí
J	journalist	jìzhě
C	flight attendant	chéngwù

Visa Extensions

Extensions of 30 days are given for any tourist visa. You may be able to wrangle more with reasons such as illness or transport delays, but second extensions are usually only granted for a week, on the understanding that you are leaving. Visa extensions take three days and cost Y160 for most nationalities and Y940 for Americans (reciprocity for increased US visa fees). The fine for overstaying your visa is up to Y300 per day.

To extend a business visa, you need a letter from a Chinese work unit willing to sponsor you. If you're studying in China, your school can sponsor you for a visa extension.

Visa extensions in Shànghǎi are available from the PSB (Gōng'ānjú; Map p114; ☎ 2895 1900; 1500 Minsheng Rd; 民生路1500号; ⏰ 9am-5pm Mon-Sat).

Residence Permit

The 'green card' is a residence permit issued to English teachers, businesspeople, students and other foreigners who are authorised to live in the PRC. Green cards are issued for a period of one year.

To get a residence permit you first need to arrange a work permit (normally obtained by your employer), health certificate (p262) and temporary 'Z' visa. If your employer is switched on you can arrange all of this before you arrive in Shànghǎi.

You then go to the PSB with your passport, health certificate, work permit, your employer's business registration licence or representative office permit, your employment certificate (from the Shanghai Labour Bureau), the temporary residence permit of the hotel or local PSB where you are registered, passport photos, a letter of application from your employer and around Y400 in RMB. In all, the process usually takes from two to four weeks. Expect to make several visits and always carry multiple copies of every document. Each member of your family needs a residence permit and visa. In most cases your employer will take care of much of the process for you. If not, check expat websites for the latest updates to the process.

WEIGHTS & MEASURES

The metric system is widely used in China. However, traditional Chinese weights and measures persist, especially in local markets. Fruit and vegetables are weighed by the *jīn* (500g). Smaller weights (for dumplings, tea etc) are measured in *liǎng* (50g).

Metric	Chinese	Imperial
1m *(mǐ)*	3 *chǐ*	3.28 ft
1km *(gōnglǐ)*	2 *lǐ*	0.62 miles
1L *(gōngshēng)*	1 *shēng*	0.22 gallons
1kg *(gōngjīn)*	2 *jīn*	2.20 pounds

WOMEN TRAVELLERS

Female travellers will encounter few problems in Shànghǎi as Chinese men are neither macho nor disrespectful of women. Shànghǎi is a very cosmopolitan city, so women can largely wear what they like. Tampons can be bought everywhere, although it is advisable for you to bring your own contraceptive pills.

WORK

It's not too difficult to find work in Shànghǎi, though technically you will need a work visa. You should arrive in Shànghǎi with enough funds to keep you going for at least a few weeks until a job opens up. Examine the classified pages of the expat magazines for job opportunities. Modelling and acting can be quite lucrative – especially if you find a decent agent – and teaching English is perennially popular. Bear in mind that most big companies tend to recruit from home, offering comfortable expat packages. See also p252.

LANGUAGE

The local language variety spoken in Shànghǎi is Shanghainese (*Shànghǎihuà*), a distant relative of the widely spoken northern Mandarin variety, *Pǔtōnghuà*. English is of limited use beyond tourist hotels, so learning some Chinese is highly recommended. Visitors to Shànghǎi have no need to grapple with the local lingo, however, as Mandarin is universally understood throughout the city, and indeed throughout China, while Shanghainese is not understood outside of its relatively small area.

Learn a few key phrases before you go. Write them on pieces of paper and stick them on the fridge, by the bed or even on the computer – anywhere that you'll see them often.

You'll find that the people of Shànghǎi appreciate your efforts to speak a little Mandarin, no matter how muddled you may think you sound. So don't just stand there, say something! If you want to learn more Mandarin than we've included here, pick up a copy of Lonely Planet's comprehensive and user-friendly *Mandarin Phrasebook*.

For some interesting reading on the growing role of Mandarin in Shànghǎi, see p36.

PRONUNCIATION
Pinyin

In 1958 the Chinese adopted a system of writing their language using the Roman alphabet, known as *Pīnyīn*. Pinyin is often used on shop fronts, street signs and advertising billboards, but very few Chinese are able to read or write more than a few words in it.

A few consonants in Pinyin may cause confusion when compared to their English counterparts:

c	as the 'ts' in 'bits'
ch	as in 'chop', but with the tongue curled back
q	as the 'ch' in 'cheese'
r	as the 's' in 'pleasure'
sh	as in 'ship', but with the tongue curled back
x	as the 'sh' in 'ship'
z	as the 'dz' sound in 'suds'
zh	as the 'j' in 'judge', but with the tongue curled back

Tones

Chinese has a large number of words with identical sequences of consonants and vowels but different meanings; what distinguishes such words are 'tones' – rises and falls in the pitch of the voice on certain syllables. The word *ma*, for example, has the following four different meanings, depending on the tone (plus a fifth 'neutral' tone, not shown):

high tone	mā	(mother)
rising tone	má	(hemp, numb)
falling-rising tone	mǎ	(horse)
falling tone	mà	(to scold, to swear)

Mastering tones can be tricky for beginners, but with a little practice it gets a lot easier.

SOCIAL
Meeting People

Hello.	你好。	Nǐ hǎo.
Goodbye.	再见。	Zàijiàn.
Please.	请。	Qǐng.
Thank you.	谢谢。	Xièxie.
Thank you very much.	太谢谢了。	Tài xièxie le.
Yes.	是的。	Shìde.
No. (don't have)	没有。	Méi yǒu.
No. (not so)	不是。	Bùshì.

Do you speak English?
你会说英语吗? Nǐ huì shuō yīngyǔ ma?
Do you understand?
懂吗? Dǒng ma?
I understand.
我听得懂。 Wǒ tīngdedǒng.
I don't understand.
我听不懂。 Wǒ tīngbudǒng.
Could you please ...?

你能不能 …?
Nǐ néng bunéng …?

  repeat that
  重复　　　　　chóngfù

  speak more slowly
  说慢点儿　　　shuō màn diǎnr

  write it down
  写下来　　　　xiě xiàlái

Going Out

What's on …?
… 有什么娱乐活动?
… yǒu shénme yúlè huódòng?

  this weekend
  这个周末　　　Zhège zhōumò

  today
  今天　　　　　Jīntiān

  tonight
  今天晚上　　　Jīntiān wǎnshang

PRACTICAL
Question Words

Who?
谁?　　　　　　Shuí?

What?
什么?　　　　　Shénme?

When?
什么时候?　　　Shénme shíhou?

Where?
哪儿?　　　　　Nǎr?

How?
怎么?　　　　　Zěnme?

Numbers & Amounts

1	一/幺	yī/yāo
2	二/两	èr/liǎng
3	三	sān
4	四	sì
5	五	wǔ
6	六	liù
7	七	qī
8	八	bā
9	九	jiǔ
10	十	shí
11	十一	shíyī
12	十二	shí'èr
13	十三	shísān
14	十四	shísì
15	十五	shíwǔ
16	十六	shíliù
17	十七	shíqī
18	十八	shíbā
19	十九	shíjiǔ
20	二十	èrshí
21	二十一	èrshíyī
22	二十二	èrshí'èr
30	三十	sānshí
40	四十	sìshí
50	五十	wǔshí
60	六十	liùshí
70	七十	qīshí
80	八十	bāshí
90	九十	jiǔshí
100	一百	yībǎi
200	两百	liǎngbǎi
1000	一千	yīqiān
10,000	一万	yīwàn
100,000	十万	shíwàn

Days

Monday	星期一	xīngqīyī
Tuesday	星期二	xīngqī'èr
Wednesday	星期三	xīngqīsān
Thursday	星期四	xīngqīsì
Friday	星期五	xīngqīwǔ
Saturday	星期六	xīngqīliù
Sunday	星期天	xīngqītiān

Banking

I'd like to …
我想 …
Wǒ xiǎng …

  change money
  换钱　　　　　huàn qián

  change travellers cheques
  换旅行支票　　huàn lǚxíng zhīpiào

  use my credit card
  用我的信用卡　yòng wǒ de xìnyòngkǎ

Excuse me, where's the nearest …?
请问, 最近的 … 在哪儿?
Qǐng wèn, zuìjìnde … zài nǎr?

  automatic teller machine
  自动柜员机　　zìdòng guìyuánjī

  foreign exchange office
  外汇兑换处　　wàihuì duìhuànchù

Internet

Is there a local internet cafe?
本地有网吧吗?
Běndì yǒu wǎngbā ma?

Where can I get online?
我在哪儿可以上网?
Wǒ zài nǎr kěyǐ shàng wǎng?

Can I check my email account?
我查一下自己的email户, 好吗?
Wǒ chá yīxià zìjǐ de email hù, hǎo ma?

  computer

电脑
diànnǎo
email
电子邮件
diànzǐyóujiàn (often called 'email')
internet
因特网/互联网
yīntè wǎng/hùlián wǎng (formal name)

Phone
I want to buy a phonecard.
我想买电话卡。
Wǒ xiǎng mǎi diànhuà kǎ.

I want to make …
我想打 …
Wǒ xiǎng dǎ …
  a call (to …)
  打电话 (到 …)   diànhuà (dào …)
  a reverse-charge/collect call
  对方付费电话   duìfāng fùfèi diànhuà

Where can I find a/an …?
哪儿有 …?
Nǎr yǒu …?
I'd like a/an …
我想要 …
Wǒ xiǎng yào …
  adaptor plug
  转接器插头
  zhuǎnjiēqì chātóu
  charger for my phone
  电话充电器
  diànhuà chōngdiànqì
  mobile/cell phone for hire
  租用移动电话
  zūyòng yídòng diànhuà or
  租用手机
  zūyòng shǒujī
  prepaid mobile/cell phone
  预付移动电话
  yùfù yídòng diànhuà or
  预付手机
  yùfù shǒujī
  SIM card for your network
  你们网络的SIM卡
  nǐmen wǎngluò de SIM kǎ

Post
Where's the post office?
邮局在哪里?
Yóujú zài nǎlǐ?
I'd like to buy (an) …

我想买 …
Wǒ xiǎng mǎi …
  aerogram
  航空邮简   hángkōngyóujiǎn
  envelope
  信封   xìnfēng
  stamps
  邮票   yóupiào

I'd like to send …
我想 …
Wǒ xiǎng …
  a letter
  寄信   jì xìn
  a fax
  发传真   fā chuánzhēn
  a package
  寄包裹   jì bāoguǒ
  a postcard
  寄明信片   jì míngxìnpiàn

Transport
DIRECTIONS
Where is/are (the) …?
… 在哪儿?
… zài nǎr?
  metro station
  地铁站   Dìtiě zhàn
  toilet
  卫生间   Wèishēng jiān
  places to eat
  吃饭的地方   Chīfàn de dìfang
  pubs
  酒吧   Jiǔbā

PUBLIC TRANSPORT
What time does … leave/arrive?
… 几点开/到?
… jǐdiǎn kāi/dào?
  the bus
  汽车   Qìchē
  the train
  火车   Huǒchē
  the plane
  飞机   Fēijī
  the boat
  船   Chuán

metro (station) 地铁(站)   dìtiě (zhàn)
taxi   出租车   chūzūchē

Is this taxi available?
这车拉人吗?   Zhè chē lā rén ma?
Please use the meter.
打表。   Dǎ biǎo.
How much is it to …?

去 … 多少钱? Qù … duōshǎo qián?
I want to go to (this address).
我要去 Wǒ yào qù
(这个地址)。 (zhège dìzhǐ).

When is the … bus?
… 汽车几点开?
… qìchē jǐdiǎn kāi?
  first
  头班 Tóubān
  next
  下一班 Xià yībān
  last
  末班 Mòbān

EMERGENCIES
It's an emergency!
这是紧急情况!
Zhèshì jǐnjí qíngkuàng!
Could you help me, please?
你能不能帮我个忙?
Nǐ néng bunéng bāng wǒ ge máng?
Call the police/a doctor/an ambulance!
请叫警察/医生/救护车!
Qǐng jiào jǐngchá/yīshēng/jiùhùchē!
Where's the police station?
警察局在哪儿?
Jǐngchájú zài nǎr?

HEALTH
Excuse me, where's the nearest …?
请问, 最近的 … 在哪儿?
Qǐng wèn, zuìjìnde … zài nǎr?
  dentist
  牙医 yáyī
  doctor
  医生 yīshēng
  hospital
  医院 yīyuàn
  (night) chemist/pharmacist
  药店 (夜间) yàodiàn (yèjiān)

Is there a doctor here who speaks English?
这儿有会讲英语的大夫吗?
Zhèr yǒu huì jiǎng yīngyǔ de dàifu ma?

I have (a) …
我 …
Wǒ …
  diarrhoea
  拉肚子 lādùzi
  fever
  发烧 fāshāo
  headache
  头疼 tóuténg

FOOD & DRINK
Useful Words & Phrases
breakfast 早饭 zǎofàn
lunch 午饭 wǔfàn
dinner 晚饭 wǎnfàn
snack 小吃 xiǎochī
eat 吃 chī
drink 喝 hē

Can you recommend a …?
你能不能推荐一个 …?
Nǐ néng bunéng tuījiàn yīge …?
  bar/pub
  酒吧/酒馆 jiǔbā/jiǔguǎn
  cafe
  咖啡馆 kāfēiguǎn
  restaurant
  餐馆 cānguǎn

Is service/cover charge included in the bill?
帐单中包括服务费吗?
Zhàngdān zhōng bāokuò fúwùfèi ma?
I don't like innards.
我不喜欢吃内脏。
Wǒ bù xǐhuān chī nèizàng.

I don't want MSG.
我不要味精。 Wǒ bù yào wèijīng.
I'll have that. (pointing out a dish)
  来一个吧。 Lái yīge ba.
I'm vegetarian.
我吃素。 Wǒ chī sù.
Not too spicy.
不要太辣。 Bù yào tài là.
Let's eat!
吃饭! Chī fàn!
Cheers!
干杯! Gānbēi!
Please give me a receipt.
请给我发票。 Qǐng gěi wǒ fāpiào.
Waiter!
服务员! Fúwùyuán!
Waitress!
小姐! Xiǎojiě!
bill/check
买单/结帐 mǎi dān/jiézhàng
bowl
碗 wǎn
chopsticks
筷子 kuàizi
(cooked) together
一块儿 yīkuàir
fork
叉子 chāzi
hot
热的 rède

knife		
刀子	dāozi	
ice cold		
冰的	bīngde	
menu		
菜单/菜谱	càidān/càipǔ	
plate		
盘子	pánzi	
set meal (no menu)		
套餐	tàocān	
spicy		
辣	là	
spoon		
勺子	sháozi	
toothpick		
牙签	yáqiān	
tissue paper		
面巾纸	miànjīnzhǐ	

Food Glossary

bīng	冰	ice
bīngqílín	冰淇淋	ice cream
cù	醋	vinegar
dòufu	豆腐	tofu
gānzàng	肝脏	liver
hànbǎobāo	汉堡包	hamburger
huángguā	黄瓜	cucumber
huángyóu	黄油	butter
hújiāofěn	胡椒粉	pepper
jiàngyóu	酱油	soy sauce
jīdàn	鸡蛋	egg
jīròu	鸡肉	chicken
làjiāo	辣椒	chilli
làjiāo yóu	辣椒油	chilli oil
lāmiàn	拉面	pulled noodles
miànbāo	面包	bread
niúpái	牛排	beef steak
niúròu	牛肉	beef
pángxiè	螃蟹	crab
qiézi	茄子	aubergine
qíncài	芹菜	celery
qīngcài	青菜	green vegetables
ròu	肉	meat
sānmíngzhì	三明治	sandwich
sèlā	色拉	salad
shāokǎo	烧烤	barbecue
shǔtiáo	薯条	chips
sùcài	素菜	vegetables
tāng	汤	soup
táng	糖	sugar
tǔdòu	土豆	potato
wèijīng	味精	MSG
xīhóngshì	西红柿	tomato
yán	盐	salt
yángròu	羊肉	lamb
yángròuchuàn	羊肉串	lamb kebab
yāozi	腰子	kidney
yāzi	鸭子	duck
yóuyú	鱿鱼	squid
yú	鱼	fish
zhōu	粥	rice porridge (congee)
zhūpái	猪排	pork steak
zhūròu	猪肉	pork

RICE DISHES 米饭

báifàn	白饭
steamed white rice	
chǎofàn	炒饭
fried rice	
jīdàn chǎofàn	鸡蛋炒饭
fried rice with egg	

SOUP 汤

húntun tāng	馄饨汤
won ton (dumpling) soup	
jīdàn tāng	鸡蛋汤
egg drop soup	
sānxiān tāng	三鲜汤
three kinds of seafood soup	
suānlà tāng	酸辣汤
hot and sour soup	
xīhóngshì jīdàntāng	西红柿鸡蛋汤
tomato and egg soup	

VEGETABLE DISHES 素菜

báicài xiān shuānggū	白菜鲜双菇
bok choy and mushrooms	
cuìpí dòufu	脆皮豆腐
crispy skin bean curd	
dìsānxiān	地三鲜
cooked potato, aubergine and green pepper	
háoyóu xiānggū	蚝油鲜菇
mushrooms in oyster sauce	
hēimù'ěr mèn dòufu	黑木耳焖豆腐
bean curd with mushrooms	
jiǔcài jiǎozi	韭菜饺子
chive dumplings	
shāo qiézi	烧茄子
cooked aubergine (eggplant)	
tángcù ǒubǐng	糖醋藕饼
lotus root cakes in sweet-and-sour sauce	

SEAFOOD 海鲜

chāngyú	鲳鱼
pomfret	
chǎo huángshàn	炒黄鳝
fried eel	
cōngsū jìyú	葱酥鲫鱼
braised carp with onion	

dàzhá xiè 大闸蟹
hairy crabs

fúróng yúpiàn 芙蓉鱼片
fish slices in egg white

gānjiān xiǎo huángyú 干煎小黄鱼
dry-fried yellow croaker

guōbā xiārén 锅巴虾仁
shrimp in sizzling rice crust

héxiāng báilián 荷香白鲢
lotus-flavoured silver carp

hóngshāo shànyú 红烧鳝鱼
eel soaked in soy sauce

huángyú 黄鱼
yellow croaker

jiāng cōng chǎo xiè 姜葱炒蟹
stir-fried crab with ginger and scallions

jiǔxiāng yúpiàn 酒香鱼片
fish slices in wine

mìzhī xūnyú 蜜汁熏鱼
honey-smoked carp

níngshì shànyú 宁式鳝鱼
stir-fried eel with onion

qiézhī yúkuài 茄汁鱼块
fish fillet in tomato sauce

qīngzhēng guìyú 清蒸鳜鱼
steamed Mandarin fish

sōngjiānglúyú 松江鲈鱼
Songjiang perch

sōngshǔ guìyú 松鼠鳜鱼
squirrel-shaped Mandarin fish

sōngzǐ guìyú 松子鳜鱼
Mandarin fish with pine nuts

suānlà yóuyú 酸辣鱿鱼
hot-and-sour squid

yóubào xiārén 油爆虾仁
fried shrimp

zhá hēi lǐyú 炸黑鲤鱼
fried black carp

zhá yúwán 炸鱼丸
fish balls

HOME-STYLE DISHES 家常菜

biǎndòu ròusī 扁豆肉丝
shredded pork and green beans

fānqié chǎodàn 番茄炒蛋
egg and tomato

gānbiǎn niúròu sī 干煸牛肉丝
stir-fried beef and chilli

guōbā ròu piàn 锅巴肉片
pork and sizzling rice crust

hóngshāo qiézi 红烧茄子
red-cooked aubergine

huíguō ròu 回锅肉
double-cooked fatty pork

jiācháng dòufu 家常豆腐
'home-style' tofu

jiānbǐngguǒzi 煎饼裹子
egg and spring onion pancake

jīngjiàng ròusī 精酱肉丝
pork cooked with soy sauce

mù'ěr ròu 木耳肉
'wooden ear' mushrooms and pork

níngméng jī 柠檬鸡
lemon chicken

niúròu miàn 牛肉面
beef noodles in soup

páigǔ 排骨
ribs

qīngjiāo ròu piàn 青椒肉片
pork and green peppers

sùchǎo biǎndòu 素炒扁豆
garlic beans

sùchǎo sùcài 素炒素菜
fried vegetables

tiěbǎn niúròu 铁板牛肉
sizzling beef platter

xiānbèi yāohuā 鲜贝腰花
scallops and kidney

yángcōng chǎo ròupiàn 洋葱炒肉片
pork and fried onions

yāoguǒ jīdīng 腰果鸡丁
chicken and cashews

yúxiāng qiézi 鱼香茄子
fish-flavoured aubergine

SHANGHAINESE DISHES 上海菜

hǔpíjiānjiāo 虎皮尖椒
tiger skin chillies

jīngcōng ròusī jiá bǐng 京葱肉丝夹饼
soy pork with scallions in pancakes

jīngdū guō páigǔ 京都锅排骨
Mandarin-style pork ribs

sōngrén yùmǐ 松仁玉米
sweet corn and pine nuts

sōngzǐ yā 松子鸭
duck with pine nuts

xiāngsū jī 香酥鸡
crispy chicken

xiánjī 咸鸡
cold salty chicken

xiǎolóngbāo 小笼包
little steamer buns

xièfěn shīzitóu 蟹粉狮子头
lion's head meatballs with crab

yóutiáo niú ròu 油条牛肉
fried dough sticks with beef

zuìjī 醉鸡
drunken chicken

HÁNGZHŌU DISHES 杭州菜

dōngpō bèiròu 东坡焙肉
Dongpo pork

héyè fěnzhēng ròu 荷叶粉蒸肉
steamed pork wrapped in lotus leaf

jiào huā jī 叫化鸡
beggar's chicken

lóngjǐng xiārén 龙井虾仁
Longjing stir-fried shrimp

mìzhī huǒfāng 蜜汁火方
honeyed ham

shāguō yútóu dòufu 沙锅鱼头豆腐
earthenware-pot fish-head tofu

sòngsǎo yú gēng 宋嫂鱼羹
Mandarin fish soup with ham and mushrooms

xīhú chúncài tāng 西湖纯菜汤
West Lake water shield soup

xīhú cùyú 西湖醋鱼
West Lake fish

CANTONESE DISHES 粤菜

bái zhuó xiā 白灼虾
blanched prawns with shredded scallion

chǎomiàn 炒面
chow mein

chāshāo 叉烧
cha siu

diǎnxīn 点心
dim sum

dōngjiāng yán jú jī 东江盐焗鸡
salt-baked chicken

gālí jī 咖喱鸡
curried chicken

guōtiē 锅贴
fried dumplings

háoyóu niúròu 蚝油牛肉
beef with oyster sauce

kǎo rǔzhū 烤乳猪
crispy suckling pig

mìzhī chāshāo 蜜汁叉烧
roast pork with sweet syrup

shé ròu 蛇肉
snake

tángcù lǐjī/ 糖醋里脊/
  gǔlǎo ròu 古老肉
sweet-and-sour pork fillets

tángcù páigǔ 糖醋排骨
sweet-and-sour spare ribs

xiāngsū jī 香酥鸡
crispy chicken

SICHUANESE DISHES 川菜

bàngbang jī 棒棒鸡
shredded chicken in a hot pepper-and-sesame sauce

dàndànmiàn 担担面
Dandan noodles

dàsuàn shàn duàn 大蒜鳝段
stewed eel with garlic

gānshāo yán lǐ 干烧岩鲤
stewed carp with ham and hot-and-sweet sauce

gōngbào jīdīng 宫爆鸡丁
spicy chicken with peanuts

málà dòufu 麻辣豆腐
spicy tofu

mápó dòufu 麻婆豆腐
Granny Ma's tofu

shuǐ zhǔ niúròu 水煮牛肉
fried and boiled beef, garlic sprouts and celery

suāncàiyú 酸菜鱼
boiled fish with pickled vegetables

yuānyāng huǒguō 鸳鸯火锅
Yuanyang hotpot

yúxiāng ròusī 鱼香肉丝
fish-flavoured meat

zhàcài ròusī 榨菜肉丝
stir-fried pork or beef tenderloin with tuber mustard

zhāngchá yāzi 樟茶鸭子
camphor-smoked duck

BĚIJĪNG & NORTHERN DISHES
京菜和北方菜

běijīng kǎoyā 北京烤鸭
Peking duck

jiāozhá yángròu 焦炸羊肉
deep-fried mutton

jiǎozi 饺子
dumplings

mántou 馒头
steamed buns

qīngxiāng shāojī 清香烧鸡
chicken wrapped in lotus leaf

ròu bāozi 肉包子
steamed meat buns

shāo bǐng 烧饼
baked rolls

shuàn yángròu huǒguō 涮羊肉火锅
lamb hotpot

sùcài bāozi 素菜包子
steamed vegetable buns

DRINKS 饮料

bābǎo chá 八宝茶
eight-treasures tea

bái pútáojiǔ 白葡萄酒
white wine

báijiǔ 白酒
white spirits

bǎiwēi 百威
Budweiser

bèikè 贝克
Becks

chá/cháshuǐ 茶/茶水
tea

dòunǎi 豆奶
soya milk

fēndá 芬达
Fanta

hóng pútáojiǔ 红葡萄酒
red wine

hóngchá	红茶	nǎijīng	奶精
Western (black) tea		coffee creamer	
jiāshìbó	嘉士伯	niúnǎi	牛奶
Carlsberg		milk	
júhuā chá	菊花茶	píjiǔ	啤酒
chrysanthemum tea		beer	
kāfēi	咖啡	qìshuǐ	汽水
coffee		soft drink (soda)	
kāi shuǐ	开水	suānnǎi	酸奶
water (boiled)		yoghurt	
kěkǒu kělè	可口可乐	xǐlì	喜力
Coca-Cola		Heineken	
kuàngquánshuǐ	矿泉水	xuěbì	雪碧
mineral water		Sprite	
lǜ chá	绿茶	yán qìshuǐ	盐汽水
green tea		salt soda water	
měiniándá	美年达	yézi zhī	椰子汁
Mirinda		coconut juice	
mǐjiǔ	米酒	zhēnzhū nǎichá	珍珠奶茶
rice wine		bubble tea	

GLOSSARY

arhat – Buddhist, especially a monk who has achieved enlightenment and passes to nirvana at death

Ba Jin – popular and prolific anarchist writer of the 1930s and 1940s. Li Feigan (his real name) is probably best known for his 1931 novel *Jiā (The Family)*.

báijiǔ – literally 'white alcohol', a type of face-numbing rice wine served at banquets and get-togethers

běi – north

biéshù – villa

bīnguǎn – tourist hotel

Bodhisattva – one worthy of nirvana but who remains on earth to help others attain enlightenment

bówùguǎn – museum

CAAC – Civil Aviation Administration of China

cāntīng – restaurant

CCP – Chinese Communist Party; founded in Shànghǎi in 1921

Chiang Kaishek – (1887–1975) leader of the *Kuomintang*, anticommunist and head of the nationalist government from 1928 to 1949

chop – carved name seal that acts as a signature

Confucius – (551–479 BC) legendary scholar who developed the philosophy of Confucianism, which defines codes of conduct and patterns of obedience in society

Cultural Revolution – a brutal and devastating purge of the arts, religion and the intelligentsia by Mao's *Red Guards* and later the *PLA* from 1966 to 1970

dàdào – boulevard, avenue

dàfàndiàn – large hotel

dàjiē – avenue

dàjiǔdiàn – large hotel

dàshà – hotel, building

Deng Xiaoping – (1904–97) considered to be the most powerful political figure in China from the late 1970s until his death. Deng's reforms resulted in economic growth, but he also instituted harsh social policies and authorised the military force that resulted in the Tiananmen Sq incident in Běijīng in 1989.

dōng – east

fàndiàn – hotel, restaurant

fēn – one-tenth of a *jiǎo*

fēng – peak

fēngshuǐ – geomancy, literally 'wind and water'. The art of using ancient principles to maximise the flow of *qì* (universal energy).

Gang of Four – members of a clique, headed by Mao's wife, Jiang Qing, who were blamed for the disastrous *Cultural Revolution*

gé – pavilion, temple

gōngyuán – park

guānxi – advantageous social or business connections

gùjū – house, home, residence

gǔzhèn – ancient town

hé – river

hú – lake

jiāng – river

jiǎo – unit of currency, one-tenth of a *yuán*

jiē – street

jié – festival

jīn – unit of measurement (500g)

jìniànguǎn – memorial hall

jiǔdiàn – hotel

jū – residence, home

junk – originally referred to Chinese fishing and war

vessels with square sails. Now applies to various types of boating craft.

kuài – in spoken Chinese, colloquial term for the currency, *yuán*

Kuomintang – *Chiang Kaishek's* Nationalist Party. The dominant political force after the fall of the Qing dynasty.

liǎng – unit of measurement (50g)
lòngtáng – narrow alleyway in Shànghǎi
lóu – tower
lù – road
luóhàn – see *arhat*

máo – in spoken Chinese, colloquial term for the *jiǎo*
Mao Zedong – (1893–1976) leader of the early communist forces, he founded the *PRC* and was party chairman until his death
mǎtou – dock
mén – gate
miào – temple

nán – south

overseas Chinese – Chinese people who have left China to settle overseas

PLA – People's Liberation Army
Polo, Marco – Italian merchant who (supposedly) visited China and the Far East in the 13th century
PRC – People's Republic of China
PSB – Public Security Bureau; the arm of the police force set up to deal with foreigners

qiáo – bridge
qīngzhēnsì – mosque
qípáo – the figure-hugging dress worn by Chinese women (also called a *cheongsam*)

Red Guards – a pro-Mao faction who persecuted rightists during the Cultural Revolution
rénmín – people, people's
Renminbi – literally 'people's money', the formal name for the currency of China. Shortened to RMB.

shān – mountain
shì – city
shìchǎng – market
shíkùmén – stone-gate house
sì – temple, monastery
Sun Yatsen – (1866–1925) first president of the Republic of China. A revolutionary loved by republicans and communists alike.

tǎ – pagoda
taichi – slow motion shadow-boxing. The graceful, flowing exercise has its roots in China's martial arts. Also called *t'ai chi ch'uan* or *tàijíquán*.
Taiping Rebellion – 1.1-million-strong rebellion (1850–64) that attempted to overthrow the Qing dynasty
tíng – pavilion
triads – secret societies. Originally founded to protect Chinese culture from the influence of usurping Manchurians, their modern-day members are little more than gangsters, involved mainly in drug running, gun running, prostitution and protection rackets.

xī – west

yuán – the Chinese unit of currency, the basic unit of RMB; garden
zhōng – middle
Zhou Enlai – an early comrade of Mao's, Zhou exercised the most influence in the day-to-day governing of China following the *Cultural Revolution*. His death triggered the Tiananmen Sq incident in 1976.

BEHIND THE SCENES

THIS BOOK

This edition of *Shanghai* was written by Christopher Pitts and Daniel McCrohan. Damian Harper and David Eimer wrote the previous edition. This guidebook was commissioned by Lonely Planet's Oakland office and produced by the following:

Commissioning Editor Emily K Wolman

Coordinating Editors Jessica Crouch, Shawn Low

Coordinating Cartographer Tadhgh Knaggs

Coordinating Layout Designer Aomi Hongo

Managing Editors Annelies Mertens, Laura Stansfeld

Managing Cartographers Shahara Ahmed, David Connolly

Managing Layout Designer Sally Darmody

Assisting Editors Kate Daly, Barbara Delissen, Melissa Faulkner, Robyn Loughnane, Martine Power

Assisting Cartographers Ross Butler, Eve Kelly, Ross Macaw

Assisting Layout Designer Kerrianne Southway

Cover Yukiyoshi Kamimura, lonelyplanetimages.com

Internal Image Research Sabrina Dalbesio, lonelyplanetimages.com

Colour Designer Paul Iacono

Project Manager Chris Love

Thanks to Lucy Birchley, Ji Yuanfang, Yvonne Kirk, Rebecca Lalor, Wayne Murphy, Raphael Richards

Cover photographs Night scene of a skyscraper in Pǔdōng, Photolibrary (top); People in a bar, Nonstock Inc/Photolibrary (bottom)

Internal photographs p3 Jorisvo/Dreamstime.com; p4 (#2) Getty Images, Scott S. Warren; p7 (#5) www .Dragonfly.net.cn; p7 (#6) Giles Robberts/Alamy; p8 (#3) Mike Goldwater/Alamy; p11 (#3) Andrew James Art (www. andrewjamesart.com); p47, p51 Daniel McCrohan/Author; p50 Yang Liu/Corbis

All other photographs by Lonely Planet Images: p2, p4 (#1), p5 (#2), p7(#1, #3), p6 (#4), p9 (#1, #2, #3), p10 (#1, #2), p12 (#1, #2), p45, p46, p48 (bottom), p49 (top & bottom), p50, p52 Greg Elms; p4 (#3) Ray Laskowitz; p5 (#1), p8 (#1) Krzysztof Dydynski; p5 (#3), p6 (#2), p8 (#2), p11 (#2) Richard I'Anson; p11 (#1) Brent Winebrenner; p12 (#3), p52 (top) Bruce Bi.

All images are copyright of the photographer unless otherwise indicated. Many of the images in this guide are available for licensing from Lonely Planet Images: www. lonelyplanetimages.com.

THANKS
CHRISTOPHER PITTS

First off, thanks to the authors of the previous edition, Damian Harper and David Eimer, who provided a solid foundation to build on. In Shànghǎi, thanks goes to roomies Claudio Valsecchi and Gerald Neumann for their insights, recommendations and introductions; Erica Ding for providing invaluable translation assistance; John Ward; He Nong; Han Yuqi; Zane Mellupe; Antonio Jiménez Rosa; Munson Wu; Elfa Huang; Shen Xiansheng; Tao Wansheng; Shen Chuanzhu; and Maria Chao. Also big thanks to coauthor Daniel for his enthusiasm, and for introducing me to Huw, Fung and Jake,

THE LONELY PLANET STORY

Fresh from an epic journey across Europe, Asia and Australia in 1972, Tony and Maureen Wheeler sat at their kitchen table stapling together notes. The first Lonely Planet guidebook, *Across Asia on the Cheap*, was born.

Travellers snapped up the guides. Inspired by their success, the Wheelers began publishing books to Southeast Asia, India and beyond. Demand was prodigious, and the Wheelers expanded the business rapidly to keep up. Over the years, Lonely Planet extended its coverage to every country and into the virtual world via lonelyplanet.com and the Thorn Tree message board.

As Lonely Planet became a globally loved brand, Tony and Maureen received several offers for the company. But it wasn't until 2007 that they found a partner whom they trusted to remain true to the company's principles of travelling widely, treading lightly and giving sustainably. In October of that year, BBC Worldwide acquired a 75% share in the company, pledging to uphold Lonely Planet's commitment to independent travel, trustworthy advice and editorial independence.

Today, Lonely Planet has offices in Melbourne, London and Oakland, with over 500 staff members and 300 authors. Tony and Maureen are still actively involved with Lonely Planet. They're travelling more often than ever, and they're devoting their spare time to charitable projects. And the company is still driven by the philosophy of *Across Asia on the Cheap*: 'All you've got to do is decide to go and the hardest part is over. So go!'

SEND US YOUR FEEDBACK

We love to hear from travellers – your comments keep us on our toes and help make our books better. Our well-travelled team reads every word on what you loved or loathed about this book. Although we cannot reply individually to postal submissions, we always guarantee that your feedback goes straight to the appropriate authors, in time for the next edition. Each person who sends us information is thanked in the next edition and the most useful submissions are rewarded with a free book.

To send us your updates – and find out about Lonely Planet events, newsletters and travel news – visit our award-winning website: lonelyplanet.com/contact.

Note: We may edit, reproduce and incorporate your comments in Lonely Planet products such as guidebooks, websites and digital products, so let us know if you don't want your comments reproduced or your name acknowledged. For a copy of our privacy policy visit lonelyplanet.com/privacy.

who all provided fantastic recommendations. Back at HQ, thanks to Emily, David and everyone else who worked on this edition. And finally, thanks to the family on both sides of the Atlantic for their endless support, and to Perrine, Elliot and Céleste – a thousand and one kisses, kung fu outfits and glitter-pink I Heart Shànghǎi T-shirts.

DANIEL McCROHAN

Firstly a massive thanks to Shànghǎi stalwarts Huw Morgan-Jones and Jake Newby for their invaluable advice on pretty much everything to do with the city. Huge appreciation also goes to Chen Feng for sharing his fascinating insights into Shanghainese culture and for introducing me to *real* Shanghainese food. And I'm hugely indebted to Julia Grindell, chief correspondent at *China Confidential*, for her tireless work in helping me put together the Economy section for this book.

Others I'd like to thank include Fung, for his help on all things arty, Gil Miller and Lolo for their travel tips and Anders Jarnkrok for giving me the history-expert nod. Thanks must also go to my colleagues Chris Pitts, Emily Wolman and David Connolly for making this project so much easier than it should have been.

As always, though, the biggest thanks go to my loved ones back in the UK and to my darling wife, Taotao.

OUR READERS

Many thanks to the travellers who used the last edition and wrote to us with helpful hints, useful advice and interesting anecdotes:

Patrick Benusiglio, Chiara Castelbolognesi, Diego Constant, Eduardo Cruz, Lai Fei, Mark Hodgkin, Susan Kelly, David McAdams, Renae McDermott, Meghan McGrath, Rena McNally, Vincent Ng, Gregory Otte, Michael Poesen, Ine Reijnen.

Notes

INDEX

INDEX

TOP PICKS

INDEX

MAP LEGEND
ROUTES

Freeway		One-Way Street	
Primary		Tunnel	
Secondary		Mall/Steps	
Tertiary		Pedestrian Overpass	
Lane		Walking Tour	
Under Construction		Walking Path	
Unsealed Road		Track	

TRANSPORT

Ferry		Rail (Underground)	
Metro		Cable Car, Funicular	
Rail			

HYDROGRAPHY

River, Creek		Canal	
Intermittent River		Water	

BOUNDARIES

State, Provincial

AREA FEATURES

Airport		Land	
Area of Interest		Mall	
Building		Market	
Campus		Park	
Cemetery, Christian		Sports	
Cemetery, Other		Urban	
Forest			

POPULATION

⊚ CAPITAL (STATE)	○	Small City
● Large City	○	Town, Village
● Medium City		

SYMBOLS

Information
- Bank, ATM
- Embassy/Consulate
- Hospital, Medical
- Information
- Internet Facilities
- Police Station
- Post Office, GPO
- Telephone
- Toilets

Sights
- Buddhist
- Castle, Fortress
- Christian
- Confucian

- Jewish
- Monument
- Museum, Gallery
- Point of Interest
- Ruin
- Taoist
- Zoo, Bird Sanctuary

Shopping
- Shopping

Eating
- Eating

Entertainment
- Entertainment
- Clubbing, Music, Sports & Activities

- Nightlife

Drinking
- Drinking
- Cafe

Sleeping
- Sleeping

Transport
- Airport, Airfield
- Bus Station
- Parking Area
- Taxi Rank

Geographic
- Mountain, Volcano
- River Flow

Published by Lonely Planet Publications Pty Ltd
ABN 36 005 607 983

Australia (Head Office)
Locked Bag 1, Footscray, Victoria 3011,
☎ 03 8379 8000, fax 03 8379 8111,
talk2us@lonelyplanet.com.au

USA 150 Linden St, Oakland, CA 94607,
☎ 510 250 6400, toll free 800 275 8555,
fax 510 893 8572, info@lonelyplanet.com

UK 2nd fl, 186 City Rd, London, EC1V 2NT,
☎ 020 7106 2100, fax 020 7106 2101,
go@lonelyplanet.co.uk

© Lonely Planet 2010
Photographs © As listed (p279) 2010

Printed by Hang Tai Printing Company, Hong Kong.
Printed in China.

Mixed Sources
Product group from well-managed forests and other controlled sources
www.fsc.org Cert no. SGS-COC-005002
© 1996 Forest Stewardship Council